The First Team

THE FIRST TEAM

Pacific Naval Air Combat
from Pearl Harbor to Midway

By John B. Lundstrom

Naval Institute Press
Annapolis, Maryland

Naval Institute Press
291 Wood Road
Annapolis, MD 21402

First Naval Institute Press paperback edition, 2005
ISBN 1-59114-471-X

The Library of Congress has cataloged the hardcover edition as follows:
Lundstrom, John B.
   The first team.
   Bibliography: p.
   Includes index.
   1. World War, 1939–1945—Aerial operations, American.
2. World War, 1939–1945—Naval operations, American.
3. World War, 1939–1945—Campaigns—Pacific Ocean.
I. Title.
D790.L8 1984   940.54′4973   84-9822
ISBN 0-08721-189-7

Printed in the United States of America on acid-free paper ∞
12 11 10 09 08 07 06 05   9 8 7 6 5 4 3 2
First printing

Dedicated to the memory of
Bernard Lundstrom, my father
and
Roger M. Rice, my brother-in-law and friend

Contents

Foreword

The wit and comradery that the British muster so well in uncomfortable circumstances sparkles in a ditty made up by Royal New Zealand Air Force types to honor the USS *Yorktown* (CV-5) at a trying time of her existence. Our flattop had put in at Tonga Tabu's out-of-the-way anchorage so divers could check the extent of underwater damage received in the Coral Sea battle. As an added layer of security for the ship during this delicate operation, some of us of her air group were temporarily based ashore in readiness to launch from a nearby meadow that served as an airfield. We listened in good heart as the serenade went on extolling that "fine tidy ship." We were pleasantly surprised that here were spontaneous sentiments that matched so well our private feelings for our stout ship, our "home plate" in fighter director lingo. Bruised but not bested, she was as clean and hearty as we could make her. There was plenty of fight left in that high-stepping girl. The divers determined that with some innovative patching she could fight some more—and she would!

By the time of this visit to Tonga Tabu, Yorktowners' impression of the war and their part in it was beginning to pall. Clearly, Japan was taking over in the western Pacific. The *Yorktown* and the *Lexington* had presented the only serious opposition to Imperial plans. Their assignment was simple: react, try to stop the most serious advances. The reactive role, aside from its built-in perils, is depressing and, over a period of time, is mighty rough on the good-humor program, especially with no end in sight. The Japanese were winning, and they seemed to be tireless. When the *Lexington*, after several weeks' absence, rejoined us in our own piece of the Coral Sea, our spirits leaped only to dive to a new low as we watched her flaming death throes and felt the bone-shattering blast that sent her to the bottom. Still there was pride and plenty of spirit in the *Yorktown*. We had carried the fight to the foe and had stopped a baleful threat to Australia. We knew great issues depended on our carrying on. There was impressive confirmation of this idea in the orders that put the *Yorktown* back to sea for the Midway battle, a patched-up ship and a scratched-together air group. There were guarded feelings about our assignment, but it was obvious our combat specialties were very much in demand.

For her Japanese attackers, the *Yorktown* turned out to be the whole U.S. fleet. She absorbed all their attentions which might have been inflicted on other ships. Her people mourn her loss but bask in the knowledge they left deep scars on the Imperial Fleet and added to her good name. For her attacks on the Japanese carriers, the *Yorktown*'s part amounted to a good half of TF 16/17 effort, sharing it only with the *Enterprise*. Thus, the *Yorktown* put in a rousing good day's work, and her air group carried on from surviving decks until the battle was done. This is history that can read like a good old sea yarn, yet it has been waiting forty years and some for a scholar of John Lundstrom's persistence to put it together as such.

Study of carrier actions in the first half year of war in the Pacific is frustrating to one who searches for credible reasons that can account for the extraordinary reversal of fortunes of the chief contenders battling at that time. Such study is less a search and more a groping in the murk where combat results do not follow the logic of numbers, experience, equipment, and whatever else might tangibly shape outcome. In a rapid succession of events toward the end of this period, our carrier forces, consistently the underdogs, came off winners. Since this result has much the aspect of an act of God, historians, with wondrous restraint, seem to have been inclined to let it go at that. Whatever the reason may have been, there remains much to be told about what was really going on in our carriers in these crucial months. This is a grievous deficiency to afflict the historical record of carrier warfare in the very months our ships sealed the fate of Japan's seaborne air power and pushed her onto the road to defeat.

The luck, miracles, and outright sacrificial performances that made May and June 1942 banner months for our war fortunes in the Pacific are mingled in sources and records that until now have wanted the attentions of a keen and resourceful scholar. Heretofore, accounts of this period have tended to be broad-brush, imprecise, and wanting in detail. Or, at another extreme there are exhaustive treatments of colorful doings taken in isolation with little or no reference to what went before or came afterward. These kinds of treatment obscure the important fact that in our aircraft carriers throughout the period, significant organizational, personnel, and material factors were at work. Some were fair solutions to severe problems; some were unadulterated trouble. In any case, they did affect the ships and squadrons. These factors must be identified and considered alongside combat events if one is to understand and grade efforts, accomplishments, and failures that shaped results.

As a fighter pilot veteran of the *Yorktown*'s entire combat career, her last year afloat, I am very grateful to John Lundstrom for the chance he gave me to help dig out and expose to light material that shows how it was in the flattops in the early months of the war in the Pacific. He gave me a chance to do something better than grumpily watching time run out, fuming the while over deficiencies of historians' treatment of this period. He also afforded me some tantalizing glimpses of material gleaned from Japanese sources and from hitherto untapped sources here at home. When it is all assembled, the account permits analysis, then assessment of the extent to which results were shaped by such things as luck, miraculous intervention, the performance of men, and, yes, the singular part the *Yorktown* and her people played in the decisive engagements of this period.

REAR ADMIRAL WILLIAM N. LEONARD (RETIRED)

Preface

In August 1973 while researching my M.A. thesis on Pacific Fleet strategy in 1941–42, I had the privilege of meeting several *Yorktown* (CV-5) veterans. Included among them were two former Fighting Squadron Forty-two (VF-42) pilots, Rear Admiral William N. Leonard and Captain William S. Woollen, both retired from the Navy. Hearing their recollections of combat at the battles of the Coral Sea and Midway, I realized immediately how little of what they related to me was recorded anywhere, and how it offered much new insight on those epic engagements. Comparatively speaking, fewer detailed official reports and documents are available on the role of the fighters in the early-1942 carrier actions than existed for the dive bombers and torpedo planes. The nature of fighter operations militated against comprehensive descriptions of their activities in single action reports, for unlike the other types of carrier aircraft, the fighters usually operated in small groups or even alone and often tallied widely differing experiences. The standard published accounts of Coral Sea and Midway left a great deal to be desired in their coverage of fighters. Consequently, it was impossible to reconstruct in detail the aerial combat that occurred in these battles.

Equally fascinating to me was Admiral Leonard's explanation of the Navy's aerial gunnery philosophy—deflection shooting—and the development of team tactics. Using Grumman F4F Wildcat fighters, the U.S. Navy's carrier fighter pilots took on the vaunted Mitsubishi A6M2 Zero fighters that had swept from the Western Pacific skies fighters flown by the British, Dutch, Chinese, and U.S. Army air forces. Admittedly the Wildcat was inferior in performance to the Mitsubishi Zero, while the Japanese naval pilots—for the most part superb aviators—enjoyed prior seasoning in combat. Yet in the hands of the U.S. Navy's flyers the Wildcats more than held their own with Zeros, particularly at Midway. American gunnery training and tactics proved better than the enemy's and fitted in well with the Grumman's strong points: firepower, protection, and overall ruggedness. In connection with the development of fighter tactics, the names of John S. ("Jimmy") Thach and James H. Flatley are well known, but nowhere was there an analysis of precisely what their contributions were. Both men exerted an influence far beyond their relatively junior ranks.

How important were the carrier fighters in the Pacific War's early operations? James Flatley stated at the time: "Fighters are absolutely essential to the success of carrier operations," and John Thach remarked: "Our aircraft carriers can be kept afloat only by fighters." The carrier fighters often participated in attacks on enemy ships and bases while serving as escorts for the rest of the air group or as fighter-bombers. On combat air patrol, they constituted the most important defense for their task force against enemy strike groups and search planes. They contested with enemy fighters for control of the air, a prerequisite for any kind of tactical or strategic success. In analyzing carrier strategy and operations, one cannot afford to ignore their impact.

From my interviews with Bill Leonard and Bill Woollen came a deep interest in the operations and tactics of the Pacific Fleet's carrier fighting squadrons from Pearl Harbor through the Battle of Midway. In the course of researching this book, I have made contact with over forty former fighter pilots and dive bomber and torpedo plane crewmen, and their response has been overwhelming, both in their eagerness to help and in the richness and essential accuracy of most of their recollections. Many had preserved original documents and photographs available nowhere else, and a few had personal diaries that they generously allowed me to use. It was the unexpected volume and quality of accounts by participants (Japanese as well as American) that allowed detailed reconstructions of the fighter actions presented in this book. The Japanese government has undertaken the publication of a massive official history (around 100 volumes) that provides a framework for studying their viewpoint of the air battles. Other outstanding Japanese sources likewise treated in great detail certain aspects of the early battles and Japanese personalities. From the Naval History Division's Operational Archives Branch and the National Archives came a large amount of reports, war diaries, correspondence, and message files, much of it not previously tapped for histories of the early phases of the Pacific War. These documents fleshed out and complemented the personal accounts and permit an overview of strategic and operational factors to place the role of the carrier fighters in its proper perspective.

Together the wide variety of sources make possible what I think is a new assessment of carrier operations in the Pacific from December 1941 to July 1942. For the first time there are comprehensive accounts of the aerial combat in these legendary carrier actions. Equally important is an analysis of how the carrier fighting squadrons were manned and equipped, offering a case study of how prewar tactical ideas and materiel had to be readapted for war, matching them in early 1942 against the best pilots the Japanese would have to offer. Finally, this book is meant to chronicle the service of the men themselves, their triumphs, trials, and tribulations that contributed to victory in the Pacific. Even as the Royal Air Force had its "Few," so did the U.S. Navy place its hopes for victory on the shoulders of a small number of aviators. The reader will probably be surprised how often the same men appear in combat after combat. It is for them in particular that I have written this book.

Acknowledgments

This book would not exist but for the interest, assistance, and encouragement of many individuals, foremost among them retired Navy men who fought in the carrier battles I have described. Indeed, the idea for this project arose during a 1973 interview with Rear Admiral William N. Leonard, and I doubt at the time he knew what he was in for. Commenting upon almost every draft, Bill has helped it grow (metastasize might be a better word!) from a short article to its present scope. Whenever I have needed his recollections or clarification of a technical point, he has enthusiastically responded. Another whose kind assistance did a great deal to launch this study was the late Admiral John S. Thach. In October 1974 I spent a delightful four days as a guest in the Thach home, going over in detail with the admiral his most distinguished career as a fighter pilot. A second trip that year involved a visit with Captain E. Scott McCuskey, and Scott has remained a good friend ever since. Other naval officers who responded to my early call for help were Vice Admiral H. S. Duckworth, Rear Admirals Oscar Pederson and A. O. ("Scoop") Vorse, Captains Brainard T. Macomber, William S. Woollen, John P. Adams, W. E. Rawie, Burt Stanley, and James G. Daniels (the last three with the loan of excellent personal diaries), Commanders Tom F. Cheek, John B. Bain, and George F. Markham, and Lieutenant Commander E. Duran Mattson. Many other participants have immeasurably aided my research, and a full list of them is given in the bibliography.

Anyone undertaking naval research has reason to thank the staff of the Naval History Division's Operational Archives Branch under Dr. Dean C. Allard, and his advice and encouragement for my research are deeply appreciated. The key documents repose there, well-organized and accessible. At the National Archives, Dr. Gibson Smith and Elaine Everley of the Navy and Old Army Records Branch introduced me to the Bureau of Aeronautics records and the so-called Flag Files (Record Group 313), which include valuable documents of the Commander, Aircraft, Battle Force, 1941–42. Ever since I happened to meet him by surprise in an elevator of the Milwaukee Public Museum (where I work), Captain Roger Pineau, past director of the Navy Memorial Museum, has given me rich insight into the Imperial Japanese Navy and warm personal interest in my research.

Other students of naval aviation have gone far out of their way to offer me invaluable assistance. Major Bowen P. Weisheit, USMCR (Ret.), director of the Ensign C. Markland Kelly, Jr. Memorial Foundation, has proved very much a kindred spirit and a good friend. He is most generously sharing with me his exhaustive research on Fighting Eight and the rest of the *Hornet* Air Group at the Battle of Midway. His efforts, beginning as they did with piecing out what the fighters did there, demonstrate fully the goal of this book—to throw new light on carrier operations as a whole. The reader will doubtless be surprised by his findings; certainly I was. I have been most fortunate to have close at hand another good friend and expert on naval aviation, Richard M. Hill, who has drafted the aircraft sideviews for this book. A former carrier pilot and specialist in aircraft markings, Dick is another who has offered help and encouragement from the beginning. A naval historian of my generation, so to speak, and also a *compadre* is Barrett Tillman, now with the Champlin Fighter Museum. Barrett and I have helped each other for years, and he was able to use my 1941–42 naval fighter research for his fine book *The Wildcat in WWII*. Other authors I would like to thank for their help include Walter Lord, Frank Olynyk (whose research into naval fighter claims has been phenomenal), Dr. Clark G. Reynolds, Dr. Lloyd Graybar, Dr. Robert E. Barde, Colonel Raymond Toliver, USAF (Ret.), Henry Sakaida, John C. Reilly, and, from Japan, Dr. Hata Ikuhiko, Dr. Izawa Yasuho, and Mr. Takeshita Takami of the War History Office.

Relatives of deceased naval aviators have been most kind in answering my calls for help. Rear Admiral James H. Flatley III has allowed me free access to his father's surviving papers. A distinguished naval aviator like his father, Admiral Flatley has read portions of the manuscript, commenting from the viewpoint of a present-day carrier fighter pilot. Commander Donald A. Lovelace II likewise provided me with a copy of his father's personal diary. It is a moving, highly informative look at carrier life during the early stages of the Pacific War and helps one take some measure of the fine men who lost their lives in that conflict. Commander Lovelace's mother, Mrs. Helen Lovelace Skaer, wrote to me of her first husband's visit home before he reported in May 1942 to Oahu. Immeasurably aiding my research on Edward ("Butch") O'Hare have been his sister, Mrs. Paul V. Palmer, and his daughter, Mrs. Kathleen O'Hare Nye. The family retains many valuable and useful documents relating to him. Mrs. George A. Hopper, Sr. provided me with an excellent portrait of her son, Ensign Hopper, who was killed in VF-3's scramble from the *Yorktown* at Midway. Richard Groves, younger brother of Ensign Stephen Groves, also killed in action on 4 June 1942, sent me information on his brother and the warship recently named for him.

A great deal of new information lies buried in Japanese-language sources, and I am very much indebted to two translators, Ota Tatsuyuki and Dr. Funahashi Akira, for making it available to me. Robert T. Maciolek copied a number of important photographs and has helped reproduce the illustrations. Several of my friends, Ronald Mazurkiewicz, Keith Johannsen, Bruce Cazel, Patrick O'Hare, and Dale Roethig, have served as sounding boards for my new ideas. Two other friends gave of their time and knowledge when this project was just beginning. They are William F. Surgi, Jr. and Kenneth Crawford of the Battle of the Coral Sea Association. Both are veterans of Coral Sea and Midway, and during my first two trips to Washington, D.C. helped me to get around and meet the people I had to know.

For this book (as well as my first in 1976), I have been fortunate in having Constance MacDonald as my editor and Beverly Baum as designer. It has been a pleasure to watch them transform a raw manuscript into the finished product.

Last of all I would like to thank the most important person in my life, my wife Sandy, who married into this project. She drafted most of the maps and sketches. Her constant support and interest have helped me to get over the rough spots and put this into print.

Special Note

All distances are given in nautical miles. Degrees of bearing are True, unless noted (M.) for magnetic. Dates present problems because of the International Date Line. I have tried to indicate with each instance the location to which the date pertains.

Japanese names are rendered in proper usage with surnames first and given names second. The only exception is in citation of Japanese authors for books that have been printed in the West.

In dealing with Japanese aircraft types, I have eschewed use of codenames such as ZEKE, BETTY, KATE, VAL, and so on, which came into general use after late 1942. For this study they are anachronistic. In their place I have used proper Japanese terminology for the main combatant types as well as Japanese model and year descriptions for all Japanese aircraft. The main combatant types and terms are:

English	Japanese	Abbreviation
Carrier fighter	*Kanjō Sentōki*	*Kansen*
Carrier [dive] bomber	*Kanjō Bakugekiki*	*Kanbaku*
Carrier [torpedo] attack plane	*Kanjō Kōgekiki*	*Kankō*
Land attack plane [medium bomber]	*Rikujō Kōgekiki*	*Rikkō*

List of Japanese aircraft mentioned in text

Aichi D3A1 Type 99 carrier bomber	[VAL]
Aichi E13A1 Type 0 reconnaissance floatplane	[JAKE]
Kawanishi E7K2 Type 94 reconnaissance floatplane	[ALF]
Kawanishi H6K4 Type 97 flying boat	[MAVIS]
Mitsubishi A5M4 Type 96 carrier fighter	[CLAUDE]
Mitsubishi A6M2 Type 0 carrier fighter	[ZEKE]
Mitsubishi F1M2 Type 0 observation floatplane	[PETE]
Mitsubishi G3M2 Type 96 land attack plane	[NELL]
Mitsubishi G4M1 Type 1 land attack plane	[BETTY]
Nakajima B5N2 Type 97 carrier attack plane	[KATE]
Nakajima E8N2 Type 95 reconnaissance floatplane	[DAVE]
Yokosuka D4Y1-C Type 2 carrier bomber	[JUDY]

Abbreviations and Special Terms

ABF	Aircraft, Battle Force
ACTG	Advanced Carrier Training Group
AirBatFor	Aircraft, Battle Force
Air Group	Unit with two or more squadrons
AlNav	All Navy
AP	Transport ship
Arrow	Direct out on a True (as opposed to magnetic) heading
A-V(N)	Naval aviator (reserve)
A-V(S)	Aviation service officer (reserve)
Bandit	Enemy aircraft
BB	Battleship
Bogey	Unidentified aircraft
BuAer	Bureau of Aeronautics
BuNav	Bureau of Navigation (later Bureau of Personnel)
Buntaichō	Division officer (command echelon in Imperial Japanese Navy)
BuOrd	Bureau of Ordnance
Buster	Fighter director term, to proceed at best sustained speed
CA	Heavy cruiser
CAP	Combat Air Patrol
CEAG	Commander, *Enterprise* Air Group
CHAG	Commander, *Hornet Air Group* ("Sea Hag")
Chūtai	Japanese aviation unit of six to nine aircraft
Chūtaichō	(Jap.) Commander of a *chūtai*
CinCPac	Commander-in-Chief, Pacific Fleet
CL	Light cruiser
CLAG	Commander, *Lexington* Air Group
CNO	Chief of Naval Operations
CO	Commanding Officer
ComAirBatFor	Commander, Aircraft, Battle Force
ComANZAC	Commander, ANZAC Area
ComCarDiv	Commander, Carrier Division
ComCarPac	Commander, Carriers, Pacific Fleet
ComCruBatFor	Commander, Cruisers, Battle Force
ComCruDiv	Commander, Cruiser Division
ComCruPac	Commander, Cruisers, Pacific Fleet

ComCruScoFor	Commander, Cruisers, Scouting Force
ComCruTF	Commander, Cruisers, Task Force
ComDesDiv	Commander, Destroyer Division
ComDesPac	Commander, Destroyers, Pacific Fleet
ComDesRon	Commander, Destroyer Squadron
CominCh	Commander-in-Chief, U.S. Fleet
ComScoFor	Commander, Scouting Force
CSAG	Commander, *Saratoga* Air Group
CTF	Commander, Task Force
CTG	Commander, Task Group
CTU	Commander, Task Unit
CV	Carrier
CXAM	Type of radar
CYAG	Commander, *Yorktown* Air Group
D	Died
DD	Destroyer
Division	With aircraft, a unit of four to nine planes
DOW	Died of wounds
EO	Engineer Officer
FD	Fighter Director
FDO	Fighter Director Officer
FO	Flight Officer
Hey Rube	Fighter director term ordering return to base
Hikōkitai	(Jap.) Carrier air unit
Hikōtaichō	Air group officer (command echelon in Imperial Japanese Navy)
IAP	Inner Air Patrol
IFF	Identification, Friend or Foe
Kanbaku	(Jap.) Short for *Kanjō Bakugekiki*: Carrier [dive] bomber
Kankō	(Jap.) Short for *Kanjō Kōgekiki*: Carrier [torpedo] attack plane
Kansen	(Jap.) Short for *Kanjō Sentōki*: Carrier fighter
KIA	Killed in action
Kidō Butai	(Jap.) Carrier striking force (literally, mobile force)
Kōkū Butai	Japanese naval air force
Kōkū Sentai	Japanese carrier division or (land-based) air flotilla
Kōkūtai	Japanese land-based naval air group
(M.)	Magnetic
MAG	Marine Air Group
MIA	Missing in action
NAP	Naval Aviation Pilot (U.S. naval designation)
NAS	Naval Air Station
OpNav	Chief of Naval Operations
Ret.	Retired
Rikkō	(Jap.) Short for *Rikujō Kōgekiki*: Land attack plane (medium bomber)
SecNav	Secretary of the Navy
Section	With aircraft, a unit of two to four planes
Shōtai	Japanese aviation unit of two to four planes (usually three)
Shōtaichō	(Jap.) Commander of a *shōtai*
Special Service	(Jap.) Officer promoted from enlisted man
Squadron	With aircraft, a unit of 18 to 36 planes
(T.)	True
Tally Ho	Fighter director term for making an intercept

TF	Task Force
TG	Task Group
TU	Task Unit
USN	U.S. Navy (referring to personnel—regular Navy)
USNA	U.S. Naval Academy (Annapolis)
USNR	U.S. Naval Reserve
VB	Bombing, dive bomber (often used for any bomber)
Vector	Direct out on a magnetic (as opposed to True) heading
VF	Fighting, fighter
VMF	Marine fighting, fighter
VMSB	Marine scouting
VOS	Observation floatplane
VP	Patrol, patrol plane (usually flying boat)
VS	Scouting, scout plane (usually dive bomber)
VSB	Scout bomber (dive bomber)
VT	Torpedo, torpedo plane
WD	War Diary
XO	Executive Officer
YE	Homing signal and transmitter
Zed	Condition of readiness just below general quarters
Zed Baker	(ZB) Homing signal receiver

Ranks Used in Text

(a) Commissioned:

ADM	Admiral
VADM	Vice Admiral
RADM	Rear Admiral
Capt.	Captain
Cdr.	Commander
Lt.Cdr.	Lieutenant Commander
Lieut.	Lieutenant
Lieut. (jg)	Lieutenant (junior grade)
Ens.	Ensign
W.O.	Warrant Officer

In U.S. Navy

Gun.	Gunner
Mach.	Machinist
Rad. Elec.	Radio Electrician

(b) Enlisted Ratings (Petty Officers):
  Aviation Ordnance Man: Chief (ACOM), AOM1c, AOM2c, AOM3c
  Aviation Machinist's Mate: Chief (ACMM), AMM1c, AMM2c, AMM3c
*Aviation Pilot: Chief (CAP), AP1c, AP2c
  Aviation Radioman: Chief (ACRM), ARM1c, ARM2c, ARM3c
  Radioman: Chief (CRM), RM1c, RM2c, RM3c
  Japanese: Aviation Petty Officer, PO1c, PO2c, PO3c
(c) Nonrated Men:
  Seaman, 1st Class (Sea1c); Seaman 2nd Class (Sea2c)
  Japanese: Aviation Seaman, 1st Class, Aviation Seaman, 2nd Class

*Reestablished 17 March 1942.

The First Team

PART I

The Early Operations

CHAPTER 1

Introduction to War

THE FIGHTING SQUADRONS: MISSIONS, MEN, AND AIRCRAFT

For the pilots of Fighting Squadron Six (VF-6), the change in orders circulated late on the afternoon of 27 November 1941 raised a few eyebrows. Operating temporarily out of NAS (Naval Air Station) Pearl Harbor, old Luke Field covering most of Ford Island in the center of Pearl Harbor, the squadron labored mightily to ready itself for another bout of training on board the aircraft carrier USS *Enterprise* (CV-6). Lt. Cdr. C. Wade McClusky, VF-6's skipper, had nineteen Grumman F4F-3 and F4F-3A Wildcat carrier fighters on strength, but the *Enterprise*'s air department told him to bring the next day only sixteen of them out to the ship. For this cruise the carrier would not have deck space for more of the fixed-wing Grummans, because marine aviators were coming on board with twelve F4F-3s of their own for "special experimental work."[1] The leatherneck pilots were fully carrier-qualified, but their sudden deployment on board the *Enterprise* was sufficiently unusual to excite comment. Scuttlebutt within Fighting Six decreed that the *Enterprise* was going to deliver the marine fighters to lonely Wake Island 2,000 miles west of Oahu.

For once rumor was entirely correct despite stringent security precautions. The situation in the Pacific had grown demonstrably tenser by mid-November 1941. The United States and Japan, hitherto not active participants in the European war, glowered at each other across the vast expanse of ocean. For the United States Pacific Fleet, based at Pearl Harbor, it was a race against time to surmount seemingly ubiquitous shortages of trained manpower and materiel and prepare for the war that appeared ever more likely as the ominous autumn of 1941 counted down. Mindful of the grave danger to the Philippines and the rest of the Far East should Japan attack, Admiral Harold R. Stark, Chief of Naval Operations (CNO), stressed the defense of the American island bases of Wake and Midway. To protect these vital outposts, Admiral Husband E. Kimmel, Commander-in-Chief, Pacific Fleet (CinCPac), sought to use Army Air Force pursuit squadrons to operate there. The Army, however, was reluctant to base its fighters on isolated small islands, as its pilots lacked the training for extended over-water flights.

When the Army refused to provide fighters, Kimmel had to turn to the slender resources of his Marine Air Group 21 (MAG-21) for fighters and scout bombers with which to garrison Wake and Midway. The swiftest means of ferrying these short-ranged aircraft to their distant destinations was to take them on board aircraft carriers of the Pacific Fleet for transport to within flight range of the islands. That put the problem squarely onto the shoulders of Vice Admiral William F. Halsey, the senior naval aviator in the Pacific Fleet. His imposing title was: Commander, Aircraft, Battle Force (abbreviated ComAirBatFor), and he had charge of the three carriers, their air groups, and related activities ashore. To those on board his flagship *Enterprise*, he was known (but not to his face) as "Wild Bill," for both his strong personality and his impressive appearance. An old destroyerman, Halsey was a latecomer to naval aviation. Already wearing the four stripes of a captain, he earned his wings in 1935 and embraced carrier aviation with the same enthusiasm and dash accorded the other great loves of his life. Ironically, he would miss the two carrier battles of spring 1942, to his deep disappointment.

On 27 November, Kimmel and Halsey decided to use the *Enterprise* to transport twelve marine fighters to Wake. They would come from Major Paul A. Putnam's Marine Fighting Squadron 211 (VMF-211) based at the Marine Corps Air Station at Ewa near Barbers Point on Oahu. To reinforce Midway, Kimmel turned to his other available flattop, the *Lexington* (CV-2). Still completing her overhaul at Bremerton in Washington State was the *Saratoga* (CV-3). She was slated early in December to sail south to San Diego to collect her air group training there and would be available to bring a second marine fighting squadron out to Oahu.

Operationally within the Pacific Fleet, Halsey commanded Task Force 2, a tactical grouping of battleships, cruisers, and destroyers centered around his flagship *Enterprise*. Originally the task force was to undertake tactical exercises in Hawaiian waters, but the secret mission changed that. In addition, the *Enterprise* Air Group was to work on night carrier landings, something to ponder for those pilots who had not yet attempted landing on board after dark. Early on the morning of 28 November, *Enterprise* pilots and aircrews left the ship moored in Pearl Harbor to man their aircraft parked at the naval air station field on Ford Island. The *Enterprise* herself stood out to sea just after dawn along with the rest of Task Force 2. Once away from land, Halsey separated the carrier, three heavy cruisers, and nine destroyers, designating them Task Force 8. They were bound for Wake and awaited only the aircraft due to fly out from Oahu.

Later that morning at NAS Pearl Harbor, eighty-three aircraft from five squadrons were readied to fly out to the *Enterprise*. First to depart were the thirty-seven Douglas SBD-2 and SBD-3 Dauntless dive bombers. Eighteen each of the thick-winged, two-seat dive bombers made up Bombing Squadron Six (VB-6) and Scouting Squadron Six (VS-6), while the 37th SBD was the air group commander's personal aircraft. The SBDs conducted searches and executed dive bombing attacks against ship and land targets. Although the two squadrons were known by different titles, bombing and scouting, there was actually little real difference in their function or employment. While the Dauntlesses circled and joined into formation, the fighter pilots manned their stubby Wildcats: sixteen from Fighting Six and twelve from VMF-211. Two pilots, one marine and the other naval, discovered to their mutual disgust that their engines would not start. Emergency measures by anxious machinist mates availed them nothing, and the two marooned aviators had to hustle over to the last component of the *Enterprise* Air Group, held to the last for just such a contingency. This was Torpedo Squadron Six (VT-6) with eighteen Douglas TBD-1 Devastators. Aged and nearing obsolescence, the TBDs with their aerial torpedoes comprised the main shipwrecking potential of the air group and also served as horizontal bombers. Open middle seats in two of the torpedo planes beckoned the two fighter pilots, and soon all eighty-one flyable aircraft were aloft and en route to the carrier. Standing alone in mute frustration were the two balky Wildcats left behind on Ford Island for repairs.

After a short flight, the air group located the *Enterprise* steaming off the Oahu coast and broke formation in order to land on the flattop now heading briskly into the wind. "The Big E," as she was affectionately nicknamed, was a massive warship (displacing 25,500 tons at war load) fashioned in the form of a self-supporting, highly mobile airfield. Her weathered wooden flight deck, 825 feet in length, together with the capacious hangar beneath, accommodated the seventy-odd aircraft of her air group. Her dive bombers, torpedo planes, and fighters constituted the main battery—the reason for her existence. All of the aircraft landed without incident.

When the pilots assembled in their respective squadron ready rooms, they had a little surprise. "Wild Bill" demonstrated that he meant business this cruise. The *Enterprise*'s Captain George D. Murray had at the admiral's direction issued "Battle Order Number One."[2] This placed the ship under "war conditions" and indicated that if the task force encountered hostile (read, Japanese) warships or aircraft, the Americans would shoot to prevent any interference with the primary mission at hand, Wake's reinforcement. Just before sailing, Kimmel had shared with Halsey a message from Stark warning CinCPac of the imminence of war. All clues vouchsafed to Washington pointed to invasion threats against Southeast Asia and the Philippines, not eastward toward the Hawaiian Islands. Halsey himself did not think the Japanese fleet would operate even as eastward as Wake, but he was taking no chances. Task Force 8's course took it just north of Japanese bases in the Marshall Islands. The *Enterprise* Air Group received orders to arm planes: bombs for dive bombers, torpedoes for the TBDs, and a full load of .50-caliber machine gun bullets for VF-6's Grummans.

Only after landing on board did Putnam's pilots learn they were bound for desolate Wake, and none had along any personal gear other than his flight kit. Putnam alone had known beforehand of their secret destination. Fighting Six in return "adopted" their friends in VMF-211 and tried to make the voyage a pleasant one for them. The marines had flown their Wildcats for only a month or so, and they had many questions about their new mounts. Specialists from Fighting Six swarmed over the marine fighters to ensure they were in top condition. When the admiral learned Putnam was short one Grumman, he told Fighting Six to "sell" one of its own F4F-3s to VMF-211 to restore the detachment to an even dozen. This left McClusky with fourteen Wildcats for the balance of the cruise. Somewhat taken aback by the Navy's solicitous behavior, Putnam remarked in a letter to his commanding officer at Ewa that he felt like the "fatted calf"[3] being prepared for the feast. In light of the fate that befell gallant VMF-211 at Wake, Putnam's analogy was not far off.

On the trip out, Fighting Six did not fly but stood Condition II (or "Zed II") alerts. Under this procedure, a division of four fighters took turns waiting on deck, pilots sitting in the cockpits, their engines warmed and ready to go. "The Big E" kept her dive bombers busy searching 300 miles ahead of the task force. Halsey's battle order and obvious attention to detail highlighted the importance and possible danger of this mission. Wake lay within bombing range (700 miles) of Japanese airfields in the Marshalls. The outward leg of the voyage, however, went so smoothly that the thought of imminent war was hard to sustain. The ships followed the diplomatic news by radio, noting the mission of special envoy Kurusu Saburo to Washington. Of more immediate concern was the fact that they crossed the International Date Line, which mysteriously did away with 2 December. For most it was the first time they had encountered this phenomenon, which would soon become commonplace for them.

Early on Thursday, 4 December, Task Force 8 neared the waters 200 miles east of Wake. Fighting Six turned out before dawn and flew its first combat air patrol of the voyage. The Grummans handled differently with the unaccustomed weight of 1800 rounds of .50-caliber ammunition per fighter. About 0700, the twelve marine fighters took off for Wake, but they failed to make contact with their escorts, seven SBDs sent aloft by the *Enterprise*. Fortunately one of the Navy's Consolidated PBY Catalina flying boats, temporarily operating out of Wake, chaperoned VMF-211 to the island. The leathernecks left with the good wishes of all of VF-6 and also with some thoughtful gifts, including at least one bottle of Scotch scrounged from a secret hoard on board the carrier.

Task Force 8's mission accomplished, Halsey turned eastward for another encounter with the date line (and two 5 Decembers). The only excitement on this part of the voyage came on the second 5 December. That morning VF-6's executive officer, Lieut. Frank T. Corbin, led an inner air patrol of fighters on the lookout for enemy submarines. Making his landing approach, he found his tail hook would not extend, preventing him from catching the arresting wires and stopping the F4F on deck. While he circled overhead, "The Big E" worked up to 20 knots, which with a brisk wind gave him 47 knots of wind over the deck. Corbin brought his fighter in and slowed without damage. That evening stronger winds forced Halsey to reduce fleet speed to 15 knots to make things easier for the destroyers bucking stiff winds and turbulent seas. He hoped the weather would not significantly delay his anticipated time of arrival back at Pearl. That was set for Sunday morning, 7 December.

Their Wake mission nearly behind them, now is a good opportunity to take a closer look at Fighting Squadron Six.[4] Formed on 1 July 1935 as Fighting One (VF-1B), the squadron first served aboard the old *Langley* (CV-1) before switching the next year for temporary duty on the far more commodious *Lexington*. Then came a new designation, Fighting Eight (VF-8B), and a new ship, the carrier *Enterprise*, then under construction. On 1 July 1937, the Navy reorganized its carrier squadrons, hoping to reduce confusion by designating them according to the hull numbers of their assigned ships. Thus Fighting Eight became Fighting Six, and the squadron insignia was a blazing red comet racing across the heavens. With the commissioning in 1938 of "The Big E," Fighting Six happily operated from the fleet's most modern flattop. In May 1939, the *Enterprise* came out to the Pacific. Fighting Six in May 1941 became the first Pacific Fleet squadron to convert from Grumman F3F-2 biplanes to Grumman F4F Wildcats, taking delivery of eighteen F4F-3As. That summer and fall the squadron worked hard to shake down the new monoplanes and get them combat-ready.

Fighting Six comprised nineteen pilots who not only flew the aircraft, but with the squadron's 120-odd enlisted men maintained the fighters in fully operational condition. Within the naval aviation squadrons were two parallel forms of organization, one scheme for flight operations and the other for administration of the squadron "on the ground." The 1941 fighting squadron had a nominal operating strength of eighteen fighters, divided for flight purposes into three divisions of six planes each, led respectively by the commanding officer, the executive officer, and the flight officer. The divisions in turn were subdivided into three sections each of two aircraft—the basic component of section leader and wingman. In July 1941 the Navy had finally gone over to two-plane sections, replacing the more cumbersome section of three aircraft. Rank did not always determine whether a pilot acted as section leader; that generally depended on flying experience and ability.

In command of Fighting Six was Lt. Cdr. Clarence Wade McClusky.[5] At thirty-nine he was advanced in age as an active fighter pilot, given the standards of that time. A 1926 graduate of the United States Naval Academy, McClusky earned his wings in 1929 and joined an earlier Fighting One [VF-1B, the "High Hats," later Bombing Three (VB-3)] for duty on board the *Saratoga*. Thereafter he saw service in patrol and battleship observation planes, but during much of the 1930s, McClusky held staff posts and taught at the Naval Academy. In June 1940, he reported to Fighting Six on board the *Enterprise* and soon became executive officer. A year later he "fleeted up" to skipper of the outfit. As CO, he was totally responsible for all operations and activities of the squadron. In the naval hierarchy, his post was equivalent to that of captain of a small warship, such as a destroyer or submarine, and within the squadron, the CO was called "captain." Level-headed, personable, and direct, Wade McClusky ran his squadron well. Ironically the mission that brought him immortality saw him flying a dive bomber instead of a fighter.

The executive officer was Lieut. Frank Corbin, who had safely landed his hook-less fighter on 5 December. A member of the 1927 Naval Academy class, Corbin first tried his hand at submarine duty before he decided he would rather soar above the waves than cruise beneath them. His wings followed in 1936, and he flew battleship floatplanes, then spent a year with Scouting Two (VS-2) on board the *Lexington*. From 1939 to 1941 he instructed fledgling pilots at NAS Pensacola, reporting in mid-1941 to Fighting Six for his first squadron duty in fighters. As second-in-command, he saw to the smooth running of the squadron.

Third in the squadron hierarchy was the flight officer, Lieut. (jg) James S. Gray, Jr. A civilian pilot while still in high school, Gray graduated in 1936 from the Naval Academy and resumed flying once he completed his obligatory tour of sea duty. In July 1939 he earned his wings of gold and a welcome posting to Fighting Six, where he rose steadily from green wingman to flight officer. Gray took his trade seriously and became a specialist on aerial gunnery. In 1941 he wrote a fundamental manual on gunnery for fighter pilots. Tall, confident, and handsome, he would achieve squadron command soon after the outbreak of the war. As flight officer, he prepared flight schedules according to available pilots and aircraft and saw to the training of junior pilots.

Other important squadron departments included engineering and gunnery. Fighting Six's engineering officer was Lieut. (jg) Roger W. Mehle (USNA 1937), who, together with his line chiefs, plane captains, and mechanics, ensured the readiness and mechanical reliability of the aircraft. The gunnery officer was Lieut. (jg) Francis Frederick ("Fritz") Hebel, in charge of machine guns, ammunition, gunsights, and other ordnance-related materiel. Completing the list of departments were communications, materiel, and personnel. Senior pilots headed each, with junior pilots and enlisted men to assist. Together they comprised a nearly autonomous fighting unit capable of operating at sea or from a land base.

Of the nineteen pilots currently on strength with Fighting Six, nearly half—nine—were graduates of the "trade school," the Naval Academy. They included a batch of five from the class of 1938 who had completed flight training in early 1941 and still were learning the ropes. Of the remaining ten, four were veterans of the old aviation cadet program (1935 to 1939, see appendix) and already held regular commissions. Of the squadron's six reservists, all but one had been on board for at least six months, and most had a year or more in fighters. The men of McClusky's outfit were efficient and somewhat cocky because they knew they were good. Like all the U.S. Navy's fighter pilots, they had enjoyed the benefits of gunnery training superior to that of any air force in the world. They learned the

VF-6, 24 Jan. 1942, *l to r standing:* Rawie, Hodson, Heisel, Provost, Flynn, Grimmell, Presley, Rich, Daniels, Criswell, Holt, Hiebert, Bayers, Hermann; *seated:* Quady, Hoyle, Corbin, McClusky, Gray, Mehle, Kelley. (Capt. W. E. Rawie, USN.)

art of deflection shooting, the skill of estimating the proper lead to hit their targets from the side, above, or below, not merely from ahead or astern. This enabled them to utilize deadly overhead and high-side firing passes—complex gunnery runs that largely negated return fire from enemy bomber formations and repositioned the fighters for another pass. Fighting Six would see considerable combat early in the war, but their chance for real glory would elude them in the Battle of Midway.

Also taking part in Kimmel's reinforcement plans was the *Lex*, the grand old veteran of the carrier fleet. In service since 1927, the *Lexington* and her sister the *Saratoga* were the longest warships afloat, each nearly 900 feet in length, their flight decks perched above converted battle cruiser hulls. They became the epitome of American carrier aviation, representing a quantum jump from the hard-working but lowly *Langley*. For this operation the *Lexington* would transport eighteen Vought SB2U-3 Vindicator scout bombers from Marine Scouting Squadron 231 (VMSB-231) from Oahu to Midway. The *Lexington*'s crew geared up to depart on 5 December for what they thought was another training cruise. The afternoon of 3 December, however, CinCPac cut orders for Rear Admiral John H. Newton to take the *Lexington*, three heavy cruisers, and five destroyers (together designated as Task Force 12) westward from Oahu to a point 400 miles southeast of Midway. There at 1130 on 7 December, the *Lexington* was to send the dive bombers to Midway. Newton led the *Lexington* force in place of his superior, Vice Admiral Wilson Brown, who was Commander, Scouting Force (ComScoFor). Brown with

Roster of Pilots, Fighting Six, 1 December 1941

Lt. Cdr.	Clarence Wade McClusky	USN	USNA 1926
Lieut.	Frank T. Corbin	USN	USNA 1927
Lieut. (jg)	James S. Gray, Jr.	USN	USNA 1936
Lieut. (jg)	Roger W. Mehle	USN	USNA 1937
Lieut. (jg)	Francis Frederick Hebel	USN	
Lieut. (jg)	Eric Allen, Jr.	USN	USNA 1938
Lieut. (jg)	Rhonald J. Hoyle	USN	USNA 1938
Lieut. (jg)	Frank B. Quady	USN	USNA 1938
Lieut. (jg)	Wilmer E. Rawie	USN	USNA 1938
Ens.	John C. Kelley	USN	USNA 1938
Ens.	James G. Daniels III	USN	
Ens.	Gayle L. Hermann	USN	
Ens.	Harold N. Heisel	USN	
Ens.	Thomas C. Provost III	A-V(N)	
Ens.	Herbert H. Menges	A-V(N)	
Ens.	David R. Flynn	A-V(N)	
Ens.	Ralph M. Rich	A-V(N)	
Ens.	Walter J. Hiebert	A-V(N)	
Ens.	Norman D. Hodson	A-V(N)	

other elements of his Task Force 3 headed for Johnston Island to conduct amphibious training exercises.

The morning of 5 December the *Lexington* eased out of her berth in Pearl Harbor, joined her consorts, and headed out to sea. A few hours later, the eighteen marine Vindicators landed on board, followed at 1100 by the first aircraft of the *Lexington* Air Group. Swinging into the landing circle were the eighteen Brewster F2A-3 Buffalo fighters of Fighting Squadron Two (VF-2) led by Lt. Cdr. Paul H. Ramsey. During recovery, the F2A-3 flown by Clayton Allard, AMM1c (NAP), came in high, floated over the deck arresting wires, and slammed into the barrier. Allard suffered only minor facial cuts, but his battered Brewster[6] had to go over the side into the sea to make room for the rest of the air group. With the *Lexington*'s own sixty-five aircraft and the eighteen marine dive bombers, even the *Lex*'s massive flight deck became congested. Unlike the latest flattops, she possessed only two flight deck elevators, and her air officer as a matter of course parked most of the aircraft on deck. Unlike Halsey, Newton was not informed of the "war warning" message and took no extraordinary measures other than routine security precautions. Consequently Task Force 12's voyage lacked, for the outward leg, the crisis atmosphere that spiced Task Force 8's run to Wake.

Fighting Squadron Two had by 1941 attained the status of a quasi-institution within the Navy.[7] Unlike the other carrier squadrons, the majority of VF-2's pilots were enlisted men with the designation of "naval aviation pilot" (NAP) as opposed to officer pilots who were "naval aviators." Organized in January 1927 as an experiment to test the effectiveness of using enlisted pilots, Fighting Two evolved into one of the Navy's elite outfits. The NAPs were determined to show the officers and everyone else how good they were. Their record was most enviable. In late 1940, for example, all eighteen fighter aircraft sported the "E" awarded for individual pilot excellence—the first time an entire squadron qualified simultaneously for that coveted honor. Just to enter the unit, competition was incredibly stiff. Appropriately, the squadron insignia was the old rating badge of a chief aviation pilot (equivalent to a chief petty officer, but abolished in 1933 as a rating), and

VF-2, 19 Dec. 1941, *l to r top row:* Allard, Carmody, Packard, Borries, Flatley, Ramsey, Bauer, Simpson, Rinehart, Barnes, Brooks; *bottom row:* Achten, Brewer, Cheek, White, Sumrall, Rutherford, Firebaugh, Baker, Gay, Runyon. (Cdr. Tom F. Cheek, USN.)

below the stripes the word "Adorimini!" (a sometime Roman legionary battle cry loosely translated as "Up and at 'em!").

On 1 December the pilot strength of Fighting Two comprised six officers and sixteen NAPs. Before the squadron was fated to see heavy combat, the powers that be had transferred all but three officers and one NAP to other units, a great pity because the squadron had become a well-trained team with its NAPs. The commanding officer was Lt. Cdr. Ramsey (USNA 1927), and his executive officer was Lieut. James H. Flatley, Jr. (USNA 1929). Number three in the hierarchy was Lieut. Louis H. Bauer (USNA 1935), the flight officer. Of the remaining three officers, Lieut. (jg) Fred Borries, Jr. was a Naval Academy graduate (1935), while the other two, Lieut. (jg) Fred H. Simpson and Ens. Clark F. Rinehart, were veterans of the pre-1939 aviation cadet program. Fighting Two's officers were all highly experienced flyers.

The sixteen NAPs were all petty officers: chiefs, first or second class, with the ratings of aviation machinist or radioman. All had been in the Navy for at least five years, but they were not as old as some sources have alleged (their average age said to be 39!).[8] Most were in their late twenties or early thirties, having received flight training in 1935 or later. After the war broke out, the chiefs received direct promotions to temporary rank of lieutenant (junior grade), while most of the rest fleeted up to warrant rank. Unlike prewar practice when warrant officers did not fly, the VF-2 machinists, gunners, and radio electricians retained their flight status. Although most did not see combat with Fighting Two, they ended up in other combat units, notably Fighting Six and Fighting Three, where they definitely made their presence welcome.

Fighting Two possessed another distinction, this one rather dubious, however. The unit was the only carrier fighting squadron still equipped with Brewster F2A Buffalo fighters. To understand why this state of affairs was detrimental to VF-2's combat effectiveness requires a discussion of naval fighter policy.[9] In the late 1930s, the U.S. Navy cautiously considered the merits of two competing monoplane fighters for service on board carriers. A true carrier fighter is not simply a land plane with a tail hook dangling from its tail. Many factors involved in sea service had to be considered. For one thing, a carrier fighter had to be robust to take repeated jolts when thudding in for a landing, when the tail hook snagged the arresting wire and jerked the aircraft violently. Pilot visibility was another important factor. When

Roster of Pilots, Fighting Two, 1 December 1941

Lt. Cdr. Paul H. Ramsey		USN	USNA 1927
Lieut. James H. Flatley, Jr.		USN	USNA 1929
Lieut. Louis H. Bauer		USN	USNA 1935
Lieut. (jg) Fred Borries, Jr.		USN	USNA 1935
Lieut. (jg) Fred H. Simpson		USN	
Ens. Clark F. Rinehart		USN	
Harold E. Rutherford	ACMM	USN	NAP
Gordon E. Firebaugh	ACMM	USN	NAP
Theodore S. Gay, Jr.	ACMM	USN	NAP
Paul G. Baker	CRM	USN	NAP
George W. Brooks	RM1c	USN	NAP
Charles E. Brewer	RM1c	USN	NAP
Doyle C. Barnes	AMM1c	USN	NAP
Howell M. Sumrall	AMM1c	USN	NAP
Donald E. Runyon	AMM1c	USN	NAP
Patrick L. Nagle	AMM1c	USN	NAP
Tom F. Cheek	AMM1c	USN	NAP
Julius A. Achten	AMM1c	USN	NAP
Clayton Allard	AMM1c	USN	NAP
Harry T. Carmody	AMM1c	USN	NAP
George A. White	AMM2c	USN	NAP
Howard S. Packard	AMM2c	USN	NAP

making his carrier landing (actually a form of controlled stall), the pilot had to be able to see over his aircraft's nose. Experience dictated that air-cooled, radial engines were superior for carrier fighters to the long, liquid-cooled inline engines. All of these attributes made for a fighter design that was heavier and less streamlined with slightly inferior performance compared to its counterparts intended solely for land-based operations.

In 1936, the Navy's Bureau of Aeronautics let out two contracts for prototype monoplane carrier fighters. One went to the Brewster Aeronautical Corporation for its XF2A-1 fighter design. The other the Navy awarded to the Grumman Aircraft Engineering Corporation for the XF4F-2 fighter. Once they had tested the two prototypes, the Navy would decide between the two designs. Brewster based its XF2A-1 around the Wright R-1820 nine-cylinder radial engine rated at 950 horse-power. The XF2A-1 made its first flight in December 1937. Meanwhile, Grumman adopted the Pratt & Whitney R-1830 series engine, a fourteen-cylinder, twin-row radial design. Grumman's entry, the XF4F-2, first flew in September 1937. After extensive testing, in June 1938 the Bureau of Aeronautics awarded a contract to Brewster for fifty-four F2A-1 fighters.

Now Brewster had the ball, but they were unable to score. Beset with management problems, Brewster experienced production difficulties that disastrously slowed the delivery of the new fighters, not endearing the company with the Navy. In all of 1939, Brewster delivered only eleven F2A-1 fighters. In December of that year, Fighting Squadron Three (VF-3) received nine F2A-1s, sufficient to reequip only half the squadron, which retained nine Grumman F3F-1 biplane fighters as well. An engine change led to the production in 1940 of the F2A-2 version, nine of which in October went to Fighting Three. That same month, Fighting Two turned in the Grumman F2F biplanes the unit had flown since 1935 and obtained F2A-2 fighters in their place. Brewster produced a total of forty-three F2A-2s for the Navy.

While Brewster failed to meet production quotas, the Grumman Corporation revamped the XF4F-2 to produce in February 1939 the greatly improved XF4F-3 fighter. As the new design's powerplant, Grumman utilized the Pratt & Whitney R-1830-76 fourteen-cylinder radial engine rated at 1200 horsepower. An important feature of that engine was a two-stage supercharger providing much-improved performance at high altitude. The Navy liked what it saw, and on 8 August 1939 gave Grumman a contract for fifty-four F4F-3 fighters. The new Grummans began coming off the production lines in the summer of 1940, most for the hard-pressed Royal Navy. Quantity production to fill American contracts began in December 1940, and first deliveries to Fighting Four (VF-4) and Fighting Seven (VF-7) took place on the East Coast around the end of the year.

By 1941 the Navy had two monoplane carrier fighters in service, but decided to go with the Grumman F4F-3 as the principal design. Lieut. John S. Thach's Fighting Three in August 1941 happily traded their F2A-2s for Grumman F4F-3 Wildcats. Lt. Cdr. Ramsey's Fighting Two, on the other hand, would have to stay with the Brewster Buffalo for the time being. In September, he took delivery of the latest model, the F2A-3. The Brewster F2A-3 Buffalo was a midwing monoplane powered by the Wright R-1820-40 nine-cylinder radial engine rated at 1200 hp. Weight empty for the aircraft was 4,894 lbs., and the plane grossed 7,253 lbs. at full load. Top speed was 278 knots (320 mph) at 14,500 feet. Climb rate from sea level was initially 2,440 feet per minute; time to 10,000 feet was 4.6 minutes (average of 2,174 feet per minute) and to 20,000 feet, 10.2 minutes (average 1,961 feet per minute). [These performance figures as for all aircraft varied slightly per individual aircraft and are meant only as a guide.] The Brewster sported only a single-stage supercharger, so high altitude performance fell off rapidly. Range was 1,190 miles at 149 knots cruise. Normal fuel capacity was 160 gallons, half carried in self-sealing fuel tanks. A CO_2 system flooded the other tanks with carbon dioxide to prevent fires. The aircraft featured armor plate and an armored windscreen to protect the pilot. Armament was four .50-caliber machine guns (two in the wings and two over the engine) with 325 rounds per gun. Two 100-lb. bombs could also be carried.

On paper at any rate, the Brewster F2A-3's statistics look little different from those of the Grumman F4F-3, to be described below. When first produced, the Brewster F2A-1 was an excellent aerobatic aircraft, a delight to fly. The Finns used that model Brewster for several years against the Soviets with good success. However, by the time the F2A-3 came into service, much additional weight had seriously compromised the original design. The F2A-3, for example, had the same powerplant as the F2A-2, but weighed 500 lbs. more. This greatly reduced maneuverability and worsened flight characteristics when compared with earlier versions of the F2A. Airframe design did not permit installation of a more powerful engine. The fighter did not prove as rugged as hoped, and there was a growing tendency for the landing struts to fail. The naval pilots also intensely distrusted the quality of manufacture of the Brewster products and discovered what looked like actual examples of sabotage done at the factory. Under such circumstances, they were reluctant to fly Brewster's airplanes. When the shooting began in the Pacific, Fighting Two was the only carrier squadron saddled with Brewsters, and they were anxious to convert to Grumman Wildcats.

Mainstay of the carrier fighting squadrons through the crucial eighteen months following Pearl Harbor was the Grumman F4F Wildcat in its various models. Squat, deep-bellied, and angular—with its distinctive, knock-knee, narrow landing gear— the F4F, along with superior combat tactics and gunnery, proved ultimately more than a match for Japanese Mitsubishi Zero fighters. The F4F-3 came in several variants, differing mainly in engine models. Basic dimensions for all variants included a wingspan of 38 feet and an overall length of 28 feet, 11 inches. Original-

Gordon Firebaugh, ACMM, and VF-2 F2A-3 Buffalo on board the *Lexington*, 19 Dec. 1941. (Capt. G. E. Firebaugh, USN.)

production F4F-3s—lacking as yet the pilot armor and self-sealing fuel tanks added mainly after the outbreak of war—had a gross weight of 7,065 lbs. The performance figures cited here are for the later production run with the R-1830-86 Pratt & Whitney radial engine, rated at 1200 hp, with pilot armor and self-sealing fuel tanks already fitted (gross weight about 7,450 lbs.). Top speed was 286 knots (329 mph) at 21,100 feet. Initial climb rate was 2,460 feet per minute; time to 10,000 feet was 4.6 minutes (average 2,174 feet per minute), to 20,000 feet, 10.3 minutes (average 1,942 feet per minute). The original version without armor or leakproof tanks was almost 400 lbs. lighter and enjoyed a slightly higher performance.

As designed, the F4F-3 featured a two-stage engine supercharger for high-altitude work, but the systems experienced teething troubles. In order not to be compromised by delays such as plagued Brewster, the Navy in March 1941 began taking delivery of sixty-five so-called F4F-3As. These were F4F-3 fighters fitted instead with the Pratt & Whitney R-1830-90 engine sporting a conventional single-stage supercharger. Original gross weight was 6,876 lbs., but when self-sealing tanks and armor were fitted, weight increased to about 7,200 lbs. Performance with the additions was: top speed 275 knots (317 mph) at 16,100 feet. Initial climb rate was 2,170 feet per minute; time to 10,000 feet was 4.8 minutes (average 2,083 feet per minute, to 20,000, 11.2 minutes (average 1,786 feet per minute). In general, performance was a little less sharp than that of the standard F4F-3, and the pilots preferred the -3s when they could get them.

Both the F4F-3s and F4F-3As as designed carried 160 gallons of gasoline in two aluminum tanks (main and reserve). In late 1941, the squadrons on the East Coast began receiving new leak-proof main fuel tanks—bladderlike, rubber contraptions that, when installed in place of the metal main tanks, offered unparalleled fire protection, but at the cost of reducing the fuel carried to 144 gallons. With self-sealing fuel tanks, the nominal range for the F4F-3 was 816 miles at 130 knots. In practical terms this meant a combat radius of about 200 miles from a carrier, but the pilots themselves did not know precisely how far they could go in an F4F-3 and return. Cockpit fuel gauges became highly unreliable with the installation of the new tanks, and pilots had to keep careful totals of minutes flown at various power settings to know what their fuel situation currently was. The lighter F4F-3A with its single-stage supercharger was a little better with respect to range. With self-sealing fuel tanks provided, the F4F-3A had a nominal range of about 920 miles at 139 knots. The Navy had not yet given much thought to developing auxiliary fuel tanks for the F4F, and the Wildcat's limited range and endurance would prove troublesome.

As main armament, both the F4F-3 and the F4F-3A featured four Browning .50-caliber M2 machine guns, two in each wing. There were 450 rounds per gun, enough for 34 seconds of fire. The Browning provided the ultimate in high rate of fire and real hitting power, even at long range. The cyclic rate was 700 to 800 rounds per minute, and initial muzzle velocity for the projectile was about 2,900 feet per minute. Unfortunately, in December 1941 the fleet did not yet have an incendiary bullet for the .50-calibers. Most of the F4Fs sported two bomb racks, one under each wing, that could accommodate one 100-lb. bomb each.

When originally delivered, the Grummans did not have factory-installed pilot armor, bullet-proof windscreens, reflector gunsights, or self-sealing fuel tanks. Tactical lessons from the air war over Europe clearly demonstrated the necessity for pilot and fuel tank protection, but most of the fighting squadrons in the Pacific went to war without those vital defenses. Eventually the F4Fs labored under about 135 lbs. of pilot armor installed behind the seat, as well as a windshield of bullet-proof glass. The armor proved to be tough enough to keep out Japanese 7.7-mm bullets and sometimes even the explosive 20-mm cannon shells. Because of the additional weight and its adverse effect on performance, some pilots considered the armor a mixed blessing, but no one who saw an aircraft burst into flames ever complained about self-sealing fuel tanks. The bladderlike tanks absorbed 7.7-mm rounds and prevented leaks, but apparently the 20-mm explosive shells could rip them open.

On 6 December, the last Saturday before the outbreak of war, Halsey's Task Force 8 worked hard bucking 32-knot winds in order to fuel destroyers. During the routine search, one of the torpedo planes spotted the *Lexington* and her consorts on the way out to Midway. That day also, Kimmel reviewed the fleet's war plans should conflict occur in the Far East. He felt, as did the rest of the high command, that Allied holdings in the eastern Pacific would be targets if Japan declared war. In that event, Kimmel planned to use his Pacific Fleet to conduct diversionary raids

	F4F-3	F4F-3A	F2A-3	Total
VF-2 (*Lexington*, at sea)	—	—	17	17
VF-6 (*Enterprise*, at sea)	1	13	—	14
(ashore at NAS Pearl H.)	—	4	—	4
VMF-211 (at Wake Island)	12	—	—	12
(ashore at MCAS Ewa)	11	—	—	11
AirBatFor Pool (at NAS Pearl H.)	4	1	5	10
	28	18	22	68

on Japanese bases in the Marshalls. He would combine the *Lexington* and the *Enterprise* into one striking force under Halsey, but retain the battleships in Hawaiian waters. Carrier fighter status in the Pacific Fleet is in the table.[10]

AIR RAID ON PEARL HARBOR X THIS IS NO DRILL

At dawn on Sunday, 7 December, Halsey's Task Force 8 was still some 215 miles west of Oahu, although the winds had abated for the most part. Halsey planned to send eighteen *Enterprise* SBD dive bombers to search 150 miles ahead of the task force as a normal precaution. Instead of returning to the carrier, the search flight would proceed directly to Pearl Harbor. The rest of the air group would follow that afternoon, taking off before "The Big E" entered port. Reveille for the pilots that morning was at 0445. On the flight deck blue-liveried plane handlers moved the eighteen Dauntlesses into launch position. Leading the mission was Lt. Cdr. Howard L. Young, a former skipper of Fighting Six. He was commander of the *Enterprise* Air Group and flew his personal SBD. Thirteen dive bombers from Lt. Cdr. Halsted L. Hopping's Scouting Six and four from Lt. Cdr. William R. Hollingsworth's Bombing Six comprised the remainder of the flight. The carrier maneuvered into the wind, and at 0618 began launching the SBDs. Three additional dive bombers followed them aloft for the tiresome duty of flying inner air patrol against submarines. Four VF-6 pilots waited on Zed II alert in their Grummans. The novelty of flying combat air patrols with full ammunition and orders to shoot had soon worn off. After the SBDs departed, the carrier settled down for a quiet Sunday morning.

It was not a quiet Sunday morning at Pearl Harbor. Beginning at 0755, 183 Japanese fighters, dive bombers, and torpedo planes tore into the unsuspecting Pacific Fleet. The attackers flew from the six fleet carriers (*Akagi, Kaga, Sōryū, Hiryū, Shōkaku,* and *Zuikaku*) of Vice Admiral Nagumo Chūichi's Striking Force operating about 240 miles northwest of Oahu. A second wave of 167 Japanese aircraft was already en route. The fleet lost five battleships sunk, and numerous other vessels sunk or damaged. Aircraft losses among the Army, Navy, and Marine Corps aviation units based on Oahu were staggering. No Navy or Marine Corps fighters made it off the ground to intercept Japanese planes. At Ewa, VMF-211 lost eight F4F-3s destroyed on the ground.

The first hint of trouble at Pearl Harbor reached the *Enterprise* at 0812. It was the electrifying message: "Air raid on Pearl Harbor. This is no drill!"[1] Brought to Halsey as he sat down to breakfast, the communication caused the admiral to think the so-called attackers were his own SBDs. Operating since 28 November on strict radio silence, Halsey had not informed Pearl that his dive bombers were coming. He had thought his aircraft would not have any trouble identifying themselves, and ordinarily they would not. The second and decisive message followed closely on the heels of the first. It left no doubt of war: "Alert! Japanese planes attacking Pearl and air fields on Oahu!"[2] After making their routine search, the *Enterprise* dive bombers ran into a hornet's nest. The skies over Pearl Harbor were full of enemy planes and intense antiaircraft fire. Young, who made it safely to Luke Field on Ford Island, tried to assemble his surviving SBDs to send them out to locate the enemy carriers. Of the eighteen, five either were shot down or made crash landings.

On board the *Enterprise*, general quarters sounded at 0830 to give truth to the rumors spreading wildly throughout the ship. The shock was brief, and like the professionals they were, the crew worked smartly to bring the flattop to full combat readiness. Plane handlers brought all fourteen of VF-6's Wildcats up to the flight

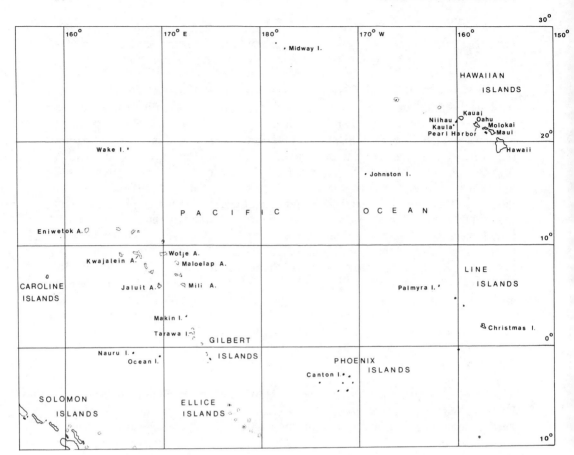

The Central Pacific.

deck. The pilots sat in their cockpits and warmed up the engines. Listening to their radio receivers, they heard a babble of urgent transmissions and felt a bit of the drama taking place at Pearl Harbor not far away. They were anxious to help. Some of the messages they overheard seemed to indicate that Japanese planes were rendezvousing over Barbers Point. Wade McClusky climbed to the bridge to speak with the admiral and Captain Murray. He hoped to take some of his fighters to Pearl to intercept enemy planes. Halsey was not yet certain what he was going to do, but whatever happened, he wanted all of his fighters available. He sympathized with VF-6's desire to fight, as he wanted nothing better than a chance to attack the Japanese.

At this juncture, however, Halsey thought it best to hold most of his meager fighter strength in reserve to defend the task force should the Japanese appear. All but four F4Fs disappeared down the forward elevator into the hangar in order to clear the flight deck. At 0915, "The Big E" sent aloft as her first wartime combat air patrol (CAP) four F4Fs led by Lieut. (jg) Fritz Hebel. Being spotted on the flight deck ready for launch were fifteen SBDs, mostly from Bombing Six. Crews swarmed around them to fuel and arm each with one 1,000-lb. bomb. Halsey decided his best course of action was to remain in his present location south of Kaula Rock. At 0921, CinCPac issued orders to Halsey to arrange to rendezvous his own Task Force 8 with Newton's Task Force 12 (*Lexington*) and Brown's Task Force 3. Halsey a few minutes later set the rendezvous at a point 100 miles west of Niihau Island well to the west of Oahu. He prayed for the opportunity to unleash a surprise counterattack of his own against the Japanese raiding force.

Messages and fragmentary reports continued to jam the air, but none provided Halsey with concrete information as to the location of the enemy striking force. Murray replaced the three SBDs on inner air patrol with three Grumman Wildcats led by Frank Corbin, VF-6 executive officer. They took off at 1015.

Meanwhile a report had come in that two enemy carriers were operating 30 miles south of Barbers Point. At 1020, the *Enterprise* started scrambling the fifteen SBDs, but before they departed, a correction was received from the heavy cruiser *Minneapolis*. The previous report of enemy flattops lurking south of Barbers Point was in error.

The fifteen SBDs circled the carrier, while Halsey and Murray decided what to do with them. From a communication sent by CinCPac, Halsey deduced that certain areas around Oahu had not received an adequate search. Consequently, he sent his dive bombers south and west of Oahu—sectors presumably not covered by Pearl-based searches. At 1055, he also sent six Curtiss SOC-3 floatplanes from his heavy cruisers to search 150 miles to the north–northeast. There was nothing else to do but wait. Halsey informed Kimmel that he was depending on shore-based aircraft to provide him with the enemy's position. He did not want to waste any more of his strike planes on searches. As if to punctuate his impatience to fight, the *Enterprise* at 1105 broke her huge battle ensign for the first time. At 1240, she launched a relief combat air patrol of four F4Fs led by McClusky, then twenty minutes later recovered the seven of Corbin and Hebel for refueling. Still in reserve as the carrier's main striking force were the eighteen TBD-1 Devastators of Torpedo Six.

With great effort, "Brigham" Young, the group commander, collected nine of his *Enterprise* SBDs at Ford Island. Around noon, he sent these veterans of the ill-fated morning search to cover sectors north and northwest of Oahu to a range of 175 miles. It was not realized that the Japanese flattops had recovered their aircraft (less the twenty-nine that had failed to return) and already steamed hard away to the northwest. Analysis of enemy radio transmissions had led CinCPac to believe the enemy carriers might be southeast of Oahu, when actually they were on the reciprocal bearing to the northwest. The *Enterprise* at 1345 relaunched nine of her SBDs newly returned from the forenoon search and sent them out again. Also that afternoon, Halsey deployed all but a few of his destroyers into a scouting line and sent them off to look for the enemy fleet.

At 1505, the *Enterprise* rotated her combat air patrol again, putting aloft a fresh six-plane division under Jim Gray. Soon after, McClusky's four planes landed on board. Everyone awaited a sighting report and the word to go. About a half hour later, warships appeared on the horizon and approached Task Force 8. They consisted of one heavy cruiser, three light cruisers, and twelve destroyers led by Rear Admiral Milo F. Draemel. Most had sortied that morning from Pearl with orders to join Halsey. Gray's VF-6 contingent was not particularly pleased to greet the new arrivals. Beginning around 1600, Draemel's nervous gunners took potshots at the circling CAP for the better part of an hour. The F4Fs fortunately escaped damage, but Fighting Six would not be so lucky that evening.

Not long after Draemel's force closed up, Halsey received what finally appeared to be the word. One of VB-6's SBDs reported sighting a Japanese carrier and cruiser only 60 miles south of Oahu, then added he was being attacked by fighters. Indicative of the confusion of that day, the SBD pilot actually had spotted only friendly forces and misidentified them. The enemy fighters turned out to be Army

A-20 light bombers. Halsey, however, had no choice but to commit his remaining strike force on the basis of the report. That location worked out to about 100 miles southeast of Task Force 8. The air strike comprised the eighteen TBDs of Torpedo Six, six VB-6 SBD "smokers" (Dauntlesses fitted with smoke generators to shield the approach of the torpedo planes to their drop points), and six F4F fighter escorts. Fighting Six's contribution was:

Aircraft	Bureau No.	Pilot
6-F-1	3906	Lieut. (jg) Francis Frederick Hebel, USN
6-F-15	3935	Ens. Herbert H. Menges, A-V(N)
6-F-5	3916	Ens. James G. Daniels III, USN
6-F-12	3938	Lieut. (jg) Eric Allen, USN
3-F-15*	3982	Ens. Gayle L. Hermann, USN
6-F-4	3909	Ens. David R. Flynn, A-V(N)

*F4F-3 on loan from Fighting Three.

In charge of the strike was VT-6's skipper, Lieut. Eugene E. Lindsey, and he apparently had orders to fly to Pearl Harbor after making his attack. The launch of the thirty planes lasted from 1642 to 1659, and they departed shortly thereafter.

Reaching the target area about an hour later, Lindsey's troops diligently searched the vicinity of the reported contact, but found nothing. Darkness intervened, and Lindsey decided to return to the ship. In the growing murk, Hebel's F4Fs happened to separate from the rest of the group. He skillfully used his Zed Baker radio homing receiver to take the escort directly back to the task force. Somewhat surprised to discover some of the strike planes overhead, Halsey at about 1950 directed Hebel to fly north to Oahu and land there. The fighters dutifully headed off into the night, bound for a blacked-out and apprehensive destination. About 15 minutes after the F4Fs departed, Lindsey's TBDs and SBDs reached the *Enterprise*. Halsey relented and allowed them to land, probably because the TBDs, still laden with their 2,000-lb. aerial torpedoes, began to run low on fuel. At 2004, the *Enterprise* turned on her lights despite the threat of enemy submarines. Few of the pilots nervously queuing up to land were night-qualified, and they faced the added distraction of coming on board with torpedoes still attached—the first night carrier landings in the U.S. Navy by armed torpedo planes. Recovery operations lasted from 2017 to 2113. The only real excitement occurred when a Devastator thumped down hard into the barrier and dropped its fish onto the flight deck. The flight deck crew corralled the sliding torpedo without any damage to the ship. Torpedo Six, at least, had flown its night carrier exercises!

Fritz Hebel at the head of VF-6's escort fighters spotted ahead of him in the blackness an island dotted with fires. Thinking it was Kauai with its burning cane-fields, he turned east and ended up over Molokai before he realized his error. The fires actually blazed on Oahu as reminders of the savage enemy attack. Checking with his pilots to make certain they had sufficient fuel, Hebel led the six Grummans across the channel west to Makapuu Point on Oahu. From there they followed the coastline south and west over Diamond Head and Waikiki toward the Pearl Harbor Channel entrance south of the harbor proper. Around 2110, Hebel noticed runway lights illuminating the Army's Hickam Field just east of the harbor channel. The lights along Hickam's northeast–southwest runway appeared a welcome invitation to land. The naval air station on Ford Island also had its runway lights on, but the thick smoke from the fires around the harbor momentarily obscured them from the VF-6 pilots. Hebel took the flight north past Hickam. The six F4Fs had descended to about 500 feet and turned on their red and green running lights. They started around the Army field, but during the circuit north Hebel noticed the floodlights at Ford Island farther north. NAS Pearl Harbor was open for business after all.

The authorities at Pearl knew of the approach of the *Enterprise* aircraft. Halsey had radioed the naval air station to expect them after dark. Rear Admiral Patrick L. N. Bellinger, commander of Patrol Wing Two, worried that ship and shore batteries might fire on the friendlies. At his direction duty officers several times circulated warnings to all ships and batteries that American aircraft were en route and would land. Bellinger was not the only one concerned about the planes. Young, the *Enterprise* group commander, had stationed himself in the Ford Island control tower along with the duty controller. He tried numerous times with the tower's low power transmitter to contact the *Enterprise* flight leader or the ship, but without success. When he started up the harbor entrance channel toward Hickam, Hebel radioed the Ford Island tower for instructions. The duty controller at Young's direction swiftly responded with orders to break formation over Ford Island at 1,000 feet with navigation lights on, then land. Young did not want the aircraft to circle needlessly and invite trouble.

The six F4Fs cruised at 500 feet with running lights prominent during the short hop over to Ford Island. They offered every appearance of executing a routine night landing. Automatically Hebel banked to the right to circle Ford Island counterclockwise and execute the usual left carrier break for landing. From the benefit of hindsight, this was a "perfectly normal" mistake, as Halsey later testified.[3] The turn swept the six F4Fs opposite the Ford Island control tower and over Drydock Channel and Battleship Row, scenes of some of the worst destruction of the raid. On board the battered ships, distraught gunners fully believed that the enemy had returned. Several warships challenged the neatly lighted intruders for proper recognition signals, and when the countersigns did not appear immediately, gunnery officers gave orders to shoot. First the battleship *Pennsylvania* cut loose with her machine guns at the low-flying aircraft. That ignited a chain reaction all over the harbor. Captain James M. Shoemaker, in charge of NAS Pearl Harbor, later remarked: "Somebody let fly, and I never saw so many bullets in the air—all tracer bullets at night." He thought Hebel's fighters had become the target of "every gun in the Pearl Harbor area, near as I could tell."[4] Even sailors with Springfield rifles took aim at the hapless aircraft, venting some of the rage they felt after the devastation of the day. Hearing the gunfire, both Admiral Kimmel and Rear Admiral Claude C. Bloch, commanding the 14th Naval District, issued immediate ceasefire orders. It was already too late for three men.

Without warning the VF-6 pilots became the focus of intense antiaircraft fire. Hebel in shock radioed, "My God, what's happened!"[5] Bullets ripped into the Grumman flown by his wingman, Ens. Herbert H. Menges, and either killed or incapacitated him.[6] Out of control, the stricken F4F stalled down and dived past Ford Island toward Pearl City, a peninsula across the channel. At the shallow angle it plowed into the veranda of "Palm Lodge," a house situated next to the water, and burst into flames. The building burned to the ground, but no one other than the pilot was harmed. Herb Menges was the first U.S. naval fighter pilot to die in the Pacific War. He joined the Navy in July 1939 for flight training and earned his wings and promotion to ensign on 1 August 1940. That November he was posted to Fighting Six, where a year of seasoning had made him into a steady and skilled fighter pilot.

Likewise hit almost instantly was the last F4F in the formation, Lieut. (jg) Eric

Allen's 6-F-12. It exploded in flames.[7] Allen had no time to gain altitude, but bailed out immediately while still very low. Seconds after he left it, the burning Grumman plunged into the water off Ford Island. As for Allen, his parachute had barely snaked open before he struck the water with a shattering impact. The fall inflicted severe internal injuries, but even worse, he had been struck in the left chest by a rifle-caliber bullet that ultimately collapsed a lung. Incredibly and with an indomitable spirit, Allen was able to make his way in great pain through the oil and debris-choked Drydock Channel past the crippled battleship *California* toward Ford Island. At the Naval Academy (he graduated in 1938), he had been a strong swimmer. Bluejackets from the minesweeper *Vireo* pulled him out of the water and rushed him to the naval dispensary. Only when they tried to clean the fuel oil from him did they realize he had been struck by a bullet. By that time it was too late. Eric Allen died at 0200 the next morning. He had qualified in early 1941 as a naval aviator and joined Fighting Six that spring. The cruise for him had begun with an ill omen: his Grumman was one of the two that would not start on 28 November.

Having lost two of their number to antiaircraft fire, the four remaining F4Fs scattered, each pilot running for his life. A five-inch antiaircraft shell smashed through Ens. Gayle L. Hermann's engine without exploding and turned the F4F into a glider. He had to make a dead stick landing on Ford Island immediately before stalling out. In the teeth of tracers and shell bursts, Hermann touched down on the runway and ended up in a small golf course off its eastern edge. Even with the familiar profile of the stubby Wildcat flickering in their sights, some machine gunners shot up Hermann's F4F-3 as he rolled to a stop. He was unhurt and stoically

Ens. Gayle Hermann's 3-F-15 (BuNo. 3982) in happier days as 3-F-9 on board the *Saratoga* in early Oct. 1941. Repaired after VF-6's disastrous 7 Dec. night landings at Pearl Harbor, 3982 flew in all of the *Enterprise*'s early raids, but was lost with VF-2 at Coral Sea. (NA 80-G-81391.)

grabbed his chute for the walk across the airfield to VF-6's hangar, but the borrowed 3-F-15 was a mess, what with a wrecked engine and eighteen "friendly" bullet holes.

Fritz Hebel swung northward, seeking a haven at the Army's Wheeler Field.[8] Stirred up by the ruckus over Pearl, Army antiaircraft batteries north of there forced Hebel to sheer off. He gunned his engine to pull away from the shooting, but the Pratt & Whitney, perhaps damaged, sputtered and died. Hebel had to find someplace to set her down quickly. In the blackness he had to settle for a canefield north of Aeia. Skidding along the broken, stubbled ground, the F4F cartwheeled, tore in two, and piled into a small gully. Part of the wreckage burst into flames. Onlookers pulled the unconscious pilot from the shattered cockpit and took him to the Army hospital at Schofield Barracks. Having suffered a severe skull fracture, Hebel died the next day. One of the most experienced pilots in the squadron, Hebel had enlisted in 1936 in the original aviation cadet program. With his wings in 1937 came a two-year tour in battleship floatplanes. Commissioned ensign in 1939 (to rank from 1937), he instructed nascent pilots in flight elimination training at the Grosse Ile (Michigan) Naval Reserve Air Base. In March 1941, he accepted a regular commission, and about that time was a welcomed acquisition of VF-6.

As soon as the sky grew livid with gun flashes and tracers, Ens. James G. Daniels switched off his lights and dived southwestward on past Ford Island toward Barbers Point. Soon he found himself at very low altitude back over the ship channel entrance. Hearing the tower trying to raise the *Enterprise* flight, he established contact, and was told to set down swiftly. Coming in from the south, he almost clipped the foretop of the beached battleship *Nevada* opposite Hospital Point, then had to endure gunfire from that ship, batteries around Hickam off to the right, and the West Loch ammunition depot. Nevertheless he landed 6-F-5 at Ford Island before the gunners could concentrate on him. As he taxied up to the flight line, a .50-caliber machine gun nearby opened up on him, but fortunately soon was silenced. Gayle Hermann appeared out of the darkness and jumped up on his wing to congratulate his friend on still being alive! The two reported to Young at the tower. He was busy trying to contact the *Enterprise* and warn her against sending any more planes to Pearl. Daniels and Hermann spent an uncomfortable night in a shot-up, vacant set of quarters wondering what had happened to the others.

The last VF-6 pilot to leave his aircraft that terrifying night was Ens. David R. Flynn, who celebrated his twenty-seventh birthday that day.[9] The best present he received was his life. Like Daniels, Flynn extinguished his running lights as soon as the shooting started. He dropped into low-level, violent evasive maneuvers, then headed south out to sea for about ten miles. His radio transmitter and receiver not working, Flynn was leery of returning to Oahu without a way of announcing his coming. Equally troublesome, his fuel was about gone. He made landfall at Barbers Point and turned north for the marine field at Ewa. About four miles short of his destination, his engine suddenly stopped. At 2130, Flynn hit the silk at 1,200 feet and chuted into a canefield. Some soldiers came along and conveyed him to Tripler Army Hospital, where he was treated for an injured back and wrist. He learned from witnesses that his F4F had actually ignited in the air as he abandoned it. The flaming Grumman crashed nearby. Luckily for Dave Flynn, no one mistook him for one of the Japanese paratroopers so widely reported, or, like Eric Allen, he might have been shot in midair.

Fighting Six on the first day of war saw no Japanese, yet sustained grievous losses: three pilots killed and four F4F-3As destroyed (with another badly damaged). For VF-6's whole first tour of war duty (December 1941–June 1942), 7

December would see the worst casualties. The authorities could only wring their hands and put the blame on faulty communications and overeager gunners, owing to the great confusion at Pearl. This in itself was little consolation for the families and friends of the men who were killed that tragic night. Had Lindsey's whole strike group gone in together to Pearl, the losses would undoubtedly have been much higher.

Unlike the *Enterprise*, the *Lexington* in Rear Admiral Newton's Task Force 12 was well away from the inferno at Pearl Harbor. The trip toward Midway had proved uneventful, and the dawn of 7 December saw Newton about 500 miles southeast of Midway. Later that morning the *Lex* was to launch the marine scout bombers to fly to Midway, then start back for Pearl. Shortly after 0815 came news that destroyed the routine of a tranquil morning at sea. The ships squared away for war. Newton on board his flagship *Chicago* decided he would take an active role in directing air operations on board the *Lexington*. At 0850, he directed her commanding officer, Captain Frederick C. Sherman, to ready a combat air patrol, a needless order because Sherman had already begun a massive respot of the crowded flight deck to facilitate the launch of Fighting Two. Then at 0923, Newton warned Sherman he might have to despatch the marines to Midway ahead of schedule. A few minutes later, Fighting Two put its first combat air patrol aloft, a division of six F2A-3 Buffaloes.

For some reason Newton was not satisfied by the defensive preparations made by the *Lexington*. At 1012 he unexpectedly ordered Sherman to launch all of his remaining fighters. Sherman complied, and the pilots of Fighting Two scurried on deck to man planes. By 1021, the *Lexington* had sent off all eleven F2As on deck, giving Paul Ramsey seventeen fighters aloft. Sherman bristled at the interference of the nonaviator Newton in running his routine air operations. He felt it was pointless to keep all of the fighters airborne unless there was a definite threat. Now there would be none in reserve ready to relieve the fighters aloft when their fuel ran low. At 1038, he signaled to Newton the suggestion that the *Lexington* launch sixteen SBDs on a full circle search to 165 miles, and added, "Unless enemy aircraft are positively identified in vicinity, consider undesirable have all fighters in air at same time."[10] Newton relented, approved the search, and permitted Sherman to reduce the strength of the combat air patrol. Sherman was anxious to launch the marines for Midway, both to bolster the defenses of that vital outpost and to relieve the congestion on his flight deck. That was no longer possible. Orders had arrived from both Kimmel and Halsey directing Task Force 12 to intercept the enemy raiding force, presumably withdrawing westward from the Hawaiian Islands. Task Force 12 would simultaneously be heading for a rendezvous with Halsey's Task Force 8.

The question of launching the marines had precluded the landing of the CAP fighters, and Sherman wanted to get them on board for fuel. There was a flurry at 1230 when the *Lexington*'s CXAM search radar detected an unknown aircraft (or "bogey") bearing 269 degrees, distance 43 miles. Fighters charged out after the contact, but soon identified it as an American PBY Catalina flying boat. Sherman decided it was high time to land most of his fighters. The *Lexington*'s harried flight deck crews cleared the flight deck aft, and shortly after 1300 the carrier recovered all but a division of the fighters. Newton at 1320 formally canceled the marine flight to Midway in order to use the marine squadron to attack the enemy should Task Force 12 locate them.

Sherman had most of his fighters on board, but the ones still aloft were getting low on fuel. Complicating matters was the *Lexington*'s crowded flight deck which took considerable time to respot for landings and takeoffs. Sherman wanted that relief combat air patrol aloft as soon as possible and decided to try an old carrier trick. At 1353, he reversed the *Lexington*'s powerful turboelectric drive and maneuvered his ship astern to secure sufficient wind over the deck.[11] Then at 1357 came the exceedingly rare sight of a stern launch, as six VF-2 Brewster Buffaloes took off over her fantail. Without having to go through a time-consuming respot of the flight deck, Sherman brought her bow into the wind and took on board his gas-starved fighters. Fighting Two maintained a combat air patrol until after dusk.

Early that afternoon Newton learned that CinCPac felt the Japanese carriers were south of Oahu, placing Task Force 12 astride their likely course of withdrawal. For the task force it looked like a real chance for combat. The *Lexington* launched a supplementary search of two SBDs at 1650, and there was a brief scare twenty minutes later when one of the planes on the afternoon search thought it spotted the enemy. The contact turned out to be a small reef near French Frigate Shoals. The supplementary search, however, could not find their way back to the carrier. Sherman first tried radio homing, then at 1800 made the courageous decision to turn on his searchlights. He had all aircraft on board by 1841. The *Lexington* was at war, and it had been a trying day, but at least her air group was spared the bloody introduction that befell their counterparts on board the *Enterprise*.

PEARL HARBOR AFTERMATH

Nightfall on 7 December found the Pacific Fleet reeling from the stunning surprise air strike on Pearl, but at least its carriers were unharmed. Vice Admiral Halsey's Task Force 8 with the *Enterprise* operated southwest of Oahu, while Rear Admiral Newton's Task Force 12 with the *Lexington* steamed southeastward away from Midway. Both carrier forces searched for enemy warships possibly withdrawing southwest toward the Marshalls. Very fortunately for the Americans, their two flattops were nowhere near the Japanese striking force, which wielded no fewer than six carriers. Vice Admiral Nagumo drew off to the northwest away from Oahu in order to skirt Midway's air patrols before turning directly for Japan.

Before dawn on 8 December, Lt. Cdr. Young assembled his operational *Enterprise* SBDs and F4Fs on Ford Island and made ready to fly back out to the ship. At first light as they were about to depart, a naval Sikorsky JRS amphibian transport took off and drew tremendous antiaircraft fire from all around the harbor. Young had to delay his flight for an hour to make certain all the batteries knew his aircraft were friendly. Accompanying Young's SBDs back to the *Enterprise* were Jim Daniels and Gayle Hermann. All the aviators brimmed over with eyewitness accounts of the destruction and confusion at Pearl. McClusky still had only a fragmentary notion as to the fate of the other four escort pilots. The two who made it out to the ship knew only that Eric Allen was being treated at the naval dispensary on Ford Island (he died early that morning). Hermann had taken a spare F4F, leaving his shot-up Grumman at Ford Island. Even so, McClusky only had ten fighters on board and kept them busy flying CAP all day.

Halsey started in for Pearl late that morning. All the searches proved negative, so it seemed safe to bring the *Enterprise* into port overnight for fuel. She despatched her air group for dispersal among several fields on Oahu. As passengers the TBDs carried a pair of VF-6 pilots to reclaim two other F4Fs left at NAS Pearl Harbor. At 1630, McClusky took eight F4Fs to the Army's Wheeler Field a dozen miles north of the harbor. There they came under the Hawaiian Air Force's 14th Pursuit

Wing (Brig. Gen. Howard C. Davidson) in line with standing orders under which the Air Corps controlled the island's air defenses. Four other F4Fs (including the two spares picked up at Pearl) landed just before dark at Wheeler.

The *Enterprise* beheld the grotesque scene at Pearl. Her crew recoiled at the specter of dead and wounded battleships, burnt planes, wrecked hangars, and the stench of fuel oil. "The Big E" enjoyed no rest, as Halsey wanted her under way before first light on the ninth. Fighting Six personnel drew two F4F-3s from the AirBatFor pool and also hoisted on board another F4F left ashore ten days before. That night jumpy sentries ashore repeatedly fired on small boats shuttling to and from the carrier's berth.

The visit to Wheeler, once the pride of the Air Corps' pursuit forces, gave the VF-6 pilots (other than the survivors of the escort mission) their first look at war. Wheeler was a shambles of bomb craters, over forty burnt fighters, bullet holes, and broken glass. After the comforts of life on board ship, war-torn Wheeler was a shock. The Army enforced strict blackout discipline, and "black as hell"[1] the night was. One definite hazard to health and life itself was promiscuous firing by trigger-happy soldiers. This discouraged the curious from moving around after dark.

The *Enterprise* sailed at 0420 on 9 December. Her mission was to guard against the return of the enemy raiders and also to chase submarines which CinCPac believed lurked north of Oahu. This would prove to be a curious voyage, and there soon would be the question of who was chasing whom. By diverting the enemy subs, the *Enterprise* would cover the return of the *Lexington* to Pearl Harbor and also the anticipated arrival of the *Saratoga* from the West Coast. Based temporarily at Wheeler, the VF-6 pilots awoke at 0400 on the ninth, if indeed they got any sleep at all that troubled night. The twelve F4Fs took off at 0615, seen off personally by General Davidson, "an old and good friend"[2] of the squadron who was sad to see them go. McClusky's pilots soon spotted the carrier a short way off Oahu. Jim Gray, for one, was most pleased to be back: "Never had fresh sea air and a clean ship stood in greater contrast to a smoking, burned out, and evil-smelling air base."[3] The ship promptly sent several fighters aloft on CAP, which they flew until noon. The rest of the day the exhausted pilots gratefully spent in their bunks. Fighting Six was still under strength with only fifteen Grummans (thirteen F4F-3As and two F4F-3s) on board.

After Task Force 8 had rounded Oahu to the north, the ships came under the scrutiny of eager eyes. Cdr. Inaba Tsuso, skipper of the Japanese submarine *I-6*, reported to headquarters the sighting of one American carrier and two cruisers heading northeast away from Oahu. The Japanese Sixth Fleet, which controlled the I-boats, immediately sent no fewer than seven submarines to pursue Inaba's contact. Joining them was at least one more I-boat from the pack that had surrounded the Hawaiian Islands.[4]

The morning of 10 December saw Bill Halsey and the Japanese submariners close to what they sought—each other. Fighting Six flew an early morning patrol, then secured on Zed II alert for the rest of the day. The admiral appeared that morning in the squadron ready room and gave the pilots a rousing "fight talk." Almost at the same time, the SBDs on search were having a time with the submarines. There were three separate contacts on the dawn search. Ens. Perry Teaff of Scouting Six happened upon the diving submarine *I-70* and so damaged the pigboat that she had to surface and could not submerge. Later that day, Lieut. (jg) Clarence E. Dickinson of the same squadron finished the job by sending the hapless I-boat to the bottom. The Japanese tried hard to return the compliment. The *Enterprise*, while maneuvering to recover aircraft, had to sidestep a torpedo.

One of the heavy cruisers, the *Salt Lake City*, shelled a surfaced submarine. The alarums, for imagined as well as real contacts, became so intense that Halsey threatened one of his junior officers that he would personally throw the fellow overboard if he came up with another panicky, unconfirmed sighting report.

The next day the task force seemed in the midst of schools of predatory enemy subs. At 0900, one torpedo zipped past only 20 yards astern of "The Big E," and there were numerous depth charging runs by destroyers on suspected contacts. Fighting Six did not fly on 11 December, but stood Zed II watches in addition to routine squadron duty. This continued for the next several days. The fighter pilots learned an important lesson—wartime service is mostly sheer boredom. Finally even the numerous sub contacts grew passé. There was recourse to the war news, most of which was bad or inaccurate (or bad and inaccurate). Fighting Six was very proud of their recent marine guests whose valiant role in the defense of Wake emerged in the news broadcasts. On 14 December, the squadron obtained a new pilot in the person of Radio Electrician Edward H. Bayers, an NAP and VF-2 veteran who served in the *Enterprise*'s ship's company. The next day in heavy seas and gusting winds, Task Force 8 finally turned south for Oahu. Both Halsey and the sub skippers had tired of the chase. The Japanese fleet commander sent most of his I-boats to harass the West Coast.

The *Lexington* also spent a bewildering time at sea in the days following Pearl Harbor, flailing away against enemies who were not there. The morning of 8 December, Rear Admiral Newton's Task Force 12 raced southeastward toward Johnston Island, fully expecting to counter an enemy dawn raid there. Fighting Two sent aloft a dawn combat air patrol, while SBDs from Scouting Two searched out 315 miles in an effort to locate enemy warships believed withdrawing toward the Marshalls. Later that morning, Vice Admiral Brown's Task Force 3 appeared on the horizon and speedily effected rendezvous. From on board his flagship, the heavy cruiser *Indianapolis*, Brown assumed command of Task Force 12. Halsey instructed Brown to withdraw to Pearl if he did not find the Japanese that morning.

Early on the afternoon of 8 December, the heavy cruiser *Portland* and a destroyer dropped out of Task Force 12 to recover a lost plane, and the rest of the ships soon left them behind. CinCPac relayed an intercept of enemy carrier plane transmissions that seemed to show the enemy flattops were well to the northwest of Oahu. That news helped Task Force 12 to relax a bit. The *Lexington* sent aloft a minimum CAP of two VF-2 Buffaloes, followed by five SBDs on inner air patrol and a special flight of fifteen dive bombers to look for a plane missing from the dawn search. All seemed quiet until 1540, when Newton's flagship *Chicago* detected on radar a number of unidentified aircraft bearing 245 degrees, distance 44 miles. The bogeys approached the task force. Ten minutes later, the *Chicago* flashed a warning to the *Lexington*: "Many bandits, bearing 255° (T.), distance 30 miles, closing."[5] Sherman sounded general quarters; on the flight deck crews readied fighters for launch and began arming available SBDs for a strike mission. Radar indicated bogeys were circling 30 to 40 miles out from the task force.

While the *Lexington* made ready to launch planes, an urgent message from the *Portland* came over the radio. She reported being attacked by enemy aircraft. Together with the destroyer *Porter*, she was still over the horizon to the north, not having rejoined Task Force 12. Adding to the confusion, at 1618 the skipper of Patrol Squadron Twenty-one (VP-21), Lt. Cdr. George T. Mundorff, then making a flight from Johnston to Pearl, radioed that his PBY Catalina flying boat had just bombed an enemy cruiser and destroyer southeast of Johnston Island. At 1620, the *Lexington* scrambled ten F2A Buffaloes from Fighting Two, followed by SBDs armed with bombs. The carrier despatched a fighter division to aid the beleagured *Portland*. After a short flight, the VF-2 pilots came upon Mundorff's PBY lurking near the *Portland* and the *Porter*. Understandably nervous, the *Portland* loosed a few rounds in the direction of the Brewsters, but fortunately did not hit any. Mundorff promptly transmitted to base that enemy fighters were attacking him! He later reported bombing a carrier that under the circumstances could only have been the *Lexington*, although she did not log any actual attacks. Satisfied that the PBY was the only aircraft in the area, the VF-2 fighters returned to their ship. Mundorff finally went on his way too, evidently wondering how the hell the Japanese got Brewster fighters. It was a bizarre case of mistaken identity all around.

Shortly before dark, the *Lexington* recovered her aircraft and settled down for a quiet night, but this was not to be. At 1850, headquarters on Johnston broadcast alarms of an enemy attack. Brown detached his three heavy cruisers and charged off to the north toward Johnston for a night action. En route they gathered up the *Portland* and the *Porter*. The *Lexington* and the rest of the destroyers followed at a more sedate 15 knots. At 1913, Brown learned that there was no enemy at Johnston, just another false alarm. The eighth of December had been rough on the nerves of Task Force 12!

For the next five days Brown operated south and west of Oahu, mainly seeking to keep out of trouble. Fighting Two flew combat air patrols on 9 and 10 December, but thereafter secured on alert status. Paul Ramsey was reluctant to fly his fighters because of defective landing struts. He would note on 11 December just before returning to port that Fighting Two had "ceased all operations until enemy contact became imminent."[6] During this cruise three more landing struts had failed, and of the seventeen F2A-3s currently on strength, there were progressive strut failures in no fewer than twelve. The squadron desperately required reinforced struts to replace those in use. A large measure of the congestion on the *Lex*'s flight deck eased on 10 December, when she sent the eighteen marine SB2U-3s of VMSB-231 to their base at Ewa. They later made a nonstop flight from Oahu to Midway.

To keep Task Force 12 at sea, CinCPac provided Brown with the fleet oiler *Neosho*, but rough seas greatly hampered fueling. Finally on 13 December Brown shaped course directly for Pearl. That morning the *Lexington* Air Group departed the ship for Ford Island. Ted Sherman sent every plane aloft carrying either bombs or, in the case of the TBDs, torpedoes. Even VF-2's Buffaloes labored under the weight of two 100-lb. bombs slung under the wings of each. Fighting Two quartered that night on Ford Island, while the *Lexington* hit port, fueled, and made ready to sail early on 14 December. Scuttlebutt had it that the task force would participate in a relief expedition for Wake Island.

THE *SARA* TO THE FRONT

At the outbreak of war, the third of the Pacific Fleet's three carriers was well out of harm's way. The *Saratoga* (CV-3), the *Lexington*'s sister leviathan, had just completed a routine refit at the Puget Sound Navy Yard. Sailing on 4 December from Bremerton, she made a brisk three-day voyage along the West Coast. The morning of 7 December, the *Sara* neared the entrance to the harbor at San Diego. There she would embark her air group based temporarily at NAS San Diego on North Island and in a few days rejoin the fleet at Pearl Harbor. In addition to the four squadrons of Lt. Cdr. Edgar A. Cruise's *Saratoga* Air Group, the flattop would also transport Maj. Verne A. McCaul's Marine Fighting Squadron 221 (VMF-221) to Oahu. North Island that fateful morning was alive with activity, as squadron personnel scurried to complete last-minute preparations to embark. Finally there was a late-morning lunch break, and as the men rested, the *Saratoga* at 1132 glided into her berth at Pier Fox on North Island.

In their ready room ashore at North Island, several pilots of the *Saratoga*'s Fighting Squadron Three (VF-3) took a breather. They were totally unprepared for the news they heard just before noon: "The Japanese are bombing Pearl Harbor!"[1] Surprise quickly changed to purposeful anger, as North Island tried to assume a warlike stance. Preparations for embarkation continued apace, and the squadrons dispersed their aircraft around the airfield in the unlikely event the Japanese should attack. Sabotage by enemy agents appeared more of a hazard.

At North Island squadron armorers worked hard at belting ammunition, while others loaded gear on board the *Saratoga*. The Army furnished two pursuit squadrons to cover the skies over North Island, while the Navy hoisted its planes on board the flattop, which was to sail the next morning. The *Saratoga* on this trip would have a total of 103 aircraft (see table).[2]

Fighting Three's skipper, Lieut. John S. ("Jimmy") Thach, could not muster a full squadron of eighteen aircraft. The first day of the war the squadron had only ten Grumman F4F Wildcats, although Thach managed to draw another from the NAS San Diego aircraft pool. This still left him short nearly half of his authorized complement of airplanes, not to mention spares. There was a chronic shortage of fighters on the West Coast and in Hawaii. Admiral Kimmel himself on 22 August 1941 had declared that the fighter situation was deplorable. As of 22 October, Thach had only six F4F-3s, and Halsey threatened the Bureau of Aeronautics that he would reequip Fighting Three with Brewster F2A-3 Buffaloes unless seventeen F4F-3s were forthcoming shortly.[3] Thach did not obtain all the aircraft he needed, and now he was off to war.

Fighting Squadron Three bore a lineage as illustrious as any aviation squadron in the U.S. Navy. Its tortuous pedigree also well illustrates the growing pains of naval aviation.[4] Formed on 10 March 1923, the squadron at first bore the designation Fighting Squadron Two (VF-2) and became the first unit in the U.S. Navy trained to operate from an aircraft carrier, with flight duty on the old *Langley* beginning in January 1925. Two years later, VF-2 became VF-6, but upon assignment to the newly commissioned *Saratoga*, the unit on 1 July 1928 changed its designation to Bombing Squadron Two (VB-2B). Flying nimble fighter bombers, Bombing Two helped to pioneer the new dive bombing tactics, earning the nickname "Helldivers." Late in 1928, the pilots adopted as their insignia cartoonist Pat Sullivan's frisky "Felix the Cat," with the famous feline toting a bomb.

The Navy still considered the squadron a fighter unit; so in July 1930, it assumed its old title of Fighting Six (VF-6B) and usually flew off the *Saratoga*. With the general reorganization of 1937, VF-6 on 1 July became VF-3 in accordance with

	Saratoga Captain Archibald H. Douglas		
Commander, *Saratoga* Air Group	Lt. Cdr. Edgar A. Cruise	1	SBD-3
Fighting Three (VF-3)	Lieut. John S. Thach	11	F4Fs
Bombing Three (VB-3)	Lt. Cdr. Maxwell F. Leslie	21	SBD-3s
Scouting Three (VS-3)	Lt. Cdr. Herbert L. Hoerner	22	SBD-3s
Torpedo Three (VT-3)	Lieut. John E. Clark	11	TBD-1s
VMF-221	Maj. Verne A. McCaul	14	F2A-3s
		1	SNJ*
Cargo	miscellaneous aircraft†	22	
		103	

*Training plane.
†No fighters included.

Lieut. John S. Thach, 1940. (Capt. O. B. Stanley, USN.)

Lieut. Donald A. Lovelace. (Cdr. D. A. Lovelace II, USN.)

the *Sara*'s hull number, three. In December 1939, the unit exchanged half of its biplane fighters for nine new Brewster F2A-1 monoplane fighters, but obtained nine other Brewsters (this time F2A-2s) only in October 1940. Unlike their compatriots in Fighting Two, Thach's pilots were able to divest themselves of the Brewsters before the war began. At NAS San Diego in August 1941, the squadron received its first F4F-3 Wildcats.

Fighting Three was a happy squadron whose tone was set by its able and amiable skipper, John Thach. A 1927 graduate of the Naval Academy, "Jimmy" Thach took to aviation eagerly and earned his wings in 1930. That year he reported to glamorous Fighting One (VF-1B), the "High Hats," on board the *Saratoga*. There he flew Curtiss F8C-4 Falcon two-seat biplane fighters. One interesting assignment was as a pilot for actors Clark Gable and Wallace Beery in the motion picture *Hell Divers*. In 1932 came shore duty at Norfolk where Thach worked as a test pilot. Two years later he joined Patrol Squadron Nine (VP-9F), operating from the seaplane tender *Wright* in the Pacific. Cruiser duty in Scouting Six (VS-6B) on board the light cruiser *Cincinnati* loomed in 1936, and Thach flew Curtiss SOC floatplanes. The next year he returned to flying boats, this time with Patrol Five (VP-5) at NAS Coco Solo, Canal Zone. Finally, in June 1939, Thach landed a billet as gunnery officer in Fighting Three, which brought him back to his real love, fighters. He soon became executive officer, and in December 1940 assumed command of Fighting Three.

Thach was one of the outstanding squadron leaders in the Navy. Age thirty-six, he was tall and soft-spoken, with a pleasant Southern drawl (hailing from Fordyce, Arkansas). A consummate fighter pilot, Thach made it a practice to greet each new pilot in the squadron with a special initiation—mock combat between the rookie and himself. In these duels, Thach often flew while eating an apple or reading a newspaper. Even so, he would easily slip on his opponent's tail, showing a cocky but inexperienced throttle jockey he still had a lot to learn as a fighter pilot. Aside from his prowess in the air, Thach was an excellent teacher, able to instill learning and confidence in his students. He was also an air tactician of the

VF-3, 5 Mar. 1942, *standing l to r:* Mason, Clark, Sellstrom, Eder, Johnson, Lackey, Haynes, Stanley, Peterson, Dufilho, Lemmon; *sitting:* Morgan, Vorse, Lovelace, Thach, Gayler, O'Hare, Rowell. (Mrs. Patricia O'Hare Palmer.)

first order. Well before the outbreak of war he conceived his famous defensive tactic known later as the "Thach Weave" (see appendix). Air combat in the South Pacific and especially at Midway would give him ample opportunity to demonstrate the validity of his tactics.

Executive officer of Fighting Three was Lieut. Donald A. Lovelace. Younger than Thach by one year and a member of the Naval Academy's Class of 1928, Lovelace likewise possessed a wide variety of naval aviation experience. Earning his wings in 1931, he spent three years in Utility Squadron Two (VJ-2S) aboard the seaplane tender *Wright*, then flew Douglas P2D-1 twin-float torpedo planes with Patrol Three (VP-3F) based at NAS Coco Solo. His first carrier duty came in the summer of 1936 when he joined Scouting One (VS-1B) on board the *Ranger* (CV-4). Still aboard the *Ranger*, Scouting One in July 1937 became Scouting Forty-one (VS-41), and Lovelace worked his way up to flight officer. Shore duty in 1939–40 at the Naval Aircraft Factory intervened; then on 6 January 1941 he became executive officer of Fighting Three. In Don Lovelace the squadron discovered a quiet, conscientious, and thoughtful leader who fitted in well with the skipper's way of running the outfit. Thach and he became close friends.

Aside from Thach and Lovelace, Fighting Three had seven other Naval Academy graduates. From the class of 1935 was Lieut. Noel A. M. Gayler, flight officer. Another Academy alumnus destined for rapid fame was Lieut. (jg) Edward H. ("Butch") O'Hare from the class of 1937. The squadron was fortunate to have three former aviation cadets, survivors of the pre-1939 program and all highly experienced fighter pilots. Indeed, the pros far outnumbered the rookies, as Fighting Three was a well-seasoned unit. By far most of the pilots had a minimum of a year with the squadron. Joining on 8 December at San Diego were two pilots fresh from Advanced Carrier Training Group, Pacific (ACTGPac), but Thach still lacked enough planes even to accommodate his experienced pilots.

Throughout the rest of 7 December and into the early hours of the next day, the dockside bustled with the loading of aircraft and other gear. On Monday

Roster of Fighting Three Pilots, 7 December 1941

Lieut. John S. Thach	USN	USNA 1927
Lieut. Donald A. Lovelace	USN	USNA 1928
Lieut. Noel A. M. Gayler	USN	USNA 1935
Lieut. (jg) Victor M. Gadrow	USN	USNA 1935
Lieut. (jg) Albert O. Vorse, Jr.	USN	USNA 1937
Lieut. (jg) Edward H. O'Hare	USN	USNA 1937
Lieut. (jg) Howard F. Clark	USN	USNA 1938
Lieut. (jg) Robert J. Morgan	USN	USNA 1938
Lieut. (jg) Marion W. Dufilho	USN	USNA 1938
Ens. Rolla S.Lemmon	USN	
Ens. Onia B. Stanley, Jr.	A-V(N)	
Ens. Howard L. Johnson	USN	
Ens. Willard E. Eder	A-V(N)	
Ens. John H. Lackey	A-V(N)	
Ens. Richard M. Rowell	A-V(N)	
Ens. Dale W. Peterson	A-V(N)	
Ens. Leon W. Haynes	A-V(N)	
Joined on 8 December:		
Ens. John W. Wilson	A-V(N)	
Ens. Edward R. Sellstrom, Jr.	A-V(N)	

morning the admiral commanding Carrier Division One broke his two-star flag on board the *Saratoga*. He was Rear Admiral Aubrey Wray Fitch, one of the few experienced aviation flag officers in the Pacific Fleet. At 0910 that morning, the *Sara* got under way bound for Pearl Harbor. Three elderly destroyers fell in ahead as antisubmarine escort, and the little task group nosed past Point Loma into the vast, unfriendly Pacific Ocean. Fighting Three pilots stood Zed II alerts for the rest of the day.

During the first few days of the cruise, there were the inevitable alarums due to early war jitters. The *Saratoga* copied a report placing a Japanese flattop off Monterey! On 9 December she had her own big false alarm. One of the SBDs on dawn search excitedly reported sighting a tanker fueling a submarine 60 miles south of the force. Fitch took no chances, but sent off a strike of twenty-three dive bombers, then took the *Saratoga* northwest away from possible danger. Meanwhile the tanker identified herself as the USS *Sepulga*, a fleet oiler, to other search planes sent to look her over. The "submarine" was a ship's boat. To cap a morning of errors, the *Saratoga*'s attack group never did find the target because the original sighting report gave the wrong position. On 10 December, CinCPac informed Fitch that Task Group 16.1, consisting of the heavy cruiser *Minneapolis* and four destroyers, had left Pearl that day to effect a rendezvous with the *Saratoga* force, now designated as Task Group 16.2, and escort it back to Pearl Harbor in order to arrive there the afternoon of 13 December.

Before dawn on 11 December, the *Saratoga*'s CXAM radar tagged a bogey dead ahead and 30 miles distant. Lovelace of Fighting Three had the dawn alert, and while he was in the hangar preparing the aircraft, the bull horn ordered him and a wingman to scramble and intercept the suspected enemy aircraft. Excited, Lovelace manned his fighter on deck, but this first chance at combat was not to be. Just before takeoff, an officer rushed over to his plane, jumped up on the wing, and told Lovelace to circle the ship until further orders. The two F4Fs departed at 0633, twenty minutes before sunrise. Following them aloft were twelve SBDs as dawn search and inner air patrol. About a half hour later, Thach led a division of four F4Fs aloft to reinforce the CAP. The hoped-for vector to pursue the contact did not materialize, and "excitement soon faded."[5] The original contact had disappeared from the screen. When Lovelace landed back on board, he was amused to see that the ordnancemen had in hopeful anticipation chalked humorous slogans on the bombs.

That afternoon Fitch learned that his escort, Task Group 16.1, would be delayed by heavy seas, postponing the arrival at Pearl by one day. There was more excitement later in the day when an SBD from Bombing Three ditched 50 miles northeast of the carrier. The crew abandoned the sinking aircraft and took to a rubber raft. Circling overhead was VB-3's skipper, Lt. Cdr. Maxwell F. Leslie, who remained there on station for two and a half hours while the destroyer *Talbot* left the task force and raced for the rescue. Leslie did not leave for the carrier until the destroyer had his men on deck. Shortly following noon on 12 December, Fitch effected rendezvous with Task Group 16.1 and headed for Pearl. The main threat to the *Saratoga* was submarines, and Kimmel was taking no chances.

CHAPTER 2

"We are in great need of a victory." The Wake Island Operation

INITIAL MOVES

The first week of the Pacific War saw the United States Pacific Fleet embattled on all sides. On 10 December, Guam's tiny garrison succumbed, while Japanese air power daily pounded Wake Island. Planners in Washington doubted the fleet's ability to repel expected invasions of Wake, Midway, and Samoa. There was no question of sending the fleet to relieve beleaguered American troops in the Philippines. Kimmel's first concern was to protect Hawaii by using his carrier task forces to patrol between Wake, Midway, and the Hawaiian Islands to prevent the return of enemy raiding forces east of the 180th Meridian. Aside from supporting the island garrisons, such patrols would also keep the *Lexington* and the *Enterprise* at sea and mobile. The fleet could no longer risk protracted stays by carriers at Pearl Harbor. Kimmel awaited the arrival of the *Saratoga* from the West Coast; then he could do something for Wake.

Wake's defenders served as a shining example for the whole Pacific Fleet. From the first day of war, the island garrison, led by a former skipper of Fighting Five, Cdr. Winfield Scott Cunningham, bravely endured severe air strikes. The remnants of Paul Putnam's VMF-211, crippled during the first surprise attack, fought magnificently with the few Grumman Wildcats they patched together. On 11 December, Wake repulsed a major enemy amphibious attack and sank two destroyers, one by VMF-211. Constant air attrition whittled away the island's air power, manpower, and supplies. Unreinforced, it was only a matter of time before the garrison would be overwhelmed by a second Japanese invasion.

Kimmel on 12 December consolidated plans to relieve Wake. Of his three carriers, the *Enterprise* in Halsey's Task Force 8 was chasing submarines north of Oahu, Brown's *Lexington* was headed for Pearl, and the *Saratoga* likewise was expected in a few days. Kimmel decided to keep Halsey at sea to cover the other two carriers while they shuttled in and out of Pearl. Since the *Lexington* was scheduled to arrive on 13 December, Kimmel earmarked her to make a diversionary raid on Japanese bases in the Marshalls. This would draw enemy attention away from the actual Wake Island relief force. The *Saratoga* drew the tough assignment of escorting the Wake relief ships. She would stop at Pearl, top off her oil bunkers, then put out to sea for Wake. On board would be the fighters of VMF-221 to bolster Wake's air strength, while the seaplane tender *Tangier* embarked troops, ammunition, supplies, and a vital radar set for Wake's garrison.

The *Lexington* rested in port one day, and on 14 December made ready to sail

Commander, *Lexington* Air Group	Lt. Cdr. William B. Ault	1	SBD
Fighting Two	Lt. Cdr. Paul H. Ramsey	21	F2As
Bombing Two	Lt. Cdr. Harry D. Felt	17	SBDs
Scouting Two	Lt. Cdr. Robert E. Dixon	14	SBDs
Torpedo Two	Lieut. Claire L. Miller	15	TBDs

as the nucleus of a new task force: Task Force 11 (the *Lexington*, three heavy cruisers, nine destroyers, and a fleet oiler) under Brown. His mission involved raids on the Japanese naval base at Jaluit in the Marshalls, although he retained discretion to substitute other targets or withdraw without attacking if necessary. CinCPac set "D-Day" (the day when reinforcements would reach Wake) as 23 December, Wake time (22 December in Hawaii), and Brown was to attack the day before. It was a difficult assignment, as Brown faced with his lone carrier what Kimmel had once intended in his prewar "Marshalls Reconnaissance and Raiding Plan" for two carrier task forces closely supported by squadrons of PBY flying boats.

The afternoon of 14 December, Task Force 11 left Pearl. Shortly before dark the *Lexington* Air Group flew out to the carrier and landed on board. It had the strength shown in the table—total, twenty-one fighters, thirty-two dive bombers, and fifteen torpedo planes, or sixty-eight aircraft, not all of them operational. Fighting Two embarked twenty-one Brewster F2A Buffalo fighters, only seventeen of which were flyable. Three others on board were awaiting major overhaul, and one needed a right main landing strut. Brown took up a southwesterly heading at 16 knots. On the way out, he encountered Task Force 16 waiting uncomfortably off Oahu.

Delays had postponed the *Saratoga*'s arrival by one day. On Sunday morning, 14 December, she drew close enough to Oahu to be able to fly off her air group before entering port herself. Thirty-one SBDs fanned out ahead to watch for submarines; then at 1112, the rest of the air group headed for NAS Kaneohe Bay just northeast of Pearl Harbor. Inbound there was a flutter when an Army B-17 Flying Fortress happened upon the formation. Fighting Three closed in belligerently, only to discover its quarry was friendly. The *Saratoga* aviators settled in at Kaneohe and discovered that Japanese dive bombers and fighters had done quite a job in the last week on the patrol plane base:

> Our first glimpse of the damage showed the skeletons of the burned and bombed PBY's. They had been piled to one side in the week since the attack. The framework of a burned hangar still stood gauntly black in the sunshine. The wreckage of two or three machine-gunned and burned cars stood beside the road. Broken glass had been cleared away but bullet holes still starred the plaster of the B.O.Q.[1]

Fighting Three just had time to eat lunch before they received orders to fly back out to the ship. The *Saratoga* would not, after all, enter port until the next day. The carrier took on board all of her airplanes but the marine fighters and the torpedo planes, which spent the night ashore.

Before dawn on 15 December, the *Saratoga*'s aircraft once again departed for Oahu, this time to NAS Pearl Harbor. Thach's fighters maintained combat air patrol over the carrier until she made ready to enter port. Satisfied that she was safe, the Wildcats peeled off to land at the naval air station. Suddenly, at 0818, a lookout on board the carrier thought he saw a submarine stalking the flattop four miles south of Barbers Point. The alarm went out by radio, bringing Fighting Three overhead in a hurry. A diligent search by aircraft and destroyers failed to turn up

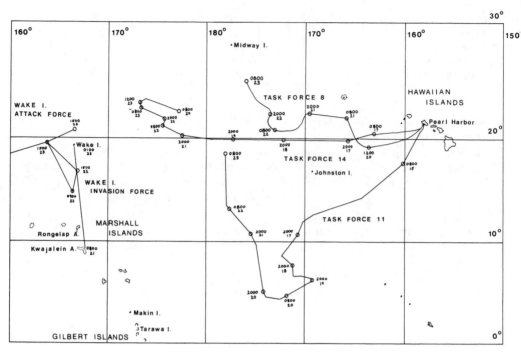

The Wake Island relief operation.

an I-boat; so the fighter pilots headed back to Ford Island, where they were surprised to find no ground crews to service their aircraft. The pilots had to refuel their own planes, and Lovelace had quite a scare when his fuel tank ran over, the nozzle squirting gasoline into his eyes. Luckily he was able to rinse them clean without any ill effects. That afternoon there was time to take a break and a closer look at the sad wreckage and sunken battleships strewn round the harbor. While the pilots relaxed that evening, the *Saratoga*'s first combat assignment began to take form.

As commander of Task Force 14, the actual Wake relief force, Kimmel designated a nonaviator, Rear Admiral Frank Jack Fletcher flying his flag as commander, Cruiser Division Six on board the heavy cruiser *Astoria*. Fitch, who was slightly junior to Fletcher, became the air task group commander. Fletcher's Task Force 14 comprised the carrier *Saratoga*, three heavy cruisers, eight destroyers, the elderly fleet oiler *Neches*, and the seaplane tender *Tangier*. Because of the *Saratoga*'s delayed arrival, Kimmel expedited matters by having the *Tangier* and the *Neches* depart on 15 December. With its faster cruising speed, the rest of the task force could easily overtake them in a few days.

Fletcher's primary task was to see that the reinforcements on board the *Tangier* and also the marine fighters on board the *Saratoga* arrived at Wake safely. Ideally, the *Tangier* was to discharge her troops and cargo, then embark evacuees from Wake and return to Pearl; but there was always the chance she just might have to run up on the beach at Wake. Kimmel postponed D-Day for twenty-four hours, setting it as 24 December, Wake time.[2] This meant that during the daylight hours of 24 December, the *Tangier* and three destroyers were to arrive at Wake. Presumably the marine fighters would fly off the *Saratoga* early that morning, and there evidently were provisions for operating one of the *Saratoga*'s two dive bombing squadrons from Wake as well, at least on a temporary basis. Meanwhile, Fitch's carrier aircraft and the marine fighters from Wake had to maintain control of the air space surrounding the vulnerable atoll. CinCPac estimated that the *Tangier* might require two days at anchor off Wake to complete unloading and loading. That placed an extremely heavy burden on the fighters, both naval and marine, whose services were critical to the success of the operation. Fletcher's oiler *Neches* was old and slow, top speed only 12.75 knots, but she was the only one available. Brown took the swifter *Neosho* with Task Force 11, but he had more ocean to cross in less time than allotted to Fletcher. Even hampered by the slow rate of advance, Fletcher could expect to reach Wake on schedule. He had the option to fuel at his discretion; obviously this meant refueling just before he expected contact with the enemy. Task Force 14 faced no easy task if the enemy mustered any real opposition.

The night of 15–16 December the pilots of Fighting Three slept on board "Sister Sara" berthed off Ford Island. Early the next morning they saw the fighters of VMF-221 rehoisted on board the carrier. Given the fragile nature of the Brewster Buffalo and the infrequent carrier landing experience of the marine pilots, no one wanted to risk any damage to the fighters. Destination was as yet unspecified, but it was difficult to dismiss Wake from one's mind. Reporting ashore to NAS Pearl Harbor, Fighting Three reclaimed their planes and stood dawn alert. Later that morning there was time to check out rookie pilots Lee Haynes, Jack Wilson, and Edward ("Doc") Sellstrom in Grumman F4F Wildcats. Thach had drawn two additional fighters from the AirBatFor pool, giving Fighting Three only thirteen F4Fs in all: ten F4F-3s, two F4F-3As and the XF4F-4, an early F4F-3 modified as an experimental, folding-wing version of the Wildcat. It was a sad commentary on naval aviation preparedness that Thach had to embark on a major combat mission with barely more than half a squadron of airplanes, one of which was on strength just for tests! The green pilots, inexperienced as they were, gave their elders more worries when, during field carrier landing practice, two of them managed to ground-loop their frisky mounts. This was an easy thing to do because of the Wildcat's narrow undercarriage. Both aircraft suffered scraped wingtips. Maintenance crews hurriedly repaired one Grumman, but they had to rush the other dockside to be hoisted on board the *Saratoga* before she sailed. They just made it. At 1215, the carrier got under way.

Lt. Cdr. Cruise assembled the *Saratoga* Air Group at NAS Pearl Harbor, and later that day led them out to the carriers, landing on board a half hour before sunset. The group's composition (shown in the table) was twenty-seven fighters, forty-three dive bombers, and eleven torpedo planes, eighty-one aircraft in all, but not all were operational. The figures for fighter strength are deceptive. The marines were to transfer to Wake, leaving the *Sara* only thirteen fighters with which to protect the task force and escort strikes.

Two days out of Pearl, Brown's Task Force 11, en route to attack the Marshalls, underwent a rather bizarre experience. At dawn on 16 December, the *Lexington* launched twelve SBDs to fly in pairs a routine search 100 miles ahead of the task

Commander, *Saratoga* Air Group	Lt. Cdr. Edgar A. Cruise	1	SBD-3
Fighting Three	Lieut. John S. Thach	13	F4Fs
Bombing Three	Lt. Cdr. Maxwell F. Leslie	21	SBD-3s
Scouting Three	Lt. Cdr. Herbert L. Hoerner	21	SBD-3s
Torpedo Three	Lieut. John E. Clark	11	TBD-1s
Attached:			
VMF-221	Maj. Verne A. McCaul	14	F2A-3s

force. Not long before 0800 there came the electrifying report that two of the SBDs had encountered a Japanese carrier bearing 210 degrees, distance 95 miles from the task force. No further messages were forthcoming from them. Brown and Sherman deduced that Japanese fighters had intercepted the two search planes, and Brown detached his oiler *Neosho*, sending her away from danger. Excited by the opportunity to sink an enemy carrier, he later remarked it was the "chance of a lifetime."[3] The *Lexington* at 0813 scrambled ten F2As from Fighting Two as combat air patrol, then started spotting a strike force for takeoff. Beginning at 0924, she launched sixteen dive bombers, thirteen torpedo planes, and seven fighters, all led by the group commander, Bill Ault.

During the launch of the strike group, the two SBDs that had originally spotted the enemy carrier returned to the task force. Once the flight deck was clear and the attack planes were en route to the target, the *Lex* at 0933 brought the two on board. Taken before "Ted" Sherman, the two pilots, Ens. Mark T. Whittier and Ens. Clem B. Connally of Bombing Two, both stated they had dive-bombed the carrier, but claimed no hits. As related by the two ensigns, the target stayed strangely dead in the water and gave no return fire. It was puzzling indeed. Finally someone remembered that on 7 December a naval tugboat towing a dynamite barge to Palmyra Island had received orders to cut it loose and return to base. Evidently that barge was the "carrier" so vigorously assaulted by the two SBDs. Sherman at 1143 somewhat sheepishly signaled Brown on board the *Indianapolis* that the target was a drifting barge.

Searching the target area thoroughly, Ault's flyers certainly found no carrier, and somewhat mystified they returned to base. The *Lexington* at 1325 recovered the attack planes, then despatched ten SBDs to look for the barge. They also could not locate it. Fighting Two flew CAP until near sunset. The two ensigns who had bombed the "carrier" had great difficulty surmounting the sarcasm of their fellow pilots, but they adamantly maintained that what they had attacked was indeed an enemy flattop. To add to the comedy of errors, the *Neosho* had disappeared over the horizon to escape the enemy "carrier," and no one knew precisely where she was. Brown dared not break radio silence to contact her. The next day the dawn search located her 41 miles to the southwest, but the afternoon search failed to sight her. Finally Brown roped in his errant oiler after dawn on 18 December and made ready to fuel before commencing his final approach to the target.

The morning of 17 December, the *Saratoga* and her escorts, one day from Pearl, overtook the *Neches* and the *Tangier*, uniting Task Force 14 for the first time. Fletcher set course for Wake at his oiler's best sustained speed, 12.75 knots. On board the flattop, Captain Archibald H. Douglas spread the word among the officers that the *Sara* was bound for Wake. The response was overwhelming, as everyone was proud of Wake's gallant defense. In the wardroom, someone put up a chart with Wake clearly outlined as the objective toward which the task force's track slowly inched. Fighting Three could not be more jubilant over the opportunity for early combat, especially at Wake. For the next several days, there would be no flying for the fighters, only the inevitable Zed II alerts. No matter, for each day the sun dipped into the ocean straight ahead of the Wake-bound ships.

Meanwhile, momentous events transpired at Pearl Harbor. By order of President Franklin D. Roosevelt, the Navy relieved Admiral Kimmel of his command pending a court of inquiry on the Pearl Harbor attack. The new CinCPac was Admiral Chester W. Nimitz, but he could not possibly reach Pearl Harbor and take command before the last week of December. On 17 December, Vice Admiral William S. Pye, commander of Battle Force, became temporary commander-in-chief, United

States Pacific Fleet, pending Nimitz's arrival. Pye's first concern, naturally, was the Wake Island operation already in progress. Fleet intelligence, trying to rebuild its estimates of what was going on in the Pacific, began to detect radio communications between Japanese land-based air units operating out of the Marshalls and powerful carrier forces evidently in the area. Wake's air besiegers flew from bases in the Marshalls. These messages seemed to indicate that the enemy had hedged his bets by assigning strong carrier reinforcements to support a second, more massive assault on the stubbornly held atoll. On 18 December (Hawaiian time), the link became more definite, when decrypts tied the Japanese 8th Cruiser Division and 2nd Carrier Division (both identified as part of the Pearl Harbor Attack Force) with the Fourth Fleet in the Marshalls. That command was responsible for the capture of Wake. One message hinted of the presence of the 5th Carrier Division as well, perhaps in the eastern Marshalls. This, if true, appeared to place four Japanese carriers at the disposal of the commander attacking Wake. Pye forwarded these estimates to Brown and Fletcher, fully remembering that Kimmel's original plans were predicated on not encountering strong opposition.

Brown on 18 December also learned from the acting CinCPac that the Japanese had apparently set up a seaplane base at Makin Atoll in the Gilberts and also occupied Tarawa south of there. In order to approach Jaluit, his primary objective, Brown would have to pass within search range of Makin and risk early detection. This could bring down on Task Force 11 not only air attacks by land-based bombers, but also counterattacks by enemy flattops possibly in the area. Task Force 11 spent 18 and 19 December fueling while slowly closing Jaluit. On 19 December Brown detached the *Neosho* to wait in safer waters. Weighing greatly on his mind was the necessity of skirting Makin in order to attack Jaluit.

For Paul Ramsey's Fighting Two, the cruise so far had proved largely uneventful, but the excitement was building at the thought of going into combat in a few days. The nineteenth of December turned out to be a day for photographs, first of the assembled squadron draped over the wings of two Brewster Buffaloes, then a group shot of the pilots (the NAPs in their denim fatigues doubling as flight gear), and finally individual poses by pilots in front of their aircraft. Little did Fighting Two know it would be months before most of them even saw the enemy!

With his other two carrier task forces now at sea, Kimmel had thought it wise to bring Halsey's Task Force 8 back to Pearl for resupply and rest. On 16 December the *Enterprise* sent her air group to NAS Pearl Harbor, then made ready to enter port. Fighting Six contributed eleven Wildcats for the flight, while four others patrolled over the carrier until she was safely in the ship channel. For those pilots flying into Pearl, thoughts of the debacle on the night of 7 December were uppermost: "The long way in past all the batteries still gives everyone a thrill."[4] The pilots had a free afternoon to poke around Ford Island and look at Japanese aircraft shot down during the raid. What they saw did not impress them. Rejoining the squadron was Dave Flynn, survivor of the tragic 7 December incident.

On 17 December, Fighting Six squared away new pilots who had ridden the *Saratoga* across from San Diego: Ensigns David W. Criswell, Howard L. Grimmell, and William M. Holt. They and the newly acquired Rad. Elec. Bayers practiced field carrier landings in Grumman F4F Wildcats. Even that training had to be curtailed the next morning for lack of fighters. McClusky had to turn over to Fighting Three, pending their return from Wake, no fewer than three F4Fs, but in turn received two others, one of which was Hermann's old F4F, repaired after being shot up on 7 December. From the AirBatFor pool, Fighting Six also scrounged a stray Brewster F2A-3 Buffalo left ashore by Fighting Two. It was one of two

The "Chiefs" of VF-2, *l to r:* T. S. Gay, Paul Baker, Gordon Firebaugh, Hal Rutherford on board the *Lexington*, 19 Dec. 1941. (Capt. G. E. Firebaugh, USN.)

VF-2, 19 Dec. 1941. (Cdr. T. F. Cheek, USN.)

McClusky was supposed to get. This time he ended up with fourteen F4F Wildcats and one F2A Buffalo. The squadron was to embark the next day. Lieut. (jg) Mehle's VF-6 engineers spent the night in a Ford Island hangar getting the newly acquired aircraft ready for duty.

Fighting Six at daybreak on 19 December turned out on alert. The *Enterprise* sailed as part of Halsey's Task Force 8. His orders were to operate south of Midway and westward of Johnston in order to support the two carrier task forces about to engage the enemy. Pye wanted Halsey to act as a backstop should the Japanese pursue either Brown or Fletcher. McClusky that morning led twelve fighters out to the carrier, including the one F2A Buffalo with VF-2 veteran Ed Bayers flying her. After two and a half hours of tiresome circling, all aircraft landed safely. With the three fighters already on board the *Enterprise*, Fighting Six for this cruise counted eleven F4F-3As, three F4F-3s, and one F2A-3. Again, a fighting squadron had to sortie without attaining full aircraft strength. The VF-6 pilots had no dope as to the objective, only that they were west-bound.

The nineteenth of December was a day of anticipation for Fletcher's Task Force 14 plodding along at the *Neches*'s best speed. Ahead the skies grew ominously overcast. Squall lines formed, and the seas turned rougher. The noon position report placed the task force 1,020 miles east of Wake and five days from the objective. Unfortunately, it began to appear that Japanese carriers might be even closer.

THE DISAPPOINTMENT

The morning of 21 December (Wake time), the Japanese added a definite new twist to the problem of reinforcing Wake. Just before dawn, forty-nine strike planes from the carriers *Sōryū* and *Hiryū* roared down on Wake to bomb and strafe suspected strong points with impunity. There was no warning, nor was there air opposition from VMF-211. Lacking radar, the island command had no idea the raiders were coming. The eighteen Zero fighters, twenty-nine dive bombers, and two torpedo planes suffered no losses, and their presence over Wake sent reverberations all the way back to Washington.

The Japanese carriers were there because of Fourth Fleet's cry for help following the abortive 11 December invasion. Admiral Yamamoto Isoroku, commander of Combined Fleet, on 15 December detached from Nagumo's Pearl Harbor Attack Force a powerful striking force of two carriers, two heavy cruisers, and two destroyers. They formed the Wake Island Attack Force under Rear Admiral Abe Hiroaki, and his air task leader was Rear Admiral Yamaguchi Tamon, commander of the 2nd Carrier Division (the *Sōryū* and the *Hiryū*). Yamaguchi's air groups comprised thirty-two Zero fighters, thirty-two dive bombers, and thirty-six torpedo planes, all manned by crack aviators. From the west, Abe's ships had descended on Wake and on 21 December launched their strikes from about 200 miles away. After recovering aircraft, Abe steamed southeast toward the ships of the 2nd Wake Invasion Force, which that day had sortied from Kwajalein Atoll in the Marshalls. Operating southeast of Wake was Rear Admiral Gotō Aritomo's Marshall Area Operations Support Force with four heavy cruisers and two light cruisers. Gotō's task was to protect the invasion convoy's right flank and also to watch (presumably with his cruiser floatplanes) for the possible appearance of an American task force trying to reinforce Wake.

Aware that at least one enemy carrier lurked off Wake, Pye in his uncomfortable role as caretaker CinCPac had good reason to reevaluate the basic plan. Significantly, the enemy appeared to be increasing his air strength, land- and carrier-based, in the critical Marshalls–Gilberts region. This boded ill for Task Force 11's diversionary raid on Jaluit, as the enemy might well detect Brown on his way in. Best to cancel the Jaluit raid altogether. Pye preferred bringing Task Force 11 north to support Fletcher's Task Force 14 near Wake. According to CinCPac estimates, beginning D+2 (26 December, Wake time), Brown should be able to put planes over Wake. Halsey with Task Force 8 (the *Enterprise*) was bound for Midway. He would act as the reserve. The afternoon of 20 December (21 December, Wake time) Pye ordered Brown to cancel the raid on Jaluit and head for Wake. He was most concerned that Brown and Fletcher fuel before going into action, as he especially feared a running battle with Japanese carriers in which fuel shortage or damaged vessels could mean disaster for the Pacific Fleet.

Ironically, the same day Pye decided to call off the Jaluit raid, Brown on his own had concluded that Jaluit would be too tough. Instead he opted to attack Makin and Tarawa in the Gilberts, the air strikes to take place the morning of 22 December (East Longitude Date). At 1600 on 20 December, he announced his new plans to the task force. Interestingly, the attack plan called for the SBD dive bombers to be relaunched as supplementary combat air patrol after returning from the strike. Six to eight SBDs were to deploy in each quadrant around the *Lexington*, circling at 1,000 to 3,000 feet and one mile out from the screening vessels. This was the first manifestation of an idea that was a favorite of Sherman.[1] He felt that SBDs could cope with enemy torpedo planes, a concept that he would pursue in the future. Almost simultaneously with Brown's issuing of his Makin–Tarawa plans, his flagship *Indianapolis* copied the CinCPac despatch canceling the Jaluit strike. At 1738 Brown changed course to the northwest and headed off at 16 knots. He was still many days from the crucial area, as it was necessary for him to skirt the Marshalls to avoid enemy air searches before heading directly toward Wake.

The morning of 20 December, Fletcher's Task Force 14 with the *Saratoga* crossed the International Date Line, propelling time ahead to 0845, 21 December. Fletcher was now on the same side of the line as Wake and around 700 miles east of there. The weather was forbidding, with a gray overcast. That day the *Saratoga*'s SBDs flew intermediate and inner air patrol, but there still was no flying for Fighting Three. That afternoon, Fletcher received a despatch from Pye that ordered Task Force 14, except for the *Tangier* and her escorts, to stay more than 700 miles from the Japanese air bases at Rongelap in the Marshalls. Pye did not want the *Saratoga* to get too close to Wake, which was a focus for Japanese bombers flying from the Marshalls. If Fletcher kept more than 700 miles from Rongelap, enemy land-based air could neither sight nor attack him. At 2000, Task Force 14 was 635 miles northeast of Wake. Fletcher held to a northwesterly course to take the task force well north of Wake in order to approach the island from that direction.

The pilots of Fighting Three awoke before dawn on 22 December to prepare for flight duties, the first since landing on board near Oahu. The weather, they discovered, was worse than before. The *Sara* pitched and rolled in turbulent seas that even washed over her massive bow. Lovelace drew the early morning patrol, taking six Grumman F4Fs aloft at 0634. His mission was to cover the task force while Fletcher fueled his destroyers from the oiler *Neches*. Cross swells combined with 16- to 24-knot winds parted several oil hoses and greatly impeded the process. Fletcher had to swing north, then northeast to try to ease sea conditions. Task Force 14 at 0800 was 518 miles northeast of Wake. They were getting nowhere or even losing a little distance during fueling, but Fletcher still held to schedule to arrive at Wake on D-Day, 24 December. Fueling delays, however, cut deeply into what time reserve he had. Still, he had no choice but to continue fueling so that his destroyers would have the fuel to steam and fight, if need be, for several days.

By midmorning, Lovelace's fighters started to have fuel problems of their own. The *Saratoga* readied Thach's 1st Division to relieve them. His six F4Fs took off at 1021, and plane handlers respotted aircraft forward on the flight deck in order to land Lovelace's CAP. Unexpectedly, Thach returned to the carrier at high speed, flew along the flight deck, and gave the emergency deferred forced landing signal (wheels up, tail hook down). His wingman was in trouble. Lieut. (jg) Victor M. Gadrow's Grumman (3-F-12) acted up, and he tried to reach the carrier for a quick landing. Suddenly the aircraft appeared to lose power and fall away. It struck the water with a great splash about 1,400 yards off the port quarter. The F4F sank immediately in the rough seas. Racing to the scene, the destroyer *Selfridge*, acting as plane guard, found nothing. Fighting Three had suffered its first casualty of the war. Vic Gadrow was a 1935 graduate of the Naval Academy and had but recently transferred to aviation after almost five years on board the battleship *Colorado*.

Earning his wings in the spring of 1941, Gadrow had reported to Fighting Three, where he was learning fast. Thach had earmarked him as a section leader. The loss of pilot and aircraft left Fighting Three with twelve Wildcats.

That same morning, 22 December, aircraft from the *Sōryū* and the *Hiryū* again attacked Wake, but this time a surprise awaited them. Two VMF-211 pilots, Capt. Herbert C. Freuler and 1st Lieut. Carl R. Davidson, were aloft and in position to intercept. The enemy strike group consisted of thirty-three Nakajima B5N2 Type 97 carrier attack (torpedo) planes [KATE] from both carrier air groups. Escorting them were six Zero fighters. The carrier attack planes formed up by divisions (*chūtai*) at 12,000 feet to execute horizontal bombing runs over Wake, the six fighters covering them from 18,000 feet. Freuler charged after six Japanese planes in close formation at 12,000 feet. He thought they were Zero fighters, but actually they were a *chūtai* from the *Sōryū* Carrier Attack Unit. Diving in, Freuler shot down two bombers, the last in a furious head-on run.[2] Exploding just in front of the F4F, debris from the second Japanese plane so damaged Freuler's Wildcat that he had to run for base. Before he could get clean away, a real Zero jumped his tail and riddled the F4F with gunfire, wounding Freuler. He crash-landed on Wake and walked away, although his airplane was done for. Davidson immediately tangled with some of the Zeros, and was seen no more. The bombers plastered suspected battery positions, then departed southwest toward their carriers. Wake no longer had any fighter support.

Fletcher spent the afternoon of 22 December fretting about fueling delays in the face of worsening weather. At noon, he had resumed his slow advance to the northwest, but conditions permitted only four of his destroyers to take their drink of oil. He hoped to fuel the rest early the next morning before commencing the second phase of the operation—sending the *Tangier* and her escorts to Wake. At 2000, Task Force 14 was 543 miles northeast of Wake. During the night Fletcher made good some of the miles lost because of the refueling and prepared to resume fueling at first light the next day. Late that evening, Fletcher received another message from CinCPac revealing Pye's misgivings about the Wake operation. Fletcher was not to take the *Saratoga* any closer than 200 miles to Wake. He could still fly the marine fighters off to Wake during the approach, but now they would have to protect the island and also the *Tangier*'s run to the objective. There was no prospect that VF-3's fighters, now numbering only a dozen, could cooperate with VMF-221 after they reached Wake. Thach's fighters would have to remain behind to defend Task Force 14.

Even so, the Japanese were not about to give the Pacific Fleet the opportunity to reinforce Wake. In the early hours of 23 December, the 2nd Wake Island Invasion Force drew up near the atoll and disembarked special naval landing troops. They stormed ashore around 0230, and by dawn, despite a gallant defense, the Wake garrison was sorely beset. At 0700, the first of twenty fighters, twelve dive bombers, and twenty-seven carrier attack planes from the *Sōryū* and the *Hiryū* appeared over Wake and pounded any signs of resistance that popped up ahead of advancing Japanese troops. Except for tiny Wilkes Island where the marines had virtually annihilated the invaders, the Japanese by 0800 had subdued all opposition. The battle for Wake was over.

Radio reports from Wake had alerted CinCPac of the presence of invasion forces. At Pearl Harbor, Pye convened his staff before dawn. They generally agreed that with the forces at hand, Wake probably could not be saved. The enemy was bound to be much stronger for the second attempt to capture the atoll. Intelligence estimated that as many as two carriers, some cruisers, and probably a pair of fast battleships lurked near Wake, although some officers thought there might be only one "small" carrier, the *Sōryū*.

Given the expected loss of Wake, the question became one of allowing Fletcher to attack the invasion ships clustered around the island. He could attack alone, or later in concert with Brown coming up from the southeast. Captain Charles H. McMorris of War Plans urged that Fletcher make a counterattack, citing a number of pertinent points to support his aggressive advice. Task Force 14 had already fueled (or should have, according to plan) and was ready to fight. The *Saratoga* this trip wielded two fighting squadrons (VF-3 and VMF-221), and McMorris fel this put the odds "strongly in her favor."[3] A swift carrier raid, he believed, would catch the Japanese unaware, as they did not know of the presence of Task Force 14 in the area. McMorris stressed that at little real risk to the *Saratoga*, there wa a major opportunity to deal the enemy a telling blow and win for the Pacific Flee a desperately needed victory.

Pye, for one, viewed the situation less sanguinely than did McMorris. Unlike some members of his staff, he thought there were at least two Japanese carrier prowling off Wake and knew that they, in combination with the fast battleship also likely to be out there, would be too much for Task Force 14 to handle Especially so early in the game he did not want to risk the loss of even one of hi own carriers. During the deliberations, a despatch from Admiral Stark offered tacit approval of the conservative approach, stating that "Wake is now and wil continue to be a liability."[4] Pye later described his feelings:

> My conclusion was that if action developed against any but unimportant naval forces at Wake it would be on enemy's terms in range of shore-based bombers with our forces 2000 miles from nearest base with inadequate fuel for more than 2 days high speed, with probable loss of any damaged ships, and might involve two task forces.[5]

Thus in Pye's view anything that Fletcher alone or later with Brown might encounter at Wake either would be too weak to count as much of a diversion, or, far more likely, would be too strong to defeat. Consequently Pye radioed a recall order to Brown and Fletcher, bringing them back to Pearl. Covering their withdrawal would be Halsey with Task Force 8 near Midway.

About 450 miles northeast of Wake, Fletcher's Task Force 14 before dawn on 23 December monitored some of the island's invasion reports. The *Saratoga* readied flight operations for six F4Fs on CAP and an outer air patrol (100-mile search) by twelve SBDs. Thach led his 1st Division aloft at 0628. After sunrise, the *Neches* resumed fueling the last four destroyers. Fortunately the seas were calmer, and refueling proceeded more swiftly than the previous day. Unaware of CinCPac deliberations, Fletcher continued to prepare for the *Tangier*'s dash to Wake, to begin on schedule later that morning. The *Neches* and a destroyer would stand off to the east in safety, while Task Force 14 went in. Fletcher would accompany the *Tangier* to within 200 miles of Wake and cover her final approach with the *Saratoga*'s air group. Presumably the marine fighters would take off at dawn on 24 December. On board the *Saratoga*, there was great anticipation, as the pilots were certain they would pitch into the enemy besiegers of Wake, including "one small carrier"[6] skulking off the island.

The first inkling of a major change for Task Force 14 occurred at 0753, when the *Astoria* copied Cdr. Cunningham's famous message referring to the enemy on the island: the issue is in doubt. Just two minutes later came CinCPac's recall order.

the product of five hours of deliberation at Pearl. Pye had sent it before he received final word of Wake's fate. According to one source, Fletcher was so exasperated at receiving the recall, that he threw his gold-braided hat to the deck.[7] Faced with a direct order, he had no choice but to comply. At 0800, he was still 430 miles northeast of Wake. To facilitate fueling, he turned north, taking advantage of better sea conditions to complete the necessary transfer of oil to his destroyers.

While Fletcher and Fitch stewed over the situation, the *Saratoga* went on with business as usual. There were relief flights to send off and planes low on fuel to recover. At 0956, Lovelace's 2nd Division from Fighting Three took off as CAP. Behind the six F4Fs came twelve SBDs from Scouting Three as the forenoon outer air patrol. The dive bomber flown by Lieut. (jg) Harold D. Shrider rolled down the flight deck, but failed to attain flying speed. Circling near the carrier, Lovelace clearly saw what happened. The Dauntless shot out over the bow, but instead of climbing away, it plummeted into the water just ahead of the ship. There was a huge splash, as the SBD disappeared into the ocean. Its tail bounced back up almost instantly, and as the aircraft balanced on its nose, the *Saratoga* brushed an outstretched wing. Shrider's SBD sank without a trace. A destroyer hurried to the scene to pick up survivors, but there were none.

Thach landed a few minutes after the mishap and learned of the recall. Reaction was understandably bitter. Everyone felt frustrated at not being able to help the Wake marines and bluejackets. They thought they were wasting a grand opportunity to deal the Japanese a stinging defeat. Talk among the officers had it that the enemy had only "one small carrier" in the area—easy pickings for the *Saratoga*. With more insight than most, Lovelace wrote in his diary, "The set up seemed perfect for those of us who did not have the complete picture of the strategical situation."[8] He, for one, was willing to give CinCPac the benefit of the doubt.

Lovelace's attitude was rare among the officers of Task Force 14. Captain Douglas of the *Saratoga*, for example, urged Fitch to contact Fletcher on board the *Astoria* and request permission for a raid on Wake the next morning to blast enemy invasion shipping there. Fitch sympathized with those who wanted aggressive action, but he left the bridge because of the "mutinous" nature of the conversation. The orders gave Fletcher no discretion, although he stayed in the area on a slow northerly heading to complete fueling. Fighting Three flew CAP for the rest of the day. At 1730, just before sunset, Fletcher with great reluctance set a southeasterly heading back toward Pearl, a little less than 1,600 miles away. At 2056, CinCPac sent amplifying orders telling Fletcher to retire toward Midway and on Christmas Day to despatch the fighters of VMF-221 to that base. The *Tangier*, as well, was to proceed to Midway.

Still east of the date line, Brown's Task Force 11 with the *Lexington* was about 750 miles southeast of Wake, when at 0745 [22 December] the carrier logged in the recall order. Brown changed course to rejoin the *Neosho* and fuel on the way back to Pearl. Halsey's Task Force 8 with the *Enterprise* was located nearly 1,100 miles east of Wake. He and his minions likewise were disgusted at the turn of events—the spectacle of the United States Pacific Fleet retreating without even contesting the fall of Wake. They thought that before recall the *Saratoga* had already closed to within striking distance (200 miles off Wake). Fighting Six's unofficial war diary lamented, "Everyone seems to feel that it's the war between the two yellow races."[9]

What were the obtainable realities of the Wake relief mission? CinCPac set D-Day as 24 December. The authorities at Pearl possessed all of the information available to Fletcher and a great deal more. Fletcher had no authority whatsoever to alter the basic plan without approval. In his "semi-official" history, Rear Admiral Samuel Eliot Morison took Fletcher to task for not scrapping the operational plan when he first learned that Japanese carrier planes had hit Wake (21 December, Wake time). According to Morison's hindsight, Fletcher should have left the *Tangier* and the *Neches* behind and rushed in at 20 knots, so he could surprise the Wake invasion forces at dawn on 23 December.[10] Morison ignores the fact that CinCPac specifically expected Task Force 14 to refuel before entering combat. Fletcher fueled in the face of poor sea conditions. Even so, he "expected to carry out the mission and have the *Tangier* and planes arrive Wake on D-Day."[11]

The attack by Japanese carrier planes on Wake and the actual second invasion decisively altered the equation in favor of the enemy. Pye had no way of knowing whether the enemy carriers would loiter around Wake in hopes of trapping an American relief force. Task Force 14 required control of the skies. Critics have failed to realize that the *Saratoga* alone just was not a match for the *Sōryū* and the *Hiryū*. McMorris cited the fact in defense of an aggressive approach, that the *Saratoga* carried two fighting squadrons. Evidently he was not aware that Fighting Three was sadly understrength (only thirteen F4Fs when it left Pearl), while the marines of VMF-221 were not much better off with fourteen F2A-3 Buffaloes. Complicating matters was the fact that the leathernecks were inexperienced in carrier operations and doctrine; certainly in a desperate battle they could not be counted upon as effective in a carrier situation as an equivalent naval fighting squadron. Once the decision was made by Pye to withdraw, Fletcher had no choice but to obey. Morison unkindly cited in his history a somewhat gratuitous comment by an unidentified cruiser captain who said, "Frank Jack should have placed the telescope to his blind eye like Nelson."[12] These were easy words for someone without the responsibility of command in that particular situation. Pye simply could not risk losing an American carrier at that time. For the Pacific Fleet in December 1941, Wake despite the valor of its defenders was indeed a liability.

CHAPTER 3

Interregnum

THE WEEKS OF FUTILITY

The fall of Wake brought a lull in active operations to the extent that the Pacific Fleet contemplated no offensive operations for the time being. Pye, ad hoc CinCPac, awaited the arrival of Chester Nimitz. In Washington, Admiral Ernest J. King was assuming the post of Commander-in-Chief, United States Fleet (CominCh). A naval aviator (wings in 1927 as a captain), King was a former skipper of the *Lexington* and in 1938–39, Commander, Aircraft, Battle Force (ComAirBatFor). He had definite ideas about employment of carriers and no qualms about implementing them.

As December came to a close, all three carrier task forces operated west of the Hawaiian Islands. Retiring from the abortive Wake relief were Task Forces 11 and 14. Rough seas dogged both Brown and Fletcher. Halsey's Task Force 8 received a new mission: protect Midway pending the arrival of the seaplane tender *Wright*. Pye held to the basic policy of shuttling the carriers through Pearl one at a time. When one carrier task force was in port, the other two would be at sea. Any other course of action would have to wait until the new CinCPac had settled in.

To help bring order out of chaos at Pearl, Halsey on 18 December had sent ashore several members of the AirBatFor staff to handle administrative duties. Important for the carrier squadrons was Cdr. John B. Lyon, structures (aircraft) officer in charge of the materiel office. He handled aircraft allocation and regulations. One of his first concerns involved aircraft markings and how they could be altered to reduce the deplorable number of mistaken-identity shootings. Naval aircraft at that time were painted dark blue on the upper surfaces and light gray underneath. Basic markings comprised small white fuselage stars (in blue circles with central red dots), one on each side behind the cockpit, and similar but larger stars on the wings (upper surface left wing, lower surface right wing). Squadron type and plane markings (in black or white numerals and letters, depending on the squadron [see appendix]) were placed on the fuselage, cowling, and wings. The nomenclature of the fuselage markings, next to the roundels, identified squadron number, type ("F" for fighting), and individual plane number within the squadron. Thus 2-F-1, for example, was the number one aircraft in Fighting Two.

On 21 December, representatives from the Army's Hawaiian Department and the Pearl Harbor–based Navy's Patrol Wing Two met to discuss what could be done to assure proper recognition.[1] They decided to put stars on all four upper and lower wing surfaces and increased the diameter of those roundels to the full

Changing insignia, probably VF-6 late Dec. 1941 or early Jan. 1942. (NA 80-G-14451.)

width of the chord. Likewise they proposed increasing fuselage roundels to the maximum size possible. To complete the new color scheme, they also recommended that the aircraft rudders be painted with thirteen equally sized stripes, alternating red and white. With the approval of CinCPac, Lyon two days later issued specific regulations for the carrier squadrons to follow in line with the 21 December conference.[2] The planes would look very colorful, if nothing else! Fighting Six's 1941 Christmas card noted: "pepermint [sic] candy sticks may be viewed on the tails of planes."[3] Squadrons repainted their aircraft according to the ComAirBatFor scheme, but in early 1942 there was a bewildering number of minor changes, which with much shifting of aircraft from one squadron to another led to a somewhat motley look among the carrier squadrons.

More important than how the fighters looked was the vital need for sufficient numbers of them. Lyon and his counterpart at NAS San Diego, Cdr. Henry R. Oster, advised their superiors to transfer Grumman F4F-3s and F4F-3As from marine fighting squadrons on the West Coast out to Pearl. The marines could more easily obtain more airplanes from Atlantic squadrons currently exchanging F4F-3s for the new folding wing F4F-4s. Thus on 26 December, Oster instructed VMF-111 and VMF-121 to turn in thirty-seven Grummans for shipment to Pearl. They arrived in January–February 1942 and were urgently required in bringing the fighting squadrons up to some semblance of authorized strength.

Brown's Task Force 11 with the *Lexington* was the first to return after the futile Central Pacific operations. Heavy seas prevented his ships from refueling and restricted flights. What missions Fighting Two did fly were mostly inner air patrol hunting enemy submarines. During one such, on 26 December and one day from Pearl, VF-2 pilot Harold E. (Hal) Rutherford, ACMM, discovered gasoline leaking into the cockpit of his F2A-3 Buffalo. He headed back to the *Lexington* and at 1113 requested permission to land. The *Lex*'s flight deck was not clear, but Rutherford could not wait. The Brewster's engine sputtered, then cut out altogether. The veteran chief deadsticked 2-F-3 into choppy seas about a mile off the carrier's port bow. The destroyer *Monaghan* fished him out suffering only minor injuries. The next day Paul Ramsey led seventeen operational F2As to NAS Pearl Harbor, and Task Force 11 docked there that afternoon.

Fighting Two discovered six new pilots awaiting its return. Lieut. (jg) Richard S. Bull, Jr., a former VF-42 pilot, had just come from Britain, where he had been an aviation observer. The five others were NAPs: Thomas W. Rhodes, RM1c, William H. Warden, AMM1c, Beverly W. Reid, AMM2c, Homer W. Carter, AOM2c, and Wayne E. Davenport, AMM2c. The squadron turned over three F2As to the AirBatFor pool for repairs and reassignment, leaving seventeen on tap. On 29 December the *Lexington* with the rest of Task Force 11 departed for a short cruise southwest of the Hawaiian Islands. Ramsey took his seventeen F2As out to the ship, but only sixteen made it. Fred Borries in 2-F-5 dropped too fast after taking the landing signal officer's cut and struck the ramp. His Brewster caromed off the stern and splashed 200 yards off the port beam. The F2A sank swiftly, but the faithful *Monaghan* recovered Borries, who sustained a cut forehead and bruised left shoulder. This cruise the *Lexington* Air Group numbered sixteen fighters, thirty-three dive bombers, and fifteen torpedo planes.

The thirtieth of December, the day Admiral Nimitz formally became CinCPac, Fighting Two ran into more trouble: another F2A cracked up on landing. The Brewster airplanes simply lacked the strength for prolonged service at sea. On New Year's eve, Task Force 11 headed in for what it hoped was action at last, as radio intelligence pointed to enemy warships supposed lurking off Johnston Island. Brown closed in for the kill, but soon learned it was another false alarm. Once again Ramsey's squadron endured a landing mishap. At this rate the F2As would not last long enough to fight! (An outcome that would have been better for everyone.) The first two days of 1942 Brown steamed back toward Oahu. On 3 January, the whole group took up residence at MCAS Ewa, where Fighting Two reported to the Army's 7th Pursuit Command for temporary duty on air defense. The *Lexington* herself would be in the navy yard for several days, while concerned specialists tried to remedy an electrical ground in one of her four main rotors. If they could not effect repairs, she would have to limp to Bremerton.

Task Force 14's turn in port came next. On the trip back from Wake Fletcher had also encountered turbulent seas. Because of the date line, the ships enjoyed two Christmas Days, and during the second, the *Saratoga* was able to send VMF-221's fourteen F2A Buffaloes to Midway. Spared combat at Wake, VMF-221's leathernecks would bear the brunt of the June 1942 Japanese air assault on Midway. The afternoon of 27 December afforded Thach the long-awaited opportunity for gunnery exercises, and he took all twelve F4Fs aloft for runs on towed sleeves. Two days later, the *Saratoga* Air Group flew to NAS Kaneohe Bay, and the ships docked at Pearl.

During their brief time ashore, Fighting Three caught up with the mail and finally had a chance to relax. The squadron sold off four F4F-3As (including three VF-6 airplanes that VF-3 did not have a chance to fly) and drew one F4F-3 in return. Also available were two F2A Buffaloes on loan from Fighting Two. In light of VF-3's previous experience with F2A-2s, these Brewsters were no problem to fly. However, on 30 December, Thach still only counted fourteen fighters (twelve F4Fs and two F2As). Little yet could be done to alleviate the near-crippling shortage of fighters with the fleet.

On 30 December, Task Force 14 changed admirals. Fletcher left his flagship *Astoria* for a new carrier task force assembling at San Diego. Taking his place was another nonaviator, Rear Admiral Herbert Fairfax Leary, Commander, Cruisers, Battle Force. He broke his two-star flag on board the *Saratoga*. Rear Admiral Fitch reluctantly went ashore as Halsey's administrative representative for Aircraft, Battle Force. Among the urgent items he handled were organization, supply, and materiel for all of the carrier squadrons shore-based on Oahu. He also saw to the organization of special carrier air service units at the various naval air stations in the Hawaiian Islands. Fitch worked diligently and successfully to bring the carrier air groups to full operating strength, but he would be sorely missed at sea.

Leary's Task Force 14 with the *Saratoga* (fourteen fighters, thirty-seven dive bombers, and thirteen torpedo planes), two heavy cruisers, and six destroyers sailed on 31 December to patrol in the Midway area. The first few days were routine, and Fighting Three worked in some excellent training on 2 January. The next day an AlNav (All-Navy) despatch from the Bureau of Navigation brought news that nearly everyone had been promoted one rank. Thach and Lovelace became lieutenant commanders, most jaygees stepped up to senior grade, and ensigns with long service added a half-stripe as lieutenants (junior grade). Quite a scramble ensued for the proper insignia and an opportunity to be sworn in by the captain. The promotions were Navy-wide and provided a more realistic rank, given responsibilities of the new war. They certainly were welcome in all of the fighting squadrons. For Thach, celebrations were dampened by illness. On 4 January he went on the sick list, and Lovelace led Fighting Three for the rest of the cruise.

Taking his turn in the Oahu revolving door was Bill Halsey, returning on 31 December after being a distant spectator to the drama at Wake. His mission of covering Midway proceeded without a hitch. Just before reaching Oahu, the *Enterprise* sent her air group to Ewa. Wade McClusky took eight F4Fs there, leaving four under Roger Mehle to patrol over the carrier on her approach to Pearl. Ens. John C. Kelley, piloting one of the VF-6 F4Fs, made a normal takeoff run up deck until he lifted off. Then the Wildcat suddenly skittered left, dropped its left wing radically, and stalled. Kelley narrow missed the deck edge, while he spiraled into the sea. Despite smashing his head on the gunsight mount, Jack Kelley scrambled free of his sinking plane to be picked up by the plane guard destroyer. Fighting Six stayed briefly at Ewa and commiserated with the marines over bottles of beer about the fate of Wake. The same afternoon, they flew on to Ford Island, where there was no New Year's liberty for them. The uninterrupted sleep they enjoyed was almost worth missing the parties. For the next few days the squadron rested ashore. On 2 January they took delivery of four F4F-3As courtesy of Thach (three were originally VF-6 planes) and turned in the orphan F2A Buffalo. Fighting Six now boasted seventeen F4F Wildcats (fourteen F4F-3As and three F4F-3s).

The morning of 3 January, Task Force 8 departed on a make-work cruise north of Oahu for some gunnery training, to cover an important convoy coming in from the States, and to have only one carrier task force in port at a time. McClusky took fifteen F4Fs out to the *Enterprise* and left two ashore for the five new pilots, Presley, Hodson, Grimmell, Criswell, and Holt, to use in field carrier landing practice. The next day, Halsey's ships carried out practice of their own, antiaircraft gunnery exercises. Flying inner air patrol (and carefully keeping well clear), the VF-6 pilots were not impressed: "If those guns ever do go into action they will probably bring down as many friends as foes."[4] Rough seas curtailed training the following two days. On 7 January, the *Enterprise* flew off her aircraft before coming into port. Fighting Six first flew to NAS Kaneohe, then hopped over to base at Ewa with their marine buddies. They landed in the rain, which was okay until the marines decided to respot the fighters. The VF-6 pilots had to brave the weather and taxi their Wildcats to new parking areas.

Again because one carrier was coming into Pearl, another had to leave. Her turboelectric drive now functioning properly, the *Lexington* sailed on 7 January, now as flagship of Task Force 11 because Brown had moved over from the heavy cruiser *Indianapolis*. CinCPac had planned originally to use Task Force 11 against enemy bases at Wotje and Maloelap atolls in the Marshalls in connection with other operations being planned, but then changed his mind; Brown's orders were to conduct the usual patrol toward Johnston. Leary's Task Force 14 operated northwest of that area. Ramsey had seventeen F2As with him on board the *Lexington*, but only fifteen were flyable. Brown set a southwest course toward Johnston Island.

The enemy was closer at hand than many realized. On 6 January while Task Force 14 started back to the southeast from Midway, a *Saratoga* dive bomber on search spotted an enemy submarine traveling eastward on the surface. The SBD attacked, but dropped an unarmed 500-pounder on the I-boat as it crash-dived. The next day the submarine still lurked nearby. Another *Saratoga* SBD pilot saw her bucking heavy seas 47 miles southeast of the task force and attacked, but again the bomb was not armed! Both days Fighting Three conducted tests and deck handling practice with the folding wing XF4F-4. On 8 and 9 January, the seas grew so tumultuous that flying was canceled. Waves washed over the *Sara*'s bows, and seawater ran into the forward elevator well. Central Pacific seas in winter did not make for pleasurable sailing! Leary continued southeasterly at a slow pace, bound for a rendezvous with Halsey's Task Force 8 set up by CinCPac to allow the *Saratoga* to exchange aircraft with the *Enterprise*. As part of this, Thach was to hand over his F4F-3s to McClusky in return for VF-6's less desirable F4F-3As.

Task Force 11 with the *Lexington*, heading southwest from Pearl toward Johnston Island, next became involved with the I-boats. Around 0630 on 9 January, lookouts on *I-18* spotted Brown's ships about 300 miles northeast of Johnston. The skipper, Cdr. Otani Kiyonori, radioed to Sixth Fleet headquarters the position, course, and speed of the *Lexington*-class carrier and cruiser he had found. That alerted the submarine command to the presence of an American carrier force operating around Johnston, and it pulled several I-boats from patrols off the Hawaiian Islands in order to pursue Otani's contact.[5]

On 10 January, unaware she had been sighted the previous day, the *Lexington* launched a routine search of twelve SBDs to proceed 300 miles ahead of the task force, while four VF-2 F2As covered the remainder of the circle with 50-mile precautionary patrols astern. At 1020, Fighting Two got its first look at the enemy.[6] Lieut. (jg) Fred Simpson and Doyle C. Barnes, AMM1c, caught sight of a Japanese submarine running surfaced about 60 miles south of the task force. The I-boat's lookouts were on the ball, and the skipper crash-dived before the two F2As could get close. Simpson hightailed it back to the *Lexington*, at 1057 dropping a beanbag message container onto the flight deck. The note inside detailed the submarine's course and speed (270 degrees, 18 knots) and position, which when plotted worked out to roughly 100 miles west of Johnston.

The *Lexington* recovered the morning search, and at 1230 sent a similar mission with SBDs and F2As. As an added bonus, Sherman also despatched two pairs of TBD Devastators from Torpedo Two. Each carried two 325-lb. depth charges. They did not have long to wait. Flying their 50-mile search, Lieut. (jg) Clark Rinehart and Charles E. Brewer, RM1c, from Fighting Two eyeballed the same I-boat, brazenly cruising on the surface now 80 miles south of Task Force 11. So as not to spook the enemy into submerging, Rinehart cleverly pulled back up sun, and at 1325 reported his position to the ship. The *Lexington* vectored to the scene two TBDs, flown by Ens. Norman A. Sterrie and Harley E. Talkington, AOM2c.

Meanwhile, Rinehart held back until he saw the two Devastators in position; then he led Brewer in a strafing run. Sterrie and Talkington approached at 2,000 feet, and at 1341 dived in. The Japanese finally saw them coming, and the I-boat began to plow under the waves. Sterrie salvoed his two depth charges just astern of the sub, but his wingman's ash cans failed to release. Attacking from the other side of the sub, the two VF-2 pilots opened fire with their Brownings at 3,000 feet, holding down the triggers as they charged in. Rinehart later described the action:

> We could see our tracers bouncing off his deck as he went down, so I know bullets were going into him. And don't let anyone tell you those .50-calibers won't tear a hole in anything they hit.[7]

The two kept shooting until they had to pull out. Brewer had an exceptionally fine view of the proceedings, as he recovered at 100 feet. The two F2As had expended 650 rounds in the run. Talkington meanwhile had swung around, and this time he put his two depth charges 50 to 75 yards ahead of the I-boat as she finally slithered under the water. From his low-level vantage point, Brewer was certain these near misses "jerked sub abruptly to the right"[8] and inflicted some damage. Afterward a small oil slick stained the water.

Joined by the other two TBDs, the four attackers carefully searched the area for another hour, but spotted no further trace of the submarine. Returning to the ship, Rinehart jotted down a short summary of the attack and put it inside a message container. His manner of delivery caused quite a stir on board the *Lexington*:

> As he swooped across the flight deck, at bridge level, he had to turn his plane on its side to avoid nicking the stack with a wing tip. Just hanging on his prop, he slid past the bridge, where everyone was taking cover, thinking he was going to crash, and neatly deposited his bean bag at the feet of Admiral Brown.[9]

For the past month, the *Lexington*'s pilots had taken some verbal abuse for the accuracy of their message drops, and Rinehart showed how he thought it should be done.

Brown detached the destroyers *Phelps* and *Monaghan* with prospects of finishing off a crippled submarine, but they found no trace of the enemy. The I-boat was marked down only as "damaged." That evening in the wardroom, Ramsey, with a smile he could not hide, "reprimanded" Rinehart for his show-off message drop, then warmly commended him for his presence of mind in not attacking immediately. It was far better that he waited and summoned those who could strike the enemy a more telling blow. Japanese records do not mention the incident, but it appears from examining their official history that the submarine *I-19* (carrying Captain Imaizumi Kijirō, commander of 2nd Submarine Division) is by far the likeliest candidate for the attack. She arrived on 15 January at Kwajalein from a patrol off the West Coast.[10]

By 10 January, Task Force 14 had been out for a dozen days, mainly a boring cruise marking time northwest of Oahu. Leary often zigzagged slowly at 7 to 12 knots to conserve fuel. Usually seas were high and skies overcast, permitting the fighters little opportunity to fly. The afternoon of 10 January, as Task Force 14 continued on a southeasterly course toward the rendezvous with Halsey, there was a remarkable deck crash. While one VT-3 TBD made its landing approach, high waves sent the *Saratoga* pitching steeply. Her stern rose abruptly, and the LSO tried to wave off the TBD, but it kept coming. Then, with a horrible rending noise, the Devastator struck the edge of the ramp and tore in half. Its engine and portions of the cockpit with the pilot, Ens. Earle C. Gillen, still strapped in his seat, clattered onto the flight deck. The rest of the shattered aircraft fell into the sea astern, killing both passengers. Dazed, Gillen unstrapped his seat belt and unsteadily tried to rise. He could not stand—the impact had broken his leg.

The next day, 11 January, seas were a little less turbulent, but the giant *Saratoga* still bounced playfully amid the "long, big swells."[11] Ready to take off on morning CAP, Lovelace waited for the signal to go, but Captain Douglas canceled all flights. Three long blasts from the stack whistle announced his decision. Pilots on deck cut engines. Again the *Sara* shipped water over her massive bow. Fighting Three spent another quiet day on routine squadron duties. At 1915, while the pilots enjoyed dinner in the wardroom, a "terrific explosion"[12] shattered the calm. The *Sara* first heeled violently to starboard, then fell back to port. A submarine torpedo had slammed into port side amidships, torn into three firerooms, and killed six firemen. At the sound of general quarters, the VF-3 pilots ran for their ready room. The *Saratoga* took on a list to port, but damage control soon had the situation under control. When she was hit, the *Saratoga* was 420 miles southwest of Pearl and holding a southeasterly course. Her assailant was *I-6*, one of the boats that had chased the *Enterprise* in December. Cdr. Inaba, her skipper, radioed exultantly that he had sunk a *Lexington*-class ship in position bearing 060 degrees, 270 miles from Johnston. Although far from gone, the *Saratoga* was in a bad way. Leary canceled the rendezvous with Halsey and set course for Pearl.

The morning of the twelfth Fighting Three joined the crowd assembled on deck to survey the damage. Fuel oil from torpedo-shattered oil bunkers had spattered aircraft parked aft on the flight deck. Metal fragments lay all over the deck courtesy of the large gash riven into the carrier's tender flank. The *Sara* could still make 16 knots, and that morning she launched SBDs on search. One of them attacked an I-boat on the surface and drove it down with a 500-lb. bomb (this time armed). To follow up the contact, she despatched seven more SBDs on a search and destroy mission. They ended up harassing an oil slick and flew on to Pearl. The *Sara* herself experienced some scary moments after 1230, when water in contaminated oil tanks caused a loss of fuel suction. The carrier drifted without power for a short time before the engineers could correct the problem. The *Saratoga* would be laid up for a long time; the question was whether she could be repaired at Pearl.

The *Lexington* also experienced a far from tranquil 11 January. Task Force 11 steaming northwest of Johnston weathered heavy swells from the northwest but encountered little wind. This made for difficult flying conditions. The morning search went all right, but poor conditions slowed the takeoffs for the afternoon mission. At 1250, a bad rain squall interrupted the launch after only four fighters and six dive bombers had gotten away. An hour later two "freak" waves broke over the *Lexington*'s bow, washed down the flight deck, and ran into the forward elevator well. A short circuit rendered both flight deck elevators inoperable. Sherman canceled further flight operations, and not until 1630 was the *Lex* able to recover the abortive afternoon search.

At 0600 on 13 January, Lovelace led most of the *Saratoga* Air Group to NAS Pearl Harbor, as the wounded carrier made ready to enter port. Thach checked into the naval hospital for treatment, while Fighting Three began shifting over to Ewa. Word had it that they would be there for a long time. In the navy yard, ship's company and workmen labored furiously to unload the *Sara* prior to drydocking her. The next day, VF-3 baggage headed out to Ewa. Lovelace sold back to Fighting Two the pair of F2As borrowed two weeks earlier. A new pilot fresh from operational training, Ens. Newton H. Mason, reported for duty. Lovelace himself finally made it out to Ewa on 15 January. There workmen were rebuilding the marine air station after massive damage incurred on 7 December. Conditions were still spartan, "but the food is OK and the sleeping is good,"[13] commented Lovelace

Task Force 11 with the *Lexington* returned on 16 January to Pearl. Nimitz

Squadron/Station	F4F-3	F4F-3A	XF4F-4	F2A-2	F2A-3	Total
VF-2 *Lexington*	—	—	—	—	17	17
VF-3 *Saratoga*	11	1	1	—	—	13
VF-6 *Enterprise*	5	13	—	—	—	18
VMF-211 Ewa	—	—	—	1	—	1
VMF-221 Midway	—	—	—	—	14	14
VF-42 *Yorktown*	18	—	—	—	—	18
BatFor Pool, PH	7	2	—	—	—	9
Cargo (en route)	—	10	—	—	—	10
Cargo (*Yorktown*)	14	6	—	—	—	20
A&R Shops, PH	—	1	—	—	3	4
	55	33	1	1	34	124

brought Brown back in order to regroup and offer support for the reinforcement of Samoa and subsequent raids on the Marshalls that were planned. Ramsey's VF-2 along with the rest of the *Lexington* group ended up at Kaneohe. There, two NAPs, Harry Carmody, AMM1c, and George White, AMM2c, left for other assignments. On 17 January, CinCPac decided to send the *Saratoga* back to the West Coast for repairs. One fighting squadron would soon be short a flight deck!

Mid-January at least saw the first arrival of replacement fighters for the fleet. Around 14 January a transport brought in seven disassembled F4F-3s and F4F-3As from the West Coast. Due in a few days were ten more F4F-3As from VMF-111 and 121 based at NAS San Diego. These airplanes would allow Fighting Three to operate at full strength of eighteen fighters and also permit Fighting Two to exchange its Brewster F2As for Grummans. The fighter strength in the Pacific Fleet as of 15 January 1942 is shown in the table.[14]

THE SAMOAN OPERATION—THE *YORKTOWN* TO THE PACIFIC

When Nimitz took over as CinCPac, he found his Pacific Fleet already committed to one major undertaking for January 1942, the reinforcement of the American garrison at Samoa. As early as 14 December, Admiral Stark had arranged for a special convoy to assemble at San Diego. It would transport the 2nd Marine Brigade to Samoa. Departure was to be in early January.

For direct escort of the Samoa convoy, Stark earmarked the aircraft carrier *Yorktown* (CV-5), then at the main Atlantic Fleet base at Norfolk, Virginia. Commissioned in 1937 as the Navy's first truly modern flattop, the *Yorktown* in 1941 had only been on loan to Admiral King's Atlantic Fleet. She had previously served in the Pacific as Bill Halsey's flagship when he first commanded Aircraft, Battle Force and concurrently Carrier Division Two. He along with the rest of the fleet had been sad to see her hasty departure in April 1941 for the Atlantic. The *Yorktown* with three battleships and numerous other vessels from the Pacific Fleet acted to beef up the naval forces that President Roosevelt was arraying to confront more effectively Adolf Hitler's *Kriegsmarine* in the North Atlantic. Her first task upon arriving on the East Coast was to dock at the Naval Operating Base, Norfolk, there to prepare for extended operations in the Atlantic. Leaving the *Yorktown* Air Group for temporary duty ashore was her fighting squadron, Lt. Cdr. Wallace W. Beakley's Fighting Five (VF-5). Beakley's troops still operated Grumman F3F-3 biplanes and were scheduled to convert to Grumman F4F-3A Wildcats. Taking VF-5's place for what was supposed to be a limited time was Fighting Squadron Forty-two (VF-42), extracted from the *Ranger* Air Group. As it happened, Fighting Five never did return to the *Yorktown*, as Fighting Forty-two took her to war and her final battles.

Formed in July 1928 as Scouting Squadron One (VS-1B),[1] the air unit that later became Fighting Forty-two was another of the old *Langley* squadrons. In 1929, VS-1B was supposed to reequip eventually with Keystone amphibian floatplanes, complete with landing gear and tail hooks. Consequently the pilots adopted as their insignia a duck sporting pontoons as footgear, but the amphibians never arrived. With the commissioning of the carrier *Ranger* (CV-4), Scouting One transferred from the *Langley* and took up residence on board. During the 1 July 1937 reorganization, the squadron's designation changed from VS-1B to VS-41 (Scouting Squadron Forty-one), identifying it as one of the *Ranger*'s two scouting squadrons (she did not have a bombing squadron). In early 1941, the Navy decided to form two fighting squadrons for the *Ranger* Air Group as well as two for the new carrier *Wasp* (CV-7). At the time, the Navy was de-emphasizing torpedo units, so that the air groups aboard those two carriers would comprise two fighting and two scouting squadrons. In peacetime at any rate, one fighting squadron at a time would serve on board, while the other stayed ashore to train pilots or was available to go out on board another carrier if need be. The *Ranger*'s regular fighting squadron, Fighting Four (VF-4, the "Red Rippers"), became Fighting Forty-one (VF-41). On 15 March, Scouting Forty-one changed its designation and type to Fighting Squadron Forty-two (VF-42). The pilots were delighted to trade their old, slow, and lumbering Vought SBU-1 biplane scout bombers for sleek, new Grumman F4F-3 Wildcats fresh from the Grumman factory on Long Island. The squadron spent the spring of 1941 getting acquainted with their new role and aircraft.

In June 1941, VF-42's executive officer, Lt. Cdr. Oscar Pederson, fleeted up to squadron command when the old skipper, Lt. Cdr. Thomas B. Williamson, finished his tour of duty. Tall, easygoing, and genial, "Pete" Pederson had graduated in 1926 from the Naval Academy. Earning his wings in 1930, he saw service in flying boats, then carrier duty (1935–36) in Scouting Four (VS-4B) on board the *Langley*. In June 1940, he reported to Scouting Forty-one, working his way up to commanding officer the next year. He had no previous operational service in fighters, but he was an experienced naval aviator and ready to assimilate fighter doctrine. His new executive officer, Lieut. Charles R. Fenton, was considerably more seasoned in fighters, and proved invaluable during the squadron's transition.

The *Yorktown*, with VF-42 now part of her air group, set sail on 28 June 1941 from Norfolk on what would be the first of four "Neutrality Patrols" in the North Atlantic. The initial pair of cruises were uneventful, but the third, in September, took the *Yorktown* into the fog-bound, rainy waters off Newfoundland, and in October and November the carrier helped escort convoys as close as 700 miles from German-occupied Brest, France. She returned on 2 December to Norfolk via Halifax and Portland, Maine. The air group at this juncture was promised extended duty ashore, while the ship herself was to undergo vital refit and upkeep after her strenuous sea duty. The fighter pilots in particular welcomed the chance for shore duty because their flying (tactics and gunnery in particular) had been curtailed while the *Yorktown* was on active operations. The need for strict radio silence, for example, prevented much training on fighter direction. The pilots were all keen to learn as much as they could about modern fighter operations. That fall they were briefed by Lt. Cdr. William E. G. Taylor, USNR, a highly experienced naval aviator who had served for a time in a Royal Navy carrier fighter squadron and as commander of the RAF's famed "Eagle Squadron."

On the fateful day of 7 December 1941, the *Yorktown* was berthed at Norfolk, while Fighting Forty-two with sixteen pilots present (another was ill) and eighteen Grumman F4F-3 Wildcats in commission operated out of NAS Norfolk's East Field.

The following pilots were with the squadron:

Lt. Cdr. Oscar Pederson	USN	USNA 1926
Lieut. Charles R. Fenton	USN	USNA 1929
Lieut. (jg) Vincent F. McCormack	USN	USNA 1937
Lieut. (jg) William N. Leonard	USN	USNA 1938
Lieut. (jg) Richard G. Crommelin	USN	USNA 1938
Ens. Roy M. Plott	USN	
Ens. Arthur J. Brassfield	USN	
Ens. Brainard T. Macomber	A-V(N)	
Ens. Elbert Scott McCuskey	A-V(N)	
Ens. William S. Woollen	A-V(N)	
Ens. Leslie L. B. Knox	A-V(N)	
Ens. William W. Barnes, Jr.	A-V(N)	
Ens. Walter A. Haas	A-V(N)	
Ens. Edgar R. Bassett	A-V(N)	
Ens. Richard L. Wright	A-V(N)	
Ens. John P. Adams	A-V(N)	

With the startling news of the Japanese attack, squadron personnel began packing to board the *Yorktown*. Although the carrier remained far from battleworthy because of the need for a refit, there were furious preparations to get under way. Naval authorities feared an attack by the Germans against the *Yorktown* and some British carriers undergoing repairs at Norfolk. Early the next morning, VF-42 laboriously taxied its aircraft down to the dock where they were hoisted on board. Three new pilots, Ens. Edward Duran Mattson, USN (a 1939 Annapolis graduate), Ens. John D. Baker, A-V(N), and Ens. Harry B. Gibbs, A-V(N) reported for duty. Mercifully the powers that be canceled the *Yorktown*'s immediate sortie, and the carrier repaired to drydock for much-needed attention to the underwater portions of her hull.

Fighting Forty-two returned to East Field for a week of hard work to ready

VF-42, 6 Feb. 1942, *l to r top row:* Mattson, Wright, Gibbs, Barnes, Baker, McCuskey, Crommelin, Adams, Bassett, Haas; *seated:* Macomber, Brassfield, Plott, Leonard, Fenton, Pederson, McCormack, Woollen, Knox. (RADM William N. Leonard, USN.)

Art Brassfield, VF-42's able engineer officer, 13 Nov. 1941. Note old telescopic gunsight on F4F-3. (NA 80-G-64709.)

their fighters for combat. Squadron mechanics installed self-sealing fuel tanks and fitted pilot armor in each Grumman, both time-consuming processes. Pederson agitated hard for permission to remove the bomb racks from his Grummans, and Captain Elliott C. Buckmaster of the *Yorktown* acquiesced. Any savings of weight and drag were profitable in terms of performance. Unfortunately, the squadron could not obtain any of the innovative reflector gunsights, nor could the clumsy old sighting-tube telescopic gunsights be used with the bulletproof windshields intended for the F4Fs. This was a serious matter because Fighting Five still was not ready to resume its place on board the *Yorktown*. Pederson's troops remained with the ship. In light of VF-42's conspicuous opportunities for early combat and the fine record her people amassed, their colleagues in Fighting Five never quite forgave them for taking VF-5's own ship to war.

While the Yorktowners labored so industriously to prepare for war, the high command worked out the details of her first mission. There was no doubt she was going back to the Pacific. As related above, the *Yorktown* was tapped to escort the Samoa reinforcement convoy departing the West Coast in January. Buckmaster received orders to proceed to San Diego via the Panama Canal. The *Yorktown* and her escorts sailed on 16 December from Norfolk, well-loaded with aircraft and other vital gear for the Pacific. On 21 December, Fighting Forty-two flew thirteen Grummans to France Field, Canal Zone, to provide combat air patrol for the flattop's passage through the canal. Lieut. (jg) William N. Leonard's F4F had the misfortune to blow a tire. He was most anxious not to be left behind, and the flight officer, Lieut. (jg) Vincent F. McCormack, managed to get new tires installed just before the carrier cleared Gatun Lock. The next day the *Yorktown* steamed north-westward into the Pacific. The VF-42 contingent at France Field took off, buzzed the canal, then hurried after their carrier now drawing away from Panama.

On 30 December, the little *Yorktown* task force approached the California coast. Fighting Forty-two along with the rest of Lt. Cdr. Curtis S. Smiley's *Yorktown* Air

Group flew to North Island to land at NAS San Diego. Later that day the *Yorktown* herself anchored safely in San Diego harbor. Assembled there were the various vessels assigned to convoy troops to Samoa: three ocean liners doubling as transports, an ammunition ship, an ex-collier, and a fleet oiler. On New Year's Day, Rear Admiral Fletcher and his staff boarded the *Yorktown*. They had flown in from Pearl to form a new Task Force 17 with the *Yorktown* as flagship. It was to be an exciting and memorable association. Fighting Forty-two's New Year's morning was not so cheerful. The Army had turned the lot of them out at 0600 for alert because of a possible enemy air attack. None materialized.

Pederson's squadron spent a hectic week at NAS San Diego making final arrangements before departing for combat. Bill Leonard and assistant, Ens. Walter A. Haas, with "intense bird dogging" ran down the necessary supplies and gear, which included: "spares for consumables, the latest kits for airframe and engine modifications, gunsights and electrical wiring and controls."[2] Leonard especially sought N2AN illuminated reflector gunsights and turned some up at San Diego. Squadron armorers had to rearrange instrument panels to fit them in and jury-rig mounts to hold the sights. These would prove hazardous to foreheads in the event of ditching, but at least VF-42 had something they could use to shoot at the enemy. Meanwhile the *Yorktown* began loading thirty-two additional aircraft as cargo to be transported out to Pearl Harbor. These included twenty F4F-3s and F4F-3As taken from VMF-111 and VMF-121, urgently needed by the fleet. The *Yorktown*'s own air group had the following organization:[3]

Yorktown Captain Elliott C. Buckmaster		
Commander, *Yorktown* Air Group	Cdr. Curtis S. Smiley	1 SBD-3
Fighting Forty-two	Lt. Cdr. Oscar Pederson	18 F4F-3s
Bombing Five (VB-5)	Lt. Cdr. Robert G. Armstrong	19 SBD-3s
Scouting Five (VS-5)	Lt. Cdr. William O. Burch, Jr.	19 SBD-3s
Torpedo Five (VT-5)	Lt. Cdr. Joe Taylor	12 TBD-1s

With a utility group of three planes and twenty-nine planes (twenty F4Fs and nine SBDs) as cargo, the *Yorktown* would have 101 aircraft for the next cruise.

The afternoon of 6 January, Task Force 17 stood out from San Diego. Fletcher's force comprised the *Yorktown*, the heavy cruiser *Louisville*, the light cruiser *St. Louis*, four destroyers, a fleet oiler, and the convoy itself of five vessels. The air group was snuggly embarked, having been earlier hoisted on board the carrier. Task Force 17 was South Pacific–bound. As the *Yorktown* passed Point Loma, the carrier went to general quarters and:

> . . . launched just about the whole VF squadron. We were told this is the way it would be—Japs just over the horizon. We got off smartly and Fletcher was pleased at our sparkiness and willingness to play any games ordained.[4]

Pederson started the voyage with eighteen Wildcats on strength, but soon he would not have nearly so many. The troubles began on 7 January. That morning VF-42 flew two morning CAPs and checked out a number of contacts. Landing from one of the patrols, Ens. Edgar R. Bassett touched down all right, but found himself enmeshed in the barrier. The arresting wire had snapped, injuring three men on deck. The next morning there was an amusing incident. Well before dawn, meteorologists on board the *Yorktown* released a weather balloon, which lookouts on board one of the cruisers misidentified as a signal for an emergency turn. The ship, and perforce the rest of the task force, turned left 45 degrees. Fletcher acted swiftly to put his ships back on course.

For VF-42 the morning CAP went smoothly, but a mishap occurred the afternoon of 8 January. At 1415, six fighters began taking off for combat air patrol. One of them, 42-F-1, flown by Ens. William S. Woollen, started down the deck as the *Yorktown*, beset by deep swells, began rolling to starboard. Almost immediately, Woollen's right wing dropped, throwing the Grumman into a violent twist to port. He added throttle, but could not regain control. After only 200 feet of run, the Grumman shot out over the portside of the flight deck and settled into the water, hitting 300 yards off the port bow. The *Yorktown* maneuvered to avoid the sinking aircraft, and soon the destroyer *Russell* had Woollen on board. A VF-42 trouble board later blamed the incident on the carrier's roll combined with torque from the Wildcat's engine.[5] Fighting Forty-two pilots carefully thought over the question of launch and asked for permission to experiment with takeoffs when the carrier placed the wind 10 degrees off the starboard bow. After such a launch, the fighter pilot would turn left to clear his slipstream from the flight deck rather than to the right as was standard practice. The Yorktowners later declared this method to be much superior to the old of heading directly into the wind and swinging to the right after takeoff. The new procedure permitted shorter intervals between fighters during launch.

The next few days, VF-42 flew routine combat/inner air patrols. The morning of 12 January and again that afternoon, the pilots on CAP simulated coordinated strafing runs on the destroyers. One pilot, however, did not complete the afternoon flight or even get well into it. Walt Haas in 42-F-3 ran through a normal takeoff until, under the new procedure, he turned left to clear his slipstream from the deck. Haas happened to look over his right shoulder, but forgot to watch his speed and climbed slightly. His unforgiving Grumman stalled, then nosed down in an uncontrollable spiral toward the water. Just as the left wing slapped the sea, Haas threw his upper body to the right side of the cockpit in an effort to keep his head away from the wicked gunsight mount. He scrambled out of the sinking plane and was soon on board the destroyer *Walke*. Fortunately Haas was not hurt badly, but he along with the rest of the squadron began to experience a great hankering for shoulder straps to restrain head and body motions from pitching them into the gunsight mount during a crash.[6]

Two days later, the *Walke* took on board another uninvited guest. Task Force 17 and its charges sailed right down on the equator, and it was hot. At 0730 on 14 January, the *Yorktown* began launching six fighters for routine CAP and more mock strafing runs on destroyers. In the midpoint of his takeoff run, Ens. Richard L. Wright in 42-F-14 noticed he just was not getting enough airspeed. It was too late to stop—his Grumman went out over the bow and immediately dropped toward the water. Wright carefully turned left to clear the carrier, then ditched 200 yards ahead. Although the *Walke* rescued him in less than ten minutes, VF-42 was now down to fifteen operational planes. For Wright's mishap there was no ready explanation; perhaps the electrical propellor pitch control was at fault.[7] That day, the task force crossed the equator, but dispensed with the high jinx common in other vessels. The VF-42 pilots were concerned with the mounting operational losses, and certainly they did not pine for the frivolities because most were not yet Shellbacks and were vulnerable to initiation.

Steaming southward from Pearl Harbor to join Fletcher off Samoa was Halsey's Task Force 8 with the *Enterprise*. On New Year's Day, CinCPac had decided to combine the two task forces to execute some sort of offensive action against enemy island bases. Prodding him the next day was an order from King, the new CominCh, calling for "some aggressive action for effect on general morale."[8] Given the circumstances, only Bill Halsey would be available. On 7 January he had returned to port. The next day Nimitz ordered him to proceed to Samoa, combine Task Force 17 with his own Task Force 8, and orchestrate simultaneous raids on the Marshalls and Gilberts, the attacks to take place the first week of February. Fighting Six along with the rest of the *Enterprise* Air Group spent a few days ashore on "unavailable status," allowing for a rest of sorts. The stay was noteworthy mainly for 10 January, when the squadron finally managed to accumulate eighteen F4F Wildcats—the first time VF-6 had operated at full strength since peacetime.

The *Enterprise* with an escort of three heavy cruisers and seven destroyers set sail the morning of 11 January. After lunch, Wade McClusky gathered eighteen pilots from Fighting Six and led them out to the ship. Rookie pilots Dave Criswell and Wayne Presley made their first carrier landings this flight, a reward for hours of field carrier landing practice. Task Force 8 at first headed due west—the destination as yet a secret to the pilots. The AirBatFor staff alerted Fighting Six to prepare for the eleven-plane "swap" with Fighting Three on board the *Saratoga*. McClusky's troops were to exchange most of their F4F-3As for F4F-3s, some of them already fitted with pilot armor and self-sealing fuel tanks, as yet unavailable to Fighting Six. The next day, McClusky learned the trade was off. The *Saratoga* had taken a fish and now limped back to Pearl. The pilots were a little dismayed at not getting the better planes, since it now appeared they would soon see some action. Halsey had changed course to the southwest and informed his people that they would head for Samoa to escort a convoy, then, in the words of VF-6, "raise a little hell up in the Gilberts or Marshalls."[9]

By 14 January, Halsey's ships were deep in the lower latitudes and uncomfortably hot weather. Fighting Six was in hot water with the air department as well. Norm Hodson on an inner air patrol had flown to the wrong sector, while Ed Bayers and Wayne Presley got lost in a rain squall. The *Enterprise* had to break radio silence to guide them back to the ship. Intelligence placed a number of enemy flattops lurking in the Marshalls, so the missing self-sealing tanks and armor looked dearer than ever. The next day as the task force neared the equator, the weather was even more torrid: "Fighter pilots flying the noon CAP with open cockpits and 150 knots of wind to cool them returned parched and dehydrated, for the wind itself was like a volcano's breath."[10] The feud with the air department persisted, as VF-6 grumbled, "They changed their minds five different times about what we'd do in what planes this date."[11] The task force crossed the equator without any particular ceremony, probably a good idea considering the mood most were in.

The sixteenth, another scorcher, was an even worse day for the task force. An SBD crashed on landing and killed the chief petty officer manning the arresting gear, while a TBD from Torpedo Six ditched, its crew missing. (They sailed an eventual 750 miles in a rubber raft and fetched up on the beach of Puka Puka.) On board ships in the task force, two sailors also died of accidental causes. The next day another SBD ditched from lack of fuel. There was no flying for Fighting Six while the *Enterprise* refueled from a fleet oiler.

The actual Samoa reinforcement went without a hitch. Both task forces converged on the lush island group. Fletcher on the night of 19 January released his fast transports for the run to Tutuila Island, the slower vessels following the next day. While the convoy disembarked troops and supplies, the carriers maneuvered off Samoa, occasionally catching tantalizing glimpses of the green tropical isles during breaks in the usually squally weather they encountered. Far to the west four Japanese carriers savagely pounded Australian defenses at Rabaul on New Britain, presaging a new Japanese thrust into the Southwest Pacific. Meanwhile, Task Forces 8 and 17 marked time accomplishing their mission of covering Samoa. Then there would be time to pay the Japanese a visit.

While southern waters beckoned Halsey and Fletcher, Wilson Brown's Task Force 11 suffered through a short but frustrating cruise in the Central Pacific. The morning of 19 January after three days in port, the *Lexington* along with the rest of Task Force 11 (three heavy cruisers and nine destroyers) sailed from Pearl Harbor to conduct a patrol in the waters northeast of Christmas Island. Nimitz desired that Brown support the other two carrier task forces when, after the Samoan operation, they made the first counterstrikes on Japanese island bases. Late that afternoon, the *Lexington* Air Group flew out to the ship. Lt. Cdr. Ramsey had sixteen F2A Buffaloes on strength with Fighting Two. While on shore he had turned in two unserviceable Brewsters and from Fighting Three received the two he had lent them. Task Force 11 took up a southerly heading. For the next few days, flight schedules called for gunnery training flights interspersed with short searches and intermediate air patrols.

In Washington, ComInCh monitored intelligence reports placing the enemy carrier striking force deep in the Southwest Pacific. The time looked ripe to launch a diversionary carrier strike in the Central Pacific. On 20 January, King suggested a carrier raid on Wake. The next day Nimitz chose Brown's Task Force 11 to deliver the surprise strike on Wake and obtain some revenge for the capture of the island. Fuel, however, would be a problem as it was during the abortive relief expedition the previous month. Brown had no oiler with him, so Nimitz arranged to send his one available fleet oiler, the venerable *Neches*, to rendezvous before the strike.

Brown received his orders the afternoon of 21 January. He was to refuel on 27 January from the *Neches*, then raid Wake with aircraft and follow with a ship bombardment if the situation permitted. To escort the old girl to the rendezvous, Brown detached the destroyer *Jarvis* and followed himself at a more economical pace. Everyone on board the ships looked forward to the opportunity of smashing the Japanese at Wake. Unfortunately, during the predawn hours of 23 January the Imperial submarine *I-72* found and sank the as yet unescorted *Neches* 135 miles southwest of Oahu. Brown learned of the loss of his oiler later that morning. Without her fuel, there was no way the task force could steam to Wake, fight, and return. Nimitz recalled Task Force 11 to Pearl. Disgusted, Brown at 1900 changed course northeastward for Oahu. Someone else would have to make the first Pacific Fleet counterattack against the Japanese.

CHAPTER 4

"This Sunday it's our turn to shoot!" The 1 February Raids

APPROACH TO BATTLE

Leaving Samoa to the marines they helped protect, the carrier task forces shaped course to the northwest toward enemy waters. Frank Jack Fletcher's Task Force 17 with the *Yorktown* took station about 150 miles astern of Bill Halsey's Task Force 8 with "The Big E." In a week they hoped to carry out the long-awaited first counterattack by the carriers of the United States Pacific Fleet. Ahead of them loomed the mysterious Japanese Mandated Islands. Halsey planned coordinated strikes against Jaluit and Mili in the southern Marshalls and also against a recent Japanese conquest, Makin Atoll in the northern Gilberts. Target date was the dawn of Sunday, 1 February. The first order of business, however, was to make for a 28 January fueling rendezvous northeast of Howland Island.

On board the *Enterprise*, Fighting Six continued its war with the ship's air department under the air officer, Cdr. A. I. Malstrom. After each tiresome inner air patrol, the fighter pilots tried to work in some much-needed aerial gunnery practice. They shot at a sleeve towed by one of the Grummans, whose pilot then had the onerous task of trying to land the sleeve on board for scoring. Fighting Six just could not drop the sleeves. A pilot in another fighting squadron described what the tow plane had to face:

> Problem for the tow pilot was to gauge position of sleeve over the deck. He was at the front end of a 500′ towline. He had been threatened with dire punishment if he dragged anything through the antenna array. Prudence weighted misses into the Pacific Ocean rather than into the ship's top hampers. [I] never hit [damaged] the ship but the ocean many times.[1]

Nimitz on 27 January modified Halsey's mission. Because it appeared that the Japanese had seriously weakened their forces in the Marshalls to support southward jabs into the Southwest Pacific, now was the time to deal them a stinging blow and deflect their effort away from Australia. Nimitz wanted the attacks "driven home,"[2] with repeated air strikes and ship bombardments against the Marshalls and the Gilberts. He authorized Halsey to extend the attacks beyond one day if feasible. To Fighting Six, heartened that day by a personal "fight talk" by "Wild Bill" himself, it seemed as if "we will now take on the whole mid-Pacific area."[3]

Halsey's staff on 27 January labored far into the night to map out a new operational plan that greatly increased the scope of the raids. Halsey decided to take the *Enterprise* and her consorts into the midst of the vaunted northern Marshalls,

Lieut. (jg) Jack Kelley's VF-6 F4F-3A being rearmed after CAP about the time of the 1 Feb. Marshalls Raid. Note the target tow can under the right wing. (NA 80-G-6334OC.)

steaming within easy striking distance of enemy airfields believed located on Kwajalein, Maloelap, and Wotje atolls. Air strikes scheduled for the dawn of 1 February were to knock out the airfields and seek out heavy ships for follow-up strikes. In addition, there would also be ship bombardments of Wotje and Maloelap. Halsey felt that if he could surprise the enemy and hit him hard initially, he could neutralize strong counterattacks while Task Force 8 remained within attack range of the enemy air bases.

To Fletcher, Halsey passed the original objectives of Jaluit, Mili, and Makin. On 28 January, Lieut. Wilmer E. Gallaher, executive officer of Scouting Six, flew to the *Yorktown* with the revised plan of attack. According to an envious VF-6 diarist, Gallaher returned with "tidings of a quiet and efficient flight deck crew and Air Plot."[4] That day, both task forces fueled independently. For those on board the *Enterprise*, the night refueling from the oiler *Platte* was most impressive. Halsey wrestled with the problem of fuel after the anticipated high-speed operations in the Marshalls. He informed Nimitz on 29 January that he would need an oiler from Pearl to meet him if he continued his attacks beyond one day.

The target names were little more than strange, exotic words to the pilots of the two carrier air groups. On 29 January, Fighting Six heard a lecture by Halsey's intelligence officer, Lieutenant Colonel Julian P. Brown, USMC. It was a sixty-minute talk, but the fighter pilots, at least, felt they still knew "not a damn thing about these islands we are about to attack."[5] Submarine observations and snippets of radio intelligence were not enough to unveil the secrets of Japan's "mystery islands."

Lifting the veil somewhat here, it would be useful to discuss the opposition as revealed in postwar sources.[6] Japanese naval forces in the Marshalls and the Gilberts fell under the jurisdiction of South Seas Force, the operational title for the Japanese Fourth Fleet—old friends because of their invasion of Wake just to the north. A portion (thirty-three carrier fighters, nine land attack planes, and nine flying boats) of Rear Admiral Gotō Eiji's 24th Air Flotilla (*kōkū sentai*) constituted the air defense of the region. The rest of the air flotilla operated from Truk and

Rabaul to the south to support the invasion of the Bismarck archipelago. The flying boats and some land attack planes conducted daily long-range searches around the major island bases to offer early warning of approaching American warships. The Japanese planned to stage in squadrons of land attack planes from widely scattered bases in order to concentrate them at the point of danger, a procedure that would prove ineffective in meeting swift American carrier raids.

The two principal aviation units within the 24th Air Flotilla were the Chitose Air Group (kōkūtai) and the Yokohama Air Group. Authorized strength for the Chitose group was thirty-six twin-engine land attack planes (medium bombers) and forty-eight carrier fighters. Somewhat inexplicably the group lay in a backwater of Imperial Navy air allocations despite its direct confrontation with the United States Pacific fleet. Its bombers were obsolescent Mitsubishi G3M2 Type 96 land attack planes [NELL], an improved version of the twin-tailed mediums that in 1937 had bombed China from bases in Formosa and the homeland. Most crews were veterans of the previous December's strikes on Wake. The fighters were not the new Zeros, but rather Mitsubishi A5M4 Type 96 carrier fighters. The Yokohama Air group was equipped with huge Kawanishi H6K4 Type 97 flying boats [MAVIS], capable of extremely long patrol missions.

It is worth a digression here to examine in detail the Mitsubishi A5M4 Type 96 carrier fighter (Type 96 kanjō sentōki, later known to the Allies as CLAUDE).[7] It was the first monoplane carrier fighter placed in service by any power. The prototype made its maiden flight in 1935, and the Imperial Navy adopted the design the following year. The new fighter featured the classic 1930s look: trim, graceful, with tapering wings, open cockpit, and fixed, neatly spatted, undercarriage. The Type 96 fighter saw combat in the fall of 1937 over China and played a vital role in assuring Japanese air superiority. The model flown in 1942 by the Chitose pilots was the A5M4, Model 24, known variously to the Allies at first as the "Type 96" or "Type 97" fighter, being easily confused with the Japanese Army's Nakajima Ki-27 Type 97 land fighter. Its powerplant was the Kotobuki-41 radial engine rated at 785 hp. Top speed was about 235 knots (270 mph) at 9,800 feet, while climb rate to that height (3,000 meters) was 3 minutes and 35 seconds (average a respectable 2,750 feet per minute). The aircraft was exceptionally light, only 3,680 lbs. loaded. Nominal range was 648 miles, and a drop tank could extend the combat radius as much as 250 miles. Installed above the engine and synchronized to fire through the propellor were two 7.7-mm machine guns. The fighter could also carry a payload of two 30-kilogram bombs. There was no pilot armor, nor were the fuel tanks leakproof. The Type 96 fighter was extremely maneuverable with a fast climb, although it was not in a class with the second-generation monoplane carrier fighters, such as the Mitsubishi Zero or the Grumman Wildcat.

Distribution of aircraft on 1 February in the Marshalls and Gilberts was as follows:

1. At Roi (Ruotta to the Japanese) in Kwajalein Atoll was the headquarters of the Chitose Air Group under Captain Ohashi Fujirō. Present were eighteen Type 96 carrier fighters led by the senior fighter pilot, Lt. Cdr. Igarashi Chikamasa, hikōtaichō (group leader).
2. At Taroa in Maloelap Atoll was a detachment of the Chitose Air Group under Lieut. Kurakane Yoshio, buntaichō (division leader) with fifteen Type 96 carrier fighters under his direct control and nine Type 96 land attack planes led by Lieut. Nakai Kazuo, buntaichō.
3. At Jaluit (Emidj) was a detachment of the Yokohama Air Group, six Type 97 flying boats under Lt. Cdr. Koizumi Sanemirō, hikōtaichō.

4. At Makin Atoll in the Gilberts was a detachment of the Yokohama Air Group, three Type 97 flying boats led by Lieut. Sakaki Isamu, *buntaichō*.

TASK FORCE 8 IN THE MARSHALLS

For Halsey's troops there was no 30 January, as they crossed the International Date Line at midnight directly into 31 January. Fighting Six flew inner air patrol and CAP all day. Worried over the lack of armor protection, VF-6's engineering department under Roger Mehle spent the day fitting ⅜-inch boiler plate as ersatz armor behind the pilot seats of all the Grummans. Dave Flynn, one of the section leaders, had the misfortune to break a finger and had to be replaced by Ens. Ralph M. Rich. That afternoon, the task force had a close call. Radar at 1350 detected an enemy aircraft 34 miles to the south, on course as if on the return leg of a search and bound for Maloelap Atoll to the southwest. As visibility at the time was fifteen miles or so, it was highly unlikely the Japanese had spotted Task Force 8 at an embarrassing moment. Halsey drew up a sarcastic message thanking the Japanese crew for missing the task force and arranged for it to be dropped the next day. One member of Fighting Six, observing his fellow pilots, noted, "There is little or no tension on board, altho' you can tell something is afoot."[1] The *Enterprise*'s executive officer, Cdr. T. P. Jeter, headed the plan of the day with this little verse:

> An eye for an eye,
> A tooth for a tooth,
> This Sunday it's our turn to shoot.
> —Remember Pearl Harbor.[2]

After dark the task force worked up to 30 knots, and the two bombardment groups peeled off to head for their targets.

Using what information they had, Halsey's staff plotted the various targets and parceled out the attack strength. Task Force 8 aimed for a 1 February predawn launch virtually in the midst of the islands they intended to hit—vital positioning for simultaneous strikes on the widely separated airfields and ship anchorages. They thought the most dangerous Japanese base was Kwajalein Atoll, a flight of 155 miles from the chosen launch point. Allocated for that target were all of "The Big E's" SBD dive bombers, thirty-seven of them, led by the group commander, Howard Young. To follow up were nine TBD Devastators from Torpedo Six, in this instance armed with bombs for horizontal attack. They would search out likely ships anchored in the atoll's lagoon. The remaining nine TBDs would stay in reserve on board the *Enterprise* to be launched for a torpedo strike should the first wave locate suitable large ship targets.

Powerful Kwajalein Atoll had absorbed all of the *Enterprise*'s dive bombers and torpedo planes; yet there remained important bases at Wotje and Taroa in Maloelap Atoll. Because no other aircraft were available, the *Enterprise* would have to utilize her fighters to attack these targets. Because she had to hold some fighters back for CAP, that meant no fighter escorts for the planes hitting Kwajalein. Twelve of the eighteen F4Fs would attack the secondary targets, while six stayed as combat air patrol. Aiding in the destruction of Wotje and Taroa would be bombardments by cruisers and destroyers detached for that purpose from Task Force 8.

Thus McClusky, VF-6's skipper, was to take the six F4Fs of his 1st Division to bomb and strafe the airfield at Wotje, only 36 miles southeast of the intended launch point. Bombarding Wotje at dawn would be two heavy cruisers and one destroyer led by a rear admiral the carrier men soon would know well, Raymond A. Spruance. Intelligence estimated that Wotje could possess a naval air group

1 February 1942 Organizations and Strengths

(a) *Enterprise* Air Group
Commander, *Enterprise* Air Group

		Cdr. Howard L. Young	1 SBD-3
Fighting Six	Lt. Cdr. C. Wade McClusky		18 F4F-3, -3A
Bombing Six	Lt. Cdr. William R. Hollingsworth		18 SBD-2,-3
Scouting Six	Lt. Cdr. Halsted L. Hopping		18 SBD-2,-3
Torpedo Six	Lt. Cdr. Eugene E. Lindsey		18 TBD-1

73

(b) Fighting Six
*Bureau no.**

		1st Division
	F-1	Lt. Cdr. C. Wade McClusky, USN, squadron commander
	F-12	Rad. Elec. Edward H. Bayers, NAP, USN
3908	F-3	Lieut. Roger W. Mehle, USN
	F-2	Lieut. (jg) Rhonald J. Hoyle, USN
3910	F-5	Lieut. (jg) James G. Daniels III, USN
3936	F-6	Ens. Walter J. Hiebert, A-V(N)

		2nd Division
3912	F-7	Lt. Cdr. Frank T. Corbin, USN, executive officer
	F-8	Lieut. (jg) John C. Kelley, USN
3917	F-9	Lieut. (jg) Gayle L. Hermann, USN
	F-18	Ens. Wayne C. Presley, A-V(N)
	F-11	Ens. Thomas C. Provost III, A-V(N)
	F-4	Lieut. (jg) Frank B. Quady, USN

		3rd Division
3920	F-13	Lieut. James S. Gray, Jr., USN, flight officer
3914	F-14	Lieut. (jg) Wilmer E. Rawie, USN
4035	F-15	Lieut. (jg) Harold N. Heisel, USN
3937	F-16	Ens. David W. Criswell, A-V(N)
3926	F-10	Ens. Ralph M. Rich, A-V(N)
3916	F-17	Ens. William M. Holt, A-V(N)

		Ens. David R. Flynn, A-V(N) (injured)
		Ens. Norman D. Hodson, A-V(N)
		Ens. Howard L. Grimmell, Jr., A-V(N)

*If known.

---

with perhaps a dozen aircraft. Lieut. (jg) Jim Daniels in McClusky's division was given a hand-held camera with which to take photos during and after the strike for assessment of damage. Simultaneously with McClusky's attack, six F4Fs led by VF-6's flight officer Jim Gray were to work over Taroa in Maloelap Atoll. That would entail a flight of about 100 miles southeast of the designated launch point. Taroa was thought to be a quieter place than Wotje, although "positive information relative to existing defenses is entirely lacking."[3] If Taroa had any aircraft at all, Halsey's experts thought perhaps a few seaplanes might be there. Following up Gray's strike would be a bombardment by the heavy cruiser *Chester* and two destroyers. Like Daniels, Gray also carried a hand-held camera to take photos of

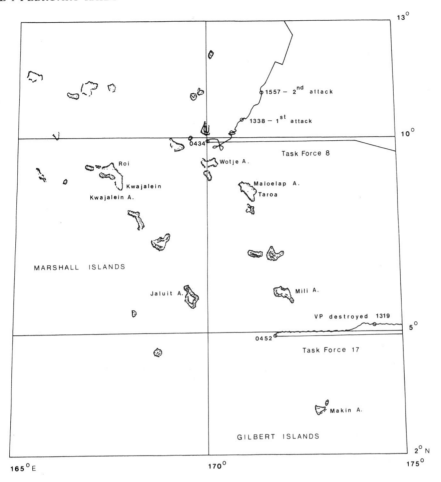

The 1 Feb. 1942 raids on the Marshalls and Gilberts.

Taroa. Upon returning to the carrier, all of the Grummans would be retained as CAP to protect the ships. Presumably the Japanese would have few aircraft flyable after widespread dawn attacks surprised them on the ground. At least that was the plan!

The approach to the target proceeded without incident. At 0300, the *Enterprise* woke the aviators and served a special breakfast for them. Flight quarters sounded at 0345, and within an hour the task force had reached the designated launch position. "The Big E" was ready to send her aircraft into the night. The busy activities attendant to the predawn launch seemed efficient and businesslike, belying the fact that this was the first set-piece carrier strike against the enemy. Frank Corbin, VF-6's executive officer, led his 2nd Division pilots out on deck to man the six F4Fs allotted as combat air patrol. They picked their way carefully through the aircraft spotted on deck:

> With props turning and strong prop wash and the danger of whirling blades in crowded quarters, the manning of airplanes was always like broken field running in a crouch.[4]

Behind the CAP fighters ranged thirty-seven SBDs waiting to depart for Kwajalein. Promptly at 0445, the launch officer brought Corbin to the line, listened to the roar of his Pratt & Whitney, then flagged him into the darkness. After the fighters took off, the SBDs followed. For her second deckload, the *Enterprise* deployed the nine bomb-armed TBD Devastators of Torpedo Six. They and one SBD delayed by engine trouble started taking off shortly after 0500.

For the VF-6 pilots scheduled to hit Wotje and Taroa there was an interval of almost an hour before takeoff. They spent the time waiting in the comfortable chairs of the fighter ready room. On deck, plane handlers spotted twelve F4Fs for launch. Each fighter sported two 100-lb. bombs, one under each wing, and a full load of .50-caliber bullets: ball, armor-piercing, tracer, but no incendiaries—none had yet made it out to the fleet. Gray's 3rd Division, facing the longer flight, departed first, Gray leading the way at 0610 into the darkness. Pilot of the fourth Grumman was Dave Criswell, making his first night launch. Passing over the bow, he swerved violently to the left. Possibly disconcerted by the lack of visible horizon, Criswell corrected his slip too vigorously. The F4F jerked into a stall, flipped over on its back, and hit the water with a tremendous splash. Criswell never left the cockpit, as the aircraft sank swiftly into the swirling black waters.[5] Appointed an aviation cadet just one year before, Criswell had completed flight training in August, then spent three months at San Diego in the advanced carrier training group there. His was the fourth life lost by Fighting Six before even meeting the enemy. The rest of the 3rd Division made it aloft without trouble and formed up behind Gray for the flight to Taroa. Following them aloft at 0616 was McClusky's 1st Division bound for nearby Wotje.

Thus by 0620 the *Enterprise*'s first wave of fifty-eight aircraft was en route in order to attack simultaneously at sunrise, a few minutes before 0700.

The Wotje Strike

With less than 40 miles of ocean to cross on the trip to Wotje, McClusky climbed leisurely to 10,000 feet in order to kill some time and also assure plenty of height from which to dive in at dawn. Wotje might have fighters; so the skipper wanted to be ready for opposition. From the light peeping in from under the eastern horizon, the VF-6 pilots had no trouble locating their atoll and its principal island. McClusky led the division into proper attack position, and by 0658 he was ready. Abruptly he pitched into a high-speed, glide bombing run, and the others had to scramble to stay with him. Beneath them, Wotje seemed to slumber. In the lagoon several naval auxiliaries and fat merchantmen swung at anchor.

Aiming for the airstrip and buildings clustered around one end of it, McClusky and his pilots each toggled one 100-lb. bomb, then climbed to attack again. Six explosions shattered the stillness. The second time around, the F4Fs drew the attention of several antiaircraft guns ashore and also fire from some of the ships in the lagoon. More bombs thudded into Wotje's hard coral surface. After releasing their payloads, the pilots swung back to strafe buildings and suspected shore batteries. Jim Daniels went low to take photos of Wotje to help assess damage and dodged antiaircraft bursts while he pointed his hand-held camera. He was later commended for his efforts. By 0714, McClusky's troops had done what they could to rough up the neighborhood. They had encountered no enemy aircraft aloft nor seen any on the ground. Leaving the island to Spruance's bombardment group rapidly bearing down from the southeast, the VF-6 pilots looked over their handiwork and chalked up several columns of smoke, including three particularly promising blazes. None of the F4Fs suffered any damage in return. As he departed, the skipper noted with satisfaction shells from the bombardment force exploding on Wotje.

Trouble at Taroa

Having already lost one of their number to accident, Gray's 3rd Division set off on a fast cruise for Maloelap Atoll about 100 miles southeast. As dawn threatened, Gray took the five F4Fs up to 15,000 feet. At 0640 they made out ahead the outline of an atoll—Maloelap by the look of it. Rocking his wings, Gray gave the signal to attack the nearest island. Pushing over into a steep dive, he released one of his 100-pounders, pulled out low over the island, and scooted out over the lagoon. Behind, he glimpsed to his chagrin only innocent palm trees and a bright, sandy beach marred only by the flash of his exploding bomb. Mistaking it for Taroa in the faint light, Gray had bombed tranquil, uninhabited Tjan, 15 miles northwest of the actual objective. His wingman, Lieut. (jg) Wilmer E. Rawie, had followed the leader in and likewise wasted one of his bombs. The other three Gray warned off before they, too, expended their payloads needlessly.

By the time he climbed back to 5,000 feet, Gray had noted the correct target off to the southeast. Impatient, he added throttle and charged off in that direction. Behind him, Rawie tried desperately to catch up, and strung out well astern of the lead section was the rest of the division, Lieut. (jg) Harold N. Heisel, Ens. Ralph Rich, and Ens. William Holt. As he neared Taroa, Gray discovered it was not the small, sleepy seaplane base described by Intelligence—far from it. Ahead was a well-equipped airfield complex resembling Ford Island. In fact, Taroa was one of the main enemy bases in the Mandates. Gray soon picked out what looked like numerous aircraft, including twin-engine bombers, parked alongside the runways.

What Gray did not see were three fighters in the process of taking off. The Japanese no longer slept on Taroa. Spotters had located the warships (one heavy cruiser and two destroyers) of Captain Thomas M. Shock's Taroa Bombardment Group silhouetted by the rising sun. They spread the alarm, turning out flight crews of Lieut. Kurakane's Chitose Air Group detachment based at the airfield. Kurakane and two others ran to the fighters waiting on alert, while mechanics started warming up the remaining fighters. Lieut. Nakai's land attack plane crews also assembled around their headquarters. On the short hop from Tjan to Taroa, Rawie happened to see two enemy fighters pass about a mile head and a few thousand feet above him. These two Type 96 fighters comprised the normal combat air patrol which had taken off at 0620, thirty minutes before sunrise. They headed out to look over the warships moving in from the east, and at 0659 swooped in on Shock's cruiser *Chester* to drop a couple of small bombs without scoring any hits.

The Japanese did not spot any of the scattered Grummans infiltrating from out of the western darkness. Gray dived in from 8,000 feet. He aimed his final bomb for the airstrip; then, anxious to put the parked bombers out of business, he pulled out low and swung back over the island to strafe. Behind the leader, the 3rd Division began its own attacks. Observers on board the *Chester*, coming in from the other side of Taroa, cheered them on:

> Tiny dots, like darting gnats from this distance, were diving over the large island, slipping across and zooming up, then wheeling and coming down. Our planes.[6]

Rawie had coaxed his Grumman up to 6,000 feet in the mad dash for Taroa, then saw his leader abruptly dive away. Following Gray in, Rawie likewise chose the airfield as his target, pulled the bomb release at 1,200 feet, then cut loose with his four .50-calibers. The bomb detonated with a satisfying flash. Recovering from his dive, Rawie scooted low over the island and headed north a short way. Just ahead and flying in the same direction were another pair of enemy fighters. Rawie

W. E. Rawie on 17 June 1942 with D.F.C. awarded for his 1 Feb. victory at Taroa. (NA 80-G-11626.)

PO3c Atake Tomita, Rawie's opponent on 1 Feb. 1942 over Taroa. (Via Dr. Izawa Yasuho.)

identified them as "Type 97's" on the basis of the wretched silhouettes he had to go by. Actually they were two of the previously described Mitsubishi A5M4 Type 96 carrier fighters, in this instance flown by Lieut. Kurakane, the senior pilot present, and PO3c Atake Tomita. Along with a third pilot, the two had manned aircraft on the first alert, had hurriedly taken off, and now were trying to get their bearings. They were unaware that American fighters were present.

For Will Rawie it was a golden opportunity to attack and score stealthily. He gunned his engine and overhauled the aircraft on the right for a surprise attack from just below. At close range, he fired a long burst that immediately struck home in Kurakane's airplane. Fifty-caliber slugs tore through the fuselage and engine, setting the Mitsubishi ablaze. Kurakane shook off his amazement and rolled his stricken fighter on its side so he could bail out. The action was visible from the *Chester*: "One specklike plane expanded magically into a ball of flame and plunged into the palms, leaving a hot red streak above it."[7] At 0704, the burning Type 96 spun into the water, leaving a patch of gasoline and debris burning fiercely as testimony to the first victory scored during the war by a fighter pilot of the U.S. Navy.

Following through on his attack, Rawie kept going straight and whizzed past Kurakane's wingman. Once he reached a point well ahead of his opponent, Rawie hauled his Grumman into a sharp 180-degree turn in order to confront his Japanese head-on. Atake found himself in big trouble—low and slow—but he grimly challenged the American all the way. Both adversaries held their head-on run to the limit; neither would be the first to peel off. The result was inevitable. In his diary, Rawie explained: "This being my first head-on approach I muffed it & pressed home too far & hit the Jap's wing with my underside."[8] The midair collision sheered off Rawie's Zed Baker homing antenna and dented the fuselage, but otherwise the imperturbable Grumman flew on as smoothly as before. Not so for Atake's Mitsubishi. The brush with the F4F had crumpled one of its wingtips and nearly ripped out the aileron. In no condition to fly, Atake had to try to set down immediately.

After the collision, Rawie found himself heading south, back toward the airfield.

He dropped low to strafe, but after a few rounds fed through his guns, all four failed to function. Concerned with this state of affairs, Rawie pulled off to try to clear them, but efforts at recharging them were useless. To make matters worse, another Mitsubishi maneuvered directly onto his tail and made its presence known through tracers zinging past the F4F's fuselage. Not seeing Atake limp away, Rawie thought his pursuer was the fighter he had just rammed, but it must have been the third Type 96 which had taken off along with Kurakane and Atake. There was no time to hang around, what with his guns out of commission; Rawie used his superior speed to draw away from his attacker, then turned west out over Maloelap lagoon and sought clouds for concealment. He flew along the island chain to the last one (Kaveni); then it was "Home, James" to the carrier.

Heisel, Rich, and Holt had followed the two lead planes into the fray. They salvoed their 100-pounders into the hangars and parked aircraft, then dropped nearly to the deck to strafe. The lack of incendiary rounds was highly frustrating. Only Rich succeeded in flaming one of the bombers ranged around the airfield. Courageously, the Chitose pilots and mechanics worked under fire to ready fighters to scramble aloft. By 0710, three more Type 96s were airborne, and within five minutes, two more with the CAP already aloft making a total of eight, not counting Atake's damaged fighter. The angry Japanese took after the VF-6 pilots at a particularly embarrassing moment. Like Rawie, the three had to deal with malfunctioning guns. Rich hauled out of the area first, totally disarmed by gun failures. Several Japanese jumped Heisel and Holt and chased them away from Taroa. Heisel, especially, had a bad time. One Japanese sent a 7.7-mm bullet directly into his main fuel tank. Fortunately the tank did not leak gasoline and ignite. Inasmuch as Fighting Six did not yet have self-sealing fuel tanks, they were as vulnerable to fire as the Japanese.

Gray himself made three long, deliberate strafing runs on the airfield before he noticed enemy fighters around. At 0718 he spotted one Type 96 fighter low over the runway, just as if it had taken off. Despite the fact he now had only one fifty-caliber working, Gray charged after the vulnerable Mitsubishi and shot it up. The Japanese came around for a downwind landing and seemed to crack up on the runway. Actually, Gray's target appears to have been Atake's crippled fighter, in bad shape after ramming Rawie. Atake touched down in a hurry, and as he taxied, his aileron fell off. Meanwhile, Gray found himself the unwilling center of attention of as many as eight Type 96 fighters now aloft and thoroughly aroused. He was alone, the other four Grummans having departed. Roaring in from several directions at once, the Japanese fell all over themselves to bag the lone Grumman. Gray quickly saw how much more maneuverable the elegant little fighters were than his F4F, and wisely refrained from trying to match turns or climbs. Instead he concentrated on countering each run as the enemy flashed past.

After a minute of frantic maneuvering, Gray turned into a head-on run with one Japanese, then rolled out to one side to avoid a collision. Appearing directly in front of his guns was a Type 96, already set up for a good side shot. Gray hurriedly adjusted his aim and shot toward the target as it spun away. It was high time for him to be on his own way, too. He fought clear, but not before the enemy had deposited with him some thirty to forty souvenirs of friendly Taroa. These Japanese bullets had peppered the tail of Gray's F4F-3A, penetrated his emergency fuel tank, and nearly severed his rudder cables. Only the Grumman's stout construction and Mehle's makeshift boiler-plate armor had brought old F-13 home. A Curtiss SOC-3 floatplane had witnessed Gray's troubles as its ship, the *Chester*, opened fire on Taroa. Gray finally left the area around 0720, just as the first of the eight-inch shells slammed into the island. All in all, this mission was a little more than Fighting Six had bargained for.

Roi–Namur and Kwajalein Island

Led by "Brigham" Young, the *Enterprise*'s SBDs flew westward in the darkness seeking the twin island of Roi and Namur on the northern edge of the large atoll of Kwajalein. At 0653 they passed what seemed just to be a small coral islet, but because of dense ground fog, they did not realize it was Roi. The Japanese, however, heard them pass and turned out the troops. Not until 0705, about ten minutes after sunrise, did Young recognize the target. He directed Halsted Hopping's Scouting Six to make the first attack. Japanese antiaircraft guns were manned, and by the time Hopping's 1st Division dived in, Type 96 fighters had begun scrambling from Roi airfield. One Mitsubishi slipped underneath Hopping's SBD as it recovered from its glide bombing run and sent VS-6's skipper spinning into the sea. Fighters bagged another SBD, while flak accounted for one as well. Scouting Six lost a fourth dive bomber, which was seen to ditch just north of Roi. The squadron bombed the island with its underwing 100-pounders, and some pilots dropped their 500-lb. bombs as well. From 0709 to 0730, ten Type 96 fighters from the Chitose Air Group had got up to contest the SBDs. Scouting Six roughed up the airfield and surrounding buildings and also claimed destruction of two or three fighters.

Young did not follow up with VB-6's eighteen SBDs because during the attack he monitored a report from a VT-6 pilot telling of two enemy carriers in Kwajalein lagoon. Gene Lindsey had led the nine VT-6 TBDs directly to Kwajalein Island on the southern rim of the huge atoll. Numerous ships swung at anchor in the lagoon north of Kwajalein Island, and right on schedule at 0658, Lindsey brought his TBDs in formation for horizontal bombing runs on the ships. Fortunately no Japanese fighters were present. Young and Bombing Six and seven SBDs from Scouting Six scurried southward from Roi over the lagoon. They found no carriers— the report had been wrong—but beginning at 0727, the SBDs attacked a rich crop of warships, submarines, naval auxiliaries, and merchantmen. Young radioed to the *Enterprise* that no enemy carriers were present, but the ship had already launched VT-6's 2nd Division, nine TBDs armed with torpedoes. Led by Lt. Cdr. Lance E. Massey, VT-6 executive officer, the Devastators reached Kwajalein well after the other friendlies had left for home. None of the Japanese fighters at Roi patrolled the southern half of the lagoon, so Massey's pilots were able to make uninterrupted torpedo drops. There were no American plane losses over the lagoon or Kwajalein proper. Altogether the attackers had damaged one light cruiser, one submarine, and seven other ships.

The Need for Follow-up Strikes

After Gray's fighters had departed, the Taroa Bombardment Group had to deal with the hornet's nest the little island had unexpectedly proved to be. The *Chester* shelled Taroa for twenty-five minutes, dueling with shore batteries and hitting the airfield area. During the bombardment, her lookouts spotted Japanese aircraft taking off from the airfield. Surprised that Taroa's air power had survived all of the attacks, Captain Shock deemed it prudent to withdraw. He no longer had any fighter support, nor did he have prospects of getting any. Not long after 0730, Lieut. Nakai led eight Type 96 land attack planes aloft (his ninth had been burned by Ralph Rich), and, at Taroa, the Type 96 fighters began landing in small groups for fuel and ammunition. Ground crews rearmed them with small bombs and sent them after the bombardment ships. The Chitose fighters and land attack planes

initiated a series of attacks on the *Chester*. The only hit came as the result of a dive by a fighter that pushed over from 8,000 feet into a steep, 70-degree descent and put one 30-kilogram bomb onto the cruiser's main deck aft. It caused superficial damage. The worst scare came around 0830 when Nakai's eight land attack planes in close formation made a level bombing run on the swiftly moving cruiser. The nearest bombs hit only 100 yards away. The attacks ceased after 0900, but Taroa had used every operational plane: all thirteen fighters and eight land attack planes. The cruiser and her two escorts sheered off to the northeast, the *Chester* recovering her four SOC float planes at 1130. Over Taroa these antiquated biplanes had survived repeated fighter attacks and even claimed one destroyed!

Of the VF-6 pilots who attacked Taroa, Rawie happened to return first to the *Enterprise*, landing around 0800. The carrier had already recovered McClusky's Wotje attackers and worked to refuel and rearm them for CAP. Halsey wanted to know what had transpired at Taroa, so Rawie was ushered into the flag shelter to tell the admiral and his staff about the surprising enemy strength at Taroa. For his victory he received warm congratulations, as well as some ribbing for ramming the second Japanese fighter. One wag later plastered on the carrier's island a drawing of Rawie's F-14 with its prop chopping the tail off an enemy fighter. The caption read, "Oh yea?! You may dodge my bullets but I'll saw you in half!"[9]

SBDs began arriving back from the Kwajalein strike, and at 0905 the *Enterprise* recovered eleven of them. With strike planes now available, Halsey intended to attack Taroa again. While Rawie helped brief the pilots, the air department quickly readied seven SBDs from Bombing Six and two from Scouting Six for the mission. Led by Lt. Cdr. Hollingsworth, VB-6 skipper, they left at 0935 without fighter escort because Fighting Six had only fifteen Grummans available. Criswell's F4F had splashed before dawn on takeoff, and two others from Gray's division returned

An *Enterprise* SBD about to depart for a raid on the Marshall Islands, 1 Feb. 1942. (NA 80-G-63339D.)

too shot-up to be patched by emergency repairs. The *Enterprise* had a dozen fighters aloft on CAP, but some ran low on fuel. Hollingsworth reached Taroa around 1030 and luckily discovered most of the fighters on the ground after their bombing attacks on the *Chester*. His pilots thought they saw about a dozen twin-engine bombers and eleven fighters dispersed in several groups around the airfield. Five Type 96 fighters intercepted the attack, but inflicted no losses on the SBDs.

Hollingsworth worked Taroa over, but Halsey was taking no chances. Of the twenty-odd dive bombers that started landing after 1000, the carrier culled out another set of nine for a third try at Taroa. Lieut. Richard H. Best, VB-6's executive officer, led eight from Bombing Six and one from Scouting Six, departing at 1035. This time three Chitose fighters were aloft and jumped Best's SBDs during their runs. They shot down one dive bomber, and Best's crews in return claimed two fighters destroyed.

Wotje proved to be a far easier target than expected because of the lack of fighter opposition. To plaster the shipping known to be there, the *Enterprise* at 1116 sent aloft under Young a strike group of eight SBDs and nine TBDs armed with bombs. Between 1220 and 1235 they executed several careful bombing attacks that left the island and its ships a shambles. In return no American planes were lost.

The Defense of the Task Force

Throughout the morning and early afternoon, the *Enterprise* buzzed with furious activity to launch, recover, and rearm her planes. For a brief time after 0730, the carrier actually had all of her aircraft aloft at one time, a rare event in combat. Fighting Six by necessity concentrated on CAP, while the dive bombers and torpedo planes flew the subsequent strikes. The task force was apprehensive, tensely awaiting expected enemy counterattacks. Conspicuous in his large white sun helmet, Halsey paced the flag bridge, keeping an eye on flight operations. At 1025, radar detected a bogey bearing 220 degrees and 40 miles. The *Enterprise* sent fighters to check it out, but they found nothing. Task Force 8 operated virtually within sight of Wotje, but no Japanese aircraft were seen. The calm was somewhat unnerving.

At 1255, the *Enterprise* launched four VF-6 F4Fs led by Corbin and six SBDs from Bombing Six to serve as anti–torpedo–plane patrol. Ready to come on board were four CAP fighters low on juice and Best's eight SBDs returned from Taroa. After they all landed, the CAP comprised seven F4Fs and six SBDs. Between 1315 and 1322, the last strike planes—the Wotje attackers—were recovered. Plane handlers parked the aircraft forward, as the *Enterprise*'s flight deck remained spotted for landings.

Stunned by a surprise Sunday attack (not a Japanese monopoly), the 24th Air Flotilla regrouped slowly. It would take many hours to fly more land attack planes in from Truk; so the burden for conducting the air counterattack fell upon Lieut. Nakai. After fruitlessly bombing the cruiser *Chester*, Nakai had radioed Captain Ohashi at Roi requesting permission to take his eight land attack planes there. Nakai wanted to rearm them with aerial torpedoes not available at Taroa, but Ohashi refused because Roi's facilities had been damaged by bombing. Thus Nakai had to circle near Taroa until after the two SBD attacks. His land attack planes came in at 1130 when it appeared the coast was clear. Ground crews worked rapidly to rearm them, lest a fourth American attack catch them on the ground. All eight of Nakai's bombers had suffered damage of one sort or another that morning, and after they landed, one was found to be unserviceable. Impatient to get away quickly, Nakai at 1210 took five G3Ms aloft and told the other two crews to leave when their planes were rearmed. Scattered clouds made it difficult to spot the American carrier force, but shortly before 1330, Nakai's five Type 96 land attack planes finally located Halsey northeast of Wotje.

The *Enterprise*'s combat air patrol operated under considerable handicaps. None of the carrier's aircraft possessed any IFF (Identification—Friend or Foe) gear, so it was extremely hard for the fighter director officer (FDO) to distinguish between the friendlies and the hostiles on radar. Serving as FDO was Lt. Cdr. Leonard J. ("Ham") Dow, the staff communications officer. Repeatedly Dow had to send F4Fs to look over suspicious contacts that proved to be returning *Enterprise* strike planes. IFF procedures at this time were very primitive, calling for the returning flight leader to break radio silence with a prearranged code to inform the ship from what direction he was coming.

Nakai unwittingly profited from the confusion in his approach to the target. Flying CAP, Rawie glimpsed the enemy bombers while they were still a good distance out from the task force. While he was warning Corbin, Nakai slipped into cloud cover. Dow had plenty of trouble trying to sort out the small Japanese formation from his own friendlies on radar plot. A few minutes later he sent two sections of F4Fs in the direction where Rawie had reported bandits. They made contact with the twin-engine bombers at 10,000 feet and 15 miles from the ships. Roaring into the attack, the Grummans again were brought up short by gun failures. Rawie, for one, had only one of his four Brownings working after his first pass. Damn discouraging not to be able to shoot at enemy planes right in front of you!

Nakai did not help matters by his recourse to highly unorthodox tactics for medium bombers. Instead of continuing with a horizontal run in tight formation as mediums were supposed to do, Nakai led his land attack planes into a shallow dive to make what ultimately became a glide bomb attack. That made it much more difficult for the fighters to complete their firing passes, as the enemy bombers picked up a lot of speed. Of the half dozen VF-6 pilots who were able to intercept, only two wingmen, Lieut. (jg) Frank B. Quady and Ens. Norman Hodson, could claim any success. Together they shot up Nakai's own plane.

The five Japanese bombers emerged from the overcast at 6,000 feet and became visible from the ships, which opened up with every five-inch antiaircraft gun that could bear. By now the land attack planes were making around 250 knots, and

Halsey's gunners greatly underestimated their speed. Five-inch bursts trailed behind the bombers, just where the fighters wanted to be. Lt. Cdr. E. B. Mott, the *Enterprise*'s gunnery officer, saw Corbin's F4F as it "popped out of a cloud, made one pass at them [the Japanese], looked at our AA fire and decided to get up in the clouds again."[10] According to doctrine, the fighters pulled off once the fleet's antiaircraft guns were on target. In this case it was likely fortunate they did so. The Grummans were ineffective because of gun failures, and the poorly aimed AA fire was more of a threat to them than to the swiftly moving bombers.

The interceptors behind him, Nakai concentrated on his glide bombing run against the carrier. Opening formation into a loose Vee, the five Mitsubishis rapidly overhauled release point, when Nakai's bombardier would signal a simultaneous bomb drop. Captain Murray discovered the enemy closing from off the *Enterprise*'s starboard bow. He rang for 30 knots and ordered her rudder put over hard left, then reversed in order to throw the ship out of its former track. At 1338, Nakai's planes released their bombs from about 3,000 feet. Following through in their runs, the big, twin-engine bombers pulled out spectacularly only 1,500 feet over the carrier. Owing to Murray's skillful ship handling, most of the bombs fell to starboard, but one 250-kilogram bomb exploded only 30 yards to port. Fragments ignited a small blaze on board the *Enterprise*.

The bombers headed away at low altitude. Suddenly one of them dropped out of formation and swung back toward "The Big E." It was Nakai. Crippled by fighters, the bomber evidently was no longer in shape to return to base, so Nakai was determined to crash it among the planes crowded forward on the *Enterprise*'s flight deck. From astern he overhauled the carrier in a flaming mockery of a landing approach. Light antiaircraft weapons opened fire at the low-flying aircraft as it approached. Seemingly at the last moment, the carrier finally heeled sharply to starboard, but the bomber did not match her turn. It appeared that the Japanese pilots were either dead or frozen at the controls. Both of Nakai's engines were ablaze. Finally his right wingtip scraped the port edge of the flight deck opposite the island and tore off the tail of an SBD (whose gun was bravely manned) parked forward. The wing ripped off at the fuselage and clattered onto the deck, spraying the area with gasoline from its ruptured fuel tank. The rest of the shattered aircraft slid into the sea. The gallant Nakai was dead, his other four planes returned to base, and "The Big E" had survived her introduction to the enemy.

After Nakai's attack, the carrier's flight deck crews respotted the flight deck to launch McClusky's four F4Fs at 1405 as relief CAP. A few minutes later, three F4Fs landed for fuel and ammo, leaving eight aloft. Near 1500, the FDO grew suspicious about a radar contact and sent McClusky's second section, Roger Mehle and Lieut. (jg) Rhonald J. Hoyle, to investigate. Anticipating a second attack, the *Enterprise* scrambled five F4Fs led by Gray, which increased to thirteen the fighters aloft. In the overcast, Mehle stumbled on an enemy twin-float seaplane. His first pass silenced the rear gunner, but the wily Japanese pilot escaped into the clouds. McClusky's own wingman, Rad. Elec. Bayers, happened upon the floatplane and made a couple of runs before it evaded him too in the murk. Finally Mehle found the enemy once more and finished what he had started. The floatplane fell in flames. It was an Aichi E13A1 Type 0 reconnaissance floatplane [JAKE] from the 19th Air Group based at Ebeye Island in Kwajalein atoll.

Later that afternoon, Nakai's two remaining land attack planes went after the *Enterprise*. They departed Taroa at 1430 and an hour later appeared on radar about 25 miles east of the task force. Radar tracked them as they came round west to

VF-6 F4F-3A (BuNo. 3917) after the 1 Feb. 1942 Marshalls Raid. F-9 was flown in combat by Ens. T. C. Provost. Note patch for battle damage incurred on left elevator. (NA 80-G-63340A.)

attack the ship from up sun. Nine F4Fs were aloft, divisions under McClusky and Gray. The Chitose crews this time executed a normal horizontal bombing approach from 14,000 feet at 140 knots. McClusky led his F4Fs out to intercept the raiders, and as they made ready to attack, the ships below cut loose with their five-inch antiaircraft guns. According to standing orders, the VF-6 pilots sheered out of range. The skipper carefully observed where the shells were bursting and by radio coached the gun directors. A black AA blossom rocked one of the two land attack planes and caused smoke to stream from its right engine. At 1557, both Japanese bombardiers released their 250-kilogram bombers as the *Enterprise* swung hard aport. They only made near misses.

Once the Japanese had drawn clear of antiaircraft fire, McClusky and company moved in again. Singling out the trailing bomber were the skipper, Mehle, and Daniels, and they roared through several individual firing passes, registering hits but not bringing down the aircraft. Finally as Daniels bored in, his bullets chopped into the silver, twin-tailed Mitsubishi and set it ablaze. The task force heard Daniels exult, "Bingo! Bingo! I got one!" The Japanese plunged into the water. For the victor, "it was both wonderful & terrifying."[11] Meanwhile, McClusky, Mehle, and Hoyle set out after the surviving bomber, which still trailed smoke from the antiaircraft hit. That one proved a tough bird, and McClusky had to call off the chase because the F4Fs were being drawn too far from the ships. He could only claim a probable kill, and his caution was justified, as the leader made it back to Taroa.

The *Enterprise* rotated her CAP at 1641, another flight operation on what was becoming a very long day. McClusky's division gratefully landed for a short rest, fuel, and bullets. At 1643, Rawie on patrol discovered another Japanese floatplane lurking in the clouds bearing 240 degrees, distance 12 miles from the carrier. He gave chase until his Grumman faltered because of prop and fuel pressure problems. The *Enterprise*'s Captain Murray was worried about an enemy dusk strike, so he arranged to land some of the CAP a little early to fuel them and send them aloft again. Shortly after 1700, Gray's division made ready to land. He himself had problems when the landing gear on his Wildcat gave way. For her dusk CAP, the carrier launched eight F4Fs, putting all fourteen of VF-6's operating Grummans in the air.

Sunset was at 1835, but a bright moon rose a few minutes later. The last of the combat air patrol landed at 1902. The clear, moonlit night transformed the ship wakes into bright silver, causing Halsey more anxiety about a possible enemy night strike. Indeed, the Japanese had flying boats out looking for the task force. At 2000, general quarters sounded when radar detected enemy aircraft at 35 miles, but they did not approach. Halsey turned northwest to take cover under a weather front. He managed to get clean away from the now less mysterious Marshall Islands.

Fighting Six claimed five enemy aircraft shot down and a sixth destroyed on the ground: three fighters, one floatplane, and two twin-engine bombers. One twin-engine bomber was damaged and another probably destroyed. The squadron lost no F4Fs in combat, but seven returned with battle damage. One F4F and pilot were lost on takeoff, and two others damaged in flight accidents. The two dive bombing squadrons together claimed a total of six enemy fighters shot down over Roi and Taroa, for the loss of five SBDs (three to fighter attack). The total *Enterprise* plane losses, therefore, were six aircraft. The next day the group counted available for flight operations a total of fifty-six airplanes (fifteen fighters, twenty-three dive bombers, and all eighteen torpedo planes).

For the *Enterprise* pilots there was much to learn from their experiences in the Marshalls. With regard to the fighters, the principal complaint was that there simply were not enough of them. Fighting Six opened the day with eighteen F4F Wildcats; by sunset there were only fourteen serviceable. The demands for fighter protection were enormous. The task force itself required a combat air patrol, the bombers needed (but did not get) fighter escorts, and there were so many targets that the fighters themselves had to execute some attacks. Young, the group commander, strongly recommended that the fighting squadrons operate twenty-seven F4Fs, even if it meant reducing the number of SBD dive bombers to accommodate them. He felt it extremely fortunate that Torpedo Six had lost none of its Devastators in combat. "Fighter protection for VT is mandatory,"[12] he wrote in his report. Both Halsey and Murray subsequently endorsed this advice.

The raids also brought out defects and deficiencies in materiel. Extremely disconcerting for the fighter pilots were the widespread machine gun failures. Investigation determined that the heavy belts of .50-caliber ammunition shifted in the trays during violent maneuvers and jammed the guns. In prewar maneuvers, the pilots rarely carried more than seventy rounds per gun; so the problem did not crop up. The *Enterprise*'s report suggested that dividers be installed in the trays to prevent the belts from displacing. The Bureau of Aeronautics was already working on the problem, having been alerted by Fighting Seventy-two in the Atlantic. The BuAer experts offered a solution on 11 March, when they sent instructions on how to modify the trays.[13]

The fighter pilots, as well as airplane drivers in the other carrier squadrons, clamored for self-sealing fuel tanks to prevent leaks and reduce the hazards of fire. Likewise, Fighting Six still awaited the arrival of factory-designed armor plate. Mehle's boiler plate was only an expediency. The lack of incendiary ammunition was a particular nuisance, especially as the pilots had discovered how readily enemy aircraft would burn if hit squarely. Special IFF radio gear was also vital, for the fighters at least, to help the fighter director officer keep track of his combat air patrol. Ideally all carrier aircraft, and those shipped on board the cruisers as well, should have IFF to alleviate the need for the CAP to chase down bogies only to discover they were friendlies.

In his report Halsey expressed admiration for the enemy aviators who attacked Task Force 8, praising the "determined manner in which the Japanese bombing planes were handled, the ferocity and accuracy of their attacks."[14] He thought it significant that naval aviators flew the Japanese bombers, rather than army pilots. With their naval experience, the Japanese pilots were thus able to execute long-range search missions at sea. He added that if the U.S. Navy likewise possessed fast, multi-engine heavy bombers, they could do the same—a dig at the Army Air Force's monopoly on the use of heavy bombers such as the Boeing B-17 Flying Fortress.

The Japanese fighter pilots, on the other hand, drew less than rave reviews from their opponents. Fighting Six's unofficial war diary concluded bluntly: "Japanese VF stinks (00's included)."[15] Some SBD crews thought at Taroa they encountered at least one Zero among the fighters that jumped them, although none actually was present. They noted the Japanese appeared surprisingly unaggressive against them once the SBDs closed up into mutually supporting formations. The elegant, pointed-winged fighters seemed reluctant to press home attacks, but contented themselves with "flat-hatting" aerobatics out of gun range. The Japanese preferred high-side runs—long-range "sniping" according to one VB-6 pilot.[16] The SBDs alone claimed six enemy fighters destroyed, and even the *Chester*'s lowly SOC-3 floatplanes reported one victory. Fighting Six in general condemned both enemy equipment and tactics. The F4F pilots found their own mounts faster and better-armed (when their guns worked!) than the obsolescent fixed-gear fighters they faced. Without a doubt, however, the enemy had the edge in maneuverability, giving thoughtful pilots pause to reflect that their own offensive tactics should emphasize hit-and-run rather than tail-chasing dogfights.

Strangely, the Fighter Unit of the Chitose Air Group did not feel chastened at all. Although not pleased about the nasty surprise attack, they were celebrating too. The unit reported the destruction of seventeen American aircraft (including three probables) for the loss (at Taroa) of one fighter shot down and another badly damaged. At Roi, ten Type 96 fighters engaged the SBDs and claimed five shot down without any loss. During VF-6's strike on Taroa, ten Type 96 fighters were on CAP or managed to get aloft in time to fight. No Chitose pilots were killed, as Lieut. Kurakane survived his abrupt parachute descent and swim as a result of Rawie's ambush. Atake was much admired for his fighting spirit in ramming the Grumman. Against the second Taroa raid, five fighters intercepted, claiming one dive bomber without any loss in return, and on the third raid, three Chitose fighters were engaged, claiming five American planes, again without loss. Big scorer at Taroa was W.O. Wajima Yoshio, with three kills to his credit.

THE *YORKTOWN*'S STRIKES

Frank Jack Fletcher's Task Force 17 transited the International Date Line shortly after 2400 on 29 January, immediately catapulting it ahead in time to 31 January. Ahead lay Fletcher's targets, Jaluit and Mili in the Marshalls and Makin Atoll in the Gilbert Islands. No search planes found the task force during the day, and at 1900, Fletcher separated his ships into two groups as ordered. Forging ahead was the Striking Group: the *Yorktown*, the heavy cruiser *Louisville*, and the light cruiser *St. Louis*. The heavy ships bent on 25 knots in order to reach the prescribed launch point at dawn. Following at a more sedate 16 knots to preserve fuel were the destroyers *Hughes, Russell, Sims,* and *Walke.* Barometric pressure continued to fall, as the ships drew deeper into the tropical low that plastered the southern Marshalls. Indeed, weather would prove more hazardous to the *Yorktown* aviators than the enemy. The basic plan was for the *Yorktown* Air Group to execute simultaneous dawn strikes against all three targets. There would be no fighter escorts, as the carrier would retain Fighting Forty-two to defend the task force. During the night the Striking Group pressed westward into the waters between the target atolls.

Flight quarters on board the *Yorktown* sounded at 0415 the morning of 1 February. Fletcher had taken his ships as close to Jaluit as Halsey wanted him to go. The carrier would conduct flight operations while the task force made tracks eastward back the way it had come. At 0452, the *Yorktown* swung eastward into the wind to launch first a combat air patrol of four fighters, then the Jaluit attack group of seventeen SBDs (the group commander and sixteen from Bombing Five) and eleven bomb-armed TBDs from Torpedo Five. The moon was out, but thick clouds to the west diffused the moonlight and made group rendezvous aloft extremely difficult. The *Yorktown* Air Group leader, Cdr. Smiley, could not gather all of his planes together, and most proceeded to the target in small groups or independently. At the time of the group's departure (0515), Jaluit lay about 140 miles to the northwest. Between 0537 and 0604, the *Yorktown* sent aloft the other two strike groups. Scouting Five's skipper, Lt. Cdr. William O. Burch, Jr., took nine of his SBDs 120 miles southeast to Makin. His executive officer, Lieut. Wallace C. Short, gathered five SBDs for the 70-mile flight northeast to Mili.

Curt Smiley's Jaluit attackers had to brave atrocious weather all the way to the target. The overcast, punctuated with violent rain squalls, ruined any opportunity for a coordinated strike and compelled the pilots to bomb from extremely low altitude. There was no air opposition, but at most the harried pilots could claim damage to a few auxiliary vessels in the harbor. Losses for this mission were high. Two SBDs simply disappeared, probably because of the weather. Torpedo Five lost four TBDs, two of which ditched near Jaluit. At Makin, Burch's pilots discovered two Japanese Kawanishi Type 97 flying boats from the Yokohama Air Group and an auxiliary vessel. They burned both aircraft anchored in the lagoon and bombed the small ship without loss to themselves. Mili proved to be barren of worthwhile targets.

Meanwhile, the *Yorktown* took the opportunity at 0637 to rotate the combat air patrol, launching six F4Fs and recovering the four aloft. A few minutes later her radar detected a bogey bearing 250 degrees, distance 25 miles. Bad weather prevented lookouts from spotting the aircraft, which evidently did not close to within sighting distance of the ships. Visibility grew poorer around the ships even though it was now after sunrise. Around 0700, the carrier encountered ahead her four destroyers, which joined formation right on schedule. His task force reunited, Fletcher settled down to await the return of his strike groups and probably the enemy as well. Around 0730 another bogey appeared on the screen. The *Yorktown* launched two Grummans to reinforce the CAP. The contact turned out to be a TBD that had separated from the strike force in the murk and felt its way back to base. Also approaching the task force were the SBDs, fresh from hitting Makin and Mili. Captain Buckmaster again attended to the CAP, sending aloft a relief of six F4Fs, and then respotted the flight deck to land the second patrol. The deck was clear to bring on board Burch's fourteen SBDs and the torpedo straggler.

After 0900 the weather, already unpleasant, turned especially grim. The wind grew in intensity, causing the carrier to roll and pitch in the turbulent seas. The

Yorktown at 0903 launched VS-5's fourteen SBDs as anti–torpedo-plane patrol, then took on board two CAP fighters and three aircraft just back from Jaluit. Twenty minutes later, eleven more from the Jaluit attack made landings, until Buckmaster had to suspend flight operations temporarily. The task force suffered the fury of a vicious rain squall. The pelting rain shrank visibility to less than 100 yards with wind gusts to 50 knots. More than one pilot found it impossible to stay aloft. At 0940, the VS-5 SBD flown by Ens. T. A. Reeves flew into the water off the carrier's port beam, and the destroyer *Walke* charged over to recover the crew in a brilliant rescue at the height of the storm. A Curtiss SOC-3 floatplane from the *Louisville* simply disappeared. Under these circumstances it was useless to maintain a CAP, and Buckmaster ordered them to land. The six fighters braved the elements to come on board at 0945 along with two strike planes. Between 1015 and 1030, all the other aircraft aloft, at least those that were coming back, returned to the *Yorktown*. Task Force 17 could do nothing but ride out the unexpectedly nasty storms.

One of the last pilots to land reported sighting an aircraft on the water 20 miles southwest of the task force's present position. Anxious to rescue his downed flyers, Fletcher at 1040 detached the destroyers *Hughes, Sims*, and *Russell* to look for that crew and other missing aviators. Westward-bound, the three tincans deployed into a scouting line, while the rest of the task forces withdrew to the east at 20 knots.[1] The three destroyers soon encountered an aircraft, but not a welcome one. Searching the storm-tossed seas was a Japanese Kawanishi flying boat, one of three that had taken off after the Americans had left Jaluit. At 1110, the flying boat's crew reported sighting two enemy destroyers bearing 105 degrees and 230 miles from Jaluit. The *Hughes* noticed the intruder and requested air support, and the *Yorktown*'s radar at 1117 pinpointed the snooper bearing 270 degrees, distance 32 miles from the task force. Buckmaster scrambled VF-42's 3rd Division led by Vince McCormack. The six F4Fs departed at 1120 and disappeared into the murk. For 20 minutes the VF-42 pilots searched diligently for their quarry, ducking thunderstorms and squall lines, but, in the vernacular, "there was no joy" as the enemy eluded them. The *Yorktown* had to recall her pilots. Likewise the Kawanishi crew from the Yokohama Air Group lost sight of the destroyers at 1145, searched the area once more, and finally reached base at 1610.

Task Force 17 passed through another thick squall line around noon. With McCormack's troops circling overhead, the *Yorktown* at 1257 launched a relief CAP of six fighters under Lt. Cdr. Fenton, then respotted the deck to recover the 3rd Division. As Fenton took off, Fletcher broke radio silence to direct his destroyers to rendezvous. The *Louisville* received permission to home in by radio its missing plane, but there was no response from the pilot. Another Japanese flying boat lurked in the area and stumbled upon the destroyers. This Kawanishi had left Jaluit at 0810 on search and evidently amplified the contact made by the other crew. At 1305 the *Hughes* piped up to warn that the snooper was back again. The Japanese next appeared over the destroyer *Russell* and endured a dose of antiaircraft fire for its troubles. The big flying boat slipped away to the north in a rain squall and headed for the *Sims*. The *Russell* radioed her a warning, a thoughtful act because this time the Japanese decided to be belligerent. Coming at the *Sims*, they released four small bombs that exploded 2,000 yards astern of the fast-moving vessel. The *Hughes* again sighted the flying boat briefly before it disappeared to the northeast.

The *Yorktown* detected the Japanese shortly after the *Hughes* broadcast the alarm. Radar placed the bogey bearing 015 degrees, distance 34 miles from the carrier. Oscar Pederson acting as FDO alerted the CAP and vectored Fenton's division by sections to locate the intruder. The bogey continued swinging around to the northeast. Finally, the *Yorktown* lookouts had it in their glasses, bearing 060 degrees, distance 10 miles. In best position to intercept was Fenton's third section, two F4Fs flown by Ens. E. Scott McCuskey and Ens. John P. Adams. They quickly pounced on the big seaplane while it was momentarily clear of the clouds. In close succession the two VF-42 pilots roared through a firing pass. The Kawanishi nosed down for speed, and with engines straining fled toward the overcast. On their initial run, the two Grummans had silenced the tail gunner. Observers on board the ships could easily see the huge flying boat, beset by two gnatlike fighters, cross ahead of the carrier, then disappear into the clouds. For the second attack, the section split. McCuskey dipped beneath the target and shot into its keel and wings, while Adams sat on its tail. Flame blossomed along the fuselage; then a violent explosion blew off the twin-ruddered tail. Flaming debris fell into the sea, leaving a fiercely burning slick on the surface. The Yokohama Air Group had lost a third Kawanishi Type 97 flying boat that day to the Yorktowners.

This was the *Yorktown*'s (and VF-42's) first aerial victory, and it took place in dramatic fashion in full view of the ship. Her irrepressible executive officer, newly promoted Captain J. J. ("Jocko") Clark, had grabbed a microphone and over the ship's loudspeaker cheered on the crew. At the sight of the flaming Kawanishi, he yelled, "Burn, you son-of-a-bitch, burn!"[2] McCuskey, to the delight of the many listeners in the *Yorktown*, soon topped that by exulting over the radio, "We just shot his ass off!"[3] At 1430 when the F4Fs landed back after the CAP, the flight deck crew mobbed McCuskey and Adams. In advance they had prepared for the first victory by fashioning a bizarre costume with a fezlike hat and a jacket "covered with tin medals, ribbons, and an ace of spades."[4] Because the two had shared in the victory, one received the hat and the other the jacket.

Originally Fletcher had hoped to launch a second strike that afternoon against Jaluit, but the weather was too miserable. The return of the morning missions had been greatly delayed, and if he sent them off again, they would have to fly back in darkness and atrocious weather. Also Fletcher wanted to fuel his destroyers in anticipation of making coordinated attacks the next day with Task Force 8. That afternoon, therefore, he decided to proceed with fueling his tincans from the heavy ships, then look forward to better flying conditions on 2 February. Fighting Forty-two braved the elements to fly CAP until dusk. As it turned out, Fletcher that evening received orders from Halsey to withdraw. The first counterattack was over. For Task Force 17 the experience was largely soured by poor weather, but the carrier and her air group eagerly awaited more opportunities to smash the Japanese.

RETURN TO PEARL

Task Force 8 gratefully concealed itself in a squall line during its retirement from the Marshalls. Halsey took the opportunity to fuel his destroyers from his heavy ships. Contrary to expectations, enough fuel remained to take them back to base. The morning of 2 February was delightfully raw and overcast, "one of the best rain squalls I've seen in years."[1] according to Rawie. With the *Enterprise* dancing in the heavy seas, no flight operations were scheduled. Aside from those on duty, the fighter pilots had a chance to rest and recount their experiences of the previous day. Despite the weather, the Japanese were out looking for them. Several times "The Big E's" radar had planes on the screen, but none of the Japanese came within sighting range. For two days after that there was no flying for Fighting Six. The task force recrossed the date line, living 2 February over again. The men were

VF-6 F4F-3A with single 100-lb. bomb is flagged away for inner air patrol from the *Enterprise*, Feb. or Mar. 1942. (NA 80-G-14540.)

amused to hear Radio Tokyo's version of the Marshall raid; according to that highly regarded source, the Americans sank one small auxiliary and killed thirty-eight civilians.

On 4 February, one day out of Pearl, "Buster" Hoyle while flying the detested inner air patrol happened upon a surfaced submarine. He dropped his single 100-lb. bomb, which exploded just forward of the I-boat. The submarine crash-dived, and a destroyer sent by Halsey to look the area over saw an oil slick. Hoyle had done some damage with his puny bomb. Fighting Six much preferred to see SBDs or especially TBDs flying antisubmarine patrol. They at least could carry a depth charge, something really capable of hurting a sub. The air department did not agree, and the VF-6 pilots continued to log many hours circling the task force on inner air patrol.

The morning of 5 February, the *Enterprise* Air Group turned out for the flight to NAS Pearl Harbor. Heavy rains dogged the trip in, but everyone made it safely. While her aviators were squaring away on Ford Island, the *Enterprise* and her consorts entered port. Sailors and workmen on board the ships and throughout the navy yard gave them rousing cheers. No doubt about it, the 1 February strikes had done wonders to boost American morale. Boosting pilot morale was word that they were getting forty-eight hours of uninterrupted rest at the Royal Hawaiian Hotel. The only thing that impinged on good times was the Army's ban on hard liquor in the islands. Summoning all of their hidden resources, Fighting Six managed to accumulate a healthy supply of intoxicants—even if some of it was refined torpedo alcohol shared with submarine crews also recuperating at the Royal Hawaiian. Gray and associates encountered some submariners not too happy to see pilots from "The Big E." They were off the *Pompano*, twice bombed by mistake on 20 December by *Enterprise* dive bombers.

On 6 February, Task Force 17 with the *Yorktown* made its first wartime appearance off Oahu. The *Yorktown* Air Group flew in to the marine field at Ewa, where the pilots secured their aircraft, had lunch, then headed off for one day at the Royal Hawaiian Hotel. When the *Yorktown* warped into harbor, her crew were shocked at the devastation wrought since they had been there the previous spring.

Their reception was somewhat pale compared with that given Halsey:

> Pearl Harbor seems to have exhausted itself cheering the *Enterprise* force. When *Yorktown* and her escorts arrived in port the following day, they attracted only moderate attention. The newsmen, with the colorful Halsey to write about, could spare few words for Frank Jack Fletcher or for the even quieter Raymond Spruance.[2]

The *Yorktown* and her aviators would in the future find themselves in the shadow of the glamorous "Big E," but Aircraft, Battle Force headquarters ashore was mighty pleased to see the *Yorktown*. She offloaded twenty F4F-3s and F4F-3As vitally needed by the fleet. The drastic shortage of carrier fighters was about to abate.

CHAPTER 5

The Battle off Bougainville:
Fighting Three in the South Pacific

With the *Saratoga* laid up for repairs, her air group in mid-January 1942 fetched up ashore on Oahu. Fighting Three settled in with the marines at Ewa and faced the prospect of flying dawn and dusk alerts for the Army's Seventh Interceptor Command responsible for air defense of the Hawaiian Islands. On 17 January, Jimmy Thach, now over his illness, rejoined the squadron and found good reason to be pleased with the situation. For the first time since the previous summer, Fighting Three obtained enough fighters to operate near authorized strength. Between 16 and 18 January, the squadron drew five Grumman F4F-3 Wildcats newly arrived from San Diego. Thach was also satisfied with flight arrangements worked out with the Army. Although his troops would fly routine dawn and dusk alerts, the rest of the time was largely their own to conduct gunnery and tactical training flights. The Army gave Thach use of air space off Oahu's north coast for gunnery exercises. It was much harder to work in gunnery training when under the Navy's jurisdiction at Pearl Harbor.

Routine alerts and training missions occupied much of the next few days. There was a mishap on 22 January. Flying the dusk alert that afternoon, the pilots had to remain aloft until well after dark because of a thick overcast and other delays. Finally they were allowed to come down. The night landings at Ewa proceeded without trouble until the third Wildcat, one of the newly arrived F4F-3s, touched down on the runway. The pilot, Ens. Lee Haynes, had neglected to lock his landing gear, and the undercarriage crumpled under the weight of the aircraft. Still moving swiftly, the fighter slid on its belly for one hundred yards and piled up on the mat close to the intersection of Ewa's two runways. Adding to Haynes's trouble was the fact that gasoline leaking from the smashed fuselage tank drain plug underneath the aircraft had ignited from sparks. Fortunately he escaped the blaze without injury. Ewa's fire fighters were on the scene quickly, but the fierce flames and exploding ammunition hindered their efforts. Meanwhile nine VF-3 F4Fs were still aloft, their fuel dwindling. The Ewa controller told the planes to land at the Army's Wheeler Field, but Oahu was totally blacked out, so that Wheeler was hard to find. Six fighters persevered and landed at Ewa. Don Lovelace followed orders and searched for the Army field. Visions of VF-6's disaster the night of 7 December came to his mind when he discovered his landing lights were burned out. He finally managed to get his wingman to turn on his own lights for identification. Fortunately, everyone got down safely that night.[1]

After flying the afternoon alert again on 24 January, the whole squadron, decked out with .45-caliber automatic pistols, piled into a schoolbus for the perilous drive across the blacked-out island. The pilots were going for, of all things, a stay at the swank Royal Hawaiian Hotel. Admiral Halsey had long been concerned about the need for his pilots to unwind and rest somewhere on Oahu. He finally settled on the Royal Hawaiian, masterpiece of the wealthy Waikiki Beach set, the aviators sharing the resort with submarine crews in port after war patrols. Life at the hotel was somewhat simpler in comparison to what it once was, but the beach was always magnificent. The pilots relaxed there until the evening of the next day. On 26 January they were back on duty at Ewa, and Thach received two more F4F-3s courtesy of VMF-121 at San Diego.

The *Lexington* had warped into port on 25 January, back after the abortive Wake raid. Paul Ramsey that morning had led his Fighting Two to NAS Kaneohe Bay. Big changes were in store for the chiefs of Fighting Two: because of the arrival of F4F-3As from VMF-111, Ramsey would finally be able to reequip his squadron with Grumman Wildcats and get rid of the maligned Brewster Buffaloes. This, however, would also put Fighting Two ashore for what ultimately would be three months. On 26 January, Fighting Two ferried its Brewsters over to Ford Island and made ready to accept eleven F4F-3As. Ramsey's sixteen operational F2A-3 Buffaloes would go to Marine Air Group 21.

On 26 January, Aircraft, Battle Force headquarters alerted Thach to prepare Fighting Three for sea duty at short notice. The *Lexington* waited in port for a few days to complete minor repairs, but CinCPac soon would have need of her. The next day, Fighting Three formally joined the *Lexington* Air Group in place of Fighting Two. The fact that U.S. naval carrier squadrons were autonomous units permitted them to be shifted from carrier to carrier swiftly and without trouble, whereas Japanese carrier aviation was not nearly as flexible in this regard. Thach took his boys to NAS Kaneohe Bay to prepare for embarkation, while Fighting Two took their place at Ewa to facilitate transfer of the Brewsters to the marines. Ramsey and Thach traded a few planes so that Fighting Three would have the best aircraft. The much-traveled XF4F-4 ended up in Ramsey's custody. On 30 January, Thach got the word. Fighting Three would fly out to the *Lexington* on the last day of the month.

The same day Thach received his orders, his new task force commander, Admiral Brown, learned of his mission from CinCPac. Task Force 11's first job would be to escort the fleet oiler *Neosho* to rendezvous with Halsey's Task Force 8, certain to be low on fuel after its foray into the Marshalls. After meeting Halsey north of Johnston, Brown was to head south toward Canton Island to cover a convoy scheduled to arrive there on 12 February. After that, Brown was to return to Pearl. Task Force 11 comprised the carrier *Lexington*, the heavy cruisers *Minneapolis* and *Indianapolis* (under Rear Admiral Thomas C. Kinkaid), seven destroyers, and the portly *Neosho*.

The *Lexington* and her consorts on the morning of 31 January set sail from Pearl Harbor. Bill Ault's *Lexington* Air Group (eighteen fighters, thirty-seven dive bombers, and thirteen torpedo planes) assembled at Kaneohe for the short hop out to the carrier. All of them landed safely on the *Lex* except for an F4F from Fighting Three—Ens. Newton H. Mason cracked up on his first carrier landing in the tricky Wildcat. He was unhurt, but the Grumman required a major overhaul. While Fighting Three made themselves at home on board their new vessel, orders from CinCPac arranged a definite rendezvous with Halsey. Task Force 11 set course southwest toward the Marshalls, that day (1 February west of the date line) being worked over by Task Forces 8 and 17.

Fighting Three took the measure of the *Saratoga*'s sister and definitely preferred the *Lex*:

> There was a different and better spirit aboard the Lex. The work on the flight deck went on with less noise and delay. The port holes were opened in the day time so that fresh air entered the ship and the evening meal was eaten in whites.
> . . . It was a good start, filled with promise for a happy cruise.[2]

Thach was especially impressed with the air department:

> The *Lexington* was a ship administered in every way to enhance the value of the air group. The training of the air group at sea in gunnery and bombing was given high priority.[3]

The first of February brought word of the previous day's attack in the Marshalls and Gilberts, with the reported loss of eleven planes. The VF-3 pilots wondered who of their friends and colleagues had cashed in the day before. The naval aviation fraternity was still relatively small, and everyone knew the seasoned pilots, at least by reputation. On 2 February, CinCPac changed Brown's mission. As it turned out, Task Force 8 had sufficient fuel to reach port; so Brown headed southward to carry out his offensive patrol off Canton. The entanglements of the government at home reached out even to the combat pilots on board their carrier. Lovelace, for one, spent much of the day working on his income taxes. The next day, *Lexington* search planes encountered 90 miles south the ships of Task Force 17 heading north toward Pearl after their offensive strikes in the Marshalls and Gilberts.

The fifth of February brought word from the task force commander that the ships would soon cross the equator. Some vessels did little in the way of line-crossing ceremonies, but the *Lexington* was famous for them. That day the Shell-backs (those who in the past had undergone the exquisite pleasure of meeting King Neptune's court) met to decide what they were going to do to the lowly Pollywogs. Fighting Three's only Shellbacks were Lovelace and Gayler. As it happened, the despised Pollywogs outnumbered the lordly Shellbacks approximately ten to one. With strength in numbers, the lowly rebelled. That afternoon they relentlessly hunted down the Shellbacks in retaliation for what the old salts were planning, tying Lovelace and Gayler to a bulkhead. Later, however, the Pollywogs repented and accepted their fate in good fun. As part of the preliminary ceremonies, they had to do all sorts of silly things. Lieut. (jg) Onia B. ("Burt") Stanley, Jr., one of VF-3's ex–aviation cadets, "marched about in heavy clothing searching the horizon for icebergs known to be in those waters."[4] Some had two Coke bottles lashed together as "binoculars."

After dinner, court convened in the wardroom to listen to the malefactors confess their crimes and to dispense penalties for the next day. The two VB-2 pilots— Whittier and Connally—who had bombed the dynamite barge in December, the Shellbacks ribbed unmercifully. At midnight Task Force 11 crossed the equator. The following morning on the flight deck there was a small Neptune party for many of the 2,000-odd Pollywogs, including running the gauntlet. Some like Stanley could smile; he had squadron duty and did not have to join in the fun. The *Lexington* was at war and could not spare the time for a really good initiation.

About noon on 6 February, Brown learned that Task Force 11 would head for the South Pacific. Specifically, his new mission was to cooperate with the newly created ANZAC Command (under Vice Admiral Leary) to destroy Japanese advances toward the New Hebrides and other vital islands on the line of communication between Pearl Harbor and Australia. The task force would come under the

The *Lexington* line-crossing ceremonies, 5 Feb. 1942, *l to r in foreground* searching for "icebergs": Burt Stanley, Lee Haynes on Marion Dufilho's shoulders; *behind*: Noel Gayler. (Capt. O. B. Stanley, USN.)

operational direction of Admiral King in Washington. At the urging of CominCh, the Army had provided troops to defend New Caledonia. The doughboys would arrive in early March, and King desired that a carrier task force cover them. Brown received orders to rendezvous with the ANZAC Squadron, a mixed force of American and Australian warships under Rear Admiral John G. Crace, Royal Navy. Brown would find Crace about 300 miles west of the Fijis. Messages received later that week fleshed out the duties of the ANZAC Command. Leary would operate from ashore, coordinating sea and air forces, while Brown (senior to Leary) would command at sea. Brown had a good idea what he was going to do. He would attack Rabaul—Japan's nascent bastion on New Britain.

While Task Force 11 steamed eastward of the Phoenix Islands, Fighting Three on 8 February suffered a fatality. Through an oversight, engine starter cartridges (a form of modified shotgun shell) used in the Wildcats were in short supply. In order to save what cartridges they had for combat, the squadron engineers rigged up "bungee" starters (an elastic line with block and tackle) to crank the engines for routine operations. During an engine run up, a block broke loose from where the line was tied on deck and struck Edward Frank Ambrose, AMM3c, a VF-3 mechanic, in the chest. He died four hours later. "For the want of a nail . . . ,"[5] Stanley wrote sadly in his diary.

The day after Frank Ambrose's death, Fighting Three began flying regular combat air patrol, generally a late morning patrol and another in the early afternoon. Given the excruciatingly hot weather, it was a relief to fly. On 10 February, the task force received reinforcements in the form of the heavy cruiser *San Francisco* and two destroyers. Eager to hit the enemy, especially with Allied defenses in Southeast Asia about to crumble, King ordered Brown and Leary to conduct offensive operations in the Solomons–Bismarck area. Task Force 11 would have the benefit of six Consolidated PBY Catalina flying boats searching out of Suva to cover its rear, while Leary coordinated the activities of Army B-17 Flying Fortresses slated to fly out of Suva or northeastern Australia.

On 14 February there was some excitement when the CAP encountered a Royal New Zealand Air Force Hudson bomber patrolling out of Suva. Task Force 11 was really in the South Pacific. Brown steamed for the rendezvous point west of Suva, taking time on the way to empty the oiler *Neosho*. There was oil to fill the *Lexington* and the destroyers, but the cruisers had to make do with 75 percent of capacity. The *Lexington* flew three SBDs to Suva to deliver messages for transmission there, and also a member of Brown's staff for a conference. In one of the messages Brown proposed raiding Rabaul; King and Leary promptly agreed. Rear Admiral Crace's ANZAC Squadron (flagship the heavy cruiser *Australia*, two light cruisers, and the American warships *Chicago* and two destroyers) hove into sight on 16 February. Despite heavy seas, Crace and his staff rode a small boat over to the *Lexington* to confer personally with Brown. Lacking oil for his heavy ships, Brown just could not spare the fuel to take Crace with him to Rabaul. Reluctantly the ANZAC ships would have to stay near Suva. The little armada separated that afternoon.

Brown's movement plan was to pass east of the New Hebrides and the Solomons to gain a position from which he would attack Rabaul from the northeast. He planned to launch an air strike on the dawn of 21 February, then, depending on the situation, send in one heavy cruiser and two destroyers to bombard the base. Leary's intelligence officer had forwarded news of Japanese naval aircraft and some shipping at Rabaul, but CinCPac added that the Japanese fleet carriers operated in the Dutch East Indies where they offered no threat to Rabaul's attackers. Brown shaped course northwestward toward the New Hebrides. On 17 February the heavy cruiser *Pensacola* and two destroyers joined the group, giving Brown a total of four heavy cruisers and ten destroyers in addition to the *Lex*. The newcomer *Pensacola* with the destroyers *Clark* and *Bagley* would comprise the bombardment group. The next day, the Australian high command estimated there were eight vessels in Rabaul's Simpson Harbor, supported by twelve fighters, twelve torpedo planes, and twenty-four medium bombers based at Vunakanau airfield outside the town. There did not appear to be anything that the *Lexington* Air Group, particularly with surprise on its side, could not handle. For good measure, Leary arranged for bomber strikes by American and Australian aircraft to coincide with the air strike and possible ship bombardment on Rabaul.

Responsible for defense of the Bismarcks region was South Seas Force, that old adversary from the capture of Wake and the Central Pacific raids. As his immediate task, Vice Admiral Inoue planned invasions of Lae and Salamaua in eastern New Guinea, as well as Tulagi in the southern Solomons. These operations he scheduled for March and April. Shortly thereafter, South Seas Force would undertake the seizure of Port Moresby on the south coast of Papua to utilize its strategic airfields. In all of these ventures, Inoue would confront Pacific Fleet carrier task forces. To provide air support for his invasions, Inoue in early February began concentrating units from his 24th Air Flotilla at Rabaul. Ultimately operating from there would be two naval air groups (*kōkūtai*), one equipped with single-engine fighters and twin-engine land attack planes (medium bombers) and the other with four-engine flying boats for long-range search missions. Headquarters, 24th Air Flotilla, likewise controlled strong air units based at Truk and in the Marshalls.

While Task Force 11 closed in unseen from the southeast, the Japanese at Truk and Rabaul nonetheless were edgy. In Tokyo the Naval Section of Imperial General Headquarters had intercepted heavy radio traffic in the Hawaiian area. They interpreted the many urgent American communications as indicating the departure of an American carrier task force. On 14 February, the Japanese sounded an alert. They were apprehensive after Halsey's and Fletcher's forays into the Mandated Islands. Compounding their nervousness, late on the afternoon of 19 February a Japanese shore station situated on a small island 160 miles southwest of Truk frantically reported two enemy destroyers. Could the enemy be bold enough to raid Truk? The alarm proved to be false, but coincidentally Task Force 11 bore down on Rabaul. The Japanese sounded another alert for 20 February.

Plans for 20 February involved searches from Rabaul by four Kawanishi Type 97 flying boats to cover an easterly sector (bearing 075 to 155 degrees) a distance of 500 miles from Rabaul. Other search missions originated at Truk and in the Marshalls to sweep the triangle formed by those two locales and Rabaul. Waiting on alert should the search spot the enemy were land attack planes and fighters. At Rabaul, the 4th Air Group had on hand eighteen land attack planes and twenty-six fighters; nine land attack planes from the Chitose Air Group (acquaintances from the 1 February raids) waited at Truk, while twenty-seven land attack planes and thirty-six fighters from the same unit were in the Marshalls. Additional Kawanishi flying boats from the Yokohama Air Group stood by at Rabaul for possible night torpedo strikes. In a pinch each big flying boat could carry two torpedoes. The Japanese were definitely ready and waiting.

Task Force 11 made an uneventful passage northward from the New Hebrides into the waters northeast of the Solomons. On 19 February, as the task force paralleled the coast of Bougainville, Thach held a pre-battle inspection of Fighting Three. Observing the hirsute countenances of some of the squadron personnel, he ordered all beards to be shaved, "so they won't be a fire hazard."[6] Flight organization of Fighting Three is given in the table. The aircraft nominally assigned each pilot on the basis of the squadron flight organization is shown, but a pilot rarely flew the assigned airplane, instead manning whatever fighter the flight leader and squadron duty officer assigned after learning from Air Plot the side number and deck position of the planes scheduled for the upcoming launch. Thus during the whole cruise Burt Stanley flew his nominally assigned aircraft (F-5, BuNo. 4009) only twice.[7] On 19 February (and also the next day), there were not sufficient aircraft for all of the pilots, as only sixteen of VF-3's eighteen Grummans were flyable.

The morning of 20 February, Task Force 11 held to its northwesterly course well north of the Solomons. Brown had not yet reached the point where he would swing to the southwest for the final approach to a target in order to attack at daybreak the next morning. The *Lexington* readied for a day of routine flight operations. At dawn she launched a precautionary search out 300 miles ahead of the task force. Flying that mission were six SBD dive bombers from Lt. Cdr. Robert E. Dixon's Scouting Two. Thach and five pilots from the 1st Division waited that tranquil morning to take off on combat air patrol when the dawn search returned. The *Lexington*'s Captain Sherman relied mainly on her CXAM radar to detect approaching enemy planes. Directing the combat air patrol aloft was the fighter

Bureau number*	Nominal Aircraft, side number	Assignment
		1st Division
3976	F-1	Lt. Cdr. John S. Thach, USN, commanding officer
	F-2	Ens. Edward R. Sellstrom, Jr., A-V(N)
	F-3	Lieut. Edward H. O'Hare, USN
	F-4	Lieut. (jg) Marion W. Dufilho, USN
4009	F-5	Lieut. (jg) Onia B. Stanley, Jr., A-V(N)
	F-6	Ens. Leon W. Haynes, A-V(N)
		2nd Division
4021	F-7	Lt. Cdr. Donald A. Lovelace, USN, executive officer
	F-8	Ens. Richard M. Rowell, A-V(N)
	F-9	Lieut. Albert O. Vorse, Jr., USN
	F-10	Lieut. (jg) Robert J. Morgan, USN
	F-11	Lieut. (jg) Howard L. Johnson, USN
	F-12	Ens. John H. Lackey, A-V(N)
		3rd Division
3986	F-13	Lieut. Noel A. M. Gayler, USN, flight officer
	F-14	Ens. Dale W. Peterson, A-V(N)
4031	F-15	Lieut. (jg) Rolla S. Lemmon, USN
	F-16	Lieut. (jg) Howard F. Clark, USN
	F-17	Ens. Willard E. Eder, A-V(N)
	F-18	Ens. John W. Wilson, A-V(N)
		Ens. Newton H. Mason, A-V(N)

*If known.

director officer, Lieut. Frank F. ("Red") Gill, a naval aviator for almost ten years. Reinforcing the fighters when necessary were SBD dive bombers acting as low-level anti–torpedo-plane patrol. That idea was a particular favorite with Sherman, who wanted to compensate for the small number of fighters available to defend the task force.

The *Lexington*'s CXAM radar silently watched the skies, and at 1000 made its first contact of the morning, showing unidentified aircraft bearing 220 degrees, distance 40 miles. They seemed to be the search SBDs returning on schedule. On deck, mechanics had six fighters warming up, while Thach's 1st Division awaited orders to man planes. At the time, the *Lexington* was on a northwesterly heading at 15 knots. Rabaul, the next day's objective, bore 453 miles southwest of the task force. At 1015, the radar detected what looked like an intruder bearing 180 degrees, distance 35 miles. Sherman ordered Thach's 1st Division to scramble. The *Lexington* swung into the wind to launch the six Grummans. Once aloft, Thach came under the control of Red Gill, the FDO. Gill instructed Thach's section to check out the contact, keeping in reserve over the task force sections led by Butch O'Hare and Burt Stanley.

Because of the importance of radar and fighter direction technique in the 20 February engagement, a summary of the art may be useful here.[8] The mission assigned to fighters on combat air patrol (CAP) was the destruction of enemy search planes and strike groups. Prewar doctrine entailed the use of airborne fighter lookout patrols to detect the approach of the enemy. A large portion of the fighting squadron was thus assigned to patrol in given sectors to spot the enemy, warn the task force, and then make interception. The process was time-consuming and highly

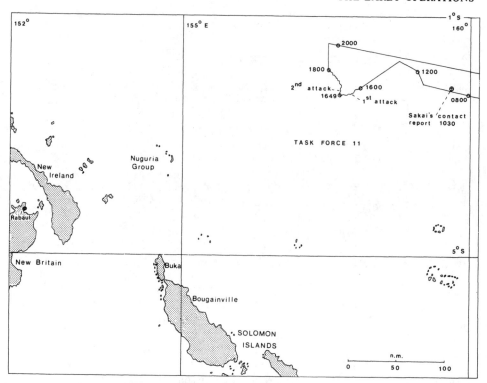

The 20 Feb. action off Bougainville.

inefficient. In 1941, the carriers shipped on board long-range search radars, notably the CXAM-1 model. Radar enabled a ship to detect the presence of, and determine the bearings and ranges of aircraft roughly within an 80-mile radius of the vessel. The most important controlling factors with regard to detection were the number of aircraft in a group and their altitude. Radar waves were ultrahigh frequency and did not dip over the horizon; they were in essence "line of sight."

Radar in 1942 had a number of features that made fighter direction more difficult. First of all, there was no clear indication of the contact's altitude. The radar operator could only offer a reasonable guess based mainly on the range of the contact (the farther out, the higher it was) and something called the "fade chart" method. Null areas existed in the electro-magnetic lobes of the waves when projected to specific areas. Thus contacts would disappear at certain ranges, depending on the target's altitude, and reappear later. Careful calibration and tests determined that only those aircraft flying at the same height faded at the same distance. For an individual radar set, these fade areas, once plotted, remained constant. The method was none too accurate, but it was the best at hand. The radars in use at the time had what were known as "A" scopes. They did not offer a visual display of the situation. Instead, the information to be intelligible had to be manually entered on a 360-degree polar plot. The flight path of a particular contact first became recognizable on the grid as a series of dots which resolved themselves when connected into a course line. Such plotting took precious time.

The unidentified aircraft or "bogeys" having been detected and plotted, it was the function of the fighter director officer (FDO) to track them, and then by addressing course, speed, and altitude orders to specific elements of the CAP (which would likewise be tracked), bring the chosen fighter elements into an intercept with the unidentified aircraft. The FDO thus held great responsibility; according to Thach, "he can win or lose the battle right there."[9] Early 1942 doctrine, adopted mainly from the British, called for the FDO to exercise the "direct method" of fighter direction. Under this procedure, the FDO used a standard vocabulary to provide all of the information to the pilots, estimating the point of contact himself. The CAP fighters needed proper initial position from which to start their firing passes, and this required visual contact with the enemy as far out as possible. With a fast-moving contact, this could be difficult. Five miles (10,000 yards) was about the limit at which a fighter pilot could spot an oncoming plane. The FDO had to make allowances for low visibility and other factors in order to bring his fighters into visual contact *ahead* of the bogey. Of necessity, the FDO had to be able to visualize the situation, taking account of the relative positions of the aircraft, then determine the proper course and altitude for the intercept.

Adding to the FDO's difficulties was the fact that his FD staff with the plot board had to work in a small, cramped corner of Air Plot within the carrier's island. There were too many distractions. Later the FDO would have his own area, but in early 1942 too often he was the orphan of the air department. Likewise handicapping the FDO's efforts was the primitive nature of fighter radios and the IFF (Identification—Friend or Foe) gear. The radios were only medium-high frequency (MHF) with a good possibility of enemy monitoring. The FDO had to hold his radio traffic to a minimum for fear of revealing his position to the enemy. Through a signal emitted by IFF gear that allowed the radar operator to identify the contact, IFF indicated to the FDO which aircraft were friendly. The device was obviously top secret, and there was apprehension that it would fall into Japanese hands. Unfortunately it was also quite scarce; only a few aircraft as yet had IFF. This meant the CAP constantly had to check out bogeys that proved to be friendly carrier aircraft or cruiser floatplanes. The malfunctioning of IFF or its outright absence often meant the FD plot was swamped with bogeys, making it impossible to keep everyone straight, as the *Enterprise* learned on 1 February.

Basic CAP organizations at this time were fighter divisions and their component two-plane sections. Each pilot and each section had an individual name–number designation for use in the radio calls. When in "hot waters," carriers commonly retained aloft during daylight one division of four to six F4Fs. The air officer usually rotated the patrols at two- or three-hour intervals. Longer flights were common, but harrowing; as Noel Gayler later noted, "the darn plane runs itself almost out of gas."[10] Patrols kept visual contact with the carrier unless ordered elsewhere. The fighters cruised at power settings for maximum endurance when on routine patrol, sometimes stepped up to two-thirds power when hunting snoopers, and of course shifted to full military power when heading off an enemy strike. CAP altitudes were variable, mainly depending on weather conditions and cloud ceiling. The pilots did not like to fly long patrols over 10,000 feet because they had to go on oxygen. Twelve thousand feet was about maximum for a standing CAP at that time, unless the FDO had good reason to believe a strike was coming in higher than that. Fighter direction, like so much pertaining to carrier combat, was still evolving into proper form. No one knew what really worked until it was tried in battle, as on 20 February.

In this case, the *Lexington*'s radar had indeed detected a snooper. That dawn three big Kawanishi flying boats had departed Rabaul to search the waters to the east. Eager eyes, excited by the previous day's alert, were rewarded with the sight of Task Force 11. At 1030, Lieut. (jg) Sakai Noboru, pilot of the flying boat covering the sector 075 to 090 degrees from Rabaul, reported to headquarters that he had spotted an enemy striking force bearing 075 degrees and 460 miles from Rabaul, with a course of 315 degrees. Skillfully shadowing the task force, Sakai remained

Famous view of Jimmy Thach (F-1) and Butch O'Hare (F-13) taken 10 Apr. 1942 off Kaneohe. F-1 (BuNo. 3976) on 20 Feb. 1942 was flown by Thach and Noel Gayler, F-13 (BuNo. 3986) by Lee Haynes and Thach. Both aircraft were lost with VF-2 in May 1942 at Coral Sea. (USN.)

Another look at VF-3 Grummans flown by Thach and O'Hare, 10 Apr. 1942. (USN.)

in the area and took cover in the abundant cloud cover nearby. Brown's intended raid was a surprise no more. What followed is a classic example of the defense of a task force by the combat air patrol.

Guided by directions from Gill, Thach and his wingman, Ens. Edward ("Doc") Sellstrom, hunted for the intruder. At 1056, Thach informed the FDO that there were heavy clouds ahead. A few minutes later, the fighter section reached the end of its navigational leg at a point bearing 205 degrees (M.) and 35 miles from the carrier. Thach observed a rain squall dead ahead and asked the FDO whether the bogey was inside. Gill replied affirmative, so Thach with Sellstrom tucked under his wing went on instruments and disappeared into the whiteness. Looking around in the murky atmosphere, Thach was startled to see the huge, four-engine Kawanishi loom just below him. In his words, the FDO had put the Japanese "right into my lap."[11] At 1100, Thach snapped off a quick sighting report and went to work. Their speed carried the two Grummans out of the squall, but the flying boat concealed itself inside. Gill radioed that the contact had just faded from the radar screen, indicating that the Japanese had dived.

There was no recourse but to search the cloud. After several excruciating minutes, the two VF-3 pilots saw the Kawanishi break into the clear around a thousand feet and hightail it for base. Thach and Sellstrom went diving after their quarry, approaching it from behind. The skipper opted to make a high-side attack, with

Sellstrom, who would follow him in, to cross over to the opposite side as he followed through the firing run. This was standard doctrine used to box in the target. By radio, Thach told Sellstrom to "bracket"; then he proceeded with his attack. As his point of aim in the long high-side run, Thach took the starboard pair of engines on the long parasol wing. His bullets chewed into the silvery wing, causing a stream of gasoline to trail in a fine, white spray. Pulling out of his run, Thach was surprised and then amused to see that Doc Sellstrom had not followed. Instead the rookie pilot had taken his instructions literally and started crossing behind the flying boat to take up position on the other side. The Kawanishi's tail gunner furiously fired his 20-mm "stinger" at Sellstrom's Grumman, forcing him to jink violently to evade angry red tracers. Now in position for a second attack, Thach dived in again from the right, with Doc roaring in angrily from the left. This time the whole wing burst into flames. Eight bombs tumbled free from underneath the stricken Kawanishi. Thach saw both Japanese pilots stand up, but they made no move to bail out. The flying boat skidded into the sea with a tremendous explosion and fire. At 1112, black smoke from the blaze was visible even back on board the *Lexington*. A great cheer went out for VF-3's and the *Lex*'s first victory. Sakai's crew had paid with their lives for the warning they had provided Rabaul.

Thach's two Grummans had barely returned to the ship when radar located a second bogey nosing around the area. This was another Kawanishi Type 97 flying boat from the Yokohama Air Group. Flown by W.O. Hayashi Kiyoshi, this aircraft had departed Rabaul at 0800 to cover the sector 090 to 105 degrees. En route, Hayashi had received orders to amplify the contact made by Sakai. On board the *Lexington*, Red Gill turned to Burt Stanley's section to chase the bogey. Stanley and his wingman, Lee Haynes, headed out. What followed is well described in Stanley's diary:[12]

"Orange Section from Romeo [Gill's radio call]—Vector 343—Buster [move at top speed]—Angels six" [altitude 6000 feet] came from the fighter control.

I acknowledged and at full speed we started north ahead of the fleet. We had hardly gone twenty miles when Haynes' plane pulled along side and began to dance energetically. He had sighted our objective. I saw it then, a sleek silver patrol boat, four-engined, tremendous even at a thousand yards.

"Tally-ho from Orange leader," I transmitted gleefully, "A BIG four engined patrol plane."

As we climbed for attack position, I checked my plane; gas switch, prop, gunsight, gun switches—The patrol plane had spotted us. Black spindles of explosives fell from the fuselage to send up white geysers a mile below. They had jettisoned their bombs in hopes that the unloaded plane could escape.

As we pulled into position Haynes could see the cannon in the waist sending up its incendiary shells, seeking our range. I was already starting my attack. A half roll and the pull-through. The sights crept up and then held steady—Now. I pressed the trigger and nothing happened. The motor continued its roar and the wind still tugged at my clothing but only the fretful sparkle of the patrol plane's rear machine gun showed that someone was firing. I had missed the Master gun switch. I was flying 3-F-7 and the switch was in a different place.

Haynes had followed me closely and while I snapped on the switch and tested the guns I noticed the tail gun was no longer firing. Good shooting Lee.

From above and behind this time as the broad wing filled the gunsight, the guns responded to the switch. The red trail of the tracers could be seen to end abruptly as they passed from sight into the wing and the pilot compartment. Another burst, longer and more accurate now, and flame burst from the inboard engine on the port side. It disappeared and reappeared as I fired once more before ducking to avoid the tail.

Ens. Burt Stanley, 1940. (Capt. O. B. Stanley, USN.)

I looked back to see it become a solid sheet flowing from the wing to the fuselage. Gray smoke traced the path of the plane as the left wing and nose began to drop. That last burst must have killed the pilots.

"Whee, we got it." I couldn't resist reporting.

Haynes had quickly followed to deliver a last blow. The nose had dipped lower until it was diving out of control— the smoke increasing with the speed. Now, nothing could save it—nothing could stop that dive.

It crashed in a burst of red and a black pall quickly covered the spot. The great ball of smoke rose slowly to reveal a circle of flame on the gasoline covered water but the wreckage was already beneath the surface. Ten men were dead and the plane, efforts of a hundred, was destroyed. But it had to be.

Likewise the task force spotted the smoke of the dead Kawanishi and registered the kill at 1218. Hayashi's crew never had a chance to contact Rabaul.

Obviously the Japanese knew of the approach of Task Force 11 toward Rabaul. Brown had to make important decisions quickly. The enemy now had twenty hours to clear the harbor and prepare for his attack. There was plenty of time for additional aircraft to stage in from Truk and the Marshalls. Limiting Brown's own options was the nagging fuel shortage in Task Force 11. Not until perhaps 24 February could he rendezvous with the fleet oiler en route from Pearl. The prevailing slight winds had caused the *Lexington* and her consorts to expend more fuel than expected during flight operations. Brown had no reserve fuel for high-speed operations should he have to fight a running battle with the enemy. By noon, Brown had decided to call off the Rabaul strike. Pugnacious Ted Sherman had urged that the raid continue, but Brown planned instead for a feint. He would change course to southwest directly for Rabaul until late that afternoon, if necessary meeting an attack by enemy long-range bombers. He hoped the presence of an American carrier task force, even if it did not actually carry out an attack, would divert Japanese attention from the East Indies. At 1337, he broke radio silence to inform King and Leary of his decision.

In Rabaul and at Truk, admirals also labored over important decisions. Rear Admiral Gotō, commanding 24th Air Flotilla, felt a raid on Rabaul was inevitable.

From the search reports, he deduced that the American carrier force would steam to within 200 miles of Rabaul and strike at dawn. Ready as his own striking force he had eighteen land attack planes from the 4th Air Group. The same unit had twenty-six fighters at Rabaul as well, but none had the range to fly 450 miles to the target and back again. Sixteen were Mitsubishi A5M4 Type 96 carrier fighters [CLAUDE], and even with drop tanks their radius of action was only 250 miles. The ten Mitsubishi A6M2 Zero fighters at Rabaul did not, as yet, have drop tanks. Some members of Gotō's staff suggested to him that they wait until the next day to counterattack, but he had determined to attack that afternoon without fighter escort if need be. At 1310, Gotō ordered the 4th Air Group to sink the American carrier reported that morning. The Yokohama Air Group was also to maintain contact with one Type 97 flying boat, and to prepare for a dawn torpedo strike the next day. At Truk, Vice Admiral Inoue arranged to concentrate his surface ship strength (four heavy cruisers, two light cruisers, and destroyers) to execute a night attack after dark on 21 February.

The 4th Air Group, led by Captain Moritama Kahiro, merits an introduction. It was very new, being formed on 10 February at Truk. Nominal strength was twenty-seven land attack planes and twenty-seven single-engine fighters, each type divided tactically into *chūtai* (divisions) of nine planes each. All three fighter *chūtai* were present at Rabaul, but only the 1st and 2nd *Chūtai* of land attack planes were there. The other nine bombers trained on Tinian. The fighter pilots came mainly from the Chitose Air Group in the Marshalls, but the bomber crews, at least those already at Rabaul, were chosen veterans who had seen combat in the Philippines and the East Indies. Between 14 and 17 February, the group had settled at Rabaul, with the bombers based at Vunakanau field.

The land attack planes flown by the 4th Air Group were a relatively new model, the Mitsubishi G4M1 Type 1, Model 11 [BETTY].[13] Powered by a pair of 1530-hp radial engines, the G4M1 sported large wings tapering almost to a point fixed to a cigar-shaped fuselage. Manned by a crew of seven, the land attack plane (in Japanese, *rikūjō kōgekiki*, abbreviated *rikkō*) was armed with four 7.7-mm Lewis machine guns, one each in nose, dorsal blister, and both beam blisters, and a 20-mm cannon in the tail. The aircraft had a maximum speed of 231 knots (266 mph) and cruised at 170 knots. Its range was phenomenal, offering a radius of action with payload of 600 miles. Around 2,000 lbs. of bombs or one aerial torpedo could be stowed inside the roomy fuselage. In common with other Japanese aircraft, there was virtually no armor or self-sealing fuel tanks. The crews themselves christened their *rikkō* with the endearing titles of *hamaki* (cigar) and "Type 1 lighter."

Unfortunately for the Japanese, 20 February would see them unable to utilize their favorite antishipping weapons, torpedoes. None had yet arrived at Vunakanau. Instead the crews would make horizontal bombing runs, and their payload would be two 250-kilogram bombs per aircraft. Leading the mission was Lt. Cdr. Itō Takuzō, a respected and experienced naval aviator holding the command rating of *hikōtaichō* (group leader). He led the 1st *Chūtai* personally from the right seat of his command aircraft, whose first pilot was W.O. Watanabe Chūzō. Joining Itō as an observer in his G4M1's spacious flight deck was another senior aviator, Lieut. Setō Yogorō. The 1st *Chūtai* lost one of its nine *rikkō* when one aircraft proved to be a dud. At the head of the 2nd *Chūtai*'s nine *rikkō* was Lieut. Nakagawa Masayoshi, a *buntaichō* (division leader). To establish contact with the American carrier force and prepare the way for a night torpedo strike, at 1400 a Kawanishi flying boat commanded by Reserve Ensign Makino Motohiro took off from the seaplane base at Simpson Harbor. Twenty minutes later, Itō's seventeen land attack

4th Air Group Air Striking Force

1st Chūtai

	1st <i>Shōtai</i>	
No. 1 plane	Lt. Cdr. Itō Takuzō, <i>hikōtaichō</i>	(O)
No. 2 plane	PO1c Uchiyama Susumu	(O)
* No. 3 plane	PO1c Ono Kosuke	(P)
	2nd <i>Shōtai</i>	
No. 1 plane	Lieut. (jg) Mitani Akira	(P)
* No. 2 plane	PO1c Mori Bin	(P)
No. 3 plane	PO2c Baba Tokiharu	(P)
	3rd <i>Shōtai</i>	
+No. 1 plane	PO1c Maeda Koji	(P)
+No. 2 plane	PO2c Kogiku Ryosuke	(P)

2nd Chūtai

	1st <i>Shōtai</i>	
No. 1 plane	Lieut. Nakagawa Masayoshi, <i>buntaichō</i>	(P)
No. 2 plane	PO2c Morita Akira	(O)
No. 3 plane	PO2c Fujimoto Takaji	(P)
	2nd <i>Shōtai</i>	
No. 1 plane	Ensign (Special Service) Ono Shin	(P)
No. 2 plane	PO2c Ishizaki Goichi	(O)
No. 3 plane	PO1c Tatewaki Hiromichi	(P)
	3rd <i>Shōtai</i>	
No. 1 plane	W.O. Kawasaki Masao	(O)
No. 2 plane	PO1c Fusetami Nobuo	(O)
No. 3 plane	PO1c Ogawa Takegorō	(O)

Note: The names of individual aircraft commanders are given, and also their duties: (P) is pilot; (O) is observer.
+Indicates aircraft returned to Rabaul.
*Indicates aircraft ditched, but crew rescued.

planes departed Vunakanau on their search and destroy mission. The flight had the composition shown in the table.[14]

With Brown's decision to abort the raid, the action focused on Fighting Three to defend the task force from possible raids. Not long after Stanley's section returned after destroying the second flying boat, radar at 1240 had a third bogey 80 miles west. The contact eventually closed to 70 miles, but by 1317 had disappeared from the screen. Thach's 1st Division remained aloft until around 1330, when the *Lexington* launched Lovelace's 2nd Division of six F4Fs as relief CAP. Aside from Lovelace, the other two section leaders were Lieut. Albert O. Vorse, Jr. and Lieut. (jg) Howard L. Johnson. At the same time, Sherman took the opportunity of despatching a second search group to the west, comprising twelve SBDs from Bombing Two. Thach's pilots came on board to some well-deserved congratulations.

The radar screen was quiet until 1542, when it displayed a contact bearing 270 degrees, distance 76 miles. In the opinion of the radar operator, the bogey appeared to be cruising at 150 knots on a heading of 090 degrees, altitude perhaps 8,000 feet. This contact evidently disappeared from the screen not long after. Gill carefully monitored the situation, but no immediate threat to Task Force 11 was visible. On patrol at 10,000 feet were Lovelace's six F4Fs. By 1600, they had been aloft for 2½ hours and began to run low on fuel. On the flight deck and ready to replace them were the six F4Fs of Lieut. Gayler's 3rd Division. To fill out the division to six, his pilots had borrowed two aircraft from the 1st Division. In a lesser degree of readiness waited the squadron's remaining four fighters.

Around 1600, Gill decided it might be wise to rotate the combat air patrol early in order to put fighters on station with full fuel tanks. Some sort of counterattack from Rabaul was not unexpected. Contacting the air officer, Cdr. Herbert S. Duckworth, he requested permission to launch Gayler's 3rd Division ahead of schedule. Duckworth checked with the captain, who approved, and at 1606 the *Lexington* turned into the wind to conduct flight operations. Hustling to respot the airplanes on deck, plane handlers pushed SBDs and TBDs aft to make room forward for the takeoff. At 1615 Gayler led his division off the deck. The six F4Fs formed up by sections for the climb to patrol altitude. Aside from Gayler, the 3rd Division section leaders were Lieut. (jg) Rolla Lemmon and Ens. Willard E. Eder. Overhead, Lovelace saw the carrier swing into the wind, and, according to procedure, knew that he should bring his fighters down for a landing. His radio receiver was not functioning, but in this routine instance there was no need for orders. As the 2nd Division descended to land, the *Lexington*'s flight deck crew pitched in to respot the deck for recovery. Prodded by the bullhorn, available fighter and SBD pilots manned planes on deck to taxi them forward, while plane handlers had to manhandle the awkward TBDs up the flight deck.

Even as Gayler's pilots manned planes, the *Lexington*'s radar at 1611 foreshadowed trouble. There was a large blip bearing 255 degrees, distance 75 miles. Plotted on the board, the bogeys seemed to approach Task Force 11, then at 1622 disappeared from the scope. Suddenly, at 1625, they were there again, and this time it looked as if the bogeys meant business. According to the plot, the contact bore 276 degrees, distance 47 miles from the ships. It was moving fast; distance at 1630 was only 24 miles. Gill immediately vectored Gayler's six F4Fs to intercept the enemy, while the bridge rang for flank speed. The *Lexington* began working up to 30 knots. There was no question of continuing with recovery operations. Parked forward on the flight deck were four F4F Wildcats and eleven VS-2 dive bombers fully fueled and representing a tremendous fire hazard should enemy bombs catch them on deck. Duckworth ordered an emergency respot of the flight deck. Those fueled planes had to get aloft!

Lovelace's pilots moving into the landing circle wondered what was up when the *Lexington* turned out of the wind and back to her base course of 234 degrees. Her bridge flashed a searchlight signal to Lovelace warning him not to come on board. Soon after, Gill gave the 2nd Division the steer. The 2nd Division pilots had already lowered their tail hooks in anticipation of recovery, but there was more important business now. Vorse and Johnson responded quickly to the vector. Lovelace, who could not hear the radio orders, got the message when his wingman, Richard Rowell, zoomed out of the landing circle. So quick was the 2nd Division's redeployment that at least one of the pilots climbed with his tail hook flapping in the slipstream.

Gayler's division never had a chance to rendezvous after takeoff; the three sections pressed ahead on their own. The main problem was the slow climb rate of their fully loaded Grummans which they tried to coax to high altitude before the enemy arrived. They only just made it. Ahead of him, Gayler discerned nine twin-engine bombers formed tightly into a Vee of Vees. Camouflaged with a combination of green and tan on their upper surfaces, the bombers appeared a new type to him—single-tailed in place of the twin-tailed "Type 96" and "Type 97" mediums vaguely depicted in recognition manuals.

The Japanese were the nine *rikkō* of Lieut. Nakagawa's 2nd *Chūtai* of the 4th Air Group. Poor flying conditions east of Rabaul, heavy clouds punctuated with rain squalls, had compelled Lt. Cdr. Itō to split his strike force into two elements each to search independently for the American carrier. Nakagawa spotted Task Force 11 first and approached to attack, headquarters logging in his contact report at 1635.

Their altimeters read 13,000 feet when Gayler and his wingman, Ens. Dale W. Peterson, made ready to attack. The Japanese formation flew at about 11,500 feet making about 170 knots. Diving into a steep high-side run, the two F4Fs at 1639 charged after one of the bombers on the edge of the formation. Tracers poured out at the Grummans from all nine *rikkō*, but the gunfire failed to deter Gayler and Peterson. Together they set their target ablaze on the first pass, and the stricken bomber careened out of formation. Using the speed they gained in their dives, the two fighter pilots made zoom climbs to regain position for a second attack. Next to arrive were Lemmon and his wingman, Lieut. (jg) Howard F. ("Spud") Clark. They likewise attained excellent position over the bombers, and with a high-side run shot down another Japanese. So far, the gunnery passes were virtually textbook quality.

Gayler's third section, Bill Eder and Ens. John Wilson, arrived on the scene after the other four pilots had begun their attacks. Eder had found that Wilson's Grumman was unable to climb as fast as his own; perhaps the powerplant was not producing the horsepower it should. Eder hung back for a time to let his green wingman catch up, but Wilson could not close the gap and soon fell out of sight. Because of the delay, Eder was unable to climb above the enemy before they were upon him. He charged in from below and behind one of the trailing bombers and fired a long burst. Three of his guns stopped functioning, and Eder broke off to clear them. Meanwhile Gayler evidently was attacking the same target from above on his second pass, his gunnery as deadly as with his first run.

Thus the initial attacks of Gayler's 3rd Division lasted from 1639 to about 1641. Lookouts on board the ships first sighted the nine Japanese bombers at 1639 in light cloud cover about 10 miles out. Then the shipboard observers saw three bombers drop out of formation in the next two minutes—one dogged by a lone Grumman from below and behind, obviously Eder. Thus it appears each of the three sections accounted for at least one bomber, with Gayler sharing the third kill with Eder. At 1641, lookouts on board the destroyer *Phelps* noticed six bombers emerge from the cloud and head directly for the task force. The 4th Air Group pilots stoically tightened formation to fill the gaps. If nothing else, this battle would impress all with the fighting spirit and determination of the Japanese. Their only defenses were machine guns and cannons manned by gunners who desperately tried to stay with the Grummans darting in and out of the edges of the formation.

With the bombers now visible from the ships, Ted Sherman brought the *Lexington* left to head her into the wind. There was frantic effort on the flight deck to launch all fueled planes. The airdales had rolled aircraft aft and rapidly made space first for the F4Fs and then for the SBDs to get off. The bull horn commanded: "Thach in 13, Sellstrom take 2, O'Hare in 15, Dufilho, 4."[15] Stanley and Haynes ran to the VF-3 ready room, only to find that all of the operational fighters were taken. They would have to weather the strike from a ship's deck—an uneasy predicament for any pilot. Some of the SBD crews had been lounging about without helmets, goggles, and other flight gear, but they manned planes just the same. Duckworth was proud of his flight deck crew:

That respot was the fastest respot ever made in carrier history. It was as if some great hand moved all the planes aft simultaneously.[16]

Thach's F4F started down the flight deck at 1643. Behind him queued the remaining fourteen aircraft, eager to get off.

The pressure of Gayler's pilots was relentless. At 1643, his wingman Peterson shot the fourth bomber out of formation, evidently the lead plane flown by Nakagawa. This occurred about the same time some of the cruisers in the screen cut loose with their five-inch antiaircraft guns, and they later received credit for damaging the lead bomber. Actually the shell bursts were as yet nowhere near the target. The loss of the *chūtai* leader's aircraft with the master bombardier seemed to confuse the other crews. In level bombing runs, the Japanese were careful to release bombs simultaneously on command in order to catch the target ship in a special bomb pattern. Now the pilots hesitated a bit in making their approach. Finally they regrouped and swung right to parallel the *Lexington*'s course, overtaking her from astern. As the bombers and interceptors did come within antiaircraft range of the ships, the VF-3 pilots disgustedly noted the shell bursts blossoming above and anywhere up to a thousand feet behind the Japanese—more of a threat to the F4Fs than the bombers. This distraction did not prevent Lemmon from sending a fifth *rikkō* spinning toward the water.

The delay by the Japanese permitted VF-3's 2nd Division to join the fray after their furious climb to altitude. They struck as the bombers rapidly neared their release point. Five pilots, "Scoop" Vorse, Bob Morgan, Howard Johnson, John Lackey, and Richard Rowell, swarmed after the bombers, disposing of cripples already shot up by the 3rd Division and cutting out of formation one of the four surviving bombers by means of slashing low-side runs. Far below, the *Lexington* at 1646 completed launching the last aircraft and opened fire herself on the enemy approaching from astern. Fighting Three had done its part to wreck the bomb run, and now it was Sherman's turn to shine. He took the 30-knot carrier into a series of evasive maneuvers. All four land attack planes dropped their bombs, but the nearest detonation to the *Lexington* was 3,000 yards distant owing to Sherman's superb shiphandling.

More thrilling to the spectators than the actual bombing was what transpired just a few minutes later. From off the *Lex*'s starboard bow, lookouts picked out a crippled bomber approaching at low altitude. Evidence indicates this was the lead plane winged by the 3rd Division at 1643. No doubt existed as to the enemy pilot's intention. He had determined to execute a *taiatari* ("body-crashing") dive onto the flight deck, a repeat performance of Lieut. Nakai's effort on 1 February against the *Enterprise*. At 2,500 yards, all of the *Lex*'s starboard 1.1-inch cannons and .50-calibers cut loose. Trying to stretch height and distance to the utmost, the Japanese pilot strove to keep his mutilated aircraft aloft just long enough to crash the carrier, but he "didn't have a chance."[17] Accurate antiaircraft fire evoked a trail of smoke from the *rikkō* still a thousand yards out. Sherman deftly kept the carrier's stern pointed toward the suicider. Just 75 yards astern over the *Lexington*'s wake, the Japanese ran out of air. At 1651, the *rikkō* smacked the water with a fiery explosion. Noted a relieved Stanley with almost humorous understatement: "He would have really made a mess of our flight deck if he had reached it."[18]

Overhead, fighters chopped away at the four land attack planes, whose pilots poured on the power to escape. Vorse and cohorts set aflame the *rikkō* they had forced out of formation before bomb release. Lovelace came upon the remaining three as they drew away from the carrier, and charged in for a low-side run on the little formation. The Japanese split up to run for home; nosed down for speed, the land attack planes quickly accelerated to 200 knots or more. Coming around to make a second pass at one of the bombers, Lovelace closed from below and behind, filling its tail with .50-caliber slugs. Then he saw another Grumman take hits, stagger, and drop away. The Japanese had drawn their first revenge.

The stricken fighter was that of Howard Johnson. Not long before, bullets had hit his engine, causing a loss in power. Although he gamely stayed in action, his fighter lost speed, and he found himself sucked dead astern of his target, easy pickings for the tail gunner's 20-mm cannon. Before Johnson could evade, the gunner had riddled his fighter with 20-mm explosive shells. Fragments cut up both of his legs. Johnson bailed out of his crippled Wildcat; at 1649, lookouts saw his chute open, as did Lovelace who radioed the carrier. The flagship then directed the destroyer *Patterson* to rescue the downed pilot.

As the Japanese tried to escape, Thach's four F4Fs climbed individually toward the fight. Red Gill, however, wanted a reserve; so he reined in Butch O'Hare and his wingman Marion Dufilho, much to their disgust. Meanwhile Thach and Sellstrom hurried to overtake the fleeing bombers. The skipper reached a point just above and ahead of a land attack plane, and turned to make a flat-side approach. Happening to look back, Thach saw one of his Grummans boring in from dead astern of the target. He tried to warn that pilot, as the newcomer was in grave danger from the bomber's 20-mm tail stinger. It was too late. As the second F4F pressed into firing range, Thach saw a 20-mm shell explode on its windshield. Pitching into a wild spin, the aircraft started down toward the water. Its pilot was Jack Wilson. Apparently his engine was still misbehaving, and lacking the speed to overtake the target for a proper, safe deflection shot, he had nevertheless charged in from astern. He did not bail out—the cannon shell probably killed him instantly. Observers on board the *Lexington* saw the fighter splash about five or six miles out. Brown detached the destroyer *Hull* to look for a survivor, but there was none.

Thach followed through on his flat-side approach, and, with hits in the engine and wingroot, flamed the bomber that had killed Wilson. Recovering from his run, Thach discovered behind and beneath him still another bomber. The Japanese took recourse to shallow dives to gain speed for their escape. Waiting until the *rikkō* had slipped underneath, Thach then dropped into a deadly overhead run. He later remarked that his first burst was "too accurate."[19] It riddled the fuselage, possibly playing havoc with the crew, but these bullets did not bring down the airplane. Realizing that the quickest way to flame this type of target was to treat an engine nacelle "as if it was a target sleeve,"[20] Thach zoomed up for a high-side run. Well-aimed bullets sent into the engine caused a wing to explode and fall off the doomed bomber. For one of his two kills, Thach shared credit with a 2nd Division pilot who was attacking the same target.

Looking at their fuel gauges, Lovelace and his pilots saw that their full power, hell-bent-to-leather climb into battle had consumed almost all of their remaining fuel. The 2nd Division was definitely *hors de combat*. The five F4Fs (less Johnson's splashed Grumman) had to land quickly or risk ditching. The *Lexington*'s flight deck was not clear for landing; the VT-2 TBDs still cluttered the stern, as the deck was spotted for launch. The 2nd Division would have to circle until weary plane handlers could push the Devastators forward again.

While Thach and friend destroyed the seventh and eighth land attack planes, an enterprising dive bomber crew also did its part to smash the 2nd *Chūtai*. The SBD pilot was Lieut. Edward H. Allen, exec of Scouting Two. He climbed toward the fray after the mad scramble from the *Lexington*, coming upon a maimed bomber that had managed to arrest its fall toward the water. With a short burst from his twin .30-caliber nose guns, Allen sent the Japanese to a fatal embrace with the sea. Meeting a second cripple, Allen maneuvered so that his rearseat man, Bruce Rountree, ARM1c, could shoot his flexible .30-caliber Browning into the *rikkō*'s belly. Flames spouted forth, giving Allen and Rountree a share in the land attack plane's destruction.

The ninth Japanese eluded fighters on its withdrawal from the area. Nosed down for speed and lightened without its bomb load and most of its fuel, the *rikkō* was hard to catch. A couple of 3rd Division pilots set out in pursuit, as did Thach in order to gather his boys back in—a difficult task, for their blood was up. Finally Thach got the F4Fs in tow and started back toward the task force. They thought the last Japanese had escaped, but the *rikkō* was so unlucky as to encounter the XO of the other *Lexington* SBD squadron, Lieut. Walter F. Henry of Bombing Two. Returning from the afternoon search, he noticed a bomber approaching from ahead. Because of his initial favorable position, Henry was able to turn onto the target's tail. It took him many miles of pursuit to ease his SBD-2 up into firing position. There was no return fire from the Japanese, although he could see crew members. One short burst from his twin .30s was sufficient to send the valiant bomber to a fiery end. The *rikkō* splashed about 80 miles west of the task force. Turning back in the direction of the *Lexington*, Henry happened upon a ditched bomber still afloat and being abandoned by its crew. Still fighting mad, he dived in to strafe the drifting *rikkō* until it exploded and sank.[21]

The 1st Chūtai *Meets Butch O'Hare*

All nine Type 1 *rikkō* of the 2nd *Chūtai* had fallen without survivors. After Lieut. Nakagawa's 1635 contact report, headquarters heard nothing further from him. With the eight *rikkō* of the 1st *Chūtai*, Lt. Cdr. Itō had monitored Nakagawa's message. He was north of the enemy's reported location and turned south to look for them. Scattered cloud cover evidently delayed the sighting, but at 1700, Itō radioed Rabaul that he had the enemy in view and would soon attack. The 1st *Chūtai* had cruised at around 15,000 feet, but anticipating the bomb run, Itō began letting down to 11,000 feet. In the process his land attack planes accelerated to about 190 knots. When he first spotted the enemy carrier, the Americans were off his right to the southwest. Itō planned to parallel the target's course and overtake it from astern. Under the circumstances had the two *chūtai* leaders actually co-ordinated their attacks, the timing could not have been better. Because most of Fighting Three pursued the first wave, only two Grummans lay between Itō and his objective.

In the midst of the first attack, the *Lexington*'s CXAM evidently had the 1st *Chūtai* on the scope at 1649 as bogeys bearing 015 degrees, distance 30 miles. At that time Itō was still looking for the target. Gill may have had these bogeys in mind when he held O'Hare's section in reserve. The first Americans to spot the second wave were lookouts on board the destroyer *Patterson*. She had dropped astern to rescue a downed VF-3 pilot, Howard Johnson. At 1656, her lookouts saw a formation of enemy aircraft apparently circling about 10 miles north. The ship flashed a warning to the *Lexington*, then went about her business rescuing the pilot bobbing conspicuously in his yellow life jacket. By 1705, the sailors had Johnson on board, and a witness recounted, "The smile on the pilot's face was a thing to remember."[22] The ship's physician treated his wounds, about thirty shrapnel cuts on both legs.

The approach of enemy aircraft from the northeast caught the *Lexington* somewhat by surprise. As related earlier, the CXAM radar with its primitive "A" scope did not offer a continuous 360-degree display. All information had to be plotted separately in order to be intelligible to the FDO. By now the scope was cluttered with contacts: the remnants of the first wave, CAP fighters, and SBDs from the recently launched anti–torpedo-plane patrol, as well as the afternoon search. At 1700, the radar showed bogeys bearing 080 degrees, distance 9 miles, but it appears now that the Japanese were not quite that close to the target. At 1702, observers on board the *Lexington* made visual contact with what they reported as six or eight bombers off the carrier's starboard quarter.

The only fighters available to the FDO were O'Hare and Dufilho, and Gill immediately ordered them to intercept. Seven other F4Fs were to the west pursuing the first wave, and Thach was trying to round them up to return to the task force. Lovelace's five F4Fs from the 2nd Division circled at low altitude around the *Lexington* awaiting the go-ahead to land. These Grummans were almost out of fuel. The carrier's hard-pressed flight deck crew worked frantically to clear the deck aft to bring them on board. The five Grummans were priceless, given the near impossibility of obtaining replacement aircraft in the South Pacific. With the second attack imminent, the fighters would have to land almost immediately or certainly ditch.

Butch O'Hare and his wingman encountered the Japanese at about 1705 only a few miles astern of the ships.[23] They thought they confronted nine twin-engine bombers deployed in a tight Vee of Vees, but actually there were eight (see sketch). Coming downhill in their shallow dive, the bombers were moving fast. Fortunately for the two VF-3 pilots, they benefited from an altitude advantage of a few thousand feet in which to set up their interception. Approaching the formation from ahead, O'Hare and Dufilho let the center Vee pass beneath them, then rolled into a high-side run to hit the right side of the formation. O'Hare singled out as his target the right trailing bomber in the right Vee, a *rikkō* most probably flown by PO2c Baba. Swiftly and devastatingly his .50-caliber slugs found their mark in the bomber's starboard engine nacelle and wingroot. O'Hare was one of the most skilled marksmen in the squadron. His initial bursts chopped into the *rikkō*'s engine, causing it to spew oil and smoke heavily. Losing power rapidly, the bomber slowed abruptly and started down toward the water.

Still in the same firing run, O'Hare had scored so swiftly that he shifted his point of aim a little farther ahead to the left trailer in the same Vee, almost certainly PO1c Mori's aircraft. To clear his first victim falling away to starboard, O'Hare had to pull up sharply, but then he was able to give his undivided attention to the second target. A few well-directed bursts hit Mori's right engine and went on through to nick the left wing tank. Trailing a thin, white stream of raw gasoline, the bomber shuddered as its speed dropped suddenly, then wheeled to the right and down out of formation. Butch later remarked that his main worry on this run was avoiding a collision with one of the cripples while he dived beneath the formation to follow through on the pass. Mori's *rikkō* had not sustained fatal damage (although it later ditched), but it did not regain formation and release bombs over the *Lexington*. Mori withdrew from the target area at low altitude.

Having extended his high-side run to shoot at the second target, O'Hare crossed on over to the left side of the Japanese formation, where he zoomed back to regain position and attack. He looked back to discover that his wingman had not followed. Dufilho, to his own intense chagrin, found that his machine guns would not function. Like the VF-6 pilots in the Marshalls, "Duff" had fallen afoul of shifting ammunition belts which hopelessly jammed the guns. In order to give his section leader an unobstructed shot at the bombers, Dufilho pulled off to try clearing his Brownings. Events rapidly left him behind.

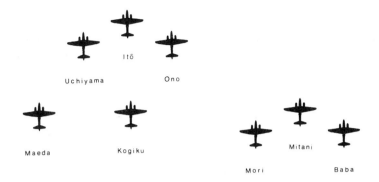

Starting his run this time from over the left side of the enemy formation, O'Hare set about destroying one by one the three aircraft in echelon on that side. With a shallow high-side run, he fired into the rearmost aircraft, taking as his point of aim the port engine nacelle. He shot until he saw flame blossom in the aircraft and the target drop out of his sights. Most likely this was the *rikkō* flown by PO1c Maeda, the 3rd *Shōtai* leader. One of the Japanese who later landed at Rabaul recounted that a Grumman just before bomb release had set his bomber ablaze. The stricken land attack plane then cut out of formation, but "miraculously"[24] a fire extinguisher smothered the flame, allowing the crew to catch up with the rest of the *chūtai* to drop bombs along with them. Maeda was the senior surviving pilot of the two aircraft that did make it back to base, and every indication is that this was his account.

O'Hare had to change course slightly as the first target in this pass (Maeda) skidded violently; then he charged after the next aircraft in line, PO1c Uchiyama's G4M1, flying behind Itō's left wing. Relentlessly O'Hare shot into the bomber's left wing and engine. As with O'Hare's first kill (Baba), the engine on Uchiyama's plane flamed up and seized, causing the aircraft to sheer sharply left into a dive. The Grumman's relatively shallow approach undoubtedly had other dividends as well, as tracers zipped through the right side of the Japanese formation. Throughout its attacks, F-15 was the sole target of every Japanese gun that could bear. From dorsal blisters, beam hatches, and tail stingers, anxious gunners blazed away, but O'Hare was oblivious to return fire. His carefully executed, high-deflection firing runs largely protected him from enemy retaliation.

As Butch started into his third firing pass, also from the left, the 1st *Chūtai* swiftly overtook the bomb release point over the *Lexington*. The warships' five-inchers had begun peppering the skies with black shell busts, but O'Hare ignored them as they appeared over a thousand feet short of their intended quarry. He could see five bombers still in formation (Itō, Ono, Mitani, Kogiku, and Maeda, who had caught up). As his next target he selected the lead bomber itself, in order to destroy the master bombardier or mess up the bomb run. Closing within point-blank range, O'Hare achieved remarkable results. His .50-caliber slugs tore into Itō's port nacelle, which flared up and exploded. Its big, twin-banked radial engine actually wrenched free of its mountings and dropped away! So violent was the blast that Japanese in other aircraft later reported their commander's plane hit directly by an antiaircraft burst. Trailing thick, black smoke, the command *rikkō* careened radically left and started down.

Itō, however, had set up his bomb run skillfully. Immediately after the *hikō-taichō*'s aircraft had dropped out of formation, the four land attack planes released their payloads over the *Lexington*. Meanwhile, O'Hare pursued a sixth target, but exhausted his ammunition after his guns had each shot about ten rounds. In the four minutes it had taken the 1st *Chūtai* to reach the drop point after O'Hare's first interception, he had singlehandedly destroyed three bombers and severely damaged two others. Under the circumstances, it is quite understandable that he thought he had downed five planes. The only damage his faithful F-15 took in return was two holes punched in the wing by "friendly" antiaircraft fire and one enemy 7.7-mm bullet in the fuselage. Japanese gunners had several times claimed his Grumman as it darted in and out at the edge of the formation.

While the enemy bore down on the *Lexington*, Duckworth proceeded with the vital job of recovering Lovelace's five Grummans. Sherman was reluctant to bring his carrier fully into the wind, as that would make the bombing easier for the Japanese. Instead he maneuvered at 30 knots with a 30-degree rudder, compounding problems for the pilots and their LSO, Lieut. Aquilla G. Dibrell. All were up to the task, and the fighters landed safely. The first thing Lovelace noticed after he touched down and cleared the barriers forward was that everyone was running for cover! There was good reason—bombs were falling. At 1709 as the last F4F, flown by Bob Morgan, crossed the ramp, Dibrell jumped into his net alongside the flight deck. With considerably more accuracy than the 2nd *Chūtai*, Itō's bombardiers nearly hit the carrier. The nearest 250-kilogram bomb struck the water only 100 feet astern of the wildly twisting *Lexington*.

The last act of the drama was about to begin. While withdrawing from the scene, the surviving 1st *Chūtai* crews watched their commander's *rikkō* spiral toward the sea. Suddenly it appeared to them that the bomber's "pilot was trying desperately to change the course of his death-descent so that the plane would head directly for the enemy aircraft carrier."[25] In a magnificent show of flying skill, W.O. Watanabe (if he was still alive and at the controls) fought to regain control of the horribly maimed aircraft. Confronted by the approaching enemy plane, observers on board the *Lexington* clearly saw the blacked port nacelle where the engine had fallen out. Itō's command markings showed prominently, reminding the Americans of their own colorfully striped rudders.

Converging from about 30 degrees off the *Lexington*'s port side, the commander's *rikkō* limped at low altitude, straining valiantly to reach the carrier. At 3,000 yards, the one 1.1-inch mount and two .50-calibers on board the *Lexington* that were able to bear cut loose ribbons of tracers. As before, Sherman tried to present the *Lex*'s stern to the proto-kamikaze. To preserve height and speed, Itō dumped his bombs into the sea. Quickly the light AA fire began to take effect, causing smoke to stream from the wing and fuselage. Perhaps bearing dead or wounded men frozen at the controls, the bomber failed to turn and match the carrier's maneuvering at 30 knots. Instead the *rikkō* held its course, passing alongside the *Lexington*'s portside and continuing to take hits. Finally the G4M1's nose dipped, first at a gentle angle, then more steeply. At 1712, the command plane plunged into the sea in a fiery explosion about 1,500 yards ahead of the carrier's port bow. Sherman had to turn sharply to avoid steaming over the blazing pyre of fuel and floating debris. The 1st *Chūtai* aviators heading away at high speed let their hearts interpret what they saw and thought the *hikōtaichō*'s aircraft had crashed into the enemy carrier, the type of gesture the Japanese so revered. Though they missed their goal, Itō and his crew died as Samurai.

Their payloads delivered, the five 1st *Chūtai* land attack planes believed still to be aloft had to run the gauntlet of seven scattered F4Fs and several SBDs poised astride the direct route to Rabaul. Holding formation were the four bombers of

(*Left*) 20 Feb. 1942, Lt. Cdr. Itō's land attack plane, its left engine shot away by Butch O'Hare, tries to crash on the *Lexington*. (NA 80-G-17034.) (*Right*) Seconds after the previous photo was taken, Itō's aircraft is about to splash. Note command stripes on the tail. (NA 80-G-17036.)

Lieut. (jg) Mitani and petty officers Maeda, Ono, and Kogiku. Far beneath them limped PO1c Mori's battered *rikkō*, shot out of formation on O'Hare's first pass. Mitani, the only remaining officer, did not make it out of the target area. Doc Sellstrom, who had scrambled with Thach, ambushed him and shot down the bomber about eight miles ahead of the ships. Again some Japanese felt that Mitani had crashed into an American ship, or hoped he had. That left three bombers in formation, with Mori flying alone. Not all of the dispersed VF-3 fighters that pursued the 2nd *Chūtai* managed to intercept the withdrawing 1st *Chūtai*. Thach, for one, was unable to set up an attack, but 40 miles out, one of the 3rd Division pilots (evidently Noel Gayler) tagged another bomber and claimed its destruction. This was either a cripple from the first or second wave trying to clear the area, or possibly an attack on Mori's lone plane. Mori later reported considerable unwanted attention on his way out from American planes that thoroughly shot up his aircraft, but the Mitsubishi continued chugging along.[26]

Meantime about 30 miles from Task Force 11, Allen and Rountree of Scouting Two latched onto the little formation of Maeda, Ono, and Kogiku, inaugurating what became a long stern chase. Allen found his SBD enjoyed a speed advantage of perhaps three knots over the lightened G4M1s. He selected one Japanese and eased into firing range, mostly using Rountree to pepper the cigar-shaped fuselage with his .30-caliber machine gun. The seemingly imperturbable bomber flew on as before, although Allen thought most of the crew killed or wounded. After chasing the bombers 150 miles into the sunset, Allen had to break off because of dwindling fuel and return to base. The anonymous Japanese account (most likely Maeda's) recounted how "enemy planes persistently stuck to our tail."[27] Allen's target was the *rikkō* flown by PO1c Ono, and the SBD apparently shot up the right engine, holed fuel tanks (with most of the gasoline leaking out), and killed at least two of the crew. Ono would not make it back to base after his forty-minute ordeal at the hands of Allen.

With the fighters aloft certain to be low on ammunition if not gasoline, Duckworth's air department labored diligently to ready the four flyable Grummans of the 2nd Division as relief CAP. While the *Lexington* was still spotted for recovery, two SBDs took the opportunity to land. Then it was the turn of the fighters to take off about thirty minutes after they had landed in such haste and danger. This time Stanley made sure he would be airborne in the event of a third wave. He pulled rank on Rowell and took his place as Lovelace's wingman. The 2nd Division departed around 1740, and Lovelace climbed to high altitude, carefully looking for more enemy planes. The skies, however, were clear.

Harried plane handlers rearranged the deck once more for recovery operations. Beginning around 1745, the nine F4Fs of the 1st and 3rd Divisions queued up in the landing circle awaiting their turns to land. What a reception they got! Topside on board the *Lexington* the whole air battle had unfolded before eager observers. Intense excitement reigned, as the fighters shot one bomber after another out of the sky. Brown later remarked that it was necessary to remind his staff this was serious business and not a "football game,"[28] so vociferously did they whoop with every kill. The star was Butch O'Hare, and as he taxied F-15 to its spot up deck, the crew mobbed him in their wild enthusiasm. So cool and professional during the actual combat, O'Hare later revealed his nervousness:

> When the fight was over I thought I'd lost my voice, I screamed in the cockpit to see if my voice was OK. It was. Only the transmitter had gone sour.[29]

After he landed, all O'Hare wanted was more bullets and a drink of water; he was ready to fight again. Someone extricated the embarrassed O'Hare from his crowd of admirers and led him up to the bridge where Brown and Sherman offered their sincere congratulations.

Shortly thereafter Brown prepared another despatch for CinCPac and Com-ANZAC. In it he reported the attack by an estimated thirty heavy bombers and added that there was no damage and plane losses were light. Preliminary accounts gave twelve to twenty enemy aircraft destroyed. Brown restated his intention to rendezvous on 22 February with the oiler *Platte*. Meanwhile, the *Lexington* made ready to close down flight operations as dusk intervened. Beginning at 1825, she landed the SBDs of the afternoon search and those hurriedly despatched on anti–torpedo-plane patrol. By 1902, the last of Lovelace's four fighters had come on board after dark, and a few minutes later, Task Force 11 changed course to 100 degrees, speed 22 knots bound for the vital rendezvous.

In Rabaul, 24th Air Flotilla headquarters had monitored Lieut. Nakagawa's contact report, then thirty minutes later copied Lt. Cdr. Itō's own sighting report. At 1815, a 1st *Chūtai* crew radioed that the bombing attack had ceased at 1730 with the sinking of one enemy warship. Tersely the communication indicated that task force defense was highly effective, inflicting the loss of several land attack planes. For the battered survivors, the flight back to base was not easy either. At 1925, PO1c Ono ditched his tattered Mitsubishi at Nugava in the Nuguria group east of New Ireland.[30] Twenty-five minutes later, PO1c Maeda and his wingman PO2c Kogiku reached Rabaul and landed safely at Vunakanau field. Riddled with bullet holes, both aircraft remained nonoperational for several days. Last of the strike still aloft, PO1c Mori executed a tricky night ditching at 2010 in Simpson Harbor. They were the only aircraft to return. The 4th Air Group had lost three senior officers and thirteen whole flight crews missing in action. Among the aviators who did return were several wounded. Fifteen *rikkō* were lost. The survivors claimed sinking one cruiser or destroyer and, possibly from a successful *taiatari* attack, the setting of fierce fires on board the enemy carrier. They also reported shooting down eight defending Grummans.

Two search planes had followed in the wake of the strike group in order to shadow the Americans for subsequent attacks. The first was the Kawanishi Type 97 flying boat flown by Reserve Ensign Makino of the Yokohama Air Group. Evidently he never made contact and was not heard from again, although the Americans nowhere claimed destruction of a third flying boat. The Yokohama Air Group thus lost twenty-nine men and three flying boats that day. At 1430 an Aichi E13A1 Type O reconnaissance floatplane [JAKE] from the *Kiyokawa Maru* Air Unit also left Rabaul. Its crew at 1815 radioed a contact report placing the Americans bearing 062 degrees and 470 miles from Rabaul. The floatplane shadowed Task Force 11 until well after dark, and at 2000 reported it was returning. Inexplicably, this aircraft also failed to materialize. Thus the air units at Rabaul lost on 20 February a total of nineteen aircraft shot down or missing.

Sorting out their battle accounts after dinner, the VF-3 pilots claimed a total of fifteen twin-engine bombers and two four-engine flying boats destroyed, with a sixteenth bomber falling to Lieut. Henry of Bombing Two. Thus they felt only two of the eighteen bombers attacking Task Force 11 had escaped. At first, shipboard observers gave Butch O'Hare credit for six bombers, but he reduced that to five. Final fighter claims were as follows:

Lieut. Edward H. O'Hare	5 bombers	(in F-15)
Lt. Cdr. John S. Thach	1 patrol plane assist	(in F-1)
	1 bomber, 1 bomber assist	(in F-13)
Lieut. Noel A. M. Gayler	1 bomber, 2 bomber assists	(in F-1)
Lieut. (jg) Rolla S. Lemmon	1 bomber, 1 bomber assist	
Ens. Dale W. Peterson	1 bomber, 1 bomber assist	(in F-5)
Ens. Edward R. Sellstrom, Jr.	1 patrol plane assist, 1 bomber	(in F-2)
Ens. Richard M. Rowell	2 bomber assists	
Lt. Cdr. Donald A. Lovelace	1 bomber assist	
Lieut. Albert O. Vorse, Jr.	1 bomber assist	
Lieut. (jg) Howard F. Clark	1 bomber assist	
Lieut. (jg) Robert J. Morgan	1 bomber assist	
Lieut. (jg) Onia B. Stanley, Jr.	1 patrol plane assist	(in F-7)
Ens. Willard E. Eder	1 bomber assist	
Ens. John H. Lackey	1 bomber assist	
Ens. Leon W. Haynes	1 patrol plane assist	(in F-13)
Did not score:		
Lieut. (jg) Marion W. Dufilho		(in F-4)
Lieut. (jg) Howard L. Johnson (wounded in action)		(in F-11)
Ens. John W. Wilson (killed in action)		(in F-9)

American losses totaled two Wildcats shot down, one pilot missing in action, and another wounded. Seven other F4Fs took damage from enemy 7.7-mm bullets or "friendly" antiaircraft fire, but none was unserviceable. Noel Gayler in F-1 had a close call when a 7.7-mm round pocked the bullet-resistant glass on the windshield, but it did not penetrate. For most of the pilots it was a long night waiting for the excitement of their first combat to dampen. After 0200, a sleepless Thach ran into his good friend O'Hare in the wardroom. Fueled by sandwiches, they relived the battle for the next few hours, mapping out its lessons for further thought before finally turning in.

The Japanese at Rabaul and Truk had no certain way of knowing that the enemy carrier force had withdrawn. After midnight on 21 February, six torpedo-laden Kawanishi flying boats departed Rabaul for a night search and destroy mission.

They failed to find the American warships and after sunrise returned to base. That morning the air units at Rabaul and Truk searched diligently for the Americans, but with negative results. Inoue arranged to fill the void at Rabaul by ordering air reinforcements. The *chūtai* of *rikkō* from the 4th Air Group temporarily based at Tinian left immediately for Rabaul. The 1st Air Group, a crack unit in the process of shifting from the Dutch East Indies to the Marshalls, also sent part of its strength to Rabaul. On 24 February the 24th Air Flotilla, using nine land attack planes and nine Zero fighters, mounted its first air strike on Port Moresby, inaugurating what would be a long and bitter struggle for air superiority over Papua. Aside from replenishing his air losses, Inoue had reason to reconsider future operations. He postponed from 3 March to 8 March the impending invasion of Lae and Salamaua. As events will show, this was an important delay for the Allies, one due primarily to the presence of the *Lexington* and the excellent marksmanship of Thach's Fighting Three. The fighters achieved an impact at the strategic level.

On 21 February, Task Force 11 held its southeasterly heading en route to the vital rendezvous with the fleet oiler *Platte*. The weather had turned squally, but the overcast helped conceal the ships from enemy searches. Before flying the morning combat air patrol, Thach in the VF-3 ready room held a detailed critique of the previous day's action. There were mistakes, and Thach discussed them. For one, the fighters had pursued the first wave too far from the ships. Thach felt he should have regrouped his squadron sooner for more complete protection of the task force. He commented upon the fact that both Grummans lost had been shot down while making zero-deflection runs from directly astern of the targets. By far, the most effective attacks against enemy medium bombers were overheads and high-sides. Materiel shortcomings included the jamming of the F4F's machine guns under certain circumstances and the low climb rate of that airplane, which lengthened the time required to make one run and climb into position for the next. Antiaircraft fire from the ships was also a hindrance. Fighting Three had understood that the ships would hold off until the last moment if the fighters were scoring well. Instead, AA fire had opened too early, and the fighters had to fly through their own AA to attack enemy bombers. The lack of IFF had made it difficult for the FDO to sort out the CAP, search planes, and the hastily launched anti–torpedo-plane patrol. The problems endured by Fighting Three in no manner overshadowed their tremendous success. Thach stressed the battle had proved "our tactics, expert marksmanship and teamwork were right."[31] Brown noted in his report, "Both attacks were very determined being continued against the most effective fighter protection."[32] The 20 February battle off Bougainville had shown that the fighting squadron warranted the confidence of the rest of the task force.

On the 21st, Fighting Three flew combat air patrol from 1030 until dark. The only enemy threat occurred at 1545, when the *Lexington*'s radar detected a bogey 38 miles north of the task force. On a westerly heading, the contact appeared to be an enemy flying boat on the return leg of its search. At the time visibility was only 10 miles, so it seemed highly unlikely that the Japanese had spotted Task Force 11. Flying the afternoon CAP was Lovelace's 2nd Division. While the F4Fs were aloft, the ships entered a rain squall. Lovelace thought he would swing around the edge of the small storm and catch the *Lexington* as she emerged on the other side. The squall was not small, however, and the F4Fs ran afoul of black clouds and severe wind gusts. Soon Lovelace found himself 40 miles out and had to tune his Zed Baker homing receiver for the correct course home. For the harassed fighter pilots, flying CAP in the tropics seemed to bring only blistering sunshine or dark, malevolent storms.

The afternoon of 22 February brought the rendezvous with the faithful ANZAC Squadron escorting the oiler *Platte*. Fueling and other such duties occupied the task force for the next three days. Brown transmitted a number of important messages to his superiors, one a detailed account of the 20 February that included the handsome mention: "Lieut. Edward H. O'Hare chiefly responsible for destruction of 6 planes."[33] Another listed operational requirements for the task force and included the delivery "as early as practicable"[34] of six additional F4F-3 Wildcats, three as replacements and three as spares. In a despatch to Nimitz, Brown surmised that because it was so difficult to surprise Rabaul, he would not attempt another such raid until reinforced by another carrier. This recommendation set into motion events that would send the *Yorktown* and the rest of Task Force 17 into the South Pacific, making operations against Rabaul likely sooner than Brown would have wished.

While Thach's Fighting Three aboard their borrowed flattop found all the action they could handle, Paul Ramsey's Fighting Two battled boredom on the beach.[35] At the end of January, Ramsey's troops had switched over to Ewa to complete conversion from F2A-3 Buffaloes to F4F-3 Wildcats. Aside from familiarization flights in their new mounts, the VF-2 pilots also stood the usual alerts for the Army air defense command. On 4 February, Ramsey moved back to Kaneohe, there coming under the control of Cdr. Harry D. Felt's *Saratoga* Air Group.

Workers at Pearl Harbor tidied the *Saratoga* for the voyage back to Bremerton for full repairs and modernization. On 7 February the giant flattop slipped out of drydock, fueled, and otherwise made preparations to get under way. The AirBatFor staff ordered Ramsey to provide ten pilots and aircraft to ride the *Saratoga* back to the West Coast. Once there, the VF-2 Detachment would report for temporary duty at NAS San Diego. Ramsey furnished ten F4Fs (mostly F4F-3As just received from VMF-111 and the lone XF4F-4), ten pilots, and sixty-two men to guard the *Sara*'s trip home. The VF-2 Detachment comprised the following pilots, all experienced:

Lt. Cdr. James H. Flatley, Jr., USN, commanding			
Lieut. Louis H. Bauer, USN			
Lieut. (jg) Fred H. Simpson, USN			
Harold E. Rutherford	ACMM	USN	NAP
Gordon E. Firebaugh	ACMM	USN	NAP
Theodore S. Gay, Jr.	ACMM	USN	NAP
George W. Brooks	ARM1c	USN	NAP
Charles E. Brewer	ARM1c	USN	NAP
Donald E. Runyon	AMM1c	USN	NAP
Patrick L. Nagle	AMM1c	USN	NAP

At Kaneohe, Fighting Two retained fifteen pilots but only two F4F-3A Wildcats. For the rest of the month, the squadron flew training flights and alerts from Kaneohe. Gradually Ramsey secured additional aircraft until he again had eighteen fighters on hand.

On 9 February, the *Saratoga* departed Pearl as flagship (so to speak) of Task Force 19 under Captain Douglas. Escorting her were four tincans. At 1800, the *Sara* sounded flight quarters and made ready to land aircraft, the VF-2 Detachment and all of Scouting Three along with the group commander, Harry Felt. Until 1820, the landings went without a hitch. Then suddenly while recovering fighters, the carrier without warning dropped speed from 22 knots to 14, causing one F4F to

110

The VF-2 Detachment on 10 Feb. 1942 celebrates the *Saratoga*'s 59,000th landing made the day before by Chief Firebaugh; *l to r*: Nagle, Flatley, Rutherford, unknown, Runyon, Firebaugh, Brooks, Gay, Brewer. (Capt. G. E. Firebaugh, USN.)

crack up on deck. The ship suspended landings until her engineers corrected the problem. At 1836, the air officer gave the go-ahead, and she brought the rest of her brood safely on board. Gordon Firebaugh, one of VF-2's chiefs, was surprised to learn he had made the *Sara*'s 59,000th landing, and the next evening received the customary cake for making a thousandth landing.

For the pilots of the VF-2 Detachment, the voyage proved highly uneventful. Indeed, Flatley's crew did no flying at all until 15 February. Early that morning the air group readied for the flight to NAS Seattle as the *Saratoga* neared the entrance to Puget Sound. Flatley led his nine aircraft (minus the damaged fighter) to Seattle. There they waited while mechanics changed the F4F tail wheels from hard rubber to pneumatic tires; then they flew south to NAS Alameda at Oakland. The next morning, the VF-2 Detachment took off for NAS San Diego. At Bremerton, the *Saratoga* went into the Puget Sound Navy Yard. She would be in limbo during a highly exciting period in the Pacific War!

CHAPTER 6

The *Enterprise*'s Central Pacific Raids

RETURN TO WAKE ISLAND

The second week of February while "The Big E" underwent normal upkeep in port, the admirals tried to determine where best to send her next. Enemy advances in Southeast Asia and the Southwest Pacific appeared irresistible. Singapore was about to fall. The dilemma facing CinCPac's planners involved selecting a target that could cause a meaningful diversion of Japanese effort, but one that would not unduly risk the fleet's precious flattops. In Washington, CominCh agitated for more offensive strikes. There were even proposals to raid Tokyo, as well as a large number of other locales. At Pearl, Nimitz finally resolved to combine the *Enterprise* and the *Yorktown* into one task force (ultimately designated Task Force 16) under Bill Halsey for the mission of attacking Wake Island and also Eniwetok in the northern Marshalls. Halsey readied the *Enterprise* and her escorts (Task Group 16.1) to sail on 14 February. Fletcher's task group with the *Yorktown* would follow a few days later.

Fighting Six had had a profitable shore leave and was ready for action. Factory-designed armor had arrived to take the place of boiler plate, but only four of the seventeen F4Fs (ten F4F-3As and seven F4F-3s) had self-sealing fuel tanks. The afternoon of 14 February, Wade McClusky led his seventeen fighters out to the *Enterprise*. Remaining on shore were Jim Daniels and Dave Flynn, both heading for new assignments. In Daniels's case, he was reporting to ACTG, Pacific to train as a landing signal officer. Replacing them in Fighting Six were two rookies, Ens. Joseph R. Daly and Ens. Roy M. Gunsolus. The day after the squadron landed on board, the air department again assigned them to fly the detested inner air patrol. So far nothing had changed on that score.

On 16 February, the aviators learned they were going to join the *Yorktown* for strikes on Wake and Eniwetok, but those orders were already superseded. The fall of Singapore the day before had caused King to relent on his call for immediate action. Fletcher's *Yorktown* force received other orders, but Halsey's Task Force 16 with the *Enterprise*, two heavy cruisers, and seven destroyers would proceed with the Wake attack. Halsey's troops had yearned to avenge their buddies at Wake ever since the island was first attacked in December. Eniwetok turned out not to be much of an objective anyway. Submarine reconnaissance missions had revealed nothing there worth attacking.

With the usual grumbling against the air department, Fighting Six flew its inner air patrols. As before, the patrols comprised five fighters, so one aircraft could

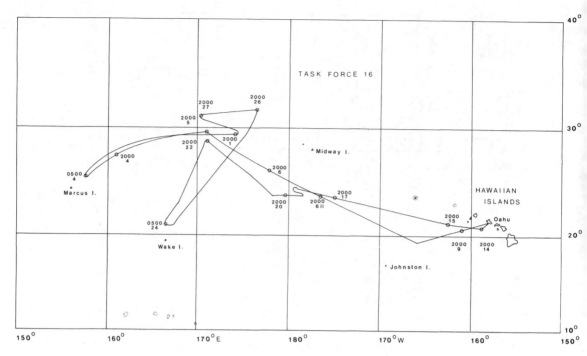

The Wake–Marcus raids, Feb.–Mar. 1942.

tow a sleeve for the rest of the division to make gunnery passes against it. The old problem of jammed guns struck with a vengeance, but there were still no ready solutions. On 18 February, "The Big E" happened to launch a scouting flight of two TBD torpedo planes, whose pilots were told not to fly into the rough weather looming ahead. Without telling the pilots aloft, the ships themselves disappeared into the cold front—a rotten trick on the two torpedo planes, which now were lost. One Devastator managed to find the *Enterprise* just before dark, but the other ditched about 60 miles away. The next morning Halsey arranged for a special search mission to locate the downed aviators and pinpoint them for a destroyer coming out to rescue them. Task Force 16 marked time until they were safely on board the tincan. Halsey's solicitude for his own men did not escape the *Enterprise*'s flyers. They knew the old man would do anything in his power to recover them if they had to go into the drink.

For Fighting Six the rest of the long approach to Wake was uneventful except for the morning of 21 February. Scheduled for inner air patrol, Norm Hodson at 0620 started down the flight deck. His F4F-3A lacked flying speed, sailed out over the bow, then settled into the waves. The plane hit about 75 yards off the *Enterprise*'s bow and sank in less than a minute. Hodson swam clear and waited for the destroyer *Blue* to pick him up; he returned to the carrier the next day. Investigation pointed to propellor pitch control problems as the cause of the mishap.[1] Fighting Six now had sixteen airplanes.

Bad weather dogged the task force on 22 and 23 February, as the air group worked out plans for the attack on Wake. The initial plan made no provision for fighter escort, but reconnaissance photographs of Wake taken by Army bombers seemed to indicate enemy fighters based there. The final plan called for a predawn launch on 24 February with thirty-seven dive bombers, nine TBDs armed with bombs, and six fighter escorts. They were to attack at 0708, ten minutes before

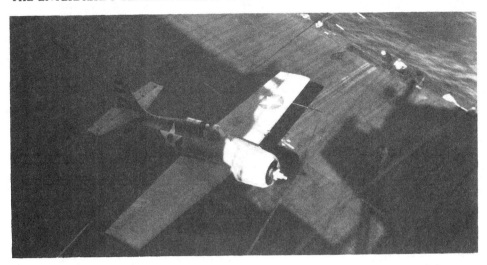

VF-6 F4F-3 taxiing on board the *Enterprise*, probably mid-Feb. 1942. The small roundel on the left wing and its absence on the upper right wing mark this Grumman as newly acquired with only its fuselage markings conforming as yet to VF-6 practice. (NA 80-G-73679.)

sunrise. At the same time, a special bombardment group of two heavy cruisers and two destroyers under Rear Admiral Spruance would shell the island. Spruance left the task force on 23 February to steam west of Wake in order to approach the island from that direction, intending to surprise the enemy garrison. Held in reserve for possible ship targets would be VT-6's 2nd Division of nine TBDs armed with torpedoes. Halsey planned to launch about 120 miles north of Wake, well within the combat radius of the Grummans. Above the *Enterprise*, Fighting Six was to maintain a CAP of at least four fighters all day long. For 24 February, Fighting Six had the organization shown in the table.

At 0430 on 24 February, the *Enterprise* sounded flight quarters, sending aviators

	1st Division (escort)
F-1	Lt. Cdr. Clarence Wade McClusky, USN, squadron commander
F-2	Rad. Elec. Edward H. Bayers, USN
F-3	Lieut. Roger W. Mehle, USN
F-4	Lieut. (jg) Rhonald J. Hoyle, USN
F-5	Lieut. (jg) John C. Kelley, USN
F-10	Ens. Ralph M. Rich, A-V(N)
	2nd Division (2nd CAP)
F-7	Lt. Cdr. Frank T. Corbin, USN, executive officer
F-8	Lieut. (jg) Frank B. Quady, USN
F-9	Lieut. (jg) Gayle L. Hermann, USN
F-6	Ens. Howard L. Grimmell, Jr., A-V(N)
F-11	Ens. Thomas C. Provost III, A-V(N)
F-18	Ens. Wayne C. Presley, A-V(N)
	3rd Division (1st CAP)
F-13	Lieut. James S. Gray, Jr., USN, flight officer
F-14	Ens. Walter J. Hiebert, A-V(N)
F-12	Lieut. (jg) Wilmer E. Rawie, USN
F-17	Lieut. (jg) Harold N. Heisel, USN
	Ens. Norman D. Hodson
	Ens. Joseph R. Daly
	Ens. Roy M. Gunsolus

scurrying to their ready rooms. Later when they emerged on deck to man planes, they encountered highly forbidding flying conditions—a pitch-black predawn, heavily overcast with intermittent violent squalls. Warming up the engines, the mechanics had to set fuel mixtures rich because of high humidity. Consequently, reflected light from the bright blue exhaust flames caused strange halos to appear in the propellor wash, surrounding the aircraft and almost blinding the pilots. Spotted up front for immediate launch were the four F4Fs of Jim Gray's 3rd Division scheduled for the first CAP. They had the dubious distinction of taking off first into the unfriendly skies. A war correspondent, Keith Wheeler, witnessed Gray's departure into the mist:

> A shadowy fighter skittered up the deck. . . . For eternal seconds the shadowy plane down there crabbed sideways. It slid across the port row of deck lights . . . the pilot wrenched it back and drummed over the bow. It dipped and the blue spots of exhaust flame vanished under the carrier's bow.
> . . . The twin blue spots came into view again and climbed away, swinging off to the right.[2]

Walt Hiebert, Will Rawie, and Harold Heisel followed their division leader into the murk. Behind them, deck crews readied the first dive bombers for launch.

Spotted first among the SBDs, Scouting Six began its takeoffs around 0600. Flown by Lieut. (jg) Perry Teaff, the second SBD suddenly veered off the deck during its takeoff run and flew into the water ahead of the carrier. Teaff had become disoriented by the halo effect. He was severely injured, and his rear gunner sank with the plane. Thereafter, the launches were slow and ragged, as the pilots tried to compensate for the terrible visibility. At the head of the second deckload was McClusky's 1st Division of six F4Fs on escort. They got off without trouble. The last aircraft of the Wake strike, a TBD, lifted off at 0647. Cdr. Young, leading the strike, was most impatient to depart, and did leave at 0650, thirty minutes behind schedule. Cloud cover and the irritatingly slow launch prevented all of the strike planes from joining up in proper formation, and confusion persisted until dawn.

Meanwhile from northwest of Wake, Spruance's bombardment group stealthily approached the island. Weather had delayed these vessels as well, and at sunrise they were still eighteen miles from the target. Halsey did not break radio silence to warn them that the *Enterprise* strike would be late. Worse, the Japanese already knew they were near. At 0707, three Japanese Nakajima E8N2 Type 95 floatplanes [DAVE] dive-bombed the cruiser *Northampton* and the destroyer *Maury*, but caused no damage. The *Enterprise*'s fighters would have been especially useful at that juncture if they had arrived on time. Glare from the rising sun in their eyes and mist over the island obscured targets and delayed the bombardment even more. Finally at 0742, Spruance opened fire on Peale Island, one of Wake's three islets. His heavy guns plastered the area, but did not knock out shore batteries, which continued to pop back at him. The cruisermen wondered just where their carrier planes were.

Departing Task Force 16, group leader Young took up a heading of 180 degrees in order to cover the 110 miles to the prearranged deployment area just west of Wake. On the outbound flight, the dive bombers (Young's command plane, eighteen from Bombing Six, and seventeen from Scouting Six) worked up to 18,000 feet, while the nine TBDs armed as horizontal bombers managed 12,000 feet. McClusky's six F4Fs took station in between at 15,000 feet, their primary duty being to escort the vulnerable Devastators. At 0750, Young reached the deployment point and made ready to attack. Visibility over the island had improved, and the fifty-one-plane strike group split up for the attack. While the TBDs began their horizontal bombing run, the SBDs raced in to bomb the airfield. McClusky looked carefully for enemy fighters, but there was no air opposition. The little seaplanes that had pestered the cruisers prudently made themselves scarce. The only Japanese aircraft in sight were two Kawanishi Type 97 flying boats anchored in the lagoon. The SBDs promptly sank them. The Japanese replied with light antiaircraft fire which did not bother the attackers overmuch, although a lucky hit downed one dive bomber from Scouting Six. No big ships were present, so the strike planes had to be content with roughing up likely looking buildings and installations.

After bombing the island, several SBDs searched the area for ship targets. One Scouting Six pilot, Ens. Delbert W. Halsey (not related to the admiral), happened upon a big Kawanishi Type 97 flying boat aloft about five miles east of Wake. The Japanese had been bothering the ships of Spruance's bombardment group in the process of finishing their shelling. Reporting his target to Young circling the island, young Halsey roared into the attack. Young in turn radioed his fighter leader, "Take that seaplane, Mac."[3]

"We'll take him," VF-6's skipper replied. Here finally was something to shoot. From 15,000 feet, McClusky led the division in a high-speed spiral toward the reported location of the enemy. En route, the F4Fs had to sidestep antiaircraft fire from the two American heavy cruisers nearby. Soon McClusky discerned the Kawanishi at 1,000 feet trying to escape. Changing his spiral into a high-side run, McClusky brought the huge wing into his sights. His first bursts tore into the left outboard engine, setting it afire. As McClusky sheered off to recover from the run, behind him his wingman Bayers made his own attack. Continuing the fine shooting of his leader, the NAP set another engine ablaze. Mehle, leading the second section, was the next to shoot. He pressed his run to the limit, and as he started to pull out near the target, he nearly became enveloped in smoke and flames. The Kawanishi had exploded, blown apart as flames touched off the fuel in the massive wing tanks. Mehle had to scramble hard to avoid the flaming mass. "I had the canopy closed," he later recounted, "but it felt as though someone had passed a blow torch over my face."[4] The other three pilots of the 1st Division never had the chance to fire. The dramatic interception took place in full view of Spruance's ships, and their crews gave Fighting Six a loud cheer. Receiving McClusky's jubilant report so quickly, Young at 0835 quipped, "You win a cigar."[5]

The fighters regrouped after their swift victory and headed for the rendezvous point east of Wake. En route they happened upon several VS-6 SBDs working over a hapless converted patrol boat. Always eager to join a scrap, McClusky headed over to strafe, but found his offer to help rudely rebuffed by the scouts, who told the fighters to go off and find their own boat. Well! The destroyer *Maury* later finished off the small auxiliary. The flight back to the task force was routine, and between 0948 and 1014, the strike planes, less the one VS-6 SBD lost at Wake, landed on board the *Enterprise*. Mehle had a surprise when he looked over his Grumman. A three-inch gash marred the smooth leading edge of his left wing. It was cut by an aluminum fitting, debris from the destroyed Kawanishi flying boat. "A fine souvenir—may be seen on request."[6] noted VF-6's unofficial war diary.

Twenty miles northeast of Wake, Spruance gathered up his bombardment ships, then headed northeast to rejoin Task Force 16. On the way they encountered another of the seemingly ubiquitous enemy patrol vessels. The *Balch* swung out of formation to deal with it, quickly sinking the auxiliary. The bombardment group also picked up a "shadower" in the form of a Kawanishi Type 97 flying boat, but the wily Japanese stayed maddeningly out of antiaircraft range of the ships. At 1043, Spruance radioed Halsey to request fighter support.

The *Enterprise* responded to Spruance's call for help by allocating a division of four F4Fs to be led by Roger Mehle. The air department could only provide a rough estimate of the position of Spruance's Task Group 16.7. They believed the bombardment group was about 100 miles southwest of the main body. At 1125, the *Enterprise* launched five F4Fs, two for CAP and Mehle's three on their search and destroy. The fourth fighter did not function properly and had to be scratched from the mission. Flying with Mehle were Ralph Rich and one of the new pilots, Joe Daly. The three soon encountered poor weather, thick cloud cover punctuated by rain squalls. They flew to where Spruance's ships were supposed to be, but no ships hove into sight. For about ninety minutes, Mehle crisscrossed the area, hoping to turn up either the cruisers or the snooper. The *Enterprise*, as it turned out, did not break radio silence to inform the bombardment group that fighters were en route. During the morning's shelling, the cruiser *Northampton*'s radar had gone haywire. Therefore Spruance had no way of knowing the fighters were close by. That afternoon the cruisermen fumed as the Japanese flying boat stuck to them, while Mehle flew in circles not far away but not in contact.

There was more trouble in store for Mehle and his two wingmen. Fuel dwindling, they finally turned in the direction of the carrier, but they did not know (nor were they told) that the main body of Task Force 16 had changed course 25 degrees to port and upped speed 3 knots. Consequently, the *Enterprise* would not be where Mehle expected to find her. Tricky winds aloft did the rest, and soon Mehle was thoroughly lost. After several hours of desperate searching, Mehle finally managed to tune in the ship's YE signal on his Zed Baker homing receiver. The three flyers approached the carrier opposite the side from which they had departed. "The Big E" at 1538 swung into the wind to land planes, and Mehle came on board at 1545 after a flight of four hours and twenty minutes. Only eight gallons of gasoline sloshed in his fuel tank. Rich followed him in, but Daly did not make it. At 1548 while on the downwind leg of his approach, Daly's engine sputtered, then cut out for good because of fuel starvation. He had no choice but to put F-2 into the sea. There was not much time, as he flew at only 200 feet. Very wisely he quickly cranked up his wheels to prevent a nose-over on ditching, let down his flaps, and lowered his seat. The Grumman stalled into a wave crest 300 yards ahead of the destroyer *Ralph Talbot*. Despite his precautions, Daly cut his head on the gunsight mount; but bobbing in his life jacket, he had no trouble staying afloat until the *Ralph Talbot* could bring him on board.[7] With the loss of Daly's Grumman, Fighting Six was now down to fifteen F4Fs.

Task Force 16 ducked into a convenient storm that shielded its withdrawal from Wake. Now there was time to compile action reports and formulate recommendations, and everyone was apologetic about the delay in getting the air group to Wake, acknowledging that had the enemy possessed fighters or bombers there, things could have been rough indeed. Again there was the usual complaint of too few carrier fighters. The admiral, Captain Murray, and Young all desired fighter strength increased from eighteen to twenty-seven. Halsey even felt that in return he would accept fewer dive bombers on board to make room, but would not reduce the number of torpedo planes because of their value against ships. Young reiterated that, "Fighter protection of VTB's, surface bombardment groups, as well as the carrier is mandatory."[8] Murray in his report concurred, noting that fighter escort for strike groups was "highly desirable."[9] Young also brought up the need for reserve pilots, particularly for the fighting squadron. He recommended at least 50 percent spare pilots on strength:

> Fighter squadrons require greater percentage of replacement and spare pilots due to *constant* combat patrols which must be maintained in addition to other missions assigned VF in action.[10]

Special problems likewise emerged with the question of fighter support for task groups operating independently of the carrier task force. When Spruance's ships rejoined on 25 February, the cruisermen expressed great displeasure at being left without air support. The whole previous afternoon, the Japanese flying boat had trailed the bombardment group. Shortly before dark, it made a move as if to attack. Simultaneously a pair of land attack planes had appeared overhead. They had sneaked in from another direction while the patrol plane had diverted everyone's attention. Fortunately the bombers had not hit anything. Captain Ellis M. Zacharias of the heavy cruiser *Salt Lake City* wrote in his report that the carrier fighters had not done their job by failing to destroy all aircraft at Wake. He urged that carriers operate sufficiently close to detached task groups to offer them air support.

Fighting Six, of course, had destroyed every enemy aircraft it saw and had made a determined effort to find the snooper shadowing Spruance's ships. As for the two land attack planes, the Japanese had evidently rushed them up to Wake from Kwajalein, refueled them, and sent them out after the cruisers. For search and destroy missions of the nature of the one assigned Mehle, the Grumman Wildcats had to have more range. The captain of "The Big E" urged that the F4Fs "be provided as expeditiously as possible with auxiliary droppable tanks attached to the wing bomb racks."[11] The fighter pilots themselves were not very happy with the type of mission given Fighting Six the late morning of 24 February, and stressed that much more planning and coordination would be necessary for success.

A VISIT TO MARCUS

On 25 February while Task Force 16 withdrew northeastward from Wake, Nimitz authorized Halsey to attack Marcus Island. Known to the Japanese as Minatori-shima, this lonely outpost lay only a thousand miles from Tokyo. The *Enterprise*'s crew was surprised to see the task force heading west, and realized something was up. As usual, Halsey sought concealment in heavy weather and braved storms most of the way to Marcus. On 28 February, he revealed his plans. The *Enterprise* with Spruance's two heavy cruisers as escort would make a high-speed run toward Marcus to reach a point 175 miles northeast of there in order to launch planes before dawn on 4 March. The air strike would consist of dive bombers only, with no provision for fighter escort. There would be one swift attack; then Halsey would withdraw.

Monday, 2 March, proved an interesting day on board the *Enterprise*. First, a nasty rainstorm sent the morning search away, compelling the ship to break radio silence to bring them back. As if that were not enough, the inner air patrol of SBDs twice during the course of the day found and bombed lone submarines. Unfortunately both turned out to be the USS *Gudgeon* on the outward leg of her second war patrol. No damage was inflicted, but another pack of submariners had reason to be angry with "The Big E." On board the carrier, VF-6 pilots watched in horrified amazement a "fancy bit of brainwork"[1] in Fly I, the air department. The air officer had scheduled a particular SBD to fly solely for an engine check and compass calibration. As its pilot decided during the engine run-up that something was amiss with this aircraft, it was struck below into the hangar for repairs.

Unperturbed, the air department then ordered another SBD launched, and its perplexed pilot had nothing to do but circle the task force for four hours before the air officer let him back on board.

On 3 March, intelligence sources revealed that Marcus might have an airfield, so Halsey changed his plans. There would be a fighter escort after all. Instead of launching at 175 miles, the *Enterprise* would close to within 125 miles of the target to accommodate the short-ranged Grummans. The strike group would consist of thirty-two SBDs (group command plane, seventeen from Bombing Six, and fourteen from Scouting Six) and six F4F Wildcats from Fighting Six. McClusky shuffled his flight organization a bit and assigned the following to the Marcus strike:

	Lt. Cdr. Clarence Wade McClusky, USN (CO)
	Rad. Elec. Edward H. Bayers, NAP, USN
F-10	Lieut. James S. Gray, Jr., USN (FO)
	Ens. Walter J. Hiebert, A-V(N)
	Lieut. Roger W. Mehle, USN
F-17	Lieut. (jg) John C. Kelley, USN

For CAP, Fighting Six would have nine F4Fs available.

As in the Wake raid, the *Enterprise* hoped to surprise the defenders by attacking ten minutes before sunrise. Going for the airfield would be the SBDs of Bombing Six, while Scouting Six handled the radio station and other likely installations. "Brigham" Young with a photo section of three SBDs of Scouting Six would look for ship targets. There was to be one pass, then a high-speed retreat to the southeast to mislead the enemy. Fighting Six would deal with any enemy air opposition and act as rear guard against any pursuit. On board the carrier, Torpedo Six acted as reserve for launch should any important ship targets be located. It was likely that some VF-6 fighters would escort the TBDs if the *Enterprise* sent them out. This would be as close to the enemy's homeland as American surface ships had dared go since the outbreak of war, although the next month they would come much closer.

The *Enterprise* and her two escorts pressed ahead to the launch point, and at 0438 on 4 March, she swung into the wind for flight operations. Weather conditions were good, far better than at Wake nine days before. Moonlight illuminated the seas around the ships, but heavy clouds loomed in the direction of Marcus. At 0446, the first SBD rolled down the flight deck. Order of takeoff was the group commander and Scouting Six, followed by Bombing Six, with McClusky's six F4Fs the last to go. Ahead of schedule, the last fighter was off by 0504. Task Force 16 changed course to 070 degrees, speed 25 knots. Swiftly the strike planes made their rendezvous, almost as fast as in daylight. At 0525, Young signaled the departure and took up a heading of 251 degrees bound for Marcus 128 miles away. The rendezvous was complete except for one fighter, the last to get off. Jack Kelley could not find the rest of the group and did not dare fly to Marcus alone. He also did not want to risk approaching the *Enterprise* without announcing himself—but to do so would mean breaking radio silence, which he would not do. He resigned himself to circling out of gun range until dawn before he could fly over to the *Enterprise* and land.

Young led the strike group in a gradual climb toward 16,000 feet. The closer the planes drew to Marcus, the deeper the overcast. With her radar, the *Enterprise* tracked the group, and via the superfrequency YE homing transmitter she communicated to Young that he was five miles north of the correct course to Marcus. This proved to be an excellent way to guide attackers through bad weather to the target, and the risk of detection was slight. A tailwind boosted airspeed, and combined with the surprisingly quick rendezvous, put the group well ahead of schedule. Suddenly around 0630, a convenient break in the clouds revealed Marcus below, the island's white runways conspicuous despite the darkness. Forty minutes remained before sun up, but Young had to strike now lest engine noise alert the Japanese. In the darkness and low-hanging clouds, it would be difficult. Nevertheless, Young gave the signal to attack.

Diving in, Bombing Six dropped several parachute flares in an attempt to illuminate the target. Uncertain whether there were any aircraft parked on the airstrip, Young tried to make contact with McClusky to tell him to strafe the field. Radio trouble prevented his raising VF-6's skipper, but Jim Gray answered the call. Young told him to check out the field, so Gray dropped low to buzz the runways. He saw no enemy aircraft. Meanwhile, the SBDs bombed anything that looked important in the moonlight and flare illumination, but could not guarantee results because of the low visibility. Antiaircraft fire was sporadic, but did account for one VS-6 SBD which ditched east of the island. McClusky and the three VF-6 pilots with him followed the last SBDs in, then circled at 5,000 feet just southeast of Marcus to cover their withdrawal. Unfortunately Gray did not know where they were and did not rejoin. At 0650 the group left Marcus behind, twenty minutes before they were scheduled to attack!

Well before dawn, the carrier's radar had detected an unidentified aircraft loitering just out of gun range. It seemed fairly certain that the bogey was a strike aircraft that had failed to join up with the rest. At 0643, about a half hour before sunrise, the Enterprise turned southeasterly into the wind to launch the four F4Fs of Frank Corbin's 1st CAP. Eight minutes later, a grateful Jack Kelley landed back on board. Routine combat air patrol activities continued, as the ship awaited the return of the strike force. Soon they too were back. Between 0837 and 0907, the *Enterprise* landed thirty-five aircraft. Only one SBD and one fighter had failed to return. Halsey changed course to 050 degrees, speed 25 knots to "haul out" of the area. At 0940, the ships upped speed to 30 knots.

Gray was still aloft in F-10, but desperately lost in the overcast. After checking out the airfield, he had been unable to latch onto either the SBDs or his fighters for the flight back to the carrier. As he had feared, the tempermental Zed Baker receiver in his Grumman was acting up. After a couple of hours of searching, he was down to his last twenty gallons of fuel, with little chance of finding the ships. Only the cold seas beckoned, his chances for survival appearing almost nil.

On board the *Enterprise* Lieut. John Baumeister, the radar officer, first assumed a bogey that appeared on his scope was an enemy plane. The contact had come from the direction of Marcus, had flown unseen past the ships, which were shielded by low-hanging clouds, and then continued on. But, very fortunately, Gray just the previous night had mentioned to his friend Baumeister that he thought the homing device in F-10 was unreliable. Suddenly realizing the bogey might be Gray, Baumeister consulted Captain Murray and received permission to transmit a short radio message to him with the correct course back to the carrier. At 0956, Baumeister had the great pleasure of seeing his Annapolis classmate land on board. After a flight of nearly five and a half hours, Gray had only nine gallons of fuel remaining. The trip back from Marcus must have seemed an eternity to him.

Fighting Six maintained a combat air patrol aloft until a half hour after sunset. The afternoon was unremarkable except for a false alarm that sent all hands scur-

Famous overhead shot of VF-6 F4F-3s and -3As on board the *Enterprise* about the time of the Marcus Raid, 4 Mar. 1942. Note VF-6 overpainting of smaller wing roundels and the variations in the number of tail stripes. (NA 80-G-17532.)

rying to battle stations. Lieut. (jg) Robin Lindsey, the carrier's assistant landing signal officer, took the opportunity to fly in the last CAP of the day. A veteran of Fighting Six, he had taken additional training to become an LSO. The senior LSO, Lieut. H. B. ("Bert") Harden, brought him and the rest of the CAP fighters on board just after dark.

The morning of 5 March found Task Force 16, as usual, in the middle of a storm front in the turbulent Central Pacific. This was satisfying to the VF-6 diarist, who described the weather as "delightfully ugly."[2] Flying was not possible, and that meant more sack time for weary pilots. Late that afternoon, Halsey rejoined his destroyers. Tokyo radio noted gravely another raid on the Greater East Asia Co-Prosperity Sphere. At Marcus, the Yankees had "killed eight people and wrecked a shanty."[3] Task Force 16 on 6 March fueled from the oiler *Sabine*. Fighting Six flew inner air patrol that day, but the next three days weather was so nasty that most flight operations were curtailed.

Combat lessons learned during the Marcus raid included the litany of no incendiary bullets, too few self-sealing fuel tanks, and the paucity of reserve pilots. In his report, Murray warned that, "on recent occasions it has been necessary to make demands upon pilots that, if continued, will unquestionably become injurious to health."[4] The obvious solution was to operate more than one carrier together, so the two flattops could alternate routine but time-consuming flying duties. Young was disappointed in the paucity of ships and aircraft at Marcus, "It is regretted that more valuable targets could not be found."[5] In his endorsement of the Marcus reports, Nimitz later reiterated his demands for proper materiel: leakproof tanks, incendiary bullets, IFF gear (which would have helped Gray on 4 March), and the like. CinCPac also agreed fully with the need for reserve pilots. Regarding the Marcus Raid itself, he had two comments. He definitely preferred the tactic of coordinating ship bombardments with air strikes, which "insures severe damage."[6] Also Nimitz noted that accurate antiaircraft fire had hindered accurate bombing. He felt that some of the fighters should have been used for strafing runs as flak suppression for the dive bombers. "It remains that preliminary ground strafing aids the main destruction by the bombers."[7] Of course, there had to be enough fighters available even to escort the strike planes to the target, underscoring the top priority of getting more Grummans on board the carriers.

The morning of 10 March, the *Enterprise* flew her air group off to Oahu, then entered Pearl Harbor. By noon, the pilots had secured their aircraft and gladly checked out for a solid week's rest at the Royal Hawaiian Hotel. Harold Heisel of Fighting Six, however, went to the Naval Hospital for allergy treatments and would miss the next two cruises. For those aviators heading for the Royal Hawaiian, the ship at Halsey's direction furnished five bottles of good whiskey, almost impossible to obtain normally on Oahu. In defiance of naval regulations, Halsey entertained a liberal policy toward moderate imbibing and the curative value of a shot for men under great strain. In his memoirs, Halsey noted that after Pearl Harbor, "I took the law into my own hands," and explained further:

> As Commander Aircraft Battle Force, I directed my representative ashore, Rear Adm. Aubrey W. Fitch, to requisition 100 gallons of bourbon for our flight surgeons to issue to our pilots. This eventually became standard practice. I don't remember if it was ever officially approved, but I do remember that "Jake" Fitch accused me of inaugurating highly unorthodox procedure and leaving him to hold the bag.[8]

The pilots did not mind.

CHAPTER 7

The Lae–Salamaua Raid

GATHERING THE FORCES

The morning of 16 February Task Force 17 left Pearl Harbor bound for southern waters. Retaining his old task force designation and without orders to join Halsey's Task Force 16, Fletcher had with him the *Yorktown*, the heavy cruisers *Astoria* and *Louisville*, six destroyers, and the fleet oiler *Guadalupe*. With Halsey alone en route to raid Wake, Fletcher assumed the role of reserve with orders to take station in the Canton Island area. From there, he could support Halsey's raids in the Central Pacific or move south to join Brown's Task Force 11 in the Southwest Pacific. That afternoon, Curt Smiley's *Yorktown* Air Group flew out from Oahu. Fresh from standing several days' alert at Ewa, Pete Pederson's VF-42 troops brought with them seventeen F4F-3 Wildcats.

The *Yorktown*'s voyage southward was routine—flight operations involved the usual searches, inner air patrols, and training exercises. The days were differentiated only by accidents, when the rare mishaps did occur. On 21 February north of Canton Island, an SBD from Bombing Five splashed while trying to land. Three days later another dive bomber, this one from Scouting Five, flew into the water during takeoff. For several days Task Force 17 marked time around the equator, awaiting the call to action. It came on 27 February, orders from CinCPac to Fletcher instructing him to join Brown's Task Force 11 in a hot spot of the Pacific: the New Guinea–Bismarcks–Solomons area. The rendezvous was to take place at noon, local time, on 6 March in the waters 300 miles north of Noumea, New Caledonia. By some oversight, Fletcher did not have the proper cyphers to decode the message. He had to send a destroyer to Canton to request that Pearl Harbor rebroadcast the despatch. By the time he received the message, he had to bend on speed in order to make the date. No matter, Task Force 17 was heading into action again.

In the wake of the abortive Rabaul raid, Brown's Task Force 11 with the *Lexington* rested in relatively safe waters northeast of New Caledonia. The ships topped off with fuel to enable them to execute another offensive sweep toward Rabaul. As related above, Brown sent a stream of recommendations and reports to his superiors, advising that Rabaul be left alone unless the attacking force numbered two carriers. Faster than he had dreamed, King and Nimitz granted his wish and hurried Fletcher down to the Southwest Pacific. Seconding their action was Leary, who on 25 February had pressed for an "early attack"[1] by both task forces on Rabaul. He felt such a raid was vital to cover the anticipated arrival of an important troop convoy at Noumea. Nimitz agreed, but warned both King and Leary that the fleet could not long support both task forces so far from base. Because of the tenuous logistical situation, Brown's task force would have to retire soon. Brown himself seemed surprised by the stir his earlier message had caused. On 26 February, he radioed Nimitz noting that despite Leary's message, now he did not even recommend a two-carrier descent on Rabaul, "under the present conditions."[2] Brown's recommendation arrived too late. In response to his original advice, Fletcher's Task Force 17 was on its way, and Rabaul was the target.

While the deliberations took place, Task Force 11 on 25 February headed southwestward toward the Coral Sea. That day was a busy one for VF-3's paintshop artist. He painted rising sun flags near the cockpit of each Grumman that had scored on 20 February repulsing the bomber attacks on the *Lexington*. O'Hare's F-15 was foremost, with five flags proudly showing his victory tally. The next day brought the carrier the first sight of land since 31 January, as the ships traversed the Santa Cruz group of islands. The destroyer *Patterson* maneuvered alongside the giant *Lexington* and by bosun's chair transferred a wounded but happy Howard Johnson. He could walk, but fragments still lodged in his skin. "It was good to have him back," wrote Burt Stanley.[3]

Fighting Three on 27 February resumed flying combat air patrol as Task Force 11 set out across the Coral Sea. The first order of business was to transfer provisions to the destroyers, already at sea longer than expected. Course on 28 February was still southwesterly, taking the ships within 250 miles of Rossel Island in waters that would become much more familiar (and deadly) in May. Brown held to his southwesterly heading until 0200 on 1 March, then swung back around to the northeast toward the New Hebrides. On 3 March, the oiler *Kaskaskia* arrived to refuel thirsty ships. That day formal orders from CominCh instructed Brown to combine Task Forces 11 and 17 as well as the ANZAC Squadron to undertake a raid on Rabaul. King suggested an approach from the east or northeast with a target date of about 10 March.

On 4 March while Task Force 11 fueled northwest of Efate, O'Hare learned to his embarrassment how much of a hero he was to his countrymen at home. The press had made a great deal of his exploits on 20 February, and the rest of the squadron could not resist joshing him about his new-found fame. "We all asked him for his autograph," Stanley wrote, but added, "He took it well and I feel he deserves the publicity he got."[4] Butch was a winner on deck as well as in the air. Don Lovelace felt that he "is very modest in a natural sort of way."[5]

The morning of 6 March saw Task Force 11 and the ANZAC Squadron still drawing fuel oil from the *Kaskaskia*, Brown having adroitly sidestepped a hurricane that had rampaged through the area. Joining the group right on schedule was Fletcher's Task Force 17. Now Brown controlled a very respectable force of two carriers, eight heavy cruisers, and fourteen destroyers. Fletcher, his staff, the *Yorktown*'s Captain Buckmaster, and his key people came on board the *Lexington* to confer with Brown and Sherman. Together they discussed the options open to them for prosecuting a 10 March attack on Rabaul. In February Brown had tried the easterly approach and discovered the Japanese ready and waiting. Now he wanted to try from the south, hoping to execute moonlight air strikes on Rabaul and also the airstrip at Gasmata on New Britain's south coast. Sherman favored the plan because of the *Lexington*'s night-trained SBD and TBD squadrons, but the *Yorktown*'s Air Officer, Cdr. Murr Arnold, had to explain that the *Yorktown*'s pilots were not night-qualified. Brown reluctantly decided on a dawn air strike against both places followed by cruiser bombardment if the situation were favorable.

As senior aviator present, Ted Sherman received command of the two air striking groups and worked out the plan, as the ships steamed westward toward the designated launch point for 10 March, 125 miles distant from both Rabaul and Gasmata. Issued on 7 March, Sherman's air operations order delegated the Rabaul strike to Cdr. Ault's *Lexington* Air Group. His force was to comprise nine F4F Wildcats from Fighting Three, thirty-one SBD dive bombers from Bombing Two and Scouting Two, and thirteen torpedo-armed Devastators from Torpedo Two. Taking on the less formidable Gasmata targets would be the *Yorktown* Air Group under Cdr. Smiley with eleven F4Fs from "VF-5" (as the plan erroneously dubbed VF-42), thirty SBDs from the two dive bombing squadrons, and twelve TBDs from Torpedo Five. For both objectives, the plan called for simultaneous launches before dawn on 10 March and the use of "normal departure," that is, by squadrons. Attacks were to take place in squadron waves, with the escort fighters in the lead. The F4Fs, each armed with a pair of 30-lb. fragmentation bombs, had the mission of bombing and strafing the airfields, then supporting the bombers when they went in. Initial attack by fighters was very much in vogue with the senior commanders. Sherman made provisions to divert half the Gasmata attack group to Rabaul if the targets there warranted the additional strength.

A CHANGE OF TARGETS

By the time Sherman distributed the Rabaul–Gasmata attack orders, events had conspired to render them superfluous. The evening of 7 March, Leary forwarded to Brown a sighting report from a Royal Australian Air Force patrol plane. The Aussies had spotted a large convoy, including one cruiser, several destroyers, and transports, steaming off Buna on New Guinea's northeast coast. Also, air reconnaissance that day over Rabaul counted some twenty-three vessels in the harbor. Clearly something was going on. The eighth of March brought definite word of Japanese invasions at Salamaua and nearby Lae up the Papuan coast from Buna. Reportedly the landing forces had disembarked from eleven ships. Meanwhile, Australian aircraft checking out Rabaul found the harbor nearly bare of shipping, in stark contrast to the previous day. They saw no worthwhile targets at all off Gasmata. Brown was a little too late to nip the invasions in the bud.

As a consequence, Brown on 8 March reviewed the options now open to him. In many ways, it was a day of frustrations. The Japanese had unexpectedly seized the initiative on New Guinea. A sudden violent rainstorm descending on Brown's little fleet had compelled him to break radio silence to warn his ships against possible collisions. Radio silence again fell by the board when one of the cruiser floatplanes (from the *San Francisco*) became lost on inner air patrol. The aircraft transmitted messages in hopes of being homed back to the task force, but in vain. Thus Brown had every reason to believe that the enemy was alerted to his presence and would be waiting for him to attack Rabaul, which in any event had few ship targets present.

Off Lae and Salamaua, the Japanese had assembled a large force of ships committed to linger in the area while unloading troops and supplies. They could not readily clear out. Therefore Brown decided to attack the vessels lying off the two New Guinea villages and conferred with Sherman and his *Lexington* people as to the feasibility of launching air strikes on the two objectives just a few miles apart. The aviation experts quickly settled upon a launch point in the Gulf of Papua. Such an approach from south of the target would be far less exposed than from the east, an area that lay under the gaze of search planes from Rabaul. The aviators acknowledged, however, that the southerly approach posed great risks. The aircraft would have to fly over the trackless jungle and jagged heights (topping 15,000 feet

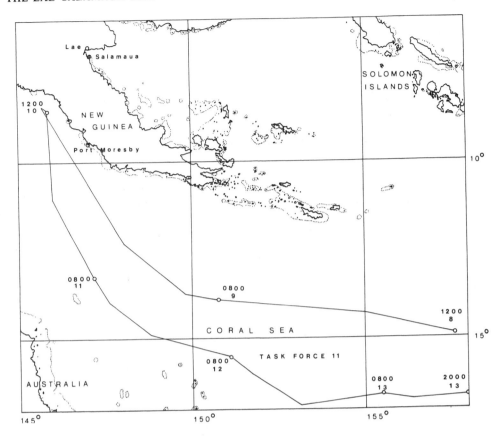

The 10 Mar. Lae–Salamaua raid.

in some places) of the rugged Owen Stanley Mountains making up the spine of Papua. To commercial pilots who had hauled gold from Lae back to Port Moresby, the Owen Stanleys were notorious for bad weather, towering cloud formations, and low visibility.

Thus the evening of 8 March plans were afoot to strike Lae and Salamaua from carriers operating in the Gulf of Papua. Target date was the morning of 10 March. While the two carrier task forces operated so far westward, Rear Admiral Crace, RN, with four heavy cruisers and four destroyers would take station near Rossel Island to cover the back door, that is, the sea approaches to Port Moresby and New Caledonia. On 9 March, the carriers and their escorts headed westward across the Coral Sea toward the next day's launch point. Eager for more information on flying conditions over the Owen Stanleys, Brown sent two officers on separate missions to obtain it personally. One of his staff, Cdr. Walton W. Smith, rode an SBD dive bomber to Townsville in northeast Australia, and Bill Ault (the *Lexington* Air Group commander) flew another to embattled Port Moresby. Both returned with valuable data. Ault ducked in at Moresby between Japanese bombing raids. From what the two officers learned, Sherman's planners determined there was a suitable mountain pass (height 7,500 feet) in line with the launch point and the objective. Often this pass cleared in the morning, say from 0700 to 1100, but thereafter the clouds usually closed in tightly. On this basis, Sherman set the launch time as 0800 on 10 March.

Sherman modified his air operations plan to fit the new circumstances. Jimmy Thach later described the basic procedure:

> An awful lot of work has to be done before an attack. Information has to be obtained and checked—geographical facts, weather forecasts, what enemy forces are where. All this information went to Captain Sherman and he had to okay the final plan. But before he published the operational order, he always consulted with all squadron commanders. If we didn't like a tentative plan, we said so. He considered everything and always came out with the best possible answer.[1]

Sherman arranged for the two carrier air groups to depart one after the other (the *Lexington*'s planes first) in order to attack, as described earlier, staggered in waves of squadrons about ten minutes apart. Going in first would be the eight F4F-3s of Thach's Fighting Three, then Bob Dixon's Scouting Two to plaster Lae and the ships located there, and finally a coordinated attack on Salamaua harbor by Bombing Two and Torpedo Two. Twenty minutes later, the *Yorktown* Air Group would repeat the process.

The use of fighters and torpedo planes posed special problems on this mission. There was worry over the short range of the F4F-3 Wildcats. The first thought was to stop briefly at Port Moresby to top off tanks, but the risk was too great that Japanese bombers might catch the F4Fs on the ground. Thus the task force would have to move in close to the shoreline to put the fighters within range of the target over the mountains. Brown and Sherman settled for a launch point 125 miles south of Lae and Salamaua. Thach worked out the fuel–distance equations and figured he had the fuel to reach the target area, fight for ten to twelve minutes, then return. Sherman's plan still called for Fighting Three's escort to carry two 30-lb. fragmentation bombs apiece. Pete Pederson's Fighting Forty-two was off the hook in that regard, as the squadron had removed its bomb racks the previous December. For Thach's troops still lugging the fuel-consuming bombs, the *Lexington*'s air department came up with a new wrinkle. To clear her deck space for heavier takeoffs, the *Lexington* would launch the fighters first, then send off all the strike planes. The deck free, the fighters would land briefly to refill their tanks and then take off again. With their faster cruise, Thach's Wildcats would soon catch up with the bombers. The *Yorktown* with her far more efficient elevator system (three to the *Lex*'s one working elevator) could keep her fighters in the hangar until necessary, then send them aloft.

The mountains would pose another sort of problem for the Douglas TBD Devastators. There was a mountain pass at 7,500 feet, but even that might be too high for Devastators laden with torpedoes to surmount. Sherman very much wanted to use at least one TBD squadron armed with torpedoes in order to inflict maximum damage on enemy ships. In the end he chose to send Jimmy Brett's Torpedo Two with torpedoes, while the *Yorktown*'s Torpedo Five was to go armed with two 500-lb. bombs apiece (half the weight of an aerial torpedo) to make horizontal bombing runs. It was still questionable whether Brett could coax his heavily laden TBDs over the one mountain pass.

The two strike groups were to have the composition shown in the table. Total plane strength for the attack was 104: 18 F4F Wildcats, 61 SBD dive bombers, and 25 TBD torpedo planes. Allocated for defense of the carriers were six F4Fs from Fighting Three, seven from Fighting Forty-two, five SBD dive bombers from Bombing Two, and four SBDs from Scouting Five.

Dawn on 10 March found the two carrier task forces maneuvering in the Gulf of Papua about 45 miles off shore, well to the west of Port Moresby. The weather

	Lexington Air Group		
Commander, *Lexington* Air Group	Cdr. William B. Ault	1	SBD-3
Fighting Three	Lt. Cdr. John S. Thach	8	F4F-3s
Bombing Two	Lt. Cdr. Weldon L. Hamilton	12	SBD-2s
Scouting Two	Lt. Cdr. Robert E. Dixon	18	SBD-2, -3s
Torpedo Two	Lt. Cdr. James H. Brett, Jr.	<u>13</u> 52	TBD-1s
	Yorktown Air Group		
Fighting Forty-two	Lt. Cdr. Oscar Pederson	10	F4F-3s
Bombing Five	Lt. Cdr. Robert G. Armstrong	17	SBD-3s
Scouting Five	Lt. Cdr. William O. Burch	13	SBD-3s
Torpedo Five	Lt. Cdr. Joe Taylor	<u>12</u> 52	TBD-1s

was excellent. The *Yorktown* at 0704 launched a combat air patrol of four F4Fs under VF-42's executive officer, Lt. Cdr. Fenton. The *Lexington* launched her strike group first. At 0749, Thach's eight VF-3 escort fighters took to the air, followed in short order by the eighteen SBDs of Scouting Two, VB-2's twelve SBDs, and thirteen TBDs from Torpedo Two. At 0822 with the deck clear, Thach's fighters descended to land on board the *Lexington* for a short snort of gasoline. The carrier sent them aloft once again at 0834, and Thach set course to overtake the remainder of the air group already en route to the target.

The *Yorktown* organized the launch of her fifty-two planes into three deckloads. From 0805 to 0815, the carrier sent aloft the thirteen SBDs of Scouting Five and the twelve bomb-armed Devastators of Torpedo Five. Following them at 0829 were Bob Armstrong's seventeen SBDs from Bombing Five. Next came the fighters. Beginning at 0846, the *Yorktown* launched Pederson's ten VF-42 Wildcats as escorts, as well as a pair of fighters for the second combat air patrol. Leading Pederson's 3rd Division on the strike was Lieut. McCormack, VF-42's flight officer. His plane failed to start, so he commandeered an F4F manned by one of the CAP pilots on standby, Ens. Bill Woollen. Without further trouble, the ten VF-42 escorts were off.

Because of their prior launch, the *Lexington* group bounded ahead of the *Yorktown* planes. The dive bombers gradually worked up to 16,000 feet. His SBD not loaded with a bomb, Ault according to plan peeled off once the dive bombers reached the mountain pass. Carefully observing weather conditions, Ault decided they were adequate to continue the mission. He would circle over the pass until the last of the strike planes had attacked and started back. If the clouds did close up, he would be in position to guide the planes back. After the actual attack, he broadcast weather and wind data for the returning pilots. Leaving the group commander behind, the *Lexington*'s SBDs started the last 45 miles to Lae and Salamaua bordering the bright blue waters of Huon Gulf just ahead.

Power settings at fast cruise, Thach's eight F4Fs overtook the torpedo-laden TBDs of Torpedo Two just as they neared the mountain pass. Jimmy Brett's pilots found they could not climb as fast as the terrain rose beneath them, and for a time it looked as if Torpedo Two might have to abort the mission. Then Brett, as Thach later wrote:

> saw a green, flat area in the sunshine—and remembered his glider training. He got his ships over this area and found an updraft of about twelve hundred feet a minute. This just washed him up over the top and got him started down the other side. As he went over, Jimmy radioed to me: "Halfway house."[2]

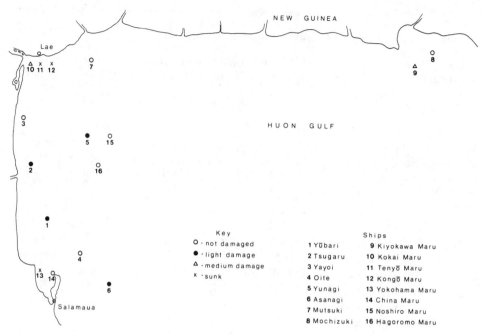

Disposition of Japanese ships off Lae–Salamaua, 10 Mar. 1942.

The fighters quickly swept past the lumbering torpedo planes, overtook the dive bombers, then pressed ahead to attack before the rest of the group. By 0920, Thach was over the target area. He quickly scanned the skies, but saw no evidence of enemy fighters. Likewise on the dirt strip at Salamaua, there were no Japanese aircraft. It began to look as if they had caught the enemy flat-footed. According to Thach, "As no fighter protection was necessary, we were left with the problem of attempting to do something else of value."[3] Splitting the escort, he sent Noel Gayler's division north to Lae, while his 1st Division checked out Salamaua for likely targets to bomb and strafe.

As Thach discovered, the Japanese forces at Lae and Salamaua were indeed unprepared for the impending thunderbolt. The move to the two New Guinea coastal settlements was one step in South Seas Force's plans to consolidate its hold in the crucial Bismarcks–New Guinea–Solomons region. Slowed five days by the postponement imposed by Inoue after Brown's abortive 20 February raid, the invasions, codenamed the SR Operation, took place without trouble on 8 March. By the afternoon of 9 March, the airstrip at Lae was ready for aircraft, and 24th Air Flotilla planned in a few days to operate fighters from there. The morning of 10 March, a total of sixteen Japanese ships operated in the Lae–Salamaua area. Anchored off Lae were the transports *Kongō Maru*, *Tenyō Maru*, and *Kokai Maru*, escorted by the destroyers *Yayoi* and *Mutsuki*. Lying off Salamaua were the army transports *Yokohama Maru* and *China Maru*. In the open waters of Huon Gulf between the two locales were the light cruiser *Yūbari* (flagship of Rear Admiral Kajioka Sadamichi, convoy commander), the large minelayer *Tsugaru*, three destroyers (the *Yūnagi*, *Oite*, and *Asanagi*), and two small converted minesweepers (the *Hagoromo Maru* and the *Noshiro Maru No. 2*). About 25 miles east of Lae and in the direction of Finschhafen was Kajioka's "Air Unit," the converted seaplane tender *Kiyokawa Maru* and the destroyer *Mochizuki*. By far the greater portion of amphibious vessels available to South Seas Force was concentrated in the Lae–Salamaua area.

While the fighters looked around for something to attack, Scouting Two approached Lae at 16,000 feet. Among the rich crop of ship targets below, Dixon singled out three fat transports. One (the *Kongō Maru*) was moored alongside the dock at Lae, and the other two (the *Tenyō Maru* and the *Kokai Maru*) were anchored about a half mile off shore. Scouting Two's eighteen SBDs attacked the ships with their 500-lb. bombs, reserving the two underwing 100-pounders for buildings at Lae. Repeatedly, Dixon's pilots hit the *Kongō Maru* and the *Tenyō Maru*, and they thought they put both on the bottom. The third transport, the *Kokai Maru*, they set on fire. Two SBDs jumped the light cruiser *Yūbari* in the act of getting under way and claimed one hit. Several others ganged up on one of the small auxiliary minesweepers and shot it full of holes. Ashore at Lae, Japanese naval base troops unlimbered four 8-cm high-angle antiaircraft guns, and one popped a VS-2 SBD flown at 200 feet by Ens. Joseph P. Johnson. The SBD splashed just off shore.

About the time Scouting Two started its dives, Gayler led his four fighters north to Lae. His wingman was Dale Peterson, and the second section comprised Scoop Vorse and Bob Morgan. They spotted the antiaircraft guns ashore giving the SBDs grief. Charging in, the F4Fs bombed and strafed the gun positions, killing the artillerymen or driving them off their guns. The pilots then proceeded to shoot up the buildings surrounding the Lae airstrip and sprinkled a few 30-lb. fragmentation bombs around for good measure. Drawing their attention after they plastered the airfield were warships getting under way in the harbor. The fighters swarmed after the *Yūbari* and her consorts trying desperately to build up speed. They concentrated on the light cruiser, one destroyer, and one of the auxiliary minesweepers. Strafing runs pushed to masthead height poured machine gun bullets into the bridges and superstructures of the target vessels. Gayler's pilots reported small fires ignited on board the destroyer and the little minesweeper.

According to plan, Hamilton's Bombing Two and Brett's Torpedo Two had orders to coordinate their attacks, but so many targets clamored for attention that both squadrons split into small detachments to go after different ships. Bombing Two's 1st Division tackled what they thought was a *Mogami*-class heavy cruiser. Actually she was the big minelayer *Tsugaru*. Two close misses by big 1,000-lb. bombs caused her "light damage." Hamilton's 2nd Division attacked the *China Maru*, one of the two transports off Salamaua, but made no hits. At 0938, VT-2's TBDs began their approaches. Three Devastators singled out the second transport lying off Salamaua, and a hit by at least one of their torpedoes put the *Yokohama Maru* onto the mud of the harbor bottom. Other TBDs went up toward Lae and attacked the transports there, but unfortunately several fish ran too deep or otherwise malfunctioned. Neither Bombing Two nor Torpedo Two took any losses.

While the *Lexington*'s strike planes worked over the ships in the harbor, Thach's four fighters at Salamaua did their job forcing the Japanese Army troops there under cover. Together with his wingman Doc Sellstrom and his second section (Butch O'Hare and Marion Dufilho), Thach strafed likely gun positions and made dummy runs to draw fire away from the vulnerable TBDs. For a time his division cruised at 8,000 feet over the target area. Enemy antiaircraft guns soon found their altitude and peppered the vicinity with black shell bursts. Thach descended to 5,000 feet and the bursts followed, but the VF-3 skipper quickly noted the Japanese gunners did not allot sufficient lead for the swiftly moving F4Fs. Fortunately the bursts always fell behind them. As the ships maneuvered wildly in the harbor, VF-3's 1st Division did its part as well. Thach's troops strafed a couple of destroyers and a small minesweeper, an experience that left Thach highly impressed with the firepower, even against ships, of his .50-caliber Brownings.

During the first phase of the attack, the Japanese managed to get only one aircraft into the fight, a Nakajima E8N2 Type 95 reconnaissance floatplane [DAVE] from the *Kiyokawa Maru* Air Unit. The little, open-cockpit, float biplane was armed only with two 7.7-mm machine guns (one fixed forward, a second flexible in the rear cockpit), but its aggressive crew was not at all reluctant to take on far more powerful aircraft. First the nimble floatplane charged after TBDs that had separated to go after ships south of Lae. In response, four VS-2 SBDs tried to corner the wily Japanese, but the slippery Type 95 evaded them all. Not only that, but the Japanese got in their own licks as well, flying, according to the Americans, with "determination and valor."[4] They rashly challenged the four F4Fs of Gayler's division, as the fighters worked over the *Yūbari*. Gayler himself discovered the enemy aircraft just ahead of him, evidently as it evaded fire from his teammate Vorse. "Noel got a glimpse of him for a few seconds, lifted his nose just enough to shoot down the Jap, then kept on with his own strafing."[5] After destroying the only Japanese plane they saw, Fighting Three moved out to cover the rendezvous of the strike planes and escort them out of the area. Now it was the *Yorktown's* turn to attack.

The *Yorktown's* strike group had no trouble crossing the forbidding Owen Stanleys and first reached the target area about fifteen minutes after the *Lexington's* planes had begun the attack. Although launched last, the VF-42 escort fighters soon caught up with the rest of the group. The fighters were organized as follows:

1st Division
Lt. Cdr. Oscar Pederson, USN, Commanding
Ens. Harry B. Gibbs, A-V(N)
Lieut. (jg) William N. Leonard, USN
Ens. William W. Barnes, A-V(N)
Lieut (jg) Richard G. Crommelin, USN
Ens. Richard L. Wright, A-V(N)

3rd Division
Lieut. Vincent F. McCormack, USN, flight officer
Ens. Walter A. Haas, A-V(N)
Lieut (jg) Brainard T. Macomber, A-V(N)
Ens. Edgar R. Bassett, A-V(N)

As the ten fighters neared the target area, one of the pilots, Edgar Bassett, faced a personal moment of truth. Ordinarily a happy-go-lucky individual and expert card player, "Red Dog" Bassett had for a long time firmly convinced himself he would not live past his twenty-eighth birthday. Then came the announcement of the strike on 10 March and the pilots who would fly. The tenth of March happened to *be* Bassett's twenty-eighth birthday, and he felt certain he would not return from the mission. Before takeoff, he solemnly left instructions as to the disposition of his personal effects.

Fighting Forty-two checked out the battle area, but like Thach's pilots before them, Pederson's escorts found little for the fighters to do. They patrolled over Lae, then Salamaua to make sure there was no air opposition, then finally separated by sections to strafe. Some of the VF-42 pilots worked over many small boats in Salamaua harbor, evidently trying to rescue personnel from the sunken army transport *Yokohama Maru*. Pederson and his wingman went low to strafe the airfield at Lae. Pulling out of a run, VF-42's skipper realized that things were far from right with his Grumman, whose engine starting shaking so violently that he feared it would fail. Japanese bases on shore and the dense jungle inland did not offer inviting spots for a crash landing.

Meanwhile the strike planes of the *Yorktown* Air Group reached the target area. First to attack were the seventeen SBDs of Armstrong's Bombing Five. Beginning at 0950, they went after the light cruiser *Yūbari* and some of the other vessels which had got under way. Next to arrive was Scouting Five, at 1005 concentrating its attacks on the transports off Lae. Torpedo Five appeared fifteen minutes later. Taylor's horizontal bombers selected as their target the converted seaplane tender *Kiyokawa Maru* 25 miles east of Lae. The TBDs made their bomb runs from between 13,000 and 14,000 feet and each dropped two 500-lb. bombs. They hit the seaplane tender at least once, inflicting what the Japanese later described as "medium damage," enough anyway to send her back to the homeland for repairs. A second *Kiyokawa Maru* Type 95 floatplane managed to intercept the TBDs and put a few holes in them. Because it dived away radically, VT-5's rear gunners thought they disabled the enemy plane. Not long after Torpedo Five attacked, the Army's contribution to the Lae–Salamaua counterattack arrived. Eight Boeing B-17E Flying Fortress heavy bombers from the 19th Bombardment Group flew up from their base at Townsville and bombed the ships in the harbor, claiming several hits. Following them were eight RAAF Hudson medium bombers from Port Moresby to complete the attack.

Thach described the raid well from the Allied point of view:

> This whole fight was a sort of picnic because we had no air opposition to speak of. We destroyed everything worth while in the vicinity.[6]

American claims amounted to five transports, two heavy cruisers, one light cruiser, and one destroyer sunk, with an auxiliary minesweeper also sent to the bottom. They also reported heavy damage to two other destroyers, two gun boats, and one seaplane tender—all for the loss of one SBD. Actually they sank three transports (the *Kongō Maru*, *Tenyō Maru,* and *Yokohama Maru*), caused "medium damage" to the transport *Kokai Maru* and the seaplane tender *Kiyokawa Maru,* and put some holes in the *Yūbari*, the minelayer *Tsugaru,* and the destroyers *Asanagi* and *Yūnagi.* Japanese casualties totaled 130 killed and 245 wounded.

On the flight back, the only pilot in real difficulty was Pederson, nursing his vibrating F4F-3 over the Owen Stanleys. If his engine let go and he had to bail out, Pederson would have very little in the way of survival gear. For this mission, the *Yorktown* had provided each pilot with a "meat cleaver and a small bottle of aspirin,"[7] little consolation indeed for facing the Papuan rain forest. Later the Navy would develop survival equipment and doctrine to a high art. Fortunately for Pederson, his F4F had enough in it to bring him back to the carrier safe and sound. Examination showed the aircraft had actually bent a strut in the engine mount.

While the strike planes made their attacks, events at the task force were routine. The *Yorktown* had six fighters aloft on CAP, while the *Lexington* served as relief. Lovelace took six VF-3 fighters aloft at 0937. Visibility was extremely good, at least 50 miles from altitude. At 1015, the ships spotted the eight B-17s en route to Lae–Salamaua. Thirty-five minutes later, the *Lexington* began landing the first of the strike planes. Brown's carriers by noon were withdrawing at 20 knots to safer waters to the southeast.

The Japanese were not through with the raiders, even if there was not much they could do to retaliate. Late that morning, 24th Air Flotilla sent a special search of three Kawanishi Type 97 flying boats to search the waters south of Port Moresby. Toward dusk, the *Yorktown*'s radar detected a bogey 26 miles distant. Both carriers prepared to scramble fighters, but the contact disappeared from the scope without closing. The ships supposed the bogey to have been an RAAF aircraft flying out of Port Moresby. Actually it was one of the Type 97 flying boats. At 1720, its crew radioed Rabaul with the report of an American carrier task force in the Gulf of Papua bearing 250 degrees and 90 miles from Port Moresby. It comprised one *Saratoga*-class carrier, two heavy cruisers, and five destroyers on course 120 degrees, speed 18 knots. Regretfully for 24th Air Flotilla, bad weather was closing in, and it was too late in the day to launch a daylight strike. The Americans had eluded retribution that day.

In his action report, Brown estimated the impact of the raid upon the enemy:

> It seems probable that our appearance off Rabaul on February 20 and our overwhelming attack at Salamaua on March 10 caused them to proceed with caution quite apart from the losses they have suffered in ships.[8]

That, at least was his hope. Pearl Harbor was not so sanguine. On 11 March, War Plans Division recorded: "Even with the damage inflicted, it is doubtful if the enemy will be greatly retarded."[9] The Pacific Fleet analysts were wrong. Even if the pilots had not sunk near all they claimed, they still inflicted on the Imperial Navy by far its heaviest losses since the outbreak of the war. The raid manhandled many of the ships that South Seas Force needed for its amphibious ventures and also raised anxiety in the Japanese high command. Vice Admiral Inoue postponed the invasions of Port Moresby and Tulagi for one month, and he had to importune Combined Fleet for carrier support. The Battle of the Coral Sea loomed closer.

In general, the commanders were pleased with the conduct of the 10 March air strike. Sherman noted the risk in flying the treacherous Owen Stanley mountains and recommended that this type of operation not be undertaken very often. Principal material deficiencies included the fogging of SBD bomb sights during dives from the cool high altitudes down to the much warmer, humid air near sea level. Some pilots made their attacks virtually blind. The *Yorktown* aircraft suffered numerous radio malfunctions, greatly hampering communications within the strike group. Not very reliable even under ideal conditions, aircraft radios largely succumbed to high humidity.

Regarding the fighters, both Brown and Sherman in their reports emphasized that the F4F-3 Wildcat's short combat radius compelled them to take the carriers closer to the shoreline than they would have liked. Both urged that droppable fuel tanks be developed to increase the radius of action. During the attack, Thach's Fighting Three carried light bombs to act as fighter bombers and flak suppression in the first wave of the attack. All of this, of course, was in line with CinCPac's recommendation that the fighters support the bombers by attacking airfields and gun positions. Thach, for one, did not like the idea of loading down F4Fs and using them as bombers. He thought they got away with it this time because no Japanese fighters were present. Thach and his crew believed that fighters should act as fighters, particularly when there was a chance for stiff air opposition. The 30-lb. bombs, they felt, were only token gestures; as Gayler later complained, "When we went over to Salamaua we carried along those little dinky bombs and they did no damage."[10] That in their eyes was the main problem—the inadequacy of the F4F Wildcat when used as a fighter bomber. For the power of the .50-caliber machine guns, however, Thach had the greatest respect. With their Brownings he thought a squadron of fighters capable of repelling an attack by a whole flotilla of destroyers.

WITHDRAWAL AND THE *LEXINGTON* HOME

The eleventh of March saw the two carrier task forces continuing to withdraw southeastward into the Coral Sea. The *Yorktown* took over routine aviation duties

(CAP, searches, and inner air patrol), while the *Lexington* flew two SBDs to Townsville to deliver by "pigeon post" a number of despatches for relay by land-based transmitters. Bogey blips appeared on the radar scopes, but none approached the ships. The next day came formal orders from CinCPac instructing Brown to provision Task Force 17 and return his Task Force 11 to Pearl Harbor. The *Lexington* was needed up north. On 13 March, another routine day, the task force happened upon a Curtiss SOC floatplane riding the waves, the same *San Francisco* aircraft lost five days before. The pilot said he planned to take advantage of the steady southeasterly trades and thereby drift close to Australia, close enough to make it with such gasoline as he had left.

Rear Admiral Crace's cruisers and destroyers arrived as scheduled at the 14 March rendezvous, bringing with him precious cargo, the fleet oilers *Neosho* and *Kaskaskia*. There were also tidings that the cruisers had lost five Curtiss SOCs two days before when all had failed to return from a search—heavy losses indeed. Brown arranged for a carrier search to try to find them, but the SBDs turned up no trace of the five missing aircraft.

Because it was obvious that Task Force 17 would remain in the South Pacific for at least one operation, Fletcher and Buckmaster reviewed their aircraft status, devoting particular attention to Fighting Forty-two. Pederson had seventeen F4F-3 Wildcats on strength, but three had unaccountably developed leaks in their self-sealing fuel tanks—effectively putting them out of commission until repaired. Lieut. (jg) Arthur J. Brassfield, VF-42's engineer officer, huddled with his chiefs and tried to fathom the reason why the tanks had gone defective. On 14 March he submitted a preliminary report on the matter, noting that the particular tanks were of the "cemented type" (seams glued together rather than vulcanized).[1] The tank problem would loom big in April. Since CominCh had instructed Task Force 11 to do everything in its power to make Fletcher's ships combat-ready, the *Yorktown* proposed to trade two of its overtime fighters for fresher F4Fs from Fighting Three and also requested additional SBDs and TBDs. In response, Sherman agreed to "sell" no fewer than twelve aircraft (six fighters, five dive bombers, and one torpedo plane) to the Yorktowners.

At 1314 on 14 March, the *Lexington* landed the two aged VF-42 F4Fs plus five TBDs carrying ten pilots to fly the trade planes. While their new mounts were being readied on deck, the VF-42 pilots enjoyed the hospitality of Thach and company in the VF-3 ready room. There they recounted their experiences on 20 February and swapped accounts of the Lae–Salamaua raid. About 90 minutes after, the *Lexington* was ready to launch the seventeen aircraft for the flight over to the *Yorktown*. It would not be an uneventful hop.

Flying one of the newly purchased Grummans, Walt Haas was amazed to find just after takeoff that his engine cut out and popped ominously. When he lost power, Haas was cruising at 400 feet about a mile from the *Lex*. At first he thought the main fuel tank was empty and switched to his reserve, but the engine died anyway. As the Grumman settled toward the water, he lowered his flaps and made at 1456 what Thach thought an "excellent water landing."[2] After impact, Haas's Grumman nosed up, then started to sink. Though stunned by a head injury from the gunsight mount, he quickly sprang out of the cockpit and broke out the life raft. Soon the plane guard destroyer, the *Dale,* had him on board. For Haas, ditching was becoming too much a regular thing; this was his second in two months. The other five Grummans made it to the *Yorktown* without any trouble, but as Bill Leonard later wrote, "This contretemps rather chilled any warm regard held for VF-3 in this swap."[3]

The loss of F4F-3 Bureau Number 4009 also gave Burt Stanley an unscheduled thrill. That aircraft, F-5, had been his faithful mount until his skipper sold it to Fighting Forty-two. Stanley thought the VF-42 pilot must have "offended her."[4] Fighting Three's experts put forward the theory that Haas had used too much manifold pressure, but VF-42's trouble board absolved Haas of any blame. They thought the fuel system was in some way defective. (The squadron would have much more experience with fuel systems in April, and that not to its liking.) The final endorsement by the authorities at Pearl ascribed the loss of 4009 to particles in the fuel lines. The mishap left VF-42 with twenty F4Fs on strength.

His ardent desire for combat still unfulfilled, Crace departed that evening bound for Suva. On 15 March, Task Force 11 fueled from the *Neosho*, while Fletcher's ships drained the *Kaskaskia*. The *Yorktown* had the duty until early afternoon, then secured from flight operations. That day, surgeons operated on VF-42's Lieut. (jg) Roy M. Plott, treating him for a painful fistula. Ill for the past few months, Plott had done little flying. After the successful operation he began a slow convalescence. Also that day, a whaleboat from the *Dale* returned Haas to the *Yorktown*. Now a somewhat battered "expert" in ditching Grumman Wildcats, he set about designing a special harness to protect his tall frame from smashing into the jury-rigged, do-it-yourself gunsight bracket that the VF-42 engineers had been forced to develop to go along with the new bulletproof windshields in the F4Fs. The squadron clamored for issue shoulder harnesses, but none was forthcoming from the Bureau of Aeronautics.[5]

Refueling finally completed the morning of 16 March, Fletcher's Task Force 17 steamed northwest toward the New Hebrides to continue with the mission of guarding the line of communication between the United States and Australia. Fletcher had with him the *Yorktown*, the heavy cruisers *Astoria* and *Portland*, and five destroyers with which to patrol the Coral Sea and assault the Japanese should they boil out of their bastion in the Bismarcks. Mercifully, the Yorktowners could not know there would be two and a half months of cruising in tropical waters capped by a desperate battle before they would limp back to Pearl Harbor.

Heading northeast the afternoon of 16 March, Brown's Task Force 11 with the *Lexington*, three heavy cruisers, six destroyers and a fleet oiler shaped course for Pearl. During the voyage the weather was generally excellent. Fighting Three did relatively little flying, offering the opportunity for some rest and a chance to catch up with the inevitable reports and paperwork. As executive officer, Lovelace wrote the citations for VF-3 pilots recommended for decorations. He also put Thach in for a Navy Cross for the 20 February action, and Sherman fully agreed. Thach himself was busy with another award recommendation. The senior officers decided that O'Hare's heroism, quick thinking, and excellent shooting on 20 February had earned him the Medal of Honor. Thach fervently concurred, and compiled the necessary supporting documents. O'Hare discovered what was happening:

> Daily Butch begged Thach not to do it. "It'll only mess things up," he insisted. "We've got no use for medals out here. I only did a job. You shot down four Nips yourself that day. I don't want to be recommended for any medal."[6]

O'Hare found that stopping the U.S. Navy once it made up its mind was a lot harder than repulsing a Japanese air attack.

On 22 March, the *Lexington* began a series of training exercises for her air group. Strike aircraft simulated an attack on the task force, while Fighting Three got in some fixed gunnery practice by shooting at towed sleeves. Sherman repeated the exercises on the two succeeding days. On 26 March as Task Force 11 neared port, the *Lexington* launched her air group at 0730 to fly to fields on Oahu. Fighting Three bade goodby to the grand old ship and headed for NAS Pearl Harbor. There they were surprised to see revetments now provided for their planes. Pilots from other squadrons crowded in to congratulate the *Lex*'s men for their successes in the South Pacific. The senior pilots reported to headquarters to brief the admirals. Lovelace found out he was to receive a squadron command—that was good. However, he was disappointed to learn his orders sent him stateside to Scouting Ten (VS-10) in the soon-to-be-formed Carrier Replacement Air Group Ten. He really wanted a fighting squadron and still worked to get one. Later that day, Fighting Three drew a week's leave at the Royal Hawaiian Hotel. There O'Hare faced an ordeal even worse than Japanese bullets—dealing with reporters and radio commentators. Usually he deferred to Thach at his side.

The *Lexington* herself arrived in port late on the morning of 26 March. Sherman took her to the Repair Basin for a short overhaul and removal of the superfluous and weighty eight-inch gun turrets located fore and aft of her island—relics of a bygone era. Now the *Lex* had need of more antiaircraft guns to help her survive in Japanese-infested waters. Her first voyage to the South Pacific was highly memorable. However, she had another date with destiny in the Coral Sea.

CHAPTER 8

The Tokyo Raid

PRELIMINARIES—INTRODUCING THE GRUMMAN F4F-4 WILDCAT

Lt. Cdr. Paul Ramsey's Fighting Two spent February 1942 ashore at NAS Kaneohe getting acquainted with their Grumman F4F Wildcats, these aircraft having replaced the obsolescent Brewster F2A-3 Buffaloes the squadron had taken to war. On board the *Lexington,* Lt. Cdr. Thach's Fighting Three had taken Fighting Two's place for what had proved to be an event-filled cruise to the South Pacific. Ramsey's squadron was working to recover from the devastating blow of the detachment of Lt. Cdr. Flatley and nine other experienced pilots to ride the *Saratoga* back to the West Coast. During February, Ramsey gradually accumulated fighters, helped mainly by the shipment of Grummans brought over on board the *Yorktown.* By the end of the month, Ramsey had garnered eighteen Grumman F4Fs for his sixteen pilots.

On 2 March, Ens. George F. Markham, Jr. reported for duty to AirBatFor headquarters at Pearl Harbor. His original orders had earmarked him to Fighting Forty-two, but that squadron was on board the *Yorktown* in the distant South Pacific. Paul Ramsey needed pilots, so headquarters detailed Markham for temporary duty with Fighting Two. He would be the first reserve officer to serve with the famed squadron. Ramsey welcomed him cordially. Fresh from advanced training at Norfolk, Markham was surprised to see himself cast as an expert on the F4F-3 Wildcat. In fact, he had logged twice as much time in that type as anyone in the squadron. The day after he reported, Markham flew his first training mission with Fighting Two. It was an interesting experience:

> The way I was taught to fly the F4F at ACTG was to conserve the engine, but in the squadron the skipper had a fighter and he was going to have his outfit fly it like a fighter and 17 of them did. Being tail end Charlie of crack-the-whip was enough for a greenie who could hardly join up properly without flying at higher MP and RPM settings than I expected. Anyway I kept them in sight and everyone was very nice to me when I got down, which was double the incentive to be more on the ball next time.[1]

Markham did well with the squadron. Ramsey made him his wingman and later appointed him acting gunnery officer as well.

Ramsey continued the regimen of training flights sandwiched in between the usual dawn and dusk alerts. On 4 March, the squadron took delivery of the first Grumman F4F-4 Wildcats, eight of them, to reach the Hawaiian Islands. The F4F-

4 was the new folding wing version of the Wildcat. On 10 March, the squadron had a total of twenty-five aircraft on the books (nine F4F-3As, eight F4F-3s, and eight F4F-4s), but eight F4F-3s were being held for Fighting Six. The next day Ramsey took Fighting Two over to the naval air station on Maui for two weeks of antisubmarine patrols off Kahului.

The second week of March found the *Enterprise* at Pearl and her aviators enjoying leave at the Royal Hawaiian Hotel. CinCPac expected that Halsey's Task Force 16 should be ready to depart about 21 March in order to relieve Fletcher's Task Force 17 with the *Yorktown* in the South Pacific. In that case, Fletcher would start north about 5 April. On 13 March, however, Nimitz received a rather strange communication from CominCh in Washington. In it King specified that Halsey's Task Force 16 be reorganized to include the *Enterprise*'s sister ship, the new carrier *Hornet* (CV-8), then en route from the East Coast to the Pacific. Halsey was to remain on standby to fly to the West Coast when the *Hornet* reached California. Somewhat puzzled, Nimitz replied the next day, noting that King's plans would conflict with his intention to relieve Task Force 17. The mystery was clarified on 19 March, when Captain Donald B. Duncan, CominCh staff aviator, arrived at Pearl to conduct a special briefing. He elucidated King's top secret plan to bomb Tokyo and other Japanese cities with Army North American B-25 Mitchell medium bombers carried on board the *Hornet*. A grandstand play, it appealed to President Roosevelt. The upshot was that Task Force 16 had to remain at Pearl until the *Hornet* got out to the Pacific. Meanwhile, Task Force 17 would have to persevere south of the equator.

After a glorious leave, Fighting Six was back in business on 17 March at Ford Island. Personnel changes had taken place in the interval. On 12 March orders had arrived naming Lt. Cdr. Corbin as commanding officer of Bombing Ten (VB-10) in the new Carrier Replacement Air Group Ten at San Diego. Jim Gray stepped up to acting executive officer of Fighting Six. The squadron on 17 March took charge of eight F4F-3s from Fighting Two and dealt off most of the F4F-3As. Three days later, the squadron with nineteen F4Fs on strength (fourteen F4F-3s and five F4F-3As) began flying alerts for the Army.

The big day for Fighting Six was 21 March. In place of Howard Young, Wade McClusky as senior squadron commander fleeted up to command of the *Enterprise* Air Group. In his place as skipper of Fighting Six, he nominated and Captain Murray endorsed Gray, who as a member of the Academy's class of 1936 was very junior for a squadron command. His appointment still had to be approved by the Bureau of Navigation, but as of 21 March, he led Fighting Six. Taking his place as executive officer was Roger Mehle, a 1937 Academy graduate who had earned his wings in the summer of 1940. He had been with the squadron for about a year and a half. Becoming the flight officer was one of the several 1938 Academy classmen in the squadron, Lieut. (jg) Rhonald ("Buster") Hoyle. Hoyle's wings had come in early 1941, and he had served briefly with Fighting Five before joining Fighting Six. All told, it was quite a shift of youth in place of experience.

Once more the *Enterprise* made ready to sail, but no definite departure date came through. On 23 March, Fighting Six moved over to the marines at Ewa, where they could work more gunnery training flights into the schedule. Com-AirBatFor decided to expand Fighting Six from a nominal strength of eighteen to the new established strength of twenty-seven fighters. To accomplish this, Gray needed quite a few more pilots and aircraft, especially F4F-4s with folding wings to save space on board ship. The only readily available source of seasoned carrier fighter pilots was Ramsey's Fighting Two, just returned to Kaneohe from its stint on Maui. On 28 March, AirBatFor headquarters passed the word to Ramsey transferring ten enlisted pilots (NAPs), the eight F4F-4s, and twenty-five men for temporary duty with Fighting Six on board the *Enterprise*. The ten pilots were:

Howell M. Sumrall, AMM1c (NAP), USN
Doyle C. Barnes, AMM1c (NAP), USN
Julius A. Achten, AMM1c (NAP), USN
Clayton Allard, AMM1c (NAP), USN
Tom F. Cheek, AMM1c (NAP), USN
Beverly W. Reid, AMM1c (NAP), USN
Thomas W. Rhodes, ARM1c (NAP), USN
William H. Warden, AMM1c (NAP), USN
Howard S. Packard, AMM1c (NAP), USN
Homer W. Carter, AOM1c (NAP), USN

About half the pilots were old VF-2 hands; the rest had joined since the start of the war. Another example of robbing Peter to pay Paul, their departure left Fighting Two with only seven pilots on strength.

Also on 28 March, Fighting Six took their first look at the Grumman F4F-4, and they would be the first to take that variant into action. It is worth a digression here to examine the development of the F4F-4.[2] The F4F-3 and its cousin the F4F-3A were fixed wing fighters, and the Navy well knew the advantages of having a service fighter whose wings could fold. With the room saved for stowage, one could operate significantly more fighters from a carrier. In 1939, the Bureau of Aeronautics approached Grumman to design an F4F-3 with the folding wings feature, and in March 1940, they awarded a contract for the prototype. The Royal Navy, likewise a purchaser of F4Fs (Martlets), was also eager to have folding wing fighters for its flattops, which had even less aircraft storage than the Americans.

The story of how Leroy Grumman used paperclips and erasers to work out the basic principle for folding the F4F's wings is well known. Instead of folding straight up, the wings devised by Grumman first rotated 90 degrees while folding back along the fuselage, a compact and highly efficient system. In April 1941, the Grumman corporation completed conversion of a production F4F-3 (BuNo. 1897) into a folding wing type designated the XF4F-4. This aircraft sported hydraulic gear to fold the outer wing panels parallel to the fuselage, but otherwise it was identical to the F4F-3. Gross weight was 7,489 lbs., about 400 lbs. more than a standard F4F-3. Neither type as yet had pilot armor or self-sealing fuel tanks installed. The Navy in May accepted delivery of the XF4F-4 and assigned it to Fighting Forty-two, then working up with F4F-3s at NAS Norfolk. The aircraft then bounced around to other squadrons, and at the start of the war was with Fighting Three at NAS San Diego.

On 11 December 1941, the Fleet Air Tactical Unit at NAS San Diego issued a report on the XF4F-4, based on earlier tests, which noted that in comparison with the F4F-3, the folding wing version was "perceptibly more sluggish in flight than the F4F-3 on account of extra weight." Nevertheless, the FATU concluded that as a "compromise," the XF4F-4 was still a "very satisfactory carrier fighter."[3] On 6–7 January on board the *Saratoga*, Thach's Fighting Three conducted further tests of the XF4F-4.[4] Under the circumstances, the XF4F-4's gross weight jumped almost 300 lbs. to 7,750 lbs. with the installation of pilot armor, full ammunition, and fuel (160 gallons). Fighting Three thought the aircraft "comparatively inferior to the F4F-3" and strongly recommended that the production model gross no more than 7,500 lbs. Other reports concluded that the hydraulic wing-folding mechanism could

Two F4F-4s from VF-6, 17 Apr. 1942, well illustrate the folding wing feature of that model Grumman. (NA 80-G-16961.)

also be dispensed with, as plane handlers could fold the wings by hand, saving more weight. So far so good. The fighter pilots would accept a folding wing F4F-4 otherwise identical to the F4F-3, but the version that ended up in the fleet turned out to be different in other, less acceptable ways.

Simultaneously with its American contracts, the Grumman corporation negotiated with the British Admiralty to produce F4Fs for the Fleet Air Arm, the F4F being called the Martlet in British service. In early 1941, Grumman contracted to produce 100 fighters, to be known as Martlet IIs. This aircraft was a variant of the F4F-3A with a Pratt & Whitney "Twin Wasp" S3C4G engine (R-1830-90) and single-stage supercharger. The first ten Martlett II fighters produced, beginning in March 1941, had fixed wings, but the rest were to incorporate the folding wing feature. The British were also unhappy with having only four Browning .50-caliber guns, and desired an increase of firepower to a minimum of six. Together with the Grumman designers but without input from BuAer, they developed a six-gun battery for the Martlet II. The new installation offered 240 rounds for each of the six guns (enough for eighteen seconds of fire) as opposed to the F4F-3's four guns with 450 rounds per weapon (thirty-four seconds of fire). The six-gun feature was also considerably heavier than the old four-gun battery. Meanwhile, Grumman perfected the wing-folding mechanism, and beginning in July 1941 produced folding wing Martlet II fighters with the six-gun installation. The gross weight of the Martlet II with factory fitted armor and self-sealing fuel tanks was 7,512 lbs., just a bit heavier than the XF4F-4 without armor or leakproof tanks.

June 1941 saw the Grumman corporation faced with two big contracts for producing folding wing F4Fs/Martlets. The British had on order the 90 remaining Martlet IIs and at least 150 Martlet IVs, identical to the II except for substitution in the IV of the lighter Wright Cyclone R-1820-40B nine-cylinder radial engine. The U.S. Navy ordered 436 F4F-4s and expected to contract for production of many more. To simplify production of the Martlets and the F4F-4s, Grumman requested BuAer permission to use the six-gun battery in both versions. Within the Bureau, considerable debate ensued over the change, but the experts in Washington agreed with the six-gun installation on the basis of superior British combat wisdom and the need for standardization to ease production. They did not, however, consult the fighting squadron skippers, most of whom would have vetoed the change, thinking they could destroy enemy aircraft with four guns and desiring maximum ammunition capacity for sustained shooting. They were satisfied with the F4F-3's four-gun battery as it was.

The new F4F-4 Wildcats with folding wings, the six-gun battery, and the Pratt & Whitney R-1830-86 engine with two-stage supercharger (the same as in the later F4F-3s) entered quantity production late that year, five being delivered in 1941 to the U.S. Navy. They also featured factory-installed armor plate and self-sealing fuel tanks, which with the six guns and the hand-activated wing-folding mechanism raised gross weight for the F4F-4 to 7,975 lbs. That was more than 700 lbs. above the F4F-3A and 500 lbs. over the F4F-3 when both of those types likewise sported armor and leakproof tanks. Compared to the F4F-3 with the same powerplant, the heavier F4F-4 naturally experienced a drop in performance. Nominal performance figures for the F4F-4 were as follows: Top speed was 278 knots (320 mph) at 18,800 feet. Initial climb rate was 2,190 feet per minute; time to 10,000 feet was 5.6 minutes (average of 1,786 feet per minute), to 20,000 feet 12.4 minutes (average 1,613 feet per minute). In acceleration and general handling it proved less perky than the F4F-3 because of increased weight. Official range was considerably under the other two variants, 720 miles at 140 knots cruise. This gave the F4F-4 an effective combat radius of perhaps 175 miles.

First deliveries of the F4F-4 went in early 1942 to fighting squadrons on the East Coast. On 4 February 1942, the Bureau of Aeronautics despatched letters to Vice Admiral Halsey (ComAirBatFor) and Rear Admiral A. B. Cook (Commander, Aircraft, Atlantic Fleet) describing the F4F-4 mainly in terms of weight limitations.[5] In the letters, BuAer chief Rear Admiral John H. Towers provided an interesting look at the Bureau's rationale for approving the F4F-4. Towers noted that the original F4F design called for a gross weight of about 6,000 lbs., and that perhaps 7,000 lbs. seemed about the safe limit for carrier landings. According to BuAer, the F4F-4's "normal" operating weight should be 7,345 lbs., with the aircraft loaded with 110 gallons of fuel (instead of 144) and four guns provided with only 200 rounds per gun (instead of 240 rounds). The two outboard guns under "normal" operating conditions would not be loaded! Towers explained:

> The airplane has provisions for six guns. This is due to the necessity for standardizing the wings of the Navy F4F-4 airplanes and the British Martlet. The extra two guns on the F4F-4 are provided as an alternate load for use with reduced fuel or as an overload item only when special circumstances demand. The British Martlet II has a Wright R-1820-40 engine which is single stage and hence lighter in weight. This permits the use of six guns by them as a normal load. By installing six guns with all ammunition (1440 rounds) and by filling the fuel tanks to capacity (144 gallons) the weight of the F4F-4 airplane becomes 7896 lbs.

Halsey on 10 February forwarded copies of the BuAer letter to all of his fighting squadrons, where its receipt must have caused some puzzlement.[6] The pilots all knew the only way to operate a fighter from a carrier in combat was to carry all of the fuel and ammunition it could hold. No one wanted to fight with only two-thirds the fuel and less than half the ammunition carried in an F4F-3! If combat was not "special circumstances" as mentioned in Towers's letter, what was? In essence, BuAer in the interests of production schedules and inter-Allied amity had provided the Navy's fighter pilots with an airplane they would not like, at least at first!

Fighting Six spent the last few days of March learning about the new model Grumman they would take into battle. They were not impressed: "The planes are like a TBD with a fish,"[7] a grave insult. On 1 April, Gray led a division of four F4F-4s out to the *Enterprise* at sea for training exercises. He observed the mock torpedo attack on the carrier by Torpedo Six, then landed on board to demonstrate to the air department the features of the F4F-4. That day the squadron took delivery of fifteen F4F-4s just arrived from the West Coast. This was the beginning of a big exchange of aircraft, so Fighting Six would have all available F4F-4s. Gray turned over most of his F4F-3s to Fighting Three and ended up with twenty-three F4F-4s and four F4F-3s. Fighting Six was the first carrier fighting squadron to attain the recommended operating strength of twenty-seven airplanes.

On 3 April with the *Enterprise* back in port, Fighting Six shifted back to NAS Pearl Harbor to install new gear and commission the factory-fresh planes. Three days later Gray shot off a rocket to Halsey offering his opinion of the Grumman F4F-4 fighter.[8] The performance of the folding wing Wildcat was "exceedingly unsatisfactory." The weight, he felt, simply was too much for the available horsepower, a fact most detrimental to the aircraft's climb and maneuverability. He noted that the F4F-4 had the "feel of a fully loaded torpedo plane." In tests, VF-6 pilots discovered that the climb rate of a fully loaded F4F-4 was only 1,500 feet per minute up to 15,000 feet. Thereafter even that anemic climb rate fell off drastically to 600 feet per minute at 22,000 feet of altitude. Gray found it took almost forty minutes and nearly half of the fuel supply to coax an F4F-4 up to 32,000 feet. Certainly, he added, the fighter would be fine against unescorted bombers and other "cold meat," but what about the seemingly magical Zero in light of claims for the climb rate, speed, and maneuverability of the vaunted Mitsubishi product? Gray requested swift replacement of the F4F-4 with a version sporting a more powerful engine.

The *Enterprise*'s veteran skipper George Murray fully agreed with the opinions of VF-6. He contributed an endorsement to Gray's letter that stated flatly: "The F4F-4 is greatly inferior to the latest Japanese fighters."[9] Murray further delineated what was the dominant idea among U.S. naval fighter tacticians:

> Under no circumstances should our fighter pilots in F4F-4 permit themselves to become engaged in tactics involving 'dog fights' with enemy fighters. Until a fighter of greatly increased performance becomes available, 'hit-and-run' tactics against any enemy opposition appear to offer the greatest probability of successful combat. Against Japanese 00 and 01 fighters, it is doubtful if the F4F-4 can ever obtain initial altitude advantage which is essential for 'hit-and-run' tactics.[10]

These criticisms of the new fighter even before it saw combat certainly did not make the Bureau of Aeronautics happy.

On 7 April, Fighting Six exchanged one F4F-4 damaged the previous day in a taxiing mishap for another F4F-3. This gave Gray a total of twenty-two F4F-4s and five F4F-3s. All hands worked diligently to get the new planes ready to fight. The same day, the *Enterprise* put the squadron on a two-hour sailing notice. The VF-6 troops were "Rarein to go!"[11] The *Enterprise* would soon be involved in a new operation, this time with the carrier *Hornet,* from whose deck flew Fighting Squadron Eight.

THE ADVENT OF FIGHTING EIGHT

The last naval fighting squadron to be formed before the outbreak of the war was Fighting Squadron Eight (VF-8), part of the *Hornet* Air Group intended for the new flattop of the same name. Launched in December 1940 at Newport News ship yard near Norfolk, the *Hornet* (CV-8) was a slightly bigger sister of the *Yorktown* and the *Enterprise*, displacing 29,100 tons at full war load. The Navy expected to commission her in the fall of 1941. Her prospective commanding officer was Captain Marc A. Mitscher, then assistant chief of the Bureau of Aeronautics and a pioneer naval aviator. Meanwhile in August 1941, pilots with postings to the nascent Fighting Eight began gathering at NAS Norfolk, and the squadron was commissioned on 2 September.[1]

Fighting Eight's skipper was Lt. Cdr. Samuel G. Mitchell, age thirty-seven, known familiarly as "Pat." He graduated in 1927 from the Naval Academy and in July 1930 qualified as a naval aviator. His first squadron duty came in battleship observation floatplanes, where he spent nearly three years before transferring in June 1933 to Patrol Two (VP-2F) operating large flying boats out of NAS Coco Solo, Canal Zone. A year later he became a student in the postgraduate course for line officers at the Naval Academy, and in September 1935, upon graduation, he reported to Scouting Four (VS-4B), first on board the venerable *Langley*, then later the *Saratoga*. In 1937 he joined Patrol Seven (VP-7F) working from Cdr. Mitscher's seaplane tender *Wright* in the Pacific, and again flew large flying boats. From June 1938 until the summer of 1941, Mitchell worked at the Bureau of Aeronautics in Washington, where he was more concerned with theoretical than practical aspects of naval aviation. In July 1941 he was promoted to lieutenant commander, and Mitscher brought him along from BuAer to take command of Fighting Eight. Genial and intelligent, Mitchell at times seemed uncomfortable in his role as skipper of a fighting squadron. Other than when he trained as a naval aviator nearly a dozen years before, he had no squadron time in carrier fighters and relatively little carrier service, none of it recent. Taking a totally new squadron and making it into a combat ready team was a formidable task, particularly as Mitchell had had no experience as an executive officer in a squadron.

Fighting Eight's first XO was Lieut. John Raby (USNA 1929). He earned his wings in 1931 and went to fighters (VF-3B) for three years of seasoning on board the old *Langley*. Subsequently he served two separate tours instructing fledgling pilots at NAS Pensacola, the last just before being ordered to Fighting Eight. Raby was a highly experienced, outstanding air leader, but circumstances decreed that he leave VF-8 for his own command before the *Hornet* headed out to the Pacific. Lieut. (jg) Stanley E. Ruehlow became VF-8's flight officer. Originally an enlisted man (and conscious of it apparently, as one VF-8 pilot found him the "stiffest" among the squadron's "trade school" officers),[2] Ruehlow qualified for the Naval Academy Preparatory class, entered Annapolis in 1931, and graduated four years later. Qualifying as a naval aviator in early 1939, he spent two years with Fighting Five on board the *Yorktown* before his posting to Fighting Eight. That summer and fall, seven other experienced pilots reported to the squadron. Two, Lieut. (jg) Fitzhugh L. Palmer, Jr. and Lieut. (jg) Richard Gray, were 1936 Annapolis graduates with fighter experience. Another with good fighter credentials was Ens. John F. Sutherland, A-V(N), who served two years with Fighting Five. Also reporting was a batch of eight ensigns fresh from advanced carrier training at NAS Miami.

Pat Mitchell and troops, the old hands and the rookies, set up shop at Norfolk. Getting airplanes to fly proved rather difficult. That fall saw rapid expansion of the air arm and acute shortages, as the Navy organized the two advanced carrier training groups. In September, the squadron obtained a few F4F-3s, and in early October a shipment of seven F4F-3A hand-me-downs from Fighting Five in the process of converting to -3s. More aircraft trickled in later. On 6 October, Lt. Cdr. Stanhope C. Ring formally commissioned his *Hornet* Air Group (himself becoming "Sea Hag," a play on the acronym of his title as Commander, *Hornet* Air Group or CHAG). The group comprised Fighting Eight, Bombing Eight, Scouting Eight, and Torpedo Eight. The *Hornet* was commissioned two weeks later.

By early November with the *Hornet* in service and working up, Fighting Eight at Norfolk had ten F4Fs and one North American SNJ-3 advanced trainer for instrument work. The young ensigns concentrated on field carrier landing practice, camera gunnery, and sundry other tasks to sharpen their skills as naval fighter pilots. The squadron awaited delivery of live ammunition to permit shooting at towed target sleeves. Sunday 7 December, and the sudden outbreak of war found the *Hornet* and her squadrons still fitting out. In the middle of December, VF-8's ensigns made their first carrier landings on board the *Hornet*, exciting times for all.

Fighting Eight on 23 December embarked on board its new carrier, as the *Hornet* made ready for her shakedown cruise. Her air group was far from combat ready. Fighting Eight with nineteen F4F-3s, two F4F-3As, and two SNJ-3s was in the best shape, but the two dive bombing squadrons had to make do with Curtiss SBC-4 Helldiver biplanes. The torpedo boys still had obsolete SBN-1s as well. Her aircraft snugly hoisted on board, the *Hornet* sailed two days after Christmas on a shakedown cruise southward to the Gulf of Mexico. The green ensigns continued practicing carrier landings, and there were some spectacular accidents. Unfortunately, the *Hornet*'s air department tended to ground rookie aviators when the youngsters fouled up solely because of inexperience. Ironically, her superior officers seemed to expect proficiency without practice, punishing mistakes by restricting flight time desperately needed to gain vital experience. That somewhat demoralized the air group. The *Hornet* returned on 31 January to Norfolk, and her squadrons went ashore.

In early February, Fighting Eight underwent an important change in personnel. Orders detached Lt. Cdr. Raby as executive officer to take command of Fighting Nine in the soon-to-be-formed Carrier Replacement Air Group Nine, also at Norfolk. Taking his place as VF-8's XO was Lieut. Edward J. O'Neill. This posting was a somewhat strange choice, obviously one of expediency, for Eddie O'Neill was the *Hornet*'s senior landing signal officer, an important member of the air department. A 1931 Naval Academy graduate, O'Neill earned his wings in June 1934, then spent nearly two years in VF-6B on board the *Saratoga*. A year in float observation planes followed, then a tour of duty (June 1937–June 1939) as an instructor at NAS Pensacola, where he qualified as an LSO. He practiced his trade on board the *Lexington* until late 1941, when he transferred to the *Hornet*. Thus both skipper and new exec had done little recent flying before joining the squadron, and that was bound to have an impact on combat effectiveness.

Things were beginning to roll regarding the *Hornet*'s departure for the war zone. On 20 February, CominCh ordered the *Hornet*, the heavy cruiser *Vincennes*, the light cruiser *Nashville*, four destroyers, and the fleet oiler *Cimarron* to leave around 1 March for duty in the Pacific. After nearly a month ashore, Fighting Eight returned to the ship on 28 February, and after some delay, the little task force (number 18), sailed on 4 March from Norfolk. The trip south through U-boat–

infested waters was routine, but with very little flying for the fighters. Task Force 18 traversed the Panama Canal on 12 March, then headed north for San Diego, where the aircraft flew ashore and the *Hornet* docked on 20 March.

Along with the rest of the air group, Fighting Eight operated from NAS San Diego on North Island while the *Hornet* was in port. There the squadrons would take delivery of new aircraft and otherwise make themselves ready for battle. Mitchell turned over to the San Diego–based ACTG seventeen elderly F4F-3s for use in training and carrier landing qualification. In return, Fighting Eight drew nineteen factory-fresh F4F-4 Wildcats from NAS San Diego. Bombing Eight and Scouting Eight gratefully exchanged their Curtiss Helldivers for some Douglas SBD-3s, while Torpedo Eight discarded the rest of its biplanes for more TBDs.

Her air group ashore to reequip, the *Hornet* departed on 23 March with a flock of rookie pilots on board ready to try their carrier qualifications before graduating from the advanced carrier training group. That afternoon, they had their chance. One of them, Ens. Frederick Mears, later recorded his impressions:

> I believe that a carrier landing is the most thrilling action sight there is in peacetime. . . . To take a fast plane, heavy with armor plate, machine guns, gas, and sometimes bombs, and set it down on a short, narrow deck requires all the attention and skill of the most experienced pilot. When the pilots have never done it before and are nervous, to say the least, it is that much more spectacular.[3]

Of the five SBDs sent aloft that afternoon, two crashed. Then the fighter pilots took their turns trying to put their tricky Wildcats down on deck. According to Mears, the "most exciting crash" was made by Ens. Robert A. M. Dibb. Bringing in old F4F-3 BuNo. 1848 for his third landing:

> . . . [Dibb] takes the cut, hits wheels first just forward of the ramp, bounces once again, and then crashes squarely into the barrier with the plane still in flight and afire. . . . a bright blanket of flame shoots from the nose over the belly of the plane as it noses up. Dibb literally dives out of the cockpit, hits the wing with his shoulder, and rolls off onto the deck.[4]

Dibb was uninjured, but the plane burned fiercely, setting the flight deck on fire. Fire fighters quickly extinguished the blaze, and young Dibb soon completed his carrier qualification in another aircraft. (Later on Dibb would play a role in the Battle of Midway and acquit himself well.) The next day the fighters tried again, and two of them splashed. The *Hornet* returned on 25 March to San Diego with a batch of (barely) qualified carrier pilots.

The presence of folding wing F4F-4 Wildcats on board the *Hornet* permitted Fighting Eight to go up to the new establishment of twenty-seven fighters, but the squadron had on strength only twenty-two pilots:

Lt. Cdr. Samuel G. Mitchell	USN	USNA 1927
Lieut. Edward J. O'Neill	USN	USNA 1931
Lieut. Stanley E. Ruehlow	USN	USNA 1935
Lieut. Bruce L. Harwood	USN	
Lieut. Fitzhugh L. Palmer, Jr.	USN	USNA 1936
Lieut. Warren W. Ford	USN	USNA 1937
Lieut. (jg) Richard Gray	USN	USNA 1936
Lieut. (jg) Lawrence C. French	USN	
Lieut. (jg) Minuard F. Jennings	USN	
Lieut. (jg) John F. Sutherland	A-V(N)	
Ens. Carlton B. Starkes	A-V(N)	
Ens. James C. Smith	A-V(N)	

Ens. George Formanek	A-V(N)
Ens. Charles Markland Kelly, Jr.	A-V(N)
Ens. Elisha T. Stover	A-V(N)
Ens. Johnny A. Talbot	A-V(N)
Ens. Humphrey L. Tallman	A-V(N)
Ens. John Magda	A-V(N)
Ens. Stephen W. Groves	A-V(N)
Ens. George R. Hill	A-V(N)
Ens. Henry A. Carey, Jr.	A-V(N)
Ens. John E. McInerny, Jr.	A-V(N)

Mitchell had to scrounge additional pilots to man the extra planes slated to arrive. From ACTG Pacific he obtained one pilot, Ens. Richard Z. Hughes, who had orders to Fighting Eight, but then nabbed four more originally slated for Jimmy Thach's Fighting Three once they completed training. The four were Ens. David B. Freeman, Ens. Morrill I. Cook, Jr., Ens. Henry A. Fairbanks, and Ens. Robert S. Merritt. Also joining the squadron was a naval reserve officer who was not an aviator, Lieut. J. H. Carlin, A-V(S). He would take over compiling most of the routine squadron paperwork, part of a program to relieve the pilots of some of their nonflying chores.

On 29 March, Fighting Eight drew an additional eleven F4F-4 Wildcats, giving Mitchell a total of thirty fighters. However, the two dive bombing squadrons between them numbered only twenty-four SBD-3s, and Torpedo Eight had only ten TBDs. The *Hornet* set sail on 30 March from San Diego and steamed northward. She arrived the next day in San Francisco Bay and docked at NAS Alameda. On 1 April, sixteen Army B-25 Mitchell medium bombers were hoisted on board, taking up a good part of the flight deck. Other than to launch fighters in an emergency, the *Hornet* could conduct no flight operations. With the B-25s on board, any VF-8 Wildcat would have to ditch if launched, as the carrier could not land any aircraft. On 2 April, Mitscher's Task Force 18 sailed from San Francisco on what would be the *Hornet*'s first combat mission, the so-called Doolittle Raid, named after the leader of the AAF bombers on board, Lieutenant Colonel James H. Doolittle.

SIX HUNDRED MILES FROM TOKYO

With the return of "Wild Bill" from his conference on the West Coast, the Hawaii-based contingent of the "Tokyo Raid" could prepare to get under way. Task Force

VF-8 May 1942, *l to r top row*: Smith, Dietrich, Freeman, Cook, Fairbanks, Jennings, O'Neill, Mitchell, Ruehlow, Gray, Magda, Sutherland, Carey, Harwood; *bottom row*: McInerny, Talbot, Ford, French, Hill, Groves, Kelly, Stover, Starkes, Hughes, Tallman. (Capt. S. E. Ruehlow, USN.)

16 left port at noon on 8 April bound for a North Pacific rendezvous with Mitscher's Task Force 18 (with the *Hornet*) heading westward from San Francisco. Halsey had with him in addition to the *Enterprise*, the heavy cruisers *Northampton* and *Salt Lake City* (led by faithful Ray Spruance), four destroyers, and the fleet oiler *Sabine*. The *Enterprise*'s air group flew out that afternoon from NAS Pearl Harbor and overtook the task force steaming northwest. Gray brought with him twenty-two F4F-4 Wildcats from Fighting Six. The air department had slung up as spares in the hangar deck overhead spaces a further five F4F-3s, giving Fighting Six twenty-seven airplanes for this cruise. Taking the place of Scouting Six on this mission was Lt. Cdr. Max Leslie's Bombing Three (VB-3), a refugee from the shore-based *Saratoga* Air Group. Fighting Six put up an inner air patrol just before dark. The unofficial war diary crooned, "Back in our own groove with no troubles."[1]

Weather northwest of the Hawaiian Islands turned cold and raw, causing the task force to wonder whether they were bound for the Aleutians. Other than that, the voyage was routine. On 10 April, CinCPac announced a sweeping administrative reorganization of the Pacific Fleet. Halsey was no longer Commander, Aircraft, Battle Force (ComAirBatFor). His new title was Commander, Carriers, Pacific Fleet (ComCarPac), which gave him jurisdiction over the administration of Carrier Divisions One and Two (plus the *Hornet*) and all aircraft embarked on board the flattops.[2] His shore representative was now Rear Admiral Leigh Noyes, in place of Rear Admiral Fitch, who took over Task Force 11 with the *Lexington*. Fighting Six spent these quiet days flying the inevitable inner air patrols and readying their brand-new F4F-4s for combat. This included bore-sighting the guns and calibrating gun sights.

The morning of 13 April there was a break in the routine when Mitscher's Task Force 18 appeared on the horizon. Mitscher had with him the *Hornet*, the heavy cruiser *Vincennes*, the light cruiser *Nashville*, four destroyers, and the oiler *Cimarron*. Halsey merged the two task forces into one Task Force 16 under his command. The Army B-25 Mitchell bombers crowding the *Hornet*'s flight deck drew much excited comment from "The Big E," and Halsey felt it was time to announce the objective. Colonel Doolittle and his Army flyers were going to execute night bombing raids on Tokyo and other Japanese cities, then proceed to

VT-6 TBDs and VF-6 F4F-3 F-8 (BuNo. 2532), 11 Apr. 1942 on the Tokyo Raid. Singled out as an early production F4F-3 by its single cowl flap, 2532 was a VF-42 aircraft until Feb. 1942. (NA 80-G-16518.)

VF-6 F4F-4, 10 Apr. 1942, showing the six-gun installation. (NA 80-G-16511.)

Another view of the *Enterprise*'s flight deck en route on the Tokyo Raid, 16 Apr. 1942. (NA 80-G-330679.)

China. The reaction in Task Force 16 was overwhelming; on board the *Enterprise*, "all hands delighted."[3]

There was no 14 April, as the Tokyo-bound Task Force 16 skipped across the date line into 15 April. That morning found them 1,400 miles east of Tokyo, skirting air searches from Marcus Island. The weather grew rougher, as strong southerly winds intervened. Fighting Six flew only an afternoon inner air patrol. Halsey's plans were to fuel his heavy ships first, then leave the destroyers and the two oilers behind, while the carriers and cruisers made a high-speed dash westward to within 500 miles of Tokyo. There on the late afternoon of 18 April, Halsey would launch the Army medium bombers on their way. Then an equally high-speed retreat on the part of the ships was in order.

Fighting Six put up a dawn air patrol with five fighters the morning of 17 April, fueling day. There was a bit of a milestone for "The Big E." At 0845 during recovery of VF-6's inner air patrol, Howell M. Sumrall, ACMM, in F-24 made the carrier's 20,000th landing. The weather certainly did not cooperate with the festivities. A strong storm center moved in from the west. At 1222, Captain Murray canceled all flights and landed all aircraft because of 41-knot, southeasterly winds and rugged seas. Task Force 16 entered a band of bad weather and would have to live with it for the next few days. Robin Lindsey, the *Enterprise*'s assistant landing signal officer, later recorded:

> God damnest weather I've ever seen. For three days the waves were so high the deck was pitching so much that I had to have a person stand behind me to hold me on the landing signal platform so I wouldn't fall down. Several times I did, and you can imagine the amazement of the pilot's face as he passed over with no signal officer there.[4]

High seas or no, Halsey was going in. At 1445, the destroyers and fleet oilers peeled off to remain behind, as the big ships started their approach to the launch point at 22 knots.

The eighteenth of April was the big day, and the ships prepared early for action. On board the *Enterprise,* there was a call at 0255 for the air department and squadron personnel. The enemy was even closer than anyone suspected. Fifteen minutes later, the *Enterprise*'s radar detected two surface contacts bearing 235 degrees, distance 10 miles. Halsey changed course to swing north of the suspected Japanese vessels, and a few minutes later they faded from the radar scope. By 0415, Task Force 16 had resumed its westerly heading.

Flight operations for Fighting Six came before dawn. The weather had improved little, if any. Robin Lindsey observed seas "so heavy we were taking water on the

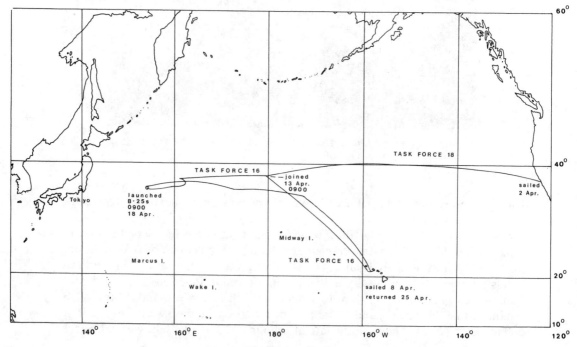

The Tokyo Raid.

Mehle's division
F-1   Lieut. Roger W. Mehle, USN
F-7   Ens. Howard L. Grimmell, Jr., A-V(N)
F-25 Lieut. (jg) Frank B. Quady, USN
F-26 Ens. Roy M. Gunsolus, A-V(N)

Rawie's division
F-23 Lieut. (jg) Wilmer E. Rawie, USN
F-24 Ens. William M. Holt, A-V(N)
F-17 Lieut. (jg) John C. Kelley, USN
F-27 Ens. Norman D. Hodson, A-V(N)

flight deck."[5] At 0507, the task force swung right to course 310 degrees into the teeth of the fierce northwesterly winds. Taking off at 0508 were eight F4Fs from Fighting Six on inner air/combat air patrol. This flight consisted of two divisions (see table). Following the fighters into the predawn darkness were three SBD dive bombers from Bombing Three to search ahead 200 miles and three from Bombing Six for engine run in and inner air patrol.

There began for the task force a series of bizarre contacts with the Japanese picket screen of converted fishing boats that patrolled the approaches to the home islands. At 0558, Lieut. (jg) Osborne B. Wiseman of Bombing Three spotted a patrol craft bearing 276 degrees, distance 42 miles. Halsey later changed course to the southwest to avoid the vessel. Wiseman after searching his sector returned to the carrier and air-dropped a message stating he thought the enemy lookouts had seen him. Further confirmation that the Japanese had detected Task Force 16 came at 0738, when the *Hornet*'s lookouts sighted a small patrol boat bearing 220 degrees, distance 10 miles. She was the little *No. 23 Nitto Maru*, a converted 90-ton whale-catcher, whose radioman excitedly tapped out a report of three enemy carriers. The contact placed the enemy flattops 650 miles east of Inubo Saki. The great secret mission was a secret no longer.

The *Enterprise* herself spotted the intruder at 0744, five miles off her port quarter. Halsey ordered the light cruiser *Nashville* to sink the enemy vessel, then instructed Mitscher to launch the B-25s immediately, hours away from the designated launch time and 650 miles distant instead of 400 miles from their targets. Halsey had no alternative. On board the *Hornet*, the air department rapidly prepared Doolittle's airplanes for takeoff. They scrounged containers to provide the bombers some extra fuel, and even used practice bombs from Torpedo Eight, filling them with gasoline instead of water. It was an emotional time for all on board.

The *Nashville* cut out of formation to deal with *No. 23 Nitto Maru*, wallowing in the heavy seas. At 0754, she fired a salvo from her six-inch main battery. Circling at 5,000 feet were the VF-6 fighters led by Mehle and Rawie, who were surprised to see the *Nashville* cut loose with her guns. Her shell splashes pointed to the hapless ex-whaler rising and falling in the heavy trough. The pilots dived in to attack. En route, Rawie caught sight of another converted fishing boat even smaller than the first, evidently the 88-ton *Nanshin Maru*. The fighters decided to get that one first. All eight of them raced in to rake the vessel with their .50-calibers. They shot the whalecatcher from stem to stern. Rawie, for one, made eleven runs and expended 1,200 rounds. It was literally the same as strafing practice, nothing heroic about it. The pilots were irritated that the helpless target refused to burn. Soon she had stopped and started settling, "wallowing in the trough."[6]

Tired of his sport, Mehle led several fighters after the first target, the one taken under fire by the *Nashville*. Shell splashes dotted the seas all around the slippery

No. 23 Nitto Maru, as the waves and her small size combined to make her an elusive target. The F4Fs did their part and thoroughly shot up the vessel. One of the VB-3 SBDs aloft happened onto the scene. Ens. J. Q. Roberts dived in from 7,500 feet after Mehle's pilots finished one of their strafing runs, but he had to abort at 3,500 feet when one of the F4Fs got in his way. On Roberts's second run, he released his bomb at 4,500 feet, but missed. At 0823, the *Nashville* with help from the fighters finally sank the tough little picket boat. The cruiser had expended 938 rounds of six-inch ammunition, highly embarrassing to her captain. Fighting Six returned to station, most of the F4Fs out of ammunition. "A bloodthirsty bunch of bastards,"[7] Rawie later quipped. The VF-6 pilots returned in time to witness the dramatic spectacle of the B-25s taking off from the *Hornet*. Rawie thought the Mitchell bombers looked especially impressive when aloft.

The *Enterprise* at 0827 launched a relief patrol of eight F4Fs in division led by skipper Gray and Lieut. (jg) Gayle Hermann. Not long after, the carrier recovered the first inner air patrol, giving Mehle's troops a chance to relax. At 0910 came a message from a VB-3 pilot reporting a Japanese light cruiser or destroyer not far away. That proved to be in error. At 0920, the *Hornet* sent the last of the sixteen B-25s aloft. Distance to Japan was almost exactly 600 miles. Task Force 16 had done its job; now it was time to turn for home. Halsey brought the ships around to a new course of 090 degrees and upped speed to 25 knots.

For the next few hours all was quiet as the task force added miles between itself and Japan. At 1107, the *Nashville* rejoined formation, as the *Hornet* busily prepared her own planes to fly now that her flight deck was free. At 1115, both carriers swung into the wind. The *Hornet* launched a CAP of eight VF-8 fighters, and the *Enterprise* despatched a special search of four SBD dive bombers. The "Big E" followed at 1127 with the launch of VF-6's third patrol (see table). Following the fighters aloft was a search of twelve SBDs (mostly from Bombing Three) to patrol astern 200 miles, and another for engine run in. Shortly thereafter, the *Enterprise* landed the fighters under Gray and Hermann and also SBDs from the morning searches. For the air department, it was a very busy day.

During the last flight operation, there came a report of an aircraft 30 miles from the task force. The *Enterprise* at 1214 had the bogey on the scope bearing 020 degrees, 35 miles. The contact, probably a Mitsubishi G4M1 Type 1 land attack plane [BETTY] on search from Japan, went on its way without sighting the ships. Meanwhile, some SBDs on search worked over three more enemy patrol vessels. The seas all around seemed to teem with these fishing boat snoopers. The CAP had another alert at 1347 with another bogey reported bearing 020 degrees, 30 miles and closing. The fighters charged in, but discovered their quarry was an SBD.

The afternoon continued with more Japanese patrol craft found near the task force. Lookouts at 1400 sighted two of them to the northwest, possibly the same

---

Hoyle's division
Lieut. (jg) Rhonald J. Hoyle, USN
Doyle C. Barnes, ACMM (NAP), USN
Rad. Elec. Edward H. Bayers, (NAP), USN
Howard S. Packard, AMM1c (NAP), USN

Provost's division
Ens. Thomas C. Provost III, A-V(N)
Beverly W. Reid, AMM1c (NAP), USN
Howell M. Sumrall, ACMM (NAP), USN
Tom F. Cheek, AMM1c (NAP), USN

pair previously attacked by Bombing Three. Led by "Buster" Hoyle and "Pappy" Provost, the VF-6 fighters swarmed over the little vessels, the F4Fs splitting their strafing runs between the two targets. It was a repeat of the morning romp. Some SBDs also joined in, while the *Nashville* closed for the coup de grâce. During the attacks, Halsey turned northwest into the wind for flight operations. The *Hornet* despatched a relief CAP of eight VF-8 Wildcats, while "The Big E" responded with eight F4Fs of her own under Mehle and Rawie. Six SBDs took off to fly over to the *Hornet*, and en route they jumped into the fight. The enemy managed one last retort. A machine gunner shot up the VB-6 SBD flown by Lieut. L. A. Smith, who later had to ditch his plane. The *Nashville*, acting the part of a destroyer, rescued both crewmen. One patrol craft sank; the other (the *Nagato Maru*) ran up the white flag. The *Nashville* picked up five prisoners from the sinking craft.

The excitement over, Task Force 16 at 1515 resumed its due-easterly course. Reports began to filter through Japanese commercial radio announcing the strike on Tokyo. Those on board Halsey's ships did not know precisely what was happening, but all things seemed to indicate their Army buddies were doing the job. At 1740, the carriers landed all aircraft aloft. That day the Imperial Navy lost five picket boats sunk, in return for shooting down one SBD. All sixteen of Doolittle's bombers hit their targets. One had to fly to the Soviet Union for internment; the rest made for China and later crashed. The use of fast, long-range medium bombers fooled the Japanese completely. They expected the American carriers to approach the home islands and launch a conventional carrier strike the next morning. The whole Combined Fleet rose to catch the raiders, but Halsey was already out of reach.

Halsey concentrated on putting as many miles as he could between Task Force 16 and Japan. The morning of 19 April, the *Enterprise* was the duty carrier, sending aloft the routine predawn inner air patrol and search. The seas were misbehaving as before; large swells kept the carriers rolling and pitching steeply. At 0558, the *Enterprise* sighted the task force destroyers. The rough seas would cause three accidents for Fighting Six that day. At 1434, while landing the third inner air patrol, the pitching flight deck dropped out from underneath Walter Hiebert's F4F-3. He floated into the barrier, nosed up, and came down hard on deck. The F4F required a major overhaul. At dusk there was more trouble. Frank Quady's F4F came in low, with the deck rising. He swerved on touchdown and ended up with his left wheel in the port catwalk. Behind him came Howard Packard, AMM1c, a transferee from Fighting Two. Packard's F4F caught the last wire, but still slammed into the barrier, messing up the propellor.

The next few days were uneventful, as the two carriers rotated flight duty. Halsey had far too much of a lead to worry about pursuit. A tragedy did occur on 21 April. One of the *Hornet* SBDs had got lost on the search. After several hours the carrier finally homed the VB-8 pilot, but, inexplicably, the SBD ditched within sight of the ships and sank immediately. Halsey had the whole task force searching the area for thirty minutes, but lookouts saw no sign of survivors. Packard had more trouble that day. While landing his F4F, he "got a little high at the ramp and ducked too hard."[8] Nosing down steeply after the landing signal officer gave his cut, Packard overreacted by pulling down his tail. His F4F hit hard and crumpled the left landing gear. According to Rawie, he "sorta splattered one plane all over the F-3 area [on the flight deck] in general."[9] The task force enjoyed two 21 Aprils because of a date line crossing, but on the second 21 April the weather was so poor there was little flying. The next day was only a little better.

By the time 23 April rolled around, Task Force 16 had entered much warmer

Erroneously designated a *Hornet* mishap, this photo actually shows Frank Quady's VF-6 F4F-4 (BuNo. 5077) in the *Enterprise*'s catwalk, 19 Apr. 1942. (NA 80-G-330670.)

waters within 500 miles of the Hawaiian Islands. The *Hornet* had the duty that day, much to the pleasure of Fighting Six. One pilot joked that the last few days made for "practically a rest cruise."[10] There was time, for example, to write reports. The *Enterprise*'s Captain Murray submitted his ship's report for 18 April. Regarding the F4F-4, Murray noted its performance was "not satisfactory."[11] Halsey the next day in his endorsement to Murray's report condemned the F4F-4 fighter for "limited range and endurance," which constituted a "serious defect."[12] CinCPac later echoed Halsey's criticisms and wrote that he "assumed that appropriate and expeditious action will be taken."[13] On 26 April, the day after the *Enterprise* docked at Pearl, Halsey sent a message to the chief of the Bureau of Aeronautics (Rear Admiral Towers) reiterating the request for drop tanks for the F4F-4s. Halsey noted that the short-legged carrier fighter "hamstrings carrier operations."[14] While he was endorsing Murray's comments, Halsey on 24 April shook the lead out of the air groups by scheduling several training exercises. It was a good morning for the strike planes to simulate attacks on the ships and for the CAP to practice their interceptions. That afternoon, however, bad weather closed in, canceling flight operations. Anyway, Task Force 16 was almost home.

The carriers shook their pilots awake early on 25 April. McClusky's *Enterprise* Air Group, for example, manned planes at 0530, but it was raining so heavily that takeoff had to be delayed. When the go-ahead did come, the deck crews could not restart eight of VF-6's twenty-four operational fighters. Wet magnetos appeared to be the culprit. Plane handlers struck the duds into the hangar to try to get them started. Gray at 0700 led the remaining sixteen fighters aloft along with the rest of the group. He was bound for Luke Field on Ford Island (NAS Pearl Harbor). At the same time the *Hornet* group formed and headed for Ewa. One careless VF-6 pilot mistakenly joined Fighting Eight and accompanied them to Ewa. Gray landed the rest of his squadron at Ford Island in a bad crosswind.

More troubles for Fighting Six were in the offing. Back on board the *Enterprise*, Rawie found himself the senior fighter pilot among the eight left on board the ship. He took charge, getting the aircraft started and organizing the flight to Pearl.

Howard Packard's cracked up F4F-3 (BuNo. 3994) on board *Enterprise*, 21 Apr. 1942. (NA 80-G-16434.)

Without his knowledge the plane handlers took his own fighter up on deck. He was late in manning his own airplane, a goof that drew the ire of the air officer. With considerable understatement, Rawie later wrote, "They kinda got sore." "SNAFU was rampant,"[15] was his other comment on the incident, which nearly cost him two days of precious leave until Gray came to his rescue. Rawie got the eight F4Fs to Ford Island without further mishap.

Nearly five months of war had dragged by, but the U.S. Navy's carrier fighters had yet to meet in combat the Imperial Navy's carrier forces with their vaunted Japanese Zeros. That situation was about to change as powerful forces gathered in the South Pacific for what would be a desperate battle in the Coral Sea.

PART II

The Battle of the Coral Sea

CHAPTER 9

Prelude to Battle

THE *YORKTOWN* IN THE CORAL SEA, MARCH–APRIL 1942

In the wake of the timely 10 March air strike on Lae and Salamaua, the two carrier forces that had made the attack parted company. Vice Admiral Brown with Task Force 11 (including the carrier *Lexington*) started northward on 16 March for Pearl Harbor, whereas Rear Admiral Fletcher's Task Force 17 with the *Yorktown* turned westward from the New Hebrides to the Coral Sea once more. Fletcher's orders were to "continue offensive action against enemy activities New Guinea area and eastward premised on information supplied by CINCPAC and COMANZAC."[1] Admiral King was especially concerned about Japanese advances toward Port Moresby and into the Solomon Islands. Like Brown before him, Fletcher came under the direct command of the distant CominCh, in Washington.

Task Force 17 comprised the carrier *Yorktown* (flying Fletcher's two-star flag), the heavy cruisers *Astoria* and *Portland,* and five destroyers. On watch for any enemy moves, the ships steamed westward toward the Coral Sea. This was a time of great apprehension for the Allies. The East Indies had fallen, and Australia was endangered:

> The atmosphere [in Task Force 17] was watchful, tense. Strong Jap forces were on the prowl, defeating Allied forces wherever encountered.[2]

Admiral Nimitz arranged to send Fletcher the fleet oilers and other supply ships necessary to keep the task force operating in the remote South Pacific. On 18 March, the men were cheered to learn that the Australians had located all five of the Curtiss SOC cruiser floatplanes lost six days before during the Lae–Salamaua operation. Their crews were safe, as the planes had fetched up on Rossel Island in the Louisiades Archipelago. The next day, the heavy cruiser *Pensacola* and the destroyer *Hammann* joined Fletcher's force.

Fletcher on 21 March informed ComANZAC (Vice Admiral Leary) that during the next two days he would fuel his ships, then patrol the Coral Sea westward to about Longitude 153 (East), or roughly south of the Louisiades. He planned to operate out of enemy air search range just south of the crucial area, looking for a likely opportunity to pounce on Japanese ships. Good information from comprehensive air searches was vital for him, so Fletcher again requested timely reports on enemy ship movements. For this he had to rely on Australian flying boats from Tulagi and Allied bombers flying out of Port Moresby and northeastern Australia.

He cautioned Leary that by 1 April he would have to retire toward Noumea for fuel and provisions.

After refueling from the fleet oiler *Tippecanoe*, Task Force 17 on 24 March headed northwestward for the Coral Sea. The ships passed about 300 miles south of the Solomons, then into the Coral Sea proper. The evening of 27 March, Fletcher detached the *Astoria* and one destroyer to cut northward toward Rossel Island, there the next day to recover the five errant floatplanes stranded the past few weeks. There being no targets reported within reach, Fletcher fueled on 28 and 29 March, then started back toward Noumea as planned. He knew it was useless to try to raid Rabaul, as the efficient Japanese air searches would spot him in plenty of time for them to clear the harbor. Indeed, earlier that week CominCh had decried repeated raids on land bases as inconsequential. King wished his carriers to destroy ships.

There was a stir on 29 March when Army aviators reported sighting thirty transports at Rabaul. Later that day, the *Yorktown* copied a message from Leary indicating that the Army had sighted Task Force 17 only 228 miles from Rabaul. That was news to Fletcher. Task Force 17 was nowhere near where the Army search plane reported it. At noon on 29 March, Fletcher's ships were about 360 miles south of Guadalcanal, putting them more than 800 miles southeast of Rabaul. Speculation on board the *Yorktown* had it that the Army flyers had turned up a small Japanese force and grossly erred in mistaking it for Task Force 17. (The Army aviators were not renowned for accuracy in recognizing ship types.) The next day, Fletcher routinely radioed his own position (some 500 miles south of Guadalcanal), adding that he was en route to Noumea to reprovision. He noted that if the Japanese did indeed move south in strength, he would swing north to deal with them.

In Washington, King monitored the messages between Leary and Fletcher. From his remote perch, imperious CominCh misunderstood the situation. Furious at Fletcher's despatch, King snapped off a message stating that Fletcher's 30 March communication was "not understood if it means you are retiring from enemy vicinity in order to provision."[3] Received the last day of March, this slur on the part of fiery CominCh caused great bewilderment on board the *Yorktown*. The Army's supposed "thirty transports" melted away, as they had not existed in the first place. According to daily air search reports relayed through Leary and carefully evaluated by Fletcher, no significant targets lay within Task Force 17's grasp. Only small numbers of Japanese filtered southward from Rabaul to Buka and Bougainville in the northern Solomons. They evidently set up a very small base at Shortland off southern Bougainville, but no one was even certain of that. If Fletcher blitzed northward, he risked detection by the excellent enemy search network, and even the meager forces would vanish. King, however, obviously wanted something done. Fletcher informed Leary (and listening CominCh) that he would attack Shortland on 6 April.

The task force spent April Fool's Day about 100 miles off New Caledonia's west coast awaiting the appearance of the oiler *Platte*. Oblivious to all the high-level machinations during the past few weeks, the *Yorktown* Air Group flew its routine patrols and otherwise worked to remain combat ready. Pete Pederson's Fighting Forty-two handled combat air patrol and some inner air patrols on lookout for subs, and even managed a few training flights as well. Many of the pilots labored to make fine hunting knives to replace the less serviceable meat cleavers provided by the ship.

The morning of 1 April, VF-42 sent aloft a division of F4Fs for CAP and also to practice coordinated strafing runs on float lights. On recovering from one pass, Scott McCuskey thought he spotted a conning tower break the surface. Diving in to investigate, he discovered instead an F4F sinking beneath the waves. It was his wingman, Johnny Adams. Experiencing a sudden loss of power, Adams had had to ditch about four miles from the *Yorktown*. It was not pleasant. Because his aircraft lacked shoulder straps, Adams upon impact had pitched forward into the F4F's jury-rigged gunsight bracket, which inflicted a large gash on his forehead and chipped several teeth. Stunned, he did not recover swiftly enough to extract his liferaft from its compartment on the dorsal fairing aft of the cockpit. Indeed, he was lucky to be alive, so swiftly did the plane sink beneath him. The destroyer *Hammann* raced over to rescue him, and later that day transferred him to the destroyer *Anderson*. The VF-42 pilots did not know why Adams's engine had failed, but they grew highly suspicious of their mounts, particularly the troublesome fuel tanks.[4]

The same day Adams ditched so painfully, Fletcher received an important CominCh directive: "Requirements for use of other task forces like yours make it necessary to continue your active operations south of equator until your force can be relieved."[5] In other words, Task Force 17 was not going anywhere else soon. Although Fletcher did not know this, CominCh had earmarked Vice Admiral Halsey's Task Force 16 for the Tokyo Raid. King added that Task Force 17 was not to draw provisions from Noumea; that locale was too exposed to enemy observation and attack. In February King had ordered an operating base organized at Tongatabu in the Tonga Islands southeast of Fiji. When Fletcher was ready, he was to withdraw there, where necessary supplies would be waiting.

On 2 April, the oiler *Platte* and a destroyer caught up with Task Force 17 west of New Caledonia. The *Yorktown*'s crew were delighted to find that the AO carried a great deal of their mail, including Christmas packages that had chased them all the way from the East Coast. Moving slowly northward, the ships that afternoon refueled and transferred provisions from the cruisers to the destroyers. Fletcher carefully evaluated the enemy situation as revealed in sighting reports and special intelligence. Unfortunately, the Japanese had faded away even with such light forces as they had used. On 4 April, Fletcher radioed Leary that he felt the 6 April strike planned for Shortland would be a waste of time. He canceled his run north in order not to tip the enemy as to his presence, then turned westward for a two-week offensive patrol in the Coral Sea.

The length of the cruise, now over six weeks with no end in sight, began to wear a little on the crews. Certain commodities had disappeared as supplies were exhausted. One carrier pilot has written of the gustatory drawbacks on long voyages:

> The food on carriers is generally quite good for the first month after stocking up and putting to sea. Thereafter it begins to deteriorate. Fresh milk disappears almost immediately, and the next to go are fresh eggs, greens, and fresh vegetables, and finally fresh meat. Officers and crew alike begin to live on powdered milk, powdered eggs, and canned fruit and vegetables and meat.[6]

Fifth April was Easter Sunday, but as one VF-42 pilot lamented, no longer did any *powdered* eggs remain in the *Yorktown*'s larder.[7] With supply facilities still primitive in the South Pacific, there was little chance of stocking up until the task force withdrew to Tongatabu.

For the next several days, Task Force 17 operated in the Coral Sea about 300 to 400 miles southwest of Guadalcanal. The ships stayed just out of enemy search radius from Rabaul, and crisscrossed the area southeast of the Louisiades through waters destined to become famous the next month. The *Yorktown*'s squadrons did their routine flying, the CAPs, IAPs, and searches, but the days, often brutally hot, assumed a sameness. McCuskey has aptly described how the pilots spent some of their off-duty time:

> Volley-ball on the forward elevator each afternoon was the order of the day. The elevator was dropped, and it was the flight deck officers and men against the flyboys. We fought, argued, razzed, needled each other—we couldn't get anyone to act as referee. It was all out—you could reach over the net; in fact the net was the really big loser.
>
> Cribbage was the most popular game, and there was plenty of time for beards, sunbathing, and just plain boredom. But there was always the possibility of going to Sydney . . . Every Sunday, there was church service on the hangar deck, and each evening there were movies in the ward room and in crew's quarters. I think we saw every movie about 10–15 times. One a few occasions, there was mail call, which was the happiest time of all.[8]

Fighting Forty-two's precarious situation vis-à-vis its aircraft worsened on 7 April. That day the nagging problem of the self-sealing fuel tanks blossomed into a real crisis, especially since the enemy was not all that far away. As Fletcher later put it, the fuel tanks began "going sour."[9] One Grumman after another was laid up because of disintegrating tank liners, and by 10 April, no fewer than seven out of the nineteen F4F-3s were inoperable. For the rest it was only a matter of time. Flying them was an experience not soon forgotten: "fuel seepage through the outer skin [of the tanks] made for scary smells."[10]

The squadron's troubles stemmed from a particular batch of self-sealing fuel tanks installed the previous December in place of the vulnerable aluminum tanks. The bladderlike tankage, made up of rubber layers reinforced with cloth, had swelled and split its seams, while the inner linings had blistered, sloughing-off pieces of material. Naturally these particles could raise hell with a fuel system, jamming fuel strainers and plugging lines, behavior that VF-42 felt explained a number of plane losses. The "cemented" type of tank, especially, turned out not to be suitable for the aromatic aviation gasoline used by the fleet, as the fuel tended to dissolve the glue and rubber making up the tanks! Owing to poor seals at the filler neck, gasoline sometimes dripped on the outer skin of the tanks, eating away at them from the outside as well. ComCarPac's materiel officer reported similar problems with F4F-3s in other squadrons.

Even if Brassfield's engineers knew what caused the deterioration, they had no way of repairing the damage. On 10 April (the same day the ship raffled off the last steak on board), Fletcher informed CinCPac of the trouble with VF-42's fighters. Meanwhile, Task Force 17 patrolled back and forth across the center of the Coral Sea. On 14 April, with the seven inoperable F4F-3s essentially unrepairable on the spot and no telling how long the rest would be flyable, he advised Nimitz of his intention to withdraw to Tongatabu if any more fighters turned "sour." Rightfully he felt the lack of fighters crippled the task force's ability to defend itself. The only recourse was to replace all of the tanks with the vulcanized variety and ensure proper sealing at the filler necks.

Fletcher's message crossed one from Nimitz stating that he had resumed operational control over Task Force 17. CinCPac told Fletcher to retire to Tongatabu for necessary supplies, then depart there on 27 April once again bound for the Coral Sea. The new orders ended the offensive patrol, and on 15 April Task Force 17 started southeast toward New Caledonia and points east. The next day another

Wildcat succumbed to bad tanks, justifying Fletcher's caution. He radioed Pearl requesting immediate air shipment of twenty-two F4F-3 self-sealing fuel tanks (enough for all fighters and three spares) from Oahu to Tongatabu. CinCPac had already made arrangements to transport the vitally needed replacements to Suva in the Fijis and replied that Fletcher should send a destroyer to bring them to Tongatabu.

On 20 April, Task Force 17 took its first really close look at a South Pacific isle. That morning the *Yorktown* flew two SBDs and two TBDs to the airstrip on Tongatabu and later dropped anchor along with the rest of the task force at Nukualofa Roads off Tongatabu. Here was the haven where the ships would refuel, reprovision, and relax before again returning to enemy-threatened waters. Already in port were the provision ship *Bridge*, the repair ship *Dobbin*, and the hospital ship *Solace*. Pederson put two F4F-3s on alert, to be shot off from the hangar deck catapults in the unlikely event the Japanese showed up. Fletcher despatched the destroyer *Walke* the 400 miles to Suva to fetch the replacement tanks. For many of the crew, there was liberty during daylight hours, and that helped restore some good humor to those who had signed on to "see the world." The small New Zealand garrison was most friendly to the Yanks, but beguiling young South Seas maidens were nowhere to be seen. Their Queen Salote had ordered them to hide in the hills!

The *Walke* returned on 22 April with the first batch of tanks flown down from Pearl Harbor. Brassfield and his machinists set to work installing them in the Grummans, a thankless task indeed. For each fighter, they had to remove access plates and over 500 screws, then push and pull the troublesome bladders into place, taking about 20 man-hours per plane. The second shipment of tanks reached Suva on 22 April and soon were brought to Tongatabu. Thus VF-42's F4Fs finally became fully airworthy, thanks to the emergency transport of vitally needed components and the unceasing labor of the squadron engineers.[11]

The morning of 24 April, a large four-engine Consolidated PB2Y-2 Coronado flying boat set down in Nukualofa harbor. Among its passengers was an officer with orders to Fighting Forty-two. Lt. Cdr. James Flatley had on 27 March received orders relieving him of command of the Fighting Two Detachment at NAS San Diego and assigning him as VF-42's new commanding officer. His totally unexpected appearance proved quite a surprise for the Yorktowners, for Captain Buckmaster had just appointed Lt. Cdr. Fenton, the XO, as CO of VF-42. Obviously there had been a foul-up somewhere. Administratively, VF-42 remained attached to the *Ranger* Air Group, as its service on board the *Yorktown* was supposed to be "temporary." On 17 February, the Bureau of Navigation in Washington had cut orders assigning Fenton to other duty (apparently command of another fighting squadron). They forwarded VF-42's copy of the orders through the *Ranger* serving in the Atlantic Fleet. The flow of paperwork being what it was, Fenton had not yet received them! Meanwhile, Curt Smiley, the air group commander, was leaving for another assignment, and Pederson was to take his place. As his successor he nominated Fenton, and Buckmaster approved, notifying BuNav by despatch. Now VF-42 had two legally appointed commanding officers.

Fenton, who was slightly senior to Flatley, had served well with the squadron for nearly a year. On that basis and in the absence of orders to the contrary, it was quite proper that he had fleeted up to skipper. Until something could be worked out in Washington, Flatley would become executive officer of Fighting Forty-two, and Vince McCormack remained flight officer. The changes in command

162   THE BATTLE OF THE CORAL SEA

took effect on 25 April. Meanwhile, Buckmaster's despatch to BuNav stirred the bureaucrats to clear up the confusion caused when Fenton failed to learn of his original orders.[12]

Both "Chas" Fenton and Jimmy Flatley had graduated in the Naval Academy's class of 1929, with Fenton sixteen numbers higher in class standing. After a year at sea, Fenton had applied for flight training, earning his wings in 1931. That year he went out to the Pacific as a scout pilot on the heavy cruiser *Augusta* and in 1933 transferred to the *Houston* in the Far East. The next summer saw Fenton at Pearl Harbor serving in Patrol One (VP-1F) piloting large Keystone PK biplane flying boats. His first carrier service followed in June 1936, when he joined Fighting Six (VF-6B) on board the *Saratoga*. The next July the "Felix the Cat" squadron was redesignated Fighting Three. From July 1939 through June 1941, he instructed at NAS Pensacola, then reported as XO of Fighting Forty-two. There his VF experience proved extremely valuable in helping the squadron make the transition from scouting planes to fighters. A steady and capable leader who was well respected and liked by his pilots, Fenton enjoyed a shipboard hobby that mirrored his meticulous approach to flying—watch repairing.

On leaving Annapolis, Flatley went to the glamor of sea duty on board the flattop *Saratoga*. From the first he had no doubt as to his choice of a specialty, applying for admission to NAS Pensacola as soon as he could. He qualified in June 1931 as a naval aviator, and that summer reported to VF-5B on board the *Lexington* for what would be a three-year tour flying Boeing F4B carrier fighters. Next came a stint in flying boats with VP-4F at Pearl Harbor. In June 1936 he was posted to VF-6B (along with Fenton) on board the *Saratoga*, but only for a year's tour. His skills in fighter aircraft sharpened, Lieut. Flatley for two years commanded the aviation unit on board the light cruiser *Omaha* in Atlantic waters. From June 1939 to August 1941, he was a flight instructor and administrator, first at Pensacola and later with "Jocko" Clark at the new Jacksonville base. In September 1941 he reported to Fighting Two on board the *Lexington* as Paul Ramsey's XO, and in

Cdr. James Flatley in his F6F on board the second *Yorktown* (CV-10). (NA 80-G-398407.)

February 1942 (as told above), he took the VF-2 Detachment on board the *Saratoga* when she limped back to the West Coast.

The hitch in getting his long-awaited squadron must have been extremely disappointing, but Flatley was not one to let it bother him. One of the truly outstanding individuals in naval aviation, he was a born leader who earned the respect (and affection) of all who served with him. A sincere, outgoing individual, he worked hard to encourage young, inexperienced pilots and bolster their self-confidence. An air tactician of the highest order as well, he sought diligently to analyze his experiences and those of others to formulate the crucial lessons of aerial combat. Although his service with VF-42 would prove brief, he made a lasting impression on those with whom he flew.

For Task Force 17 the week at Tongatabu passed swiftly. The men had the chance to stretch their legs ashore, and the ships obtained vitally needed provisions. The morning of 27 April, the *Yorktown* and her consorts got under way. Scouting Five lost an SBD-3 when Lieut. (jg) Arthur L. Downing had to ditch; the *Walke* recovered the crew. The CAP got into the act at 1241, when the *Yorktown* scrambled four F4Fs to hunt down a bogey that proved to be another huge PB2Y-2 flying boat. Fletcher set a westerly course bound for the Coral Sea. He had one carrier, three heavy cruisers, six destroyers, and the fleet oiler *Neosho*; and help was also on the way in the form of Task Force 11 with the *Lexington*. Trouble was brewing in the Coral Sea, and CinCPac was moving the *Yorktown* and the *Lexington* there to deal with it.

FIGHTING TWO TO THE SOUTH PACIFIC

By April 1942, Fighting Two had certainly felt the effects of the shortage of experienced carrier fighter pilots in the Pacific Fleet. Lt. Cdr. Ramsey had seen his squadron totally transformed from the crack outfit he had led at the outbreak of the war. First, in February, came the departure of the Fighting Two Detachment (under Jimmy Flatley) for stateside duty. Then, in March, Fighting Six grabbed ten NAPs for temporary duty, leaving Ramsey with seven pilots and a collection of careworn F4F-3As. With his carrier *Lexington* back in port on 26 March, Ramsey received orders to reembark Fighting Two as part of the *Lexington* Air Group. He had only a few weeks to get ready while the *Lexington* was in the yards. Meanwhile Fighting Two as usual operated out of NAS Kaneohe under control of the Army's 7th Interceptor Command. The squadron stood alerts and flew training missions.

On 1 April, Vice Admiral Brown hauled down his three-star flag from the *Lexington* and departed for shore duty as commander of the Amphibious Force. Replacing him as commander of Task Force 11 was Rear Admiral Fitch, ashore reluctantly since December as the AirBatFor administrative representative. He was glad to be free of shore duty and its red tape. Fitch expedited the *Lexington*'s refit, aware that CinCPac would soon have need of her. Indeed, on 2 April, Nimitz deliberated as to whether it might be best to return Task Force 11 to the South Pacific to operate with Task Force 17. On 10 April, Nimitz instructed Fitch's Task Force 11 to sail five days hence. Initially he was to transport fourteen Brewster F2A-3 Buffalo fighters of Maj. Luther S. Moore's Marine Fighting Squadron 211 (VMF-211) to the naval air station on bleak Palmyra Island. Thereafter the task force was to rendezvous with the old battleships of Task Force 1 and exercise with them in the vicinity of Palmyra and Christmas islands until 4 May, when the battleships were to return to Pearl Harbor. This was not just a training cruise. Task Force 11 had to be ready to undertake any combat mission assigned by

CinCPac. This meant, among other things, that Ramsey had to scrape together a goodly number of experienced fighter pilots to fill the depleted ranks of Fighting Two, and he needed them quickly.

For Paul Ramsey, the return to sea duty on board the *Lexington* would bring to a close two and a half months of enforced time on the beach and would offer his first real opportunity for combat. A 1927 Naval Academy graduate (along with Jimmy Thach and Pat Mitchell), Ramsey earned his wings in February 1930. His first squadron service came in VF-3B on board this same *Lexington*; the next year he switched to VF-6B with the *Saratoga*. After a tour as a Pensacola instructor and a stint in battleship float observation planes, Ramsey in 1936 joined VP-11F with the seaplane tender *Wright* in the Pacific. This began an extended tour in flying boat squadrons working out of Pearl Harbor and Seattle. He eventually became executive officer of VP-41. On 1 July 1941 came his promotion to lieutenant commander and a really choice assignment, command of Fighting Two. Ramsey continued the tradition of excellence fostered in that famed unit, but to his regret most of his pilots were transferred before he could lead them into battle. A jovial individual, for this cruise he sported a finely developed handlebar moustache, a survivor of VF-2's old jest of growing moustaches and keeping them until they had shot down a certain number of Japanese planes.

On Oahu, the only group of trained VF pilots turned out to be Thach's Fighting Three newly returned from the South Pacific, and the only solution to Ramsey's problem was to transfer on temporary duty the personnel needed by Fighting Two. On 12 April Ramsey received from Thach no fewer than twelve pilots and fifty-six men, as well as nineteen F4F-3 Wildcats so VF-2 would have the better airplanes. Originally Ramsey had hoped to reequip with F4F-4 Wildcats, but the shipment did not arrive in time. Ramsey handed over seventeen F4F-3As into Thach's custody and retained one F4F-3A. Reporting for temporary duty with VF-3 was one NAP, Wayne Davenport, AMM2c, who would return in late April to the States. Ramsey drew another F4F-3 from the fleet pool, giving him a total of 21 Wildcats (twenty F4F-3s and one F4F-3A). In addition to Thach's loan, four pilots reported in from ACTG, Pacific: Ensigns William W. Wileman, John Bain, and George Hopper, and an enlisted pilot, Robert F. Kanze, AP2c (see squadron organization).

The senior VF-3 officer joining Ramsey was Lieut. Noel Gayler, who became VF-2's executive officer. One of the top men in his 1935 Annapolis graduating class, Gayler was a relative latecomer to aviation, earning his wings in the fall of 1940. He reported to Fighting Three and became an apt pupil of Jimmy Thach. On 20 February, his division had intercepted the bombers first, and he shot down one enemy plane personally and assisted in the destruction of two others. He got another Japanese plane on 10 March over Lae. Handsome and confident, Gayler was an officer with a future; as a four-star admiral he served as commander-in-chief, Pacific during the final stages of the Vietnamese War, retiring in 1976. Fighting Two's flight officer was an old hand with that squadron, Lieut. Fred Borries. Also a member of the 1935 class, "Buzz" Borries was renowned throughout the Navy for his exploits on the gridiron. A naval aviator since 1939, Borries had served with Bombing Two before switching in early 1940 to Fighting Two.

The *Lexington* on 14 April hoisted on board the fourteen F2A-3s of VMF-211, ironic since these were the same aircraft that Fighting Two had discarded. The next morning the task force got under way from Pearl. The *Lexington* Air Group flew out that afternoon, the seventy aircraft landing without incident. For the next several days, Task Force 11 (comprising the *Lexington*, the heavy cruisers *Minneapolis* and *New Orleans*, and seven destroyers) steamed routinely on a southerly

I. Fighting Two Pilot Assignments, April 1942

<table>
<tr><td colspan="2" align="center">1st Division</td></tr>
<tr><td>F-1</td><td>Lt. Cdr. Paul H. Ramsey, USN (CO)</td></tr>
<tr><td>F-2</td><td>Ens. George F. Markham, Jr., A-V(N)</td></tr>
<tr><td>F-3</td><td>Lieut. (jg) Paul G. Baker, USN</td></tr>
<tr><td>F-4</td><td>Ens. William W. Wileman, A-V(N)†</td></tr>
<tr><td colspan="2" align="center">2nd Division</td></tr>
<tr><td>F-5</td><td>Lieut. Albert O. Vorse, Jr., USN*</td></tr>
<tr><td>F-6</td><td>Ens. Edward R. Sellstrom, Jr., A-V(N)*</td></tr>
<tr><td>F-7</td><td>Lieut. (jg) Robert J. Morgan, USN*</td></tr>
<tr><td>F-8</td><td>Ens. John H. Lackey, A-V(N)*</td></tr>
<tr><td colspan="2" align="center">3rd Division</td></tr>
<tr><td>F-9</td><td>Lieut. Fred Borries, Jr., USN (FO)</td></tr>
<tr><td>F-10</td><td>Lieut. (jg) Marion W. Dufilho, USN*</td></tr>
<tr><td>F-11</td><td>Lieut. (jg) Clark F. Rinehart, USN</td></tr>
<tr><td>F-12</td><td>Ens. Newton H. Mason, A-V(N)*</td></tr>
<tr><td colspan="2" align="center">4th Division</td></tr>
<tr><td>F-13</td><td>Lieut. Noel A. M. Gayler, USN (XO)*</td></tr>
<tr><td>F-14</td><td>Ens. Dale W. Peterson, A-V(N)*</td></tr>
<tr><td>F-15</td><td>Lieut. (jg) Howard F. Clark, USN*</td></tr>
<tr><td>F-16</td><td>Ens. Richard M. Rowell, A-V(N)*</td></tr>
<tr><td colspan="2" align="center">5th Division</td></tr>
<tr><td>F-17</td><td>Lieut. Richard S. Bull, Jr., USN</td></tr>
<tr><td>F-18</td><td>Ens. John B. Bain, A-V(N)†</td></tr>
<tr><td>F-19</td><td>Ens. Willard E. Eder, A-V(N)*</td></tr>
<tr><td>F-20</td><td>Ens. Leon W. Haynes, A-V(N)*</td></tr>
<tr><td>F-21</td><td>Ens. George A. Hopper, Jr., A-V(N)†
Robert F. Kanze, AP2c, USN†</td></tr>
</table>

* Transferred from Fighting Three 12 April 1942.
† Newly reported from ACTGPac 11 April 1942.

II. *Lexington* Air Group, 15 April 1942

(CLAG)	Commander, *Lexington* Air Group	Cdr. William B. Ault, USN	1 SBD-3
(VF-2)	Fighting Two	Lt. Cdr. Paul H. Ramsey, USN	21 F4F-3, -3As
(VB-2)	Bombing Two	Lt. Cdr. Weldon L. Hamilton, USN	18 SBD-2, -3s
(VS-2)	Scouting Two	Lt. Cdr. Robert E. Dixon, USN	18 SBD-3s
(VT-2)	Torpedo Two	Lt. Cdr. James H. Brett, Jr., USN	12 TBD-1s

course. Elsewhere momentous events rocked the Pacific theater. Halsey's Task Force 16 with the *Enterprise* and the *Hornet* approached the Japanese home islands to launch Doolittle's Army bombers, while naval intelligence (largely on the basis of deciphered enemy messages) began to discern the enemy's intention to invade Port Moresby and the Solomons.

On 18 April, the *Lexington* drew within air ferry range of Palmyra, and at 1300, she launched the fourteen marine Buffaloes for their rendezvous with what would prove to be exceptionally primitive living conditions and boredom on isolated Palmyra. Task Force 11 then steamed for its scheduled meeting with the battleships of Task Force 1. At 2212, though, Fitch received orders from CinCPac canceling the training mission. Instead, he was to proceed at economical speed to a point about 200 miles north of the Fijis. That led to speculation about likely operations in the South Pacific.

The change in mission meant that the *Lex* would dip below the equator, and preparations began for line-crossing ceremonies. Her Shellbacks conspired to take revenge for the fiasco in February during the last crossing, when the Pollywogs had rebelled. On 19 April came VF-2's first flight of the cruise, when Ramsey led seventeen F4Fs aloft on a training mission. Also that day additional orders reached Task Force 11. CinCPac directed Fitch to rendezvous with the fleet oiler *Kaskaskia* about 300 miles northeast of the Fijis. There was no definite news, but the Coral Sea began to loom big in people's minds. That evening, the Shellbacks convened their "court" to pass judgment on those lowly individuals who were about to meet King Neptune and traverse the earth's belt line.

The real hazing came on 20 April as the *Lexington* neared the line. Most of VF-2's pilots were already Shellbacks and entitled to join in on the fun. This left only the newly reported ensigns, George Markham, Bill Wileman, John Bain, and George Hopper, along with the sole enlisted pilot, Robert Kanze, to swell the ranks of the despised Pollywogs. Hapless individuals dressed in winter flight gear trod the flight deck on lookout for icebergs, or donned other outlandish costumes to face fiendish tortures devised by the remorseless old salts. The rites culminated in their running the gauntlet down the whole length of the *Lexington*'s flight deck. It was all in good fun (if not in good taste). During the day, VF-2 pilots flew one hop in concert with the TBDs on a torpedo training mission. Strangely, those scheduled to fly were all Shellbacks, leaving the Pollywog pilots free for their initiations. Finally at 0158 the next morning, the *Lexington* did cross the equator, and there were many sore-backed sailors who would not readily forget their first trip over the line.

On 21 April, Fighting Two began flying periodic inner air patrols on lookout for submarines plying the warm equatorial seas. That day, definite word came through, as CinCPac arranged for Task Force 11 to rendezvous on 1 May with Fletcher's Task Force 17 about 250 miles northwest of New Caledonia. It was the Coral Sea for certain. Events of note during the trip south from the equator included the 25 April rendezvous with the *Kaskaskia*, a big gunnery training mission on 30 April, and a ditching by Scouting Two the same day. Fighting Two had worked in some refresher training on the voyage south from Pearl Harbor, allowing the squadron to shake down and assume a measure of combat readiness. Now they waited for some action.

CHAPTER 10

Opening Shots

CORAL SEA PRELIMINARIES

The last day of April saw two American carrier task forces converging on a lonely point in the waters of the eastern Coral Sea, there because the high command believed, on the basis of radio intelligence, that the Japanese had begun a major push in the South Pacific, initially for Port Moresby and the Solomons, but with wider secondary objectives. According to staff estimates, upward of a half dozen enemy carriers with suitable escorts would likely be rampaging among Allied bases in the South Pacific. To blunt the attacks, Admiral Nimitz resolved to commit his own powerful carrier forces, designating Fletcher with the *Yorktown* and the *Lexington* to handle the defense of Port Moresby. Reinforcing him in mid-May would be Task Force 16 (the *Enterprise* and the *Hornet*) under Vice Admiral Halsey, who would take overall command of the carriers.

Not long after dawn on 1 May, Fletcher's Task Force 17 joined with Fitch's Task Force 11 at the predesignated rendezvous north of New Caledonia. Fletcher sent Fitch's ships south to meet the heavy cruiser *Chicago* and a destroyer in order to refuel from the *Tippecanoe*, while Fletcher's own vessels topped off from the oiler *Neosho*. Fletcher played a waiting game, as his intelligence sources informed him the enemy offensive was still in its early stages. His plan was to remain hidden by keeping radio silence and staying out of Japanese air search range until the enemy surface forces had tipped their hand and advanced beyond the ready reach of supporting land-based air at Rabaul. Meanwhile logistics was a very important consideration for Fletcher, as he was distant from bases where he could readily obtain fuel. His only link was the fleet train of oilers shuttling to and from Oahu.

On 2 May, Task Force 17 completed fueling, but Fletcher was disappointed to learn that Fitch did not expect to do so until 4 May. Not wanting to remain south of the critical area that long, Fletcher decided to take his own task force north toward the Louisiades, Fitch to rejoin on 4 May at the rendezvous set for Rear Admiral Crace's Task Force 44 (the old ANZAC Squadron) heading out from Brisbane. That would complete Fletcher's assigned force. That afternoon there was a flurry of excitement when two VS-5 SBDs spotted a submarine only 32 miles north of the ships. Three TBDs bombed the I-boat with uncertain results. The rest of the day and through much of the next, Task Force 17 steamed northward, zigzagging at speeds slow enough to permit the destroyers to top off from the oiler *Neosho*.

Fighting Forty-two Squadron Organization, 1 May 1942

Aircraft*

1st Division
F-1	Lt. Cdr. Charles R. Fenton, USN (commanding officer)
F-2	Ens. Harry B. Gibbs, A-V(N)
F-3	Lieut. (jg) William N. Leonard, USN (materiel officer)
F-4	Ens. William W. Barnes, Jr., A-V(N)
F-5	Lieut. (jg) Richard G. Crommelin, USN (personnel officer)
F-6	Ens. Richard L. Wright, A-V(N)

2nd Division
F-7	Lt. Cdr. James H. Flatley, Jr., USN (executive officer)
F-8	Ens. John D. Baker, A-V(N)
F-9	Lieut. (jg) Brainard T. Macomber, A-V(N) (communications officer)
F-10	Ens. Edgar R. Bassett, A-V(N)
F-11	Lieut. (jg) E. Scott McCuskey, A-V(N) (gunnery officer)
F-12	Ens. John P. Adams, A-V(N)

3rd Division
F-13	Lieut. Vincent F. McCormack, USN (flight officer)
F-14	Ens. Walter A. Haas, A-V(N)
F-15	Lieut. (jg) Arthur J. Brassfield, USN (engineer officer)
F-16	Lieut. (jg) E. Duran Mattson, USN
F-17	Lieut. (jg) William S. Woollen, A-V(N)
F-18	Ens. Leslie L. B. Knox, A-V(N)
F-19	(spare)
	Not flying (ill):
	Lieut. (jg) Roy M. Plott, USN

*Nominal aircraft only.

Orders finally arrived from Washington to clear up the confusion of who commanded VF-42. On 28 April, BuNav confirmed Fenton as CO of VF-42, directing that previous orders (which had not even reached the *Yorktown*) be canceled. On 1 May, the Bureau directed that Flatley be detached from VF-42 to return to San Diego and take command of a newly created squadron, Fighting Ten—part of Carrier Replacement Air Group Ten. That ended the awkward situation caused by Flatley's unexpected appearance and was fair to both men. Captain Buckmaster instructed Flatley to get packed and board the *Neosho* that evening. The oiler was scheduled to leave for Pearl in the next few days and at least might be able to drop him off at Fiji or Samoa, where he could obtain air transport. Flatley persuaded Buckmaster to let him remain temporarily with the squadron as XO and fight in the upcoming battle. There was no way Flatley was going to miss that if he could help it![1]

Fletcher carefully monitored contact reports from Allied aircraft searching the Bismarcks and Solomons. Finally at 1900 on 3 May came the news he awaited. Aircraft on 2 May had spotted enemy ships off Santa Isabell Island closing in on the small Australian base at Tulagi, already evacuated. Fletcher thought the opportunity to hit the invasion force worth changing his rendezvous plans. At 2030, he detached the *Neosho* and a destroyer to make the scheduled meeting and inform Fitch and Crace of developments. Meanwhile the rest of Task Force 17 (the *Yorktown*, three heavy cruisers, and six destroyers) headed north at 27 knots toward Guadalcanal in an effort to reach by dawn a suitable launch point for an attack on Tulagi.

On board the flattop, her crew felt the old girl pick up speed, obviously heading somewhere important. Scott McCuskey, for one, headed for the ready room. There he learned that Guadalcanal and Tulagi were the destinations, but no one seemed to know much about the target area. The ship was preparing photostat copies of an old Admiralty chart to hand out for the mission next day. That evening Mc-Cuskey searched the ship's library for any information on the Solomons. All he could find was a book about Guadalcanal stating that the island had been renowned for its ferocious cannibals, but that happily missionaries had tamed the natives. McCuskey did not know it, but on 4 May he would become much more closely acquainted with Guadalcanal and its inhabitants.

TULAGI STRIKE

The dawn of 4 May saw Task Force 17 operating about 100 miles south of Guadalcanal. During the night the ships had entered a cold front that brought thickly overcast skies punctuated by intermittent rain squalls. A southeasterly wind gusted to 35 knots. This definitely was not ideal flying weather, but the *Yorktown* planners welcomed it as excellent concealment for the task force and the surprise attack they hoped to spring on Tulagi. The *Yorktown* had available a total of sixty operational aircraft: eighteen F4F-3 Wildcats, thirty SBD-3 dive bombers, and twelve TBD-1 torpedo planes. The Tulagi strike group would comprise twenty-eight dive bombers and twelve torpedo planes organized as follows:

Scouting Five	Lt. Cdr. William O. Burch, Jr.	13 SBD-3s
Bombing Five	Lieut. Wallace C. Short	15 SBD-3s
Torpedo Five	Lt. Cdr. Joe Taylor	12 TBD-1s

The SBDs each lugged one 1,000-lb. bomb, while the Devastators this time carried one aerial torpedo apiece. Task Force 17 would launch from about 100 miles south of the target area. The attack plan included no provision for fighter escorts, as Fletcher and Buckmaster believed it necessary to retain all of VF-42's fighters in direct defense of the task force, thinking it unlikely that the Japanese would have an effective fighter defense over newly occupied Tulagi.

On board the *Yorktown*, preparations had proceeded smoothly for the attack. Buckmaster was particularly pleased at the efficient way in which his crews before dawn and without deck lights had armed and spotted aircraft on deck. At 0631, the carrier sent aloft on CAP the six F4Fs of Lieut. McCormack's 3rd Division. While the fighters circled the task force, the *Yorktown* then launched the Tulagi attack force in two deckloads: first Taylor's TBDs, then the SBDs led by Burch and Short. The attack squadrons used normal departure, which meant that each squadron formed up on its own and made its way independently to the target. No air group commander was aloft. The newly appointed *Yorktown* Air Group commander, VF-42's old skipper Pete Pederson, remained on board at Buckmaster's express order. He was the only fighter director officer whose competence Buckmaster respected. In this instance, the *Yorktown*'s captain felt that fighter direction duty was more important than leading the air group in action. Pederson vehemently disagreed, but there was nothing he could do about it.

The flight north was uneventful. Crossing Guadalcanal's sharp ridges, the strike planes broke into clear air and found weather conditions in the target area to be excellent. Bill Burch, whose Scouting Five was in the lead, discerned Tulagi on the horizon shortly after 0800 and saw numerous Japanese ships in and around the harbor. What he had discovered was the Tulagi Invasion Force under Rear Admiral

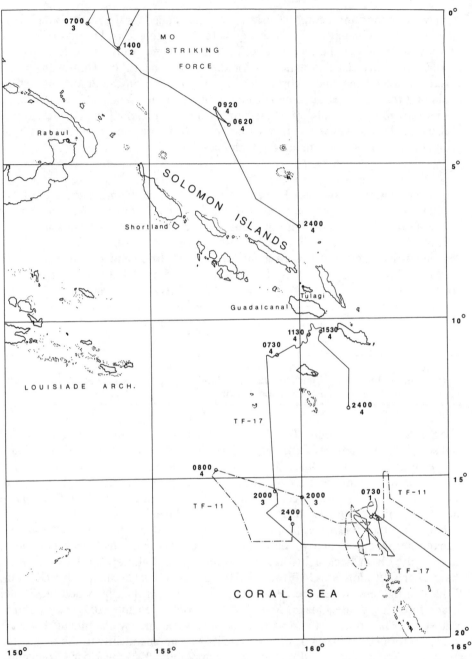

Carrier operations, Coral Sea, 1–4 May.

Shima Kiyohide, and the Japanese were busy unloading supplies and erecting a seaplane base at Tulagi. Shima's flagship, the large minelayer *Okinoshima*, lay at anchor in harbor with one destroyer nested on either side for fueling. Two large transports, surrounded by numerous small craft, swung at anchor. Two small sub-chasers were in attendance. Just recently having left the harbor and steaming northwestward were three auxiliary minesweepers bound for Shortland. Shima's flying boats searched to the northeast and east of Tulagi, and his only immediate air support would prove to be small floatplanes.

The Yorktowners achieved complete tactical surprise. Starting at 0815, Burch's thirteen SBDs swarmed after the *Okinoshima* and her two consorts, the destroyers *Kikuzuki* and *Yūzuki*. Diving in from 10,000 feet, the VS-5 pilots thought they scored four hits on a "light cruiser." They experienced great difficulty in bombing because their chilled telescopic sights fogged as they entered warmer, humid air below 7,000 feet. On board the three enemy vessels, crews worked frantically to raise steam and get under way. The targets took no hits from VS-5's attack. Next came Taylor's Torpedo Five. Three TBDs singled out the transport *Azumasan Maru* anchored off Tulagi's northeast shore, while nearby, two others took after the transport *Kōei Maru* riding at anchor off the little islands of Gavutu and Tanambogo. The TBDs scored no hits, mainly because of faulty torpedoes. Torpedo Five's main body deployed to make an anvil attack on the minelayer and the two destroyers. One torpedo did run true and slammed into the *Kikuzuki*. Her crew had to beach her. Bombing Five split up to go after several ships. Fifteen 1,000-lb. bombs hurtled through the air, but made no direct hits, again because of fogged bombsights.

Meanwhile at 0844, the *Yorktown* took the opportunity to rotate her CAP, launching Lt. Cdr. Fenton's 1st Division of six VF-42 fighters. About a half hour later, strike planes began returning to the task force. To clear the flight deck, the *Yorktown* sent aloft VF-42's 2nd Division led by Lt. Cdr. Flatley, giving her twelve fighters airborne as CAP for the recovery and rearming of the strike group. Beginning at 0931, the *Yorktown* landed all forty strike aircraft without mishap. Quickly debriefing the pilots, the air department totaled up the targets and reported damage. Fletcher decided to launch a second strike as soon as the planes could be rearmed and refueled. As yet, no enemy search planes had turned up, and from the urgent messages streaming out of Tulagi, the attackers had raised quite a fuss. At 1036, the *Yorktown* despatched fourteen VB-5 SBDs with orders to scout west and northwest of Florida Island before turning back south for Tulagi. About a half hour later, Burch led thirteen SBDs from his Scouting Five out to attack Tulagi, and on his heels were eleven TBDs from Torpedo Five. Her decks clear of bombers, the *Yorktown* at 1127 recovered VF-42's 1st Division, leaving Flatley's six on patrol. At noon, the carrier got around to launching McCormack's six F4Fs, restoring the CAP to twelve. For Fighting Forty-two, the day was proving to be only routine flying.

Near tiny Savo Island, Bombing Five overhauled the three small converted minesweepers bound for Shortland. Direct hits by the massive thousand-pounders sank two of them, while effects from near misses roughed up the third, the *Tama Maru*. Meanwhile, Shima had ordered his ships to clear the area. At 1210, Burch found the *Okinoshima* just outside Tulagi harbor. Scouting Five attacked and claimed two hits, but the smartly handled, 20-knot minelayer came through unscathed. At 1215, someone in Scouting Five sang out over the radio, "Jap seaplane. Jap seaplane. Ya got your gun out my friends?"[1] A Japanese Mitsubishi Type 0 observation floatplane [PETE] tried to intervene in the dives, but one of Burch's SBDs shot it down for its trouble.

Fighter Sweep to Tulagi

Throughout the morning of 4 May while the *Yorktown*'s strike planes merrily chased the Japanese ships out of Tulagi, her fighter pilots flew normal CAPs and stayed clear of the SBDs and TBDs as they shuttled to and from the flight deck. At 1242 in a quiet interlude, the *Yorktown* came around into the southeasterly trades and brought in Flatley's six F4Fs for fuel and a blow. This left McCormack's division aloft in increasingly nasty weather, while waiting on the flight deck on standby were Fenton's six F4Fs. Ready to man them if required for an alert or taxiing forward were pilots whose duty it was to remain in the squadron ready room until needed to move aircraft.

Shortly before 1300, the eleven TBDs of Torpedo Five once more tackled the *Okinoshima*, but the sleek minelayer handily evaded all the fish. Again, a Type 0 floatplane from the same unit as the first, the *Kiyokawa Maru* Air Group, tried to challenge the attackers. The torpedo planes reported the presence of enemy planes, but were in no real difficulty. A couple of them chased the Japanese aircraft back to its roost at Makambo Island in Tulagi harbor. No TBDs were lost during the attack, but one flown by Lieut. Leonard H. Ewoldt missed rendezvous and became separated from the rest of the squadron.

The *Yorktown* carefully monitored the radio traffic, and Buckmaster at 1303 heard from VT-5's chatter that enemy aircraft were harassing the torpedo planes at Tulagi. Responding quickly, he ordered four F4Fs to be launched and sent posthaste to Tulagi to deal with the enemy interceptors. Meanwhile, the air officer directed that the remaining F4Fs be sent down the forward elevator into the hangar in order to clear the deck for the swift recovery, rearming, and launch of strike planes en route back to the carrier. In the ready room, the VF-42 pilots got the word via the sound-powered phone to man aircraft. The bullhorn alerted flight deck personnel to ready F4Fs by starting engines. Expecting merely to taxi fighters up deck, the VF-42 pilots jumped into the cockpits of the nearest Wildcats and awaited orders. Four would have a surprise in store. Instead of their being led to the elevator, the airdales coached them into launch position. Roy Plott, acting as the VF ready room duty officer, rushed out holding a chalkboard bearing orders for the four to proceed to Tulagi. Plott raised the board so that each of the pilots could copy the course and distance to the target. That was all.

At 1311 with a wave of his flag, the launching officer despatched the four F4Fs one by one. Not until they joined in formation did the pilots recognize one another and work out who flew with whom. The four were Bill Leonard in command, Edgar Bassett on his wing, Scott McCuskey, and, on McCuskey's wing, Johnny Adams. No one was fully prepared for the mission. McCuskey, for one, had been subbing for one of the 1st Division ready pilots who had been released to grab a quick lunch. He neglected to bring his chartboard and navigational gear with him on deck because he had no idea a combat mission was pending. After the F4Fs departed, the *Yorktown* began recovering twelve SBDs from Scouting Five and nine from Bombing Five in order to use them in a third attack.

Leonard set a brisk pace that made the other three pilots nervous, but all realized that in order to do any good at Tulagi, they had better get there in a hurry. Crossing the band of nasty weather stirred up by the cold front, they emerged into bright sunlight near the south coast of Guadalcanal. Leonard led his fighters directly across the middle of that soon-to-be-infamous isle, then turned northwest over Sealark Channel toward Tulagi. With Guadalcanal's mountainous spine behind them, the F4Fs had let down to 4,000 feet, looking for action.

By the time the fighters reached the combat area, the *Yorktown* strike planes had already disposed of both Japanese seaplanes and departed for home. Looking around for someone to protect, Leonard flew northwest along the coast of Florida Island. At 1350, three enemy seaplanes suddenly appeared at 1,500 feet on an opposite heading. The newcomers were three Mitsubishi F1M2 Type 0 observation floatplanes from the *Kamikawa Maru* Air Group. The Japanese commander at Shortland had sent them south posthaste to assist in the defense of Tulagi. To

Bill Leonard in 1942-style flight gear, including the troublesome throat mike. Photo taken in fall 1942. (RADM W. N. Leonard, USN.)

signal his attack, Leonard rocked his wings and dived in after the Japanese. His wingman Bassett followed. From both sides of the Japanese formation deployed in line-astern, the two F4Fs made simultaneous high-side runs. As his target, Leonard singled out the second floatplane in line, while Bassett took the trailer. Leonard's quarry pulled into a tight, climbing turn to scissor the Grumman roaring in from above. Leonard's four .50-calibers overwhelmed his opponent's pair of 7.7-mm weapons. Blossoming flames, the floatplane started for the water.

Recovering from his attack, Leonard was surprised to see that the Japanese leader had whipped around tightly and ended up clawing his tail. Wait a minute! Floatplanes were not supposed to be able to do that. Tightening his own turn, Leonard offered his pursuer only a full deflection shot, then added throttle and accelerated away from danger. Up above the Mitsubishi once again, Leonard dropped into another steep attack, which the Japanese likewise countered with a scissors for a head-on approach. The results were the same as before—scratch one floatplane. Meanwhile, "Red Dog" Bassett had forced the third Japanese to break off and try to escape at low altitude. Bassett overhauled the fleeing enemy and shot him down over Tulagi.

Amazed, Leonard compared the performance of the enemy floatplanes with U.S. naval float observation types such as the obsolete Curtiss SOC. The reason for the F1M2's "tigerish" nature lay in the fact that the sleek biplane sported an 875-hp radial engine. The two VF-42 pilots might have run into much more trouble if the Japanese had tried violent evasive maneuvers, rather than countering the more powerful Grummans with conventional scissors tactics. In head-on runs, they were no match for the F4Fs. With his report, Leonard submitted a surprisingly accurate sketch of this new Japanese aircraft type, later dubbed PETE.

When Leonard and Bassett dived away, McCuskey and Adams did not follow. McCuskey saw no enemy aircraft and could not receive orders by radio because of a bum receiver. Aware that enemy fighters probably were nearby, he thought it best to maintain altitude as top cover until he was certain the division would not be jumped. The two VF-42 pilots took a quick look around, then dived in to find the leader. Just northwest of Florida Island, McCuskey and Adams came upon the hurt minesweeper *Tama Maru*, a 264-ton converted whalecatcher, limping north after being worked over that morning by Bombing Five. With several strafing runs, the two Grummans thoroughly shot out the hapless little *Maru*. Her captain ran his vessel aground at Hanesavu on Florida Island, about fifteen miles northwest of Tulagi. The *Tama Maru* finally sank two days later.

The old Japanese destroyer *Yūzuki* (commissioned in 1927) offered herself as the next victim. Escaping from Tulagi, she had separated from the *Okinoshima* and steamed northwest toward Savo Island. McCuskey and Adams roared through a couple of strafing runs, drawing only a feeble response from the *Yūzuki*'s anti-aircraft guns. Leonard and Bassett then appeared after their fight with the *Kamikawa Maru* floatplanes. At the leader's direction, the division took strafing formation, and using the tactics previously practiced during the cruise made four coordinated runs in succession against the destroyer. Each Grumman pilot opened fire at about 3,500 feet and pressed within masthead height before pulling out. They concentrated their tracers on the *Yūzuki*'s bridge, machinery spaces, and torpedo mounts. Heavy .50-caliber slugs riddled the vessel, starting fires and holing oil bunkers. A thick trail of fuel oil lay in the destroyer's wake. During the first two runs, Leonard noticed some return fire, but he saw no response on the final two passes. At 1410 when the fighters broke off, they left the tincan in such bad shape that she had to crawl back to Rabaul for emergency repairs. Bullets had killed her skipper, Lt. Cdr. Tachibana Hirota, and nine of his crew, while another twenty were wounded. The destroyer *Uzuki*, detached from the Port Moresby Invasion Force, had to replace the *Yūzuki* in the invasion of Ocean and Nauru islands scheduled for 15 May.

On board the *Yorktown*, the air department worked feverishly to refuel and rearm the twenty-one SBDs which had begun landing around 1319. Fletcher intended to make a third attack, and at 1325 sent a message to his cruiser commander, Rear Admiral Smith, indicating his desire to detach two heavy cruisers and two destroyers to proceed to Tulagi "to mop up damaged ships at daylight."[2] Smith nominated his flagship *Astoria* and the *Chester*. Just before 1400, the *Yorktown* launched the twenty-one SBDs for the third strike against enemy ships near Tulagi. About twenty minutes later, the carrier launched Fenton's six F4Fs as relief CAP, then landed sixteen aircraft from the second strike and McCormack's six F4Fs from the CAP. It was getting late in the day for further air operations, especially since the weather south of Guadalcanal turned even squallier as the ships paralleled Guadalcanal's south coast on an easterly heading. Further damage would have to be inflicted by Smith's warships if Fletcher went ahead with his plan to send them to Tulagi.

His own duty completed, Leonard led his division of F4Fs on course directly for the task force. They cut across the western tip of Guadalcanal and headed southeast into the Coral Sea. South of the big island, the VF-42 pilots happened upon an orphan, the missing VT-5 TBD flown by Lieut. Ewoldt; he had lost his way with neither his radio nor his Zed Baker VHF homing receiver working properly. Ewoldt joined the fighters happily, as it appeared they knew where they were going. A difficult problem now confronted all the aviators. The thick cloud cover began a thousand feet or less above the water and broke into the clear only above 2,000 feet. If the pilots remained under the clouds, they would be able to see the ships—if they came into visual range. Flying below the clouds, however, would put them too low to use their Zed Baker homing devices, which, being VHF equipment, were useful only at line-of-sight altitudes. If the pilots climbed high enough to pick up the *Yorktown*'s YE/ZB homing signal, that would put them well above the clouds and unable to see any ships. For the time being, Leonard thought it best to fly just beneath the cloud layer, and at McCuskey's suggestion, he deployed the division into a scouting line, the TBD in the center and a section of F4Fs spread out on either side. The aircraft opened a wide interval to search out a larger expanse of ocean.

Already aloft well over three hours, Ewoldt now became very worried about his fuel supply. Finally he signaled Leonard that he was going to turn back toward Guadalcanal, as he felt he no longer had enough gasoline to reach the carrier. Ewoldt also beckoned Adams over to tell him of his decision. While this was going on, Leonard himself decided to waste no more time at this altitude. He wanted to take his division above the cloud layer and tune in the *Yorktown*'s YE homing signal on the Zed Bakers. Unfortunately both Adams and McCuskey were involved in communicating with the torpedo plane and failed to notice Leonard's signal. Once the leader's section had climbed into the overcast, they lost touch with the other pilots. Reaching a suitable altitude on top, Leonard remained tuned to the CAP frequency while Bassett, as directed, succeeded in tuning in the homing signal. Using hand signals, Bassett headed the two fighters in the proper direction.

When Adams and McCuskey had finished conferring with Ewoldt, they looked about only to discover that the rest of the division had vanished. McCuskey was not too certain about his own fuel supply. In the hasty launch, he had failed to note the time of departure, and so did not know just how long he had been flying. The F4F's fuel gauges were notoriously unreliable, and McCuskey was unsure whether he and his wingman had the fuel required to search for the task force. Ruefully he saw the TBD turn back in the direction of Guadalcanal. The Devastator's large liferaft could comfortably hold the two VF-42 pilots as well as Ewoldt's crew, whereas the F4Fs carried only small rubber boats stowed in the dorsal fairing behind the cockpit, and it was by no means certain during a ditching that the pilots would have the time or opportunity to remove them. Ewoldt, as it turned out, lacked the fuel even to reach Guadalcanal. At 1536, he radioed the ship (evidently, like McCuskey, he had a functioning radio transmitter but a nonworking receiver) and then put the TBD into the water a few miles off Guadalcanal's south coast.

While Ewoldt, McCuskey, and Adams tried to figure out what to do, the *Yorktown*'s third strike had come and gone. At 1500, Bill Burch with twelve SBDs from Scouting Five arrived over Tulagi and attacked the only undamaged vessel still there, the anchored transport *Azumasan Maru*. Burch thought he secured one hit, but the ship sustained only minor hull damage from near misses. On the way out, the SBDs strafed a subchaser outside the harbor. Bombing Five overtook the transport *Kōei Maru* picking up survivors near Savo, but Short left her alone and followed a broad streak of oil on the water. This led them to the *Yūzuki* and the *Okinoshima* steaming off Russell Island. The nine SBDs attacked the *Okinoshima*, but again the big minelayer led a charmed life and took no hits. Around 1515, the SBDs turned back for the carrier, the last *Yorktown* planes to leave the target area. Beating them back to the flattop were Leonard and Bassett. "Red Dog" unerringly led his division leader to the task force, and the two F4Fs landed at 1542. There was no sign of the other two F4Fs, McCuskey and Adams.

After the TBD ditched, McCuskey opted for another try to reach home plate. He led Adams south on the same heading that Leonard had taken upon leaving Guadalcanal. The return flight began to look more dubious by the minute. Suddenly Adams enthusiastically signaled by hand requesting the lead. McCuskey gave it to him, believing that his wingman might have radio contact with the *Yorktown*. To McCuskey's amazement, Adams instead of taking a likely heading for the ship turned almost 180 degrees to fly north. After a few minutes, he swung east for a short time, then finally settled on a southeasterly heading. Adams, in fact, had broken through the static and conversed with the group commander. Back on board the *Yorktown*, Pederson had on radar what he thought were the two errant F4Fs. To be certain, he instructed Adams to fly a box before giving him the proper course to the task force. His receiver not working, McCuskey was not party to the conversation and could only watch and wonder what on earth his wingman was trying to do. He concluded that Adams had become totally disoriented. Not much fuel remained, and McCuskey felt there was no way the two could search out the carrier and still return to land if unsuccessful.

Charging up alongside his wingman, McCuskey signaled him to relinquish the lead. Adams refused. McCuskey then made it perfectly plain over the radio that he would brook no insubordination from his wingman. Both of them were going back to the beach. Adams turned to follow him. He was not about to fly off and leave his section leader, but followed "the book" and stayed with him. McCuskey made a sweep along Guadalcanal's southeast coast looking for a suitable place to land. A narrow rocky beach near Cape Henslow looked fine, so McCuskey cranked his landing gear halfway down to serve as a cushion and started in. On the sand, he expertly set down the F4F without much trouble. He radioed Adams that the landing was easy and added as a humorous conclusion, "Let's go native!"[3] This was to encourage Adams, who had taken a gunsight bracket in the teeth when he had ditched on 1 April.

All along, Adams had maintained contact with Pederson and kept him abreast of the situation. He checked his chart (something McCuskey did not have) and correctly determined that the landing site was near Cape Henslow. Pederson gave him permission to land, so Adams likewise lowered his gear part way and made a flawless touchdown. On running up to his wingman to congratulate him, McCuskey was mortified to learn that Adams had indeed raised the ship and knew the way home. For Scott McCuskey it was "the worst moment of the war."[4] He had put two irreplaceable fighters (under the circumstances) up on the beach. His own Grumman (Bu.No. 3972) was one of the six VF-42 aircraft with the secret IFF gear, so he immediately removed the device, crushed it, and threw the pieces into the surf.

While McCuskey destroyed the top secret gear, Adams spotted a band of natives coming toward him on the beach. There was nothing the two could do but act friendly, hoping all the stories about South Seas cannibals were not true. The red-stained teeth of the Guadalcanalers was a little disconcerting, but these betelnut chewers turned out to be most hospitable. Every single one of them, "including the smallest child,"[5] shook hands with the two fighter pilots. Through sign language, McCuskey and Adams obtained coconuts, and the locals led them along the beach until they came to a fresh stream. It looked like a good place to camp, so the two strung out a parachute as a tent and began "setting up housekeeping for the duration."[6] Certainly they had no expectations of an early rescue. Their hosts seemed especially excited when they learned their two guests were Americans, as they were well acquainted with an American missionary priest on the island.

Fletcher had no intention of leaving any aviators behind if there was a chance they could be rescued. Because Task Force 17 had held an easterly heading that day, by 1600 when the two F4Fs crashed-landed at Cape Henslow, the ships were only 42 miles south of there. First Fletcher ordered the destroyer *Perkins* to search for the crew of the downed TBD, and at 1610, also instructed the destroyer *Hammann* to rescue the two pilots who had landed at Cape Henslow. He canceled the planned attack on Tulagi by Smith's cruisers. After the two destroyers cut out of formation, the *Yorktown* completed the day's air operations. At 1628 she launched Flatley's 2nd Division with six fighters to fly the dusk CAP, then landed Fenton's six F4Fs and twenty-nine SBDs from the two dive bombing squadrons. At 1747 with darkness closing in, the *Yorktown* recovered Flatley's fighters and closed up shop for the night. Total aircraft losses that day were three: the two F4Fs and one TBD. After sunset, Fletcher changed course to 130 degrees and sped off at 23 knots for his rendezvous with Task Forces 11 and 44 and the fueling group at "Point Corn."

The *Hammann*'s skipper, Cdr. Arnold E. True, steamed north at 30 knots, and about 80 minutes later arrived off Cape Henslow in a rainstorm. Because of shallow water, he could bring the destroyer no closer than about three miles from shore. The *Hammann*'s lookouts sighted the two Grummans squatting on the lonely beach and also noticed a white marker (the parachute) about a quarter mile down the coast. At 1750, the *Hammann* launched a whaleboat commanded by Ens. Robert F. P. Enright, D-V(G), USNR, with orders to recover the two pilots and see to the destruction of their aircraft. Enright conned his boat to within about 150 yards of shore, but the heavy surf and rugged coastline brought him up short.

Yelling "Dingy! Dinghy!," one of the natives ran up to McCuskey and Adams and pointed to the warship lurking off shore. Worried that the vessel was Japanese, Adams looked her over but soon recognized her as the *Hammann*, the tincan that had hauled him on board when he ditched on 1 April. McCuskey's first thought was to burn the two aircraft, and he took off running while holding a lighted cigarette and a piece of paper to use as tinder. A rain squall soon extinguished that idea. By the time he returned to the stream where Adams waited, the whaleboat was well on its way. The two VF-42 pilots broke out their small rubber rafts, while Enright, caught in the swirl of the incoming tide, tried to stay off the shallow beach. The little rafts could not overcome the surf and make it out to the boat. A line tied round him, Coxswain George W. Kapp went over the side to swim to the beach. He made contact with McCuskey and Adams, and the whaleboat crew then hauled all three men back to the craft.

Enright's orders to destroy the aircraft were explicit, so he guided the boat along the beach and worked his way as close to shore as he dared. The crew pumped submachine gun bullets into the two imperturbable Grummans, but as McCuskey explained, there was little chance of igniting the fuel because of the self-sealing fuel tanks. He volunteered to swim back to the beach carrying a can of flares, and to try to set them aflame that way. The effort was almost McCuskey's last. Caught in the heavy surf, he encountered a fast undertow, became fouled in the line which he had to untie, and only just made it to shore before succumbing to complete exhaustion. After resting to regain some strength, he walked over to the aircraft which by this time were sitting in the sea, washed by the incoming tide. As if to prove Murphy's law, water had leaked into McCuskey's sealed can of flares, and they were useless. After all of the frustrations of that long day, this was almost too much to take.

Not knowing what had happened to McCuskey in the darkness, those in the boat had more problems when the line wrapped itself around the whaleboat's propellor and stopped the engine. While the crew paddled furiously to keep her away from the rocks, Albert/S. Jason, BM2c, jumped overboard with a knife and a hacksaw, with which he managed to remove the rope. Kapp then tried to swim a second time to the beach, but had to turn back. Finally Jason volunteered to go and made it to shore with a line and a flare pistol tucked safely away. He found McCuskey sitting dejectedly in the cockpit of his aircraft, trying to figure how in blazes he could destroy the two very wet Grummans. So determined was he to torch the F4Fs that Jason had to argue him out of firing the flare pistol directly into the fuel tank nozzle—a dangerous proposition indeed. Unable to destroy the aircraft, McCuskey and Jason abandoned them to the rising tide and swam out to the whaleboat. By means of the line Jason had brought, the crew pulled the two men in. At 2048, the whaleboat finally returned to the destroyer. Hospitably, the *Hammann*'s crew made the pilots welcome, gave them dry clothes, fed them, and showed them to bunks.[7]

Task Force 17 was elated at the reported destruction of shipping round Tulagi. The aviators claimed sinking two destroyers, one transport, and four small gunboats, beaching one light cruiser, and inflicting heavy damage on one seaplane tender and one destroyer. They shot down five floatplanes. Against this was the loss of three of the *Yorktown*'s aircraft. Actual results were not so impressive. The Yorktowners sank the destroyer *Kikuzuki*, the minesweeper *Tama Maru*, and the No. 1 (*Wa* 1) and No. 2 (*Wa* 2) Special Duty Minesweepers. The *Okinoshima* and the destroyer *Yūzuki* incurred what the Japanese described as "minor damage," although the *Yūzuki* had to be replaced in her next scheduled mission. CinCPac later placed the blame for the poor accuracy of the *Yorktown*'s pilots on faulty materiel (fogged bombsights) and the lack of bombing practice necessitated by their carrier's long sojourn in the South Pacific.

GATHERING STORM: 5–6 MAY IN THE CORAL SEA

Jubilant at the presumed success of his Tulagi strike, Fletcher during the predawn hours of 5 May steamed southward for the rendezvous with Fitch's Task Force 11, Crace's Task Force 44, and the fueling group. The destroyers *Hammann* and *Perkins* followed some distance behind. After an extended search, the *Perkins* had been unable to locate the crew of the downed TBD, but Ewoldt was later rescued. The *Hammann* had on board VF-42's McCuskey and Adams, fresh from their adventures on Guadalcanal.

Task Force 17 the morning of 5 May emerged from the gloomy overcast of the cold front into excellent weather. The *Yorktown*'s SBDs fanned out to search astern of the task force to determine whether any Japanese were in pursuit. At 0740, one search pilot reported an enemy submarine bearing 285 degrees, distance 150 miles, and on course toward the task force. The ship later sent out three TBDs to look for the contact, but they found nothing. Only a few minutes after the SBD contact report was received, the enemy appeared much closer to Task Force 17. At about 0750, the *Yorktown*'s CXAM radar detected a bogey bearing 252 degrees, distance 30 miles. No CAP fighters had yet taken off, so Buckmaster scrambled four VF-42 F4Fs from McCormack's 3rd Division. Loath to break radio silence, Pederson gave McCormack a steer before takeoff, telling him to head out on a course of 275 degrees (M.) at 2,000 feet and proceed 25 miles if necessary.

Reaching the end of his navigational leg, McCormack at 0810 discerned ahead the cause of all the bother. The bogey turned out to be a Japanese Kawanishi Type 97 flying boat, one of nine from the Yokohama Air Group which searched for the ships that had attacked Tulagi the previous day. The big plane cruised at 700 feet, unaware of the ambush McCormack was setting up. The division leader and his wingman, Walt Haas, flew over the snooper to gain favorable attack position. Art Brassfield, leading the 2nd section, dived in toward the target's starboard bow.

After firing on his opposite run, Brassfield recovered on the same side. Next came McCormack with a shallow high-side attack from left of the Kawanishi. Finished shooting, he pulled out over the enemy's long parasol wing and climbed away. Smoke trailed from two of the Type 97's four radial engines. Following his leader, Haas duplicated his attack.

Just as Haas pulled out, the Kawanishi suddenly nosed down, flame shooting from all four engines. Coming around for his second shot was Brassfield, while his wingman, Duran Mattson, was beginning his first run. There was no time for that. Fire spread along the center wing section and into the fuselage of the patrol plane. Never recovering from its dive, the Kawanishi plunged into the water, its burning debris raising a large pillar of smoke. The entire action had taken less than 30 seconds. Ammunition expenditure on the part of the fighter pilots was remarkably low: McCormack 100 rounds, Haas 120 rounds, and Brassfield 40 rounds, while Mattson never had a chance to shoot.[1] The Japanese flying boat splashed about 15 miles from Task Force 11 at the rendezvous and 27 miles from Task Force 17. American opinion had it that the snooper likely was trailing Task Force 11. Whatever the Japanese was doing, no contact report from the flying boat reached base. When 5th Air Attack Force headquarters later failed to raise the flying boat by radio, they correctly assumed enemy fighters had shot it down.

Welcomed by the specter of the flying boat's funeral pyre, Task Forces 11 and 17 made visual contact at 0816. Fletcher began fueling his own ships, first by transferring oil from the Neosho to the heavy cruisers, then by having the destroyers draw fuel from the cruisers. That day the Hammann rejoined and later the Perkins, and the two wayward VF-42 pilots ended back on board the Yorktown. It appeared to McCuskey that "everyone on the ship seemed after his scalp."[2] In a verbal chewing out by VF-42's skipper, Fenton took his section away from McCuskey and temporarily grounded him. He took McCuskey to task for not following Leonard into the overcast, but staying back with Ewoldt. Most of the frustration stemmed from the fact that two virtually irreplaceable Grummans lay rusting on the beach. Really at fault in this incident was the hasty nature of the launch without proper briefing. McCuskey was to be deckbound for two days.

The fifth of May was important to Fletcher because of the special intelligence information received that day from CinCPac. One message placed the Japanese fleet carriers far to the north near Bougainville, and the second indicated the enemy flattops were expected to approach Port Moresby (likely from the southeast) and launch a strike on either $X-3$ or $X-2$ Day. CinCPac had good reason to believe that X-Day, thought to be the landing date against Port Moresby, was 10 May, meaning that the carrier strikes on Port Moresby might take place on 7 or 8 May. Based on the information furnished, Fletcher and Fitch deduced that the Japanese convoy would proceed south from Rabaul, traverse the reef-studded Louisiade Archipelago, and approach Port Moresby in time to land troops on 10 May. The Japanese fleet carriers Shōkaku and Zuikaku, they expected, would stay relatively close to the invasion convoy, both to protect the ships and to take position to launch the ordered air strikes on Port Moresby. Fletcher planned to complete his fueling on 6 May, then head northwest toward the Louisiades in order to offer battle on 7 May. On the whole, 5 May was a quiet day for Task Force 17.

For Task Force 17, 6 May was to be another fueling day in anticipation of meeting the Japanese in the next few days. Fletcher's vessels steamed on a northwesterly heading, while the Lexington handled the dawn search, sending SBDs northward 275 miles. At 0700, Fletcher promulgated his operations order 2-42. This combined Task Forces 11 and 44 into one large Task Force 17. Fitch, as Com-

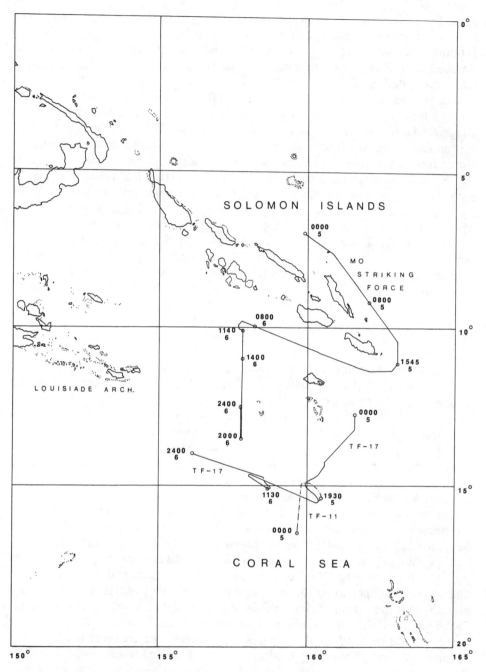

Carrier operations, Coral Sea, 5–6 May.

mander, Task Group 17.5 (Air), took direct command of the two carriers *Lexington* and *Yorktown*, while the heavy cruisers and destroyers were divided among Task Group 17.2 (Attack) under Rear Admiral Thomas C. Kinkaid and Task Group 17.3 (Support) under Rear Admiral Crace, RN. A half hour later, Task Force 17 changed course to the southeast to resume fueling. The weather was fine as the ships remained just south of the band of overcast skies and rain showers on the edge of the cold front.

Around 1015, the *Yorktown*'s radar detected a bogey lurking in the bad weather to the north. The carrier scrambled fighters to fly CAP, and during a mix-up, Bill Leonard ended up with another section leader, his roommate Lieut. (jg) Richard G. Crommelin, flying on his wing. The *Lexington*'s FDO, Lieut. Gill, veteran of the 20 February fight, took over directing the CAP. The fighters hunted diligently through a terrible overcast ranging in some places from 1,000 feet up to 27,000 feet, but they were unable to overtake the snooper. Spotters on board the heavy cruiser *New Orleans* actually sighted the Japanese aircraft as it momentarily broke into the clear. Fletcher discontinued fueling and made ready to fight, but the enemy did not close. Perforce, Fletcher resumed fueling, giving his cruisers fuel to make up for the oil they had provided the destroyers. He knew the enemy had spotted him, but it was important to ready his vessels for the coming battle. That afternoon, the *Lexington*'s SBDs again searched 275 miles to the northwest, but likewise sighted no enemy ships.

The battle that Task Force 17 expected on 7 May almost took place a day earlier.[3] The Japanese search plane that spotted and skillfully tracked Task Force 17 was one of five Kawanishi Type 97 flying boats that had taken off from Tulagi at 0630. The aircraft first reported the Americans at 1000, giving their position as bearing 192 degrees, distance 420 miles from Tulagi. Its crew issued excellent contact reports (not all of which were received back at headquarters owing to atmospheric conditions) and maintained contact until after 1400. They were the only members of the Yokohama Air Group to spot the American carriers during the Battle of the Coral Sea and live to tell of it. The 5th Air Attack Force tried to organize dusk torpedo strikes by Tulagi-based flying boats. One Kawanishi left there at 1400 to try to make contact to shadow the enemy carriers, in order to guide the rest of the dusk strike force to the target. However, they failed to locate Task Force 17 before darkness intervened.

Operating where he was, out of air attack range of Rabaul and well southwest of Tulagi, Fletcher knew the enemy had his location, and he accepted the risk of a long-range attack by flying boats. He did not believe any Japanese carriers were within range. On the contrary, his intelligence sources placed all three enemy flattops thought to be in the area (the *Shōkaku*, the *Zuikaku*, and one supposedly called the *Ryūkaku*) well to the northwest near Bougainville. American intelligence and Fletcher were wrong. The two big flattops of the Japanese 5th Carrier Division (the *Shōkaku* and the *Zuikaku*) under Rear Admiral Hara Chūichi were that morning only about 300 miles north. Part of Vice Admiral Takagi Takeo's MO Striking Force, the carriers marked time while the rest of the ships refueled. Their mission was to attack and destroy any Allied naval opposition to the invasions of Port Moresby and Tulagi (MO Operation). Delays had placed them on 4 May out of support range of Tulagi, allowing Fletcher to get away with his counterattack on the Tulagi Invasion Force. On 6 May, however, the Japanese carriers were well placed to surprise Task Force 17 if they were only to get the word and act on it.

Fifth Air Attack Force at 1050 broadcast the news that the American carrier force had been found. The news caught MO Striking Force in the midst of fueling, and Takagi's ships could not leave immediately. Finally Hara's carriers and two destroyers started south at noon, speed 20 knots. Takagi would follow with his two heavy cruisers and the rest of the tincans when he could. The third Japanese carrier present, the light carrier *Shōhō* (whose name the Americans misread as "Ryūkaku"), offered close support to the Port Moresby Invasion Convoy plodding southward from Rabaul toward the Louisiades, which the ships expected to traverse on 7 May. Other Japanese forces built a seaplane base at Deboyne in the Louisiades, but all were out of reach of the Americans except for Hara's small pursuit force.

Interestingly, as his carriers rapidly cut down the distance between himself and

Fletcher, Hara was not especially anxious to offer battle on 6 May. Entering the band of poor weather, Hara feared that his aircraft would not find the Americans, or that the enemy carriers had moved out of range. The contact reports sent by the Kawanishi on the scene were not received by Hara. The last Hara knew, the Americans were heading south away from him, whereas Fletcher generally stayed in the same area, steaming slowly during fueling and zigzagging to guard against submarines. Under the circumstances, Hara did not launch an air search that afternoon to seek out the Americans. Instead he preferred to remain hidden until the next morning, then surprise the enemy carriers. Ironically, had Hara launched his search, his pilots would have found Task Force 17 operating out in the clear. At 1930, he radioed Takagi and suggested a rendezvous at Point "A" about 280 miles south of Tulagi, to take place at 0700 the next morning. Thirty minutes later, Hara reversed course and headed north. Not until after the war did he learn that at 2000 the Americans were only 70 miles south!

Oblivious to the threat bearing down on him from the north, Fletcher continued fueling until around 1800 (Hara was 90 miles north), then sent the *Neosho* and the destroyer the *Sims* south to what he thought were safe waters. The rest of Task Force 17 swung around to the northwest to head for Rossel Island and the other Louisiade islands. Fletcher thought the Japanese invasion convoy, supported by the three enemy carriers, would cut through the Louisiades via Jomard Pass, either on 7 May or the day after. His plan of action was first to destroy or neutralize the Japanese flattops, then knock out the transports. To do this, he had to locate the carriers as early as possible on 7 May. Fortunately for him, the Japanese did not act more aggressively on 6 May!

THE INSCRUTABLE ENEMY

The evening of 6 May as Task Force 17 headed toward almost certain battle, the U.S. Navy's pilots realized how little they really knew about their Japanese counterparts on board the *Shōkaku* and the *Zuikaku*. So many questions came to mind. How good were the Japanese carrier pilots? What tactics did they use? How were the squadrons and groups organized? Was the Zero fighter as deadly as the U.S. Army and British pilots warned? What did a Zero even look like? The *Lexington* and *Yorktown* aviators would be facing part of the enemy's "first team," and the U.S. Navy's flyboys were supremely confident they could take on Japan's best and destroy them despite their lack of knowledge about the enemy. However, to understand the carrier battles reconstructed below, it will be necessary to analyze Japanese carrier doctrine and introduce opponents.

In most respects, Japanese naval aviation evolved in similar fashion to its great trans-Pacific rival, the United States Navy, but there was one important exception. The Imperial Navy's Air Arm (*Kaigun Kōkū Butai*) developed into a complete air force well before the Pacific War by creating a strong, land-based air contingent flying medium bombers as well as carrier planes and other aircraft of a more nautical nature. After World War I, the Imperial Navy had assumed the task of defending the sea approaches to Japan and her possessions. Concomitant with this responsibility was the necessity of expanding from a purely naval into a major land-based air force as well, a strategically more complex role than that of the U.S. Navy even including aircraft serving with the U.S. Marine Corps. During the China Incident (1937–41), the *Kaigun Kōkū Butai* demonstrated it could wage a major land-based air offensive right alongside (and in competition with) the Imperial Japanese Army Air Force. In no conceivable way did the use of strong naval air contingents deep within China fulfill purely naval requirements. The Imperial Navy's Air Force had become a complete counterpart to the Japanese Army Air Force. That was why from February 1942 to well within 1943 the United States Pacific Fleet could rampage the length of the Great East Asia Co-Prosperity Sphere's eastern flank without encountering a single Japanese Army aircraft.

In May 1942, the Imperial Navy wielded a mighty fist of six fleet carriers and a similar number of light or converted flattops. The First Air Fleet (*kōkū kantai*) under Vice Admiral Nagumo Chūichi was the principal carrier command. In battle, Nagumo usually led between four and six fleet carriers with their escorts, his operational command being known as the *Kidō Butai* (literally, "Mobile Force," better rendered as "Striking Force"). The carriers themselves comprised carrier divisions (*kōkū sentai*), corresponding to the land-based air flotillas (also *kōkū sentai*). With the fleet carriers, each division contained two flattops. In the Imperial Navy, the concept of the carrier division was much more important, as opposed to its purely administrative function in the U.S. Navy. Before the war, the Japanese adopted multi-carrier formations as a means of massing carrier air power into one or two coordinated strikes, epitomized by the attack on Pearl Harbor. They initiated "group training," meaning that the aircraft from one carrier division trained closely together, underscoring the fact that the aircraft within a carrier division formed a coherent unit, a "wing" to borrow a foreign term. In 1941–42, the Japanese achieved a far higher level of coordination in integrating aircraft from different carriers than did the Americans.

Japanese carrier aviation paralleled the organization of the land-based naval air units already described. In place of the land-based air group or *kōkūtai* was the aircraft carrier herself. The aviators, mechanics, armorers, radiomen, and other aviation personnel all served as an integral part of the ship's company with the rest of the flattop's crew. They did not belong to separate, independent squadrons like those in the U.S. Navy. Consequently the flying units could not switch from carrier to carrier with the ease of American squadrons, nor could they operate independently ashore. To replace losses, it was necessary to transfer individuals from other aviation units instead of assigning a new air group. Thus heavy losses could cripple a Japanese carrier.

The carrier air unit (*hikōkitai*—U.S. equivalent, "air group") took its name from its parent ship and made up the actual flying element operating off the ship. Aloft, the air unit was commanded by a *hikōtaichō* (group leader), one of the two flight command ratings within the naval air system. Usually lieutenant commanders or very senior lieutenants, *hikōtaichō* were qualified to lead air strikes made up of aircraft from their own carrier divisions and from others as well. They also retained direct command over a portion of the strike group, depending on the type of aircraft they flew. Japanese carrier pilots early in their career specialized in one of the three types of carrier aircraft: dive bomber, torpedo plane, and fighter, and they retained this specialty even as *hikōtaichō*. On the vertical tail surfaces of their personal aircraft, three broad stripes denoted their command rating. A fleet carrier could have on board more than one *hikōtaichō* (the flagship *Akagi*, for example, had three); if so, the senior *hikōtaichō* led the *hikōkitai* or carrier air unit.

Within their air units, the fleet carriers featured three types of flying units or squadron equivalents: one equipped with dive bombers, the second with torpedo planes, and the third with fighters. Like the air units themselves, these squadron equivalents bore the same name as the parent carrier. At this time, light carriers usually had only one type of strike plane (either torpedo planes or dive bombers) in addition to the carrier fighters. These squadrons all existed only as tactical organizations within their respective *hikōkitai*. They were not autonomous and did

Imperial Japanese Naval Aviation Organization

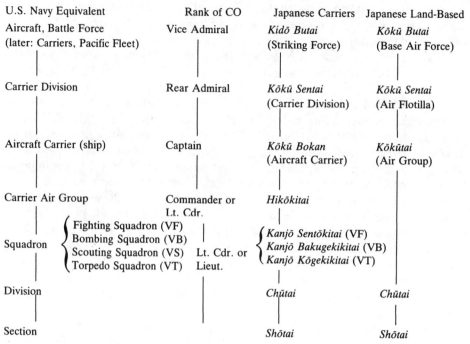

U.S. Navy Equivalent	Rank of CO	Japanese Carriers	Japanese Land-Based
Aircraft, Battle Force (later: Carriers, Pacific Fleet)	Vice Admiral	*Kidō Butai* (Striking Force)	*Kōku Butai* (Base Air Force)
Carrier Division	Rear Admiral	*Kōku Sentai* (Carrier Division)	*Kōku Sentai* (Air Flotilla)
Aircraft Carrier (ship)	Captain	*Kōku Bokan* (Aircraft Carrier)	*Kōkutai* (Air Group)
Carrier Air Group	Commander or Lt. Cdr.	*Hikōkitai*	
Squadron { Fighting Squadron (VF) Bombing Squadron (VB) Scouting Squadron (VS) Torpedo Squadron (VT)	Lt. Cdr. or Lieut.	{ *Kanjō Sentōkitai* (VF) *Kanjō Bakugekikitai* (VB) *Kanjō Kōgekikitai* (VT)	
Division		*Chūtai*	*Chūtai*
Section		*Shōtai*	*Shōtai*

not serve away from their ships. Within the squadrons, two basic subunits appeared for flight operations: the *chūtai* (division) of six or nine aircraft and the *shōtai* or section of three aircraft. Commanding the squadrons and divisions were officers, usually lieutenants, with the command rating of *buntaichō* or division leader. In most cases on board light carriers, the senior *buntaichō* also led the carrier air unit. Within the squadrons were usually two or three *buntaichō*, at least one per *chūtai*. In air strikes, senior *buntaichō* occasionally led aircraft from other carriers as well as their own. As their command insignia they sported two stripes on the vertical tail surface of their aircraft.

Its dive bombers, the Imperial Navy called "carrier bombers" (*kanjō bakugekiki*, abbreviated *kanbaku*). Thus the carrier bomber unit was known as the *kanjō bakugekikitai*. The standard carrier bomber was the Aichi D3A1 Type 99 carrier bomber [VAL].[1] A graceful, trim airplane sporting elliptical wings and neatly spatted fixed landing gear, the two-seat Type 99 *kanbaku* sported a payload of one 250-kilogram bomb. In performance it was roughly equivalent to the Douglas SBD Dauntless, but less rugged. Nominal strength for a carrier bomber unit was twenty-one airplanes (eighteen operational and three spares), organized tactically into two *chūtai* of nine planes each.

The other type of strike aircraft operating from Japanese carriers was the so-called carrier attack plane (*kanjō kōgekiki*, conveniently shortened to *kankō*). Operating as either a torpedo plane or a horizontal bomber, the carrier attack plane offered dual strike capability. The carrier attack unit (*kanjō kōgekikitai*) had a paper strength of eighteen operational aircraft and three spares (except in the *Kaga* with twenty-seven operational *kankō* and three spares) organized into three *chūtai* of six aircraft each. The basic torpedo plane was the Nakajima B5N2 Type 97 carrier attack plane [KATE].[2] Adopted in 1937, the big, three-seat Type 97 was superior to the U.S. Navy's TBD-1 Devastator in such criteria as speed, climb, and range. Even more important, Japanese aerial torpedoes proved much more rugged and reliable than their American counterparts, allowing much higher release speeds and altitudes.

The Japanese term for carrier fighter was *kanjō sentōki* (abbreviated *kansen*); hence the carrier fighter unit was the *kanjō sentōkitai*. On board fleet carriers, carrier fighter units had a nominal strength of twenty-one aircraft (eighteen operational and three spares), while most light carriers shipped between twelve and sixteen fighters on board. The normal twenty-one–plane units consisted of two *chūtai* (divisions) each with nine fighters. The unit commander (usually a *buntaichō*) led the 1st *Chūtai* personally, while the junior *buntaichō* took the 2nd *Chūtai*. Usually the fighter squadrons had only two *buntaichō*, as officer pilots were scarce. Each *chūtai* in turn comprised three *shōtai* (sections), made up of *shōtaichō* (section leader) and two wingmen. The three spare fighters more often than not were conspicuous by their absence due to shortages in aircraft and pilots. However if they were present, the unit could form a seventh *shōtai* or, more likely, distribute them among the other *shōtai*, making some four rather than three planes. Under certain conditions, Japanese fighters also operated in pairs.

The standard Japanese carrier fighter was the Mitsubishi A6M2 Type O carrier fighter, Model 21 [ZEKE], known popularly as the Zero fighter (in Japanese, *Reisen*) from the last digit of its year of adoption, 1940 or 2600 in the Japanese calendar.[3] The Zero fighter became the pride of the Imperial Navy and served almost as a symbol of the empire's fighting spirit. The fighter pilots themselves hearkened back to the Samurai and compared their Zeros with "master craftsmen's Japanese swords."[4] The designer of the Zero, Horikoshi Jirō, later wrote:

> As a result of our pilots' figurative demand for the blades and the arts of the old masters, the Japanese fighters were the lightest in weight and amongst the most maneuverable of the world's fighters. Our pilots sought tenaciously to master every trick of the superior fighter pilot, and they became well known for their prowess.[5]

First conceived in 1937, the Zero prototype underwent flight tests in the spring of 1939. The pilots were extremely pleased with the new aircraft. In July 1940, fifteen Zeros went to China for operational testing, and on the basis of experimental results, the Imperial Navy officially adopted the type as the A6M2 Type O carrier fighter, Model 11. Late in 1940, the factory redesigned the wingtips so they could fold back one meter to permit easier stowage on board carriers. This modification became the Model 21, put into quantity production in February 1941. In 1940–41, Zero fighters literally swept the Chinese Air Force from the skies, suffering in return only the lightest losses.

Sleek and smooth, with long, tapering wings and a large, streamlined cockpit canopy, the Zero looked every inch a fighter. Powered by a 950-hp Sakae-12 fourteen-cylinder radial engine, the Model 21 registered a top speed of about 288 knots (331 mph) at 14,930 feet. Climb rate was exceptional, initially 2,750 feet per minute, but the airplane required only five minutes, 55 seconds to reach 16,400 feet (average 2,770 feet per minute) and 7 minutes, 27 seconds to attain 19,685 feet (average 2,642 feet per minute). The aircraft was light, only 5,313 lbs. loaded, and it was exceptionally maneuverable with quick acceleration. Internal fuel comprised 137.25 gallons of gasoline, with provisions in the original design for a specially streamlined drop tank holding up to 87.5 gallons more. The Japanese used their drop tanks extensively, even for CAP missions. Normal fuel load, including drop tank, was 182 gallons. Consequently, range and endurance were excellent, 1,010 miles without auxiliary fuel and up to 1,675 miles with a full drop tank. This gave the Zero fighter a combat radius of up to 300 miles from a carrier and well over 500 miles from a land base.

In the criteria of protection and armament, the Zero differed radically from American fighter designs. Always offense-minded, Japanese pilots did not feel the need for pilot armor, not wishing to encumber their machines with excessive weight. They desired a highly maneuverable, agile fighter that, if properly employed, could fly out of trouble. In 1939–40 as the fighter worked up for service, few in the Imperial Navy realized the potential of leak-proof fuel tanks, and they did not pursue the concept. Thus the Zero became vulnerable to gunfire if an opponent could score, creating a great fire hazard. In May 1942, U.S. naval fighter pilots began using incendiary bullets which increased the risk of fire. Zero pilots most often went to their deaths in flames or fiery explosions. Horikoshi considered the lack of armor and self-sealing fuel tanks one of Japan's worst blunders of the war. Light losses in aerial combat over China had lulled naval analysts into thinking their crack pilots (among the best-trained in the world) and magnificent fighter aircraft were nearly invulnerable. They failed to heed the experiences of the Germans and British in Europe, who found that armor and self-sealing tanks were absolutely vital in a protracted air struggle.

The Mitsubishi designers chose a mixed armament of rifle caliber (7.7-mm) machine guns and big 20-mm cannons for the new Zero fighter. They styled such armament as "all purpose" believing that it could deal with bombers as well as single-seat targets. Mounted in the fuselage decking behind the engine were two Type 97 7.7-mm machine guns synchronized to fire through the propellor. The Type 97, a modified Vickers design, had a muzzle velocity of 2,460 feet per second and a cyclic rate of 1,000 rounds per minute. With 680 rounds per gun, there was plenty of shooting time. Fitted in each wing was one Type 99 20-mm cannon, Model 1, a Swiss Oerlikon type produced by license in Japan. Lightweight, reliable, and firing explosive shells, the cannon was thought capable of bringing down enemy aircraft with minimal hits. Its cyclic rate of fire was 520 rounds per minute, but there were only 60 rounds per gun. Initial muzzle velocity with the short-barreled cannons was only 1,970 feet per second—low for an aircraft automatic weapon. A selector switch on the control stick permitted the machine guns to be fired with the cannons or separately. Common procedure was to open with the machine guns for sighting, then cut in with the 20-millimeters when the bursts were on target. The Japanese soon discovered their armament was not as effective as they hoped. Unaided, the 7.7-mm bullets were rarely enough to bring down rugged American planes, but it took great skill to score consistently with the cannons. Because of the Oerlikon's low muzzle velocity, the trajectory was high. With only 60 rounds per cannon, Japanese pilots could not afford to waste their shots. Because of aiming difficulties, the effective range was perhaps 200 meters. On the whole, Japanese were fairly good gunners, often riddling their targets with 7.7-mm bullets. Trouble was, the 7.7's usually failed to penetrate armor plate or defeat self-sealing fuel tanks, whereas the 20-mm explosive shells could do the job, but owing to the nature of the weapon such decisive hits were rare.

Task Force 17's most dangerous opponents in the Battle of the Coral Sea would be the aviators of the 5th Carrier Division and of the light carrier *Shōhō*. As such they merit a detailed introduction.[6] The 5th Carrier Division's *Shōkaku* and *Zuikaku* were the two newest fleet carriers in service, commissioned respectively in August and September 1941. Their air units came into existence on 1 September

1941, and they hurriedly prepared with intense training sessions for the attack on Pearl Harbor. On 7 December, aircraft from the 5th Carrier Division participated in both waves attacking Pearl Harbor; indeed, the *Zuikaku*'s *hikōtaichō*, Lt. Cdr. Shimazaki Shigekazu, commanded the second wave of 167 aircraft. The 5th Carrier Division next saw action in January 1942 in connection with the capture of Rabaul, and in April participated in Striking Force's great raid against Ceylon. At the time of the MO Operation, the 5th Carrier Division's aviators were well trained and had combat experience, but they were not considered the equals of the air units of the 1st and 2nd Carrier Divisions. From the Japanese viewpoint, the 5th Carrier Division air units themselves had not flown together for very long, and they needed one good battle to bring them in line.

In the *Shōkaku* and *Zuikaku* Fighter Units, nearly all of the pilots had more than two years of flight experience. The *shōtaichō* (section leaders) were almost all China veterans, warrant officers and first-class petty officers with many hours in the air. Indeed, one *Zuikaku* fighter pilot was a well-known personality. Iwamoto Tetsuzō, PO1c, had emerged in 1941 as the Imperial Navy's leading China ace with fourteen kills. He survived the Pacific War with about 80 reported victories, making him the Navy's top living ace.

As with Iwamoto the vast majority of Japanese naval pilots were noncommissioned officers. Indeed, the *Shōkaku* and *Zuikaku* Fighter Units each had only two officers. Both unit COs, Lieutenants Hoashi Takumi of the *Shōkaku* and Okajima Kiyokuma of the *Zuikaku*, had just assumed command in April after serving as their unit's junior *buntaichō*. They were well acquainted with each other, having graduated from the same class at Eta Jima (1935) and flight training class in 1938. Both saw combat in China before the war and fought in the early Pacific actions beginning with Pearl Harbor. Promoted to junior *buntaichō* in their place were a second matched pair of officers: Lieutenants Yamamoto Shigehisa (*Shōkaku*) and Tsukamoto Yūzō (*Zuikaku*). Both were graduates of the 1938 Eta Jima class and went to the same flight class, earning their wings in April 1941. By Japanese standards they were still a bit green, but they learned quickly.

For the two 5th Carrier Division fighter units, the MO Operation had commenced with an unusual assignment, that of air ferrying to the land-based Tainan Air Group at Rabaul a badly needed reinforcement of nine Zero fighters. Vice Admiral Takagi had orders to fly off the nine Mitsubishis to Rabaul on 2 May as MO Striking Force passed east of there en route to the Solomons. The Tainan group had no spare pilots, and the carrier fighter units were expected to fly the Zeros to Rabaul, then return by carrier attack planes also provided by the *Shōkaku* and the *Zuikaku*. It was a seemingly simple task, but it would cause no end of trouble for the MO Operation. The morning of 2 May the carriers launched the nine Zeros and seven *kankō* to bring back the pilots, but the weather was so poor that they could not fight their way the 240 miles to Rabaul and had to abort. Takagi canceled that day's attempt and loitered in the area in order to try again the next day. That move delayed the whole timetable for MO Striking Force and ultimately put Takagi out of supporting distance of Tulagi when Fletcher struck there on 4 May. Meanwhile, the second ferry attempt went more poorly than the first. Not only did the sixteen aircraft again have to turn back because of storms, but one of the *Shōkaku* Zeros had to ditch. Takagi finally gave up for the time being and moved south, but too late to help Tulagi on 4 May. He was going to try again on 6 May after swinging around the Solomons, but the sighting of Task Force 17 that day spoiled that idea. The Imperial Navy suffered greatly from the lack of spare air units or pilots to use on such missions.

Japanese Carrier Plane Strength, Night 6 May

5th Carrier Division		
Shōkaku Air Group		
Lt. Cdr. Takahashi Kakuichi (H)	1 Type 99 VB	(1)
Shōkaku Carrier Fighter Unit	18 Zero VF	(18)
Lieut. Hoashi Takumi (B)		
Shōkaku Carrier Bomber Unit	20 Type 99 VB	(18)
Lieut. Yamaguchi Masao (B)		
Shōkaku Carrier Attack Unit	19 Type 97 VT	(19)
Lieut. Ichihara Tatsuo (B)	—	—
	58	(56)
plus 3 Zero fighters for Tainan Air Group		
(Rabaul)		
Zuikaku Air Group		
Lt. Cdr. Shimazaki Shigekazu (H)	1 Type 97 VT	(1)
Zuikaku Carrier Fighter Unit	20 Zero VF	(19)
Lieut. Okajima Kiyokuma (B)		
Zuikaku Carrier Bomber Unit	22 Type 99 VB	(17)
Lieut. Ema Tamotsu (B)		
Zuikaku Carrier Attack Unit	20 Type 97 VT	(16)
Lieut. Tsubota Yoshiaki (B)	—	—
	63	(53)
plus 5 Zero fighters for Tainan Air Group		
(Rabaul)		
MO Main Force		
Shōhō Air Group		
Lieut. Nōtomi Kenjirō (B)		
Shōhō Carrier Fighter Unit	8 Zero VF	(8)
Lieut. Nōtomi	4 Type 96 VF	(4)
Shōhō Carrier Attack Unit	6 Type 97 VT	(6)
Lieut. Nakamoto Michitarō (B)	—	—
	18	(18)
Total operational planes 127		

Key:
(   ) operational planes
(H) *hikōtaichō*
(B) *buntaichō*

Zero VF	A6M2 Type 0 carrier fighter
Type 97 VT	B5N2 Type 97 carrier attack plane
Type 99 VB	D3A1 Type 99 carrier bomber

The air unit on board the carrier *Shōhō* had not yet seen combat, as that ship had until then only been used to ferry aircraft. The air unit was commanded by the senior fighter pilot, Lieut. Nōtomi Kenjirō, *buntaichō*. He was a 1934 graduate of the Naval Academy and completed flight training in 1938. His *Shōhō* Fighter Unit comprised only nine Zeros and four old Type 96 carrier fighters, reduced by one Zero on 2 May when PO2c Tamura Shunichi ditched fatally. Some in the high command requested that the 5th Carrier Division transfer three Zeros and their pilots to the *Shōhō* to beef up air strength. Takagi and Hara declined, complaining their own fighter units were not up to strength. The chronic shortage of pilots and aircraft for the front line units despite relatively light losses up to this point began to have a detrimental effect on Japanese combat effectiveness.

CHAPTER 11

7 May 1942

THE BATTLE OFF MISIMA

At sunrise on 7 May, Task Force 17 was nearing the end of its overnight run to the northwest. Now the Louisiades were close by, and somewhere to the north, Fletcher and Fitch expected to find the Japanese invasion convoy protected by its powerful escort of three aircraft carriers. Fletcher's plan was to launch a search mission of his own that, in conjunction with whatever patrols General MacArthur's land-based aircraft would make, hopefully would locate the various enemy task forces in time for the *Yorktown* and the *Lexington* to throw their strike groups against the Japanese flattops. This was the first time two carrier forces had confronted one another in battle and no one was certain what the outcome would be. In the event the opposing carriers neutralized each other, Fletcher thought it necessary to have a separate task group ready to deal with the enemy invasion convoy should it attempt to force Jomard Passage through the Louisiades. He decided to detach Crace's Task Group 17.3, two heavy cruisers, one light cruiser, and three destroyers, to head westward and guard Jomard Passage.

Task Force 17's operational air strength that dawn amounted to 36 fighters, 70 dive bombers, and 22 torpedo planes—a total of 128 aircraft ranged upon the decks of the *Yorktown* and the *Lexington*. The *Yorktown* had the duty and readied a search of ten SBDs from Wally Short's Bombing Five. They were to fly single-plane searches out 250 miles covering the north–northeasterly quadrant. The *Yorktown* launched the ten SBDs at 0619. Weather in the vicinity of the task force was still good, but clouds were slowly closing in. The search pilots soon encountered increasing overcast north of the ships. The pilot flying the 067-degree heading met the worst of the thick clouds and squalls. He returned after covering only 165 miles, but the remaining aircraft flew their searches as ordered.

At 0625, Fletcher sent Crace's Support Group westward, while the rest of Task Force 17 remained in the waters south of Rossel Island. Now came the wait for the results of the search. The *Lexington* beginning at 0703 sent aloft on CAP four VF-2 Wildcats led by Noel Gayler and six SBDs (four from Scouting Two and two from Bombing Two) as the inevitable anti–torpedo-plane patrol. The task force then changed course to 355 degrees, speed 20 knots, to approach Rossel. Plane handlers brought the strike aircraft up on the flight decks, and mechanics made them ready for swift launch should the search planes report. In their ready rooms, pilots waited for the word to man planes. Task Force 17 was ready to fight; all that was needed was the location of the Japanese.

U.S. Navy's Carrier Plane Strength, Dawn 7 May

Lexington Air Group			
(CLAG)	Cdr. William B. Ault	1 SBD-3	(1)
Fighting Two	Lt. Cdr. Paul H. Ramsey	21 F4F-3, -3As	(19)
Bombing Two	Lt. Cdr. Weldon L. Hamilton	18 SBD-2, -3s	(17)
Scouting Two	Lt. Cdr. Robert E. Dixon	17 SBD-3s	(17)
Torpedo Two	Lt. Cdr. James H. Brett, Jr.	12 TBD-1s	(12)
		69	(66)
Yorktown Air Group			
(CYAG)	Lt. Cdr. Oscar Pederson		
Fighting Forty-two	Lt. Cdr. Charles R. Fenton	17 F4F-3s	(17)
Bombing Five	Lieut. Wallace C. Short	18 SBD-2, -3s	(18)
Scouting Five	Lt. Cdr. William O. Burch, Jr.	17 SBD-2, -3s	(17)
Torpedo Five	Lt. Cdr. Joe Taylor	13 TBD-1s	(10)
		65	(62)

Daybreak, 7 May, also found the Japanese eager for battle, confident they would soon wipe out the American carrier force. According to prior arrangements, MO Striking Force arrived at 0600 at Point "A," 280 miles southwest of Tulagi. Hara's carriers launched twelve Type 97 carrier attack planes to search in pairs a sector bearing 180 to 265 degrees, out 250 miles from the force. Hara felt strongly the Americans would be found to the south rather than westward tucked beneath the Louisiades, and advised his task force commander, Vice Admiral Takagi, to head south after launching the search. His hunch would prove most unfortunate. On board the *Shōkaku* and the *Zuikaku* deck crews manhandled strike planes in position for swift launch should the search reveal enemy carriers within attack range.

Other Japanese commands also despatched searches covering most of the western Coral Sea. MO Main Force with the light carrier *Shōhō* operated northeast of Misima Island and provided close support for the transports of the Port Moresby Invasion Force plodding southward toward Jomard Passage. At 0600, the two heavy cruisers *Kinugasa* and *Furutaka* in the waters just north of Rossel Island launched four Kawanishi E7K2 Type 94 reconnaissance floatplanes [ALF] to cover the southeast quadrant 150 miles out from Rossel. At Deboyne, the Support Force with the seaplane tender *Kamikawa Maru* operated a temporary seaplane base, from which several floatplanes departed at 0630 to search the southeast quadrant from Deboyne. Thus from missions originating at Rossel and Deboyne, the Japanese blanketed the crucial waters south of the Louisiades. The new base at Tulagi sent four Kawanishi Type 97 flying boats from the Yokohama Air Group out 650 miles southwestard into the Coral Sea. The 5th Air Attack Force at Rabaul used three Mitsubishi Type 1 land attack planes to search 700 miles southeast of Rabaul. The Japanese had every reason to expect their intricate search network would turn up the American carrier force lurking in the area.

With so many Japanese planes aloft and looking, it did not take long for one to find the enemy. At 0722, the radioman of one of the two *Shōkaku* carrier attack planes flying the 180-degree bearing from MO Striking Force tapped out the words reporting American ships bearing 182 degrees, 163 miles from his carrier. Hara was jubilant. That was just where he expected the enemy would be. Impatiently he waited for more information. Finally at 0745, the search crews amplified their report, noting: "The enemy carrier force consists of one carrier and one cruiser as main force and three destroyers, course 000 degrees, speed 16 knots."[1] That cinched it for Hara. With the enemy carrier only 150 miles south, Hara knew he had to

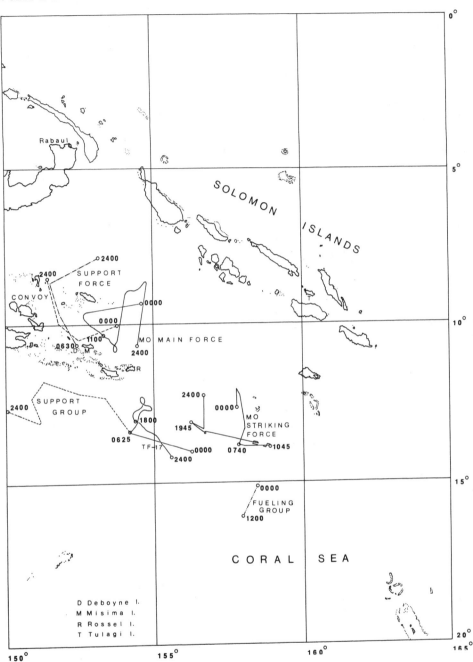

Task force operations, Coral Sea, 7 May.

attack immediately. With Takagi's concurrence, he ordered his strike groups to take off. MO Striking Force's attack comprised seventy-eight planes (eighteen fighters, thirty-six dive bombers, and twenty-four torpedo planes), organized as shown in the table.

The Japanese strike planes began taking off at 0800 and departed fifteen minutes later. Even while they formed up, the *Zuikaku* monitored an amplifying report from the search planes shadowing the target. At 0810, they radioed that they had also sighted an enemy fleet oiler escorted by a heavy cruiser. From the location

Strike leader: Lt. Cdr. Takahashi Kakuichi (H)

Carrier Bomber Group Lt. Cdr. Takahashi

Shōkaku Carrier Bomber Unit	Lt. Cdr. Takahashi	19 Type 99 VB
Zuikaku Carrier Bomber Unit	Lieut. Ema Tamotsu (B)	17 Type 99 VB

Carrier Attack Group Lt. Cdr. Shimazaki Shigekazu (H)

Shōkaku Carrier Attack Unit	Lieut. Ichihara Tatsuo (B)	13 Type 97 VT
Zuikaku Carrier Attack Unit	Lt. Cdr. Shimazaki	11 Type 97 VT

Air Control Group Lieut. Hoashi Takumi (B)

Shōkaku Carrier Fighter Unit (escort carrier attack group)	Lieut. Hoashi	9 Zero VF
Zuikaku Carrier Fighter Unit (escort carrier bomber group)	Lieut. Okajima Kiyokuma (B)	9 Zero VF

provided in the contact report, Hara deduced that the oiler and her escort were 25 miles southeast of the carrier force previously reported. Actually, the two *Shōkaku* search crews had blundered. No American carrier task force was in that location. Task Force 17 was over 300 miles to the northwest. What the Japanese had spotted and mistakenly reported as a carrier was the faithful *Neosho* with the destroyer *Sims* as escort. Fletcher had parked them in what he supposed was a safe area. Thus both carrier admirals made mistakes due to misconceptions. MO Striking Force had launched its knockout blow southward against an oiler and a destroyer, while the most feared opponent actually lurked almost due west.

Ironically at the very time MO Striking Force sent its seventy-eight planes against the phantom American carrier to the south, other Japanese search planes found Task Force 17 south of Rossel Island. First contact came at 0810, when lookouts on board Crace's Support Force, heading on its independent mission to the west, noticed a Japanese floatplane lurking on the horizon. Ten minutes later, the radioman of the No. 1 *Furutaka* plane reported sighting an American task force bearing 152 degrees, 150 miles from Deboyne. Its composition was one carrier, one battleship, two heavy cruisers, and nine destroyers, course 030 degrees, speed 20 knots. Beginning at 0830 in two separate messages, a *Kinugasa* floatplane radioed the sighting of one possible carrier, one battleship, two heavy cruisers, and seven destroyers bearing 180 degrees and 82 miles from Rossel Island. The two position reports were only 14 miles apart, and checking their charts, South Seas Force staff felt both aircraft had located the same American force. When they heard from MO Striking Force that the Japanese flattops had launched their attack planes, the staff was highly gratified, not realizing that Hara's strike had gone south and that the force near Rossel would not be hit. The Japanese had made a big error.

The morning of 7 May turned into a fighter director's nightmare. Task Force 17 either operated adjacent to a band of thick cloud cover or actually disappeared into it from time to time. Red Gill, the *Lexington*'s FDO, handled the CAP for both carriers this day, although only the *Lex* had launched any fighters as yet. The *Lexington* fighters were equipped at least partially with the vital IFF gear, but the *Yorktown*'s VF-42 had only a few sets to go around. Thus cluttering the radar were numerous unidentified aircraft, but actually friendlies: Curtiss SOC cruiser floatplanes on inner air patrol, the *Lexington*'s anti–torpedo-plane patrol, and returning *Yorktown* search planes. The fighter pilots wasted considerable effort investigating these contacts. Given the circumstances, Gayler's 4th Division had more than it could handle that morning.

The first real inkling of trouble came around 0833, when the *Lexington*'s radar detected a bogey bearing 270 degrees, distance 25 miles. The contact was circling.

Gill delegated Gayler's second section leader, Lieut. (jg) Howard Clark, to check out the bogey, but soon had to recall him because "higher authority"[2] (evidently Captain Sherman) felt the contact was friendly because it circled. When the bogey persisted in circling without approaching, Gill asked for permission to loose "Spud" Clark's section after it again. Clark undertook what Gill later described as a "heart-breaking chase,"[3] but could not overhaul what Gill felt certain was a Japanese snooper. At the edge of the weather frontal zone, Clark encountered heavy, dark clouds offering ready concealment for an enemy plane. At 0859, the bogey faded from the radar screen, but Gill concluded that the enemy had found Task Force 17. In reality, three or four Japanese floatplanes from the 6th Cruiser Division shadowed Task Force 17. Only occasionally did one of these low-flying snoopers trespass on radar, but Gill knew they were out there.

At 0855, the *Lexington* despatched reinforcements for the CAP in the form of VF-2's 2nd Division, four F4Fs led by VF-3 veteran Lieut. Albert Vorse. Not long after, another of the seemingly ubiquitous bogeys appeared on radar. To trap it, Gill deployed three fighter sections, arranging for each to converge on the target from a different direction. The fighters never did corner the wily Japanese. Finally the bogey withdrew to 45 miles and left the screen. Again the bad weather acted as perfect cover for the enemy. Returning *Yorktown* search planes also did their part to confuse the situation. Twice Gill had to direct pairs of sections to orbit on station some 10 to 15 miles out in the path of oncoming bogeys. He cautioned his pilots not to lose sight of the task force, or they could become lost in the worsening weather. The Japanese hung around until just after 1030, but meanwhile other events captured the attention of Task Force 17.

Even while the Japanese looked for him, Fletcher's own aircraft sought possible targets. At 0735, one of VB-5's SBDs reported two Japanese heavy cruisers northeast of Misima Island. They would be the *Furutaka* and the *Kinugasa*, whose planes later snooped Task Force 17. At 0815, however, came the big contact, but for reasons unintended by the SBD crew. The *Yorktown* copied a message that placed two carriers and four heavy cruisers in position Lat. 10° 03' South, Long. 152° 27' East, course 140 degrees, speed 18 to 20 knots. The position was about 200 miles northwest of Task Force 17. The *Yorktown* relayed the sighting to the *Lexington* at 0835. Both Fletcher and Fitch felt certain the SBD pilot had found the two vaunted carriers of the 5th Carrier Division, the *Shōkaku* and the *Zuikaku*. They were about where the Americans had expected them to be.

Under the circumstances, Fletcher decided to commit his full air strike force to battle. At 0915, Fitch, as commander, Task Group 17.5 (Air), promulgated his operations order number one, citing the Japanese carriers as the main objective. Because of the distance involved—at 0915 Task Force 17 was 210 miles from the target—the *Yorktown*'s air people were not certain whether Fitch would send along the short-legged fighters and torpedo planes. A query at 0920 produced a reply that Fitch was sending everything he had. Activity on the two flight decks was intense as both the *Yorktown* and the *Lexington* made ready to launch.

In accordance with air operations order number one, the carriers of Fitch's Task Group 17.5 readied their strike groups with the mission of destroying the two Japanese carriers located about 200 miles north. This was the first time (in a battle of so many "firsts") that the carrier air groups would be committed against what were believed to be well-defended targets, namely, opposing carriers. Facing its first acid test was the Navy's fighter escort theory, and it was none too sophisticated because each fighting squadron and air group generally used its own procedures. Only through hard-earned combat experience bought at the price of many lives throughout 1942 did the experts hammer out a definite escort policy for use by all the squadrons.[4]

With regard to the launching of strikes, prewar regulations specified three types of departure. "Urgent departure" required that individual aircraft sections leave the area immediately after launch, effecting such rendezvous as practicable en route to the target—that is, not very much. With "normal departure," the squadrons completed their own rendezvous, but did not linger to complete group rendezvous unless it could be done on the way to the target. This procedure allowed the fighters assigned to escort specific squadrons to join up and accompany them to the target. Complicating everything was the unfortunate fact that the attack planes and fighters all cruised at different speeds. Grumman F4F Wildcats for maximum range throttled back to between 130 and 140 knots—speeds not too uncomfortable for the SBDs. The TBDs, however, lumbered along between 100 and 110 knots and perforce remained below 6,000 feet. "Deferred departure" involved an attempt to form the whole group into one tactical unit before departing for the target. The squadrons circled the carrier until all aircraft had taken off, gradually joining in formation according to squadrons for the flight to the target. The procedure was time-consuming and particularly rough on the fighters, which had the shortest range of all. Sometimes with group cruise formations, the F4Fs had to cut back to speeds approximating maximum endurance, and that was far too slow to be effective in combat. This would cause many problems at Coral Sea and Midway.

The prewar manual USF 74 (Revised) defined the duty of escort fighters: "sight, report and counterattack enemy planes which threaten the formation escorted."[5] The basic escort unit was the section, and section leaders, once they spotted enemy fighters, were told to counter them with "direct plane for plane attack."[6] Fighters had to render continuous protection to the bombers. Thus they could not become embroiled in fighter melees which would draw them away from their charges. Escorts had to make their countermoves and rejoin formation as quickly as possible. They had to be wary of enemy fighters decoying them away from the bombers so other interceptors could dive in. It was a definite contradiction: to fight and yet stay with the bombers.

Prewar escort doctrine apparently counted on the fact that most of the fighting squadron would be committed to escorting the strike group. For example, Fighting Two in December 1941 practiced doctrine drawn up by Paul Ramsey with twelve of its eighteen fighters on escort duty.[7] With a numerous escort, the prewar manuals had recourse to two types of escort deployment, "close" and "high." The close escort comprised those fighters that provided direct protection to the bombers. They were to take station 1,500 feet above and usually just behind or on the flanks of the bomber formation. The high escort was to fly well above the formation in order to catch interceptors before they could make their firing passes on the bombers. In a sense, this concept was similar to the Luftwaffe's idea of "free chase," in which escort fighters ranged ahead and cleared the way for the bombers.

The ratio of strength between close and high escorts depended primarily on the number of fighters available in the first place. Other factors included the ability of the bombers to defend themselves and visibility that would allow the high escort to maintain contact. Close escort always drew the highest priority. The concept of close escort applied to protecting both dive bombers and torpedo planes; ideally each type would have its own close escort and perhaps a high escort as well. However, USF 74 (Revised) of April 1941 noted that escorts for torpedo planes were "not normally desirable"[8] except in two instances: for suspected strong enemy fighter defenses and for set-piece attacks in which torpedo planes remained outside the target area until the proper moment for their attack.

Against this theoretical background, we will see how the carrier air groups applied their doctrine the morning of 7 May. The overriding point is that in no instance was there a "high escort." There simply were not enough fighters. Of the thirty-six operational F4Fs, the carriers allocated half, eighteen, to the strike. The *Lexington* launched her aircraft first, beginning at 0926. Her strike group had the following organization:

Commander, *Lexington* Air Group (CLAG) Cdr. William B. Ault		
CLAG Command Section	Cdr. Ault	3 SBDs*
Fighting Two	Lt. Cdr. Paul H. Ramsey	10 F4F-3s
Bombing Two	Lt. Cdr. Weldon L. Hamilton	15 SBD-2, -3s
Scouting Two	Lt. Cdr. Robert E. Dixon	10 SBD-3s
Torpedo Two	Lt. Cdr. James H. Brett, Jr.	12 TBD-1s
		50

*CLAG SBD, one from VB-2, one from VS-2.

The *Lexington* group opted for deferred departure. Thus the squadrons formed up near the carrier, took group formation, and left as a unit, albeit divided into several elements. Climbing to 16,000 feet for the flight out were the ten SBDs of Bob Dixon's Scouting Two and Bombing Two's fifteen SBDs under "Ham" Hamilton. Providing close escort for them was Fred Borries's 3rd Division of four F4Fs from Fighting Two. Maintaining contact from medium altitude (around 10,000 feet) was Bill Ault with his command section of three SBDs. Providing their close escort was a section of VF-2 fighters under Ens. Bill Eder. Finally at low altitude came the twelve TBDs of Jimmy Brett's Torpedo Two with Paul Ramsey's four F4Fs in close support. The *Lexington* Air Group departed at 0947. As they left, the *Lex* brought on board Gayler's four CAP fighters and one VB-2 SBD from the anti–torpedo-plane patrol.

The *Yorktown* began launching at 0944, and her air group had the following composition:

Fighting Forty-two	Lt. Cdr. James H. Flatley, Jr.	8 F4F-3s
Bombing Five	Lieut. Wallace C. Short	8 SBD-3s
Scouting Five	Lt. Cdr. William O. Burch, Jr.	17 SBD-3s
Torpedo Five	Lt. Cdr. Joe Taylor	10 TBD-1s
		43

The group used a variation of normal departure worked out by Murr Arnold, the air officer, and Pederson, the deckbound group commander. The two contrived a way of getting the strike group to arrive together at the target without expending the exorbitant amount of fuel entailed in using deferred departure. They were willing to experiment. The twenty-five SBDs of Scouting Five and Bombing Five took off first and began a slow climb to 18,000 feet. They were instructed to circle the ships for the time being. Next to go were Joe Taylor's torpedo planes, which formed up at 500 feet and immediately left for the target. About fifteen minutes later, VF-42's eight escort fighters took off and separated into two elements. Vince McCormack, the flight officer, took his four F4Fs to climb and join the dive bombers. In the confusion of the launch, McCormack's wingman, Walt Haas, failed to make his rendezvous and joined the torpedo escort instead, giving Flatley five F4Fs but McCormack only three.

Together the SBDs and F4Fs departed at 1013. The TBDs had about a twenty-minute headstart, but the dive bombers and fighters cruised so much faster (130 knots versus 100 knots) that it would not take them long to catch up. A hand-held Aldis light operated by a crewman in one of the TBDs helped attract Flatley's attention and made his link-up with the torpedo planes that much easier. Having spotted the TBDs lumbering just above the wave tops, Flatley took station up sun and 6,000 feet above them. McCormack's dive bomber escort completed the climb to 18,000 feet along with the SBDs. Thus the last of the ninety-three strike planes were on their way to the target.

Her flight deck free, the *Yorktown* took the opportunity to launch four VF-42 F4Fs as her first CAP flight of the day. Led by skipper Chas Fenton, the Grummans took off at 1019. The *Yorktown* stayed into the wind to begin recovering her SBDs which had returned from the morning search, including the pilot whose report had precipitated the launch of the strike groups. Surrounded after he landed by those curious for further details, the SBD pilot himself was dumbfounded at the mention of Japanese carriers. He had spotted what he thought were two heavy cruisers and two destroyers and had phrased his message accordingly. A quick check revealed a coding error on the pilot's cipher pad. No, he had not found any carriers! It was a traumatic moment for Fletcher and his advisors, who first thought of recalling the strike groups. That, however, would be very risky in the event of a Japanese carrier strike on Task Force 17. Fortunately, Fletcher had in hand a sighting report received at 1012 from Army search planes. MacArthur's aviators had sighted one carrier, ten transports, and sixteen other warships only 30 miles from the original erroneous target. At 1053, the *Yorktown* radioed her strike group redirecting the planes to the targets located by the Army.

During the deliberations over what to do with the strike group, the *Lexington*'s radar at 1041 revealed a bogey bearing 045 degrees, distance 41 miles. To intercept the contact, Gill turned to Fenton's second section, Dick Crommelin and Ens. Richard Wright, vectoring them out along a heading of 055 degrees (M.). In that direction the visibility decreased so rapidly that the two pilots had to fly on instruments. Overhauling a snooper in this soup would be pure luck, but Crommelin and Wright had it. After proceeding about eight miles, they broke into a clear space, and across on the opposite side perhaps seven miles off was the unmistakable configuration of a Kawanishi Type 97 flying boat. The Japanese cruised at 1,500 feet, an easy kill if it could be surprised. It was another flying boat from the Yokohama Air Group operating out of Tulagi. Headquarters had pulled it off its morning search to follow up the contacts made by the floatplanes.

Throttles blocked forward, the two VF-42 pilots roared in, hoping to catch the enemy before he could turn and disappear into the overcast. Seeing their approach, the Japanese started to run for safety. The Grummans managed one high-side pass as the target ducked into the clouds; then they split up to chase the Kawanishi into the white void. In a crazy game of hide-and-seek, the fighters got only snap bursts as the big flying boat worked its way through the cloud. In his report Crommelin likened the attacks to "dogfighting tactics as maneuvers were of a necessity very radical."[9] Finally the Japanese ran out of cloud and emerged in the open at about a thousand feet. The pursuers glimpsed their quarry at the same time, Wright screaming in from above and behind, while Crommelin rolled into a high-side run from the left. With a clear shot at the target, the issue was no longer in doubt.

Fifty-caliber slugs ripped through tender engines and fuel tanks, spraying gasoline and spreading flames. Mortally stricken, the Kawanishi started for the water. On board the American ships, lookouts saw its funeral pyre about ten miles northeast and registered the time of the kill as 1100.

Task Force 17 waited in anticipation, first for the results of its attack and second for the expected enemy counterattack. Certainly the Japanese knew the location of Fletcher's ships. Around 1100, the *Yorktown* launched ten VB-5 SBDs (those who had searched that morning) to serve as anti–torpedo-plane patrol and then reinforced the CAP with four F4Fs led by Bill Leonard. Near the *Lexington*, a VB-2 SBD pilot signaled the need for a deferred forced landing, and the *Lex* rapidly cleared her flight deck aft, landing the stricken dive bomber at 1113. Then she launched Gayler's four VF-2 fighters as relief CAP and recovered Scoop Vorse's fighter division and the remaining SBDs (four) from her own anti–torpedo-plane patrol. Thus by 1130, Task Force 17 had aloft twelve F4Fs (four from VF-2, and eight from VF-42) as CAP and ten SBDs from Bombing Five as anti–torpedo-plane patrol. The *Lexington* worked to reservice her four fighters and six SBDs. The anticipated Japanese attack, however, failed to materialize.

The Attack on the Shōhō

About forty minutes after departing Task Force 17, the strike planes of the *Lexington* Air Group crossed over the northwestern tip of Tagula Island. Below lay a myriad of small islands and reefs making up part of the Louisiade Archipelago. To Hamilton leading Bombing Two, the sight of little brown and green islands meant the group had left the menacing overcast behind. Below the dive bombers, Torpedo Two came into view. The skies cleared rapidly as the aircraft left Tagula behind. Hamilton shifted his squadron behind Scouting Two, which was to attack first. Nearing the reported position of the two enemy carriers, Hamilton began scanning the horizon with a pair of binoculars despite the buffeting by his SBD. Around 1040, he discerned ship wakes some 40 miles to the north. He signaled Dixon, who in turn notified group leader Ault and Brett with the torpedo planes. The group turned to the right. Narrowing the range, Hamilton distinguished the outline of a flight deck, indicating at least one carrier in the enemy task force. There also appeared to be two or three heavy cruisers and one or two destroyers.

What Hamilton had discovered was the Japanese MO Main Force providing close escort for the convoy, which was out of sight but not far away. On board the *Shōhō*, Captain Izawa Ishinosuke made ready to land his convoy air patrol of four Zero fighters and one carrier attack plane. The light carrier was proceeding with preparations to launch a strike against the American carriers located to the south. As relief CAP, the *Shōhō* sent aloft three fighters flown by W.O. Imamura Shigemune in a Zero fighter and PO2c Aoki Chikao and PO2c Inoue Takeo flying Type 96 carrier fighters. With the CAP aloft, Izawa landed the four Zeros and one carrier attack plane. Unlike the big fleet carriers, converted flattops such as the *Shōhō* (formerly the submarine tender *Tsurugizaki*) took an inordinately long time to conduct flight operations due to design limitations. Apparently the carrier attack planes scheduled for the mission were being armed with torpedoes while sheltered in one of the *Shōhō*'s two small hangar decks. After the *Shōhō* recovered her aircraft, MO Main Force changed course to the northwest. At that time they were just northeast of Misima Island. Suddenly at 1050, the screams of lookouts warned of enemy planes approaching from off the port bow.

According to plan, the *Lexington* Air Group split up to execute a set-piece, coordinated attack—the first by American carrier aircraft against a Japanese capital ship. Leading his command section of three SBDs, Ault headed directly toward the carrier to make the first attack. Above and behind were VS-2's ten SBDs, whose job it was, according to the complicated air doctrine of the time, to soften up the target and suppress antiaircraft fire. Bombing Two swung off to the east to wait for the slower torpedo planes to catch up and make a coordinated strike with them. Staying well over Bombing Two was the VSB escort led by Buzz Borries.

Escorting Torpedo Two, Ramsey's fighter division cruised at 5,000 feet. Not far from Misima Island, the VF-2 pilots encountered a Japanese twin-float seaplane on an opposite heading and low over the water. Ramsey signaled his second section, led by Lieut. (jg) Paul G. Baker, to break off and deal with it. Diving in, Baker and his wingman surprised the floatplane at 500 feet, Baker's guns forcing the seaplane to set down a few miles off Misima. Not having time to confirm his kill, Baker turned back to join Ramsey, but did not do so before the attack on the carrier. About a half hour later when they flew past the site of Baker's first combat, there was no evidence of a kill. Ramsey later theorized that the aircraft either sank or was able to fly away, and consequently could give Baker credit only for a probable. Baker's opponent was evidently a Kawanishi E7K2 Type 94 reconnaissance floatplane from the 6th Cruiser Division. Since that unit lost four aircraft on 7 May (including a couple to the *Yorktown* SBDs on search), it is more than likely that Baker got one of them. His target was probably heading for the temporary base at Deboyne when Baker attacked.

On the *Shōhō*'s bridge, Izawa watched the American dive bombers split up and noticed the first three charge in. At 1107 he ordered his helmsman to make a sharp turn to port. There was plenty of room in the formation for him to make his countermoves, as MO Main Force had spread out into a wide diamond with the *Shōhō* in the center and four heavy cruisers (the *Aoba*, *Kinugasa*, *Furutaka*, and *Kako*) cruising 1,500 meters off each of the flattop's corners. Astern of the formation as plane guard was the destroyer *Sazanami*. On board the carrier, her flight deck crew worked feverishly to ready several Zeros for immediate launch. Ault approached at medium altitude, around 10,000 feet, and beginning at 1110, his three SBDs pushed over in their dives. Disconcerted by the target's sudden turn, all three pilots missed with their 500-lb. bombs, although Ault claimed one hit. No Japanese fighters were in position to intercept, as they were busy chasing Scouting Two. Ault regained altitude to observe his group attack. Eder's section covered the group commander all the way, but the two VF-2 pilots saw no enemy fighters.

During Ault's attack Dixon had taken Scouting Two's ten SBDs around to the north to take advantage of the sun and wind direction, and in the process the squadron gradually let down from 16,000 to 12,500 feet. Antiaircraft fire from the vessels below was not bad. Just as Dixon rolled into his dive, the two Type 96 carrier fighters jumped his lead section and tried to mess up the dives, but once the SBDs had popped their dive brakes, the fighters overshot. The Mitsubishis had to spiral in and shoot at any SBD that flashed in their gunsights—a continual distraction to the dive bomber pilots intent on hitting the carrier below.

Ignoring the fighters buzzing around him, Dixon concentrated on the carrier. As if reading his mind, Izawa continued his turn to port, completing a full circle. Thus instead of steadying up on a southeasterly course into the wind to launch planes, the *Shōhō* again swung to port, putting her crosswind to the attacking SBDs. To his disgust, Dixon saw the target execute the perfect evasive maneuver to foil his dive. Instead of attacking lengthwise along the whole flight deck, his pilots now had only her narrow beam—a much smaller target. Even worse, W.O. Imamura intervened in his Zero. Attacking VS-2's 2nd Division under Lieut. Edward Allen, Imamura slashed in from above and behind, his bullets nearly shooting away the control wires of Ens. Anthony J. Quigley's S-9. Pulling out at 2,000 feet, the SBD pilots had aimed their bombs toward the carrier, but all of the 500-pounders missed, the closest sending up a geyser about 20 meters from the *Shōhō*'s side. Scouting Two reported three hits on the carrier.

According to plan, Dixon's SBDs were supposed to regain height and dive a second time in order to drop their two underwing 116-lb. bombs on screening ships as a means of flak suppression for the attack of Bombing Two and Torpedo Two. The Japanese fighters kept them too busy to do so. Imamura cornered Allen's SBD just as he was pulling out of his dive and sent the hero of the 20 February fight into the water just astern of the *Shōhō*. The two Type 96 carrier fighters likewise shot up several of the SBDs. Only one VS-2 pilot, Ens. John A. Leppla, attempted a second dive. He attacked a cruiser and reported a hit, but none of the screening ship was damaged. Like the prewar smoke screen tactics, the idea of carrying small bombs to plaster escorting ships proved impractical in the face of even light fighter opposition.

Bathed in the water cast up by the splash of near misses, the *Shōhō* took the opportunity to launch three Zero fighters led by the group commander, Lieut. Nōtomi. They went aloft at 1117, just as Scouting Two finished its attack. Gratified that no damage was incurred, the Japanese sternly prepared for another onslaught. More *Lexington* planes waited to attack, and the *Yorktown* Air Group came into view. The *Shōhō* indeed faced a terrible ordeal. Izawa stayed with the same maneuver that had brought him success before, making another sharp turn to port.

From 16,000 feet Hamilton had watched Scouting Two press its attack. He was not certain how many hits they scored, if any, but he could see no evidence of fire on board the carrier. Bombing Two had to wait until the torpedo planes had moved into position for a coordinated attack. Fighting Two's VSB escort remained a few thousand feet over Hamilton's SBDs to watch for Japanese fighters diving in, but the enemy interceptors were all much lower than the escort and generally invisible from so far above.

Finally at 1118, Bombing Two got the signal to go in. Hamilton likewise had let down to 12,000 feet to begin his squadron's dives. The fifteen SBDs started pushing over as the *Shōhō* completed her second circle and momentarily lay in the wind axis, a good attack position. Passing 8,000 feet, Hamilton attracted one of the Type 96 fighters which stayed with him all the way down, but VB-2's skipper had more important things to concern him. Nearing 2,500 feet, he pulled the release handle and sent his 1,000-lb. bomb toward the target. Leveling out close to the water, Hamilton saw his thousand-pounder strike the center of the flight deck just forward of the after elevator and detonate with a spectacular explosion. Another VB-2 heavy bomb slammed home farther forward than the first hit, and both set off intense fires. The persistent fighter dogged Hamilton until his rear gunner finally drove it away. Lieut. (jg) Robert B. Buchan, another VB-2 pilot, reported his rearseat man downed a Japanese fighter. The squadron was not bothered further and lost no aircraft. Withdrawing to the east to rendezvous his planes, Hamilton looked back to observe the *Shōhō*'s plight, ''a spectacular and convincing pageant of destruction,''[10] as he later wrote. Bombing Two claimed five hits, and they netted two.

Hamilton could well be proud of his squadron's performance. The two 1,000-lb. bombs wreaked tremendous damage, fanning fatal fires in the upper hangar where armed and fueled aircraft fed the flames. Thick, black smoke streamed from the affected area and hid the *Shōhō*'s stern. The smoke and plumes of water raised by near misses served as excellent cover for the approaching torpedo planes. Izawa saw the TBDs closing from his starboard quarter, but other than order a turn to starboard, he could do nothing. The lead torpedo planes had already released their fish.

Brett's Torpedo Two had slowly approached the target from the southwest. They were still some distance out when Scouting Two attacked, and cursed the low speed of their Devastators. If the cruisers posed little threat to the SBDs, they were a definite hazard to the TBDs flying only a few thousand feet over the waves. Brett thought the antiaircraft fire from the two nearest cruisers so severe that he changed course around to the north to attack the carrier from abeam through the widest gap in the screen. When the *Shōhō* persisted in circling to port, Brett resolved upon an "anvil" attack against both her bows. He signaled his 2nd Division under Lieut. Edwin W. Hurst to make the standard split behind the target's stern. Six TBDs thereby would circle in toward each bow. Any direction the carrier turned, so went the theory, she was bound to present a hitting opportunity. Easily sketched on a blackboard, the tactic was most difficult to execute, given the lumbering TBDs and possible enemy countering maneuvers. Torpedo Two at 1115 began to descend from 4,000 feet down to 100 feet, the mandatory release altitude for their balky torpedoes. Torpedo Two was going in.

Antiaircraft fire was a necessary obstacle to Brett's crews, but Fighting Two saw to it that enemy fighters kept clear. As the TBDs started their final approach, a couple of Japanese fighters went after them. Ramsey did not see them, but Baker did. He and his wingman were trying to catch up after downing the floatplane a few minutes before. Diving in from 3,000 feet, Baker's section made a long high-side approach and surprised the two Type 96 fighters before they could fire at the torpedo planes. Caught unaware, the Mitsubishis had recourse to all sorts of "violent maneuvering consisting of loops, rolls, and vertical banked turns."[11] Baker, a highly experienced pilot, wisely refrained from chasing tails, but kept his speed up, fired snap bursts when he could, and regained altitude advantage. He claimed the destruction of two Type 96 fighters, and his attack certainly kept the enemy away from Torpedo Two. Meanwhile, Ramsey had secured a vantage point nearer to the *Shōhō*. He and wingman George Markham encountered no enemy fighters, but flew in the midst of clumps of black AA bursts that forced them to sheer away. The skipper carefully observed the attacks on the *Shōhō*, and his recollections were very valuable in assessing the results and lessons of the strike.

As the *Shōhō* headed southeasterly into the wind, Brett's TBDs drew up near her stern. The 1st Division crossed her stern in a wide arc around her port side, while Hurst's six planes swung to starboard. Above them, Bombing Two pressed its devastating attack. At 1119, Brett released his torpedo from off the *Shōhō*'s port quarter. Fanning out, the remaining TBD pilots curved toward the target, launched their fish, and sheered off to avoid antiaircraft fire. As each torpedo cut into the water, it threw out a huge splash before (hopefully) righting itself at the proper depth and heading for the target.

Torpedo Two's strike, the first for an American squadron against an enemy carrier, was a masterpiece. Lieut. (jg) Leonard W. Thornhill's fish was the first to slam home. His torpedo struck the *Shōhō*'s starboard quarter, the blast half hidden by smoke already raised by VB-2's bomb hits. The explosion wrecked both electrical and back-up manual steering systems, forcing the ship to hold to a steady south-easterly heading. On the port side, Lieut. (jg) Lawrence F. Steffenhagen's torpedo struck just aft of amidships, followed in short order by that of Lieut. Robert F. Farrington smashing into the port bow. Another pilot of Brett's 1st Division sent his torpedo into her port side just forward of amidships. Gunner Harley Talkington made the fifth torpedo hit. His fish detonated aft of amidships on the starboard side, causing a huge pillar of water to mushroom far above the flight deck. Torpedo Two claimed nine hits and got five.

The *Shōhō* was doomed as the five torpedoes found their mark. They tore huge holes in her hull and destroyed both fire and engine rooms. The carrier lost headway rapidly. Water flooded her lower spaces, knocking out power and causing a list. In the hangar decks and topside, fires of great intensity isolated repair parties, while below deck water poured in unchecked. The *Lexington*'s strike had effectively eliminated the Japanese light carrier *Shōhō*. Any more damage merely added to the "pageant of destruction" inflicted upon the hapless vessel.

The *Yorktown* Air Group cruised about fifteen minutes behind their counterparts from the *Lexington*. Around 1100 they sighted the Japanese task force about 20 miles northeast of Misima. In the previous few minutes Fletcher had changed their objective, redirecting the *Yorktown* planes to the targets reported by the Army search planes. That relieved the group of the necessity of searching for a second enemy carrier. The Yorktowners were all pleased to see the weather clear up. Anxious to secure altitude advantage over any interceptors attacking his charges, Flatley led his Grummans up to 10,000 feet. Even from that height he had a good view of Torpedo Five flying low over the bluish-green sea.

Leading the twenty-five SBDs of the two *Yorktown* squadrons, Bill Burch attained attack position near the *Shōhō* about the time Bombing Two completed its dives. Peering down from 18,000 feet, Burch could see only a "small" fire aft as the *Shōhō* completed her third circle and started to turn to starboard to counter Torpedo Two. From that height the great amount of damage wrought by Bombing Two may have appeared slight, but its effects were real. Burch observed the carrier steady up in the wind and assumed she would launch additional fighters. He did not know that hits by Torpedo Two had already crippled her steering gear. Radioing Taylor of Torpedo Five, Burch told him he was going to take his dive bombers in immediately. Taylor protested, saying it would be five minutes before his TBDs could make their final approach. Burch was adamant. He knew a target steaming into the wind lay in perfect dive bombing configuration.

At around 1125, Burch's seventeen VS-5 SBDs pushed over into the attack. Burch ignored three Zeros (Lieut. Nōtomi's newly launched *shōtai*) that made runs against the string of dive bombers, and concentrated on his target. All the way down, the SBD pilots had the carrier dead in their sights, as she made no attempt to maneuver. One by one they released their bombs and flattened out low over the water. Fifteen 1,000-lb. bombs fell onto and around the *Shōhō*. One VS-5 pilot had mistakenly jettisoned his payload before the attack, and another had to toggle his bomb into the sea after it would not release in his dive. Scouting Five claimed nine hits and two damaging near misses. Wally Short's eight VB-5 SBDs followed Burch into the attack, beginning their dives at around 1130. The increasing amount of smoke enshrouding the target made it difficult to assess hits, but Bombing Five felt it secured six on the carrier.

Unable to maneuver, the *Shōhō* was helpless. In rapid succession three powerful 1,000-lb. bombs pounded the bow and flight deck forward, shattering the wooden deck and igniting more fires. Other bombs slammed in farther aft. Japanese sources report possibly eleven bomb hits by both *Yorktown* squadrons. The *Shōhō* finally stopped. Repair parties battled frantically to stem fires and sought to evacuate the extremely high number of wounded. The flight deck turned into a raging inferno along its entire length. The last SBD pilot to dive, Ens. Thomas W. Brown of

Bombing Five, thought the *Shōhō* was finished and instead attacked one of the heavy cruisers. Although Brown and other *Yorktown* observers were certain they saw the cruiser roll over and sink, no other Japanese ships were damaged, according to Japanese sources.

During the approach to the target, VF-42's McCormack with three F4Fs had taken station at 17,500 feet to protect the dive bombers. After the SBDs went in, McCormack made a shallow dive astern of Bombing Five to cover the withdrawal at low level of the SBDs. The escorts, however, lost sight of the dive bombers during the descent. McCormack happened to spot a melee going on below and twice dived on targets that turned out to be, on closer inspection, American aircraft. During the withdrawal of Scouting Five, two planes described as "Type 98 VSB" attacked the last section and slightly damaged two SBDs. These misidentified fighters were most likely Nōtomi's Zeros which had followed the dive bombers down. Bombing Five was not hit at all. Neither squadron lost any aircraft during the actual attack.

The last element of the two air groups to reach the scene was Torpedo Five. Guided by Flatley from his vantage point at 10,000 feet, Taylor closed the target from wave top level. Flatley himself had a splendid view of the attack on the *Shōhō*. He quickly realized the carrier was finished and felt there should have been an officer present in tactical command of the *Yorktown* Air Group. At least eight SBDs and six TBDs, he thought, should have been diverted for attacks against the other warships present. In later operations, Flatley made due allowance for a strike coordinator.

Torpedo Five also felt the effects of antiaircraft fire from the enemy heavy cruisers. Taylor had to change course around one of the cruisers in order to take aim on the carrier's starboard bow. Masked completely in black smoke, the *Shōhō* exposed only a small portion of her bow. The TBD crews noticed only two small antiaircraft guns still firing. At 1129, they began their torpedo runs against her starboard side. Releasing from extremely close range, Torpedo Five claimed ten hits from ten fish. Japanese records indicate at least two torpedoes struck her starboard bow, although in the confusion others probably hit farther aft or were detonated by debris. Taylor withdrew to the east and mixed in with the rendezvous of Torpedo Two. He collected five TBDs from his own squadron and four from Torpedo Two, while five of his aircraft joined Brett and eight VT-2 TBDs for the flight home. Ramsey and his wingman Markham moved in overhead to escort Torpedo Two back to the *Lexington*.

The TBDs departed the scene unmolested by enemy fighters because of the alert action of Flatley's VF-42 escorts. While the TBDs made their drops, his five Grummans patrolled at 10,000 feet on the lookout for trouble. Not until the torpedo planes had attacked did a couple of *Shōhō* fighters regroup from evading Paul Baker and converge on Torpedo Five. Flatley eyed them before they could start after the dispersed and highly vulnerable TBDs. Leading his division into a steep, spiraling dive, he picked up considerable speed during the descent. Behind Flatley were his two wingmen, Ens. John D. Baker and (by mistake) Walt Haas, and the second section of Lieut. (jg) Brainard T. Macomber and Edgar Bassett (of 4 May fame).

Selecting one of the Type 96 fighters below, Flatley steepened his dive into an overhead attack. Catching sight of his adversary, the Japanese pilot resorted to aerobatics to try to evade: "steep wingovers, rolls, and loops at low altitude."[12] Screaming in at a 60-degree angle, Flatley opened fire, his bullets churning up large splashes on the surface of the Coral Sea. With a proper overhead approach, Flatley had decisively pinned his opponent. There was little the Japanese could do to escape. Using the spray from his bullets hitting the water, Flatley walked his slugs into the enemy fighter wildly flipping back and forth barely 100 feet over the sea. By the time the Grumman pulled out at 500 feet, its quarry had taken fatal damage and flew into the water. Flatley had executed a flawless hit-and-run attack and used his speed to climb and regain altitude advantage. Macomber had seen the Japanese respond under attack and thought the Type 96's maneuverability "incredible,"[13] but the enemy pilot's aerobatic skill had availed him nothing.

At the sight of Grummans diving in, the Japanese fighters had scattered. Only John Baker was able to latch onto one and used the speed he accumulated in the dive to chase it. Strangely, none of the Japanese attempted at this time to climb away. Flatley later noted that they appeared "confused."[14] Of his own division, only he regained altitude advantage. The other four VF-42 pilots split up, Baker occupied with his target, and the others also remaining at 2,000 feet or below looking for opponents of their own.[15]

Making a shallow dive, W.O. Imamura entered the scrap, and he was in no way "confused." Brainard Macomber spotted the newcomer, who passed beneath him on an opposite heading. At first glance the enemy aircraft appeared to be a two-seater scout because of the long glass cockpit canopy. Macomber charged after what looked like cold meat and made a standard attack from above and behind. The Zero, for that was what it was, turned smoothly and countered the diving F4F with an opposite run. A swift head-on pass with lively bursts of machine gun and cannon fire from his opponent quickly corrected Macomber's thoughts of how easy this fight would be. After the two aircraft flashed past one another, Macomber was dismayed to see the Japanese turn back much more quickly than could his F4F when the two fighters started to scissor for another head-on confrontation. Cutting inside Macomber's turns the Japanese inevitably worked his way onto the Grumman's tail. Macomber was too low to dive away, so he had to stay put and fight it out.

Fortunately for Macomber, help was at hand. Bassett, his wingman, happened to see the Japanese maneuver toward his section leader's tail. He, too, thought the aircraft was some sort of bomber, just as the VS-5 crews identified the Zeros that went after them as "VSB" types. At any rate, it was Bassett to the rescue. Moving up swiftly behind the preoccupied Japanese, he fired a long burst. At the first sight of enemy tracers, the Zero rolled out and away, then poured on the speed in a fast dive toward the water. Bassett saw white smoke stream from underneath his target—seemingly good evidence of damage. Coming around for a second pass on his supposedly disabled target, Bassett was surprised to see the enemy plane drawing away from him.

Looking for something to attack, Haas had after Flatley's first skirmish climbed slightly above the battle area. Then he happened to notice a Japanese plane break free of the melee and head in his direction. An F4F was in distant pursuit—Bassett chasing the Zero that had beset his section leader. The Mitsubishi ceased to smoke as soon as the Grumman had been left behind. Because of his location and altitude advantage, Haas found himself in good position to stalk the fleeing Zero. Diving in, he quickly overhauled the Japanese from behind for a good stern shot. Evidently unaware of the danger, the Zero pilot flew a straight course only a few hundred feet above the water. Reaching effective range, Haas fired a long burst that caught the Japanese by surprise:

> He [the Japanese] then slow rolled, attempted a steep climbing turn to the right and directly into my sights at which time I opened fire using a spraying burst setting him aflame.[16]

Lieut. (jg) Walt Haas about 8 June 1942 on board the *Hornet*. He was the first USN/ USMC fighter pilot to shoot down a Zero. (From Cdr. John Ford's *The Battle of Midway*.)

Haas had hit the Zero squarely in the fuselage. The pilot tried to bail out. Having barely got the canopy open, he stood up in the aircraft, but the Zero plowed into the water and disintegrated. Both Macomber and Bassett witnessed the splash. Haas's kill was the first Zero fighter shot down during the war by a fighter pilot of the U.S. Navy or Marine Corps. It went into the records as a Type 96 fighter because of the confusion of aircraft recognition. At this stage of the war, the F4F pilots did not really know what a Zero looked like. Japanese sources indicate this was the aircraft flown by W.O. Imamura, a highly experienced veteran of the air fighting in China.

Within a few minutes, the sharpshooting Haas secured his second victory of the day. After dueling with a Type 96 fighter, John Baker had finally obtained a tail position and opened fire. Smoking from wings and tail, the Japanese pulled into a barrel roll; then the sleek fighter fell gracefully away toward the water. Baker drew up short, expecting to watch his victim splash. Instead, his erstwhile quarry recovered smoothly at low level and hightailed it away. Along with another Grumman, Baker gave chase, but the opponent's clever ruse had gained him much distance. Unfortunately for the Japanese, Haas lurked above, ready to repeat his success. As he dived in for a stern shot, his increased speed carried him into close range. A touch on the trigger sent bullets into the Type 96 fighter. The Japanese never knew what hit him because the Mitsubishi exploded almost immediately. Only then did Haas, and Baker who was following, realize that the Japanese had led them into aircraft fire from one of the dark gray warships. As it was, the cruiser emitted only weak, inaccurate gunfire, and the two F4Fs escaped damage.

After regaining altitude advantage Flatley looked around for more opponents, then happened to spot another Japanese fighter. This time the Japanese saw him coming and immediately climbed away. Flatley's opponent was a Zero, and even with the increased speed of a zoom climb, the F4F-3 had little chance of overtaking the Mitsubishi. The fight broke up soon afterward. Fighting Forty-two's encounter with the *Shōhō* Fighter Unit ended in a decisive victory for the Americans. Haas shot down one Zero fighter and one Type 96 carrier fighter, while Flatley destroyed a second Type 96 fighter—all without the loss of a single Grumann. The VF-42 pilots noted with surprise the extreme maneuverability of the Japanese fighters, but it was evident from the way they burst into flames that they lacked self-sealing fuel tanks. That latter discovery provided an excellent boost to American morale. Several times the Japanese had started to smoke as if afire, only to make miraculous getaways. When they added throttle, they released smoke from their exhausts, and this deceived the American pilots. Flatley warned, "Set them on fire before you take your guns off of them."[17] Given proper tactics and good gunnery, he was confident he could destroy the enemy quickly despite the maneuverability of their aircraft.

As VT-5's torpedoes delivered the coup de grace into the *Shōhō*'s starboard side, Izawa at 1131 ordered all hands to abandon ship. Less than four minutes later, the *Shōhō* slipped under the waves. In the water were 300 survivors from a crew that had numbered over 800. Rear Admiral Gotō Aritomo, commanding MO Main Force, could not stop to rescue them. Shaken by the fierce American air strike of nearly 100 aircraft, Gotō ordered his ships to withdraw at high speed to the north. Not until 1400 did he feel it safe to detach the *Sazanami* to pick up survivors. The destroyer found only about 200, including Captain Izawa.

Japanese plane losses on combat air patrol amounted to three fighters—one Zero and two Type 96 fighters, flown by W.O. Imamura, PO2c Aoki, and PO2c Inoue. Almost certainly they fell to Flatley and Haas, who by far had the best shots. Lieut. Nōtomi led the other three Zeros to Deboyne, where they ditched in the lagoon. Together they claimed a total of four American planes shot down and another unconfirmed. A fourth *Shōhō* fighter pilot, PO2c Kuwabara Hachirō, died on board the carrier during the attack.[18]

By 1140, the two American air groups had organized themselves into a number of separate units for the flight back to the carriers. The VSB escorts covered the dive bombers, and McCormack picked up a stray VF-42 Wildcat from the torpedo escort. The flight back was largely uneventful except for one of the *Yorktown* dive bombers. In a combative mood, Ens. J. W. Rowley took off after one of the Japanese fighters heading to Deboyne. He could not catch it, and by the time he broke off pursuit, he had lost sight of the rest of the group. After wandering around the area, he later stumbled on Rear Admiral Crace's Support Group. All they could do was provide him with the right heading for Port Moresby. Lacking enough fuel, Rowley came up short and ditched just off the Papuan coast, where he and his gunner were later rescued. His SBD proved to the the *Yorktown*'s only loss for the mission. At 1210, Bob Dixon sent a prearranged message to Task Force 17, one that greatly heartened those on board:

Scratch one flat top! Signed Bob.[19]

In this way the carriers knew the attack had been successful and that the planes were on their way home.

High noon also saw MO Striking Force's air attack groups homeward bound, but they did not consider the mission much of a success. The Japanese strike planes had reached the reported target area by 0915 and looked in vain for the American carrier. Finally at 1051, the two *Shōkaku* search crews owned up to the fact there was no American carrier in the area, just the fleet oiler and the destroyer. To further smirch their performance, they had lingered too long in the area and lacked the fuel to return. Instead the two carrier attack planes headed for Indispensable Reef and ditched there. The next day the destroyer *Ariake*, detached by Takagi for that purpose, rescued the two crews. Their reports had placed Takagi and Hara in a grave situation because from other search messages it was plain that American carriers operated south of the Louisiades and posed a dire threat to the invasion convoy. MO Striking Force desired that its attack group return as quickly as possible so that the force could proceed westward at high speed and launch a second strike at long range that afternoon, before darkness ended all chance of dealing with the American carriers on 7 May.

By 1115, Lt. Cdr. Takahashi determined there definitely was no American carrier nearby and released the carrier attack group and its escorts to return to the carriers. His dive bombers would attack the oiler and accompanying destroyer. At 1126 he began his attacks. He led four carrier bombers against the destroyer *Sims*, and they scored three direct hits on the radically maneuvering tincan. The remaining thirty-two carrier bombers made slow, deliberate dives against the *Neosho* and inflicted at least seven hits, including a flaming crash by one of the *Zuikaku* carrier bombers. Noon found the *Neosho* adrift without power and perilously listing 30 degrees to starboard. Only her extensive compartmentation and tanks kept her afloat. For the loss of one carrier bomber, the Japanese had sunk one destroyer and fatally crippled a fleet oiler.

AFTERNOON REASSESSMENT

The returning strike groups showed up on Task Force 17's radars between 50 and 60 miles out. IFF equipment in the *Lexington* planes indicated the approaching aircraft were friendly. Encountering the warm frontal zone's thick clouds once more, the pilots tuned in their Zed Baker homing receivers. The SBDs had the signal as far as 75 miles, but the fighter pilots had trouble discerning the transmissions until they drew within 25 miles of the ships. The weather over Task Force 17 had definitely changed for the worse. The overcast had closed in solidly, sprinkled with intermittent rain squalls, while the east–southeasterly winds had picked up to 12 to 22 knots with gusts to 30 knots. The *Lexington* at 1234 cleared her flight deck for recovery by launching Vorse's four VF-2 F4Fs as relief CAP and seven SBDs as anti–torpedo-plane patrol. From 1239 to 1316, the *Lexington* brought on board ten fighters, twenty-six SBDs, and twelve torpedo planes from her strike group and also Gayler's four F4Fs from the CAP. The *Yorktown* in the same period recovered eight F4Fs, twenty-four SBDs, and ten TBDs from her strike, and also landed VF-42's 1st Division of four F4Fs from the CAP. Total plane losses for the mission were three SBDs, two from the *Lexington* and one *Yorktown* plane. Aloft on air patrol were eight F4Fs and seventeen SBDs.

Debriefing the aircrews, the analysts decided the groups sank one Japanese carrier and one light cruiser, with damage to one heavy cruiser. The carrier was variously described as a *Kōryū*-class or modified *Ryūjō*-class light carrier, but by process of elimination, they settled on the *Ryūkaku* (actually the *Shōhō*) as the victim of the strike. The six defending Japanese fighters had been very active. The *Lexington* pilots reported engaging ten to twelve fighters, while the *Yorktown* crews noted the presence of six Type 96 fighters and three "VSB" types. Total American claims amounted to five fighters and one VSB to F4Fs, and five fighters and one VSB to the dive bombers. Actual Japanese losses were three fighters shot down.

Flight deck crews worked feverishly to refuel and rearm the strike aircraft, while the aviators were debriefed and took a well-deserved breather. By 1420, Fitch reported, both air groups were ready to go again. Ted Sherman especially urged that a second strike be sent after the rich crop of targets known to be near Misima. Fletcher, however, was concerned that the two Japanese fleet carriers had not been located either by his own searches or by aircraft operating out of New Guinea and Australia. If he sent his SBDs out on an afternoon search, there still was little chance his strike groups could follow up, attack, and return before dark. Even worse, the frontal zone dogging the task force would make it very difficult for the strike planes to find Task Force 17 on their return. Better to hold the groups and wait for suitable objectives the next morning. For the rest of 7 May, Task Force 17 would conceal itself under the thick blanket of clouds, her fighters poised to deal with any strike the enemy might send.

Learning the bitter news of the *Shōhō*'s loss, Vice Admiral Inoue overseeing the MO Operation responded with a change in plan. He ordered the cruisers and destroyers of MO Invasion Force to prepare a night attack against the American task force. The Port Moresby invasion convoy was to withdraw temporarily to the north, hopefully avoiding any attacks. Inoue urged MO Striking Force to attack the American carriers. To Takagi and Hara, the sinking of the *Shōhō* came as a great blow. At noon Hara had announced preparations to launch at 1400 an attack against the American carriers operating southeast of Deboyne. The only thing required for this was the speedy return of his own strike group. At 1230, the first aircraft appeared overhead—nine Zero escorts and twenty-four carrier attack planes that on Takahashi's orders had not attacked the *Neosho* and the *Sims*. Lugging their torpedoes, the carrier attack planes came on board without incident. The only problem was that for MO Striking Force to conduct flight operations, the carriers had to steam southeast into the constant trade winds—away from the direction they wanted to go, namely, west. Around 1300, Takahashi's *Shōkaku* carrier bombers turned up, all nineteen in good condition, and with them Lieut. Okajima's nine Zeros, but there was no sign of Lieut. Ema Tamotsu's sixteen *Zuikaku* carrier bombers. Hara fidgeted on the *Zuikaku*'s bridge as it became evident that Ema's pilots had lost their way in the poor weather surrounding MO Striking Force. There was no telling when they would return, but Hara could not run off and leave them. The longer the carriers held to their Point Option course to the southeast, the farther they went from the American carriers to the west.

Search planes responded to the need for the Japanese to know the enemy's position. At 1240, one of the Deboyne-based seaplanes reported sighting one battleship, two heavy cruisers, and three destroyers bearing 175 degrees, distance 78 miles from Deboyne, and on course 310 degrees, speed 16 knots. The charts revealed this force to be almost directly south of Deboyne and a definite threat to the invasion convoy waiting north of the Louisiades. In actual fact this Japanese search crew had located Crace's Support Group heading northwest toward Jomard Passage. They submitted a highly accurate report except for the easy mistake of misidentifying one of the heavy cruisers as a battleship. At 1315, however, one of the Japanese land attack planes flying out of Rabaul radioed a sighting report placing American carriers bearing 205 degrees, 115 miles from Deboyne. There they were, all enemy ships apparently operating south of the Louisiades! Inoue's South Seas Force staff thought these two sighting reports had revealed the presence of two American task forces, both heading westward from where the search planes had spotted them that morning. According to a 1410 estimate, the staff placed the American battleship force slightly farther east than the American carriers, but both groups operated westward of a line bearing 180 degrees from Deboyne.

The Japanese could not have been more wrong. The Rabaul land attack plane had not sighted Task Force 17, which still was southeast of Rossel Island—much farther east than where the Japanese thought it was. What the Rabaul aviators had found was Crace's Support Group, which had no carriers. Even then, they greatly erred in their position estimate, putting the American "carriers" about 40 miles southwest of where Crace actually was, or over 150 miles west of the correct position of Task Force 17. This was a disaster for the MO Operation, leading to no end of trouble. From that time on, Crace's Support Group served as a magnet for Japanese search planes.

On board the *Zuikaku*, Hara had to postpone the 1400 launch of his strike groups, as the *Zuikaku* carrier bombers had still not turned up. Hara, like Fletcher, had to face the prospects of a night return and landing if he intended to launch a second strike that day. His staff investigated the possibility of organizing a picked force, mostly the division and section leaders, for a night strike. Shortly before 1500, however, full details of the sighting reports southwest of Deboyne reached MO Striking Force. Based on the 1410 South Seas Force estimate, Hara's staff put the enemy carriers far out of range of any air strike the Japanese carriers could launch that day. They thought the enemy carrier group was 430 miles to the west, with the battleships about 50 miles closer. According to reports, the battleships, at least, seemed to be heading away at 20 knots. Therefore, on Hara's advice Takagi radioed at 1500 that MO Striking Force would not launch a second strike that day. He intended to home his lost carrier bombers, then steam westward at high speed in order to launch an air strike the next morning.

For the most part the Japanese were ill served by their search planes, but one command at least had a fair idea of what was actually happening. At 1449, Lieut. Minematsu Hideo, in charge of the seaplane base at Deboyne, radioed his own estimate of the situation. He thought the Americans had divided into two groups, one with one battleship, two heavy cruisers, and three destroyers, and the second with two carriers, two heavy cruisers, three light cruisers, and nine destroyers. As for the location of the first group (the one without carriers), Minematsu provided the position as of 1240 as sent by one of his own *Kiyokawa Maru* planes. For the enemy carrier group, he eschewed later reports and gave the 0945 location as reported by one of the 6th Cruiser Division floatplanes. This was the most accurate evaluation of all, but there is no indication higher headquarters ever took notice of the report.

With so many search planes buzzing around the Support Group, Crace was bound to have trouble. He was painfully aware he had no fighter support. His situation was much like that of Rear Admiral Spruance's bombardment force on 24 February off Wake, but Crace's opposition would be much more dangerous. At 0915 a force of twelve torpedo-armed Mitsubishi Type 1 land attack planes had departed Rabaul. They were from the *Lexington*'s old friends, the 4th Air Group. These strike planes were escorted by 11 Tainan Air Group Zero fighters and headed for the original 0830 contact made with Task Force 17 southeast of Rossel Island. They had the radius of action to hunt the American carriers, but not far from the target area, the torpedo planes were redirected by headquarters to the west. Task Force 17 radars evidently had them on their screens beginning at 1242, bearing 290 degrees, distance 75 miles, and heading away to the southwest.

Also looking for the Americans south of Deboyne were twenty Mitsubishi Type 96 land attack planes armed with bombs. They were from a unit newly arrived at Rabaul, the Genzan Air Group The torpedo-armed land attack planes found nothing at the position reported by the Rabaul search plane. The strike leader released his Zero escorts to return to New Britain. On their own, the fighters happened upon Crace's Support Group. Finally around 1430, the torpedo planes and bombers also found Crace and attacked. In a sharp skirmish, the Japanese thought they sank a "*California*-type" battleship and damaged another battleship and a cruiser. Crace's well-handled task group actually sustained no damage, and splashed four Type 1 land attack planes besides![1] Crace, however, was hardly happy at the prospects of facing over thirty enemy bombers without fighter cover of his own. At 1526, he radioed Fletcher, stating that fighter support was essential for him to complete his mission. To add to his troubles, three U.S. Army bombers came over and dropped their bombs on the task group, fortunately not coming anywhere close to the ships. That night Crace retired southward, then moved to take position southeast of Port Moresby to cover its approaches, should the Japanese advance beyond the Louisiades. Fletcher, holding to radio silence, did not reply. Under the circumstances, it was far better for the Allies that the Japanese had found the Support Group and left the remainder of Task Force 17 alone. Fortuitously, Crace's ships emerged from the operation unscathed, but Crace vehemently called for air support in the future.

THE JAPANESE DUSK ATTACK

So far nothing had gone right! The Japanese admirals of MO Striking Force were dejected and ashamed that afternoon of 7 May. The Americans had sunk the light carrier *Shōhō* and even now could be smashing the invasion convoy. Admiral Inoue had temporarily postponed the Port Moresby invasion—the whole MO Operation might be jeopardized, and all MO Striking Force had done was sink an oiler and a destroyer. The situation facing Takagi and Hara did not appear favorable. Search reports placed the American carriers far to the west, out of range of any possible strike that day by Hara's flattops.

Shortly after 1500, the mood suddenly changed. The *Zuikaku* monitored a message relayed from one of the floatplanes supposedly shadowing the enemy carriers. According to this report, the Americans had altered course and steamed southeast. Staff officers bent over their charts and determined that if the Americans held to an easterly course, MO Striking Force just might be able to attack them at twilight. The strike group would have to return and land after dark, so it would have to be a picked force like the one discussed earlier that afternoon. No fighters would escort. The strike would be made at dusk, and, besides, the Zero fighters did not have the homing receivers so vital for navigation after dark.

Gambling that the Americans would sail within range, Hara ordered the *Shōkaku* and the *Zuikaku* to ready their strike planes. Anything was better than doing nothing. Not trusting entirely to search reports, he arranged for a precautionary sweep westward 200 miles by eight carrier attack planes. If they left soon, they could return before dark and would not require night-qualified pilots. While they took off, at 1515 the errant *Zuikaku* carrier bombers finally made it back from the morning strike—a flight of seven hours. Two of the aircraft cracked up on landing. Lieut. Ema and five of his pilots got a nasty surprise when they reported to *Zuikiku's* air officer. They were going on another long search and destroy mission into the same sort of rotten weather that had plagued their earlier flight. Their fatigue would be evident when they did finally sight the American carriers.

Around 1600, the air staff gave the selected crews a final briefing. They placed the two American task forces between 330 and 360 miles to the west. If the enemy held his present course and speed, by 1830 the distance between the two opposing carrier forces would drop to 200 miles. The pilots were told to fly a heading of 277 degrees to a distance of 280 miles. The strike group comprised twenty-seven aircraft (twelve dive bombers and fifteen torpedo planes), all flown by highly experienced crews (see table). The launch was complete at 1615, and the dusk strike force took its departure five minutes later.

The wretched Japanese search reports had mistakenly identified Crace's Support Group (which had no carriers) as the American main body, and put the American

Strike Leader	Lt. Cdr. Takahashi Kakuichi (H)
Carrier Bomber Group	Lt. Cdr. Takahashi
Shōkaku Carrier Bomber Unit	Lt. Cdr. Takahashi
	6 Type 99 carrier bombers
Zuikaku Carrier Bomber Unit	Lieut. Ema Tamotsu (B)
	6 Type 99 carrier bombers
Carrier Attack Group Lt. Cdr. Shimazaki Shigekazu (H)	
Shōkaku Carrier Attack Unit	Lieut. Ichihara Tatsuo (B)
	6 Type 97 carrier attack planes
Zuikaku Carrier Attack Unit	Lt. Cdr. Shimazaki
	9 Type 97 carrier attack planes

carriers 360 miles west of MO Striking Force. On the contrary, at 1600 Task Force 17 operated in a thick overcast only 190 miles west of the Japanese carriers. Frequent squalls at times hid the *Lexington* and the *Yorktown* from each other. Gill and his FD plot on board the *Lexington* welcomed the breather that afternoon from the bogeys that had plagued them earlier. The CAP pilots, however, had a far from easy time with the weather: "Twas a rugged afternoon to be flying the wily Wildcat,"[1] one later quipped. At 1502, trouble threatened to break out anew as another bogey appeared on the screen, but it did not approach. Both Buckmaster and Sherman took the opportunity to rotate their combat air patrols. The anti–torpedo-plane patrol of seventeen SBDs Fitch deemed useless in the low visibility, so the carriers brought them back on board, after launching the relief CAP. At 1520, the *Lexington* sent aloft VF-2 divisions under Ramsey and Dick Bull, then landed Vorse's four Grummans and seven SBDs. The *Yorktown* likewise launched four F4Fs under McCormack and brought on board Leonard's four F4Fs and ten SBDs.

The *Yorktown*'s radar at 1648 revealed an unidentified aircraft bearing 250 degrees, distance 18 miles. The bogey evidently did not register on the *Lexington*'s scope, so Pete Pederson on board the *Yorktown* took over fighter direction. He sent McCormack's division out after the contact, but in the poor weather the fighters failed to find the enemy. Six minutes later, the *Yorktown*'s lookouts spotted a Japanese seaplane bearing 315 degrees, distance 9 miles. McCormack again went tearing after the enemy, but the Japanese escaped in the clouds, last appearing on the radar at 27 miles, bearing 345 degrees. Japanese sources are unclear whether the aircraft sent a contact report. It appears the airplane was a Type O reconnaissance floatplane from the *Kamikawa Maru* Air Group based at Deboyne.

Task Force 17 went undisturbed until 1747, when the *Lexington*'s radar displayed a contact bearing 144 degrees, distance 48 miles. The radar operator thought the contact represented a formation of aircraft flying at low altitude, perhaps 1,500 feet, and moving at high speed in the general direction of the task force. On station Gill had eight F4Fs from Fighting Two and four from Fighting Forty-two. Trouble was the F4Fs were beginning to run low on fuel. Gill checked out the sections and found they averaged sixty gallons of fuel—not enough for a distant intercept in low visibility unless he could carefully coach them into the target. At first he vectored Ramsey's four Grummans and also McCormack's four, but he soon recalled McCormack. The *Yorktown* fighters lacked IFF, and Gill had trouble distinguishing them from the bogeys. The VF-42 pilots were already on instruments, so poor was the visibility in the growing twilight. Thus Ramsey's four F4Fs headed out, and the other eight fighters stayed over the ships. Gill also requested permission to scramble other F4Fs from both carriers. His superiors agreed because they suspected this contact finally represented the long-awaited Japanese counterattack.

On board both flattops, orders came at 1750 via the ready room phones, sending fighter pilots scurrying deckward to man F4Fs warmed up and ready for launch. Gayler on board the *Lexington* made ready to take six Grummans aloft, while on board the *Yorktown* Flatley had eleven planes with him. Running to his fighter, Flatley was slightly taken aback to find another pilot sitting in it. It was McCuskey, grounded because of the 4 May fiasco. McCuskey asked for a fighter to take aloft. Flatley gently ordered him out: "As much as I wanted to take him, I knew that to relax discipline at this point would ruin the whole idea behind punishment, so I had to shake my head."[2] His Grumman repossessed, Flatley led the eleven F4Fs into the air. Just after they left, however, McCuskey discovered mechanics in attendance around another Wildcat in the hangar. He guarded it jealously until he received permission from his superiors to fly. With his departure some minutes later, the *Yorktown* had all sixteen operational fighters aloft, which with the *Lexington* troops made a total of thirty F4Fs to defend the force.

Disappearing in the murk, Ramsey's four Grummans charged out to the south to intercept the bogeys. Gill gave them a couple of course changes that jockeyed them right on the target. The waning daylight filtered through the thick clouds, making for precarious visibility. About 30 miles out, Ramsey noticed below a formation of nine Japanese aircraft cruising at about a thousand feet. Leading was a Vee of five followed by two sections each with two planes. Ramsey thought they were Zero fighters. Diving in from 5,000 feet, he singled out one of the trailing sections and motioned his second section, led by Paul Baker, to take the other.

With wingman Ens. George Hopper in tow, Ramsey rolled into a long high-side run, taking aim at the rearmost Japanese on that side. He opened fire at 700 yards, and started hitting almost immediately. To his surprise, the target was reluctant to make violent evasive maneuvers once his red tracers zipped past. Ripped by Ramsey's accurate shooting, the Japanese flamed up dramatically, giving VF-2's skipper the chance to shift his aim to the surviving enemy in that section. Pressing his attack to the limit, Ramsey nearly brushed his second target as he pulled out, but the results were the same—another fiery victim spinning toward the dark sea. Hopper never even had a chance to shoot while his leader had flamed the two enemy planes. After executing his perfect strike, Ramsey climbed to regain altitude advantage.

Making a similar attack on the other enemy section were Baker and his wingman, Ens. William Wileman.[3] Baker torched one Japanese outright, while Wileman took after the other aircraft in the section and shot it up. He last saw it streaming gasoline as it disappeared in the clouds. Meanwhile Baker continued his run and chased a target in the Vee. These Japanese finally scattered as the Grumman tore at them from the rear. Fighting Two's deadly ambush had destroyed three enemy aircraft and crippled a fourth. At 1805 Ramsey exulted to the FDO that he had downed two enemy fighters.

Ramsey's targets were not Zero fighters at all, but rather nine Type 97 carrier attack planes of the *Zuikaku* Carrier Attack Unit led by *hikōtaichō* Shimazaki. Caught in the overcast, the Japanese strike group had spread out, probably forming a scouting line of sorts to help locate the American carriers. By 1800 they were still about 100 miles east of their reported objective, and certainly were not ready for combat. Because of the rain squalls, they had closed their cockpit canopies, and gunners had tucked away their flexible 7.7-mm Lewis machine guns. Suddenly from the deepening gloom angry red tracers had ripped through their midst, and Japanese planes exploded in flames. Those pilots who had survived VF-2's onslaught fled into the clouds. One crew at 1803 radioed the *Zuikaku*, "Enemy fighters have completely destroyed the attack group!"[4]

Before the *Zuikaku* torpedo planes could escape in the murk, they lost another of their number, but drew revenge with the loss. Baker charged after the five aircraft in the Vee, and separated from his wingman who was busy with another enemy plane. Making a run against his target, Baker closed in for the kill. Then he either collided with the target, or his bullets detonated the torpedo warhead. Bill Wileman, his wingman, glimpsed a sudden brilliant flash reflected in the clouds. Whatever happened, F-15 was not seen again.

Searching the area for another quarry, Ramsey evidently saw the fruits of Baker's and Wileman's efforts. At 1808 he reported the destruction of two more enemy fighters and three minutes later added a fifth to the tally. On board the *Lexington*, Gill ordered Ramsey's division to return immediately, as their fuel was getting critically low. Already strapped for fuel, the F4Fs had flown 40 miles out from the ships. Baker's absence was not immediately noticed, and would add to the confusion of an already perplexing day. At any rate, Lieut. (jg) Paul G. Baker, NAP, USN, was dead. In the Navy since 1929, Baker had made an outstanding record as an enlisted man that enabled him to attend flight training and earned him his wings in 1935. He became one of the crack NAPs of Fighting Two, and fleeted up to lieutenant (junior grade) from chief petty officer in March 1942. A dapper, well-liked individual, he would certainly be missed. With him went fifteen Japanese pilots, observers, and radiomen in the five *Zuikaku* carrier attack planes destroyed in Ramsey's ambush. Like Baker, these men were all highly experienced, elite aviators, and MO Striking Force would dearly miss them. Their numbers included the *Zuikaku* Carrier Attack Unit's CO, Lieut. Tsubota Yoshiaki, *buntaichō*, and a junior *buntaichō*, Lieut. Murakami Yoshito.

After Ramsey had departed on his intercept mission, Gill deployed the newly launched CAP fighters. To back up Ramsey, Gill sent seven VF-42 Grummans led by Flatley. On his wing were John Baker and Ens. Harry Gibbs, in the second section were Brainard Macomber and Edgar Bassett, while comprising the last section were Lieut. (jg) William Woollen and Ens. Leslie L. B Knox. Over the *Yorktown* Gill retained McCormack's four F4Fs and newly launched sections led by Leonard and Crommelin. Guarding the *Lexington* were ten fighters under Gayler and Bull. With visibility so precarious, Gill did not risk sending more fighters out to hunt the Japanese.

Gill's orders sent Flatley out along a heading of 240 degrees (M.), altitude 2,000 feet ("Angels 2"). Flatley had no idea what type of target he sought and assumed it was one of the ubiquitous snoopers that had plagued the task force most of the day. At 1808, about 30 miles south of the ships, the VF-42 pilots discerned ahead of them in the rain clouds two orange blobs dropping toward the sea. They knew the *Lexington* fighters were somewhere nearby, and by their handiwork, Fighting Two appeared hard at work. Just then a formation of six aircraft briefly exited the clouds, slid directly beneath Flatley's fighters but on an opposite heading, and disappeared to the north. Flatley at first thought they were VF-2 fighters headed back. He may have heard Gill's recall order and knew Ramsey had started back to the ships. Suddenly suspicious, however, Flatley radioed to ask what the targets were, and Ramsey piped in that they were enemy fighters.

Flatley's third section had the best look at the airplanes that had passed underneath, and they saw them for what they were—Japanese, red meatballs and all!

Without orders, Les Knox dropped out to attack, probably worried that the enemy had slipped between them and the carriers. Bill Woollen followed in order to support his wingman. The two VF-42 pilots jumped a small formation of what turned out to be torpedo planes, actually the second element of the carrier attack group—six *Shōkaku* Type 97s led by the unit commander, Lieut. Ichihara Tatsuo, *buntaichō*. On his first pass, Knox sent one Japanese spinning toward the water; then the enemy split up. Knox and Woollen separated, each taking a Japanese section in pursuit. Woollen chased after three torpedo planes, but they likewise dispersed. Soon Woollen found himself behind his target at wave-top level, flying through storms into the increasing darkness. He riddled the big, three-seat aircraft but could not down it. Finally realizing his chase had taken him almost 60 miles from the ships, Woollen dropped out, tuning his Zed Baker homer to guide him back to Task Force 17.

After splashing the first Japanese, Knox renewed his attack. He was never heard from again. Japanese records show he shot down a second torpedo plane. One of the rearseat men may have winged him, or, more likely, he became lost with a malfunctioning radio and Zed Baker. His fate remains unknown. A native of Brisbane, Australia, Knox had joined the U.S. Navy in April 1939 as a seaman recruit. Later that year he worked his way into flight training and was promoted to ensign in April 1940. For his actions on 7 May, he earned a posthumous Navy Cross. The *Shōkaku* Carrier Attack Unit lost two aircraft shot down and one badly damaged. In the latter, bullets had killed the pilot, forcing the observer in the middle seat to take control. He piloted the Nakajima close to MO Striking Force, but had to ditch. Among the pilots lost was Lieut. Hagiwara Tsutomu, a junior *buntaichō*. At heavy cost, Fighting Forty-two had done its part to cripple the Japanese torpedo strike force.

Flatley would have followed up Knox's attack had he not almost simultaneously flushed a small group of enemy dive bombers below him. They scattered as the Grummans dived in, but at 1,000 feet Flatley cornered a carrier bomber desperately trying to reach cloud cover. The division deployed in loose line-astern to make shallow high-side runs in succession. Responding defiantly, the Japanese rear gunner cut loose with his 7.7-mm Lewis gun. He also released some sort of explosive device, most likely a flare, which detonated with a bright flash right in the path of the fighters. Flatley, John Baker, and Gibbs in turn fired on the target, but failed to down the twisting dive bomber. Fourth to dive was Macomber, who used a high-rear approach. He found it getting so dark that it was difficult to determine precisely the type of plane he was attacking. He saw no return tracers, so the brave gunner may have been hit. Macomber fired a two-second burst that shattered the target, blowing off its tail in spectacular fashion. The aircraft Macomber destroyed was a Type 99 carrier bomber from the *Zuikaku* Carrier Bomber Unit. Macomber would see more of that unit later in the evening.

Looking around for more targets, Flatley could find none. Regrouping his division, he flew toward where Woollen and Knox had disappeared. After about 25 miles on that course, Flatley decided any more pursuit would be useless. Putting Baker on his left, Flatley instructed him to tune in his Zed Baker and guide the planes back to the ships, while he himself guarded the fighter circuit for possible new vectors. Like Bassett on 4 May, Baker skillfully determined the proper heading and led the five F4Fs directly back to the *Yorktown*.

The air battle lasting from 1803 to 1815 cost the Japanese heavily—seven carrier attack planes shot down outright, an eighth that ditched later, and one carrier bomber. As soon as the Grummans had drawn off, Takahashi and Shimazaki conferred by radio and called off the attack. Hopelessly dispersed into small groups, the strike planes jettisoned their bombs and torpedoes, then turned for home. Even then they had to face a night return through very bad weather. They had recourse to their radio direction finders which operated at medium high frequency (about 2400 kc.), roughly the same as American CAP radio transmissions, and this would lead to trouble for the Japanese.

Act II of the drama of the 7 May night strike took place over the American carriers. By 1830, the sun had set, and through the heavily overcast skies, only a faint light still shown in the west. The carriers had the task of gathering their fighters and recovering them as soon as possible. Given the poor visibility surrounding Task Force 17, this was not simple. Ramsey's three F4Fs landed on board the *Lexington* at 1835, followed by Bull's division of four Grummans. The *Yorktown* endeavored to land McCormack's four F4Fs, now aloft for nearly four hours. While this recovery of the low-fuel fighters progressed, Leonard led one VF-42 section out at Gill's orders to check out several bogeys, but he made no contact with the enemy. Soon Flatley's division returned and joined the fighters circling around the *Yorktown* and the *Lexington* waiting for the signal to land. For most of the pilots, it would be the first time they had tried landing on board a carrier after dark. Confusion reigned, as Grummans inadvertently cut each other out of the landing circle because of the darkness. Their inexperience caused an inordinate number of waveoffs, so the landings took considerable time.

Suddenly the enemy was there! Around 1840, carrier bombers from the Japanese strike group sighted Task Force 17. Their pilots, unobserved, closed in for a better look and did some quick figuring. At 1845, one of the Japanese radiomen tapped out, "Enemy sighted, bearing 160 degrees and 110 miles from Rossel Island, course 230 degrees."[5] There, at last, were the American carriers. It was the first time Japanese carrier pilots had sighted the American flattops during the war—but they had already dumped their bombs. In 1942 no deliberate special attack ("kamikaze") policy prevailed, and the Japanese could only resume their flight home. No one in Task Force 17 knew of their presence.

Through the coming and going of this first group of carrier bombers, the *Lexington* and the *Yorktown* carried on with the recovery of their fighters. With the landing circle so crowded, the landings were unusually hectic. One of the first VF-42 pilots to come in forgot to lower his tail hook. The landing signal officer failed to catch the error in the darkness, and the F4F sailed into the barrier, causing minor damage. A short delay ensued as the flight deck crew removed the Grumman and made quick work of rerigging the barrier. Perhaps seven or eight Grummans from VF-42 and a few from VF-2 still waited to land.

Just about to come on board the *Yorktown*, Macomber had to sheer off when the LSO gave him a waveoff because the deck was not clear. He climbed back to 1,000 feet and circled the ship. Just after 1850, he glimpsed an aircraft on the *Yorktown*'s starboard side signaling the ship by means of a hand-held Aldis lamp. This was not standard procedure at all, and Macomber thought instantly the intruder was Japanese. In the near blackout, three more Japanese dive bombers had stumbled upon Task Force 17. Evidently their pilots entertained second thoughts about their navigation and tried to find out whether the ships below were friendly by flashing a recognition signal. The ships did not turn on their searchlights in response, but neither did they open fire, adding to the uncertainty of the Japanese pilots.

Switching off his own running and approach lights, Macomber crossed over past the *Yorktown*'s starboard side. Easing up behind the strange aircraft, Macomber soon noticed there were three of them deployed in Vee formation. Two showed

Ens. Brainard Macomber on board the *Ranger,* May 1941. His F4F-3 is still in the colorful prewar marking scheme. (USN.)

their running lights, but the third displayed only a tail light. Because of the hurried nature of the launch, Macomber did not have his chartboard with navigational data or the proper setting for his Zed Baker receiver. Not wanting to lose track of the task force by a prolonged chase into the night, he determined to close in for one firing pass, then swing 180 degrees and turn back toward the *Yorktown*. Charging his guns, he drew up behind the right aircraft in the Vee, coming in from just below the target. Only its tail light revealed its presence, and it was too dark to judge distances. Consequently Macomber came too close and flew into the carrier bomber's slipstream. The turbulent air rocked the Grumman violently and ruined Macomber's shot. He then shifted over to the center aircraft and flicked his trigger. Only two guns responded, but the sight of their tracers was enough to scatter the Japanese. One of the rear gunners replied with a burst, tracers arcing out from his Lewis gun. The Japanese dropped into a left spiral and swung beneath the F4F. Because the target was still silhouetted by the faint light in the west, Macomber had a clear look at the Type 99 carrier bomber's elliptical wings and meatball insignia. With no time to waste, Macomber continued turning left 180 degrees to take up the proper heading back to the carrier. Alerted by the sight of tracers, observers in the task force saw three enemy planes cross from the west past the *Yorktown*'s starboard side ahead of her bow over to her port side. These Japanese just kept on going eastward into the darkness.

Macomber was the only American to fire on this second Japanese group to converge on Task Force 17 within a span of fifteen minutes. Meanwhile, the *Lexington* at 1856 completed landing her six fighters, and the *Yorktown* was back in business again. At 1857, the destroyer *Dewey* in the *Lexington*'s screen reported six Japanese aircraft buzzing the landing pattern. A third group of carrier bombers, perhaps two or three, had appeared overhead and circled to determine whether the vessels below were their own. The screening destroyers first noticed them, but their skippers were hesistant to open fire. At 1904, Captain Alexander R. Early, commanding Destroyer Squadron One, queried the carriers by TBS radio to learn whether they had any aircraft aloft other than square-winged Grummans. Shortly thereafter, one of the Japanese buzzed the *Lexington* and flashed out a recognition signal by lamp. On board the carrier there was little doubt the aircraft was Japanese, but Sherman, concerned for the fighters in the landing pattern, refused to fire.

Nearly all the aircraft circling over Task Force 17 were F4Fs waiting to land, about five or six from VF-42. The barely discernible stars on their wings and fuselages gave them no immunity. One pilot wrote in his report, "Ships in the formation commenced firing at anything."[6] First some destroyers opened up; then the heavy cruiser *Minneapolis* followed suit. Only Sherman on board the *Lexington* and Captain Gilbert C. Hoover, commanding Destroyer Squadron Two, kept their ships from shooting, for fear of hitting F4Fs by mistake. Circling at 300 feet off the *Yorktown*'s port quarter and awaiting his turn to land was Dick Wright. A cruiser behind him opened fire. Wright dived and came at the *Yorktown* from her starboard side, taking care to fly level with the flight deck so he would be recognized. Suddenly at 1910, the *Yorktown*'s entire starboard battery blazed, most of her 20-mm guns directed at Wright's Grumman. He thrust his control stick forward to duck under the tracers and nearly flew into the water. He called the ship and was probably the pilot who complained, "What are you shooting at me for? What have I done now?"[7] Wright turned into the groove for landing and came on board without further trouble. "The plane was not damaged," he wrote in his report, "but I aged five years at least."[8] (In addition to nearly being shot down by his carrier, Wright was distinguished in another way. He "sported a very authentic Fu Manchu mustache and acquired the nickname 'Fu Manchu.' " In spite of his "hairy aberration," "Fu Manchu" was "very steady, much respected"[9]—and very lucky that May night.)

Another VF-42 pilot was not so fortunate. Ens. William W. Barnes, Jr., flying as Leonard's wingman, had his F4F riddled by .50-caliber bullets that pierced the cockpit and severed an oil line. Hot lubricant drenched the unhappy Barnes, and a slug lodged in his parachute back. Despite the damage to his fighter, he later landed on board safely, but the Grumman was in no shape to fly the next day. Another victim of mistaken identity was Woollen, who had return alone by means of his Zed Baker after his combat with the *Shōkaku* torpedo planes. Around 1900, he took two waveoffs during his first two night landing attempts, and was about to try again when the pandemonium erupted. Astern of him one destroyer reached out with 20-mm fire, but the tracers fell below and behind him. Then a nearby cruiser joined in. Prudently Woollen extinguished his lights and climbed to 1,000 feet to give the gunners a chance to cool down. Then he resumed his spot in the landing circle and set down without further ado. Macomber was also patronizing the landing circle when the *Yorktown*'s starboard 20-millimeters intervened. He sought refuge between the *Yorktown* and a cruiser on her port beam, trusting to his lights to identify him. However, the *Yorktown*'s after port 20-mm battery chased him away. The *Yorktown*'s gunners later claimed one aircraft shot down, but their only success was Barnes.

It took time to sort out the VF-42 CAP after it had scattered. The last F4F did not touch down on the *Yorktown*'s flight deck until 1930. One of the pilots, however, was still aloft and in desperate trouble. Like everyone else, John Baker had dodged the gunfire erupting in Task Force 17, but in the process, he lost sight of the ships. Apparently Baker could transmit radio messages, but could not receive any. He had used his Zed Baker to guide Flatley's division back to the *Yorktown*, but thereafter ran afoul of one of the real defects in that equipment. To use the Zed Baker, he had to change frequencies on his radio receiver, and once tuned away from the CAP frequency, it was very difficult to tune back on it. His Zed Baker did him no good under the present circumstances. As another VF-42 pilot put it, "ZB was not good close in."[10] Thus Baker could neither rely on his homing device nor receive instructions.

Adding to the confusion was his surname. The *Lexington* communicators lost valuable time trying to determine which Baker this was, not knowing of the death of Paul Baker of Fighting Two. By the time they sorted the two out, John Baker was no longer on the radar screen. Gill later thought he had Baker on the screen at 1913, bearing 305 degrees, distance 24 miles, but that is unlikely. It is doubtful Baker would have got that far away in just three minutes after the ships opened fire. Pederson on board the *Yorktown* took over trying to communicate with him, but could not establish contact. There was nothing the ship could do for him. Finally at 2028, Pederson regretfully had to tell Baker to try for Tagula Island, giving him the course of 320 degrees (M.), distance 120 miles. With a 25-knot tailwind and what fuel he had left, there would have been a chance for him to make it—if he heard the CO. To this day, the details of John Baker's fate remain unknown. Appointed an aviation cadet in March 1941, Baker earned his wings that September and joined Fighting Forty-two the day after war broke out. He was one of three pilots lost by the fighting squadrons that strange evening of 7 May.

"Strange" indeed describes that evening. Enemy aircraft on three separate occasions had buzzed Task Force 17. Despite reports that the Japanese had actually tried to land on board, it appears far more likely they were puzzled and descended to check their navigation. The crews were night-trained and expected their carriers to illuminate with landing lights according to normal doctrine. The Japanese probably flashed something like "Turn on the lights," or perhaps a special recognition code. They later complained that American radio communications greatly interfered with their radio direction finding/homing devices. It is quite possible the American CAP radio transmissions inadvertently drew the Japanese to Task Force 17 or just jammed their homers. Obviously the day's two missions had taken a toll on the aviators, particularly the *Zuikaku* carrier bomber pilots, aloft since 0800 with only one hour's doubtful respite.

That evening Hara tried every means to prevent the calamitous loss of the whole Japanese strike group with its skilled, virtually irreplaceable pilots. Shortly after sunset, the Japanese carriers began homing transmissions, and at 1840, Hara suggested to Takagi that MO Striking Force deploy into a special formation to facilitate illumination for landing. Within a half hour, the Japanese ships had changed course to the southeast into the wind. The two big flattops steamed abreast of each other with four destroyers astern and two cruisers and one tincan ahead. Each ship awaited the signal to turn on its searchlights which all lined up in a special pattern to help the pilots judge their landing approaches. Now all that was needed was the return of the aircraft. The Japanese decision to illuminate was extremely courageous with the enemy so near, and foreshadowed Pete Mitscher's similar action in June 1944 during the Battle of the Philippine Sea.

The first aircraft landed at 2000, but the rest floundering in poor weather took up to two hours more to straggle back. Eighteen aircraft (eleven carrier bombers and seven carrier attack planes) landed on board the *Shōkaku* and the *Zuikaku*— a magnificent performance by superb aviators beset by fatigue.[11] They were justly

Fighter Credits, 7 May 1942

(a) Morning 7 May	
Fighting Two	
Lieut. (jg) Paul G. Baker	2 Type 96 fighters
	1 floatplane (prob.)
Fighting Forty-two	
Lt. Cdr. James H. Flatley	1 Type 96 fighter
Lieut. (jg) Richard G. Crommelin	½ Type 97 flying boat
Ens. Walter A. Haas	2 Type 96 fighters
Ens. Edgar R. Bassett	1 VSB
Ens. Richard L. Wright	½ Type 97 flying boat
(b) Evening 7 May	
Fighting Two	
Lt. Cdr. Paul H. Ramsey	2 Type 00 fighters
	1 Type 00 fighter (prob.)
Lieut. (jg) Paul G. Baker	1 Type 00 fighter
Ens. William W. Wileman	1 Type 00 fighter
	1 Type 00 fighter (prob.)
Fighting Forty-two	
Lieut. (jg) Brainard T. Macomber	1 Type 99 VSB
Lieut. (jg) William S. Woollen	1 VT damaged
Ens. Leslie L. B. Knox	1 VT destroyed

proud of their abilities, but intensely frustrated at not being able to smash the American carriers. The *Shōkaku* carrier attack plane with the observer at the controls ditched at 2118, and the two ill-fated crew were not recovered. Looking over the losses that evening, Hara was appalled. Nine aircraft had failed to return—all manned by crack aviators including three *buntaichō*. The torpedo strike force had suffered near crippling losses (five from the *Zuikaku*, three from the *Shōkaku*). Thus the interceptions by Ramsey's VF-2 division and Woollen's VF-42 section had significantly reduced Japanese torpedo attack potential. The Japanese aviators themselves reported the confirmed destruction of two Grumman fighters and added another as probable.

Once the shock had worn off of seeing enemy planes apparently trying to land on his flagship, Fletcher realized the Japanese carriers had to be within 200 miles of him and that they knew his exact position. Not long after 1900, both CinCPac and ComSoWesPacFor in Australia forwarded translations of intercepted Japanese sighting reports of two American carriers. Fletcher carefully considered sending his heavy cruisers and some destroyers for a night surface attack, but rejected the idea. If the surface attack force did not locate the enemy flattops before dawn, then they would be extremely vulnerable to air strikes. Fuel was another consideration because of the supposed loss of the *Neosho*. Task Force 17 would have to conserve fuel for the next several days. Sound tactics dictated that Fletcher keep his task force together. At 2124, he radioed CinCPac to report the sinking of one large enemy carrier and one cruiser that morning near Misima. Fletcher also noted that the sinking of his fleet oiler would "cripple my offensive action and may cause my withdrawal in a few days." He sketched his plans for the next day: "I am operating to attack carriers in the morning, must then fuel destroyers and will continue oppose enemy movement toward Moresby."[12] The fuel for his tincans would come from the heavy ships.

At 2200, the *Lexington* signaled the flagship that her radar at 1930 had detected aircraft circling as if landing, bearing 090 degrees and 30 miles from the task force. No explanation was given as to why it took two and one-half hours to provide this information to the task force commander. Fletcher decided to discount this tardy intelligence. The *Yorktown*'s radar had not picked up any circling aircraft, and he did not believe the Japanese carriers were that close. Besides, his own radio experts, using the single bearing emitted by the enemy homing devices, had deduced the Japanese might be either to the east or to the west on reciprocal bearings a distance of 140 miles away. CinCPac intelligence at 2131 radioed Task Force 17 that radio direction finding stations placed the Japanese signal bearing 233 degrees from Oahu. This was vague for Fletcher's purposes, but added to the belief the Japanese lay eastward of him. In retrospect, it appears that the *Lexington*'s radar had picked up Japanese carrier aircraft circling in order to tune in their homing signals. The closest the two carrier groups drew to each other was about 100 miles at 2000. Thereafter, the range opened as MO Striking Force steamed southeastward into the wind in order to land planes, while Task Force 17 headed south.

Shortly before midnight, Fletcher informed Fitch he did not intend to launch a night surface attack on the target supposedly picked up on the *Lexington*'s radar. Instead he would tackle the enemy carriers first thing next morning. At 0025, 8 May, Fitch concurred. Because of the proximity of the enemy flattops (probably two, Fitch thought) and because their course and speed were unknown, Fitch advised a full 360-degree air search at dawn to locate the enemy quickly no matter what direction he had taken. The crucial sector was the northern semicircle, which should be searched to 200 miles, while to the south the planes would have to proceed only 125 miles to find them in the unlikely event the enemy had steamed south. Task Force 17's air strike groups would be readied for immediate launch after the departure of the search planes.

Fifteen minutes after Fitch's message, Fletcher replied with his agreement to the full-circle dawn search. He added that Task Force 17 would head west, probably to narrow the distance to Crace's Support Group watching Jomard Passage. Should the carrier exchange on 8 May be favorable to the Americans, then Task Force 17 just might have a shot at the invasion convoy. Besides, more radio intelligence pointed to the certainty that the Japanese carriers were east of Task Force 17. Fletcher instructed Fitch to determine the exact course and speed for the dawn search's Point Option, which would govern to best advantage the morning's air operations.

The several Japanese commanders involved in the increasingly complex MO Operation independently spent the evening of 7 May trying to figure out what was going on. Vice Admiral Inoue, commanding South Seas Force from his headquarters at Rabaul, deduced that the main American carrier–battleship forces were southwest of Rossel or Deboyne. As explained above, these reports all referred to Crace's multinational Support Group, while Fletcher's carriers remained hidden well to the east. Inoue at 2040 issued a general directive postponing the Port Moresby landings two days to 12 May. He canceled a proposed night attack on the American carriers and instructed MO Main Force to detach the heavy cruisers *Kinugasa* and *Furutaka* to reinforce MO Striking Force. As for Takagi's MO Striking Force (the *Shōkaku*, *Zuikaku*, and company), it was to reach position Lat. 13° South, Long. 155° East to launch a dawn search, locate the American carrier force, and then destroy it by air attack. Things would be just fine after MO Striking Force had dealt with the American carriers.

Inoue's directive reached Takagi and Hara while their carriers recovered the dusk strike group. Hara had already learned the American carriers were located much farther east than he had believed when he launched his planes. His pilots informed him of sighting the enemy carriers at 1900 in position Lat. 13° South,

Long. 154°40′ East (very close to the actual position of Task Force 17). The enemy force comprised two carriers, two battleships, three cruisers, and six destroyers, and were presently located only about 100 miles west of MO Striking Force. At 2120, Hara radioed Rabaul his estimate of the situation. The South Seas Force staff immediately replied, "Is the position correct?"[13] They could not imagine in light of the other reports that the enemy was situated so far to the east. Hara amplified his earlier report, adding not only was the position report correct, but the enemy carriers were a "*Saratoga*-type" and a "*Yorktown*-type." Hara stated, "It is difficult to imagine that this is a different group from the other already sighted."[14] This squared with the fact that a small night attack force of three Kawanishi flying boats had flown to the location reported by South Seas Force, and by 2035 had found nothing.

On board his flagship *Zuikaku*, Hara was busy assessing the results of the day's battles and planning for 8 May. Plane losses that day were heavy; two carrier bombers and ten carrier attack planes had failed to return (most compliments of Task Force 17 fighters), not to mention the loss of the *Shōhō*. Hara advised Takagi it would be best to head south or east that night in order the next morning to operate on the flank of the American carrier force. This ran contrary to Inoue's 2040 directive, which essentially instructed the Japanese carriers to approach and offer direct support to the invasion convoy. Hara felt his own plan justified, first because Inoue had based his on faulty information, and second because it would be better tactically for MO Striking Force to take a flank position rather than interpose itself between the Americans and the Port Moresby Invasion Force.

Takagi thought differently. No doubt realizing that he was the one held primarily responsible for the failure to destroy the American carriers, he was less than enthusiastic about again disregarding his superior's orders. As soon as he could (at 2210), Takagi changed course to 000 degrees to head north for Inoue's dawn search point. At midnight, Takagi issued his orders, instructing Hara's 5th Carrier Division to launch its dawn search from the indicated point and cover sectors south and southwest of there out to 250 miles. Upon receipt of this missive, Hara's staff immediately realized the origin of the search would be very close to the last reported enemy position. Because of this and because the American course and speed were unknown, MO Striking Force would be compelled to launch a 360-degree search for the same reasons Fitch had to. The staff pointed out to Hara that such a full-circle search would require many carrier attack planes. In light of their heavy losses, anything past a minimal search would cripple the 5th Carrier Division's ability to make torpedo attacks. Hara tried to substitute cruiser search planes in lieu of some of his carrier attack planes, but Takagi refused. His own staff had forecast choppy seas that morning. Hara quickly offered another suggestion. He advised that the search launch point be shifted 120 miles farther north to enable the carriers to dispense with any searches to the north. Air searches by Base Air Force from Rabaul and Tulagi would cover their rear. Moving farther north would also coincide with Inoue's unspoken intention of concentrating his offensive units and would speed up the rendezvous of the two cruisers reinforcing MO Striking Force. At 0040, Takagi signaled his agreement to Hara's course of action.

Thus the stage was set for the great confrontation on 8 May. The prudent Inoue had retired his invasion convoy and escorts in order to let the two opposing carrier forces battle it out for victory in the Coral Sea. Once the enemy carriers had been sunk or routed, the MO Operation could resume. Fashioned into two prongs, MO Invasion Force would provide escort for the convoy, while MO Striking Force ranged along the left flank would annihilate Allied land-based air units and facilitate the invasion of Port Moresby—if the American carriers were destroyed.

CHAPTER 12

The Carrier Battle of 8 May

THE SEARCHES

The warships of MO Striking Force glided northward through the predawn blackness of 8 May. Below decks, mechanics readied the aircraft for the dawn search, while exhausted flyers tried to get a few hours of uninterrupted sleep before facing the rigors of another day's fighting. On board the *Zuikaku*, Hara's staff devised the morning search plan and at 0420 issued the appropriate orders. At 0600, the *Shōkaku* was to launch four and the *Zuikaku* three carrier attack planes to search a sector bearing 140 to 230 degrees from MO Striking Force. Search radius would be 250 miles. After their departure, the carriers would ready the air groups for maximum strike. Aircraft strength on board the *Shōkaku* and the *Zuikaku* amounted to 109 (not counting eight Zeros reserved for the 5th Air Attack Force), of which only 95 (37 Zero fighters, 33 carrier bombers, and 25 carrier attack planes) were operational. Dawn saw MO Striking Force still within the warm frontal zone, which meant thick clouds and low visibility. The carriers reached the designated launch point at 0600, but the seven search planes did not get off until 0615. At 0700, MO Striking Force changed course to the southwest, speed 18 knots, to head for the rendezvous with the two heavy cruisers. They joined up fifty minutes later.

Complementing the carrier searches were several aircraft from the 5th Air Attack Force flying from bases at Rabaul and Tulagi. Three Kawanishi Type 97 flying boats from the Yokohama Air Group at Tulagi took to the air at 0630 to sweep much of the northern Coral Sea. From Rabaul four land attack planes departed to search the Louisiades area. Also at Rabaul waited a strike group of torpedo-armed land attack planes, but soggy runways made their takeoff doubtful. It appears the floatplanes at Deboyne remained in reserve for use in amplifying contacts and shadowing American warships once they were sighted.

Task Force 17 change course to the west at 0116, several minutes after detaching the destroyer *Monaghan* to look for survivors from the *Neosho* and the *Sims*. (The *Neosho* drifted until 11 May, when the destroyer *Henley* found her, took off survivors, and sank the hapless vessel.) Shortly after 0500, Fitch posted the search assignments. His Task Group 17.5 with the *Lexington* and the *Yorktown* had a total of 128 aircraft, of which 117 (31 fighters, 65 dive bombers, and 21 torpedo planes) were flyable. Because of the need for a full-circle search, no fewer than eighteen SBDs would have to be used. This day the *Lexington* drew search duty. Ted Sherman decided to use most of Scouting Two, twelve SBDs, to search the crucial northern sectors out 200 miles, while six SBDs from Bombing Two would search 150 miles to the south. Upon their return, all of them would be refueled and relaunched as anti–torpedo-plane patrol to help compensate for the lower number of available CAP fighters.

First light around 0600 found Task Force 17 clear of the heavy cloud cover that had concealed it the previous day. The ships now operated in an area of modified polar air south of the warm frontal zone. This meant almost unlimited ceiling and visibility, with few clouds. At 0625, the *Lexington* sent off the morning search, also taking the opportunity to launch four F4Fs under Paul Ramsey for combat air patrol. Ramsey had reorganized Fighting Two slightly, taking Bill Eder's section from Dick Bull's 5th Division and attaching it to his own 1st Division to fill the vacancy incurred with Paul Baker's death.

At 0652, Fitch directed the *Yorktown* to launch four fighters for CAP and eight SBDs as the standing anti–torpedo-plane patrol. The *Lexington*, her early morning flights taken care of, began respotting the flight deck for launch of the strike group as soon as the search report came in. Thirty minutes later, the *Yorktown* still had not launched the air patrols, and Fitch wanted to know why. Actually the *Yorktown* had not copied the original message; so Murr Arnold, the air officer, had already begun readying the attack group for launch. After a slight respot, he was able to get the four fighters and eight SBDs aloft at 0730. Leading VF-42's contingent was Jimmy Flatley, with Brainard Macomber as his second section leader. The squadron had only thirteen Grummans in commission, but the mechanics promised another later that morning. The eight SBDs were from Scouting Five and consisted of divisions under Lieut. Roger Woodhull and Lieut. Stockton Birney Strong. After completing the *Yorktown*'s flight operations, the task force changed course to 125 degrees, speed 15 knots in order to close Point Option, the position given to the search SBDs where they could expect to find the carriers upon their return.

Flying northward, the pilots of Scouting Two encountered increasingly heavy cloud cover as they penetrated the weak warm front wherein MO Striking Force lurked. Visibility was from two to fifteen miles, with widespread local rain showers interspersed with violent squalls. A 15- to 18-knot southeasterly tail wind added to the difficulty of estimating positions. Fortunately scattered pockets of open sky enabled one of the pilots to spot the enemy. At 0820, Lieut. (jg) Joseph G. Smith happened to catch sight of MO Striking Force. Reporting by voice to assure the quickest transmission of his find, he sent the following message to the *Lexington*:

Contact, 2 enemy CV's, 4 CA's, many DD's, bearing 006 degrees, distance 120 miles from Point Zed, course 120, speed 15.[1]

Below him the Japanese carriers were pointed into the wind, strike groups poised on deck ready for launch, waiting only for word from their search planes. Smith cleverly concealed himself from the Japanese combat air patrol while he continued to shadow their ships.

Welcome news soon reached the Japanese as well. At 0807, the *Lexington*'s CXAM radar had detected a bogey bearing 330 degrees, distance 22 miles. It appeared to be an aircraft flying very low and at goodly speed along a heading of 240 degrees. Red Gill, the *Lexington* FDO, sent fighters after the bogey, but the Grummans could not make visual contact. Finally at 0816, the contact faded from the screen. Although he had no evidence for his assumption, Gill felt certain an enemy plane had eyed Task Force 17. All he could do was recall his fighters on station. The patchy cloud mass to the north gave snoopers ample cover in which to evade the CAP and watch the task force. Up to this point, only the large flying boats seemed really vulnerable to the CAP.

The radar contact indeed was a Japanese plane, the *Shōkaku* carrier attack plane

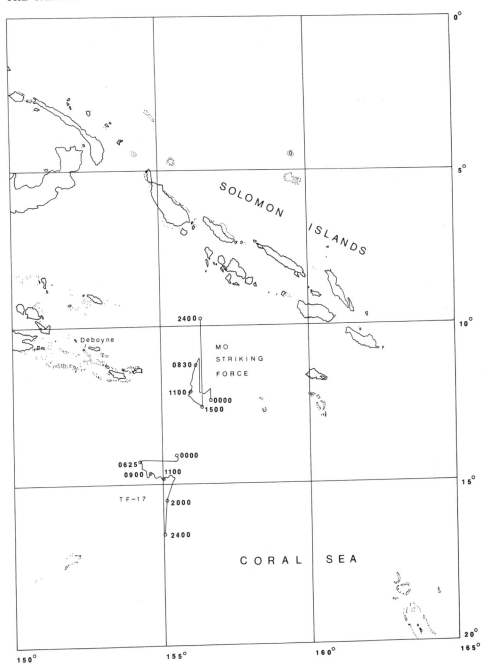

Carrier operations, Coral Sea, 8 May.

flying the 200-degree bearing from MO Striking Force. This time the 5th Carrier Division had some of its best men flying search, and the results showed it. Commander of the successful search plane was W. O. Kanno Kenzō, riding the middle seat of the big torpedo plane. At 0822, he radioed base:

Have sighted the enemy carriers.

followed by:

Location of enemy carriers 205 degrees and 235 miles from your position, course 170 degrees, speed 16 knots.[2]

Hara on board the *Zuikaku* had the messages in hand at 0830 and 0840, respectively. Meanwhile Kanno maneuvered his aircraft closer to the American task force for a better look. He transmitted information on weather, visibility, and enemy course changes. So successful was he in eluding detection that Gill never did have him on radar after 0816. Task Force 17 was not aware of his continued snooping until they monitored some of his contact reports.

With the American carriers now located, the Japanese worked feverishly to complete the launch of the strike group. Carrier attack planes armed with 800-kilogram aerial torpedoes were brought up from the hangars, while plane handlers on deck completed arming the carrier bombers with 250-kilogram bombs. Mechanics started engines and soon had them idling smoothly. Gathered around their senior officers near each carrier's superstructure, the aircrews listened to an address by their captain, then received a short but intense briefing by the *hikōtaichō* and the *buntaichō*. Lt. Cdr. Takahashi and the other air leaders made a great effort to raise spirits. In spite of the leadening fatigue and intense frustration of the previous night, all were ready to fight.

Shortly after 0900 came orders from the carrier air officers to man planes, and the aviators scurried over the flight deck. At 0910, the *Shōkaku* and the *Zuikaku* both began launching aircraft. Crewmen lined up on deck and in the carrier islands to wave their caps and shout "Banzai" as each strike plane started up the deck. With usual Japanese efficiency, the aircraft rapidly formed up, and Lt. Cdr. Takahashi took his departure at 0915 on a heading of 196 degrees. His strike force comprised sixty-nine aircraft: eighteen fighters, thirty-three carrier bombers, and eighteen torpedo planes. After the launch, Hara suggested to Takagi that MO Strike Force close the range in order to shorten the return flight of the strike planes. Takagi concurred, and at 0915, the ships changed course to 200 degrees and worked up to 30 knots to follow the aircraft into battle.

THE ATTACK ON MO STRIKING FORCE

The Japanese completed their launch first, but the Americans would make the first attack. Joe Smith's contact report reached the *Lexington* at 0820, but only in a garbled form: "2 CV, 4 CA, 3 DD."[1] The enemy's position and the originator's call sign did not come through because of poor atmospheric conditions. This incomplete message put Fitch in a great quandary, as he did not know whether the message was authentic. Smith was busy dodging Zeros and rain squalls, but at 0833, his gunner was able to send the contact report by key:

Contact 2 CV, 4 CA, many DD, bearing 006, distance 120 miles, speed 15 at 0820.[2]

Another VS-2 pilot repeated the message by voice for benefit of the ship, as did Bob Dixon, the squadron commander.

On board the two American carriers, the strike groups waited at condition one, full readiness. While Fitch and his staff evaluated Smith's reports, the flagship at 0837 relayed a startling message to the *Lexington*: "Believe we have been sighted by enemy carrier plane."[3] Radio intelligence on board the *Yorktown* had begun intercepting Kanno's radio messages. Only one decision could be made. Fitch at 0838 ordered the *Lexington* and the *Yorktown* to launch their strike groups. Both he and Fletcher knew the importance of getting their planes aloft before an enemy strike could come in. Smith's contact reports looked like the real thing.

Initially there was some confusion as to whether the contact reports referred to "Point Zed" or the actual position of Task Force 17. The search pilots had received orders to relay the enemy's location with reference to a specific location, "Point

Zed," rather than transmit the bearing and distance from Task Force 17. This would prevent the Japanese from deducing the task force's position if they intercepted the message. In this instance, however, Smith's messages were incomplete, leaving the two admirals unsure of his meaning. Here they underestimated Smith, as he flew the mission and transmitted his reports exactly as briefed.

In light of the uncertainty over the meaning of the message, Fitch at first declined to send the short-ranged torpedo planes with the strike group; but upon exchanging TBS messages with the *Yorktown,* he agreed that Smith's communications must refer to Point Zed. This placed the Japanese carriers bearing 028 degrees, distance 175 miles from Task Force 17. Fitch then included the two torpedo squadrons with the strike groups. Buckmaster, however, was worried about the range, especially for the sake of the fighters. At Buckmaster's suggestion, Fletcher at 0847 instructed Fitch to change the strike groups' Point Option to shorten their return flight. Fitch responded by proposing that Task Force 17 head north toward the enemy after the *Lexington* had recovered the morning search. The actual distance to the enemy was about 210 miles, a fact that would have given Fitch pause had he known. Fortunately the opposing carrier admirals had independently chosen to steam toward one another to narrow the range. Thus the *Yorktown* strike group, the first to find its objective, would have to fly only about 170 miles to reach the target. Fitch ordered each of his two groups to concentrate on one Japanese carrier.

The *Lexington*'s and *Yorktown*'s flight decks teemed with activity as plane handlers maneuvered the heavily laden strike aircraft into launch positions. Engines were warmed up and ready to go. In their ready rooms, pilots scribbled last-minute notes on the latest enemy position and their own vital Point Option. Then came the orders by phone to man planes. The *Yorktown* launched first, starting at 0900. The *Yorktown* strike group had the following organization:

VF-42	Fighting Forty-two	Lt. Cdr. Charles R. Fenton	6 F4F-3s
VS-5	Scouting Five	Lt. Cdr. William O. Burch, Jr.	7 SBD-3s
VB-5	Bombing Five	Lieut. Wallace C. Short	17 SBD-3s
VT-5	Torpedo Five	Lt. Cdr. Joe Taylor	9 TBD-1s
			39

Tactically the *Yorktown* group divided into two elements. Bill Burch, the senior dive bomb leader, was to take the twenty-four SBDs (each armed with one 1,000-lb. bomb) to 17,000 feet and cruise at 130 knots. His orders from Pederson (again deck-bound as fighter director) were to fly to the target independently of Torpedo Five, but to coordinate his dive bombing with the torpedo planes. Escorting the SBDs was a section under VF-42's skipper, Chas Fenton. Joe Taylor's Torpedo Five and escorts comprised the second element, Taylor opting to keep his lumbering TBDs just off the wave tops, flying at 200 feet to help protect against fighter attacks. The Devastators cruised at 105 knots. Their escort consisted of a four-plane division led by Bill Leonard with Bill Woollen as second section leader. The Grummans climbed to 2,000 feet and deployed with Leonard's section on the right over Torpedo Five and Woollen's pair on the left. Setting power for maximum range put the fighters' cruise at 130 knots, and in order to keep station over the slower TBDs, the Grummans made gentle "S" turns to cut down their actual rate of advance. Leonard preferred keeping his speed up instead of throttling back to 105 knots and plodding along with the torpedo planes. "Hanging on their prop" like that would place the Grummans at a disadvantage if they had to go into action swiftly. The *Yorktown* group departed at 0915.

8 May 1942, Fighter Pilots Escorting the Strike Groups

	Claims
(a) Fighting Forty-two	
1. Escorting the dive bombers:	
Lt. Cdr. Charles R. Fenton, USN	1 VB probable
Ens. Harry B. Gibbs, A-V(N)	—
2. Escorting the torpedo planes:	
Lieut. (jg) William N. Leonard, USN	1 VB probable
Lieut. (jg) E. Scott McCuskey, A-V(N)	1 VF
Lieut. (jg) William S. Woollen, A-V(N)	2 VF, ½ VT
Ens. John P. Adams, A-V(N)	½ VT
(b) Fighting Two	
1. Escorting the group commander:	
Lieut. Richard S. Bull, Jr., USN (MIA)	—
Ens. John B. Bain, A-V(N)	1 VF
2. Escorting the dive bombers (did not reach target):	
Lieut. Albert O. Vorse, Jr., USN	
[Ens. Edward R. Sellstrom, Jr., A-V(N)—did not take off]	
Lieut. (jg) Robert J. Morgan, USN	
Ens. John H. Lackey, A-V(N)	
3. Escorting the torpedo planes:	
Lieut. Noel A. M. Gayler, USN	2 VB, 1 VF probable
Ens. Dale W. Peterson, A-V(N) (MIA)	—
Lieut. (jg) Howard F. Clark, USN (MIA)	—
Ens. Richard M. Rowell, A-V(N) (MIA)	—

The *Lexington*'s lead strike plane rolled down the flight deck at 0907. Bill Ault organized his group in a manner similar to that of the day before, again having recourse to deferred departure to get the various squadron formations on the way with minimum separation. The group had the following composition:

Commander, *Lexington* Air Group (CLAG)	Cdr. William B. Ault	
CLAG Command Division	Cdr. Ault with 3 SBDs of VS-2	4 SBD-3s
VF-2 Fighting Two	Lieut. Noel A. M. Gayler	9 F4F-3s
VB-2 Bombing Two	Lt. Cdr. Weldon L. Hamilton	11 SBD-2,-3s
VT-2 Torpedo Two	Lt. Cdr. James H. Brett, Jr.	12 TBD-1s

As before, the *Lexington* strike group divided into three tactical elements, each with a fighter escort. Climbing to high altitude (18,000 feet) were Hamilton's eleven SBDs, each armed with one 1,000-lb. bomb. Through an oversight, these dive bombers had not been fueled to capacity, carrying only 220 rather than 250 gallons of gasoline. The fuel was ample to take the squadron to the reported target and back, but the deficit certainly lessened Hamilton's flexibility. Scoop Vorse was to have four F4Fs to escort Bombing Two, but just before launch he lost his wingman, when Doc Sellstrom's Grumman was struck in the tail by another aircraft's prop. Damage was slight, but there was no time to fix it, and Sellstrom remained behind. The SBDs cruised at 110 knots, while Vorse's three F4Fs flew at 130. Vorse also resorted to "S" turns to stay with the less speedy SBDs.

Ault's command division of four SBDs (each also carrying one 1,000-lb. bomb as payload) ascended to take station at 15,000 feet, where Ault hoped to maintain visual contact with Bombing Two above and Torpedo Two below. He intended to keep his strike group in sight (hence deferred departure) the whole flight so all elements would attack in coordination. Ault's fighter escort was to be a two-plane section led by Dick Bull. On the flight deck, Bull's Grumman had failed to start, so he ran over to his wingman's fighter and took it instead in order to get off with the rest of the group. The displaced wingman, Ens. John Bain, sat in Bull's balky F4F with a number of VF-2 mechanics in close attendance. They succeeded in starting the Pratt & Whitney, and at 0925, Bain took off last of all. He overtook Bull about 25 miles north of the ships and slipped into formation above Ault's four SBDs. Bull throttled back to the power setting for maximum endurance and settled on an air speed of about 120 knots. Ault's SBDs cruised at 110 knots.

Jimmy Brett's twelve TBDs slowly worked their way up to 6,000 feet, there joined by Noel Gayler's four-plane fighter division. Just before launch, the *Lexington*'s air officer, Cdr. Duckworth, had conferred with Gayler. Worried about the endurance of the F4Fs on such a long mission, he ordered Gayler to attack any incoming enemy strike planes and harass them all the way back to Task Force 17. Gayler cruised at 105 knots along with the TBDs, deploying his section over one side of Torpedo Two and Howard Clark's section on the other.

With the departure at 0925 of the *Lexington* strike group, Fletcher's air attack was on the way. It comprised fifteen fighters, thirty-nine dive bombers, and twenty-one torpedo planes, total seventy-five aircraft. In line with American carrier air doctrine at the time, the two groups did not form into a wing under a designated commander. Instead the groups each flew as individual squadrons to the target, attacking independently of each other. Both groups proceeded northward along the briefed 028-degree heading and soon entered the weak, warm frontal zone with its low visibility and squalls. The weather and the Yorktowners' headstart precluded any chance that the two air groups would be able to coordinate their attacks. The subsequent air battle over MO Striking Force took place as two distinct actions, separated by about 40 minutes.

Bob Dixon, VS-2 commander, who happened to be flying the search sector adjacent to Joe Smith, thought Smith might have erred somewhat in locating the target's position. In this he was correct, as Smith had placed MO Striking Force about 40 miles south of where it was. Dixon decided to investigate, and after covering his own sector thoroughly, headed for the contact at 0830. About an hour later, he finally sighted the Japanese carriers. At 0930, he sent this message:

> Contact. 2 CV, 2 DD bearing 000 degrees, distance 160 miles from Point Zed.[4]

He soon amplified his message by giving the Japanese course and speed (180 degrees, 25 knots), but it appears that neither of Dixon's reports was received by Task Force 17. For the next seventy-five minutes, Dixon shadowed MO Striking Force, darting in and out of rain squalls at low altitude so he would not be spotted. He broke off contact at 1045 only after his fuel had run low. Meanwhile, Smith had turned back immediately after discovering his radio was malfunctioning. On the way back he encountered the *Yorktown* torpedo planes and their fighter escort:

> Smith's voice radio was OK for short range and his directions and refinement of target position came in loud and clear as he flew alongside the TBDs of VT-5. Mighty helpful and heartening it was.[5]

Joe Taylor now had the correct course to the enemy, which would go a long way in negating the ill effects of the bad weather.

On board the *Zuikaku,* Hara continued monitoring Kanno's excellent contact reports. At 0940, Kanno warned that thirty or more enemy planes were headed toward MO Striking Force, alerting Takagi and Hara to the likelihood of imminent attack. The Japanese had allocated nineteen Zero fighters (ten from the *Zuikaku,* nine from the *Shōkaku*) for combat air patrol. Three from the *Zuikaku* under the China ace, PO1c Iwamoto Tetsuzō were already aloft, their pilots trying not to lose sight of their ships in the murk. For reinforcements in the event the enemy strike group appeared, the carriers had the remaining thirteen Zeros poised for swift takeoff.

The Japanese air officers had to coordinate their combat air patrol without the incalculable advantage of early warning by means of radar. Standard procedure was to retain most of the fighters on deck until the enemy had been spotted, then scramble the remaining Zeros for a close interception. Thus the Japanese CAP system required high visibility to operate at best efficiency. To complicate matters, local atmospherics on 8 May interfered with Japanese radio communications, making it difficult to vector the CAP. Of course, bad weather generally served as an effective shield to conceal MO Striking Force, perhaps even preventing American air attack altogether. However, if the Americans did manage to locate the Japanese, the advantages of poor visibility shifted their way, as the Japanese could not properly direct their fighters. So it was on 8 May.

MO Striking Force had a good scare at 0948, when Iwamoto aloft reported enemy planes approaching from the south. The *Shōkaku* rapidly launched six Zeros. Soon it was learned the bogeys were returning Japanese search planes. The *Shōkaku* decided to recover two of the Zeros just scrambled, led by Ens. (Special Service) Abe Yasujirō and replace them with three under PO2c Miyazawa Takeo. Between 1015 and 1027, the *Shōkaku* maneuvered independently to conduct air operations, and in the process MO Striking Force's formation loosened greatly. Taking the lead were three destroyers; then came the heavy cruisers *Myōkō* (Takagi's flagship) and *Haguro* of the 5th Cruiser Division. The *Zuikaku* sailed about 10,000 meters ahead of the *Shōkaku*, and nearly that same interval separated the *Shōkaku* from the heavy cruisers *Kinugasa* and *Furutaka* bringing up the rear. Circling 13,000 feet above the *Shōkaku* were two Zeros led by PO1c Okabe Kenji. At low level were five Zeros in two *shōtai* led by PO1c Minami Yoshimi and PO1c Miyazawa. Patrolling over 20,000 feet above the *Zuikaku* was her 13th *Shōtai* of three Zeros under PO1c Iwamoto. MO Striking Force was in the process of crossing a large open space within the overcast, thus allowing Iwamoto to climb so high and still see the ships below.

The Yorktown *Strike Group*

With their faster cruising speed, the *Yorktown*'s SBDs bounded ahead during the flight north to the Japanese carriers. Following them were Fenton's two protesting Grummans. Fenton discovered that the dive bombers actually climbed faster than his fighters after the F4F pilots had throttled back for maximum range. He had to be very careful of fuel consumption, severely aggravated by the costly climb to 18,000 feet. To add to his troubles, visibility rapidly decreased the farther north they went, making it difficult to keep station on Burch's SBDs. About halfway to the target area, Fenton happened to notice out to one side a flight of aircraft heading in the opposite direction—the enemy strike group! He had neither the fuel nor orders to investigate. Some of the SBD pilots saw the Japanese as well, but they likewise could do nothing but fly their mission and hope fondly that there would be friendly flight decks still in service after the Japanese had done their worst. Not long after his near encounter with the enemy, Fenton finally lost track of the SBDs in the clouds. He and his wingman, Harry Gibbs, pressed on to the target area alone in hopes of overtaking the dive bombers before they dived.

After a flight of only an hour and fifteen minutes, Burch was rewarded with the sight of MO Striking Force. At 1032, The *Yorktown* SBDs spotted what they thought were two carriers, a battleship, three heavy cruisers, and four light cruisers or destroyers crossing an open area on course 190 degrees, speed 20 knots. The *Yorktown* pilots had been aided by the enemy's mad dash at 30 knots and a brisk tailwind. Burch carefully led his twenty-four SBDs closer to the ships, using cloud cover to conceal his approach. Skirting the edge of a cloud mass, Burch moved to take position upwind of the Japanese force. By 1049, he had attained excellent position just southeast of the enemy carriers, where he waited impatiently for Torpedo Five to arrive so the two elements could coordinate their attacks for maximum shock value and mutual protection. As the lumbering Devastators were still some distance away, the SBDs had to wait, circling at the edge of the clouds. From their perch at 17,000 feet the crews could see to the north and below a number of Zeros circling lazily at perhaps 12,000 feet over the nearest flattop. MO Striking Force continued steaming southward at high speed, and the *Zuikaku* and her escorts began to disappear into the black squall line marking the southern terminus of the open area. Soon both Japanese carriers, the only targets worth attacking, would be lost to view inside rainstorms. Over the radio Burch fretted, pleading with Taylor to "Bear a hand because time's a wastin!"[6] He could do nothing until Taylor replied that he had spotted the target.

While enemy dive bombers milled about nearly overhead, the Japanese were oblivious to their presence. The *Shōkaku* completed air operations by 1030 and warily waited for something to happen. The Zeros spotted by Burch over the *Shōkaku* were Okabe and wingman PO3c Tanaka Yoshizō; Iwamoto flew at much greater height over the *Zuikaku*. At lower level near the *Shōkaku* were the five Zeros led by PO1c Minami and PO1c Miyazawa. Ready to take off was Ensign (Special Service) Abe and PO1c Kawanishi Jinichirō. Likewise poised on board the *Zuikaku* for instant launch was the *Zuikaku*'s fighter leader, Lieut. Okajima, with four Zeros of his large 11th *Shōtai*.[7]

Alarms suddenly shattered the calm in MO Striking Force. Lookouts had finally picked out the American aircraft circling nearby, and the *Zuikaku* radioed a warning

Japanese Combat Air Patrol in the First Attack (versus *Yorktown* Air Group)

(a) Aloft: 10 Zeros

Zuikaku Fighter Unit, 1st *Chūtai*, 13th *Shōtai*

No. 1	PO1c Iwamoto Tetsuzō	
No. 2	PO1c Itō Junjirō	
No. 3	Sea1c Mae Shichijirō	

Shōkaku Fighter Unit, 2nd *Chūtai*
1st *Shōtai*

No. 1	PO1c Okabe Kenji	
No. 2	PO3c Tanaka Yoshizō	

2nd *Shōtai*

No. 1	PO1c Minami Yoshimi	
No. 2	PO2c Ichinose Hisashi	KIA

3rd *Shōtai*

No. 1	PO1c Miyazawa Takeo	KIA
No. 2	PO3c Komachi Sadamu	
No. 3	Sea1c Imamura Kōichi	

(b) Launched during attack: six Zeros

Zuikaku Fighter Unit, 1st *Chūtai*, 11th *Shōtai*

No. 1	Lieut. Okajima Kiyokuma, *buntaichō*	
No. 2	PO1c Komiyama Kenta	
No. 3	PO2c Sakaida Gorō	
No. 4	PO2c Kuroki Saneatsu	

Shōkaku Fighter Unit, 2nd *Chūtai*, 4th *Shōtai*

No. 1	Ens. (Special Service) Abe Yasujirō	
No. 2	PO1c Kawanishi Jinichirō	

to the fighters overhead. Almost simultaneously, Iwamoto spotted the intruders, estimating their altitude at between 16,000 and 19,000 feet. Okabe, with a poorly functioning radio, did not learn of the enemy's presence. Below, the *Shōkaku* heeled sharply to port to come directly into the wind, while flight deck crews hastened to bring the two Zero fighters into launch position. The *Zuikaku* likewise swung into the wind to launch fighters, but Okajima's *shōtai* would have to face the added hazard of taking off directly into the teeth of a squall.

Burch, waiting at 17,000 feet just south of the carriers, finally got the word he wanted. At 1057, Taylor radioed, "OK Bill, I'm starting in."[8] Torpedo Five had sighted the enemy, so the SBDs could attack. Burch rolled into his dive so abruptly that his two wingmen had to hustle to stay with him. Below he could see the nearest flattop getting ready to launch planes! Wally Short, leading VB-5's seventeen SBDs, found himself in poor position to make a dive bombing attack on the only carrier still visible. He resolved to take his squadron back around in a wide circle to realign the SBDs for a proper dive. Meanwhile, Burch aimed for the *Shōkaku*'s starboard bow, his SBDs so close that she had to suspend the launch and immediately maneuver to evade bombs. The *Shōkaku* opened up with her 12.7-cm guns and 2.5-cm rapid fire cannons. Shells bursting above him finally alerted Okabe to the presence of enemy planes, but Burch's seven SBDs shot past him so quickly that he decided to go after the dive bombers he saw still circling overhead.

From his vantage point above the enemy planes, Iwamoto saw several dive bombers separate from the main formation and tear after the *Shōkaku*. His two wingmen close behind, Iwamoto raced in to intercept. Aided by his fast dive, Iwamoto overtook the SBDs passing 11,000 feet. He ripped into a firing pass on the lead bomber, which happened to be Burch's Dauntless, opened with his 20-mm cannons at close range, and flashed past, certain that he had downed the American. His two wingmen, PO1c Itō Junjirō and Sea1c Mae Shichijirō, ganged up on the second dive bomber in VS-5's string, flown by Ens. John H. Jorgenson. Oblivious to the enemy fighters buzzing around him, Burch plummeted at a 70-degree angle, lining up his sights on the rapidly moving carrier. As the SBDs dropped below 8,000 feet, they encountered the warm, moist air above the sea. That brought back their old bugbears, fogged sights and blurred windscreens, with a vengeance. According to Burch, his pilots "bombed from memory."[9] As each pilot drew within 2,500 to 2,000 feet of the target, he released his 1,000-lb. bomb and flattened out low over the water. One by one the seven heavy bombs struck the sea, throwing huge water geysers far higher than the *Shōkaku*'s bridge. Seawater showered the flight deck, but the carrier suffered no harm from Scouting Five's spirited but nearly blind attack.

Diving in from southwest to northeast against the *Shōkaku*'s starboard side, the SBDs of Scouting Five turned left after pulling out and made for a low cloud bank to the northwest. While recovering from its dive, Jorgenson's SBD was struck in the left wing by a heavy AA shell, and though the shell passed through without detonating, the shock nearly flipped the dive bomber on its back. As Jorgenson righted his mutilated plane, three Zeros assailed him from above and behind, their 7.7-mm bullets peppering his wings and cockpit and wounding him in the leg. The three pilots were Iwamoto, Itō, and Mae, who had followed the lead SBDs in their dives and caught Jorgenson before he could get away. Finding himself very low and being drawn away from the crucial area, Iwamoto called off the pursuit and led his *shōtai* back toward the *Shōkaku*. He was gratified to see her steaming bravely ahead, as yet untouched by enemy bombs.

Scouting Five's ordeal was not over. Before the SBDs could reach the sanctuary of the overcast, they encountered Okajima and his three wingmen from the *Zuikaku*. The four had just experienced a harrowing launch from within the center of a squall and headed northward into the clear from their carrier. They came at Jorgenson and several other SBDs from head-on, exchanging swift machine gun bursts with them before parting company in opposite directions. The *Zuikaku* pilots had pressing business in the form of Bombing Five, which was just beginning its attack on the *Shōkaku*. Safe in the clouds, Burch took stock of his squadron. All seven SBDs were there, but several had taken hits, and Jorgenson's was a flying wreck. Fortunately, the self-sealing fuel tanks had handled numerous 7.7-mm hits without leaking. Scouting Five's attack had lasted from about 1057 to 1100. The pilots claimed three hits on the carrier and the destruction of four Zeros. As told above, the *Shōkaku* took no damage, and no Zeros were shot down.

A definite lull took place between the dives of Scouting Five and Bombing Five because of Short's need to regain a proper attack position. Torpedo Five was still several miles away, but driving hard toward the target. The *Shōkaku*'s Captain Joshima Takaji took the opportunity to steady up on a southeast course into the wind and launched Abe's and Kawanishi's Zero fighters. Scouting Five's attack could not have been pleasant for them, waiting as they did on deck in fully fueled aircraft! The *Zuikaku* Zeros, seven under Okajima and Iwamoto, were busy harassing VS-5's withdrawal.

While Bombing Five completed its circle and realigned itself for the attack, Okabe's two *Shōkaku* Zeros climbed swiftly after them. Short began his dive at 1103, and the VB-5 SBDs went after the *Shōkaku*, twisting and turning far below. Okabe's fighters hit the tail of Short's formation just after the lead SBDs pushed over. The Japanese tried all sorts of fancy maneuvers to slow themselves and stay with the diving SBDs after their pilots had popped their dive brakes. Thus it was Lieut. Sam Adams's 3rd Division in the rear that bore the brunt of the attacks. Reaching the moist air close to the sea, VB-5 pilots also had to cope with the frustration of obscured sights, the "outstanding materiel defect"[10] of the battle according to CinCPac. The *Shōkaku* glided through the water at close to 34 knots. Her evasive maneuvers compelled the SBD pilots to press their dives to the limit, to wait until the flight deck loomed large below them before pulling the release handles for their 1,000-lb. bombs. One by one the SBDs attacked and recovered around 2,000 feet. Several bombs exploded near the carrier, sending huge splashes into the air. Then around 1105, one 1,000-lb bomb struck the *Shōkaku* on her port side forward, close to the bow. The blast crumpled the flight deck, temporarily disabled the forward elevator, and ignited an intense fire in the bow.

In the 3rd Division a VB-5 pilot was determined that nothing—neither Zeros, antiaircraft guns, nor fogged bombsights—would prevent him from getting his hit. Lieut. John J. ("Jo Jo") Powers firmly believed in diving low for success, even risking damage from the bomb blast. While he dived, one of the *Shōkaku* fighters evidently scored a 20-mm hit in Powers's fuel tanks, sending gasoline streaming out to catch on fire. Bullets likewise wounded both Powers and his gunner. His aircraft in flames, Powers still continued his attack and did not bail out, taking his SBD well below 1,000 feet before dropping his heavy bomb. Other pilots glimpsed his aircraft stagger as it finally pulled out at 200 feet. All was then hidden by the explosion of his bomb striking home. Powers hit the *Shōkaku* on her starboard side abaft the island, the bomb igniting intense blazes both on the flight deck and in the upper hangar deck, ensuring once and for all that the *Shōkaku* would conduct no more flight operations in this battle. Powers did not make it out of his dive; he splashed nearby. His bravery earned him a posthumous Medal of Honor.

The SBDs of Bombing Five withdrew at low level toward the cloud cover to the northwest, following the path of Scouting Five. One of the pilots found to his chagrin that his bomb had failed to release. Dumping it into the sea he probably wondered just why he had bothered to come along on this particular jaunt. Like Burch's crews, Bombing Five had to run the gauntlet of Zeros dogging their retirement. Okabe had stuck with the SBDs and was joined by Abe, who had made a perilous scramble from the *Shōkaku* after VS-5's attack. Okajima's four Zeros already waited for VB-5 on that side of the task force. Sticking overwhelmingly to high-astern and shallow high-side attacks, the Zero pilots aimed carefully for their enemy's fuselage—the many 7.7-mm hits sustained by the SBDs giving proof of their marksmanship but also testifying that the self-sealing cells would hold. In addition to Powers, another SBD from Bombing Five, flown by Ens. Davis E. Chaffee (a replacement pilot only with the ship since Tongatabu) was lost to fighter attack. Bombing Five drew nine of the sixteen Zeros aloft away from the oncoming torpedo planes. The pilots claimed three hits on the target (they actually made two) and claimed seven Zeros, although none was lost to SBDs.

Approaching MO Striking Force from the southeast were the nine TBD Devastators of Torpedo Five. They hugged the waves, flying at only 200 feet, while 2,000 feet over them were their four VF-42 fighter escorts. From his wave-top vantage point, Taylor saw both the *Zuikaku* and the *Shōkaku,* and decided to have a go at the latter, the trailing flattop, because her screen looked much looser than the vessels covering the *Zuikaku.* Such a lessening of antiaircraft fire meant a great deal to pilots hunched in TBD seats and condemned to make their torpedo runs "low and slow." At first Torpedo Five approached the target while cruising in two parallel division columns. Around 1103, the same time Bombing Five opened its attack, Taylor turned to port and descended to fifty feet, increasing the speed of his TBDs to 110 knots. The torpedo pilots started fanning out to line abreast so they could make their individual torpedo runs.

The VF-42 escort fighters followed VT-5's maneuver. On the right was the division leader's section, Leonard and his wingman Scott McCuskey, the latter restored to full flight duty. Flying on the outside of Taylor's turn, the two Grumman pilots had to add throttle to stay in position. To the left was Woollen's section, himself and Johnny Adams, who slowed up because they were inside the turn. All four VF-42 pilots were ready for action, fuel mixtures set on rich and guns charged. Indeed, Leonard was surprised that enemy fighters had not yet put in an appearance. He contemplated making a strafing run on the nearest screening vessels in order to draw fire away from the TBDs.

Suddenly several black flak bursts angrily blossomed ahead of and beneath the Grummans. Looking up, McCuskey, Leonard's wingman, glimpsed Japanese fighters (he thought there were three) to his left front, flying loose line abreast at 2,800 feet. The Zeros flew on an opposite heading. Actually there were two: PO1c Minami and wingman PO2c Ichinose Hisashi. They comprised one of the two *shōtai* of *Shōkaku* Zeros which prowled at low level looking for torpedo planes which might threaten the carrier. The other was led by PO1c Miyazawa. Minami saw Leonard's section about the same time McCuskey had spotted his. The nearer Mitsubishi fishtailed to cut speed and swung gracefully into a high-side run on McCuskey's F4F. The Zero passed almost directly over Woollen's section on the other side of the TBDs, but evidently the Japanese did not spot either Woollen's two F4Fs or Torpedo Five at 50 feet. Ichinose banked to follow his leader.

McCuskey, the target of the attack, had no time to warn Leonard by radio or do anything but turn up into his attacker to try to spoil his aim by offering only a full deflection shot. McCuskey was flying in right echelon, stepped up loosely behind his section leader. He gunned his Grumman into a sharp, climbing turn to the left, greatly aided by the speed he had accumulated in turning to follow the TBDs. Closing the range swiftly, the diving Japanese cut loose with cannons and machine guns, sending tracers just where McCuskey would have been had he not reacted so quickly. The Japanese could not manage sufficient lead to hit the turning F4F, nor could McCuskey swing around enough to take his own shot at the Zero as it pulled out of its pass. McCuskey had "bitched" his first attacker; now he had to get ready to do it again instantly.

Leonard glanced over his left shoulder just in time to see two Zeros charging toward him in close succession. Then one of them jumped his tail. The first attacker had dived on past McCuskey and found himself directly behind a second Grumman. Leonard did not understand why the Japanese did not pop him then and there with the easy stern shot, but he was not about to give his Oriental opponent a second chance. He swung into a tight turn to present the Mitsubishi with a full deflection shot, giving the enemy pilot a choice—break off and make another pass or maneuver to stay on the F4F's tail. Leonard knew that if the Zero tried to remain on his tail in a full turn, there was no way the Japanese could draw enough lead to hit. Fortunately for Leonard the enemy did scramble to stay behind him and could not shoot. Leonard managed to hold out for one or two frantic circles before he disappeared into a convenient cloud. His gambit was valid only briefly. He knew trying to turn circles with a Zero was definitely "non-habit-forming."[11]

The second Zero roared in close behind his leader. McCuskey nosed down to gain speed, then with a twisting climb carefully turned up into the second Zero flown by PO2c Ichinose. This maneuver ruined the shot, as the enemy pilot did not open fire on the F4F. Ichinose reefed his Mitsubishi into an abrupt chandelle to regain altitude for another pass. The Zero slowed in the process and seemed to hang momentarily above the F4F. McCuskey lined up his sights for a full deflection shot, putting the pipper in the track he expected the Zero to follow. He pressed the trigger, and his four Brownings raked the Mitsubishi from stem to stern, causing it to stagger and fall off awkwardly into a dive. The Zero rolled over on its back and with guns blazing (likely with Ichinose dead at the stick), it flew full tilt into the water. Almost immediately after his victory McCuskey was attacked by another Zero (one of PO1c Miyazawa's wingmen). He handled that third bandit the way he evaded the other two, by turning into his opponent. Again successful, McCuskey ducked into the clouds after the Zero flashed past.

While Minami attacked two Grummans (but lost his wingman Ichinose), Miyazawa's *shōtai* happened upon the scene. The *shōtai* immediately split up. One of the wingmen, most likely PO3c Komachi Sadamu, chased McCuskey into a cloud; below, Miyazawa and probably Sea1c Imamura Kōichi discovered torpedo planes about to attack the *Shōkaku*. They dived in. Soon to join them was Minami, who had broken off from the fight with Leonard after claiming the Grumman. Unfortunately for the Japanese, the two F4Fs flown by Woollen and Adams were in the way, and these two VF-42 pilots proved equally tough customers in a fight. From the way the Zeros behaved as they dived in, Miyazawa and Imamura evidently had not spotted the other two Grummans. Nor had Woollen and Adams seen the fight with Leonard's section. The first they knew of enemy fighters in the area was the spectacle of Zeros diving in front of them in order to attack the TBDs.

Woollen and Adams themselves dived after the Zeros to draw them away from the torpedo planes, now making their final approach. Adams successively brought two Zeros into his sights, but both times the Japanese abandoned their TBD targets and reefed into quick climbing turns. Adams could not draw sufficient lead to open fire. He later realized that in his inexperience he was trying to get too close to his target before shooting. Woollen was the hunter. First he shot down PO1c Miyazawa's Zero. A little later he hit another Zero with a telling burst. That was Minami, and Woollen had put a bullet into his fuel tank—from which trailed a narrow white stream of raw gasoline. Woollen had come perilously close to flaming Minami's Zero. None of the Japanese could concentrate on the TBDs because they had to evade the lunges of the two Grummans maneuvering above them. Miyazawa had made a couple of passes against Torpedo Five and was posthumously credited with shooting down two torpedo planes, the last one by ramming it.

Returning from their pursuit of Scouting Five, Iwamoto and his two wingmen from the *Zuikaku* had regained altitude in anticipation of meeting a second wave. Then, below, they spotted what appeared to be four Grummans roughing up a pair of Zeros. One of the Japanese was in dire straits, and the other was trying to protect him. Thus Iwamoto's *shōtai* had come upon the melee between Leonard's division and Minami's *Shōkaku shōtai*. Iwamoto's three Zeros immediately dived in to help their comrades. Iwamoto later wrote in his diary that he shot down one of the Grummans on the first pass, his wingmen together ran down another, and two Grummans escaped. Evidently Iwamoto attacked Woollen, but did not shoot him down. As for the Grumman supposedly destroyed by Itō and Mae, that was McCuskey, and he also survived the fight, as we will see. The melee broke up soon after Iwamoto's Zeros intervened, but with the TBDs continuing their attacks unharmed. The fight was a distinct victory for VF-42, as they kept the Zeros off the TBDs, shot down two Mitsubishis, and badly damaged another, all without the loss of any Grummans.

While the VF-42 pilots battled the Zeros, Torpedo Five prosecuted its attack on the *Shōkaku*. The two divisions, one led by Taylor and the other by Lieut. Edwin B. Parker, formed a single line abreast of nine TBDs, each pilot making his own run against the *Shōkaku*'s port beam and bow. They released torpedoes beginning around 1108 at ranges between 1,000 and 2,000 yards from the target. Above them the SBDs of Bombing Five were completing their attack. The torpedo crews witnessed both bomb hits, but because of poor equipment, their own attack was not so heartening. Three torpedoes were seen to run erratically, but the crews wrongly believed that three other fish hit the target. Evidently they mistook the near misses of 1,000-lb. bombs for torpedo hits. Antiaircraft fire was heavy and accurate, badly damaging one TBD. Taylor led his squadron eastward toward a squall, whose concealment "undoubtedly saved us."[12] Woollen and Adams regrouped just after the dogfight and found the TBDs shortly before they entered the clouds. Sliding into formation a short time later was Leonard, who saw the TBDs drawing away from the target, the torpedo brace straps dangling underneath the lumbering Devastators. Together the three VF-42 pilots escorted Torpedo Five out of the area, but there was no sign of Scott McCuskey.

McCuskey had been playing tag with some Japanese. After leaving the third *Shōkaku* Zero behind by disappearing into a cloud, McCuskey climbed about 800 feet, then changed direction and came out once more into the open. There to his surprise was a Zero almost directly ahead of him. He took one quick look behind to make certain his own tail was clear, then moved to attack. However, by the time he jerked his head back, the situation had changed drastically. The Japanese in front of him had spotted him and pulled into a tight, climbing turn. McCuskey turned back for the cloud with the Zero already peppering his tail. McCuskey wanted to head in the direction the rest of the division took, so he reversed course and exited the clouds once again. This time two Zeros lurked in the clear, and like a pack of dogs chasing a fox, they pursued him back into the murk. He tried twice more to leave in that direction, but always the Zeros barred his escape. The two Japanese were almost certainly Itō and Mae, the two *Zuikaku* wingmen.

Finally McCuskey felt he had no recourse but to dive away. He dropped beneath the cloud bank and flew into a dark rain squall directly ahead in order to use the thunderstorm to conceal his climb. By the time he passed 7,000 or 8,000 feet, the buffeting became very severe, and he was unable to maintain a southerly heading back toward Task Force 17. Then he developed vertigo and had to release his controls to let the Grumman stabilize itself. The Grumman plummeted to within 100 feet of the water before McCuskey pulled out of the dive. Nearby, he saw a Japanese destroyer's wake, and that helped him to orient himself. He turned again in the direction of home and throttled back for maximum range, greatly regretting not having shot the Zero he had encountered outside the cloud. Had he done so, he felt he could have rejoined his division and proceeded home in style, not feeling so thoroughly chastened by Zeros as he did. As events would show, this trip he would not make it all the way to home plate.

The last element of the *Yorktown* Air Group to reach the target area was Fenton's fighter section. The skipper appeared over MO Striking Force just as the last of the SBDs had dived and scuttled away at low altitude under the cloud layer. Fenton and Gibbs descended to 7,000 feet, took another look around, then set course for Task Force 17. By 1115 when the last *Yorktown* aircraft departed, the carrier *Shōkaku* appeared in bad shape, her crews battling fierce fires. The *Yorktown* pilots claimed six 1,000-lb. bomb hits and three torpedo hits on a carrier they believed was the *Kaga*. SBD crews reported eleven Zeros destroyed, while VF-42 claimed three (one to McCuskey, two to Woollen). Total air group losses in the target area amounted to two SBDs from Bombing Five. The crews described the stricken enemy carrier as burning fiercely at the bow with a flame resembling an "acetylene torch,"[13] apparently fueled by aviation gasoline. They thought the carrier was a goner.

The *Yorktown* Air Group had no chance to rendezvous for mutual protection on the flight back because of the low visibility in the thick cloud cover. Burch collected five SBDs from Bombing Five in addition to the seven from his own Scouting Five. Following them were nine SBDs from Bombing Five in one group. Taylor's Torpedo Five came through the attack nearly unscathed. In addition to their three VF-42 fighter escorts led by Leonard, a shot-up VB-5 SBD, flown by Ens. Benjamin G. Preston, accompanied the TBDs. Then alone came McCuskey, depending on his own navigation to return him safely to the task force. Finally Fenton and Gibbs cruised southward at 7,000 feet. It is remarkable that none of the pilots lost his bearings in the overcast, especially as it appears that no one, except for Fenton, climbed high enough to pick up the carrier YE homing beacon.

On board the *Shōkaku*, damage was heavy and casualties were high because of the intense blast and fires generated by the two bomb hits. The thousand-pounders tore hell out of her topside, disabling the flight deck, the anchor winch, and other auxiliary gear, but the carrier was not affected in any material fashion. She could still steam at over 30 knots, there was no underwater damage, and her gunnery systems were fully operable. Even so, it was a shock to see her "spouting flames" as she was. Hara groaned when his flagship *Zuikaku* emerged from the rainstorm and beheld the pall of smoke over the *Shōkaku*, "burning furiously."[14] Other matters, however, sought the attention of MO Striking Force. At 1116 came word from the Japanese strike group that they were attacking the American carriers.

This was followed nine minutes later by a report that they had sunk the carrier *Saratoga*, the enemy's largest. That was more like it! The news served as an excellent tonic for Japanese morale, frustrated by the errors and reverses of the past few days. Let the "Yankees" attack again, and they would receive what they deserved.

In the skies over MO Striking Force, the Japanese combat air patrol regrouped. Iwamoto's *shōtai* was low on fuel, so he arranged to land on board the *Zuikaku* to rearm and refuel—a risky venture when the carrier was inside the squall line. Minami, his fighter in desperate condition, also landed on the *Zuikaku*. He later had the chance to thank Iwamoto, his rescuer and old friend. Apparently Lieut. Okajima's four Zeros also came on board for fuel and ammunition. The *Zuikaku*'s Captain Yokogawa Ichihei then sent Okajima and Iwamoto aloft, warning them to be watchful for a second attack. The pilots were to be especially careful to deal with enemy torpedo planes. The *Shōkaku* CAP comprised six Zeros organized into three *shōtai*: the 1st of PO1c Okabe and PO3c Tanaka, the 3rd of PO3c Komachi, and Sea1c Imamura, and the newly launched 4th of Ens. Abe and PO1c Kawanishi.[15]

The *Lexington* Strike Group

The *Lexington* Air Group faced trouble almost from the time it left the ship. At 0945, one of VT-2's TBDs, flown by Lieut. (jg) Steffenhagen, developed engine trouble. Brett ordered him back to the ship. Steffenhagen jettisoned his torpedo and came on board the *Lexington* at 1030. Decreasing visibility played havoc with Ault's cruising deployment, intended to keep his squadrons in visual contact en route to the target. In the white void, VF-2's Scoop Vorse lost sight of Bombing Two while his division was making one of its periodic S-turns to cut down the rate of advance. After a few minutes' search, Vorse and his wingmen, Bob Morgan and John Lackey, reluctantly turned back toward Task Force 17. They lacked navigational information as to the location of the target. Vorse climbed to 22,000 feet before he tuned in the carrier's YE homing signal and set the proper course home. The three fighters arrived back in time to help defend Task Force 17 against enemy attack.

Even worse for Ault, Hamilton with VB-2's eleven SBDs could no longer maintain visual contact with the TBDs far below. He decided it was useless to remain at 18,000 feet completely socked in by the overcast, so he led the squadron in a slow descent to try to locate the rest of the group. Some of the TBD crews saw the dive bombers briefly, but the clouds closed in once more and hid them from view. Hamilton eventually leveled out at 1,000 feet, but never rejoined the other *Lexington* planes. Likewise Ault's command division and escorts descended to about 6,000 feet, taking station just under the cloud base where they could keep Torpedo Two in view.

Around 1120, the *Lexington* flyers reached the end of the navigational leg, 200 miles. Originally briefed according to Smith's erroneous position estimate, they could find no enemy carriers, but fortuitously the Japanese flattops had steamed southward at high speed for two hours and were not too far away. His fuel not yet critical, Ault started a box search. He ordered the group to swing slightly left to a heading of 000 degrees, intending to fly a few minutes on that course, then turn 90 degrees to the left, and finally (if need be) another 90 degrees to the left to complete three sides of a square before turning for home. Hamilton monitored the conversation between Ault and Brett, and maneuvered Bombing Two in similar fashion, but without success in finding either the enemy or the rest of the group. Bombing Two operated under the nagging handicap of not having been fueled to capacity, and Hamilton began to worry about running short of gasoline. He radioed his misgivings to Ault.

After heading a short while to the north, Ault as planned swung to the west. That was the key. About 1130, he sighted an enemy task force about 15 miles farther west. The Japanese force included at least one carrier which he could see and fortunately crossed an open space surrounded by overcast. Smoke hung in the air, evidence of the *Yorktown* Air Group's earlier visit. Ault ordered the planes with him to circle briefly while he tried to contact Bombing Two to coordinate the attack. Hamilton most regretfully could not comply. He was close by, but deep in the clouds even at only 1,000 feet. Without any common reference points, Hamilton had no chance of joining Ault unless he just happened to find the enemy. Nevertheless, Ault resolved to attack with the forces at hand: four dive bombers, eleven torpedo planes, and six F4Fs. Poor weather had effectively robbed him of eleven SBDs and three F4Fs. As his tactical plan, Ault would hit the carrier first with his SBDs to draw the CAP away from the more vulnerable torpedo planes. With his two fighter escorts close by, Ault forged ahead with his four SBDs, arranging to approach from a different direction from that of Torpedo Two, following at its slower pace and circling around to the south. Ault's options were limited by intermittent clouds; in some spots the ceiling was much lower than 6,000 feet.

Evidently the Japanese discovered the intruders about the same time they located MO Striking Force. The *Zuikaku* radioed a warning to the 13 Zeros. Abe and Okabe with four *Shōkaku* Zeros circled at 13,000 feet over the *Shōkaku*, and Komachi's two Zeros remained at low altitude. Okajima's four *Zuikaku* Zeros were low looking for torpedo planes, but Iwamoto's three patrolled at 19,000 feet. He was able to spot the *Lexington* planes soon after he was alerted to their presence. Iwamoto saw the Americans split into two groups and went after one of them. His choice turned out to be Ault's SBDs flying at 5,500 feet with Bull's two VF-2 F4Fs cruising 400 feet above and 1,000 feet behind them. Diving in at high speed, Iwamoto surprised the *Lex* people.

Japanese Combat Air Patrol against Second Attack (*Lexington* Air Group)

All aloft: thirteen Zeros

Zuikaku Fighter Unit, 1st *Chūtai*

　　　　11th *Shōtai*
No. 1　　Lieut. Okajima Kiyokuma, *buntaichō*
No. 2　　PO1c Komiyama Kenta
No. 3　　PO2c Sakaida Gorō
No. 4　　PO2c Kuroki Saneatsu

　　　　13th *Shōtai*
No. 1　　PO1c Iwamoto Tetsuzō
No. 2　　PO1c Itō Junjirō
No. 3　　Sea1c Mae Shichijirō

Shokaku Fighter Unit, 2nd *Chūtai*

　　　　1st *Shōtai*
No. 1　　PO1c Okabe Kenji
No. 2　　PO3c Tanaka Yoshizō

　　　　3rd *Shōtai*
No. 1　　PO3c Komachi Sadamu
No. 2　　Sea1c Imamura Kōichi

　　　　4th *Shōtai*
No. 1　　Ens. (Special Service) Abe Yasujirō
No. 2　　PO1c Kawanishi Jinichirō

The first Dick Bull and John Bain knew of the presence of enemy fighters was the startling sight of angry red tracers zipping past their wings. The two Grummans shuffled along at 120 knots, the sleek Zeros coming in so much faster that the two VF-2 pilots could do nothing to evade the first attack. Flashing past at high speed, the Zeros climbed away in front of the two Grummans. Bain hauled up his nose for a shot and fired a short burst, but the Japanese had already opened the range dramatically. Bain's bullets fell far short. He saw only two Zeros attack Bull and himself, so one of Iwamoto's trio may have made a run against the SBDs. The Zeros caused no losses this time. The SBDs dipped down early, and Iwamoto called off his pilots in order to regroup, as it looked as if the Americans were going to settle for some target other than the *Shōkaku*. Iwamoto was not at all impressed with the Americans during this attack.

Ault decided to execute a shallow glide bomb attack on the *Shōkaku* rather than climb above the overcast for a normal dive bombing run. In this case the SBDs did not use their dive brakes; rather the pilots hoped for as much speed as they could get in order to foil the aim of enemy antiaircraft. The flat glide-bombing run from 5,500 feet put them in gun range a lot longer than a steep dive from 18,000 feet. The shallow approach took them well under the four *Shōkaku* Zeros patrolling at 13,000 feet. Certainly the tactic fooled Iwamoto, so the actual bombing took place without fighter interference. One after another the SBDs charged at the carrier, pulled their bomb releases and recovered at 2,000 feet. They dropped three 1,000 lb. bombs, one of which at about 1140 struck the *Shōkaku* on her flight deck starboard just abaft the island. Ault's troops reported two hits on the carrier. As the four joined up at low altitude to withdraw, they discovered that one pilot, Ens. John D. Wingfield, had been unable to release his bomb. When told that he still had the bomb, Wingfield swung out of formation and returned to the target. The others last saw him heading toward the *Shōkaku* to do what he had come to do. The three remaining SBDs turned for home.

Bull and Bain, the two VF-2 fighter pilots, followed the SBDs in their dives in order to cover their withdrawal. As the Grummans leveled off at low altitude after the attack, a pair of Zeros started after them with a hit-and-run attack from above and behind. This time they saw the enemy coming, and Bull knew what to do. Bain later wrote, "We had considerable speed and had seen them in time to make a hard turn as they approached firing range."[16] The Zero that had singled out Bain's F4F had picked up too much speed and overshot its target, pulling out ahead of him in order to climb away. With his increased speed, Bain was able to stay close behind the Zero for a low deflection shot at medium range. As his bullets tore into the climbing Zero, it staggered and spun toward the water. The Japanese who intercepted the escort section were most likely Ens. Abe and PO1c Kawanishi from the *Shōkaku*, and it appears Bain badly damaged Kawanishi's Zero.

In countering the Mitsubishi, Bain had lost sight of the SBDs as well as all contact with his section leader. It is possible that one of the Zeros shot down Bull's Grumman; no *Lexington* pilot ever saw him again or heard him transmit on radio. A 1936 graduate of the Naval Academy, Bull had earned his wings three years later. Joining Scouting Forty-one (VS-41) on board the *Ranger*, he saw them through their transformation to Fighting Forty-two and thus had many close friends with the fighters on board the *Yorktown*. In the summer of 1941 he went to England as an observer to record aviation developments. The outbreak of war in December ended that, and Bull joined Fighting Two on 27 December. "A good man, liked, respected," Bull was another who would be missed.

After shooting down his Zero, Bain gained altitude and passed through the

John Bain in a photo taken about 8 June 1942 on board the *Hornet* after his second confirmed Zero kill. (Cdr. J. B. Bain, USN.)

overcast. Breaking into the sunlight around 8,000 feet, he noticed a Zero above and behind him. The Japanese responded quickly with a high-astern attack. Bain countered by turning up into his opponent for a head-on shot. A long burst by Bain's four Brownings persuaded the Japanese to break off his run. The Zero rolled out before coming to grips, and Bain climbed on past him. The two pilots swiftly initiated a scissors, each fighter trying to maneuver onto the tail of the other. Bain soon discovered the Zero was beating him to the turns, so he dropped his nose and unashamedly ran for the safety of the clouds. His opponent was another of the *Shōkaku* Zeros guarding the skies just over its carrier.

Brett's Torpedo Two at an altitude of 6,000 feet started across the clear space, coming at the enemy carrier from the south. Deployed on either side of the TBDs and slightly above was a section of two VF-2 Wildcats, one led by Gayler and the other by "Spud" Clark, both on detached duty from Fighting Three. Without warning, several Zeros tumbled out of nearby clouds and confronted Gayler and his wingman, Dale Peterson. At first Gayler hoped to draw the enemy's attention to keep the Zeros away from the vulnerable TBDs, but in this he was too successful. The Zeros were just too fast, knifing in and out with their slashing hit-and-run attacks which shattered the cohesiveness of the escorts. Hampering the Grummans was the fact that they had been cruising at 105 knots right along with their charges. They had no time to accelerate to a semblance of combat speed before the enemy was upon them. Their speed was too slow to be effective, as the F4Fs had to have 130 knots or more to maneuver handily. Soon it was every man for himself. Gayler glimpsed Clark and his wingman, Richard Rowell, disappear into a cloud—Zeros right on their tails. As for Peterson, he likewise was no longer in sight. The Japanese may have gotten him on the first pass. Gayler's opponents were four Zeros of Okajima's *Zuikaku shōtai*. In its action report, the *Zuikaku* later reported Okajima as intercepting a force of twelve fighters and thirty-two torpedo planes!

Gayler was desperate. A couple of Japanese had singled him out, mauling him from above and behind. They zoomed in so fast that Gayler had no chance to retaliate, as each of his opponents flashed past after shooting and climbed away. He resolved to use his low speed as an asset, however briefly. Watching as an attacker dived in from behind, Gayler snapped open his landing flaps just as the Zero reached its firing point. This abruptly slowed the Grumman and forced the Mitsubishi to overshoot more rapidly than its pilot intended. Gayler had swiftly deduced that his enemy was not trying to maneuver onto his tail for an extended shot, or such low-speed antics would have been suicide against the vastly more nimble Zeros. Ducking into the clouds at the first opportunity, Gayler left his pursuers behind. A little later, he found himself facing a lone Zero and initiated a scissors. Surprisingly the Japanese did not beat him to the turns, possibly because of damage inflicted earlier, and Gayler was able to set up a shot. The Zero dived away, and Gayler claimed a possible kill. Once again, he found himself alone in thick overcast.

The sacrifice of the torpedo escort drew four Zeros away from Torpedo Two which pressed its attack on the carrier. Okajima's pilots dispersed Gayler's division and apparently shot down both wingmen, Peterson and Rowell. Dale Peterson had earned his wings in April 1941 and was posted to Fighting Three in July. He had already earned the Navy Cross for his excellent performance on 20 February 1942. Richard Rowell's wings came in August 1940, and in November of that year, he joined Fighting Three. He also saw combat on 20 February as Don Lovelace's wingman. Early in the afternoon of 8 May Gayler heard Howard Clark transmitting on the radio, so he knew Clark had survived the ambush. He could not, however, establish contact with Clark. In return for the two F4Fs shot down, the *Zuikaku* Zeros took a few hits, but lost no aircraft shot down. The fight again demonstrated the vital need for auxiliary fuel tanks which would have allowed the Grummans to cruise at a sufficient speed to reduce the vulnerable period necessary to accelerate to usable combat speed.

While Gayler's division fought and half of them died, Brett went after the target with a "high level" approach. This meant that Torpedo Two would spiral in from medium altitude by means of a shallow dive, in the process increasing speed to around 180 knots. It was necessary to release their Bliss-Leavitt aerial torpedoes at a speed no greater than 115 knots and altitude no higher than 50 feet; otherwise they would be certain not to function properly. A high-speed approach would at least take the TBDs away from the Zeros busily fighting the escort. Taking advantage of cloud cover, Brett tried to conceal his approach by cutting through a cloud mass that served to screen his planes from the fire of the warships supporting the carrier. Descending through the overcast, the eleven TBDs emerged in the clear a few miles off the *Shōkaku*'s port bow. Immediately the flattop opened fire with her 12.7-cm guns against these new attackers. Captain Joshima ordered the helm put hard over for a radical turn to starboard away from the oncoming torpedo planes. The TBD crews could see thick, black smoke billowing from around the carrier's island—evidence of recent attention by Ault's SBDs.

Iwamoto and his two Zero wingmen caught sight of the American torpedo planes when they were three to four miles out from the target. Diving in, Iwamoto's immediate prey turned out to be two Devastators flown by Ens. Tom B. Bash and Ens. Norman Sterrie. Bash and Sterrie had inadvertently separated from the rest of Torpedo Two and broke into the open about a mile ahead and far to the left of the other nine planes. The *Shōkaku* heeled over to starboard to turn away from her attackers. Not having the speed to overtake the swift carrier and attack from off her bow, the two ensigns had to follow her through her 180-degree turn, hanging on her stern. The three *Zuikaku* Zero pilots braved their own antiaircraft fire to make a number of rapid firing passes against the two isolated TBDs, but they did not down either of the Americans. Disregarding the Zeros pumping 20-mm tracers past his ears and the *Shōkaku*'s disconcerting gun flashes, Bash pressed his attack and released his torpedo from about 600 yards off her port quarter. The *Shōkaku* had completed her 180-degree turn and now headed in the direction opposite the one she was taking when the squadron first sighted her. Bash took his lumbering Devastator right to the wave tops to avoid the attentions of the two *Zuikaku* Zeros chasing him; he had no opportunity to see what his torpedo might have done. Sterrie, though harried by a Zero on his tail, approached within 400 yards of the ship's starboard quarter before dropping his torpedo. He observed the rest of Torpedo Two coming from his right and turned to make a dummy run to draw fire away from them.

Brett and the other eight pilots of Torpedo Two saw the two ensigns pursue the *Shōkaku* around in her tight turn to starboard. This maneuver had set up the opportunity for a direct squadron attack against her starboard side. The *Lexington*'s TBDs fanned out for individual runs against the *Shōkaku*'s starboard side, each pilot choosing his own angle of attack and approaching to what he thought was optimum range to release his torpedo and break away. The classic "anvil" attack from both bows lacking, the *Shōkaku* easily turned away and outran the slow, erratic torpedoes. All nine fish missed the target, although Torpedo Two claimed five hits. Withdrawing eastward, Brett collected his squadron as best he could in a "running rendezvous." The torpedo attack proper lasted from 1142 to 1150. According to Iwamoto's professional eye, the Americans did a poor job because they had released their torpedoes over a thousand yards from the target. "Japanese torpedo planes would never have performed so poorly,"[17] he wrote, not realizing the advantages his countrymen held with better aircraft and aerial torpedoes.

The Iwamoto *shōtai* continued harassing the TBDs as they left the immediate target area. Two Zeros stuck with Bash's TBD, but help came in an unexpected manner. Fighting Two's Bain, from the CLAG command division escort, had descended through the cloud base after evading the Zero above. Breaking into the clear, he watch a lone TBD make its torpedo run and withdraw at 500 feet. Bain dived in to join up with the TBD, but behind it he noticed a Zero closing in from astern and about a thousand feet above. Bain hauled his Grumman into a chandelle and cut loose with a long-range burst. Evidently the Japanese did not like the situation, for he made a quick wingover and headed away for easier game. Bash in his report happily noted that a *Lexington* fighter had shot a Zero off his tail. The other Japanese in pursuit of Bash made three or four more swift runs, then rolled out to go after another TBD about a half mile to the right. Bash retired on his own, turning south into the clouds. Lieut. Hurst, VT-2's executive officer, also was unable to join up with the rest of the squadron, and set his own course for home. Brett succeeded in rendezvousing the other nine TBDs about 20 miles east of the target. Sliding into formation behind them was Bain, who had followed one of the TBDs in. If Torpedo Two thought they had fighter protection in the form of the lone Grumman, they were to be disillusioned. In his four combats, Bain had used all his ammunition, and his fuel ran low. Perforce, he throttled way back for maximum endurance and tagged along with the TBDs.

While Torpedo Two attacked, Ault's four SBDs retreated in another direction. Not long after, Wingfield departed for a second go at the target. Okabe's *Shōkaku* Zeros found the others and roared in. Several quick, slashing attacks forced the dive bombers to scatter into the clouds. Okabe's pilots probably were out of 20-mm ammunition by this time, but they peppered the sturdy SBDs with 7.7-mm rounds. Ault's SBD took heavy damage, with bullets wounding both him and his gunner. He was not able to rendezvous the division. Both he and Ens. Harry Wood became separated and did not determine the correct course back to Task Force 17. No one ever saw Wingfield again. Ultimately only the fourth SBD pilot, Ens. Marvin M. Haschke, made it back to the *Lexington*.

The VT escort leader, Gayler, thrashed around inside the clouds for several minutes after fighting the *Zuikaku* Zeros, seeking in vain the rest of his division. Then, breaking into a clear space, he witnessed a rare sight. Below him steamed the *Zuikaku*. Unbothered by antiaircraft fire, he took the unique opportunity of deliberately circling the Japanese flattop at a thousand feet. She appeared totally undamaged. Obviously the strike groups had missed this choice target completely. To the north Gayler saw in the distance a number of enemy warships, including one on fire. He persevered in his efforts to contact his pilots by radio, but without success. Clark was likewise transmitting, but Gayler could not establish communications with him. Finally Gayler turned south toward Task Force 17. Ten minutes later he happened upon Haschke's lone SBD and joined up. Gayler later remarked that he was happy to see Haschke for the help in navigation, whereas Haschke was pleased to have the Grumman around as fighter protection.

Not far away but socked in by thick clouds, Hamilton's Bombing Two was an unwilling bystander to the attack of the rest of the *Lexington* Air Group. Able to follow the approach and attack of the TBDs through their radio chatter, Hamilton tried desperately to locate the target, but to no avail. Indeed, he may narrowly have missed being intercepted by enemy fighters, according to a note in Iwamoto's diary. After fighting the TBDs, Iwamoto spotted what he thought were sixteen Grummans, and underneath them several Zeros. He feared that the sixteen American fighters would ambush the Zeros below, but the Americans turned back into the clouds. It is hard to see how this incident could have involved anyone on the American side but Bombing Two. Around noon, Hamilton resolved to return to the task force because of the dwindling fuel supply. He waited twenty minutes before jettisoning bombs in hopes of running across a worthwhile target.

On board the *Shōkaku*, Captain Joshima had had enough. The third bomb hit underscored the fact that the *Shōkaku* was no longer an asset to the Japanese in this battle, as she could not conduct flight operations. At 1150, he recommended to Takagi and Hara that the *Shōkaku* be detached to head north for repairs. His superiors agreed, and at 1210 she changed course to 050 degrees and sped off at 30 knots. Accompanying her were the heavy cruisers *Kinugasa* and *Furutaka* and two destroyers. Led by Ens. (Special Service) Abe, three *Shōkaku* CAP Zeros maintained air patrol over her as she withdrew. Her crew had suffered extremely heavy casualties, amounting to 109 dead and 114 wounded. Around the *Zuikaku*, her Zeros clustered to await recovery. That carrier at noon finally launched the three Zeros of her 12th *Shōtai* (W.O. Sumita Tsuyoshi) as relief CAP to augment the patrol, but they did not see action.

The *Lexington* strike group claimed a total of two 1,000-lb. bomb hits and five torpedo hits on a large Japanese carrier. Naturally the pilots thought they had inflicted fatal damage on the target, which they described as "settling fast."[18] Aircraft losses in the target area amounted to three F4F Wildcats from Fighting Two, most likely shot down by Zeros. Other *Lexington* planes, however, were desperately lost in the overcast and would not make it back to the ship. The air group had scattered beyond redemption in the relentless clouds and withdrew singly or in small groups.

Sixteen Zeros from the *Shōkaku* and the *Zuikaku* participated actively in the defense of MO Striking Force, and their losses were two fighters shot down and two more shot up. Japanese claims were extremely high, something like thirty-nine

PO1c Okabe Kenji of the *Shōkaku* Fighter
Unit. (Via Dr. Izawa Yasuho.)

planes shot down! The *Zuikaku* Fighter Unit reported shooting down thirteen
fighters, six dive bombers, and three torpedo planes, while the *Shōkaku* fighter
pilots claimed five fighters, nine dive bombers, and two torpedo planes, not counting
probable kills or damaged aircraft. High scorer in Japanese reports was Okabe
Kenji, credited with three fighters and three dive bombers shot down, and one of
each of those types as probables.[19] As far as can be determined, the Japanese
fighters actually shot down two SBD dive bombers and three F4F fighters in both
attacks. The Japanese certainly were enthusiastic claimers.

"HEY RUBE"—THE ATTACK ON TASK FORCE 17

While the *Lexington* and the *Yorktown* strike planes took off to attack the enemy
carriers, Rear Admiral Fletcher at 0908 turned over temporary tactical command
of Task Force 17 to Rear Admiral Fitch. His aviation expertise would be vital in
view of the likely Japanese counterblow. Along with the escort fighters, the *Lexington* around 0920 launched a relief CAP of four F4Fs under Buzz Borries. She
remained in the wind to recover Ramsey's four VF-2 F4Fs from the first CAP and
ten SBDs (six VB-2, four VS-2) newly returned from the morning search. Lack of
IFF gear in the CAP and search planes caused confusion as usual, the fighters
having to investigate numerous contacts that turned out to be friendly planes. At
no time did CAP threaten Kanno's *Shōkaku* search plane carefully shadowing the
force. The *Yorktown* maneuvered into the wind to launch at 0941 Vince Mc-
Cormack's four-plane VF-42 division for the CAP. She then took on board Jimmy
Flatley's four fighters.

Red Gill soon had work for McCormack's section. He sent them northward
after a bogey first detected at 0932, 39 miles out. The contact by 0948 had closed
within 25 miles, but the fighters could not find the bogey. Things heated up at
1000, when a VS-2 SBD returning from the search broadcast an alarm: twelve
unidentified aircraft bearing 270 degrees, distance 60 miles from Point Zed, which
worked out to bearing 355 degrees, 45 miles from Task Force 17. On board the
Lex, crews worked frantically to refuel the aircraft recently taken on board. The

Yorktown thought enemy aircraft a good deal closer than that. At 1003 she signaled the force that lookouts had sighted aircraft bearing 015 degrees, distance 15 miles and closing. A somewhat perplexed Gill replied that he had nothing on radar, but to play it safe he reoriented the CAP, sending out the two VF-42 sections launched not long before. At 1007, Fletcher instructed Fitch to launch additional aircraft and noted bandits moving in from 270 degrees. This looked like the long-expected enemy air strike.

While Task Force 17 pressed the alarm button, a hapless intruder worked its way to within sighting distance of the ships. At 1008, *Yorktown* lookouts excitedly reported a large seaplane on the horizon, bearing 040 degrees. It was another Kawanishi Type 97 flying boat from the Yokohama Air Group, the fourth to apppear in as many days. Again the Japanese had pressed their luck too far. Within a minute of the report, McCormack had sighted the flying boat. He and his wingman Walt Haas were getting to be old hands at this, having downed a Kawanishi on 5 May.

After a short "Tallyho," the two Grummans quickly overtook the lumbering Kawanishi. McCormack executed a steep high-side run from the right, Haas following close behind. The first attack started the flying boat smoking. McCormack zoomed back for altitude advantage, charged in from the left, fired, and recovered to the right. Haas stayed with his leader all the way. Together they had the enemy dead to rights. The clumsy flying boat simply could not evade the swift Grummans barking at its heels. The third attack pumped bullets into the target's vulnerable engines and fuel tanks atop the long parasol wing, and the Kawanishi literally exploded in Haas's face as he finished his third pass. A war whoop from McCormack announced the enemy's demise. The ships could plainly see smoke from the burning oil patch marking where the Kawanishi had splashed. Despite heavy return fire from the flying boat's turrets and gun hatches, the Japanese had put only one 7.7-mm round into the wing of one of the F4Fs. Tulagi headquarters had vectored the Kawanishi onto the target in order to amplify the contact reported by Kanno. Unfortunately, the flying boat proved too vulnerable for such work; Tulagi never received the contact report.

Even while the CAP destroyed the one enemy aircraft in the vicinity, alarms continued in Task Force 17. At 1011, the *Lexington* warned of Zero fighters bearing 025 degrees; evidently this was a misidentification by the CAP of returning SBDs. The *Yorktown* a minute later piped up with a report of enemy bombers closing from the west. Beginning at 1012, Ted Sherman scrambled the ten SBDs (six from Bombing Two, four from Scouting Two) for service on anti–torpedo-plane patrol. His pet idea of using Dauntless dive bombers as ersatz fighters would receive the definitive test that morning. Doctrine decreed that the *Lexington* SBDs deploy loosely into a semicircle around the carrier's bow (VB-2 to starboard, VS-2 to port) and cruise 6,000 yards out at an altitude of 2,000 feet. The *Yorktown*'s SBD pilots did not favor the idea of an anti–torpedo-plane patrol and would much rather have flown on the strike.

As the SBDs roared down the *Lexington*'s flight deck, it dawned on both fighter director officers that no enemy strike group lurked in the vicinity. At 1015, Gill advised both carriers to keep their fighters on standby to await developments, and shortly thereafter the task force relaxed. The *Lexington* SBDs trickling in from the morning search apparently had triggered all the false alarms. Five of them from Scouting Two converged on the ships, and beginning at 1020, the *Lexington* brought them on board. Also waiting his turn to land was Steffenhagen, with the misbehaving TBD from Torpedo Two. He landed at 1030, at which time the task force changed course to 028 degrees, speed 15 knots to narrow the distance to the target.

A few minutes later, two more SBDs appeared on the horizon, and the *Lexington* recovered them at 1050. Words fail the describe the atmosphere of ominous anticipation permeating Task Force 17 as these events took place.

At 1055, the *Lexington* and *Yorktown* radars simultaneously registered what appeared to be a large group of bogeys bearing 020 degrees, distance 68 miles and closing. Such a strong contact had to portend the long-expected enemy carrier strike on Task Force 17. On CAP, Gill had eight fighters aloft, organized as follows with their section radio calls:

VF-2	3rd Division
"Doris Red"	Lieut. Fred Borries, Jr., USN
	Lieut. (jg) Marion W. Dufilho, USN
"Doris White"	Lieut. (jg) Clark F. Rinehart, USN
	Ens. Newton H. Mason, A-V(N)
VF-42	3rd Division
"Wildcat Brown"	Lieut. Vincent F. McCormack, USN
	Ens. Walter A. Haas, A-V(N)
"Wildcat Orange"	Lieut. (jg) Arthur J. Brassfield, USN
	Lieut. (jg) E. Duran Mattson, USN

As Borries's four F4Fs had been aloft for ninety minutes and McCormack's division for seventy, Gill felt neither could manage a long-distance interception with the fuel at hand. The eighteen SBDs on anti–torpedo-plane patrol did not fall under his control. At 1058, Gill received authorization to scramble the nine F4Fs waiting on standby. A minute later he broadcast the call "Hey Rube!,"[1] the old carnival barker phrase officially put to use in the fighter direction vocabulary. It meant the CAP aloft was to return to station over their respective carriers. Trouble was coming fast.

The *Lexington* at 1100 brought her bow southeasterly into the wind to launch five F4Fs from Fighting Two and five VS-2 SBDs for anti–torpedo-plane patrol. The fighters comprised the skipper's reorganized 1st Division:

"Agnes Red"	Lt. Cdr. Paul H. Ramsey, USN
	Ens. George F. Markham, Jr., A-V(N)
	Ens. Edward R. Sellstrom, Jr., A-V(N)
"Agnes White"	Ens. Willard E. Eder, A-V(N)
	Ens. Leon W. Haynes, A-V(N)

Ramsey had given the deck-bound Sellstrom another fighter and added him to his section. The FDO at 1101 chimed in with orders for Ramsey's division to proceed out along the 020-degree (M.) heading for 30 miles, taking the opportunity to climb to 10,000 feet on the way. Two minutes later he added the imperative "Buster," which meant Ramsey was to fly at maximum sustainable speed. At 1107, Gill modified his orders. Separating the division, he instructed Eder's "Agnes White" section to go low to chase torpedo planes while the skipper's "Agnes Red" section continued climbing.

Flatley's 2nd Division from Fighting Forty-two took off at 1103 from the *Yorktown*. He had with him the following:

"Wildcat Red"	Lt. Cdr. James H. Flatley, Jr., USN
	Lieut. (jg) Richard G. Crommelin, USN
"Wildcat Blue"	Lieut. (jg) Brainard T. Macomber, A-V(N)
	Ens. Edgar R. Bassett, A-V(N)

Flatley awaited orders for two minutes after takeoff, then tried to hasten the FDO with an impatient "Let's go!" Gill told him to climb to 10,000 feet and wait on standby, "until we see what develops." The Grummans began climbing, but at 1108, the FDO changed his mind. Gill instructed Flatley to "Vector 020°, Angels 1, Buster," which meant to proceed along the 020-degree magnetic bearing at 1,000 feet altitude and top sustained speed. Flatley did not copy the whole transmission and asked Gill whether it was "Angels 1000 or 10,000." Gill apologized and told him Angels 1, distance 15 miles.[2] Flatley naturally assumed he was hunting low-flying torpedo planes and kept especially good lookout ahead and below. He took his fighters down to 2,500 rather than 1,000 feet in order to retain some altitude advantage over any torpedo planes they might encounter.

Thus the FDO formed his defending fighters into two elements: about half (nine) to intercept the enemy between 15 and 20 miles out, while the rest (eight) constituted a second line of defense over the ships. Of the nine he vectored out, he instructed six to approach at low level to attack torpedo planes. That would be a crucial mistake.

While Task Force 17 arrayed its defenses, Lt. Cdr. Takahashi's strike group had already spotted the ships. His sixty-nine planes were organized as shown in the table. On its return flight, the superlative *Shōkaku* search crew under W. O. Kanno ran across the Japanese strike group. Worried that intermittent cloud cover might delay discovery of the target, Kanno flew up alongside Takahashi's *kanbaku* and guided him directly to within sighting distance of the American task force. At 1105, Takahashi spotted the enemy ships at what he estimated was 35 miles. The target securely in sight, Takahashi released Kanno and his crew, now getting low on fuel, to return to MO Striking Force, taking with them the gratitude of all in the strike group. They all appreciated the importance of Kanno's gesture, which was much like the action of VS-2's Joe Smith in directing Torpedo Five to MO Striking Force.

As Takahashi drew closer to the target, he discerned two American carriers and rapidly devised his plan of attack. He would take his Carrier Bomber Group, thirty-three *kanbaku* at 14,000 feet, to a point upwind (southeast) of the target before diving in. This meant a detour around to the east. Lt. Cdr. Shimazaki with the eighteen torpedo-armed carrier attack planes (*kankō*) cruised at around 10,000 feet. He was to charge directly toward the enemy carriers and in the process let down swiftly from 10,000 to around 4,000 feet as his approach altitude. Lieut.

Strike Group Leader	Lt. Cdr. Takahashi Kakuichi (H)
Fighter Striking Group	Lieut. Hoashi Takumi (B)
Shōkaku Fighter Unit, 1st *Chūtai*	Lieut. Hoashi
	9 Zero fighters
Zuikaku Fighter Unit, 2nd *Chūtai*	Lieut. Tsukamoto Yūzō (B)
	9 Zero fighters
Carrier Bomber Group	Lt. Cdr. Takahashi
Shōkaku Carrier Bomber Unit	Lt. Cdr. Takahashi
	19 Type 99 carrier bombers (*kanbaku*)
Zuikaku Carrier Bomber Unit	Lieut. Ema Tamotsu (B)
	14 Type 99 carrier bombers
Carrier Attack Group	Lt. Cdr. Shimazaki Shigekazu (H)
Shōkaku Carrier Attack Unit	Lieut. Ichihara Tatsuo (B)
	10 Type 97 carrier attack planes (*kankō*)
Zuikaku Carrier Attack Unit	Lt. Cdr. Shimazaki
	8 Type 97 carrier attack planes

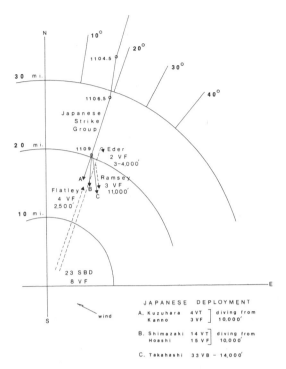

CAP and strike group deployment to 1112.

Hoashi's eighteen Zero escorts would support the torpedo planes, as presumably they would draw most of the opposition. At 1109, Takahashi signaled his tactical deployment, and the strike group broke formation, with each element heading to do its job over the target.

On the flight out, Ramsey's "Agnes Red" section climbed steadily through patches of cloud cover toward its assigned station and altitude. Suddenly at 1109 just over 20 miles out, Sellstrom radioed excitedly:

> Skipper! Eleven o'clock right up from you. Can't you see them straight up from you?[3]

Doc had caught sight of the Japanese strike group just before it deployed into separate carrier bomber and torpedo elements. Sellstrom later recounted that the strike group comprised fifty to sixty aircraft stacked in layers from 13,000 feet to 10,000 feet, with fighters on top, then dive bombers, some more fighters, and on the bottom torpedo planes. His assessment was pretty accurate.

Of immediate concern to Ramsey were the aircraft making up the enemy's highest level. Above and to his left front he picked out two massive formations, one behind the other. Each formation appeared to be a great Vee of Vees composed of eighteen aircraft. The lead Vee of Vees, perhaps still 4,000 to 5,000 feet above the three Grummans, seemed to be dive bombers, but, more ominously, the rear Vee of Vees, another 2,000 feet or so higher in altitude than the first, had the look of escort fighters. The skipper's "Agnes Red" section was still situated between the task force and the oncoming Japanese, but just barely. At only 10,000 feet, Ramsey felt he was in no position to try to intercept enemy planes still several thousand feet above him. If he rushed pell mell at the bombers from underneath (a poor attack), Ramsey reasoned that the much more numerous Japanese escort would jump him. Actually Ramsey had happened upon Takahashi's Carrier Bomber Group of thirty-three dive bombers, and they were unescorted. Evidently it did not occur to him to relinquish altitude and dive after the torpedo planes. Instead he led the three Grummans underneath the enemy formations, crossed from west to east, and started climbing to the level to the lowest Vee of Vees.

On board the *Lexington*, Gill eavesdropped on the radio chatter between Ramsey and his pilots and knew they had spotted the enemy. At 1111, he warned the rest of the CAP:

> Keep a sharp lookout. Agnes Red is attacking now.[4]

Gill vitally needed to know the enemy's altitude, but Ramsey at the moment was concerned with the Zeros he thought were above him:

> Watch those fighters on our starboard quarter.

Gill radioed, "Paul did you hear me?" Ramsey replied:

> Affirmative. There are nine heavy [garbled transmission?] bombers and fighters. We are going to chase bombers.[5]

Climbing at the maximum rate—which was not spectacular in a fully loaded Grumman—"Agnes Red" fell behind the Japanese in what would be a long stern chase back toward Task Force 17.

The other two fighter elements vectored out for distant interception did not encounter the Japanese at all because of their low altitude and cloud cover. En route to his station, Flatley momentarily thought he had found the enemy, but the two Wildcat sections Red and Blue actually had happened upon the *Yorktown*'s anti–torpedo-plane patrol. At 1111, Flatley's division reached its designated station 15 miles out, but saw no enemy. Two minutes before, Gill had warned that torpedo planes were approaching from 020 degrees (M.), distance 35 miles, so Flatley assumed the Japanese were still ahead of him. Bill Eder's "Agnes White" section, detached from Ramsey's division, hunted through the overcast and also missed the torpedo planes which passed above. Eder later remarked, "Regarding my combat on the 8th, I remember mostly clouds!"[6] He realized the Japanese had probably slipped past unseen, and led his wingman, Lee Haynes, back toward the ships. Evidently Woodhull and Strong, leading VS-5's anti–torpedo-plane patrol, also came to that conclusion and turned to take station about five miles north of the ships.

The Japanese Torpedo Attack

As *hikōtaichō* Shimazaki approached the target, he worked out his tactical deployment. His eighteen carrier attack planes made a shallow dive from 10,000 feet to 4,000 feet. Ahead Shimazaki discerned the unmistakable silhouette of a "*Saratoga*-type" carrier and decided to concentrate the torpedo attack on her. Heretofore Task Force 17 had steamed northward to shorten the distance its own strike planes would have to cover on their return, but at 1112 Fitch, acting in tactical command, changed course to 125 degrees. This placed the oncoming attackers off the ships' port sides. Shimazaki would hit the bigger carrier, the one he thought was the *Saratoga*, with fourteen carrier attack planes and send four torpedo planes as a gesture against the smaller, *Yorktown*-class carrier. The previous night's disastrous loss of torpedo planes must have weighed heavily on his mind. The nine mising *kankō* (all with elite crews) would have enabled him to launch full attacks against both American carriers.

Organization and Claims, Japanese Escort, 8 May 1942

Fighter Striking Force   Lieut. Hoashi Takumi, *buntaichō*

Shōkaku Fighter Unit, 1st *Chūtai*

1st *Shōtai*

Lieut. Hoashi Takumi, *buntaichō*	1 VF conf., 1 VF prob.
PO1c Nishide Korenobu	2 VF conf., 1 VF prob.
PO3c Horiguchi Shunji	2 VF conf.

2nd *Shōtai*

Lieut. Yamamoto Shigehisa, *buntaichō*	4 VF + 1 VB conf.
PO1c Matsuda Jirō	3 VF + 1 VB conf.
PO2c Sasakibara Masao	2 VF + 1 VB conf.

3rd *Shōtai*

W.O. Hanzawa Yukuo	4 VF conf.
PO1c Yamamoto Ichirō	1 VF + 3 VB conf.
Sea1c Kawano Shigeru	2 VF conf.

Zuikaku Fighter Unit, 2nd *Chūtai*

14th *Shōtai*

Lieut. Tsukamoto Yūzō, *buntaichō*
PO1c Kiyomatsu Ginji
PO2c Okura Shigeru (ditched at Deboyne)

15th *Shōtai*

PO1c Makino Shigeru
PO2c Nakata Shigenobu
Sea1c Nisugi Toshitsugu

16th *Shōtai*

PO1c Kanō Satoshi
PO1c Kamei Tomio
Sea1c Kurata Nobutaka

Total *Zuikaku* claims:	15 VF + 14 VB conf.
Grand total, escort claims:	36 VF (+ 2 prob.)
	20 VB

Drawing closer to the ships, the Carrier Attack Group executed its primary deployment. Shimazaki signaled the *Zuikaku* Carrier Attack Unit's 2nd *Chūtai* (four *kankō* under Lieut. Satō Zen'ichi, *buntaichō*) to branch off to the west to attack the *Yorktown*. Covering the four torpedo planes were the three Zeros of the *Zuikaku*'s 16th *Shōtai* (PO1c Kanō Satoshi). To tackle the "*Saratoga*," Shimazaki loosed Lieut. Ichihara's ten *Shōkaku* torpedo planes directly toward her massive bulk. Ichihara was to send part of his force around her bow to catch her in an anvil attack, while Shimazaki's own four *Zuikaku kankō* constituted the other pincer to entrap the "*Saratoga*" between. Escorting the "*Saratoga*" strike force were the remaining fifteen Zeros (six from the *Zuikaku* and nine from the *Shōkaku*). Letting down to 4,000 feet, the Carrier Attack Group would make its approach at that height before the final dive toward launch altitude (150–250 feet).

Struggling far above the torpedo planes was Ramsey's section "Agnes Red" in its futile attempt to overtake the Japanese dive bombers. Sitting on the skipper's wing, Sellstrom became increasingly impatient at the inability of the Grummans to come to grips with the Japanese. He knew from his experiences on 20 February that the F4F-3s with their low climb rate just would not be able to overhaul the enemy dive bombers before they attacked. Ironically, Doc had much more time in Grumman Wildcats than Ramsey, his squadron commander, who in the last two months had just become acquainted with them when Fighting Two discarded its Brewster Buffaloes. Far below, Sellstrom saw the enemy torpedo planes heading toward the task force. He tried to draw Ramsey's attention to them, but the skipper was intent on catching the dive bombers. A courageous but impetuous pilot, Sellstrom determined to risk Ramsey's ire and break formation to dive after the torpedo planes, giving them the priority their ship-wrecking potential merited. Certainly Ramsey was not pleased to see his wingman dive away without permission, to go after goodness-knows-what. The move put Sellstrom in the "dog house," but that did not bother him if there were Japanese to attack.

Streaking in from 12,000 feet, Sellstrom picked up plenty of speed and scored before the enemy had time to react. He singled out a torpedo plane, and at 1116 sent it spinning in flames toward the water. His victim was a *Zuikaku* carrier attack plane from Shimazaki's own 1st *Chūtai*. The interception took place about four miles out. Responding quickly were the three Zero fighters of the *Zuikaku*'s 15th *Shōtai* (PO1c Makino Shigeru). They overhauled Sellstrom, still close to the torpedo planes, and started a wild dogfight. Shimazaki has left a vivid account of the action:

> Our Zeros and enemy Wildcats spun, dove, and climbed in the midst of our formation. Burning and shattered planes of both sides plunged from the skies.[7]

Twice Sellstrom worked into head-on runs with Zeros and held the firing passes to the limit. In the short, sharp skirmish he claimed two Zeros as well as the one torpedo plane. The Japanese were equally certain they were fighting three Grummans and claimed at least one. Actually, the sole loss during this portion of the fight was the one *Zuikaku* torpedo plane, the first blood drawn by the defenders.

A minute after Sellstrom's furious attack, it was the turn of Scouting Five on anti–torpedo-plane patrol to feel the sting of *Zuikaku* fighters. Deployed loosely in pairs, the eight SBDs turned up between the two groups of *Zuikaku* torpedo planes, but in position to intercept neither. There was no way the SBDs, cruising at 1,500 feet, could overhaul faster-moving torpedo planes with altitude advantage. The *kankō* were past before the SBDs could react. Some of the VS-5 pilots never even saw them. Suddenly there was trouble. Birney Strong glanced up to behold the sickening sight of three Zeros peeling off into an overhead attack on his dispersed SBDs. They were the three fighters of Lieut. Tsukamoto's *Zuikaku* 14th *Shōtai*, surprised to find nine "Curtiss bombers" (as the Japanese called the Dauntlesses) flying in their area. Their amazement brief, they tore into Strong's division. On the first pass, Tsukamoto and his wingmen shot off the tail of Ens. Kendall C. Campbell's SBD, then blasted a second Dauntless from the sky. They kept the surviving SBDs too busy to join forces for their mutual defense. Joining in the fight were PO1c Kanō's three *Zuikaku* Zeros, and they went after Woodhull's four SBDs as well. For the next several minutes, the *Zuikaku* Zeros made life miserable or impossible for Scouting Five, eventually accounting for four SBDs, flown by Lieut. (jg) Earl V. Johnson, Ens. Samuel J. Underhill, Ens. Edward B. Kinzer, and Ens. Campbell. In return Scouting Five claimed four Zeros shot down, one to Lieut. (jg) Stanley W. Vejtasa (later a renowned ace with Flatley's Fighting Ten). The Japanese, however, lost no fighters in this combat.

Just outside the destroyer screen the Japanese torpedo plane group executed its final deployment against the *Lexington*. Ichihara's *Shōkaku* Carrier Attack Unit was divided into two attack elements: the 2nd *Chūtai* (four planes) under Lieut. Iwamura Yoshio and Ichihara's own 1st *Chūtai* (six planes). To his left Ichihara sent Iwamura's 4 planes to the south around ahead of the task force in order to curve back toward the *Lexington*'s starboard bow. They comprised one half of the pincers. The remaining six *Shōkaku* Type 97s charged directly for the *Lexington*'s port bow. To their right, Shimazaki's 1st *Zuikaku* Chūtai with three *kankō* forged ahead to launch their torpedoes off the *Lexington*'s port bow as the other arm of the anvil attack. Satō's four *Zuikaku* torpedo planes took on the *Yorktown* alone.

The *Lexington* anti-torpedo plane patrol (fifteen SBDs) had spread out in a large crescent around their carrier's bow. Several of them had left their patrol stations and headed north at low level looking for the enemy. Now to the north on the carrier's port side were seven from VS-2 and five from VB-2. More fortunate than their *Yorktown* counterparts, they would enjoy altitude advantage over the enemy torpedo planes descending close to the water to drop their fish. At least in the beginning, they also had fewer Zeros to contend with. As will be explained later, *hikōtaichō* Takahashi had just summoned at least six, most likely all nine, *Shōkaku* escort Zeros to high altitude to protect his carrier bombers. This left at lower level only the three Zeros from the *Zuikaku*'s 15th *Shōtai* (PO1c Makino) busily chasing Sellstrom back toward the ships. The *Yorktown* anti–torpedo-plane patrol, to its detriment, had absorbed the remaining six *Zuikaku* fighters.

Several SBDs of Scouting Two were in excellent intercept position to the north right outside the screen. Suddenly enemy torpedo planes appeared among them, diving through to reach their launch positions. Time was short, and in a few seconds the torpedo planes were beyond them, but a number of SBDs had the height and speed to charge after them. Several VS-2 pilots, including Lieut. (jg) William E. Hall and Ensigns Arthur J. Schultz, Jr., John A. Leppla, and Robert E. Smith, had the opportunity for good shots and claimed the destruction of five torpedo planes before release. All told, Scouting Two succeeded in flaming three carrier attack planes, including Iwamura's, and reduced the *Shōkaku*'s pincer to two planes. Then the Zeros appeared. (More will be heard of Scouting Two's scrap when the air melee north of the ships is described.)

Thus the combat air and anti–torpedo-plane patrols destroyed three of the eighteen Japanese carrier attack planes. Antiaircraft fire would have to do the rest. Tracking the oncoming enemy planes on radar, the ship gunnery officers as a rule held their fire from the five-inch guns until lookouts verified the targets—that morning between 5,000 and 7,000 yards away. For close-in defense, the carriers wielded a formidable array (for early 1942 at any rate) of 1.1-inch, 20-mm, and .50-caliber automatic weapons. Their gunners tried their best to put a curtain of steel in front of the attackers. Not entirely trusting the effectiveness of antiaircraft fire, the two carrier captains, Ted Sherman of the *Lexington* and the *Yorktown*'s Elliott Buckmaster, relied primarily upon smart ship handling to evade bombs and torpedoes. Prior to the attack, Task Force 17 worked up to 25 knots, but it reserved full speed (32 to 33 knots) until the actual assault in order to help keep formation. The screening vessels held to only a general scheme of maneuver, whose primary aim was to stay close enough to (but not in the way of) the carriers to support them.

Lacking the numbers required for the feared anvil tactic, Satō directed his four *Zuikaku* carrier attack planes directly for the *Yorktown*'s port bow. At 1118, her lookouts caught sight of the four around 7,000 yards out, setting her five-inchers blasting away at them. The gunnery control officers soon found how difficult it was to track the speedy *kankō*. Past the heavy cruiser *Minneapolis* swept the *Zuikaku* aircraft, the cruiser aflame with muzzle flashes. Noting torpedo planes off his port bow, Buckmaster responded by ringing up emergency flank speed, then ordered full right rudder to keep the *Yorktown*'s stern pointed toward her attackers. Deep inside the screen, the four Japanese let down close to the water. Black five-inch shell bursts bracketed the little formation, as the *kankō* pressed into launch range about a thousand yards out. One of the torpedo pilots released his fish, and suddenly flames engulfed his entire fuselage. The stricken aircraft held on course about 100 yards, then spun out of line and splashed between the *Yorktown* and the heavy cruiser *Chester*.

The three surviving *Zuikaku kankō* persevered to within 500 yards of the swiftly turning carrier, and at 1119 launched their torpedoes. The well-handled *Yorktown* evaded all three fish, whose menacing wakes streaked along the ship's port side. Possibly one other *Zuikaku* torpedo plane splashed in the immediate target area, another victim of antiaircraft fire. Reports note that just after release, one torpedo plane trailed smoke, then with a radical wing over to the right, flew into the water off the *Yorktown*'s port quarter. The remaining Japanese withdrew westward, taking with them a claim for two torpedo hits on the *Yorktown*. In the fury of the attack, some Japanese thought they saw one of their *kankō*, crippled by antiaircraft fire, plunge into a light cruiser, setting it aflame. In any case, the brave little attack force suffered 50 percent casualties to AA. On the way out an SBD attacked one of the survivors and killed the aircraft commander, W. O. Niino Tamorio.

Using a form of the anvil approach, the Japanese contrived to catch the *Lexington* in between groups of converging torpedo planes. Attack groups boring in from each bow would force the huge carrier to hold a relative straight course, as a turn toward one group to comb the torpedo wakes would present the other a torpedo pilot's dream shot. Shimazaki's three *Zuikaku* carrier attack planes and the two *Shōkaku kankō* curving around the *Lexington*'s port bow served as the pincers, while the other six *Shōkaku* torpedo planes attacked her port bow. The trained crews with their high-speed Nakajima Type 97 carrier attack planes were capable of such coordinated maneuvers, and the CAP was in no position to intervene. On this, their first opportunity to sink an American carrier, the crews of the 5th Carrier Division were not about to let their "*Saratoga*" escape them.

With his three *Zuikaku kankō*, Shimazaki charged the *Lexington*'s port bow. Cutting in front of the *Minneapolis*, they eased down to within 150 feet of the shining waves. Nearing launch point, they released torpedoes at 1118. Watching carefully, Sherman was confronted with the man-of-warsman's nemesis: enemy planes boring in on both bows. Those to port (Shimazaki) were closer, so Sherman turned away from them. The *Lexington* and her sister the *Saratoga* were the longest warships in the world and tantalizingly slow in answering the helm. The turn to starboard seemed an eternity. Amazed by the volume of antiaircraft fire, Shimazaki dived even lower until he and his two wingmen barely skimmed the wave tops and just missed colliding with the ship. He later noted:

> In fact, when I turned away from the carrier, I was so low that I almost struck the bow of the ship, for I was flying below the level of the flight deck. I could see the crewmen of the ship staring at my plane as it rushed by.[8]

Sherman also had to take into account the torpedo planes threatening his starboard bow. The *Shōkaku* pincer had coordinated well with Shimazaki's run from the north, this despite an encounter with Scouting Two that had cost two of the four planes. The blazing *kankō* splashed near the lead ships in the screen. The two survivors angled to their right toward the target's starboard bow and launched torpedoes. Barely had the *Lex* begun swinging to starboard to evade Shimazaki's fish, when Sherman had to try to turn away from this new group instead. Ordering left full rudder, Sherman discovered that the overall result of this contretemps was that his ship steamed essentially in the same direction as before. The misery of this outcome was that more torpedo attackers remained, and even now they closed for the kill.

The Japanese timed their anvil attack well. The torpedoes launched first by the two pincers missed: Shimazaki's three fish zipped alongside the target (one to starboard, two to port), while those from the two *Shōkaku kankō* ended up astern of the *Lexington*. However, they had set the old girl up, and she was in a position that favored the six *Shōkaku* torpedo planes now closing her port side. Again Sherman saw several groups of torpedo planes materialize as little specks off his port bow, and he brought the *Lexington* hard to starboard to turn away from this second wave.

Fortunately Scouting Two had spared the *Lexington* the attack of three of the remaining six *Shōkaku kankō*. Ichihara's 2nd *Shōtai* on the right flank had come in on Shimazaki's left. VS-2's Bill Hall flamed the *shotai* leader, Lieut. Yano Norio. At any rate, the two survivors changed their minds and veered to their right after the *Minneapolis* instead of left toward the *Lexington*. Captain Frank J. Lowry had put the heavy cruiser into a sharp turn to starboard to follow the *Lexington* in her first turn to starboard. The two errant *Shōkaku* pilots launched off the *Minneapolis*'s port bow. Lowry held his radical turn and handily evaded both fish. These Japanese later reported two hits on the "battleship."

Ready to take advantage of the *Lexington*'s predicament was Ichihara's own command *shotai* of three *Shōkaku* carrier attack planes. They were the main event, appearing off the *Lexington*'s port bow about the same time the two pincers completed their attacks. Sherman had already ordered a second turn to starboard, but the huge flattop was slow to respond to her helm. Seemingly undeterred by the storm of gunfire directed at them, the three *kankō* flattened low over the water and raced toward the *Lex*'s port bow. Finally she began swinging to port, but the Japanese stayed right with her. Ichihara's crews closed well within one thousand yards, making their drops from about 250 feet altitude at ranges around 700 yards. The first torpedo plunged too deep into the water, failed to correct, and passed harmlessly beneath her keel. At 1120, though, the Japanese scored. One torpedo struck the *Lexington* forward, and a second hit opposite the island, causing tremendous explosions and shudders throughout the ship. Ichihara's 1st *Shōkaku shotai* pilots managed to turn away successfully. Yano, already hit by Hall, flew into a web of tracers from the *Lexington*'s formidable light antiaircraft battery. Streaming gasoline, then fire, the *kankō* rolled over on its back and splashed with an explosion of bright flames close to the carrier's port bow.

The first Japanese Type 91 800-kilogram aerial torpedo detonated in the vicinity of the port forward gun gallery. The concussion damaged the hydraulic lift holding the two main flight deck elevators, dropping them an inch or so onto their safety catches and jamming them at flight deck level. The shock of the explosion also buckled the port stowage gasoline tanks storing highly inflammable aviation fuel. Fumes from several small leaks were compressed by water filling the flooded areas around the tanks, and gasoline vapors spread undetected into surrounding compartments. Damage control personnel rapidly inspected the port gasoline fuel system, detected no major leaks, but shut it down anyway as a precaution. An ominous development took place in the Internal Communications (IC) Motor Generator Room, situated between the big port and starboard stowage gasoline tanks. Damage from the torpedo hit wrecked the compartment's ventilation system, forcing the watch to evacuate. Unfortunately they were compelled to leave the electric motors operating in order to power the IC room.

The second hit, port-side amidships opposite the island, caused more apparent damage than the first. Striking near the firerooms, the blast fractured piping in three of them and ruptured the principal port water main, reducing water pressure

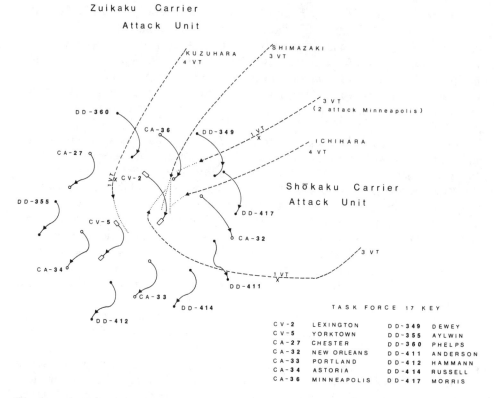

The torpedo attack on Task Force 17, 1118–1121.

forward. The three firerooms began filling with water, forcing engineering to shut down the boilers. Without the affected boilers, the *Lexington* could still make 24.5 knots. They were later pumped dry and could have been relighted if necessary. The blast also opened several fuel oil bunkers to the sea, causing a large oil slick. Flooding of several port-side compartments brought a list of 6 to 7 degrees, later offset by shifting ballast to the starboard side.

In his report, Rear Admiral Kinkaid offered a vivid description of the *Lexington* carrying on after the torpedo attack:

> Great clouds of smoke were pouring from her funnels and she was listing to port. Her speed was reduced only momentarily, the list was corrected promptly and she continued on at 25 knots and seemed to be under control. Great pools of fuel oil covered the surface of the water in her wake, and the air was filled with the sweetish odor of it mixed with the acrid fumes of gun powder.[9]

The Dive Bombing Attack

The first Japanese dive bomber did not push over in its dive until some three to four minutes after the torpedo planes had penetrated the screen, because *hikōtaichō* Takahashi had led his thirty-three carrier bombers around to the southeast to take station upwind of the target. This course swept him ahead of the task force. During his approach, the sight of Grummans trailing him (Ramsey's "Agnes Red" section) or others circling near the *Lexington* (Borries's VF-2 "Doris" division) must have alarmed Takahashi. He evidently ordered his escort leader, Lieut. Hoashi, to come

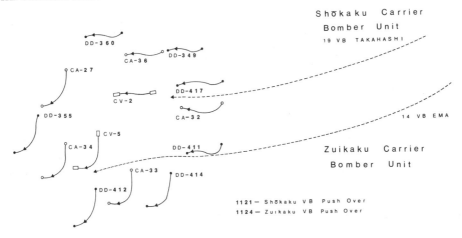

The dive bombing attack on Task Force 17, 1121–1124.

to his aid. At least six *Shōkaku* Zeros started climbing immediately, and three more followed some distance behind. They had peeled off before the carrier attack planes reached the outer screen. Their rapid climb rate gave the Zero pilots plenty of time to attain a position from which they could cover the carrier bombers before they attacked.

Stacked at 8,000 feet over the *Lexington* was Borries's division of four F4Fs made up of his own section "Doris Red" and Clark Rinehart's "Doris White." Borries must have seen the enemy dive bombers approaching and climbed to meet them. At 1116 he alerted Rinehart: "Come over here and join Marin [*sic*] and I on the port side."[10] "Marin" was Marion Dufilho, Borries's wingman, and the two were to the north off the *Lexington's* port side. Concentrating his division, Borries gained altitude toward the dive bombers, hoping to hit them before they attacked. Reaching 12,000 feet, still well under the carrier bombers, Borries was brought up short by Zeros. Six *Shōkaku* fighters ripped into the four Grummans. Reluctant to dive away in an evasive maneuver and thus lose his shot at the dive bombers, Borries kept his division at altitude and slipped into a Lufbery Circle to the left. The Japanese promptly mixed in, staying right with the Grummans.

Just a few minutes before Borries's encounter with the *Shōkaku* Zeros, the FDO had vectored VF-42's section "Wildcat Orange" (Art Brassfield) to proceed out along the 020-degree (M.) line and orbit at 15 miles. That left McCormack's section "Wildcat Brown" circling alone over the *Yorktown*. Heading out, Brassfield likewise found himself below and west of the enemy dive bomber formations. He turned parallel to their course while still in front of them and began climbing to their level. Reaching 12,000 feet, he saw the four VF-2 Grummans tussle with six Zeros and assume a Lufbery. Not able to overtake the dive bombers at any rate, Brassfield and his wingman, Duran Mattson, raced in to help their buddies in Fighting Two. Brassfield roared at the circle head-on. It was in his words, "pass a Grumman, shoot at the Jap, pass another Grumman, shoot at another Jap,"[11] in a crazy parody of a merry-go-round.

As Brassfield rushed in to help Borries and Rinehart, his own wingman found himself in deep trouble. During the climb, Mattson had flown in very loose formation on his leader's tail. Suddenly a string of Zeros flashed in at him in a succession of swift individual firing passes on his F4F. This was the third *Shōkaku shōtai* putting in an appearance. Brassfield was too busy with the Lufbery to notice Mattson's plight. After the initial passes, one of the Zeros maneuvered to stay on Mattson's tail for an easy, low deflection shot. Tracers zipped past both sides of his cockpit. *That* was too much! Mattson felt that if he did not do something immediately, the Japanese would shoot him down. He dropped into a tight left spiral, but the Zero stuck with him, riding easily on his tail and alternately shooting up the Wildcat's left and right wings. Mattson tried tightening his turns and even popped his landing flaps, but to no avail. His only alternative was to break contact and dive away at high speed. Gaining speed and distance, Mattson disappeared into the cloud base below 6,000 feet. Later when he checked his tail at low altitude, he saw no sign of the Zero that had followed him down.

While one Zero chased Mattson away from the fight, the other pair of *Shōkaku* pilots made ready to intrude on the Lufbery. They drew up unnoticed behind Brassfield, who concentrated on his head-on flurries with the Zeros in the Lufbery, and shot up his right wing. Glancing behind him, Brassfield discovered just how bad a spot he was in—Zeros tucked in tight on his tail. Like Mattson, he also had to dive to escape. Free of outside interference, the *Shōkaku* Zeros tore into Borries, forcing the dissolution of the Lufbery. The Japanese escort had soaked up the attentions of the interceptors and cleared the way for the dive bombers to approach the task force without interference.

One of the most respected dive bomber leaders in the Imperial Navy, Takahashi had never before faced such worthy opponents as the *Lexington* and the *Yorktown*. He chose for his *Shōkaku kanbaku* the nearer (and larger) flattop, the one he thought was the *Saratoga*, and signaled Lieut. Ema to take the *Zuikaku* Carrier Bomber Unit westward to attack the *Yorktown*-type carrier. Undisturbed by defending fighters, the nineteen *Shōkaku* carrier bombers deployed into a long string in final preparation for their dives. Once the actual attack commenced, individual *shōtai* leaders would lead their sections in from different bearings in order to confuse the antiaircraft gunners. Right now there was no need to do so. The *Lexington* had not yet spotted the dive bombers concealed cleverly in the sun.

Takahashi's assault on the *Lexington* began at 1121, when the lead *kanbaku* pushed over from 14,000 feet and aimed for her port bow. The flattop was in the process of completing the 180-degree turn to starboard begun during the torpedo attack, and now she steamed crosswind to the west. When first spotted by lookouts, the Japanese carrier bombers were already well into their dives. Despite the short notice, the *Lexington*'s massive antiaircraft battery reacted with a storm of fire. The first few *kanbaku* to attack received relatively little opposition, but those immediately after encountered an inferno of tracers. Usually noted for balky functioning and frequent jams, the 1.1-inch guns, of which the *Lexington* had forty-eight, for once performed, in the words of Gunnery Officer Lt. Cdr. Edward J. O'Donnell, "beyond expectations."[12] Seemingly indifferent, the Japanese pilots daringly held their dives to within 1,500 feet, then released their bombs and pulled out.

The first bomb to hit the *Lexington*, apparently one of the initial drops, struck the corner of the flight deck port-side forward, penetrated a thin metal plate under the wood planking, and entered the five-inch ready ammunition service locker. Detonating almost on impact, the 242-kilogram high-explosive "land bomb" emitted a huge sheet of bright reddish flame rising as high as the stack. The blast killed the entire crew of No. 6 five-inch gun, putting it out of commission. Fires flared up on deck and below, but repair parties soon contained them. The flight deck bulged slightly, but remained usable.

As the *Lexington* headed crosswind away from the attacking dive bombers, their dives became increasingly shallow, giving the antiaircraft gunners more time to shoot and also affecting the accuracy of the pilots. The Japanese smothered the *Lexington* with their near misses, some so close that even the *Lexington* men thought that additional torpedoes had struck her. One such bomb exploded deep in the water next to the hull. Above the waterline, the blast stove in the 20-mm gun platform in the gig boat pocket, and below, fragments penetrated two compartments and flooded them. Some near misses had actually passed through openings in the superstructure, notably one armor-piercing bomb that barely cleared the space between the bridge and the stack. Among this blizzard of projectiles, only one other bomb hit. This second bomb, dropped during a shallow dive, came in high and hit the port side of the massive smoke stack well above the flight deck. Fragments sprayed the area, raising havoc with crews manning .50-caliber machine guns on both sides of the stack. The hit also jammed the ship's siren, which continued to shriek throughout the attack. It appears the ship's own antiaircraft fire shot down one carrier bomber and roughed up several others. All in all, the *Lexington* suffered rather light damage in the dive bombing attack.

Antiaircraft fire was not the only peril the Japanese dive bombers had to face. After escaping from the Zeros that had jumped him at 12,000 feet, VF-42's Brassfield happened to catch sight of a carrier bomber diving on the *Lexington*. Using his superior speed, Brassfield drew up behind the *kanbaku* for a quick shot as the range narrowed swiftly. His bullets started the Japanese smoking, but that was not enough. Brassfield spiraled in to cut his speed and swung back for a second go at the target. By the time he pulled out at 3,000 feet in the midst of the *Lexington*'s fire, he had had the satisfaction of seeing the dive bomber flare up spectacularly in flames. It fell into the sea off the *Lexington*'s port bow. Either because of Brassfield or the *Lexington*'s AA, two *Shōkaku* carrier bombers were seen to dive on the *Lexington*, pull out short, and switch over to the *Yorktown* farther west, becoming the tail end of the attack on that ship.

Over the *Yorktown* waited a fighter section in relatively good position to intercept. McCormack and Haas of VF-42's section "Wildcat Brown" had received no orders from the FDO while the enemy strike group approached, so the two Grummans remained over the carrier. Evidently they did not spot the small torpedo attack against their flattop. Worried about a possible dive bombing attack, McCormack at 1121 told Haas to start climbing. Even while the fighters gained altitude, Lieut. Ema led his fourteen *Zuikaku* carrier bombers toward the *Yorktown*. He deployed his squadron into a long line in anticipation of attacking the carrier. Below, Buckmaster had had all the warning he needed by watching the dive bombers hit the *Lexington*. The *Yorktown* had worked up to over 30 knots and now headed south (crosswind). He was ready to use violent maneuvers to evade the bombs.

At 1124, the first *Zuikaku kanbaku* peeled off to dive. Meanwhile, McCormack and Haas just had passed 13,000 feet when they spotted below and slightly ahead the long string of enemy dive bombers waiting for their turn to attack. Rolling his F4F on its back, McCormack charged into the middle of the line with a short overhead run. He poured bullets into a target in the center of the formation, then pulled out to one side, approaching a second Japanese swiftly from the rear. Ignoring his opponent's rear gun and the *Yorktown*'s antiaircraft fire, McCormack closed to point-blank range and claimed the dive bomber when it fell away out of sight. Haas tackled the middle of the line and spiraled down along with the Japanese, corkscrewing his Grumman to loose a burst against any *kanbaku* that flicked across his gunsight. He then stayed at low level and mixed it up with retreating enemy planes. McCormack, on the other hand, headed back overhead to guard against a second wave of dive bombers.

Although the *Zuikaku* carrier bombers did not lose any of their numbers to fighter attack, McCormack's ambush certainly did not help their accuracy against the *Yorktown*. The Japanese pilots pressed their dives to the fullest extent, hurtling toward the *Yorktown* at angles of 70 degrees or more and not pulling out until below 1,000 feet. They claimed between eight and ten hits on a "*Yorktown*-type carrier," but they actually got only one, because of the crosswind dives, Buckmaster's skilled shiphandling, and section "Wildcat Brown." At 1127, one 250-kilogram "ordinary" bomb (semi-armor-piercing) struck the center of her flight deck forward of the middle elevator. Leaving a clean twelve-inch hole in the flight deck, the bombing penetrated four more decks (totaling almost two inches of steel) and detonated in an aviation storeroom situated on the armored deck. The force of the blast destroyed the compartment and the surrounding area, stove in hatches up to the hangar deck, and damaged bulkheads. Small fires ignited in several locations, venting dense, black smoke to the flight deck. Bomb fragments pierced the air intakes to three firerooms, forcing their temporary evacuation and briefly restricting the ship's speed to 25 knots.

Through their near misses, the Japanese inflicted a surprising amount of damage on the *Yorktown*. One 242-kilogram high-explosive bomb passed over the flight deck at a shallow angle, cut walkway lines under the starboard bow, then detonated in the water about fifty feet from her hull. Fragments holed the ship in four places. Another 250-kilogram bomb exploded deep in the water close port-side amidships and caved in a seam under the armored deck, opening a fuel oil bunker to the sea. Near misses seemed virtually to smother the carrier with water. The heavy smoke billowing out of the bomb hole in the flight deck gave the impression the *Yorktown* was much harder hit than she was. Engineering soon ventilated the three firerooms, put them back in service, and raised speed to 28 knots.

The *Yorktown* received assistance from one of the three wayward VF-2 escort pilots who had originally gone on the attack. Scoop Vorse's rump division escorting Bombing Two had lost contact with the SBDs and had to return to base. Vorse climbed high to use his Zed Baker homer. After a lengthy flight, he suddenly found himself over the task force and in the midst of five-inch antiaircraft shells bursting all around. Switching radio frequencies, Vorse picked up Gill's transmissions. Far below, he spotted a Japanese dive bomber about to attack the *Yorktown* from her starboard quarter—one of the two *Shōkaku kanbaku* that had switched over to the *Yorktown* after first diving on the *Lexington*. Flashing in from above, Vorse cornered the lone Japanese just after it pushed over into its dive. His bullets tore into the target. No flame erupted, but the .50-caliber slugs chopped off the *kanbaku*'s left wing and sent the mutilated aircraft flipping out of control toward the sea. Its bomb tumbled loose and raised a huge splash 300 yards off the *Yorktown*'s port beam, while the bomber and its fluttering wing fell into her wake. Vorse looked around for his two companions, but apparently they had missed his sudden break into an attack and were not in sight. Minus their leader, Bob Morgan and John Lackey separated to look for other game. The remaining *Shōkaku* carrier bomber attacked the *Yorktown*, but failed to score a hit.

The Japanese believed they had dealt mortal blows to at least one and probably both American flattops. Indeed, Takahashi at 1125 radioed that they had sunk the "*Saratoga.*" The strike crews claimed a total of nine torpedo and ten bomb hits on the "*Saratoga*," and two torpedo and eight to ten bomb hits on the *Yorktown*. Actually, as we have seen, they had not hurt Task Force 17 nearly so badly. Now the Japanese would have to fight their way back out the cordon of defending aircraft, already embroiled in several melees with escort Zeros.

The Scramble to Withdraw

Throughout the attacks on the *Lexington* and the *Yorktown* and for perhaps fifteen minutes thereafter, several wild free-for-alls raged between the defending F4Fs and SBDs on the one hand and the enemy Zeros, carrier bombers, and torpedo planes on the other. It made for a most confused melee while the Japanese forced their way through the American CAP and anti–torpedo-plane patrol. Basically there were three separate actions, although the composition of the combatants by no means stayed the same. The best way to describe them is to cover them in sequence and to give the cast of characters.

The "Low-Level Dogfight." This action involved the *Lexington* anti–torpedo-plane patrol and a number of VF-2 and VF-42 Grummans versus the retreating enemy strike planes and some Zero escorts. It took place low over the water just north of Task Force 17. American participants included the fifteen *Lexington* SBDs from Scouting Two and Bombing Two along with the following pilots:

VF-2
Lieut. Albert O. Vorse, Jr., USN
Ens. Leon W. Haynes, A-V(N)
Ens. Edward R. Sellstrom, Jr., A-V(N)

VF-42
Lieut. (jg) Arthur J. Brassfield, USN
Ens. Walter A. Haas, A-V(N)

Known Japanese Zero participants:

Zuikaku, 2nd *Chūtai*
     15th *Shōtai*
PO1c Makino Shigeru
PO2c Nakata Shigenobu
Sea1c Nisugi Toshitsugu

Shōkaku, 1st *Chūtai*
     2nd *Shōtai*
Lieut. Yamamoto Shigehisa (B)
PO1c Matsuda Jirō
PO2c Sasakibara Masao
     3rd *Shōtai*
PO1c Yamamoto Ichirō

Initiating the low-level dogfight were Sellstrom and the VS-2 SBDs intercepting the Japanese torpedo planes making their runs on the *Lexington*. Joining battle with them were three *Zuikaku* Zeros under PO1c Makino. One Japanese fighter ended up in hot pursuit of Sellstrom and latched onto his tail. Unable to shake the Mitsubishi, Doc finally found himself running at full power only 500 feet above the water. His only way out was to head for the nearest ship and hope that "friendly" antiaircraft gunners would brush the Zero off his tail, that is, before they managed to hit the Grumman. No doubt the vessel's gunners reported both the stubby F4F and its sleek Zero pursuer as torpedo planes, but they forced the Japanese to sheer off. Sellstrom made good his escape.

Joining the fight against the dispersed VS-2 SBDs after the fighter Lufbery broke up at 12,000 feet were four *Shōkaku* Zeros. They jumped the Dauntless flown by William Hall, riddling his aircraft and wounding him painfully in both ankles. Hall, however, was not about to give up. His aggressive counterattacks earned him the Medal of Honor. The Japanese also crippled the SBD flown by Lieut. (jg) Roy O. Hale. Coming to his aid was another tough VS-2 pilot, John Leppla. Leppla and his gunner, John Liska, ARM3c, charged after any Zeros within reach. Probably wounded, Hale at 1129 tried to land on board the *Lexington*. The carrier bombers had just pulled off, but the ships' gunners were wary of a second wave. As it approached the *Lexington*'s stern, the SBD was hit by a torrent of antiaircraft fire from the *Lexington* and surrounding vessels and splashed off the cruiser *New Orleans*'s starboard bow. The crew did not survive. One SBD had a long fight with a Zero that killed the rear gunner, John O. Edwards, ARM2c, but the pilot, Lieut. (jg) Chandler W. Swanson, escaped even though the Japanese had nearly shot away his control wires. Ens. Robert Smith, who had shot down two *kankō*, had better luck and escaped the Zero which attacked him.

Ens. Frank R. McDonald of Bombing Two had a nasty encounter with a Zero that put a bullet into his right shoulder and wounded his gunner as well. Fighting the pain and his own battered SBD, McDonald also sought a haven in the *Lexington*'s direction and had to run the gauntlet of antiaircraft fire for a deferred forced landing. The *Lexington* was turning still fully 120 degrees out of the wind, when at 1134 McDonald approached with hopes of landing. Ignoring a waveoff, the SBD "in a wild diving turn"[13] slammed into the flight deck, broke an arresting wire, then bounced over the corner of the deck and into the sea. Both aviators scrambled free of their sinking SBD and awaited rescue by the destroyer *Morris*.

Makino's three *Zuikaku* Zeros had stayed only a short time, but Yamamoto's *Shōkaku* pilots stayed low and kept fighting. In their excitement they claimed no fewer than six dive bombers—three to Yamamoto Ichirō alone—as well as ten Grummans. SBD pilots found game in the presence of enemy strike planes retreating low over the water. Ens. Richard F. Neely of VS-2 claimed two torpedo planes and did splash one *Shōkaku kankō*. Joining the fight were several SBDs from Bombing Two. Lieut. (jg) Robert Buchan overhauled a *Shōkaku* torpedo plane and shot it down. His synchronization gear functioned so poorly that he shot holes in his own propeller! Likewise Ens. John M. Clarke attacked a retiring carrier bomber and dumped it into the sea. Conversely Ens. Robert P. Williams was jumped by a carrier bomber after it had attacked the *Lexington*. Flying side by side the two rear gunners exchanged fire like two eighteenth-century naval frigates, then the aircraft flew away in different directions. After missing out intercepting incoming torpedo planes when all of his guns jammed, Lieut. (jg) Paul J. Knapp chased a withdrawing *Zuikaku* carrier attack plane for several miles before he realized he had no way to harm it.

Another participant of the low-level melee near the *Lexington* was VF-2's Lee Haynes, Eder's wingman in section "Agnes White." The two had returned to the vicinity of the task force after fruitlessly hunting torpedo planes in the clouds, and arrived back just as the torpedo attack went in. They separated from each other when Eder climbed after one target which proved to be a Zero, while Haynes spotted two torpedo planes much lower down. His targets were a pair of carrier attack planes that had just released torpedoes against the *Lexington* and sought escape to the north. They may have been the two Nakajimas that had attacked off the *Lex*'s starboard bow. In any case, Haynes attacked at low altitude and heavily damaged one torpedo plane, receiving credit for a probable kill.

Near the *Yorktown* there occurred a series of low-altitude combats. Pursuing *Zuikaku* dive bombers after they had hit his carrier, VF-42's Walt Haas happened upon a Zero low over the water. He charged after it, only to discover a second Mitsubishi on his tail. He headed into antiaircraft fire from the ships, hoping like Sellstrom before him that the gunners would recognize him and concentrate on his pursuer. However, he quickly found that their fire was aimed at him, and he raced for the sanctuary of a nearby cloud. Emerging from the other side, Haas flushed a retreating carrier bomber just above the wave tops. A quick burst sent the *kanbaku* spinning into the sea. Haas tried to overtake another Zero from behind, but the Mitsubishi had too good a lead. Haas broke off and headed back toward the ships. Scoop Vorse, diving in after shooting down the *Shōkaku* carrier bomber over the *Yorktown*, pulled out low near the ships, and was surprised to see a Zero fly directly across his front. Making only a slight turn, Vorse adjusted his aim and fired a long burst. He saw the Zero smoke and thought he got it.

Also fresh from his kill of a *Shōkaku kanbaku*, Art Brassfield leveled out not far from the *Lexington*. To his dismay, he caught sight of three Zeros in formation perched just above him. He hoped the enemy had not noticed him, but no such luck. The leader peeled off to make a firing pass. Reacting quickly, Brassfield hauled into a climbing turn to scissor his attacker and upset his aim. He succeeded. The Zero flashed past him in a dive, then appeared to pause ahead of the Grumman as the Japanese tried to climb away. Brassfield swiftly brought up the nose of his aircraft to give the Zero proper deflection, then gave it a proper burst. Evidently damaged, the Japanese fell away out of view.

Brassfield had no time to watch the fate of the enemy leader, the other two Zeros having scrambled onto his tail. From close astern they thoroughly shot up Brassfield's Grumman. "The 7.7 bullets were clattering on my armor plate," he later wrote. "Then there was a hell of a thing, much noise and smoke in my cockpit."[14] One of the Japanese had punched a 20-mm explosive round through the left side of the cockpit. The cannon shell brushed Brassfield's left elbow, then detonated in the clock on the instrument panel, shrapnel perforating his left knee. To add to his troubles, it ignited a small but smoky fire in the cotton supply he kept to stuff in his ears. Fortunately a convenient cloud beckoned, and Brassfield slipped inside to elude his pursuers. Later examination revealed his F4F to have ten holes in the fuselage, including one in his main fuel tank, which did not leak— a tribute to the self-sealing design.

The Medium-Altitude Melee. Above the low-level fight raged a series of separate encounters at medium altitude (12,000 feet and under) between CAP fighters and Zeros from the *Shōkaku* Fighter Unit. Known participants are listed in the table (p. 262).

The medium-altitude melees originated with the break-up of the Lufbery Circle at 12,000 feet, when eight *Shōkaku* fighters tore into Fred Borries's four Grummans. Three of the *Shōkaku* fighters soon descended to join the low-level fighting, but five led by the unit commander Hoashi stayed high to battle Grummans. Trouble for the Americans was that the Zeros fought as a team against mostly isolated F4Fs.

Nothing definite is now known of the subsequent actions of the VF-2 sections "Doris Red" (Borries and Dufilho) and "Doris White" (Rinehart and Mason).

American:

VF-2

Lt. Cdr. Paul H. Ramsey, USN
Lieut. Fred Borries, USN
Lieut. (jg) Marion W. Dufilho, USN
Lieut. (jg) Robert J. Morgan, USN
Lieut. (jg) Clark F. Rinehart, USN
Ens. Willard E. Eder, A-V(N)
Ens. Newton H. Mason, A-V(N)
Ens. George F. Markham, Jr., A-V(N)

VF-42

Lieut. (jg) E. Duran Mattson, USN
Ens. Edgar R. Bassett, A-V(N)

Japanese:

Shōkaku Fighter Unit, 1st *Chūtai*

        1st *Shōtai*

Lieut. Hoashi Takumi, *buntaichō*
PO1c Nishide Korenobu
PO3c Horiguchi Shunji

        3rd *Shōtai*

W.O. Hanzawa Yukuo
Sea1c Kawano Shigeru

"Doris Red" ended up on board the *Lexington* after a very hard time with Zeros. It is not certain whether Borries and Dufilho claimed any victories. Both pilots in "Doris White" failed to return from this battle, and apparently no Americans saw them go down. Clark Rinehart entered the Navy in 1937 in the original aviation cadet program and earned his wings the next year. All of his subsequent service was in *Lexington* squadrons, first Bombing Two, then, from 1941, Fighting Two with a commission in the regular Navy. He earned praise for his strafing of the enemy I-boat on 10 January. Appointed an aviation cadet in February 1941, Newton Mason received his first operational posting after earning his wings to Fighting Three in January 1942. The eighth of May saw his first and only combat. Almost certainly both VF-2 pilots fell at the hands of *Shōkaku* Zero pilots. The five Japanese between them claimed eleven Grummans confirmed and two likely shot down without loss to themselves.

Also at medium altitude, VF-42's Duran Mattson (Brassfield's wingman in "Wildcat Orange") found himself tangling with the agile Zeros in similar peril and frustration. After diving away from the first Zero to jump on his tail, Mattson eluded his pursuer in the clouds and recovered with a zoom climb. As he broke into the sunlight above the cloud bank, he flew into the midst of several more Zeros. Turning into a head-on run with one Mitsubishi, he discovered another shooting up his tail. The only solution was to run for the clouds, and Mattson made it. Then, automatically, he made another zoom climb to regain altitude and realized as he emerged into the clear how stupid it was to climb right back into trouble. Luck was with him, for the sky was clear.

Joining on Mattson's wing was another separated VF-42 wingman, Edgar Bassett from Flatley's division. The two looked back in the direction of Task Force 17 and saw antiaircraft bursts and other evidence the Japanese were still around. Suddenly a *shōtai* of Zeros flew across their front, and the Japanese eagerly attacked. Mattson and Bassett both turned into their opponents to scissor. In his opposite attack, Mattson shot up one Zero, but as usual a second rode his tail. Again, Mattson had to dive away in order to brush the Zero off inside the clouds. Separating from him, Bassett also escaped the Zeros.

Inside the cloud, Mattson cleared his tail and maneuvered to make his zoom climb toward a different area. Back in the open and climbing, he spotted the Zeros, now below and moving away. Nosing over to gain speed, Mattson slowly overhauled the trailing Mitsubishi from above and behind. As he was about to shoot, his target noticed the Grumman stalking it from astern and reefed into a tight, climbing turn to the right. Mattson fired a snap burst, then used his diving speed to try to follow the twisting Zero into its tight, climbing spiral. Inevitably the F4F stalled out with the Zero still above and ready to swoop on its tail. Letting his nose drop, Mattson started to dive away. Beneath him he found another Japanese in good position to be attacked. As he scissored the Zero, it turned up into him for a head-on shot. Mattson fired and held the trigger until he dived past. He thought he inflicted mortal damage on this Zero, but had no time to confirm his victory. His original quarry was already close on his tail, and Mattson just headed on down toward the friendly refuge of the cloud layer.

Zooming out of the clouds once again, Mattson found the sky above him clear, but not far away another formation of Zeros leaving the area. Making an underneath-astern approach, he fired into the trailing Zero, then dived away swiftly. The Japanese did not follow. Mattson later acknowledged his debt to the clouds: "If it had been a clear day, I'm sure I would have quickly died."[15] He also felt most grateful to the "Grumman Iron Works" for providing him with a fighter that could really take it. His F4F had no fewer than twenty-one hits by 20-mm cannon shells and numerous 7.7-mm holes; its vertical stabilizer and colorful red and white striped rudder were in tatters. No doubt his Grumman was claimed numerous times as kills by Lieut. Hoashi's *Shōkaku* pilots.

Bob Morgan, one of the three VF-2 pilots who had returned prematurely from the strike, had a fight similar to that of Mattson. While the other two F4Fs in his division became involved with the dive bombing attack on the *Yorktown,* Morgan tussled intermittently with Zeros for the next several minutes. He used hit-and-run and hide-in-the-clouds in order to make repeated attacks. Whenever he made a firing pass, one or more of the Japanese would jump on his tail and chase him back into the overcast. Morgan then would fly blind for a few moments. When the opportunity presented itself, he charged out of his place of concealment, traded shots with the waiting Zeros, and again ran back to safety. Despite running very low on fuel, he succeeded in returning to the ships and reported the destruction of one Zero.

Another *Lexington* pilot battling solo at medium altitude was Bill Eder. On returning to the task force after his fruitless hunt for torpedo planes, he sighted enemy aircraft above and climbed at the same time his wingman Haynes dived away after other targets. From underneath Eder stalked a Zero, but the Japanese turned into him for a head-on run. Both opponents opened up at long range. Eder noticed the 20-mm shells reaching out toward him, but the tracers fell short, whereas his own bullets bracketed the target and struck home. He claimed the Zero as it roared past trailing smoke. Next Eder saw what he thought was an enemy Type 96 or 97 fighter and made his run from abeam. His shells caused the target to smoke heavily, but the Japanese took refuge in neighboring clouds. His target likely was a Type 99 carrier bomber, as the dive bombers were the only aircraft present with fixed landing gear and wheel spats.

Last to enter the melee from high altitude were Ramsey and Markham of Fighting Two. Because of initial poor positioning by the FDO, Ramsey was unable to catch the enemy carrier bombers before they dived. Instead he and his wingman followed them back toward the task force and climbed to 17,000 feet en route. From that height and with scattered clouds, it was difficult to discern targets below. Not until after the dive bombing attacks did Ramsey finally spot a lone Japanese fighter flying far below at around 4,000 feet. He later reported it as a German "ME-109," which the enemy was rumored to have. According to another fighter pilot, his misidentification was:

> Not as bad a mistake as it sounds. Zero had an out-sized propellor spinner and compact radial engine. From some angles the general visual impression was of a long nose, *i.e.* in line engine. Later familiarity with Zero in all its aspects eliminated this kind of mis-identification.[16]

Motioning for his wingman to follow, Ramsey dived in at high speed. He opened fire from above and behind his target, holding down the trigger as he rapidly closed the range. It surprised him that this Japanese did not blaze up, in contrast to those he fought the previous evening. Ramsey recovered below in order to zoom up to altitude for another attack. Markham took over from astern of his skipper. He saw his tracers hit, but the Zero then turned very tightly and scooted into a cloud. Markham stayed on his tail and followed him into the whiteness, only to lose sight of the Japanese and his leader as well. Ramsey later reported the target was smoking heavily, but as it did not burn, he claimed only a probable with an assist for Markham. Slightly above him, Ramsey noticed another Japanese fighter flying just over a cloud. He turned to make a low-opposite approach, fired, then claimed the Zero as it fell away out of sight. Fighting Two's skipper spotted no other targets and took station over the task force. Markham likewise located no enemy planes and later rejoined Ramsey over the *Lexington*.

Flatley's Dogfight.

American participants:
Lt. Cdr. James H. Flatley, Jr., USN
Lieut. (jg) Richard G. Crommelin, USN
Lieut. (jg) Brainard T. Macomber, A-V(N)
Ens. Edgar R. Bassett, A-V(N)

Japanese:
Zuikaku Fighter Unit, 2nd *Chūtai*
    14th *Shōtai*
Lieut. Tsukamoto Yūzō, *buntaichō*
PO1c Kiyomatsu Ginji
PO2c Okura Shigeru
    15th *Shōtai*
PO1c Makino Shigeru
PO2c Nakata Shigenobu
Sea1c Nisugi Toshitsugu
    16th *Shōtai*
PO1c Kanō Satoshi
PO1c Kamei Tomio
Sea1c Kurata Nobutaka

The third distinct air battle took place northwest of Task Force 17 and involved the four F4Fs of Jimmy Flatley's VF-42 division. Scrambled at the news of the enemy's approach, Flatley had headed out at low level under orders from Gill. He fully expected to intercept Japanese torpedo planes, but saw none. At 1115, Gill ordered Flatley up to "Angels 10," 10,000 feet, probably to take on dive bombers reported by Ramsey as headed for the ships. This thoroughly confused the VF-42 pilots as to what they were to intercept. Climbing, Flatley's division cut through the scud around 6,000 feet and beheld the panorama of a modern sea battle: wildly maneuvering ships, black antiaircraft bursts, and burning aircraft. At 1119, Flatley reported he was astern of the ships and nearing 10,000 feet altitude. Impatiently he demanded: "Give me something to do!"[17] By this time the FDO had lost control of the situation—his radar display ablaze with contacts—and could only tell Flatley to hurry back as the enemy was attacking.

Searching the area for targets, Flatley at 1123 caught sight of several Zeros beleaguring SBDs about five miles north of the ships. The Japanese were six fighters from the 14th and 16th *Shōtai*, *Zuikaku* Fighter Unit, led by the junior *buntaichō*, Lieut. Tsukamoto. In the last five minutes they had shot down four of the eight VS-5 SBDs on anti–torpedo-plane patrol without sustaining any losses of their own. Busy making runs on the surviving Dauntlesses flying at between 5,000 and 6,000 feet, they did not notice Flatley's approach from above.

With a call of "Bandits! Enemy fighters down here. Let's go!,"[18] Flatley led the four F4Fs into a shallow, high-speed dive, hoping to bounce the Zeros with a swift surprise attack. He and his wingman Dick Crommelin singled out one Mitsubishi leveling out at 6,000 feet after shooting up an SBD. To the two Grummans screaming in with a high-side attack, the target presented a full deflection shot as it crossed from right to left in front of them. Allotting sufficient lead, Flatley at 400 yards triggered a ranging burst, then paused until the Zero loomed at 200 yards before shooting in earnest. Tracers from a three-second burst straddled his target, and the Zero spun away out of sight. Adhering to his doctrine of hit-and-run tactics, Flatley steepened his dive and used his speed to make a zoom climb to regain altitude advantage.

Crommelin was eager to shoot as well. Concentrating intensely on the Zero, he loosed a two-second burst as the Japanese flashed through his sights. In the process, however, he lost contact with his leader, not noticing that Flatley in diving had drawn behind and beneath him. More Zeros prowled at his level or below, and Crommelin charged after them. Macomber and Bassett followed the lead section into the fight and saw the Zeros scatter. Both pilots separated in order to engage Zeros individually.

Regaining altitude, Flatley climbed above the scene of his first fight, but could locate neither his division nor the enemy. He turned toward the task force, looked in that direction for a time, but, sighting no enemy, headed back in the direction he had come. He came upon three Zeros cruising in formation below. It appears likely these were PO1c Makino's 15th *Zuikaku shōtai* moving northwest to rejoin the rest of their 2nd *Chūtai*. Flatley immediately attacked, following his principle, "Never hesitate to dive in."[19] He took as his quarry the trailing Japanese and hurtled in from above and behind. As he drew into range, his target, evidently warned by one of the others, swung sharply toward the F4F and pulled into a steep, climbing turn. This spoiled Flatley's aim, but he was intent on staying with the Mitsubishi. He drew the stick back and hauled his Grumman into a tight zoom climb.

The G forces proved too much, and for a second or two Flatley blacked out. Regaining vision, he found his excessive speed had taken him from behind the Zero to up alongside the climbing Japanese. The enemy pilot worked to chop his own speed to drop back behind the F4F for an easy stern shot. More trouble loomed for Flatley because his steeply climbing F4F rapidly neared a stall—air speed fell to 110 knots and less. Spinning out at the top of the climb would put him at the mercy of the Zero jockeying onto his tail. Thinking quickly, Flatley executed a half loop. While upside down, he saw the other two Japanese clawing after him. The only thing to do was to complete the loop and dive away at high speed. He held the dive until the waves grew in his sights, then withdrew at high speed, twisting to prevent a good shot from astern. Evidently the Zeros did not follow, for when he looked back, his tail was clear. Flatley encountered no more enemy aircraft, nor did he find the rest of his division.

Crommelin had a series of adventures with three or four *Zuikaku* Zeros. Losing contact with Flatley in the first dive, he discovered another Zero below him and off to one side. Corkscrewing to cut his speed and close in behind for a good shot, he fired one burst with unobserved results and quickly left the Japanese behind. Recovering at 3,000 feet, he started climbing, but picked out just ahead another Zero flying in the same direction he was. Adding throttle, Crommelin roared in from astern and triggered a long burst. Startled by red tracers, the Zero flipped into a climbing left turn. With his zoom climb, Crommelin had the speed to overtake and keep firing while he climbed steeply. Smoke pouring out its cowling, the Mitsubishi dived out of sight, leading Crommelin to believe he had set the Zero ablaze. At that moment he discerned another Japanese beneath him, this time heading away. Rolling out of his climb, he spiraled down onto the target's tail, his speed enabling him to close the range swiftly. Likewise at first sight of the broad bands of tracers, the Zero pilot pulled into a steep climbing turn to the left— apparently the standard Japanese defensive maneuver. Crommelin gave him a good burst and was certain he had heavily damaged, if not destroyed, the enemy. He saw his bullets tear chunks out of the Mitsubishi, which nosed down and spun out of its climb.

So far Crommelin had been the hunter, shooting at four Zeros in succession and claiming two of them. As he leveled out, he heard gunfire and jerked his head back to see a Zero dancing in firing position close behind. He utilized his own standard defensive maneuver, a high-speed dive, and left the Zero behind. Evidently the Grumman's quick pushover, a maneuver that could cause a Zero's engine (served by a float-type carburetor) to cut out, had been sufficient to shake the Japanese riding his tail. Pulling automatically into a zoom climb, Crommelin un- wittingly flew right back into the gang of Zeros he had just fought. The *Zuikaku* boys were as surprised as he was. The next two or three minutes Crommelin flipped wildly about, loosing snap shots at any Japanese who flicked across his sights. No Zero was able to jump his tail and stay there long enough for a telling burst. The Japanese admired the F4F pilots for this type of violent maneuvering. Somehow Crommelin fought clear of the melee and resumed climbing.

Again gunfire sounded ominously behind him. One of the Zero pilots had seen Crommelin break away and stalked him, easing close on his tail. The eager Japanese blazed away with machine guns and cannons. Dropping his nose swiftly, Crommelin fled toward a small cloud. Entering the white refuge, he banked sharply in a 180- degree left spiral and exited underneath. The Zero was still with him, but thankfully farther back—at 500 yards, beyond effective range. Diving once again, Crommelin accelerated to speeds at which the Grumman's superior control offered him an advantage. When he thought he had enough knots, he turned radically to one side to present his opponent with a full deflection shot. The maneuver also set him up for a counter should the Zero overshoot and pass by. The enemy, however, was no longer in sight, so Crommelin sought altitude once again. He noticed two or three aircraft in the area and determined they were friendly.

As his Grumman moved skyward, Crommelin happened to see oil on his left wing and ruefully realized he was in trouble. He sought out a flight deck and spotted the brave *Lexington* in the distance. The Pratt & Whitney soured and seized noisily as the oil pressure failed, turning the Grumman into a glider. Evidently enemy bullets had either holed one of the wingroot oil coolers or nicked an oil line. When his engine quit, Crommelin was still two or three miles off the *Lexington*'s port side. Reporting his plight at 1133 by radio, he glided to try to ditch ahead of the *Lexington* formation. Reacting calmly, he made what he modestly called, "a fairly smooth water landing,"[20] his Wildcat remaining afloat long enough for him to retrieve his liferaft. The huge *Lexington* and her escorts bore down on the rubber boat. On board the *Lexington*, correspondent Stanley Johnston noticed him:

> He is just off our starboard bow and only 100 yards from our track. As we sweep past him, I can see him on his knees wildly cheering and waving at us.[21]

The destroyer *Phelps* cut out of formation and at 1144 brought Crommelin on board.

In the first attack, Brainard Macomber, leading Flatley's second section ("Wildcat Blue"), spotted a lone Zero flying above the rest. He went after the Mitsubishi by using a hit-and-run pass from high astern. Macomber hoped to make his run swiftly and regain altitude advantage, but the Japanese saw him coming and pulled into a climb. Much more cautious after his near-disastrous encounter the day before with the *Shōhō* Zero, Macomber was loath to surrender altitude advantage. Likewise he began to ascend, moving into what became a circling, climbing match with the Mitsubishi. He expected his opponent to outclimb him, but instead the Zero seemed content to stay below and across the diameter of the spiral. Macomber grew increasingly puzzled over the failure of the Japanese to attack or do anything other than climb.

Climbing at full throttle, maximum rpm, and a low air speed, Macomber's engine overheated and began to miss. By the time he passed 14,000 feet, he felt he had sufficient altitude to dive away if necessary. Dropping his nose, he stalled into a turn down across the circle toward the enemy. As the F4F swung around, the Zero countered adroitly by turning up into Macomber for a head-on shot. A second later, the Japanese changed his mind and easily moved away by holding his tight, climbing turn as Macomber shot from long range. Continuing his dive, Macomber flashed past the Zero and left it behind, if indeed the Japanese tried to pursue. Recovering at low altitude, he looked for but could locate no other targets. Later he joined up with Flatley over the task force. "The Zero very effectively removed me from the fight," he later recounted, "although I have never been able to understand his seeming lack of aggressiveness."[22] One logical explanation is that the Japanese had run out of ammunition.

Very little is known of Bassett's activities during this fight. He followed Macomber in and evidently attacked one of the Zeros milling around in the area, but the Japanese neutralized him as well. Later he was to be found in the direction of the task force and joined on Mattson's wing. As told earlier, the two then picked a fight with several Zeros. Both had to evade Japanese countermoves. Bassett subsequently reported his fuel and ammunition in good shape, and following the fight he remained on duty over the task force for another ninety minutes.

From the opening shots, what was a division of four VF-42 fighters became four separate aircraft fighting alone without support, ultimately outnumbered more than two to one. Flatley's division claimed a total of three Zeros destroyed (two to

Crommelin and one to Flatley) and at least three more damaged. In return, the division lost Crommelin's F4F shot down, but the pilot was uninjured. As related previously, it appears most probable that the four F4Fs had tangled with the nine Zeros of the *Zuikaku*'s 2nd *Chūtai*. In this fight (as in all the rest over Task Force 17) no Zeros were shot down, although one did not reach its carrier. PO2c Okura Shigeru from the *Zuikaku*'s 14th *Shōtai* flew to Deboyne and ditched there safely. The remaining eight *Zuikaku* Zeros as well as all nine *Shōkaku* Zeros returned to MO Striking Force.

Task Force 17 Regroups

As the air attack abated and the Japanese strike planes withdrew from the area, Task Force 17 took stock of damage and losses. With her escort of two heavy cruisers and four destroyers, the *Lexington* steamed northward after the dive bombing attack. Sherman brought her to starboard to come into the wind, as several damaged aircraft waited to come on board. At 1139, two badly shot up VS-2 SBDs took the opportunity to land. One was flown by Hall, who was shot through both legs, and the other by Swanson, with his dead rearseat man. A quick look convinced flight deck personnel that both Dauntlesses were unserviceable. Damage control at 1142 reported the small flight deck fire port-side forward to be extinguished, and the flattop readied to recover more aircraft. Quick to land were two pairs of fuel-starved F4Fs flown by Borries and Dufilho (CAP section "Doris Red"), and Vorse and Lackey from the aborted strike escort. Eight SBDs also thudded down on deck: six from Scouting Two (including skipper Dixon just returned from the morning search) and two from Bombing Two.

The *Lexington*'s damage control parties worked hard to put her back in order. Her engineering officer arranged to transfer fuel oil from port to starboard to counteract her list, while fire fighters handled the blaze burning under the flight deck near the port-side forward gun galleries. Duckworth, the air officer, realized his two flight deck elevators were out for good because of damage to their hydraulic system. Having no access to the hangar deck would make things a bit cramped when his own strike aircraft returned. To make some room, he ordered Hall's and Swanson's SBDs stripped and jettisoned over the side. He also was quite concerned with the aviation gasoline fueling systems. The port fuel lines were out of commission as a result of the forward torpedo hit, but the starboard lines were intact. Duckworth took no chances and suspended all refueling until all fires were extinguished. He arranged careful inspections for both fuel systems, which detected no major leaks. Gasoline, however, trickled from small leaks in the port stowage tanks, and fumes collected in certain areas forward in the ship—constituting an unseen but critical danger. From the outside at least, the *Lexington* seemed in fine shape, her appearance marred mostly by the heavy oil slick trailing in her wake. After landing planes, she swung back to port and headed northeast along the Point Option course. At 1220, Fitch reported to the task force commander that the *Lexington* had taken two torpedo hits, possibly more, but noted all fires were reported out and that the ship could steam at 24 knots. There seemed reason for optimism in Task Force 17.

To one highly interested observer, the *Lexington* began to look remarkably healthy after the pounding his strike planes had dealt her. *Hikōtaichō* Takahashi had lingered near the American task force, evidently to watch his "*Saratoga*" go under. That expected event failed to occur, and with alarming rapidity the carrier increased speed and conducted flight operations. At 1217, he instructed his radioman to tap out a message to MO Striking Force: "Cancel sinking report of *Saratoga*.

Wait."[23] Takahashi then apparently turned for home, no doubt disgusted at the turn of events, traveling as fast as he dared in order to present his superiors with vital new information about the results of his strike.

Screened by three heavy cruisers and three destroyers, the *Yorktown* moved southward rapidly during the dive bombing attack, and in the process separated from the *Lexington* group. The *Yorktown*'s lone bomb hit did not affect flight operations, and the resulting fires were soon out. She could make at least 25 knots with prospects for more once damage control had finished their work. At 1131, the carrier's CXAM radar suddenly quit. Because the *Lexington* was not transmitting over the fighter circuit, Pederson told the CAP to "Protect the force!"[24] Two minutes later, the *Yorktown* instructed the *Chester*'s radar officer to handle fighter direction, not an easy chore, but canceled the order at 1141. Gill returned to the air soon after that, and both carriers proceeded with the reorganization of the CAP and preparations to recover their strike planes returning from MO Striking Force.

Launched over two hours before, McCormack's VF-42 division labored under a critical fuel shortage, not to mention that two of the Grummans were shot up. Both McCormack (section "Wildcat Brown") and Brassfield ("Wildcat Orange") requested permission to "pancake" (land on board), Brassfield taking priority because he was wounded. At 1139 he descended into the landing circle, lowered his tail hook and wheels, but discovered his flaps would not work. Warning the ship about his flaps, he flew along the *Yorktown*'s starboard side, then banked left across the bow to begin the downwind leg of his landing approach. Then he heard over the radio, "Get that one going across the bow!" Looking around, he discovered that *he* was the one they were going to get. Expecting a storm of antiaircraft fire, Brassfield was relieved to hear:

> . . . the southern drawl of our gunnery officer [Lt. Cdr. Ernest J. Davis] say, "Oh, let's don't shoot down that one. That's one of ours."[25]

At 1141, Brassfield landed safely, displaying his noted finesse despite his wounds and the absence of landing flaps.

Around 1145, the *Yorktown* took on board four F4F Wildcats. First to land were the two pilots of section "Wildcat Brown," McCormack and Haas. McCormack was surprised to have his engine die from fuel starvation while the aircraft still sat in the arresting gear. Following them was Mattson, Brassfield's wingman in "Wildcat Orange," his F4F so badly shot up the air officer immediately consigned it to the hangar deck. Also coming on board was a VF-2 orphan, Ramsey's errant wingman Sellstrom. The air department likewise hoped to recover the SBDs from the anti–torpedo-plane patrol, but evidently the survivors were not ready to land. The *Yorktown* changed course to the northeast to rejoin the *Lexington* about seven miles away.

A total of twenty Grumman F4F fighters and twenty-three Douglas SBD dive bombers participated in the defense of Task Force 17. Their losses totaled three F4Fs (two from VF-2, one from VF-42) and five SBDs shot down, while another SBD was lost in a landing accident on board the *Lexington*. Other fighters and dive bombers damaged beyond repair managed to land on board the carriers. American aerial victory claims amounted to ten fighters, four dive bombers, and one torpedo plane for Fighting Two and Fighting Forty-two, while the three dive bombing squadrons reported the destruction of six fighters, one dive bomber, and ten torpedo planes, for a grand total of thirty-two enemy planes. From a correlation of Japanese and American sources, it appears reasonable that the F4Fs actually

Fighter Credits, 8 May 1942, Combat Air Patrol

Fighting Two:	
Lt. Cdr. Paul H. Ramsey	1 ME-109
	½ ME-109 prob.
Lieut. Albert O. Vorse, Jr.	1 VSB
	1 Type 00 fighter
Lieut. (jg) Robert J. Morgan	1 Type 00 fighter
Ens. Willard E. Eder	1 Type 00 fighter
	1 Type 96 fighter (prob.)
Ens. Leon W. Haynes	1 VT prob.
Ens. Edward R. Sellstrom, Jr.	2 Type 00 fighters
	1 VT
Ens. George F. Markham, Jr.	½ ME-109 prob.
Fighting Forty-two:	
Lt. Cdr. James H. Flatley	1 Zero fighter
	1 Zero fighter damaged
Lieut. Vincent F. McCormack	1 Type 99 dive bomber
	½ Type 97 flying boat
Lieut. (jg) Richard G. Crommelin	2 Zero fighters
	2 Zero fighters damaged
Lieut. (jg) Arthur J. Brassfield	1 Type 99 dive bomber
	1 Zero fighter
Lieut. (jg) E. Duran Mattson	1 Zero fighter damaged
Ens. Walter A. Haas	1 Type 99 dive bomber
	½ Type 97 flying boat
Ens. Edgar R. Bassett	1 Zero fighter (assist)

shot down no Zeros, but perhaps splashed three dive bombers and one torpedo plane, while the SBD crews accounted for no Zeros, but downed one dive bomber and five torpedo planes—total ten Japanese aircraft destroyed by aerial engagement. American antiaircraft fire from the ships likely destroyed one dive bomber and two torpedo planes. Many other Japanese planes sustained heavy damage from all causes, as out of the strike group seven ditched and twelve were later jettisoned.

RETURN OF THE STRIKE GROUPS

Both American and Japanese carrier striking groups had attacked their intended targets, and by noon the aircraft had started back toward their own carriers. As they flew essentially within the same air corridor, there were bound to be altercations between the two sides. First to fall to enemy fighters was the *Shōkaku* carrier attack plane commanded by Kanno Kenzō. He had made the heroic decision to guide the Japanese strike force to the American carriers he had located several hours before. Kanno departed only after Lt. Cdr. Takahashi had sighted the targets. Desperately conserving his fuel for the long return flight to *Shōkaku*, Kanno saw his luck run out when he encountered elements of the *Yorktown* Air Group on the way back from their own attack. About halfway between the two carrier task forces, Bill Woollen and Johnny Adams happened to spot an enemy torpedo plane approaching from ahead and beneath them. Diving in, the two VF-42 pilots executed a shallow high-side pass in succession. Kanno's pilot, PO1c Gotō Tsuguo, responded with a climbing turn in order to escape into cloud cover, but the F4Fs had the speed to overtake from astern. Together they shot the torpedo plane down in flames. The brave Kanno and his two crewmen perished. Recognizing their valor, the Imperial Navy on 1 January 1943 awarded the three men a posthumous letter of commendation personally signed by Admiral Yamamoto.

Fighting Forty-two's skipper Chas Fenton and his wingman Harry Gibbs were feeling frustrated at not being able to rejoin the *Yorktown* dive bombers before they attacked. Cruising in intermittent cloud cover on the flight back to Task Force 17, they happened upon a pair of Japanese dive bombers approaching from the south. The two *kanbaku* were part of the returning strike group, which never had a chance to rendezvous and gain fighter escort. The two Grummans dived in for a high-opposite attack. Flashing past at high speed, Fenton saw he had started one carrier bomber smoking and losing altitude, but he had neither the fuel nor the inclination to investigate whether his target had actually splashed. Consequently he reported only a probable kill, but in retrospect it appears likely he and Gibbs did contribute to the heavy losses sustained in this battle by the *Shōkaku* Carrier Bomber Unit.

Accompanying the torpedo planes, VF-42's Bill Leonard carefully shepherded the shot-up SBD piloted by VB-5's Ben Preston. Leonard had seen Woollen and Adams break off and return shortly thereafter, but he did not see their kill. Soon, however, he would have his own chance. As the little formation neared Task Force 17, Leonard caught sight of a Japanese dive bomber approaching at low altitude and on an opposite heading. Leonard left formation and maneuvered to make a firing run. Surprisingly, the Japanese pilot made no move to evade the Grumman's bullets, acting almost as if he were resigned to death. Leonard quickly inflicted mortal damage on the *kanbaku*. Trailing thick smoke, the carrier bomber fell off on one wing and started down toward the sea. Leonard did not have the fuel to follow his opponent and confirm the victory. Instead he wanted to rejoin his crippled SBD charge; so he noted a probable victory only.

The aircraft claimed as unconfirmed by Leonard did indeed splash in the Coral Sea. There is little doubt that Leonard's victim was *hikōtaichō* Takahashi, the senior Japanese pilot on the mission. He met his end while racing back to MO Striking Force to report that the attack was not so successful as first thought. With his death, the Imperial Navy lost a most courageous and valuable leader. Admiral Yamamoto acknowledged Takahashi's contributions in a special letter of commendation issued 1 January 1943. In it he reviewed Takahashi's career as *Shōkaku* Air Group leader from the Pearl Harbor attack through the Battle of the Coral Sea. Ironically, at the moment Takahashi died, the senior U.S. naval air leader at Coral Sea, Cdr. Ault, was badly wounded, trying to set his own best course back to his carrier *Lexington*.

In the *Lexington*'s Air Plot, Red Gill tried to make sense of his CAP's situation, a difficult undertaking because many of the aircraft lacked IFF gear. At 1149, he instructed the *Yorktown* fighters to join up if they could with their *Lexington* counterparts, so his FD plot could distinguish them. Not spotting any VF-2 Grummans, Macomber latched on to Flatley over the ships. His wingman Bassett retained enough fuel and ammunition to patrol effectively. Still aloft from VF-2 were Ramsey, Markham, Eder, and Haynes from the original CAP, as well as Morgan from Vorse's errant escort division. Most of the fighters were running low on juice, and the carriers would have to recover them soon.

Bill Burch with twelve SBDs from both dive bombing squadrons led the parade of *Yorktown* strike aircraft flying back to Task Force 17. Not long past noon, Burch, cruising peacefully at 6,000 feet, was surprised to spy six Zeros approaching from ahead. The prospect of facing more Mitsubishis, these from the enemy strike group, did not thrill him after the beating they had dealt his squadron over the *Shōkaku*. At 1203, he piped up on the radio to summon aid from the task force. Radar located Burch 30 miles due north of Task Force 17. Gill lacked the numbers, with only eight fighters airborne, to send the CAP that far to the rescue, but he sent his Grummans 10 miles north to meet the strike group and escort them in. Fortunately the Zeros never sighted Burch's SBDs.

A few minutes after his scare, Burch sighted the task force, still in disarray from the air attack nearly an hour before. Murr Arnold, the *Yorktown*'s air officer, hoped to rotate his CAP and instructed Flatley and Macomber to land before recovery operations for the strike group made launching impossible. The two came on board around 1215, and following them in were the four surviving SBDs from VS-5's anti–torpedo-plane patrol. The deck crew worked diligently to rearm and fuel the two Grummans and one other for immediate launch. Meanwhile, the *Yorktown*'s brass completed their preliminary assessment of her damage. At 1222, her radar and FD plot happily reopened for business. Four minutes later, Buckmaster radioed Fitch that the *Yorktown*'s maximum speed was 25 knots because of three boilers temporarily out of service, compliments of one enemy bomb hit. However, her flight operations were not impaired, and she would have no trouble accommodating her strike group then gathering near the ship.

Flatley with two wingmen (one of them VF-2's Doc Sellstrom) took off at 1231 as relief CAP. Deck crewmen rapidly cleared the flight deck aft for recovery. Burch's VS-5 contingent was the first to touch down. Six landed safely. "Yogi" Jorgenson tried to lower his wheels, but the battered SBD dropped off radically to the left. He had no way of making a suitable landing approach and reported he was going to ditch. At 1248 his SBD slid into the water near the destroyer *Aylwin*, which rescued him and his rear gunner. Bombing Five's fourteen SBDs were the next to come on board. Lieut. (jg) Floyd F. Moan, flying a badly shot-up SBD, discovered during his landing approach that his flaps had failed. He could not pull out in time and crashed into the rear of the island. Fortunately he and his rearseat man were not critically injured. The rest of Bombing Five landed safely. Following them were the nine TBDs of Torpedo Five, along with Preston's shot-up SBD from Bombing Five and five VF-42 escorts (Fenton, Gibbs, Leonard, Woollen, and Adams). By 1300, the *Yorktown* had recovered a total of five F4Fs, twenty-one SBDs, and nine TBDs from her strike group. With the strike planes on deck, Edgar Bassett took the opportunity to land for fuel. Later joining him was Flatley's VF-42 wingman, who found that his Grumman was acting up. Counting Flatley's own F4F aloft, Fighting Forty-two found itself with only seven F4Fs in operational condition.

The *Lexington*'s strike group had attacked a good deal later than the *Yorktown*'s, and as yet there was no sign of them. On board the *Lex*, air officer Duckworth still awaited word that all fires were extinguished before refueling the fighters and dive bombers waiting on deck. At 1233, Central Station reported all fires out, although a minor blaze still smouldered in the admiral's cabin. Drawing from the starboard fuel system, Duckworth's crews filled the fighters, then turned to the SBDs. The *Lexington* swung into the wind to launch aircraft. Engineering had put her on an even keel by shifting ballast, and had pumped the three firerooms dry. Things looked much better for the old warrior. Topside, five F4Fs from Fighting Two made ready to go on CAP. Borries and Bill Wileman formed one section ("Doris Red"); Vorse, Lackey, and Robert Kanze, AP2c, the other ("Doris White"). Duckworth assigned Kanze to Sellstrom's old Grumman, hurriedly repaired after being damaged in a deck mishap earlier that day. Starting at 1243, the five F4Fs took off and formed up over the carrier. Almost ready to follow were seven SBDs from Scouting Two and two from Bombing Two.

But as things proceeded so smoothly above deck, dire happenings in the recesses of the ship sealed her fate. Fumes from the small leaks in the port stowage gasoline tanks penetrated several compartments surrounding the evacuated IC Motor Generator Room. At 1242, a deadly omen was observed. Someone detected fumes in the CPO mess not far from the IC Motor Generator Room and cleared out the watch. Five minutes later, apparently sparks from the untended electric motors touched off gasoline vapors in a tremendous explosion that swept into the surrounding compartments killing twenty-five men, including most of the crew of Central Station. Main Control aft, normally a propulsion machinery control station, had to take over directing damage control. Because of crippled internal communications, the bridge lost steering control and had to telegraph orders to the men handling the auxiliary "trick wheel" further aft. Fumes and combustibles fed intense fires in the area surrounding the explosion. Hampered by low hose pressure in the port fire main, fire fighters had to brave dense smoke and intense heat. As the fires steadily grew, numerous small explosions wracked the area. Topside, Duckworth felt the massive 1247 explosion, which vented through the bomb elevator. He continued refueling SBDs for a short time, then shut down the entire system. Launching of the fueled dive bombers proceeded, and Bob Dixon led aloft seven SBDs from his Scouting Two and two from Bombing Two.

In the midst of the launch and the *Lex*'s turmoil, an orphan from the *Yorktown*'s strike group appeared. Scott McCuskey, one of VF-42's escort pilots, was relieved to see the *Lexington*'s familiar silhouette on the horizon. On the flight back from the Japanese task force, he had had to find his own way and throttled way back to conserve fuel. He faced the prospect of ditching if he did not spot the task force soon. Recognizing the *Lexington*, he made for her because she was closer than the *Yorktown*, and at 1255 he landed on board. Called immediately to the bridge, McCuskey was asked about the *Yorktown*'s strike and told Fitch that the Yorktowners had plastered one carrier. McCuskey thought that the *Lexington*'s brass were highly concerned over the prospects of a second Japanese strike. Meanwhile, the *Lexington* took on board five other F4Fs running very low on fuel. They were flown by Ramsey, Markham, Eder, Haynes, and Morgan. Duckworth respotted the fighters for launch, waiting only for the go-ahead to fuel them. McCuskey's F-2 was spotted number one for launch, so that he could fly over to the *Yorktown*. Meanwhile the *Lexington* waited tensely for the return of her own strike group.

On the *Yorktown*'s bridge, Fletcher and his staff formed their estimate of the situation based on first reports from the strike pilots. They had noted the presence of two enemy carriers, one of which, by the most conservative estimate, they had hit with at least two 1,000-lb. bombs and two torpedoes. Depending on what the *Lexington* planes did, that meant one unhurt enemy flattop. After attempting to direct Army Air Forces bombers from Australia onto the undamaged Japanese carrier, Fletcher at 1304 provided CinCPac with his estimate and added, "Enemy had superiority in fighters."[1]

Having enlightened his superiors, Fletcher mapped out his own course of action. Fitch on board the *Lexington* still retained tactical control, but he grew more preoccupied with the *Lexington*'s deteriorating condition. First step was to complete recovery of the strike groups, then evaluate the chances for a second strike that afternoon. The *Yorktown*'s planes were back, but the *Lex*'s were still en route. The *Yorktown*'s operational air strength comprised only seven fighters, eleven dive bombers, and eight torpedo planes. Her magazines held only seven aerial torpedoes. It was doubtful she could spare any fighters to escort a second strike. Clearly the *Yorktown* appeared in no condition to attack again immediately, and the *Lexington* Air Group was probably in the same fix. Fortunately the *Yorktown* herself continued to improve. Fires under the three inactive boilers were relighted, allowing her 30 knots once more. An oil slick trailing conspicuously in her wake was the only outward sign she had been hit.

The presence of an undamaged enemy carrier weighed heavily on Fletcher's mind. From radio intercepts, the *Yorktown*'s communicators had determined that the unhurt Japanese flattop was accommodating the aircraft of her damaged sister as well as her own. Given the unknown situation of the *Lexington* Air Group and the *Yorktown*'s weak plane strength, Fletcher decided to break off battle for the day. At 1315, he signaled Fitch:

> In view of enemy fighter plane superiority and undamaged carrier, I propose retiring. What do you think?[2]

Fitch at 1324 replied "Affirmative," and Fletcher responded:

> Tomorrow may rearm this ship with your planes and renew attack.[3]

In the meantime he again radioed Australia the location of the undamaged Japanese carrier in the hope that MacArthur's B-17s would attack her.

Shortly after 1300, the first elements of the overdue *Lexington* strike group appeared to the north of Task Force 17. Arriving back about the same time were Hamilton's eleven VB-2 Dauntlesses, which had seen no combat, and the little formation of VF-2's Noel Gayler and VS-2's Marvin Haschke, both of whom had seen much fighting. On the way back, Gayler had a welcome opportunity for revenge. He had encountered a pair of enemy dive bombers returning from the strike on Task Force 17. Peeling away from Haschke's SBD, Gayler used his initial good position to make several firing passes and claimed both *kanbaku*. No doubt he contributed to the heavy losses taken that day by the *Shōkaku* Carrier Bomber Unit. A few minutes later the two Americans spotted two other sections of carrier bombers, but by this time Gayler could not spare the fuel to attack them.

Nearing the task force, Gayler was saddened to hear Clark, his second section leader, radio that he was ditching. Lost in the clouds after the melee with the *Zuikaku* Zeros, Clark was unable to find his way back home. He was never heard from again. Another of the 1938 graduates of the U.S. Naval Academy, "Spud" Clark earned his wings in early 1941 and joined Fighting Three in April of that year. Well liked and able, Clark was another fighter pilot beaten not by the Japanese, but by the weather.

Hamilton's eleven SBDs, followed by Gayler and Haschke, landed on board the *Lexington* between 1322 and 1328. Heralding their arrival was a particularly violent explosion up forward on the *Lex*. Damage control parties labored in vain to contain the fires ahead of the forward elevator. Almost the whole of the hangar deck had to be abandoned because of the acrid smoke that filled it.

Fitch had recovered most of his dive bombers, but none of the short-legged TBDs had yet appeared. He was worried about them. Fletcher from his vantage point on board the *Yorktown* had seen the *Lexington* aircraft return. At 1334, he instructed Fitch: "As soon as all planes are recovered or hope given up, head south–southwest at best practicable speed,"[4] Fitch responded by saying he would head north to shorten the distance his returning TBDs would have to cover. His 1341 reply crossed one from Fletcher asking when the air task group commander proposed to retire southward away from a possible enemy strike. Fitch answered he would change course when all aircraft were recovered.

The object of Fitch's concern, Brett's Torpedo Two, was indeed on the way. Nine TBDs flew together, with John Bain's lone VF-2 Grumman tagging along. Two other TBDs were returning independently. The only other elements of the *Lexington* strike group still aloft were three SBDs flown by the CLAG Bill Ault, Harry Wood, and John Wingfield. All three had scattered in the overcast and were hopelessly lost.

Brett's little contingent had quite a scare at 1230 about 50 miles south of MO Striking Force. They stumbled upon enemy planes above them returning from pounding Task Force 17. Four Zeros peeled off to attack. In response, Brett led his nine TBDs down to wave-top level and deployed them tightly into a staggered plane line with both of the wing formations stepped down. This permitted all nine rear gunners to bear against fighters attacking from high-astern. Meanwhile a pair of Zeros drew up a few thousand feet over each side of VT-2's formation, and the leader rolled out to make a high-side run. He flashed in, threw some shells into the TBD formation, then recovered by crossing over to the other side. Brett coached his gunners onto the fighters, cautioning them to allot enough lead. The Japanese restricted their attacks solely to predictable successive high-side runs by individual Zeros. Torpedo Two gunners put some bullets into two Mitsubishis and claimed both. Good gunnery discouraged the enemy from coming too close, and the tight formation baffled all attempts to stampede the TBDs. Likely as not, the Japanese pilots also ran low on fuel and ammunition, and doubtless they were anxious to resume their own flight home. After three or four runs, they broke off battle. Torpedo Two had good reason to be proud of its fight.

During the attacks, Bain had taken his F4F out of range to clear the field for the rear gunners. He took station scraping the wave tops about half a mile off to one side. Fortunately no Zeros bothered him. His actions engendered considerable ill feeling among the TBD crews, who saw an F4F escort sheer away in the face of enemy fighter attack. They did not realize that Bain had no ammunition and could do nothing for them but be shot down if he intervened. Also his fuel situation was critical. Bain's radio had not functioned throughout the entire mission, and he could not inform Brett of his situation.

After repulsing the four Zeros, Brett concentrated on nursing the short-ranged TBDs all the way home. Only 20 miles short of the carriers, one Devastator finally drained its tanks and started toward the water. Lieut. (jg) Thornhill and his crew scurried out of their sinking plane and inflated their big liferaft. Fletcher subsequently despatched the destroyer *Dewey* to look for them, but her lookouts found no trace. Brett was extremely worried that Thornhill's fate might befall the eight TBDs still with him. Finally, around 1400, his goal hove into sight on the horizon. When friendly aircraft approached the task force, the ships expected them to execute a few special maneuvers in order to identify themselves to anxious anti-aircraft gunners. Brett simply did not have the fuel to spare, so he took his formation straight in. They gave the ships quite a scare, and several opened fire, thankfully without hitting any of the aircraft. Almost simultaneously the two stragglers, TBDs flown by Lieut. Hurst and Ens. Bash, reached the task force as well, and the *Lexington* made ready to land them all. By 1414, the *Lexington* had brought on board Bain's Grumman and ten TBDs. That made a total of five F4Fs, twelve SBDs, and eleven TBDs from her original strike group—all that were coming back. Three SBDs were aloft lost in the clouds.

Back from the attack on the *Shōkaku*, afternoon of 8 May 1942. VT-2 TBD is taxiing up the *Lexington*'s flight deck, while in background John Bain's VF-2 F4F-3 is about to land. (NA 80-G-16806.)

While the *Lexington* torpedo planes closed the task force, Fletcher determined his course of action for that evening and the next day. He planned to transfer all of the *Lexington*'s operational aircraft to the *Yorktown*, then detach the crippled *Lexington* and suitable escort directly to Pearl Harbor. Should the Japanese resume their advance on 9 May, Fletcher would fight his one carrier against the enemy's one unhurt *Shōkaku*-class flattop. At 1352 he informed CinCPac of his plans. His decision to release the *Lexington* proved to be wise. At 1355, she signaled the *Yorktown* that all her fires were not out, and Gill at 1406 had to turn over fighter direction duties to Pete Pederson on board the *Yorktown*. The *Lexington* could no longer train her radar. The CAP still comprised six F4F's from VF-2 and Flatley's lone Wildcat from VF-42. Ten SBDs from the *Lexington* handled anti–torpedo-plane patrol, while four others landed on board the *Yorktown* for fuel.

With the *Lexington*'s own condition worsening, Fitch and his staff poured over pilot reports and intelligence intercepts. During his debriefing, Gayler remarked that he had flown over what undoubtedly was an undamaged enemy fleet carrier, and VT-2's executive officer, Lieut. Hurst, likewise indicated he had spotted an enemy carrier task force about 20 miles south of the target he attacked. Radio intercepts of enemy air traffic seemed ominous, combined with concern over the reportedly large numbers of Japanese aircraft that had attacked Task Force 17 and defended their own flattops. It appeared possible that more than one intact enemy carrier lurked out there. At 1422, Fitch radioed Fletcher: "Strong indications additional enemy carrier has joined up." [5] The flagship quickly passed the word along to CinCPac. From previous CinCPac intelligence reports, Fletcher had learned that the carrier *Kaga* was at sea; her location was unspecified, but she could possibly be in the Truk area. Earlier that week, Allied search planes had reported sighting the *Kaga* near Bougainville, in fact mistaking the light carrier *Shōhō* for her. *Yorktown* pilots insisted the carrier they had pounded that morning was the *Kaga*.

Faced with the prospect of overwhelming enemy carrier superiority, Fletcher had to reevaluate his situation. His aircraft strength, particularly in fighters, was so low that a second strike would likely prove futile. A night attack by his surface warships appeared equally vain. On the morrow Japanese carrier planes could sink them at will, and the fuel situation, particularly with the loss of the oiler *Neosho*, did not permit extended high-speed operations. Consequently Fletcher felt he had to withdraw. He informed Rear Admiral Crace's Support Group of the presence of two enemy carriers nearby and also sent CinCPac a revised statement of damage. He believed his two air groups had hit one enemy carrier with at least four torpedoes and three 1,000-lb. bomb hits, which left the Japanese flattop "burning badly." [6]

While Fletcher agonized over the decision to withdraw, the last act in the drama of the *Lexington* strike group played to sympathetic listeners in Task Force 17. Not long after 1400, the *Lexington* copied a shaky transmission from Ault reporting that both he and his gunner were wounded. CLAG inquired whether the ship had him on radar. Soon after, the *Lexington* had to shift all communications over to the *Yorktown*. Ault did not register on the *Yorktown*'s radar. Wood, another lost *Lexington* SBD pilot, piped in that he was heading for land. He requested credit for a bomb hit if CLAG had reported two. Wood could hear some of Ault's transmissions, enough to tell that the group commander was far away. The *Yorktown* could do nothing for the wounded Ault, and he knew it. At 1454, Ault offered his farewell to his shipmates and to his ship:

From CLAG. OK, so long people. We got a 1000 lb. hit on the flat top.[7]

He was never found, nor was Wingfield from Scouting Two. Wood was more fortunate. He reached Rossel Island and along with his gunner was later rescued. The last aircraft from the *Lexington* strike group had finally left the skies. The group therefore lost a total of eight planes: three F4Fs shot down, one F4F ditched, three SBDs and one TBD also ditched.

Had it been up to Takagi and Hara, they gladly would have included the *Kaga* in MO Striking Force, but she was still in Japan. They were left with one undamaged carrier, the *Zuikaku*, as the *Shōkaku* and her escorts had already departed northward. At 1230, the *Shōkaku* ordered her aircraft to land on board the *Zuikaku*. About the same time the strike leaders began radioing base about the conditions of their squadrons. Either things were pretty confused, or losses were catastrophic. At 1240 Takagi decided to retire north after recovering the strike planes. This would give him a chance to regroup and reassess the situation. About twenty minutes later the first planes began straggling back to MO Striking Force. They came a few at a time, with the result that the *Zuikaku*'s recovery operations lasted until 1430. She took on board a total of forty-six aircraft from the two groups: eight Zeros, twelve carrier bombers, and four carrier attack planes of her own, and nine Zeros, seven carrier bombers, and six carrier attack planes from the *Shōkaku*. Because of their battle damage with consequent risk of fouling the *Zuikaku*'s precious flight deck, no fewer than seven aircraft ditched: one *Zuikaku* Zero, five carrier bombers (two *Zuikaku*, three *Shōkaku*), and one *Zuikaku* carrier attack plane. Another shot-up *Shōkaku kanbaku* pilot found his own crippled flattop instead, ignored waveoffs, and cracked up on her flight deck. The total of missing or ditched strike planes amounted to twenty-two: one fighter, thirteen carrier bombers, and eight carrier attack planes.

With the landing of the remnant of the strike group, Takagi and Hara assessed the situation and their own capability of launching a second strike. The returning crews were adamant that they had sunk the *Saratoga*-type carrier, and Takahashi did not survive to dispute them. About the *Yorktown*-type carrier they were not so sure, but the staff assessed damage as three bomb hits, enough to cripple or even sink the American carrier. Their victory, as they called it, came at a terrible price. Even of the aircraft that returned (not to mention the twenty-two that did not), many were not ready to fly. During the landings, *Zuikaku* deck crewmen pushed shot-up aircraft over the side totaling three Zeros, four carrier bombers, and five carrier attack planes, in order to make room for the rest. To his horror, Hara found only nine dive bombers and torpedo planes ready to attack again, although he could give them a strong fighter escort. Later that day the *Zuikaku* reported as operational twenty-four Zeros, nine carrier bombers, and six carrier attack planes. In the hangar and likely to be ready in a day or two sat an additional Zero, eight carrier bombers, and four carrier attack planes. Taking into account his plane strength and the fact that his logistical situation was even worse than that of Task Force 17, Takagi's decision, broadcast at 1500, to break off battle is perfectly understandable. MO Striking Force (or what was left of it—the *Zuikaku*, two heavy cruisers, and one destroyer) turned north to rendezvous with its fleet oiler.

Jubilant at the reports claiming the destruction of two American carriers, Vice Admiral Inoue at Rabaul likewise had to face a major setback because of MO Striking Force's high plane losses. He postponed the MO Operation entirely, but ordered the occupation of Ocean and Nauru islands to proceed as planned. MO Striking Force was to proceed northeastward and support that operation. Thus with the withdrawal of the contending forces, the Battle of the Coral Sea was over. Task Force 17 had accomplished exactly what was expected of it, the defense of Port Moresby. Fletcher's force had blunted the first of several expected Japanese thrusts into the South Pacific. The only trouble was that Task Force 17 had got itself grievously bloodied in the process.

THE LOSS OF THE *LEX*

After the *Lexington* had recovered the last of her strike group, her aviators congregated on deck, hoping that damage control and repair would progress sufficiently for them to resume flight operations. The plane handlers had shifted all of the aircraft aft, and optimistically spotted the eight F4F fighters for takeoff. No one was more eager to go than VF-42's orphan McCuskey, whose faithful F-2 was spotted number one. He along with some VF-2 pilots hoped for the word to man planes.

The *Lexington* about 1430 on 8 May after recovering VT-2 and escort. Down by the bow, she does not as yet show any external evidence of the fires that soon will engulf her. (NH 76560.)

At 1442, however, a second major explosion wracked the massive flattop. Its blast lifted the forward elevator a foot or more above the flight deck and sent smoke and steam gushing from the ship. An intense fire erupted inside the already smoke-filled hangar deck, setting one aircraft ablaze as the flames spread aft. Three minutes after the explosion, Sherman signaled the *Yorktown*: "*Lexington* has serious explosion," followed at 1452 by: "This ship needs help."[1] Some on board fully agreed with their captain. Topside, McCuskey was amazed to see three sailors run up to his Wildcat and snake out the small liferaft stowed just behind the cockpit. Sherman hoisted the breakdown flag. Soon afterward all power failed in the forward half of the ship. The *Lexington* was in danger of succumbing to the flames growing in her bow. All her aviators could do was wait on the flight deck and try to be of assistance to the crew.

It soon became obvious that the *Lexington* required assistance in order to save lives. At 1505, Fletcher sent the destroyers *Phelps, Morris,* and *Anderson* to stand by the stricken carrier. At the same time he made ready to reassume tactical control from Fitch. To regroup and prepare for a possible second enemy strike, the air department thought it advisable to rotate the CAP. To add to the uncertainties, the *Yorktown*'s radar had been cutting out, and she alerted the heavy cruiser *Chester* to maintain a continuous radar watch. At 1512, the *Yorktown* turned into the wind to despatch a relief CAP of four VF-42 F4Fs (Fenton's section "Wildcat Black" and Leonard's "Wildcat White") and ten SBDs from both Bombing Five and Scouting Five as anti-torpedo-plane patrol. About fifteen minutes later, she recovered the old CAP (one F4F from VF-42, six from VF-2) and anti-torpedo-plane patrol—eight VS-2 and two VB-2 dive bombers. Checking the bureau numbers of the VF-2 F4Fs, the *Yorktown*'s air department probably had a laugh. F4F BuNo. 1865 was one of the old VF-42 fighters dealt off on 14 March to VF-3 as "overaged." It had fought at Coral Sea and returned home. Aloft, the *Yorktown* immediately put Fenton to work checking out the carrier's YE homing transmitter which appeared to be malfunctioning. Fenton and his wingman flew about 15 miles out to check the strength of the signal.

The explosion that finally settled the question of the *Lexington*'s fate occurred at 1525. It blew out plating near the firerooms and damaged the boiler uptakes. Water pressure in the hangar deck fire curtains also failed, releasing a great surge of flame. It became necessary to evacuate the forward machinery spaces, cutting power in more areas, thus severing the only link between the bridge and steering control. Sherman then attempted to steer his giant carrier by her engines only. With sickening speed the inferno swept aft. Damage control managed to flood ammunition and bomb magazines, but all they could do with the torpedo warheads was play hoses on them to keep them cool. At 1538, the ship reported the fire as out of control. Eventually the blaze severed all connections with Main Control, ending all attempts to steer the ship. The *Lexington* careened wildly through the formation as escort vessel hustled out of her way. By 1600, the flattop slowed and began circling. Sherman ordered the men to leave the lower spaces and come up on the flight deck. Her powerplant secured, the *Lexington* let off steam and came to a stop. Then she drifted helplessly, broadside to the gentle swells of the Coral Sea.

Concerned over the very real possibility of a second Japanese strike, Fletcher had to reckon with the fact that the *Lexington* no longer could stay up with the rest of the task force. At 1601, he separated Task Force 17 into two groups. Operating with the *Lexington* would be Kinkaid's Task Group 17.2, two heavy cruisers and three destroyers. His mission was to stand by the crippled flattop,

Carrier Planes, Task Force 17 about 1600, 8 May 1942

Aloft or on board		(Operational)	Missing, ditched, or jettisoned, 8 May
(a) On board the *Lexington*			
CLAG (missing in action)			1 SBD-3
VF-2	8 F4F-3s	(7)	6 F4Fs
VB-2	12 SBD-2, -3s	(11)	1 SBD
VS-2	2 SBD-3s	(1)	5 SBDs
VT-2	11 TBD-1s	(10)	1 TBD-1
(VF-42)	1 F4F-3	(1)	—
	34	(30)	14
(b) Aloft or on board the *Yorktown*:			
VF-42	13 F4F-3s	(7)	1 F4F-3
VB-5	15 SBD-3s	(10)	2 SBD-3s
VS-5	12 SBD-3s	(5)	5 SBD-3s
VT-5	12 TBD-1s	(8)	0
(VF-2)	6 F4F-3s	(6)	—
(VB-2)	5 SBD-2, -3s	(5)	—
(VS-2)	8 SBD-3s	(8)	—
	71	(49)	8

Total Carrier Plane Losses on 8 May (including on board the *Lexington*)
16 F4F-3, -3As
28 SBD-2, -3s
13 TBD-1s
57

rescue her crew, and sink her if need be, or escort her southward if she could be saved. As the *Yorktown* group moved off to the south, her radar evidently picked up a contact. At 1700, the *Yorktown* scrambled seven F4F Wildcats from both Fighting Two and Fighting Forty-two. As they clawed skyward, she warned the task force: "Prepare to repel air attack." The *Chester* offered to vector fighters, but Pete Pederson declined, noting that his radar was now "fairly reliable."[2] The alarm proved false, but that did little to reduce tension in Task Force 17.

Meanwhile, the destroyer *Morris* moved up alongside the *Lexington* after she hove to, and passed hoses up to the flight deck in a vain effort to fight fires. With rescue ships on hand, Sherman directed that the wounded be evacuated, and at 1652, ordered all squadron and air department personnel to embark on board the *Morris*. Under the circumstances, most of the aviators did not get the word to leave until Sherman soon after ordered all hands to abandon ship. That unhappy event took place at 1707. By that time, the *Lexington*'s list to port had increased to 7 degrees, and her fires roared unabated. She was doomed, and Sherman had no assurance that the flames would not set off torpedo warheads in the mezzanine deck over the after part of the hangar deck. Explosions there would threaten the 2,500-odd sailors crowded on deck and also the safety of the surrounding rescue ships.

The *Lexington*'s crew went over the side in an orderly manner, either hand-after-hand down lines or (for the adventurous) by diving fifty feet into the water. Screening ships sent whaleboats and launches to rescue the men in the water. For the most part, aviation personnel abandoned ship over her port and starboard quarters. Many took with them rubber rafts salvaged from the aircraft on deck. Correspondent Stanley Johnston remembered one such case:

Smoke curls around F4F-3s on the doomed *Lexington*'s flight deck, late afternoon, 8 May. Scott McCuskey's (42-) F-2 is spotted first on the extreme right, identified by its single cowl flap, characteristic of an early-production F4F-3 (BuNo. 2531). (NA 80-G-16802.)

One crew chief in Ramsey's squadron got into his little rubber boat and commenced to paddle away, his cap at a jaunty angle and his flare pistol at his side. Ramsey whistled to him and the man sculled his way back to ask:

"What do you want, skipper?"

"Nothing," said Ramsey. "Just wanted to say you look fine and that it's only 400 miles to Australia."[3]

Among the aviators leaving the ship were the following fighter pilots:

Fighting Two:
Lt. Cdr. Paul H. Ramsey, USN, CO
Lieut. Noel A. M. Gayler, USN, XO
Lieut. (jg) Robert J. Morgan, USN
Lieut. (jg) Marion W. Dufilho, USN
Ens. Willard E. Eder, A-V(N)
Ens. Leon W. Haynes, A-V(N)
Ens. John B. Bain, A-V(N)
Ens. George A. Hopper, Jr., A-V(N)
Ens. George F. Markham, Jr., A-V(N)
    Fighting Forty-two:
Lieut. (jg) E. Scott McCuskey, A-V(N)

All the fighter pilots safely reached the escort vessels, but Fighting Two lost one enlisted man either killed in the blast or missing in the water:

Virgil L. Weeks, PhM2c, USN[4]

Evacuation of the crew took the better part of an hour, and they departed just in time. Around 1800, an enormous blast exploded amidships, followed in short order by another, even bigger detonation farther aft. Fire had worked its way aft among the planes parked on deck, setting most ablaze. Now this explosion blew the aft elevator apart and tossed several aircraft into the air. The stern was a mass of flames. In spots the *Lexington* soon glowed cherry red, as the fire relentlessly consumed the vitals of the ship. Sherman and his department heads bravely remained on board to conduct a final inspection. From the main body, Fletcher despatched the destroyers *Phelps* and *Dewey* to assist in the rescue. Filled to capacity with survivors, several other destroyers rejoined the flagship. Overhead, the crews of the circling aircraft watched the awesome death throes of the flaming *Lexington*, accented by the deepening darkness. According to Bill Leonard, one of the CAP pilots:

> Fires, explosions large and small, debris blowing over the side made her look like hell afloat. It was a sad sight.[5]

Called back to the *Yorktown* for recovery, the ten SBDs and eleven F4Fs found it "plenty dark" by 1818 when the last of them landed on board.

Fletcher at 1826 signaled to Kinkaid conducting the rescue that the rest of Task Force 17 would hold a course of 225 degrees at 14 knots (less zigzagging) until 2000, then head for a rendezvous point. There Kinkaid would be able to rejoin after sinking the *Lexington* with torpedoes. Sherman waited until 1830 on board the inferno his vessel had become. He was certain he left no living crew on board. A whaleboat from the *Hammann* with Ramsey on board recovered the *Lexington*'s captain from the water. In the night sky, the *Lexington* burned brightly, a beacon of flame and towering black smoke visible for many miles. After carefully checking the waters for survivors, the rescue ships cleared off, having brought 2,770 men (92 percent of her complement) to safety. At 1841, the *Phelps* received orders to sink the *Lexington*, and between 1915 and 1952, she sent five torpedoes into the flaming mass so persistently still afloat. Finally just after 1952, the *Lex* rolled over to port and slipped beneath the waves. As she disappeared from view, a tremendous underwater explosion rent the sea. The concussion reverberated as far as 20 miles, where it was felt among the ships of the main body. The *Phelps*, near the catastrophe, was so shaken, her skipper thought she had been torpedoed.

Kinkaid's task group rejoined Task Force 17 at 2037, and Fletcher set a southwesterly course. On everyone's mind that gloomy evening was the loss of the *Lexington*, one quarter of the total American carrier strength in the Pacific. Not knowing of the carrier's loss, Admiral Nimitz back at Pearl had drafted a congratulatory message praising Task Force 17's "glorious accomplishments," which were the "admiration of the entire Pacific Fleet."[6] To the weary participants in the Battle of the Coral Sea, the words would sound a little hollow because the gallant old *Lex* was not there to share in them.

CHAPTER 13

Coral Sea Aftermath

"WE ARE ALL SHORT OF OIL, RUNNING LIKE HELL."[1]

The dawn of 9 May found Task Force 17 continuing its southerly retreat into the expanses of the Coral Sea. The day was lonely without the reassuringly massive bulk of the *Lexington* rounding out the formation. It was still hard to believe the great carrier had burned, then disappeared into the depths. The *Yorktown* still manifested evidence of her wounds of the previous day. Staining her wake was a persistent trail of fuel leaking from her tanks. Fuel needs for the ships in company became a major problem after the loss of the *Neosho*. Aside from fueling in southern Australia, Fletcher would have to look to Tongatabu, Fiji, or Samoa as a source of fuel unless he could achieve underway replenishment from the oilers and tankers CinCPac was busily trying to round up for him. Several of his destroyers were in a bad way, but they would have to wait until the task force secured respite from alarms and emergency maneuvers in order to transfer fuel from the *Yorktown* and the cruisers to the short-legged tincans. Fletcher knew that Halsey's Task Force 16 was en route to the Coral Sea, but it looked as if the enemy lay between him and Halsey's two fleet oilers.

The *Yorktown* at dawn sent off several pairs of SBDs from both Scouting Five and Bombing Five as morning search. Their mission was to canvas the northern semicircle to determine whether the Japanese were in close pursuit. The *Yorktown*'s contingent of thirteen operational F4F Wildcats stood ready to fly CAP. Shortly after 0900 came an electrifying message from one of the scouts. The SBD pilot reported sighting an enemy carrier task force, but his message cut out in mid-transmission as if the sender had been attacked by enemy fighters. His section mate completed the report, which informed Fletcher that a Japanese carrier force bore 310 degrees, distance 175 miles from Task Force 17. The report gave the enemy's course as 110 degrees, that is, headed toward the Americans, and a speed of 25 knots. The *Yorktown* at 0922 went to general quarters, broadcast the alarm, and raised fleet speed to 27 knots. She scrambled part of her fighters for combat air patrol and readied a strike of SBDs. Leading the mission, made up of four *Lexington* survivors, was VS-2's Bob Dixon. They would proceed without escort because of the need to retain fighters to defend the task force. Fletcher comandeered a plane and pilot from Scouting Five, and at 1000 sent the SBD off with his staff gunnery officer, Cdr. Walter G. Schindler, in the rear seat. Schindler's destination was Rockhampton, Australia, 350 miles west of the task force, where he was to contact General MacArthur and arrange for an Allied bomber strike on the reported Japanese carrier force. Maintenance of security through strict radio silence dictated this form of "pony express."

Task Force 17 suffered an anxious morning. Dixon's strike force of SBDs departed, but could not find the target. An analysis of the reports later determined that the search pilots, suspecting the worst, had mistaken the surf-beaten Lihou Reefs as a carrier force kicking up spray in headlong pursuit. "They called it as they saw it,"[2] wrote one Yorktowner. At 1151, the *Yorktown* suffered a plane loss when a VS-2 SBD flown by Ens. Lawrence G. Traynor of Scouting Five ditched near the carrier. The destroyer *Morris* recovered Traynor and his gunner. That afternoon, with enemy pursuit now far less likely, Fletcher arranged for the destroyers to transfer *Lexington* survivors to the less crowded cruisers. Even this operation was interrupted by bogeys appearing on radar. They proved to be Army B-17 Flying Fortresses staging in from Noumea to Townsville, Australia. The Army also sent a strike force of fourteen bombers to hit the carrier force erroneously reported earlier that day. The Army flyers looked diligently for the enemy, but of course they were not there; so at dusk the bombers returned to Townsville.

The afternoon of 9 May, Fletcher received an important directive from CinCPac, in which Nimitz told him to return the ships of the "old" Task Force 17 to the West Coast "if practicable," otherwise to Pearl Harbor.[3] Kinkaid with the screening vessels formerly belonging to Fitch's Task Force 11 had new orders to join Halsey's Task Force 16 at the earliest opportunity. Fuel would be available at Tongatabu if Fletcher desired to regroup there. The next day Fletcher decided he would stop at Tongatabu. That evening, he turned eastward after having swung well south of New Caledonia. To free Kinkaid's ships for service with Halsey, survivors transferred by coal bag to the heavy cruiser *Chester* and some of the destroyers for transport to Tongatabu. The afternoon of 11 May, Fletcher detached Kinkaid with the heavy cruisers *Minneapolis*, *New Orleans*, and *Astoria* and three destroyers to proceed to Noumea, while the rest of the task force pressed on for Tongatabu. Kinkaid was to stop briefly at Noumea, then join Halsey approaching from the northeast, while the *Astoria* continued on to Tongatabu. Task Force 17's trials in the Coral Sea were over.

Admiral Inoue's decision to postpone the MO Operation reached Tokyo late on 8 May, causing great consternation within Combined Fleet staff. They were irate that Inoue had broken off battle, letting the American warships withdraw unmolested. In Tokyo they did not know how grievously battered were the Japanese carrier air groups or that MO Striking Force was desperately low on fuel. At 2200, Admiral Yamamoto peremptorily ordered Inoue to "destroy the enemy."[4] No doubt flustered by the unexpected and firm imperative in the Combined Fleet response, Inoue's staff just before midnight on 8 May reviewed the situation and ordered Takagi's MO Striking Force (built around the carrier *Zuikaku*) to search on 9 May after fueling.

Embarrassed twice while trying to fuel, MO Striking Force had not taken a full drink of oil since sailing on 1 May from Truk. On 9 May Takagi joined up with his fleet oiler *Tōhō Maru* and spent the whole day fueling. Hara surveyed the plane situation on board the *Zuikaku* and found only forty-five aircraft from both groups still operational: twenty-four Zero fighters, thirteen carrier bombers, and eight carrier attack planes. Late on 9 May, Takagi once more steamed southward into the Coral Sea, doubtful he would find anything after the chastisement his flyers had dealt the Americans on 8 May. The 10 May dawn search revealed only an American oiler (the *Neosho*) drifting out of control. That target was not worth another strike. Shortly past noon, Takagi reversed course and struck north for the Solomons. He still had some fighters to deliver to Rabaul—a seemingly innocuous mission that had caused the MO Operation no end of trouble! After that he was to act in support of the South Seas Force's next operation: the twin invasions of Ocean and Nauru islands northeast of Rabaul. The afternoon of 10 May, Combined Fleet formally acknowledged defeat of the MO Operation by postponing the invasion of Port Moresby until summer. The Imperial Japanese Navy had suffered its first major strategic setback of the war.

TASK FORCE 16'S ANABASIS TO THE SOUTH PACIFIC

Back in late April while Fletcher's Task Force 17 stood ready to give battle in the Coral Sea, Bill Halsey's Task Force 16 with the *Enterprise* and the *Hornet* triumphantly returned from taking Jimmy Doolittle's Army B-25 Mitchell bombers to a launch point within 650 miles of Japan. Halsey entered Pearl Harbor on 25 April, but he would not tarry long. Nimitz needed his carriers in the Coral Sea. The Tokyo Raid proved a grand gesture, but deprived Nimitz of half his carrier strength at a time when they would have been far more valuable in the South Pacific. As shown previously, both King and Nimitz worried that the threat to Port Moresby presaged a widespread enemy offensive into the South Pacific, probably with carrier raids on Australia, New Caledonia, Fiji, and Samoa. With every flattop he could muster, Nimitz intended to counter the Japanese thrust. Fletcher with the *Yorktown* and the *Lexington* had the first round, the defense of Port Moresby. Thereafter Halsey, as senior commander, would take tactical command of all the carriers in order to defend the lifeline to Australia.

On 28 April, Nimitz flew back to Pearl after conferring with King in San Francisco. CominCh not only had agreed with Nimitz's concern for the South Pacific; he ordered CinCPac to retain at least two carriers there until further notice. Halsey's own orders, issued on 29 April, gave his mission to "check further advance of the enemy in the NEW GUINEA–SOLOMON area by destroying enemy ships, shipping, and aircraft,"[1] adding that if profitable targets appeared in the Gilberts, Halsey should be prepared to smash them on his trip down to the South Pacific. Likewise on the way, Halsey's carriers were to deliver twenty-one marine F4F-3 Wildcats for the new air base on Efate. Long-range planning seemed to dictate that Halsey could count on retaining Fletcher's Task Force 17 (with the *Yorktown*) until about mid-May and Fitch's Task Force 11 (the *Lexington*) till perhaps 1 June. CinCPac, however, was making arrangements to resupply both of those task forces should there be need to keep all four carriers for an extended stay in the South Pacific.

Back from the cold Empire waters, the pilots of Fighting Six, based temporarily on Ford Island, and Fighting Eight, billeted at Ewa, enjoyed a day or two of well-deserved rest at the Royal Hawaiian Hotel, eight of the NAPs celebrating recent promotions to warrant rank. The squadrons reopened for business on 27 April. That day, two of VF-6's borrowed NAPs, Mach. Doyle C. Barnes and Mach. Tom F. Cheek, left to join Jimmy Thach's Fighting Three at Kaneohe. Replacing them were a pair of rookies fresh from the West Coast, Ens. Melvin C. Roach and Ens. Mortimer V. Kleinmann, Jr. Also that day, Fighting Six parted with the last five F4F-3s and one slightly bent F4F-4 and took delivery of six new F4F-4s. The squadron now sported a full complement of twenty-seven folding wing F4F-4s, a fact that did not thrill skipper Jim Gray, who had had little but acerbic comments about that particular Wildcat.

On 26 April Fighting Eight at Ewa lost an experienced fighter pilot in Lieut.

Fitzhugh L. Palmer, Jr., transferred to Jack Raby's Fighting Nine on the East Coast. Joining the squadron in his place was another recently graduated fighter pilot, Ens. Alfred E. Dietrich. Fighting Eight's skipper Pat Mitchell and a number of his troops went over to Kaneohe to look up Mitchell's classmate Thach and talk of fighter tactics. Thach filled them in on VF-3's experiences in the South Pacific. On 28 April, both the *Enterprise* and the *Hornet* air groups were alerted to embark in 48 hours. Scuttlebutt pointed to a South Pacific destination, particularly as the flattops were tabbed to transport in a southerly direction the twenty-one F4F-3s of Major Harold W. ("Indian Joe") Bauer's Marine Fighting Squadron 212. The *Enterprise* would take ten and the *Hornet* eleven of the fixed wing leatherneck fighters.

The last day of April, Pearl Harbor buzzed with activity as Task Force 16 put out to sea. Escorted by three destroyers, the *Enterprise* and the *Hornet* sailed that morning to conduct training exercises northwest of Oahu. The remainder of the task force would join later that afternoon. Fighting Six slept on board "The Big E," then went ashore where their aircraft had remained. Some pilots were able to spend the morning lounging at the pool, but others, led by XO Roger Mehle, had different business. Mehle took ten F4Fs out to the *Enterprise* and landed shortly past noon. There they were on hand to witness a spectacular crack-up. While landing, a VS-6 SBD flown by Ens. J. C. Lough slammed into the flight deck. Round the front cockpit its fuselage ripped in half. Two parachute flares dropped out of the battered airplane, ignited, and wafted to the stern where they burned on deck. That afternoon, the *Enterprise* launched nineteen SBDs and two F4Fs (Roach and Kleinmann) for carrier landing qualifications. Toward dusk, Gray led VF-6's remaining fifteen F4Fs out to the ship, and they came on board without incident, giving Fighting Six twenty-seven F4Fs for this cruise.

At Ewa, the *Hornet*'s air group likewise formed up that afternoon for the hop out to the carrier. Lieut. Bruce L. Harwood, VF-8's hard-working engineer officer, had an unlucky landing. His Grumman was "pretty well wrecked as he bounced, hit the barrier with his wheels and the island with a wing, flipping him clear over on his back."[2] Leroy Grumman had made his aircraft tough, the headrest fortunately preventing all but slight injuries to Harwood's tall frame; but F4F-4 Bureau Number 5122 was in sad shape, leaving Fighting Eight with twenty-six operational fighters. At 1737, the *Hornet* took her place with the *Enterprise*, and the two flattops, surrounded by four heavy cruisers, eight destroyers, and two fleet oilers, were South Pacific–bound, base course 205 degrees, speed 15 knots.

For this cruise Halsey's staff resumed the procedure of alternating the routine flight duty between the two carriers. This allowed the off-duty flattop to work in valuable training flights. Under this scheme, one carrier took the late morning, afternoon, and the next day's dawn flights, then spent the remainder of the second day off duty. The fighter pilots greatly preferred such an arrangement, as it gave them time for routine squadron duties as well as gunnery flights. Rawie penned in his diary, "We are finally getting this ship organized, so that the pilots get a little relaxation."[3]

On May Day, the *Hornet* drew early duty, turning out VF-8 pilots and thirteen SBD crews for predawn launch. The flight went poorly for Mitchell's troops. Two of the scheduled Grummans turned out to be duds and had to be replaced by both standby fighters. Ens. Stephen W. Groves, flying one of the replacement aircraft, started down the flight deck at 0452, but he could not coax flying speed out of his Wildcat. It sailed out over the bow, lost altitude, and smacked into the water about 500 yards off the *Hornet*'s port bow. Out of his sinking mount in a flash,

"Shady" Groves swam hard, aware that the flattop was bearing down on him. The *Hornet* nearly brushed the swamped aircraft. Moving in to recover the pilot was the plane guard destroyer, the *Monssen*. Investigators later theorized that the propellor governor malfunctioned.[4] That reduced Fighting Eight to twenty-five operational planes.

The next morning the *Enterprise* handled the predawn flights. Four VF-6 pilots flew inner air patrol, and SBDs searched 200 miles ahead of the task force. The *Hornet* as scheduled took the duty at 0800 and maintained the inner air patrols. At 1115 while launching a relief IAP, the gremlins again struck Fighting Eight. Taking off as part of an eight-F4F patrol was Ens. Charles Markland Kelly, Jr. Low manifold pressure plus the fact that Kelly had not lowered his flaps sent his Grumman into the drink. According to a witness, Ens. Elisha T. ("Smokey") Stover, "Kelly went charging down the deck and dropped off the bow as if an elevator had fallen out from under him."[5] The Wildcat splashed only 200 yards ahead of the swiftly moving *Hornet*, and Kelly also showed some Olympic-style swimming to get out of the way. In this case the carrier rammed the still floating F4F and sank it, but Mark Kelly was safe.[6] The faithful *Monssen* took him on board where he was greeted at the rail by another *Hornet* castaway, Shady Groves. The two learned they would remain on board the tincan for several days, each with only "one set of dried out clothes."[7] For young aviators who had had no sea duty other than on board their carrier, it proved to be a fascinating look at the surface Navy and its ways. Mitchell, however, now had only twenty-four airworthy F4Fs; at this rate Fighting Eight would have none left for combat!

For the next several days, flight operations proceeded as planned, as the task force crossed hundreds of miles of lonely seas. On 3 May, the fighter jinx switched from Fighting Eight to Fighting Six, and there it stuck, bedeviling Gray for the rest of the cruise. That morning in squally weather, Mehle "creamed" plane F-19 with a "perfect 3 point landing (prop, wingtip, and one wheel)."[8] The other wheel, the right gear, had crumpled on touchdown, and the result was a Grumman in

Enterprise SBDs, 3 May 1942. (NA 80-G-16519.)

need of major overhaul. On 4 May westward of Palmyra Island, the task force copied Fletcher's despatch reporting his successful Tulagi strikes. Obviously events in the Coral Sea had heated up, and Halsey wanted to get there faster. He raised the fleet speed of advance to 16.5 knots, enough with deductions for zigzagging and flight operations to make good 360 miles a day along the track.

The carrier not on duty was able to conduct valuable training. On 4 May, for example, the *Enterprise* despatched on one mission a force of fourteen fighters, twenty-six dive bombers, and nine torpedo planes, mainly to test the use of SBDs on anti–torpedo-plane patrol. That day also, Rawie took time to reflect on wartime conditions and "The Big E." His words applied to all of the carriers:

> I'm amazed at the way the ship keeps up. She's still as clean and neat as a year ago, more informal, but paint is still applied here and there, and with no inspections she's still clean and neat as a glass marble.[9]

The fifth of May brought another crossing of the equator, the first for the *Hornet*, which celebrated with the usual "nonsense." That vessel also sent aloft a training mission of twelve fighters, eighteen dive bombers, and nineteen torpedo planes for gunnery and bombing exercises. Later that day, Halsey's air staff unexpectedly gave the *Enterprise* the duty again and told the *Hornet* to try the training flights once more. Word on board the *Enterprise* was that "Wild Bill" did not care for the *Hornet*'s performance and made them do it again.

The Fighting Six hex reappeared at 1428 on 5 May as the *Enterprise* took on board fighters from inner air patrol. Homer W. Carter, AP1c, one of the NAPs borrowed from Fighting Two, had the misfortune to bounce his Grumman on touchdown. His tail hook skittered over number three and four wires as the p!ane rebounded upward. Nosing down, Carter's Grumman skidded through number two barrier, which sheered off the landing gear and swung the aircraft around. The F4F ended up canted steeply into the port catwalk, its nose facing the ship's stern. To add to Carter's troubles, the slide along deck buckled his main fuel tank. As

H. W. Carter's VF-6 F4F-4 (BuNo. 5176) ends up in "The Big E's" catwalk, 5 May 1942. (NA 80-G-14454.)

spilled fuel ignited, the *Enterprise* had a real emergency on her hands, but quick action by the flight deck fire-fighting crew saved the pilot and extinguished the blaze in less than a minute. Rawie echoed everyone's sentiments when he praised them as a "damn fine crew."[10]

More news of the battle raging on the Coral Sea reached the task force on 7 May. Halsey learned that the *Lexington* had taken heavy damage in an engagement with enemy carriers. As always, CinCPac intelligence bulletins kept him apprised of the latest situation estimates from Pearl. The notice received that day informed him of likely Japanese plans to invade the islands of Ocean and Nauru later that month. These islands, situated west of the Gilberts, were included in his operating orders, and the forecast was of great interest to Task Force 16. There was no 8 May, as the task force crossed the date line directly into the ninth day of the month. This came as somewhat of a shock to Ens. Thomas C. Provost III of Fighting Six. "Pappy" Provost's birthday was 8 May, and he had evidently missed it somehow. The squadron consoled him with a special birthday party replete with prodigious servings of ice cream.

By 10 May, Halsey had a clearer picture of what had occurred in the Coral Sea. Fletcher's Task Force 17 with the maimed *Yorktown* had withdrawn for good, and the Japanese had retired as well. Port Moresby was safe for the time being, owing to Task Force 17's efforts, so there was no need to hurry. Of more immediate concern were continuing CinCPac revelations of enemy plans to seize Ocean and

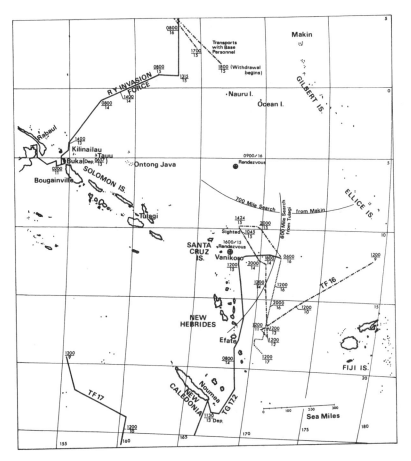

The Ocean–Nauru operation.

Nauru. Pearl thought the actual invasion forces, expected to depart from Jaluit in the Marshalls, would be rather weak. Instead, it was the Japanese covering force that drew Halsey's attention. It appeared possible that MO Striking Force, centered around the *Zuikaku,* would head northeast from the Solomons to support the invasions. Halsey would have liked nothing more than a reckoning with her. Trouble was, she would be difficult to surprise. CinCPac warned him that the Japanese conducted long-range searches, radius 700 miles, within the triangle Makin–Ellice–Solomons. From Tulagi, flying boats searched out 600 miles. Like Fletcher before him, Halsey had to bide his time until the enemy had poked his nose a good way out before Task Force 16 could pounce.

On 10 May, Halsey's ships themselves were eyeballed by a snooper, but this time a friendly one. A Royal New Zealand Air Force Hudson bomber operating out of Nandi, the Fijis, looked them over. Task Force 16 was definitely in the South Seas now. The fighting squadrons spent a routine day. Their aircraft painters covered over with blue the colorful red and white striped tails and also whited out the red dots in the national insignia on fuselage and wings, this in conformance with a new directive from CinCPac.

Task Force 16 on 11 May drew up northeastward of Efate, optimistically code-named Roses—a definite misnomer for that foul malarial island. Halsey attended to his first item of business, the delivery of VMF-212. Along with the usual morning search, the *Enterprise* sent aloft two dive bombers and a marine SNJ training plane to check out Efate's airstrip. Wade McClusky in one of the SBDs reported at 0815 that the field was definitely not suitable for fighters. Halsey at 0830 sent Bauer's twenty-one Wildcats to Noumea, an easy flight westward from the task force's current location. With him Bauer took several messages for radio transmission from shore, so Halsey would not have to risk tipping off the enemy. One of the messages instructed Rear Admiral Kinkaid with his Task Group 17.2 of Coral Sea veterans to join him as soon as possible. For that day and part of the next, Halsey intended to mark time eastward of Efate and await developments to the north. He drained one of his two fleet oilers and retained the other in the Noumea area as a floating reserve. While fueling, the *Hornet* took back her two wayward aviators when the *Monssen* came alongside and by bosun's chair returned Groves and Kelly to Fighting Eight. Fueling completed, the task force spent a quiet night.

The morning of 12 May brought Halsey the news he expected. CinCPac informed him that part of the Ocean–Nauru invasion force had already set sail from Rabaul. Indications pointed to 14 May as the date of the landings. Halsey sent two SBDs to Efate as pigeon post to deliver a message for transmission, in it requesting air reconnaissances of Ontong Java, Tauu Island, and Kilinailau Island—all north of the Solomons—because he might conduct "offensive operations in that area."[11] Task Force 16 headed northwest at 15 knots. Clearly, Halsey intended to find the Japanese covering force, destroy the *Zuikaku* and her consorts, then deal with the invasion convoy.

Only a few hours later on 12 May, new information from CinCPac reached Halsey and forced him to change his plans. Because the American submarine S-42 had sunk the *Okinoshima* (finally!), flagship of the Ocean–Nauru Invasion Force, the Japanese had postponed the landings until 17 May. Thus there was no need for Task Force 16 to race northward at this time and risk detection. Under the circumstances, Halsey decided to remain south of Efate for a while. Even more disappointing was the word that Combined Fleet had ordered the *Zuikaku* home, making Halsey's main opposition the half dozen heavy cruisers of the 5th and 6th Cruiser Divisions—important targets but not in league with a fleet carrier.

VF-6 12 May 1942, *l to r standing*: Bayers, Holt, Grimmell, Hodson, Daly, Warden, Gunsolus, Rhodes, Sumrall, Kleinmann, Carter, Roach, Packard, Allard, Hiebert, Achten, Presley, Reid; *sitting*: Rich, Provost, Kelley, Mehle, Gray, Hoyle, Quady, Hermann, Rawie. (Capt. W. E. Rawie, USN.)

By 13 May the bored fighter pilots, tired of flying interminable inner air patrols, felt that Task Force 16 was fated forever to steam in circles east of Efate. Looking for adventure, VF-6's "Buster" Hoyle hitched a ride in the rear seat of one SBD flying pigeon post to Efate. To his chagrin, the SBD air-dropped its message and did not land. In this communication, Halsey set a rendezvous for Kinkaid's task group near Vanikoro in the Santa Cruz Islands. Task Force 16 finally started northward, ostensibly to give battle, or as a VF-6 diarist quipped, "heading north to hot weather and hot water."[12] During the afternoon search, two SBDs, one from Bombing Six and the other from Scouting Six, failed to return.

The morning of 14 May the *Hornet* handled the precautionary 200-mile search, while twenty-one *Enterprise* SBDs fanned out in a special mission to look for their downed mates. Neither search was positive. On board the two carriers it became evident that something was in the wind. Base course was 351 degrees, inciting speculation that they might circle in to hit Rabaul. Actually Halsey was finalizing his plans for tackling the Ocean–Nauru covering force. Shortly he expected results from reconnaissance flights over Ontong Java, Tauu, and Kilinailau to determine whether enemy seaplanes operated there. To inform Kinkaid of a new rendezvous, he would use the destroyer *Benham* as pony express to meet Kinkaid at 15 May at the old rendezvous. His orders directed Kinkaid to a new meeting place, this time at 0900 on 16 May at a point between and roughly 300 miles south of both Ocean and Nauru. Meanwhile, Halsey could spare the time to maneuver in an attempt to elude the daily enemy air searches out of Tulagi, Makin, and Rabaul. There was a good chance that he, if not Kinkaid, could arrive unseen at the rendezvous point.

Developments at Pearl Harbor, to be discussed in detail later, compelled Halsey the evening of 14 May to alter his plans radically. Halsey received two radio messages from CinCPac. The first forwarded a warning from a concerned CominCh in Washington. Ernie King did not want Task Force 16 to operate beyond the range of Allied land-based aircraft (a motley and scattered collection of search planes and fighters!) "until necessity requires such operations to oppose major enemy offensive or unless especially favorable results are to be expected."[13] King did not want Task Force 16 sailing within range of enemy land-based air units, even though Halsey had nearly fifty Wildcats to defend his ships. Nimitz tacked on the proviso that the CominCh warning applied to enemy strike planes (such as the medium bombers based in Rabaul and the Marshalls) and not to the ubiquitous flying boats, in themselves relatively harmless except as eyes for the enemy. Halsey thought King's order far too restrictive, but even so he could expect "especially favorable results" if he ambushed the Ocean–Nauru covering forces and routed the convoy. Nimitz's second communication, however, changed all thought of that. CinCPac's message was for Halsey's eyes only, a secret order that told Halsey to make certain the enemy sighted him the next day, then withdraw. Nimitz did not want the task force to attack the Ocean–Nauru covering force. He wanted them to return north to Pearl, but he could not come out openly and order Halsey back.[14]

In compliance with Nimitz's intentions, Halsey that evening changed course to the northwest, aiming directly for the Tulagi search zone. Nimitz could count on Halsey's complete discretion in this matter. Halsey did not have to send a second ship to warn Kinkaid of the change in plans. After the enemy located Task Force 16 the next day, he would be free to break radio silence and tell Kinkaid of another meeting place. The order must have been very puzzling to "Wild Bill," but he knew it was important to CinCPac and kept it quiet.

Succinctly, Task Force 16's unspoken mission on 15 May was to "get sighted and scram." All night the ships steamed at 15 knots toward Tulagi. The *Enterprise* had the flight duty that morning, and Fighting Six at 0526 put up a combat air patrol of four Wildcats, followed shortly by a mixed inner air patrol of two F4Fs and two SBDs. The routine dawn search sent other SBDs 200 miles to the northwest, the launch made more interesting by a submarine scare. While the planes took off, the *Enterprise* careened in a hard right turn. By 0800, Tulagi lay to the northwest, distance 475 miles. Shortly before 0900, the *Enterprise* sent aloft relief flights: a second CAP with four fighters and two F4Fs as inner air patrol. Scheduled to follow were two SBDs from Scouting Six. The first to depart, flown by Ens. William R. Pittman, smacked into the water just off the carrier's bow. Pilot and radioman swam clear to be picked up by the destroyer *Ellet*. Somewhat bemused, the air officer canceled the launch of the second SBD. That morning, winds were unusually calm, with virtually no velocity, so that flight operations were rather tricky.

Aloft, the first CAP and the fighter half of the first inner air patrol grew a little anxious. They had been flying close to four hours, and the F4F-4 had earned no plaudits for long endurance. Finally at 0908, the flight deck was clear, and the six VF-6 fighters queued up in the landing circle. The third Grumman to land was flown by Mach. Julius A. Achten, one of the experienced NAPs on loan from Fighting Two. Upon initial touchdown, his Grumman bounced high enough for the hook to skip two wires. Dropping again, the F4F bounced a second time and sailed over both wire barriers. While still in flight, Achten's right wing scraped the island. Wobbling, the F4F thudded down on its left gear which collapsed, but his speed sent Achten skidding far forward along the deck. The Grumman slid into a group of planes being parked well forward. Tragically, the propellor struck and killed James T. Freund, Sea1c, a VT-6 plane handler who was parking Grumman F-10. The impact knocked down another airdale, who fortunately escaped serious

The fatal deck crash on board the *Enterprise*, 15 May 1942. On the right is Mach. J. A. Achten's F-21 (BuNo. 5079). (NA 80-G-16970.)

injury. Achten was unhurt, but both his F-21 and the F-10 (with crumpled tail and right wing) would require major overhaul before either flew again.[15]

At 1008 the audience for which Halsey had produced this charade put in its appearance. The *Enterprise*'s radar detected a contact bearing 250 degrees, distance 39 miles. Analysis of this radar plot demonstrated that the bogey, almost certainly a flying boat operating out of Tulagi, was carefully snooping the task force. At 1035, the contact bore 315 degrees, distance 80 miles, and it seemed to hold that range thereafter. Cryptanalysts on board the *Enterprise* tackled radio messages from the enemy aircraft to its base.

There was no need for Task Force 16 to continue closing the Solomons, so at 1045, Halsey changed course to 000 degrees, as if to make directly for the now obsolete 0900, 16 May rendezvous some 270 miles north. Of course, he had no intention of going there, but he wanted to entertain the enemy for a while yet. The *Enterprise* at 1118 launched its third CAP of the day, eight F4Fs led by Gray, along with a relief inner air patrol of two F4Fs and two SBDs. Because of the lack of wind, the SBDs had to leave their depth charges behind. Lt. Cdr. Dow, the FDO, vectored Gray's Division in pursuit of the bogey lurking 70 to 80 miles out. Overall visibility was extremely high. Some 40 to 50 miles away, Gray was surprised to be able to see the task force behind him—white streaks on the deep blue ocean. As for the Japanese, they ran whenever fighters tried to come after them. Throughout the day, the CAP tried a number of times to corner the wily flying boats, but to no avail. Halsey had the alarming thought the enemy might have airborne radar, but he was wrong. Japanese skill in tracking the task force and avoiding interception was due to keen eyes, not radar waves.

Halsey's sudden appearance east of Tulagi made just the sort of impact CinCPac desired. A frustrated Inoue had looked forward to a smooth seizure of Ocean and

Nauru (his RY Operation) after the setbacks in the Coral Sea. The RY Invasion Force, one light cruiser, one fast minelayer, two destroyers, and two transports, was finally at sea, moving northeast from Rabaul. Farther north and about 200 miles ahead of them was the covering force: Takagi's much used MO Striking Force now shrunk to two heavy cruisers and a few destroyers. Other South Seas Force warships were deployed much closer to Rabaul. Z-Day, the landings at Ocean and Nauru, Inoue scheduled for 17 May.

The morning of 15 May, the Yokohama Air Group detachment at Tulagi had sent three Kawanishi Type 97 flying boats to search the waters 600 miles east of base. At 1015, one crew tapped out this startling message:

> Sight two enemy carriers with four cruisers and six destroyers, bearing 098 degrees from base, distance 445 miles. Enemy base course 270 degrees, speed 14 knots.[16]

This report electrified South Seas Force. Just to make certain his troops had not spotted some reefs or islets in the Santa Cruz group and jumped to the wrong conclusion, the Yokohama detachment commander told his men to verify the contact. They not only repeated the message, but explained in exasperation that enemy fighters were actually in pursuit of them! For the next several hours, this crew and that of another flying boat vectored onto the scene maintained contact with Task Force 16 and kept their superiors accurately informed—a massive improvement since the recently fought battle.

Inoue feared an air strike on Tulagi or Rabaul, conceivably early the following day. Rear Admiral Yamada, commanding the 5th Air Attack Force at Rabaul, ordered the Yokohama group at Tulagi to execute a night torpedo attack with flying boats. He arranged to stage fighters from Lae back to Rabaul. At 1350, Inoue suspended the RY Operation and ordered his surface forces to gather about 300 miles north of Rabaul to be in position to offer night battle should the Americans close in. Stripped of his own flattops, Inoue felt especially vulnerable to American carrier raids.

About the same time Inoue postponed the RY Operation, the *Enterprise* labored

A VF-6 F4F-4 being disengaged from the arresting gear on 15 May. The aircraft shows the new marking scheme dispensing with striped tails and red balls in the roundels. (NA 80-G-14376.)

More from the "worst operating day in VF-6 history," 15 May 1942. Walter Hiebert is being helped from his F4F-4 (BuNo. 5048) after hitting the barrier. (NA 80-G-14455.)

to launch her fourth CAP and IAP. At 1345 eight F4Fs for CAP and the usual two pairs of fighters and dive bombers for IAP began taking off. Scheduled to follow were thirteen SBDs for the afternoon search 200 miles to the northwest. Fighting Six's plague of accidents continued. Ens. William Holt started a normal takeoff run in his Grumman. Just forward of the stack, his right wing unaccountably lifted his right wheel off the deck. Holt swerved violently to the left, flew over the port corner of the flight deck, and dropped away in a sickly 180-degree spin toward the water. His left wing knifed into a wave crest, causing the F4F to cartwheel. Knocked out by the rough ditching, Holt fortuitously revived when water poured into the cockpit. He scrambled out in time, lucky to suffer only a headache, bruises, and a cut arm. The destroyer *Maury* had him on board in a few minutes. If the gremlins were appeased on VF-6's behalf, they gave no sign. Landing at 1406 with the third CAP, Ens. Walter Hiebert put F-13 into the barrier after his tail hook failed to snag an arresting wire. The result was another major overhaul.[17]

Halsey decided enough was enough. At 1424, he ordered Task Force 16 to "haul out" at 20 knots, course due east. The Japanese snoopers tarried long enough to see that the carriers headed away before they started the long return flight to Tulagi. Halsey broke radio silence to set a new rendezvous for Kinkaid, this one well to the south. Fortunately for Fighting Six, the rest of that ill-starred day's flights were routine. Sunset saw the task force about 180 miles northeast of Santa Cruz, and at 1900, Halsey changed course again to head for familiar waters near Efate. The ides of May turned out to be the "worst operating day in VF-6 history,"[18] with one fighter lost and three major repair jobs. Five crashes by *Enterprise* aircraft set a one-day record for "The Big E." Without firing a shot, Fighting Six had shrunk to only twenty-one flyable F4F-4s. That day, the *Hornet* was just a bemused spectator. CinCPac, however, had earned a big victory without fighting.

Halsey had fulfilled Nimitz's desire to put a good scare into the Japanese, but

The USS *Hornet* (CV-8) in the Solomons, 15 May 1942. (NA 80-G-14866.)

as of early 16 May as he headed away from the enemy at 20 knots, he did not know what the devil was going on. The *Hornet* took over duty from an *Enterprise* (especially VF-6) reeling from the previous day's accidents. She sent a search 200 miles northwest to make sure nothing trailed them. At 0600, Kinkaid's long awaited Task Group 17.2 (the *Minneapolis*, the *New Orleans*, and three destroyers) finally joined up, and the combined task force took up a southerly heading. Ahead lay a tropical weather front that forced the *Hornet* to recover all aircraft for a time. Halsey's first concern was to refuel his thirsty ships, then await developments. At 1600, he received the all-important message from Pearl Harbor. Nimitz had recalled Task Force 16 back to Hawaii. CinCPac intelligence learned that Inoue on 16 May had formally postponed the RY Operation. Task Force 16's presence in the South Pacific was no longer required; Nimitz had other vital tasks for the *Enterprise* and the *Hornet*.

"DESIRE YOU PROCEED TO THE HAWAIIAN AREA."[1]

As the *Yorktown* departed the Coral Sea on course for Tongatabu, a long-range debate raged between King and Nimitz with regard to the deployment of her air group and the refugee *Lexington* flyers. CominCh was extremely concerned about the defenses in the South Pacific because he believed the Japanese would soon resume their offensive stabs toward Port Moresby, New Caledonia, and the Fijis. The Army Air Forces, he felt, had failed to supply adequate numbers of aircraft to protect these vital locations, so King thought it was necessary to use Pacific Fleet aircraft to do the job. On 12 May he suggested to Nimitz that some *Yorktown* and *Lexington* aircraft, pilots, and ground crews be left at New Caledonia and in the Fijis. Worried about risking his precious aircraft carriers, King added that it might be better to keep the flattops in the rear and fight their air groups from the threatened shore bases. He wanted to retain the *Yorktown* and *Lexington* aviation personnel in the South Pacific to help prepare bases so that the Task Force 16 air groups could more easily operate from such places as Noumea, the Fijis, and Efate.

The thought of stranding his carrier squadron personnel in the South Pacific was totally unacceptable to CinCPac. Strong indications had reached Nimitz that the Japanese planned major offensives in the Central and North Pacific, with Midway and possibly even Oahu as the targets. His first order of business was to convert King to this viewpoint, a difficult task because of CominCh's fixation with the South Pacific. Nimitz on 13 May replied forcefully to King's proposals. He desired that the *Yorktown* return to Pearl Harbor and there bring the *Yorktown* Air Group back up to strength:

> This group will be useful pending *Yorktown* repairs for assisting the still inadequate defense of Oahu and will be available for *Yorktown* as soon as her repairs are finished.[2]

As for the *Lexington* survivors, Nimitz had already made arrangements to send most of them directly back to the West Coast. Thus were the *Yorktown* and *Lexington* fighter pilots spared from languishing in the South Pacific. Certainly King at this time would have preferred them there.

There is no space here to discuss at length the reasons why King and Nimitz differed in their estimates of Japanese intentions. This is treated in my book *The First South Pacific Campaign*. What is important here is that Nimitz skillfully engineered circumstances that would permit him to recall his carriers to the Central Pacific where he vitally needed them to deal with expected Japanese attacks late in May or early in June. That was why he sent highly unorthodox, secret orders to Halsey to abandon the ambush of the RY Invasion Force and be sighted by the Japanese. King eventually agreed for the most part with Nimitz's estimate of the situation, and the carriers did return in time to sortie in the defense of Midway.

On 15 May, Task Force 17 reached the familiar waters of the Tonga group and made ready to enter Tongatabu's Nukualofa anchorage where fuel and supplies waited. During the voyage back, the *Yorktown*'s hard-working mechanics and ordnancemen had brought to operational status fifty-five of the sixty-nine aircraft still on board: fifteen fighters, thirty-one dive bombers, and nine torpedo planes. At 0730, Fighting Forty-two flew ten fighters to the airstrip on Tongatabu as air defense. It is likely that some *Yorktown* SBDs operated from there as well, and at least one TBD, Joe Taylor's T-1 from Torpedo Five, "which he flew around because he had fuel to spare and nurses to impress."[3] The fortunate pilots were pleased to find sixty cases of beer thoughtfully provided by the New Zealanders!

In Nukualofa Roads, the *Yorktown* and her consorts worked to ready themselves again for sea. Joining them on 16 May was Rear Admiral Smith with the *Astoria* after his short stopover at Noumea. On 17 May, the *Lexington* survivors began transferring to the transports *George F. Elliott* and *Barnett* for the trip to San Diego. Fletcher also provided the heavy cruiser *Chester* to escort them to the West Coast. As of 16 May, Fletcher himself had orders from CinCPac to return to Pearl Harbor at his "best sustained speed" when his force was ready for sea. Fitch was to return to San Diego, there to re-form Task Force 11 with the *Saratoga* as his flagship.

During the sojourn at Tongatabu, there came a parting of the ways between those fighter pilots who would stay with the *Yorktown* and those returning to the States. Fighting Forty-two formally detached Lt. Cdr. Flatley, who would take command of the new Fighting Ten at San Diego. Also leaving the squadron was Lieut. (jg) Plott, still recuperating from illness. Five of the six Fighting Two pilots who had landed on board on 8 May were slated to leave for the West Coast. Among them, Scoop Vorse and Doc Sellstrom, at least, asked to be allowed to remain on board and ride the *Yorktown* to Pearl to rejoin Jimmy Thach's Fighting Three at Kaneohe. Their orders were firm, however, and off they went. The following Fighting Two and Fighting Three pilots took ship for San Diego:

VF-2	VF-3
Lt. Cdr. Ramsey	Lieut. Gayler
Lieut. Borries	Lieut. Vorse
Kanze, AP2c	Lieut. (jg) Dufilho
	Lieut. (jg) Morgan
	Ens. Eder
	Ens. Lackey
	Ens. Haynes
	Ens. Sellstrom

Rejoining Fighting Forty-two was the much-traveled Scott McCuskey, while three *Lexington* survivors who had original postings to Fighting Forty-two finally made it to the squadron at Tongatabu. They were Ensigns Markham, Bain, and Hopper. Riding the *Yorktown* to Pearl was another ex–VF-2 pilot, Ens. Wileman, who had orders to Fighting Six.

The morning of 19 May, Fitch and his staff embarked on board the heavy cruiser *Chester,* which became flagship of his little Task Group 17.6, that ship and the two transports. That afternoon, the *Yorktown* eased out of the narrow anchorage, gathered her escorts, and headed out to sea. In her wake fuel oil still trailed from damaged fuel bunkers that could not be repaired short of the drydock at Pearl. Her planes flew out from Tongatabu and landed on board. The voyage from Tongatabu would prove refreshingly routine, mainly a time to write reports and recount at length what had happened in the Coral Sea. The *Yorktown*'s crew expected a stopover at Pearl for fuel and provisions, then hopefully a few months in a stateside yard while the *Yorktown* mended her wounds and underwent full refit. CinCPac, however, had far different ideas in mind, in which the old warrior would face her sternest trials.

Fitch's Task Group 17.6 steamed in company with the main body of Task Force 17 until the dawn of 21 May, when it was time for them to go their own way to San Diego. Sharing a cabin with his good friend Bob Dixon in one of the transports, Jimmy Flatley devoted most of his time to compiling a detailed squadron doctrine for Fighting Ten, one that reflected Flatley's careful analysis of the Coral Sea air battles. Meanwhile the miles slipped by peacefully, while Fletcher's ships closed the distance to Pearl. On 26 May, one day short of the destination, Fletcher offered this sentiment to the proud seamen of Task Force 17:

> On this the one hundredth day since our departure from Pearl, I wish to congratulate all hands upon the successful operations, the splendid seamanship, the remarkable engineering performance and the fine spirit which has marked each of the hundred days.[4]

The homecoming in Japan of the two carriers of the 5th Carrier Division was not so auspicious. On 14 May, the Naval General Staff in Tokyo assessed aviation casualty reports from the *Shōkaku* and the *Zuikaku,* concluding that "neither ship can possibly be used in the next operation."[5] The *Shōkaku* reached Japan 17 May, and the experts decided repairs would take up to three months. The *Zuikaku* likewise arrived at Kure four days later, undamaged, but with her air group in tatters. The Japanese lacked advanced training units equivalent to the American advanced carrier training groups, nor were there any replacement carrier air groups that could be transferred onto the *Zuikaku.* Her air group would have to draw green pilots fresh out of training, integrate them into the squadrons, and season them before the group would be combat ready again. This process would take two to three months according to Japanese reckoning. Thus Task Force 17 had accomplished a great deal, depriving the Combined Fleet of two fleet carriers for its "next operation"—but the Japanese high command was so overconfident of success, they felt they did not need the *Shōkaku* and the *Zuikaku* anyway!

Even with the orders received the evening of 16 May instructing him to return to Pearl, Halsey could not depart immediately. He had to gather his oilers and other detached forces in order to fuel before setting off to the north. The seventeenth of May was overcast with occasional squalls as Task Force 16 headed southward past Efate. Halsey sent two *Enterprise* SBDs there as pigeon post to deliver messages. That day orders from CinCPac told him not to attack targets in the Gilberts during his homeward passage. Nimitz desired that his redeployment to Hawaiian waters remain undetected by the enemy. The morning of 18 May, Halsey rendezvoused with his fueling group, and at 0915, he set base course as 035 degrees—Oahu-bound. That evening, Halsey received another prod from Nimitz: "Expedite return."[6]

Like the previous day, 18 May was generally rainy. The VF-6 pilots learned some definite information regarding the recent fight in the Coral Sea and were surprised by VF-2's high losses. Looking at his own aircraft with some misgivings, a VF-6 diarist gibed, "Hope we get rid of these F4F-4's before we have adventures of that kind."[7] On the way back, Halsey kept a steady 17 knots. The cruiser Curtiss SOC floatplanes handled some of the search and IAP duties, giving the carriers more time for training. On the trip down, the task force had lost 8 May, but this time over the line, they gained another 20 May. With relief, the VF-6 diarist recorded crossing "back into God's hemisphere."[8] The task force enjoyed good weather all the way to Pearl.

One day short of Pearl, Fighting Six suffered another tragedy on a voyage riddled with accidents. The *Enterprise* on 25 May did not have the duty, so Captain Murray scheduled a training mission with fifteen F4Fs, thirty-two SBDs, and fourteen TBDs. Lieut. (jg) Gayle Hermann, a survivor of VF-6's Pearl Harbor mishap, flew one of the Grummans assigned to gunnery training. Under the right wing he carried a tow can holding the target sleeve and line. At 0802 just after lifting off the flight deck, Hermann went into a tight right turn, but stalled into a slow right spin. His F4F splashed off "The Big E's" starboard bow. The plane sank with the pilot still inside, but soon after, Hermann floated free. He was unconscious, evidently sup-

An F4F-4 from VF-6 lifts off on 18 May from the *Enterprise*. The fuselage roundels have been enlarged since 15 May. (NA 80-G-7725.)

A view of the *Enterprise*'s flight deck on 18 May, the day Bill Halsey was told to "Expedite return" to Pearl Harbor. (NA 80-G-14120.)

ported by the buoyancy of his parachute pack. The *Ellet,* the plane guard destroyer, raced in to make the rescue. One of her officers, Ens. Charles F. Darnell, dived over the side to bring the pilot in, but before Darnell could swim to him, Gayle Hermann without regaining consciousness rolled out of his chute straps and sank out of sight. The *Ellet* searched the area for one hour, but to no avail.[9] It was a tough blow to the squadron, as Hermann had been one of the stalwarts, an ex-aviation cadet with a regular commission and three years in Fighting Six. A review board later determined he had attempted the sharp turn before he had the speed to do it safely.

CORAL SEA COMBAT LESSONS

The Battle of the Coral Sea offered so many "firsts" for the U.S., that it is difficult to list them all. For the purposes of this study, it was the first acid test of naval carrier doctrine, and as such proved immensely important in shaping ideas. Unfortunately, the defense of Midway loomed so soon after that there was very little opportunity for other commanders to study and apply the lessons learned so dearly at Coral Sea. For Midway, the *Yorktown* aviators were the only ones in a position to profit from their hard-earned Coral Sea experiences, and their excellent performance at Midway demonstrated the value of those lessons.

Coral Sea provided the U.S. naval fighter pilots with their introduction to the vaunted Japanese Zero fighter. The VF-2 and VF-42 pilots respected the enemy fighter, particularly its tremendous maneuverability, but the Mitsubishis did not intimidate them. On the basis of their first combat experiences, the pilots felt their Grumman F4F-3 Wildcats were equal to the Zeros in speed and climbing ability and superior in firepower and protection, being inferior only in maneuverability. Flatley stated their feelings best:

The F4F-3 properly handled can best the enemy carrier based fighters encountered so far. This includes the type 'Zero.'[1]

The F4F-3's principal defect, they thought, was radius of action. The escort fighters, in particular VF-2's troops, got into trouble on 8 May because they had throttled way back to save fuel. In that condition they were just not prepared to meet enemy fighters. To extend their range, the Wildcats had to have droppable fuel tanks. Of course, the fighter pilots much preferred a definite superiority in all areas of performance versus the Zero, and several requested delivery of the Vought F4U-1 Corsair, with greater speed, climb, and maneuverability than the F4F-3.

Thus with the F4F-3, fighter tactics proved to be the key in beating the Zero. Well demonstrated at Coral Sea was the need for altitude advantage for hit-and-run attacks. Flatley carefully analyzed his own combats and those of the other VF-42 pilots. In his action report for 7 May, he offered "Hints to Navy VF pilots." He conceded far superior maneuverability to the lighter, more agile Japanese fighters, but explained how that could be overcome:

> The most effective attack against a more maneuverable fighter is to obtain altitude advantage, dive in, attack, pull up using speed gained in dive to maintain altitude advantage. The old dog-fight of chasing tails is not satisfactory and must not be employed when opposing the Jap.[2]

With the hit-and-run attacks, Flatley cautioned: "If your target maneuvers out of your sight during your approach, pull out and let one of the following planes get him."[3] The attempt to stay with a Japanese fighter for extended maneuvers could forfeit the F4F's altitude advantage. From a superior altitude, Flatley was confident of taking on any adversary. "Never hesitate to dive in,"[4] he urged the other pilots.

One of the main reasons the F4F pilots had a hard time was that they separated from each other and failed to give mutual support. The *Yorktown* action report offered a good postmortem for the troubles of 8 May:

> Do not become separated from your formation. . . . The planes that did become separated were so busy maneuvering to get Jap fighters off their tails that they had time for nothing else.[5]

Mutual protection was something very difficult to achieve without a firm idea of how to do it, but the pilots made a commitment to try to stay together. Macomber and his wingman, Bassett, promised each other they would not separate in the next battle. Others did the same.

One thing everyone agreed on was the need for more fighters on board the carriers. Under the present circumstances, there were simply not enough to go around. Fletcher himself was acutely aware of the small number of F4Fs, especially as it appeared the enemy had many more Zeros available. Word had it that CinCPac was increasing squadron complement to twenty-seven fighters, feasible because of the use of folding wing F4F-4s. Pederson, the *Yorktown* Air Group commander, thought twenty-seven the minimum number necessary and added, "36 would be none too many if we are to engage Japanese carriers on equal terms."[6] He sketched an ideal carrier group with thirty-six fighters, thirty-six dive bombers, and sixteen torpedo planes. The fighting squadron would have twenty-seven fighters operational and nine spares, with thirty-three pilots on strength. This would enable the CAP to operate in groups of eight, rather than two to four as at Coral Sea. Additional fighters would also allow larger escorts for the strike planes. No doubt about it, the carriers had to have more fighters.

Escort operations on 7 and 8 May saw some surprises and fostered grave misconceptions on the part of some distant analysts who lacked all the facts. Despite taking the major share of credit for damaging or sinking both carrier targets those two days, neither Torpedo Two nor Torpedo Five lost any aircraft shot down. There were, of course, very special reasons for this. On 7 May, the *Shōhō*'s air defense was weak, only six fighters, and the Grumman escorts prevented them from ganging up on the TBDs. The next day the escort fighters likewise did their job, but Fighting Two paid the price with three pilots lost on the torpedo escort mission. Poor visibility and the dispersed Japanese combat air patrol also contributed to keeping torpedo plane losses to a minimum. Strangely, it seemed the Zero pilots often preferred tussling with the escorts rather than charging after the torpedo planes.

Despite their own good fortune at Coral Sea, the TBD pilots had no illusions as to the vulnerability of their poorly armed and unarmored Devastators. The *Yorktown*'s action report stressed, "it is essential that they [the TBDs] be furnished with fighter protection."[7] Pederson went on to recommend that the torpedo escort (four to eight fighters depending upon anticipated opposition) deploy themselves up sun and at least 5,000 to 6,000 feet above the torpedo planes, visibility permitting. This would be an effort to duplicate the excellent results achieved on 7 May by Flatley's escorts. In his own report for 7 May, Flatley added that if the torpedo planes were cruising well above the water (4,000 to 6,000 feet), he thought it better to put the escort fighters down sun and only 2,000 feet above the TBDs so they could cover the sun lane. Otherwise it would be too easy for Zeros to dive past the F4Fs unseen in the sun's glare. There were two methods of approach used by torpedo squadrons, and both were employed on 8 May. Taylor took Torpedo Five in low, below 500 feet to prevent steep high-side and high-astern attacks. Brett, on the other hand, led Torpedo Two into a "high level" approach, around 6,000 feet, so the TBDs could spiral in at high speed before recovering below 100 feet in order to chop speed below 115 knots for the actual torpedo release. Brett felt his style of approach would give the enemy CAP "time for only one run"[8] while the TBDs pushed home their attack. Both VT leaders agreed that close fighter support was absolutely imperative for them to complete their mission.

Strangely, the Douglas SBD dive bombers suffered the heaviest strike plane losses at Coral Sea. This led distant analysts to infer that the dive bomber escort needed beefing up, even at the expense of the torpedo planes. Again, specific reasons existed why the SBDs took it on the chin. Most of the intercepts came after they dived in. The SBDs drew so much attention because they arrived first in the target area, something that would not happen the next month at Midway. Japanese fighters jumped them or the escorts and largely left the torpedo planes alone.

Equally important, the dive bomber escorts on both 7 and 8 May failed to protect their charges. On 7 May, VF-2's VSB escort cruised at 18,000 feet and stayed well behind the lead attack element, Scouting Two. Apparently they did not spiral in with the SBDs, but remained at high altitude looking to engage any Zeros at their height. There were, of course, no Japanese at those lofty altitudes, and the escort understandably never did discern the interceptors far below. Lt. Cdr. Dixon of Scouting Two summed up the situation in his report:

> VF *must accompany* the groups to be protected. Their mere presence in a combat area means nothing in the present short, violent carrier air group attacks.[9]

The *Yorktown*'s dive bomber escorts did follow the SBDs in, but they waited until all of the SBDs had dived before doing so themselves. By the time these fighters entered the battle area, the combat was largely over. Thus both groups of VSB escorts gave priority to protecting the pushover points even though no opposition was there. Something very similar would happen to Fighting Six on 4 June at Midway.

On 8 May, the VSB escorts of both groups lost sight of the dive bombers because of poor visibility, and returned separately. Aside from Cdr. Ault's command section, the SBDs had no support whatsoever in the target area. Covering Ault was Bull's VF-2 section, but Zeros took out both F4Fs before the actual attack. The Japanese pounced on the *Lexington*'s SBDs after they made their dives. Considering how much attention they drew from defending fighters, the SBDs did well. They could protect themselves much better than could the TBDs.

Regarding VSB escort, the *Yorktown* report advised that the fighters take station 2,000 to 4,000 feet above and up sun of the SBDs. They were to spiral in around their charges to support them during the actual attack and the vulnerable period of their withdrawal. Dixon of Scouting Two offered more detailed suggestions. He thought that half of the VSB escort should deploy 1,000 feet over the center of the SBD formation to intercept head-on attacks. When the lead dive bombers pushed over, these fighters were to descend with them and cover their pull-outs, circling that area if need be. The rest of the VSB escort was to take station 1,000 to 2,000 feet above and behind the SBD formation to prevent attacks from astern. They would stay at high altitude to protect the dive point until the last SBD had pushed over. Then these fighters could follow them in to protect the trailing division. All of this, of course, was predicated on having sufficient fighters to divide up into different groups.

The admirals as well as the fighter pilots were disappointed in the combat air patrol's failure to break up the 8 May enemy strike before it attacked Task Force 17. This was the first occasion the CAP had to oppose a powerful enemy carrier strike group with fighter escorts. As such, it was an important test of fighter direction doctrine, and several important problems emerged in the FDO's handling of the situation: the altitude assigned to the fighters, the distances they were out, and the separation of the fighters into numerous small groups. What must be remembered in a discussion of the 8 May CAP is that this was the first time an FDO had to cope with such a complex attack. Contacts flooded the radar plot. Prewar maneuvers and limited wartime training did not offer the FDOs the chance to practice such intricate intercept problems. Battle required the FDO to know what he was doing—there was no time for indecision.

On 8 May, Red Gill initially deployed his fighters at 10,000, 8,000, and 1,000 feet. The loudest post-battle complaint was that the Grummans nowhere achieved altitude advantage over the enemy dive bombers before they pushed over. Indeed, both Fitch and Sherman recommended in their reports that the CAP habitually be deployed at 20,000 feet to ensure height advantage over enemy dive bombers and fighters. Sherman personally believed the CAP should comprise two elements: a high CAP at 20,000 feet and an anti–torpedo-plane patrol (of fighters if there were enough, otherwise SBDs as an expedient) cruising at 3,000 feet and situated 3,000 yards out from the screening ships. The *Yorktown*'s Pederson desired a more flexible distribution of the CAP. The FDO should send fighters to 20,000 feet only if the altitude of the enemy strike group was unknown and there was ample visibility. Visibility was vital, for at 20,000 feet the CAP might not spot enemy planes passing far below. Gill had previously addressed himself to the problem of CAP altitude. Drawing on his own experience as a naval aviator as well as the opinions of VF-2 pilots, he agreed with the old truism that it was often easier to see a plane from below than from above. He kept his high CAP at 10,000 feet so they could see each way more easily. The main drawback involved the relatively low climb rate of the F4F-3 Wildcat, something the FDO and others, especially on board the *Lexington,*. did not take into account. The way Gill used his high CAP, the fighters simply could not climb quickly enough to take position over the Japanese carrier bombers. Coral Sea certainly did not provide answers as to what altitudes the CAP should fly.

Most fighter pilots were critical of the FDO's decision to intercept fairly close to the task force. Gill's scheme evidently involved a long-range interception only by Ramsey's five F4Fs. He held Flatley's division in abeyance for three minutes before sending his four Wildcats out low to a distance of 15 miles. Gill reinforced Ramsey with three sections climbing to 12,000 feet; they acted as a second wave to make contact only a few miles out. He fragmented the CAP into several groups intercepting in piecemeal fashion. Fitch in his report stressed it would be best to vector the CAP as quickly as possible, so the fighters could make swift contact with the enemy strike and fight all the way back to the ships. The *Yorktown*'s air analysts also wanted to intercept as far out as feasible, at least 30 miles distant from the task force. They were willing to take a calculated risk in order to have the time to do a good job in disrupting the attackers. The risk was that some enemy aircraft might slip through unseen. Some of the fighter pilots thought they could intercept as far as 50 miles out, but conceded this happy event would require a great deal of coordination with the FDO and a miraculous performance by radar.

Given the agreement to hit the enemy a good deal farther out, how should the fighters deploy? At Coral Sea there is no doubt the F4Fs were unduly dispersed; in no instance was a group of intercepting fighters larger than four. Yet, Gill had tried to rectify the mistakes made on 20 February when nearly all of the CAP was in one group and missed countering a second wave of attackers. However, his complex deployment of first line, second line, and reserve proved to be beyond the ability of his equipment and training to control. The *Yorktown*'s Grummans, for the most part, lacked IFF gear. They as well as the numerous SBDs on anti–torpedo-plane patrol cluttered the radar screen. Gill could not coordinate the activities of several small fighter elements, and nowhere did the FDO achieve a decisive concentration of fighters. As Noel Gayler complained,

> The way we have been operating, we'll intercept them first with two planes then holler like hell for help and if we're lucky maybe we'll get more planes on the scene, eventually.[10]

From his FD plot on board the *Yorktown*, Pederson followed the 8 May air battle in detail. Gill's major mistake, he felt, was trying to control too closely the course of the air battle. In his opinion Gill did not keep the CAP informed of the bearings and altitudes of the various elements of the enemy strike group. Pederson thought, as did Flatley, that the FDO should have relayed to the CAP all the information he had. Most of the pilots had no real idea what they were supposed to intercept and became confused as to what the FDO wanted them to do. The fighter pilots themselves were not blameless because Gill repeatedly and in vain asked for information as to the strength and altitude of the enemy planes. Thus the pilots required additional training in order to report promptly to the FDO precisely what they saw. Only in this fashion could he have a decent idea what was happening.

The *Yorktown* action report stressed the need for improving the physical layout of the FD plot and radar. The FDO and his staff required their own area, private and ample for their needs. Also important was a special communications network to secure and disseminate information swiftly. With the medium high frequency (MHF) radios in use, the FDOs always risked revealing their presence to the enemy by breaking radio silence. Thus they had to have superfrequency radios with a reliable range of 50 miles. The *Yorktown*'s report also reiterated the need for IFF gear for all aircraft, so the FDO could tell all the players on his scoreboard. Trouble was, the next desperate battle would take place before much could be done to implement these recommendations.

PART III

The Battle of Midway

CHAPTER 14

Getting Ready for Midway

THE REORGANIZATION OF FIGHTING THREE

In the middle of April, Jimmy Thach found himself in rather strange circumstances. His squadron boasted a full complement of airplanes, but Thach was the only pilot permanently on strength with the unit! This had come about mainly because Thach had lent twelve pilots and most of his maintenance crews to Paul Ramsey's Fighting Two on board the *Lexington*. The *Lex* departed Pearl on 15 April never to return. Other VF-3 pilots left for stateside duty, including the executive officer, Don Lovelace, for a squadron of his own. Their replacements, fourteen rookies, failed to appear, either still completing training or drawn off to other units. Pat Mitchell's Fighting Eight had scooped up many of them in late March when he struggled to fill out his squadron to the new twenty-seven-plane complement.

For a time, Thach's executive officer was Butch O'Hare, but he soon departed under special orders to the West Coast. Reunited with his family, O'Hare traveled to Washington, and, after a few days rest, on 21 April he went to the White House where President Roosevelt presented him with the Medal of Honor for his gallantry on 20 February. Rita Wooster O'Hare placed the coveted medal around her husband's neck. That day he also received special promotion to lieutenant commander. Overwhelmed by the intense response accorded one of the country's first war heroes, O'Hare took a well-deserved leave before reporting back to Oahu.

Thach had plenty to do to keep himself busy at Kaneohe. On 16 April, the materiel officer on the ComCarPac staff instructed him to take delivery of twenty-one factory-fresh Grumman F4F-4 Wildcats. This shipment had not arrived in time to permit Fighting Two to reequip with the new model Grumman. Thach made ready to turn over the eighteen F4F-3A Wildcats presently on strength to Marine Fighting Squadron 212 at Ewa. The last of them went to the marines on 29 April. Meanwhile, Thach amused himself by test-flying each of his new fighters. Fighting Three, such as it was, remained at NAS Kaneohe. Another old *Saratoga* squadron, Torpedo Three, operated from there as well, and at the end of April a third rejoined the Kaneohe circle. Max Leslie's Bombing Three returned ashore after going out with the *Enterprise* for the Tokyo Raid. Ostensibly the *Saratoga* flyers awaited the reappearance of their own flattop still undergoing repair and refit at Bremerton. The *Saratoga* was expected to rejoin the fleet sometime early that summer.

Toward the end of April, Thach acquired a wingman when Ens. Robert Dibb arrived at Pearl. Just turned twenty-one, "Ram" Dibb, survivor of the spectacular crash on the *Hornet* the previous month, had orders to Fighting Three after qual-

Jimmy Thach and company at NAS Kaneohe Bay, early May 1942, *l to r*: Cheek, D. C. Barnes, Berger, Dibb, Thach, Conatser. (Cdr. T. F. Cheek, USN.)

ifying at the ACTG in San Diego. He benefited greatly from an unusually close association with his new commanding officer, for under the circumstances Thach could devote a great deal of time to training Dibb. To put up a whole division of fighters, he commandeered the services of two experienced VB-5 pilots, both cast upon the beach for health reasons until the *Yorktown*'s return from the South Pacific. They were Lieut. (jg) Charlie N. ("Tex") Conatser and Lieut. (jg) Nels L. A. Berger. Two real fighter pilots reported in after 26 April when the *Enterprise* docked at Pearl Harbor. Mach. Doyle ("Tom") Barnes and Mach. Tom Cheek were NAPs from Fighting Two who had served temporarily with Fighting Six on the Tokyo Raid. New orders sent them to Thach at Kaneohe, where they were very welcome. With Barnes and Cheek on board, Thach was able to work in some tactical training while bringing Dibb along in his familiarization with fighters.

In response to Halsey's 26 April message stressing the need for drop tanks for the F4Fs, NAS Pearl Harbor decided to wait no further for the Bureau of Aeronautics to act. Engineers at Pearl worked up a forty-two-gallon belly tank and fastened the "tub like attachment"[1] to the underside of F4F-4 BuNo. 5050. On 9 May, Rear Admiral Noyes shipped 5050 to Thach for tests: landing, takeoff, suction, and release of the drop tank. Thach reported back on 20 May, noting that the tank had functioned well. He indicated that such a tank could increase a CAP mission to four or five hours, but advised that three hours was quite enough for that duty. He felt the tanks valuable for strike missions, where the extra flight time would be crucial.[2]

Thach had his hands full after 20 May when seven young ensigns joined the squadron: Horace A. Bass, Mark K. Bright, Harold J. W. Eppler, Robert C. Evans, Van H. Morris, Daniel C. Sheedy, and Milton Tootle, Jr. Five of the seven had original orders to Fighting Eight—so Thach returned the favor to Mitchell for taking his pilots two months before. The new arrivals were fresh from ACTG and very inexperienced. Finding them especially deficient in gunnery training, Thach

Thach's new F4F-4s at Kaneohe, 5 May 1942. (*Upper photo*: NA 80-G-13201; *lower photo*: NA 80-G-64829.)

scheduled training flights so they could shoot at towed sleeves. Thach worked closely with his new pilots, flying very tight wing on each as he made his gunnery run, coaching them so they could hit their targets. Sheedy, for one, was extremely disappointed with his initial scores, but with Thach's guidance he started hitting and gained confidence. Thach was a talented teacher, very patient, and the results showed it. Intensive tactical training would have to come later. Now he could only show the rudiments of his "beam defense" maneuver, later dubbed the "Thach Weave" (see appendix). Conatser and Berger returned to their SBDs, while old hands Barnes and Cheek proved invaluable in helping to train the ensigns. Thach expected to have ample time to work with his inexperienced charges until the return of his old pilots, whom Ramsey had borrowed for Fighting Two. Then he could integrate the whole squadron into a fighting team.

Unbeknownst to Thach, forces had been set in motion that would change his rosy expectations. CinCPac's decision to send the *Lexington* aviation personnel (including the VF-3 pilots) directly to San Diego placed Thach's old team out of reach for the time being. Faced with the prospect of desperate battle at Midway, Nimitz had to have the *Yorktown* (if she could be made battleworthy) to reinforce the *Enterprise* and the *Hornet* in defense of the island. However, Noyes, Halsey's administrative representative ashore, was concerned about the condition of the *Yorktown* Air Group in light of the losses inflicted at Coral Sea, not to mention the enervation of their sustained sojourn at sea. The Yorktowners had not enjoyed a tour of shore duty for nearly a year.

Noyes examined the resources available to him to reconstitute the *Yorktown* Air Group if need be. As of 21 May, fifty-three carrier aircraft were on strength with carrier squadrons on Oahu:[3]

22 F4F-4s	Fighting Three (only 11 pilots)
18 SBD-3s	Bombing Three
13 TBD-1s	Torpedo Three
53	

As replacements, ComCarPac had twenty-seven F4F-4s, sixteen SBD-3s, and three TBD-1s. At NAS Alameda near San Francisco, three squadrons awaited transport across to Pearl Harbor:

Fighting Five	Lt. Cdr. Leroy C. Simpler	18 F4F-4s
Fighting Seventy-two	Lt. Cdr. Henry G. Sanchez	20 F4F-4s
Torpedo Eight Detachment	Lieut. Harold H. Larsen	21 TBF-1s

These units were not expected to arrive in time to sortie with Task Force 16.

Considering the urgent situation, Noyes thought it best to reorganize the squadrons in the *Yorktown* Air Group. He would replace Bill Burch's Scouting Five, which had suffered high losses at Coral Sea, with Leslie's Bombing Three. He also would switch Torpedo Three, now under Lt. Cdr. Lance Massey, for Joe Taylor's Torpedo Five. No second squadron of dive bombers was available to take the place of Wally Short's Bombing Five. Short's troops would remain on board the *Yorktown*, but Noyes directed that they temporarily change their designation from Bombing Five to Scouting Five to prevent confusion with the ex-*Saratoga* bombing squadron about to serve alongside them. This name change did not make VB-5 personnel very happy!

The question of the *Yorktown*'s fighting squadron presented special problems. Alone of the Pacific Fleet's carriers, she had not yet exchanged the fixed wing F4F-3 Wildcats for the folding wing F4F-4s that would enable her to operate at least twenty-seven fighters. That reinforcement was long overdue. Deficiencies in fighter strength, which had hamstrung operations in the Coral Sea, would not be repeated at Midway if Noyes could help it. The *Yorktown*'s Fighting Forty-two under Charles Fenton, however, had not yet made acquaintance with the model F4F-4 Wildcats, none of which had served on board. At Kaneohe Thach had had a month to work up with F4F-4s, but Fighting Three had only eleven pilots on strength, most of them rookies. His little band of eleven was the only source of carrier fighter pilots available in the Hawaiian Islands. If the *Yorktown* was to fight at Midway, she could stay in port no more than two or three days—too little time for Fighting Forty-two as a unit to reequip with the unfamiliar F4F-4s and also absorb more pilots in order to operate twenty-seven planes.

Under the circumstances, Noyes would do to Fenton and company what he had done to Thach the previous month. He decided to incorporate into Thach's rump of a squadron a strong nucleus of pilots from Fighting Forty-two to beef up the *Yorktown*'s fighter contingent to its required operating strength of nearly thirty pilots. The third week of May, Thach received word that he would take Fighting Three out to the *Yorktown* to depart around the end of the month. He was to take charge of a large batch of fighter pilots from Fighting Forty-two already on board the *Yorktown* and also utilize VF-42's enlisted crew who would turn their hats around and become the maintenance magicians of Fighting Three. The news that his rookies faced imminent combat certainly gave a new impetus to Thach's "charm school." He also knew that the next battle would be his last as skipper of Fighting Three. According to orders cut on 11 May, O'Hare upon his return in late June would assume command of Fighting Three. Thach had served with the squadron for nearly three years, and a new assignment was coming.

THE CARRIERS IN PORT

Tuesday, 26 May, was "fly in day" for the air groups on board the *Enterprise* and the *Hornet*, as Bill Halsey's Task Force 16 neared Oahu after its uneventful and somewhat baffling cruise to South Pacific waters. Shortly after breakfast, the pilots manned their aircraft and awaited the signal to go. The *Enterprise* began launching about 0730, and Jim Gray took the nineteen flyable Grummans of his Fighting Six on the short flight to Luke Field on Ford Island. Efforts to land the whole air group created considerable congestion, so it took time to settle in. After squaring the squadron away, the pilots learned they had thirty-six hours of R & R at the Royal Hawaiian Hotel, welcome news indeed. Gray himself had reason to celebrate. That day he received orders from the Bureau of Navigation assigning him as permanent commander of Fighting Six. He got his squadron well ahead of others in the Naval Academy class of 1936.

The pilots of the *Hornet*'s Fighting Eight likewise experienced delays in getting their twenty-four F4F-4s to their destination, the marine field at Ewa. "Due to the eternal circling necessary to rendezvous and stagger in behind the CHAG (Cdr. Ring) and the torpedo planes,"[1] it took two hours for the 50-mile flight. After they settled in at Ewa, the *Hornet* pilots got an unwelcome surprise. Instead of the two-day liberty they were expecting, Ring confined the whole group to Ewa. The pilots were to alternate in standing alerts from an hour before sunrise to an hour past sunset. That this was Ring's decision alone is not indicated, but is rather doubtful; however, he had to face the pilot resentment:

> As a result there was much grumbling and a near "mutiny" against the CHAG; a couple of pilots getting in trouble through talking too much and expressing their opinion of CHAG to his face.[2]

Ring grounded several SBD pilots for insubordination. The *Hornet* Air Group was not exactly a band of brothers. The upcoming Battle of Midway would reveal serious flaws in the group's combat effectiveness and cohesiveness.

The ships of Task Force 16 followed their aircraft into Pearl Harbor, and by noon the two flattops had safely moored off Ford Island. Halsey went ashore to make his arrival call on CinCPac. Nimitz listened to his report, then put him on the sick list. A skin disease had made Halsey's life miserable for about a month. His nerves were frazzled, and there was no way he could properly exercise command. In his place Halsey nominated his cruiser commander, Rear Admiral Spruance. Later that day Spruance broke his two-star flag on board the *Enterprise* as commander, Task Force 16. A non-aviator, Spruance retained in the *Enterprise* Halsey's own ComCarPac staff to advise him. The *Hornet* likewise faced a change

"The Big E"—the *Enterprise* at Pearl Harbor, late May 1942. (NA 80-G-66121.)

in comand of sorts, as Pete Mitscher was slated for promotion to rear admiral and another job. The *Hornet's* next skipper, Captain Charles P. Mason, had reported on board but had not as yet assumed command. Because the task force would linger in port only two days before departing to battle, Mitscher would remain captain of the *Hornet*, while Mason went along for the ride.

For the pilots of Fighting Six "recuperating" at the Royal Hawaiian Hotel and elsewhere around Oahu, the morning of 27 May brought unexpected orders: report back to the ship no later than 1830 that evening. Word had it "The Big E" would sail the next day. It certainly would be only a brief stopover, only three days all told in port. Nimitz himself hinted to the squadron late that morning that the upcoming voyage could offer some excitement. CinCPac boarded the carrier to

Awards ceremony on board the *Enterprise*, 27 May 1942. Roger Mehle steps forward to receive his D.F.C. from Admiral Nimitz. On Mehle's right is Wade McClusky. (NA 80-G-7742.)

decorate, among others, McClusky and Mehle with Distinguished Flying Crosses for their gallantry on 1 February in the Marshalls. Pinning the decoration on Mehle's gleaming whites, the admiral remarked, "I think you'll have a chance to win yourself another medal in the next several days."[3]

On the 27th, VF-6's duty crew exchanged six banged-up F4F-4s for eight new Grummans delivered to the squadron on Ford Island. There were two changes in personnel. Leaving the squadron for duty in CASU-1 was "Nick" Carter, AP1c, while joining was the first VF-6 officer who was not a pilot: Lieut. (jg) J. Born, A-V(S), an aviation service officer who would take over most of the administrative functions that were stealing valuable time from the pilots. Fighting Eight's duty officer on board the *Hornet* turned in the fighter creamed by Bruce Harwood the previous month and hoisted on board four replacement F4F-4s. One of those aircraft and also one supplied to Fighting Six were equipped with the experimental belly tank installation tested by Thach. Noyes ordered that the two fighting squadrons each have one such F4F-4 to conduct further tests, and also provided twenty-seven change sets and fifty-four drop tanks per squadron. They were to convert their other F4Fs when authorized by BuAer to do so.[4] As it happened, the squadrons were too busy at Midway to worry about testing belly tanks.

The *Yorktown*'s "fly in day" came the morning of 27 May, as the battered flattop approached the Oahu coast. Her air group flew what operational planes they had to Ford Island. Still trailing oil from the wounds received at Coral Sea, the *Yorktown* entered the ship channel around 1400 and maneuvered into the repair basin. Naval inspectors gave her a careful examination and decided she could be patched in a short time, but certainly not made whole. An army of storekeepers and their working crews from the ship's company swarmed over the *Yorktown* to reprovision the ship. That afternoon, the *Yorktown* pilots hung around Ford Island and swapped stories with their colleagues from the *Enterprise*, with the inevitable sad catalog of classmates and friends lost at Coral Sea. The Yorktowners had known something was afoot when their damaged flattop made for Pearl rather than some comfortable West Coast yard. Thus they expected to draw a few replacement pilots and fresh aircraft, grab a little rest, then head out to sea once more for another shot at the Japanese. So what if they had just been away for 101 days!

Frank Jack Fletcher and his cruiser division commander, "Poco" Smith, went ashore to confer with CinCPac. Having monitored CinCPac's intelligence bulletins, Fletcher knew a major effort was in store. He filled Nimitz in on what happened in the Coral Sea and received the latest estimates on enemy intentions to attack Midway and the Aleutians. Nimitz assigned him tactical command of the two carrier task forces when they rendezvoused off Midway. Spruance joined the conference, and together the admirals mapped out the basic plan for defending Midway. Fletcher discovered that his air group on board the *Yorktown* would be reorganized. Highly confident of the ability of his flyers, Fletcher asked whether his old squadrons could be retained on board, reinforced rather than replaced. Nimitz had to deny his request. When Frank Jack returned to the *Yorktown*, he let Pederson know in no uncertain terms of his irritation at the breaking up of the team that had seen him through the dark days in the Coral Sea. Pederson felt some remorse because he thought he was unwittingly responsible. Just after Coral Sea, he had recommended to ComCarPac that the air group deserved shore duty as a well-earned rest. After Fletcher finished with him, Pederson stormed ashore to protest the reorganization to Rear Admiral Noyes himself, but Noyes was adamant. Meanwhile, the *Yorktown* aviators repaired to the local BOQ and were restricted to base on alert—"No Royal Hawaiian for these chaps!"[5]

The morning of 28 May, the *Enterprise* disembarked her aviators and prepared to get under way. The flyers checked in at the Ford Island field; then those off duty spent a pleasant interlude around the pool. Meanwhile, their *Hornet* counterparts smarted under their enforced isolation at Ewa. Moreover, their separation from the bars of Honolulu had not dampened their enthusiam for drinking. In the officer's club, the pilots of Torpedo Eight concocted a drink known as the "Barber's Point cocktail," and it was deadly. Shortly after sunrise on 28 May, VT-8's skipper, John Waldron, tenderly woke his charges (and likely the rest of the base) by firing a full magazine from his .45-caliber pistol out through the barracks door.

The sortie of Task Force 16 was an impressive sight to spectators ranged round Pearl Harbor. First came the sleek destroyers to guard against lurking submarines, then the portly, heavily laden fleet oilers, followed by the cruisers of the screen. Finally the stars of the show, the *Enterprise* and the *Hornet*, emerged from the harbor. Watching them go was Halsey, an unwilling occupant of his sick bed at the naval hospital. At least he felt Task Force 16 was in good hands—Spruance was his close friend and the best man for the job. The fighter pilots missed "Wild Bill" and were a little wary of the cruiser admiral now commanding the two carriers, but they were so anxious for some action they cared little who was on the flag bridge.

Sorting out his pilots and aircraft, Gray readied his twenty-seven Grumman F4F-4 Wildcats for the flight out to the ship. Reporting that day to Fighting Six was a welcome face, Lieut. (jg) Harold Heisel, returning after his hospitalization for an allergy attack. In place of NAP Carter, who had left the squadron, came Ens. James A. Halford, A-V(N), fresh from operational training and prepared to tackle his first carrier landing on board the *Enterprise*. Ready to greet the troops on board ship was another new VF-6 pilot, Bill Wileman, formerly of Fighting Two with a kill at Coral Sea to his credit. Wileman had ridden the *Yorktown* back from the South Seas. That afternoon Fighting Six joined the rest of the air group for the short flight out to the *Enterprise*. The first plane in the groove was the TBD flown by Lt. Cdr. Lindsey, skipper of Torpedo Six. As it loomed over the ramp, Lindsey's Devastator stalled, veered off to port, and struck the water near "The Big E's" port quarter. The three crew members scrambled out before the TBD sank, but Lindsey had sustained serious injuries to his face and chest. The destroyer *Monaghan*, the plane guard, raced over to pick up the swimmers. It seemed doubtful the battered Lindsey would fly any time soon. The remaining *Enterprise* planes landed without incident.

The *Hornet* flyers at Ewa likewise became embroiled in the turmoil inherent in getting a whole carrier air group ready to depart. Mitchell's Fighting Eight had no personnel changes to record, and soon had twenty-three Wildcats aloft and pointed toward the *Hornet*. The air group had to leave one aircraft behind when the group commander's SBD proved to have a balky engine. Ring commandeered the aircraft of VS-8's executive officer, the irrepressible Lieut. William J. ("Gus") Widhelm, while Widhelm tried to make "Sea Hag's" Dauntless air-worthy. Instead, Gus ended up riding out to the ship in the middle seat of one of VT-8's Devastators. By 1800, the men of both air groups had settled in on their respective flattops and awaited word of the mission that had cut short their rest on Oahu.

The morning of 28 May while Task Force 16 put to sea, the *Yorktown* aviators learned the gory details of the reorganization (some would say dismemberment) of their air group. Going ashore were Scouting Five and Torpedo Five, while for the duration of the next cruise, Bombing Five had to take the temporary designation of Scouting Five. Fighting Forty-two felt the ax. Lt. Cdr. Fenton, the skipper, and the XO, Lieut. McCormack, would remain on Oahu to take custody of a batch of new pilots being sent out from the West Coast. The squadron had nineteen-odd (including VF-2's fighters) F4F-3s, not all flyable. The other sixteen VF-42 pilots had orders detailing them for temporary duty with Fighting Three at Kaneohe. Their response was shock and dismay. They were not at all pleased to be going into combat without their own leaders and squadron identity. The critical situation that brought about this severe change demonstrated its necessity, but that did not lighten the blow. The fighter pilots trooped down to the seaplane base on Ford Island and boarded a flying boat for the short hop out to Kaneohe.

While awaiting his new batch of pilots, Thach was delighted to see a friend. Don Lovelace reported in for temporary duty with Fighting Three, carrying in his pocket the permanent orders he had so long wanted—command of a fighting squadron. While stateside he had succeeded in changing his orders from commander of Scouting Ten to commander of Fighting Two. He was to reassemble the NAPs and rebuild the squadron. After a welcome home leave, he had sailed on 15 May from San Francisco, unaware that the *Lexington* survivors had been routed to San Diego. His transport docked earlier on 28 May at Pearl. Reporting in, Lovelace learned that Thach was heading out shortly with a mixed of bag of pilots. His own VF-2 could not assemble as a unit for several weeks; so Lovelace volunteered his services in his old spot as executive officer of Fighting Three. Rear Admiral Noyes agreed, and Thach could not have been happier to have his good friend back to help mold Fighting Three into a cohesive unit.

After their own enthusiastic greeting, Thach and Lovelace went to meet the VF-42 contingent when the flying boat arrived at Kaneohe. The *Yorktown* flyers they knew by reputation only, never having served with them. Bill Leonard recollected the introductions:

> One of the pleasant surprises was the warm greeting we received from J. Thach and D. Lovelace. After about 20 seconds of this treatment we were all theirs![6]

Thach was extremely interested in their accounts of the Coral Sea air battles, particularly impressions of Japanese Zero fighters, which he had yet to encounter. The rest of 28 May he allowed the VF-42 inductees to relax and look over their new F4F-4 Wildcats. The CASU-1 (Carrier Air Service Unit) at NAS Pearl Harbor issued VF-3 five more Wildcats, giving Thach a full complement of twenty-seven. Kaneohe was a busy place. The *Yorktown*'s LSO, Lieut. "Soupy" Campbell, gave the ex-*Saratoga* pilots as well as the rookies some field carrier landing practice and also took the opportunity to familiarize himself with the landing characteristics of the F4F-4.

Fighting Three now comprised twenty-eight pilots, twenty of them experienced. Flight time ranged from Thach's 3,500-plus hours down to the 300-odd hours accumulated by the green ensigns. Aside from the VF-42 old hands, however, most of the others had only served together for a short time. Circumstances allowed little time to get acquainted, virtually none in the air. Even the VF-42 vets had to get accustomed to new commanding officers, not to mention some strangers as wingmen when Thach organized his squadron.

Assessing the Grumman F4F-4 fighter, Thach had found it heavier and less responsive than the fixed wing F4F-3 version. Talking with his VF-42 pilots confirmed his fears that the F4F-4's ammunition supply (240 rounds per gun) was insufficient. On 28 May, he wrote the Bureau of Aeronautics offering his opinion that the gun battery in the F4F-4 was unsatisfactory.[7] Four guns with at least 400, but preferably 500 rounds per gun appeared much better. Thach would have been

VF-3 F4F-4s in revetments at Kaneohe, 29 May 1942. F-5 is BuNo. 5167. F-10 (BuNo. 5149) was flown by Art Brassfield on 4 June when he shot down four Japanese dive bombers on one mission. (NA 80-G-61533.)

irate had he known that BuAer only made the change in response to British pressure for six guns. The newly arrived VF-42 pilots took their first F4F-4 familiarization hops on 29 May and tried a couple of practice carrier landings. Leonard's first impression of the new fighter was:

> Compared with the early bird F4F-3, these -4s had a better fit and finish. Quality of fabrication had improved. A good gunsight installation and better plexiglass in the canopy were all pluses. It had the same engine and weighed about 800 pounds more. This made for discontent when we remembered our experiences with the Zero.[8]

Thus none of the VF-42 crowd was overly pleased with the F4F-4s.

At Pearl Harbor the dockyard workers and her own ship's company labored diligently to ready the *Yorktown* for battle. They put temporary patches on her leaks, shored up blast-weakened areas, installed new equipment, and reprovisioned the vessel. On 29 May the old girl slipped out of drydock, fueled, and made ready to sail on the thirtieth. Ship's company had very little chance for liberty, but they were promised a long stateside rest after the *Yorktown* fought one more battle. Just arrived 29 May to witness the *Yorktown*'s preparations were the two big transports *Hammondsport* and *Chaumont*, laden with the men and aircraft of Fighting Five, Fighting Seventy-two, and the Torpedo Eight Detachment. Aside from six new Grumman TBF-1 Avenger torpedo planes rushed to Midway, none of the newly arrived squadrons would fight the next battle. Their time would come that summer of 1942.

The morning of 30 May, the rebuilt *Yorktown* Air Group readied pilots and aircraft at Kaneohe for the flight out to the ship. Under her Captain Buckmaster, the *Yorktown*, still showing the effects of Coral Sea, put to sea that forenoon as the nucleus of Fletcher's Task Force 17. Along with the other squadrons, Fighting Three departed Kaneohe and soon found the ships off the Oahu coast. In order of divisions, the F4Fs circled the task force awaiting their turn to land. Duran Mattson in the 4th Division had a nasty surprise. His Pratt & Whitney suddenly coughed and cut out from fuel starvation. The Kaneohe ground crews had neglected to refill the main tank after the previous day's flights! He shifted to the small supply in his reserve tank and restarted his engine. The 4th Division would be the last of the fighters taken on board. Any delay in landing, and Mattson faced the prospect of a swim.

When Thach touched down on the flight deck and cleared the arresting gear, plane handlers swarmed around his F4F-4 to guide it forward in anticipation of folding its wings before parking it updeck. Like their pilots, the enlisted crew of Fighting Forty-two had been mysteriously inducted into Fighting Three, and they had never seen the new F4F-4. Supervising the individual plane captains for the unfamiliar procedure of folding the wings was Milton Wester, ACMM, one of Brassfield's "bull" chiefs. All Wester had to go on for the F4F-4 was one copy of the preliminary erection and maintenance manual—not enough to show the plane captains and him, sight unseen, how to fold the wings properly. Before Thach could retract his flaps, his plane captain and crew had unlatched the wing lock and folded the wings, tearing the flaps. The crews were under great pressure to get the fighters stowed away because the other squadrons waited to come on board. Realizing the difficulty, Thach jumped out of his cockpit and explained to the troops how to fold the wings correctly. Aside from the first two F4F-4s—whose flaps could be replaced by spares—the wing foldings went without a hitch.

Leading his 3rd Division, Lovelace touched down smartly, taxied forward over the folded barriers, then waited for the plane handlers to conduct him forward to his parking spot on deck. His wingman, Ens. Robert C. Evans, one of the rookies, followed the XO in. After the LSO gave the cut, his F4F dropped its nose too sharply. Gaining speed, Evans made a fast, updeck landing and did not snag an arresting wire. A high bounce at touchdown floated the F4F across the barrier, whereupon it smashed onto the back of Lovelace's aircraft, its propellor tearing into the XO's cockpit, fracturing his skull, and severing the carotid artery. Although medical help arrived almost instantly, the flight surgeon could do nothing to save Lovelace—he died a few minutes later. Young Evans was not seriously injured, but this freak accident had brutally robbed the squadron of one of its most experienced leaders and warmest individuals, the person Thach had counted on the most to bring the outfit together.

The tragic mishap tied up the flight deck for several minutes, as the deck crew worked frantically to clear the wreckage. Both aircraft were so badly damaged that they could not be repaired on board ship. For Mattson with his fuel dwindling rapidly, it was a very trying situation. He could not wait his turn to land, but instead gave the distress signal for deferred forced landing, flying with his wheels up and tail hook down along the carrier's port side. This gave him priority. Still, ten minutes more elapsed before the flight deck was usable. When Mattson finally did come on board, he had less than five minutes' gasoline in his tank. The remaining landings took place without incident.

After the squadron squared away on board ship and ate lunch, Thach summoned his pilots to their ready room. In a quiet but determined manner, he explained the situation. Despite the fact that the squadron had not flown together, they had a job to do, a vital and difficult task that must be done. Don Lovelace's death hurt mightily (Thach more than the others realized, because of the closeness of their friendship), but that could not be helped. As for the coming battle, the fighters had to protect the carriers at all costs. He voiced his concern over the F4F-4's reduced ammunition supply, but stressed that the fighters had to stop enemy torpedo planes short of their release points even if this meant ramming them. He outlined the procedure. The fighter was to move in from below and pull up so the prop cut through the torpedo plane's empennage. This was not merely pre-battle rhetoric, as the pilots could see their skipper was deadly serious. His impressive presentation helped the VF-42 pilots take the measure of their new commander.

Because of Lovelace's death, Thach that afternoon reorganized the squadron. He appointed Leonard, the senior VF-42 pilot present, as his executive officer, and taking Leonard's place as flight officer was Dick Crommelin. Both were 1938 graduates of the Naval Academy, had earned their wings in early 1941, and had reported to Scouting Forty-one before it became Fighting Forty-two. Both likewise had seen heavy combat at Coral Sea, with Crommelin taking a swim on 8 May. He was one of the five famous Crommelin brothers, all naval officers: John, Henry, Charles, Richard, and Quentin. In light of what Thach faced in getting Fighting Three ready for battle on short notice, he could not have desired better subordinates than Leonard, Crommelin, or his engineering officer, Art Brassfield.

With the exception of Thach, Barnes, and Cheek, all division and section leaders were pilots of the *Yorktown*'s VF-42. The new flight organization and nominal plane assignments were as shown in the table. The squadron possessed twenty-five operational Grumman F4F-4 Wildcats, one of which was kept in the hangar as a spare.

MIDWAY—THE WAITING

"You will have the opportunities to deal the enemy heavy blows." CinCPac to Task Force 16, 28 May 1942.[1]

Once safely at sea, the carrier pilots learned more about the mission upon which they had embarked. The two carrier task forces were heading northwest to counter a powerful Japanese force seeking to capture Midway Island. Word filtered down to the pilots that CinCPac expected an enemy striking force of four to five carriers, escorted by three or four battleships and a suitable screen, to batter Midway with air strikes in connection with an amphibious assault. Another enemy contingent, likely with carriers as well, threatened the Aleutians. Task Force 16, to be joined

	1st Division			3rd Division	
F-1	Lt. Cdr. Thach (CO)		*F-13	Lieut. (jg) Leonard (XO)	
†F-2	Ens. R. A. M. Dibb		*F-14	Ens. J. P. Adams	
*F-3	Lieut. (jg) B. T. Macomber		*F-15	Lieut. (jg) W. A. Haas	
*F-4	Ens. E. R. Bassett		*F-16	Ens. G. A. Hopper	
F-5	Mach. T. F. Cheek		F-17	Mach. D. C. Barnes	
†F-6	Ens. D. C. Sheedy		†F-18	Ens. M. Tootle	
	2nd Division			4th Division	
*F-7	Lieut. (jg) Crommelin (FO)		*F-19	Lieut. (jg) Brassfield (EO)	
*F-8	Ens. J. B. Bain		*F-20	Ens. H. B. Gibbs	
*F-9	Ens. R. L. Wright		*F-21	Lieut. (jg) E. D. Mattson	
*F-10	Ens. G. F. Markham		†F-22	Ens. H. A. Bass	
*F-11	Lieut. (jg) E. S. McCuskey		*F-23	Lieut. (jg) W. S. Woollen	
†F-12	Ens. M. K. Bright		*F-24	Lieut. (jg) W. W. Barnes	

Supernumerary
†Ens. H. J. W. Eppler
†Ens. R. C. Evans
†Ens. V. H. Morris

*VF-42 veteran.
†Rookie.

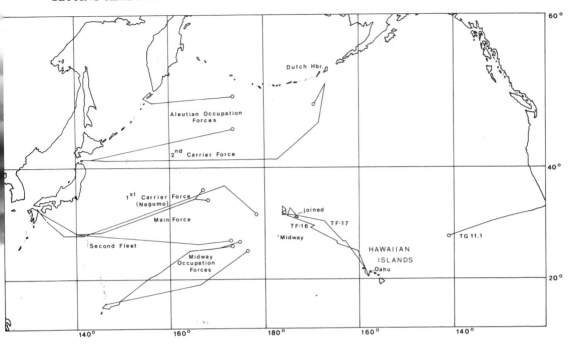

The Midway campaign, movements to 0000, 4 June.

by Task Force 17, would lie in wait north of Midway to launch a surprise counterblow against the Japanese flattops while they were preoccupied with hitting
Midway. Midway's land-based aircraft were to locate and track the Japanese carriers, then aid in their destruction. Naturally the pilots did not discover that this
incredibly valuable estimate of Japanese intentions emanated largely from brilliant
cryptanalysis of enemy naval cyphers, but the higher-ups told them as much as
they dared.

Upon departing Oahu, Task Force 16 steered course 340 degrees, speed 16
knots, for the run out to Midway, Spruance planned to take position about 350
miles northeast of Midway, there to rendezvous on 2 June with Task Force 17.
The day after departure, 29 May, the *Hornet* had the duty. Four pilots from Fighting
Eight flew inner air patrol on the lookout for I-boats, while the *Hornet*'s SBDs
conducted an intermediate air patrol out of sight of the ships. One dive bomber,
flown by Ens. R. D. Milliman from Scouting Eight, failed to return from the
mission. On 30 May the weather worsened rapidly as Task Force 16 entered a cold
front passing over Midway. No flying took place that day, and the pilots welcomed
the respite to give them time to complete routine preparations for combat. The
last day of May, Spruance fueled his cruisers and destroyers under cover of inner
air patrols courtesy of Fighting Six. The *Monaghan* took the opportunity to transfer
the injured Gene Lindsey and his two crewmen back to the *Enterprise*. Lindsey
went to sick bay, leaving Lieut. Arthur V. Ely, his exec, in temporary command
of Torpedo Six. As the ships had moved beyond the Pearl Harbor long-range
search umbrella, the carriers inaugurated routine searches by the SBDs. The first
of June saw no better weather than that of the last few days. The *Hornet*'s morning
search encountered heavy cloud cover, and Spruance canceled the afternoon flight.
Gray tried to work in a training flight for Fighting Six, but that too had to be
scrubbed. Task Force 16, fidgeting uncomfortably in tense anticipation, had nothing
to do but wait.

For three days after their departure from Pearl, Fletcher's Task Force 17 steamed northwest for the rendezvous with Task Force 16. The pilots were privy to the same daunting intelligence summaries offered their counterparts with Spruance, but circumstances kept them too busy to worry much about it—the pilots, mechanics, and ordnancemen of Fighting Three worked feverishly to ready their brand-new planes for combat. The principal problem concerned the machine guns and sights of most of the squadron's F4F-4s. The planes did not have their gunsights aligned or the guns boresighted. Indeed, more than half of VF-3's Browning .50-calibers still swam in factory cosmoline. Back at Kaneohe, Thach never had the manpower to prepare the planes. On board the *Yorktown* the ordnancemen under C. C. McCarty, ACOM, had to take each fighter individually onto the flight deck and, using a stand, raise the F4F's tail to put it in a horizontal attitude, aiming the aircraft at a boresight pattern target supported by a structure (wind battens) 200 to 300 feet down the deck. The gun bores and gunsights were aligned to converge on the target and fastened securely. After the sights and guns lined up in the correct boresight pattern, they were clamped into place and test-fired over the side of the ship. McCuskey, the gunnery officer, made sure that the fire converged properly and the guns maintained alignment while firing by watching the tracers through the gunsight, and many pilots saw to it that their assigned aircraft checked out OK. The last aircraft was not readied until late 3 June after a monumental effort by the squadron's ordnancemen. Captain Buckmaster insisted the squadron retrieve all of the fired brass for salvage!

Spruance's Task Force 16 maintained position roughly 350 miles northeast of Midway awaiting the arrival of Fletcher's forces, the weather only marginally better than it had been the past few days. The second of June was cold and rainy under heavily overcast skies as the region north of Midway endured the influence of a stalled high pressure weather system and its associated front. The *Enterprise* acted as duty carrier, despatching at 0643 a search by SBDs and an inner air patrol by very reluctant VF-6 pilots. The air staff canceled the scheduled afternoon search, as it was pointless in the poor visibility dominating the skies to the northwest. At 1150, two SBDs launched from the *Yorktown* appeared over Task Force 16 and air-dropped a message to Spruance instructing him to meet Task Force 17 at Point "Luck."

The admiral released to the ship's companies of Task Force 16 a summary of what was expected to happen, so all hands finally realized the gravity of the situation. He also indicated what their response would be:

> If presence of Task Forces 16 and 17 remains unknown to enemy we should be able to make surprise flank attacks on enemy carriers from position northeast of Midway.[2]

Naval intelligence forecast that the Japanese would most likely hit the Aleutian Islands the next day, heralding the opening of their offensive. The tension was certainly beginning to have an effect. One VF-6 pilot wrote in his diary:

> I think I can see a definite shortening of nerves—a little tighter & snap more easily—some people a little more grim & quiet—& idle chatter is rampant—all evidence of strain.[3]

There was amazement and some doubt concerning the credibility of all the intelligence estimates, but no one doubted there would be one hell of a fight if the Japanese did indeed show up.

At 1600, Fletcher's Task Force 17 appeared on the southern horizon and joined Task Force 16, 325 miles northeast of Midway. Fletcher formally assumed tactical command of the Striking Force, which comprised three carriers, seven heavy cruisers, one light antiaircraft cruiser, and fifteen destroyers. His carrier air strength amounted to 221 operational aircraft. During the waning afternoon light, Fletcher brought the two task forces together and arranged for Spruance to keep station about 10 miles off. Thus CinCPac had deployed the crucial force in his plan to save Midway.

On 3 June, the *Yorktown* drew the tasks of providing the precautionary air searches and combat air patrol, and launched twenty SBDs to search north, northwest, and northeast for 200 miles. The scout pilots encountered bad weather all along the way. Fletcher depended primarily upon the Midway-based patrol planes to warn him of the Japanese approach. Spruance's carriers were poised to launch an attack if the enemy turned up early. That morning a PBY flying boat from Midway spotted the Japanese transport force about 700 miles west of Midway, and the news soon reached Fletcher. So far it appeared that the enemy operated according to plan. Also that day came word that Japanese carrier planes had struck Dutch Harbor in the Aleutians, further reinforcing the credibility of CinCPac's estimates. If the Americans continued to forecast enemy intentions so accurately, then the main striking force of four or five carriers would come charging in next morning.

The third of June was also the day when the carrier aviators settled their plans for the all-important air operations expected on 4 June. The air staffs on board the *Enterprise* and the *Yorktown* conferred by blinker about the handling of the combat air patrol.[4] For battle, the plan was to separate the two task forces by 25 miles: close enough, it was thought, for mutual fighter support, yet sufficiently distant to prevent one snooper from discovering both carrier forces. Under such circumstances, the two carrier admirals agreed that Lt. Cdr. Leonard Dow, ComCarPac's communications officer with Spruance ón board the *Enterprise*, would handle fighter direction for all three flattops. However, if Task Force 17 operated on its own, Pederson, the *Yorktown* Air Group commander, was to direct the *Yorktown*'s fighters as usual.

The two task forces exchanged fighter organization printouts, so both Dow and Pederson would know the radio calls for all the fighters. The *Enterprise* became "Red base," and her fighters used the designation "Red" and their number in the squadron organization as identification. Likewise the *Hornet* was "Blue base," and the *Yorktown* "Scarlet base." Both fighter director officers used the same radio frequency, which would cause some confusion. Also some differences in fighter direction vocabulary cropped up, which also proved troublesome. There simply had been no time for the two to confer in person before the hasty departure from Pearl. Fighting Six's Wildcats were fully equipped with IFF devices which made them easily recognizable to Air Plot, but the *Hornet*'s Fighting Eight was only partially equipped. The *Yorktown*'s Fighting Three had relatively few F4Fs with IFF, so her air officer, Cdr. Arnold, arranged for VF-3 to shuffle plane assignments to put one IFF-equipped plane in each fighter section. Unfortunately very few other carrier aircraft carried IFF at all, so the FDOs could count on wasting much valuable time vectoring fighters to eyeball suspicious contacts that later would prove to be friendlies.

As important as the procedure for the CAP were the arrangements made for launching the strike groups. According to plan, Task Force 16's two air groups would constitute the main air striking force, to be held in reserve until the Japanese carriers showed up. The *Yorktown*'s planes on 4 June were to act as search planes, if needed, and as a strike reserve. Thus Spruance would despatch all available aircraft but F4Fs reserved for CAP, an air strike force of perhaps twenty fighters, seventy dive bombers, and twenty-nine torpedo planes. The *Yorktown*'s contribution to the strike would depend on circumstances.

The bane of 1942 American carrier aviation, the failure to combine or coordinate strike groups from different carriers, would be especially evident at Midway. ComCarPac staff on board the *Enterprise* made no attempt to work out a plan whereby the *Hornet* and *Enterprise* air groups would attack in concert. Instead, each was on its own. The "book," *USF-74 (Revised)* of April 1941, provided for a "wing" organization of two carrier air groups led by the senior group commander, but no evidence exists that anyone proposed to implement this procedure at Midway. This in the peculiar circumstances, i.e., lack of opportunity to practice what the "book" preached, was perhaps fortunate because the senior air group commander was the *Hornet*'s Stanhope Ring, who had had no combat experience. Thus for Midway, each American carrier air group was largely on its own. The ComCarPac staff acted primarily to determine attack strength, the form of departure, and targets.

Interestingly, all three American carrier air groups in the Battle of Midway devised different schemes for the employment of their escort fighters—a clear illustration of the primitive nature of escort doctrine. The air tacticians relied upon their own limited combat experience (if any), sketchy and vague reports of the recent Coral Sea fighting, or rigid, prewar air doctrine. The combat pilots from the different carriers had no chance to confer with one another, especially to sound out the *Yorktown* pilots who had fought in the Coral Sea. One thing was definite. The overriding responsibility of the fighters was to protect the carriers. At Coral Sea, the ratio of escort to CAP fighters was fifty–fifty or better. At Midway, the ComCarPac staff limited Task Force 16's fighter escort to ten fighters per carrier. The *Yorktown*'s original plan called for eight escorts out of a fighter strength of twenty-four operational planes. All this was in line with CinCPac's stated policy to preserve the carriers.

Of the three, the *Hornet*'s air group was the least experienced. On 31 May, Ring (the "Sea Hag") met with Mitscher, Captain Mason, Cdr. Apollo Soucek (the air officer), the four squadron commanders, and their flight officers. The conference dealt with plans for the massive air strike the *Hornet* expected to launch in the next few days. She would likely despatch at one time virtually all of her attack aircraft. The ideal procedure, all felt, was "group attack," in which the dive bombers coordinated their attacks with the torpedo planes to provide the mass necessary to confuse the enemy and divide his defenses. The trick was getting the whole air group to the target, so they could attack at the same time.

At the meeting, VT-8's skipper, John Waldron, requested close fighter support for his vulnerable TBDs. Ring and the two VF-8 pilots present, Pat Mitchell and his flight officer Stan Ruehlow, strongly advised that at least some of VF-8's Wildcats accompany the torpedo planes as close escort. Mitscher, however, was adamant that the escort fighters would climb to high altitude and stick close to the dive bombers. He pointed out that the main task of the fighting squadron was to guard the *Hornet* from attack. Therefore only a few (ten) could be spared for escort duty. These ten were too few, he felt, to divide between the SBDs and TBDs as Fletcher's carriers did at Coral Sea. There the *Lexington*'s fighter escorts suffered heavy casualties, as did the dive bombers. Coral Sea experience seemed to point to shortcomings in the F4F Wildcat vis-à-vis Japanese Zeros. To deal effectively with the Mitsubishis, the Grummans necessarily required substantial altitude advantage. On the basis of all these factors, Mitscher decided his fighters would stay with the dive bombers. Thus if circumstances permitted a fighter escort, those F4Fs would offer close support to the SBDs.

Torpedo Eight was deeply disappointed over the lack of direct fighter protection. Not fooled by rosy estimates, Waldron had no illusions as to the vulnerability of his Devastators. If Wildcats faced a disadvantage fighting the nimble Zeros at low altitude, what chance had his clumsy TBDs? Waldron carefully explained to his crews the reasons why they would not have fighter protection, but that did not make the dose any easier to take. He observed that the SBDs might draw many Zeros away, as they with their faster cruise would arrive in the target area first. But he added:

> However as you can well see this is not the same kind of protection which would be afforded VT if adequate VF could be supplied to go in with VT and whose sole mission was to see to it that nobody interfered with VT until they could drop their pickles.
> *THEREFORE* you pilots and you gunners must be prepared to shoot it out with the Japs.[5]

Waldron warned his squadron, "Be prepared this time for all their VF to jump on VT,"[6] a tragically prophetic statement.

At the conference the *Hornet* flight leaders worked out the launch scheme and procedure for flying to the target. Because of the high number of aircraft involved, the launch would require two deckloads. The first would comprise the CAP fighters (eight F4Fs plus two standby), the ten escort fighters, and all thirty-four *Hornet* SBD dive bombers. Whatever room was left on the flight deck after all these aircraft were spotted could be given to a few of VT-8's TBDs. Half the dive bombers would carry one 500-lb. bomb apiece; the rest that could be spotted farther aft and with more deck space to work with were to get off with one 1,000-lb. bomb slung under each. After the fighters and SBDs had lifted off, plane handlers could bring out of the hangar the remainder of VT-8's fifteen TBDs. While the torpedo planes made ready to take off, the SBDs and their fighter escorts would begin the long climb to 20,000 feet. If time permitted, the SBDs and F4Fs would circle until the TBDs were ready to depart. Then they would cruise at 110 knots, while Waldron's troops were to climb to 1,500 feet and head out at 100 knots. Ring's high-level contingent hoped to maintain visual contact with the torpedo planes far below during the flight out.

The timing for the launch of VF-8's escort fighters is of great interest. Mitchell's ten Grumman F4F-4s were to take off first, right along with the CAP fighters. Then, using precious fuel, they would have to circle for the thirty or so minutes necessary to launch the rest of the strike group. Considering the limited combat radius of the Wildcat, such a procedure drastically cut down their actual radius of action. The *Hornet*'s launch plan was conventional and doctrinaire, failing to take into account the unusual circumstances involving two deckloads. Either Mitscher and the *Hornet* air department were unaware of the limited combat radius of the F4F-4 Wildcat, or Mitchell was not forceful enough in stating the case for his fighters. The other two carriers took special precautions on 4 June to conserve the fuel of their escort fighters. The *Hornet* did not, and the result was disaster for Fighting Eight.

The *Enterprise* Air Group pilots were more experienced than their *Hornet* counterparts, but they too had yet to take part in a carrier slugging match. On board "The Big E," there evidently was no formal conference regarding the strike procedure. Captain Murray opted to launch his dive bombers as the main element of

Fighting Eight, Tentative Organization, 4 June 1942

1st Division
Lt. Cdr. Samuel G. Mitchell, USN (CO)
Ens. Johnny A. Talbot, A-V(N)

Lieut. (jg) Richard Gray, USN
Ens. C. Markland Kelly, Jr., A-V(N)

Ens. John Magda, A-V(N)
Ens. John E. McInerny, Jr., A-V(N)

2nd Division
Lieut. Stanley E. Ruehlow, USN (FO)
Ens. George R. Hill, A-V(N)

Lieut. (jg) Minuard F. Jennings, USN
Ens. Humphrey L. Tallman, A-V(N)

Ens. George Formanek, Jr., A-V(N)
Ens. Stephen W. Groves, A-V(N)

3rd Division
Lieut. Edward J. O'Neill, USN (XO)
Ens. Carlton B. Starkes, A-V(N)

Lieut. Warren W. Ford, USN
Ens. Morrill I. Cook, Jr., A-V(N)

Lieut. (jg) Lawrence C. French, USN
Ens. James C. Smith, A-V(N)

4th Division
Lieut. Bruce L. Harwood, USN (EO)
Ens. Henry A. Fairbanks, A-V(N)

Lieut. (jg) John F. Sutherland, A-V(N)
Ens. Henry A. Carey, Jr., A-V(N)

Ens. Elisha T. Stover, A-V(N)
Ens. David B. Freeman, A-V(N)

Supernumerary:
Ens. Richard Z. Hughes, A-V(N)
Ens. Robert S. Merritt, A-V(N)
Ens. Alfred E. Dietrich, A-V(N)

27 Grumman F4F-4 Wildcats

---

the first deckload, to be preceded only by fighters for combat air patrol. Afterward, the flight deck would be respotted with ten F4F Wildcats from Fighting Six led by skipper Jim Gray and the fourteen TBDs from Torpedo Six. The SBDs were to circle until the fighters and torpedo planes had taken off; then all were to depart together. Wade McClusky, the air group commander, was to take the dive bombers to high altitude, while VT-6's Devastators flew close to the water, but again it was hoped the two elements could maintain visual contact and coordinate their attacks.

In determining how to deploy the ten escort fighters, McClusky gave wide latitude to VF-6's skipper to work out the escort scheme. Better than anyone, Gray knew the likely limitations of the F4F-4 in an escort role. He had protested loudly and vehemently when Fighting Six took delivery of its first F4F-4s in March. Gray especially deplored this Wildcat's low climb rate and general sluggishness when compared even to the F4F-3s and F4F-3As his squadron had taken into combat.

Unlike the *Hornet*'s Fighting Eight, Fighting Six had the benefit of someone who had seen combat at Coral Sea: Bill Wileman, formerly of the *Lexington*'s Fighting Two, who had joined VF-6 on 28 May. He related what he knew of duels between F4Fs and Zeros at Coral Sea and confirmed Gray's belief that the Zero

Fighting Six Organization, 4 June 1942

1st Division

F-1	Lieut. James S. Gray, Jr., USN (CO)
F-2	Ens. Joseph R. Daly, A-V(N)
F-27	Ens. Melvin C. Roach, A-V(N)
F-3	Ens. Walter G. Hiebert, A-V(N)
F-4	Mach. Julius A. Achten, USN (NAP)
F-5	Ens. Ralph M. Rich, A-V(N)
F-6	Ens. Wayne C. Presley, A-V(N)

2nd Division

F-7	Lieut. (jg) John C. Kelley, USN
F-8	Ens. Norman D. Hodson, A-V(N)
F-25	Ens. Mortimer V. Kleinmann, Jr., A-V(N)
F-9	Lieut. (jg) Harold N. Heisel, USN
F-10	Mach. Clayton Allard, USN (NAP)
F-11	Mach. Howell M. Sumrall, USN (NAP)
F-12	Mach. William H. Warden, USN (NAP)

3rd Division

F-13	Lieut. Roger W. Mehle, USN (XO)
F-14	Ens. Howard L. Grimmell, Jr., A-V(N)
F-19	Ens. William W. Wileman, A-V(N)
F-15	Lieut. (jg) Frank B. Quady, USN
F-16	Ens. Roy M. Gunsolus, A-V(N)
F-17	Ens. Thomas C. Provost III, A-V(N)
F-18	Rad. Elec. Thomas W. Rhodes, USN (NAP)

4th Division

F-26	Lieut. (jg) Rhonald J. Hoyle, USN (FO)
F-20	Howard S. Packard, AP1c, USN (NAP)
F-21	Lieut. (jg) Wilmer E. Rawie, USN
F-22	Ens. William M. Holt, A-V(N)
F-23	Rad. Elec. Edward H. Bayers, USN (NAP)
F-24	Mach. Beverly W. Reid, USN (NAP)

Supernumerary:
Ens. James A. Halford, Jr., A-V(N)

27 Grumman F4F-4 Wildcats

---

could outperform the Wildcat, particularly when the enemy enjoyed altitude advantage. Gray questioned Wileman closely about the loss on 8 May of VF-2's Dick Bull, a classmate of his at the Naval Academy and a close friend, whose flying ability Gray had respected. Wileman also told of the pounding taken by the SBDs and the startling fact that neither torpedo squadron lost a TBD in combat. On 8 May, both VT-2 and VT-5 had used clouds to mask their approach. No one stressed, however, that the main reason the TBDs escaped so lightly was that their fighter escorts soaked up most of the Zeros.

Gray decided that his escort force had to approach the target at high altitude in order to secure vital advantage over defending Zeros. In light of what he thought had happened at Coral Sea, he considered the dive bombers the most vulnerable. Yet, unlike Mitscher, he did not want to leave the TBDs unsupported. That would fly in the face of combat wisdom accrued even in "The Big E's" early raids. Likewise he thought his ten fighters too few to divide. To solve his dilemma he consulted Art Ely, VT-6 executive officer in temporary command in place of the injured Gene Lindsey. Gray told Ely he would proceed to the target at high altitude along with the dive bombers. However, he would be alert to dive in, should the torpedo planes run into heavy fighter opposition. If Ely thought he needed fighter support, he simply was to radio, "Come on down, Jim."[7] Hearing that distress call, Gray's ten Wildcats would dive in and take the Zeros by surprise. The plan seemed to offer the best way of supporting both the SBDs and the TBDs, especially since Gray estimated the SBDs would, because of their faster cruise, reach the target area first and attack while the TBDs started their approach. Gray would be able, he expected, to see the dive bombers safely to their pushover point, then dive in to help Torpedo Six. That squadron, incidentally, expected close fighter support, and the morning of 4 June Lindsey briefed his crews to that effect.

The *Yorktown*'s aviators were not so certain as their colleagues in Task Force 16 as to what their tasks on 4 June would be. They knew that Fletcher intended to use them in a search and support role, whereas Spruance would launch immediately when the enemy carriers were located. Fletcher wanted no surprises such as befell him on 7 May at Coral Sea when impulsive reaction to erroneous search reports nearly squandered Task Force 17's main strike. Like the men in Task Force 16, the *Yorktown*'s pilots had been briefed as to what the admirals expected the enemy to do at Midway. They knew there likely would be an attack on the Japanese carriers the next morning.

As for the escort force, Buckmaster gave Thach eight of the twenty-five F4F-4s available to use in that manner. Thach decided to join McCuskey's section from VF-3's 2nd Division to the six of his 1st Division to form two divisions of four planes each. The next question concerned the deployment of this fighter escort. After dinner on 3 June, Thach with VB-3's skipper Max Leslie and Lem Massey, Torpedo Three's new commanding officer, talked informally in Leslie's cabin. Thach asked each where he thought the escort should go, and was highly amused to hear that Leslie wanted the F4Fs to accompany the torpedo planes, while Massey insisted they escort the dive bombers. Thach ended this "Alphonse and Gaston" routine, as he put it, by stating he would decide where he would go. Having sounded out *Yorktown* personnel, especially Leonard, who led the VT escort on 8 May at Coral Sea, Thach felt the torpedo squadron faced more danger. Therefore his fighters should stay with Torpedo Three. He thought it risky to separate his eight fighters into a VSB escort for the SBDs and a VT escort for the TBDs. There just were too few to go around.

Gray has provided a vivid recollection of the activities of his men the night before Midway:

> There were no religious services so far as memory serves. We were too busy. Guns were loaded bullet by bullet with loving care (several of us lost out on sure kills in previous actions when nothing happened as triggers were pressed). Firing circuits were checked. No dirty airplanes ever flew from *Enterprise* in these days. Plane captains took pride in keeping their aircraft gleaming and sleek. Many bought wax with their own money to outdo the others. Charts and plotting boards were cleaned and prepared for the morning's data. By the time all of the preliminaries were in hand most were too exhausted to do more than turn in and go quickly to sleep.[8]

Over in the *Yorktown*, Fighting Three did have one reason to rejoice. The evening of 3 June the squadron had put into commission the last F4F-4 Wildcat that required its guns boresighted. Now the squadron was ready to fight.

CHAPTER 15

The Battle of 4 June

THE OPENING MOVES

Midway—The Waiting Is Over

As Wednesday turned into Thursday, 4 June, Fletcher's Striking Force steamed southward at an economical 13.5 knots, the two carrier task forces remaining about 10 miles apart. First light (around 0430) was to see Striking Force at a point bearing 013 degrees, 202 miles from Midway. This constituted the famous flank ambush position planned by Nimitz, Fletcher, and Spruance. They expected the Japanese carriers to roar down on Midway from the northwest and launch a massive air strike at dawn to pummel the island's defenses. At least they hoped their intelligence actually forecast what the Japanese would do! While the enemy busied himself with Midway, Fletcher planned to seek out the enemy carriers and crush them with a powerful counterstrike of his own. That morning his three carriers had a total of 221 operational planes: 79 fighters, 101 dive bombers, and 41 torpedo planes (see table).[1]

Reveille came early on board the three American flattops. Roused at 0130, the pilots and aircrewmen shuffled off to their squadron ready rooms to lounge there in the soft reclining chairs. Assembled and ready they were, but there was no need yet to prevent them from dozing off. Between 0300 and 0400, the pilots went down to breakfast in relays. Some later remembered the wardrooms as especially quiet and subdued; others thought the breakfast chatter was normal.

On board the *Yorktown* flight quarters sounded well before dawn. Fletcher thought it best to send ten SBD dive bombers to search the northern semicircle to a radius of 100 miles. This was a precautionary scouting effort designed to detect the enemy carriers should they approach Midway from the north or northeast. The short search radius of 100 miles was sufficient because Fletcher's carriers at launch time would be over 200 miles north of Midway. If the Japanese, as expected, planned to hit Midway at dawn, perforce they would have to be well within 300 miles of the target. The *Yorktown*'s Fighting Three readied a combat air patrol for launch at the same time. Dick Crommelin's 2nd Division drew the predawn assignment.

In the quiet darkness, the air department prepared the seventeen planes on the flight deck—six Grummans and ten SBDs from Wally Short's "Scouting" Five. Night takeoff conditions proved to be ideal, with excellent visibility and a tranquil sea. The wind blew out of the southeast at a gentle five knots. This southeasterly

American Carrier Air Groups, Dawn, 4 June 1942

Task Force 16: *Enterprise* Air Group		On hand	(Opera- tional)	
Commander, *Enterprise* Air Group	Lt. Cdr. C. Wade McClusky	1	(1)	SBD-3
Fighting Six	Lieut. James S. Gray, Jr.	27	(27)	F4F-4
Bombing Six	Lieut. Richard H. Best	18	(15)	SBD-2, -3
Scouting Six	Lieut. W. Earl Gallaher	18	(17)	SBD-3
Torpedo Six	Lt. Cdr. Eugene E. Lindsey	14	(14)	TBD-1
		78	(74)	
Hornet Air Group				
Commander, *Hornet* Air Group	Cdr. Stanhope C. Ring	0•	(0)•	SBD-3
Fighting Eight	Lt. Cdr. Samuel G. Mitchell	27	(27)	F4F-4
Bombing Eight	Lt. Cdr. Robert R. Johnson	19	(19)	SBD-3
Scouting Eight	Lt. Cdr. Walter F. Rodee	16	(15)	SBD-3
Torpedo Eight	Lt. Cdr. John C. Waldron	15	(15)	TBD-1
		77	(76)	
Task Force 17: *Yorktown* Air Group				
Commander, *Yorktown* Air Group	Lt. Cdr. Oscar Pederson	1	(1)*	SBD-3
Fighting Three	Lt. Cdr. John S. Thach	27	(25)	F4F-4
Bombing Three	Lt. Cdr. Maxwell F. Leslie	18	(17)	SBD-3
Scouting Five†	Lieut. Wallace C. Short	18	(16)	SBD-3
Torpedo Three	Lt. Cdr. Lance E. Massey	15**	(12)	TBD-1
		79	(71)	

Grand Total:	On hand	(Operational)
Fighters	81	(79)
Dive bombers	109	(101)
Torpedo planes	44	(41)
	234	(221)

•CHAG flying a VB-8 aircraft.
*CYAG aircraft used by Scouting Five.
**Includes one VT-5 aircraft.
†Temporary redesignation of Bombing Five.

breeze was to prevail throughout the day, troublesome for the Americans. In order to conduct flight operations, the flattops had to steam at high speed southeasterly into the wind, which under the circumstances led them away from the enemy. This increased the distance the strike planes would have to fly. At 0431, the *Yorktown*'s flight deck officer flagged the first fighter down the deck. The remaining aircraft followed in short intervals, and as they climbed, their wing lights and blue exhaust flames shone in the darkness. Soon first light creased the eastern horizon, the beginning of the day that would see the end of Japan's supremacy in the Pacific.

At Midway other aircrews also took to the skies before dawn. Fully anticipating an air strike later that morning, the island commander despatched his PBY Catalina flying boats to search for the enemy and likewise sent the Army B-17 Flying Fortresses to attack the Japanese transport convoy located the previous day. His other attack planes and fighters he readied for departure at a moment's notice. Midway was as prepared as it could be to face the enemy's onslaught.

The object of all this careful concern on the part of the Americans appeared on schedule. Vice Admiral Nagumo Chūichi's *Kidō Butai* (Mobile or Striking Force) lurked in the darkness 240 miles northwest of Midway. It was a superb fighting force with four fleet carriers (the *Akagi, Kaga, Sōryū,* and *Hiryū*), two battleships, two heavy cruisers, and eleven destroyers. The *Shōkaku* and the *Zuikaku* were originally supposed to participate, but Fletcher's flyers had knocked them out at Coral Sea. The four flattops present mustered a total of about 228 operational aircraft: 73 Zero fighters, 74 carrier bombers, and 81 carrier attack planes (not counting 21 Zero fighters of the 6th Air Group intended for Midway), all flown by what the Imperial Navy considered its best aviators.[2] On the flight decks of the four carriers, a total of 108 aircraft (36 fighters, 36 carrier bombers, and 36 carrier attack planes) under Lieut. Tomonaga Jōichi, *hikōtaichō* and commander of the *Hiryū* Air Group, prepared to take off and attack Midway.

The Japanese operational plan was complex, replete with many separate task forces. Its ultimate aim was to bring the U.S. Pacific Fleet's carriers into decisive battle and crush them. Opening the offensive was a diversionary sweep by the light carriers *Ryūjō* and *Junyō* into the Aleutians; they attacked Dutch Harbor on 3 June. Following that and other air strikes, Japanese troops were to occupy Attu and Kiska. The northern attacks were meant to confuse the Americans and set them up for the main assault in the Central Pacific. Nagumo's *Kidō Butai*, acting as an advanced guard, had the task of smashing Midway's air defenses and supporting landings first on little Kure Island (60 miles northwest of Midway) on 5 June and then backing up the main amphibious attack on Midway to take place on N-Day, 6 June. The Japanese hoped the American fleet would sortie in strength and attempt to recover Midway. Operating behind Nagumo's carrier force and the Midway Invasion Force was Main Force under Admiral Yamamoto himself. Divided into two groups, Main Force comprised seven battleships along with escort forces. To the Midway–Aleutians operations the Japanese committed by far the vast majority of the Combined Fleet.

At 0430, Nagumo's carriers started launching the 108 aircraft of the Midway strike force. They hoped to attack the island by surprise and overwhelm defending aircraft before most could get off the ground. Around this time Nagumo also sent off a tardy, somewhat halfhearted search by seven aircraft, mostly from his battleships and cruisers. They were to look for enemy warships in the Midway area— believed by the Japanese to be a rather unlikely presence. Covering the eastern semicircle, six aircraft were to go out 300 miles, the seventh only 150 miles. Several search planes were late getting off. Nagumo did not suspect it, but Fletcher's carriers waited just 215 miles east of him.

On board the American carriers, things settled down after the *Yorktown* completed flight operations. Both task forces turned to the northeast and marked time awaiting developments. Around 0440, Air Plot set the teletypes in the squadron ready rooms clattering with the first report of the day, a message relayed by Midway noting that four PBY flying boats had earlier that morning executed a successful night torpedo strike on the enemy transport force. Silence once more descended, as anticipation grew more intense. The pilots knew that search planes from Midway busily sought the Japanese carriers, but they themselves could do nothing until the Midway flyers had pinpointed the enemy for them.

Suddenly at 0534 the carriers heard on voice radio the electrifying words, "Enemy carriers."[3] Maddeningly, there was no further clarification. Eleven minutes later, another PBY reported, "Many planes heading Midway."[4] This presumably referred to the expected Japanese air strike on the island. Things at this murky stage appeared to be going according to the situation estimates. Spruance at 0600 ordered Task Force 16 to come around to 330 degrees to remain within its designated area. Fletcher's Task Force 17 continued northeast to close Point Option, where her search planes expected to find her on their return. Three minutes later came the long hoped-for word. Fletcher and Spruance simultaneously received the text of a message sent at 0552 by a PBY: "Two carriers and battleships, bearing 320 degrees, distance 180, course 135, speed 25."[5] A quick glance at the charts placed the enemy bearing 247 degrees, distance 175 miles from the American carriers. This position report sent by the PBY was in error. The enemy striking force was actually a good 200 miles southwest of Fletcher's carriers.

There they were, at least two of the four or five carriers the Japanese were supposed to have. Their reported location was a good one from which to conduct an air strike on Midway. Fletcher made his decision. At 0607, he signaled Spruance:

> Proceed southwesterly and attack enemy carriers as soon as definitely located. I will follow as soon as planes recovered.[6]

Spruance swiftly brought Task Force 16 around to head southwest toward the enemy at 25 knots. Consulting his air staff, he reviewed the options open to him. He desired to launch his attack at the earliest possible moment, subject to limitations of the range of his fighters and torpedo planes, as well as the direction of the wind. The light southeasterly wind would compel Task Force 16 to steam away from the target at high speed while launching planes. Browning, the chief of staff, suggested a launch time of 0700, to which Spruance immediately agreed. If the Japanese continued on the reported course and speed, at 0700 they would bear 239 degrees, 155 miles from Task Force 16.

Fletcher's Task Force 17 held its northeasterly heading in order to close its Point Option and recover the morning search. These SBDs had vouchsafed no sighting reports, so Fletcher could reasonably assume his northern quadrant was secure. What bothered him was that Midway's search had uncovered only two enemy carriers. CinCPac intelligence estimates had warned that the Japanese carriers could conceivably operate in two separate groups. For the time being Fletcher thought it best to wait and see whether Midway's PBYs and B-17s turned up the other flattops. This was in line with the role assigned to the *Yorktown*: search and reserve. Shortly before 0630, the ten VS-5 SBDs converged overhead as scheduled. The *Yorktown* sent aloft six VF-3 fighters of Brassfield's 4th Division as relief CAP, then landed Crommelin's six Wildcats and VS-5's ten dive bombers. Flight operations completed, Fletcher came around to 240 degrees and bent on 25 knots to follow after Spruance.

The Launch of Task Force 16's Strike Groups

Intercepted on radio, the news of the PBY's sighting report of two enemy carriers sent Spruance's Task Force 16 racing southwestward (course 240 degrees). Both the *Enterprise* and the *Hornet* were cocked like loaded pistols—aircraft on deck ready to launch and pilots, garbed and gloved, waiting restlessly in the ready rooms scribbling down navigational information and listening for orders to man planes. Spruance did not immediately transmit his intention for an 0700 launch to the *Hornet*, and Mitscher did not know quite what was happening. At 0615, the *Hornet* Air Plot sent the ready room teletypes clattering orders for the combat air patrol fighters to man planes, and shortly came the word for the escort pilots to head out on deck as well. On the loudspeaker, Mitscher warned his people:

> The enemy main body is now attempting to take Midway. We are heading toward Midway to intercept and destroy them.[7]

Then came orders for all strike pilots, except for Ring and the four squadron commanders, to man planes, but Air Plot soon called them back to their ready rooms. The *Enterprise* showed no indication she was about to swing into the wind for launch, so the *Hornet* backed down and waited tensely.

At 0638, the *Enterprise* by blinker light began transmitting the go-ahead to launch at 0700. The air groups were to use deferred departure; that is, all aircraft within a group were to rendezvous into their base formations and leave together. En route they were to employ search–attack procedure to seek out the enemy, logical since the sighting reports might be inaccurate. Once the target was located, each group leader was to select one enemy carrier and attack. No specific Point Option course was provided, but the message gave Spruance's intention to steam to within 100 miles of the enemy. Given the enemy's plotted position, that meant a return to the base course of 240 degrees after launching was completed. The orders to the *Hornet* also provided no definite course for the aircraft to fly in order to find the Japanese carriers.

On the *Hornet*'s bridge, Mitscher convened a quick conference with Ring and the four squadron commanders, while the SBD and TBD crews manned planes (the VF-8 pilots were already on deck). Cdr. Soucek, the air officer, and a few others probably were also present. The *Hornet* brass discussed what course to fly in searching for the enemy, based on the latest information from Air Plot. The evidence strongly indicates that they decided to send the *Hornet* strike group west on a heading of 265 degrees, instead of to the southwest (240 degrees), Task Force 16's base course.[8] What reasoning this followed is not apparent in the fragmentary sources on that conference, but a few suggestions can be made. Spruance's orders called for search–attack procedure by the strike planes, indicating he was not certain *all* of the Japanese carriers were located where the PBY had found *two* of them. Mitscher and his people may have wanted to cover the area north of where the *Enterprise* thought the target area was in order to find the Japanese if they were a little farther away from Midway. It would have been highly unlikely that the enemy carriers were significantly closer to Midway than where the *Enterprise* planes were to search. Waldron differed with the proposed heading of 265 degrees, evidently thinking that both the *Hornet* and the *Enterprise* plans were incorrect. He had his own ideas about where he would go.

A few minutes before the scheduled launch, the ships of Task Force 16 split into two groups, each centered around one of the two carriers. That permitted each flattop to maneuver independently to conduct flight operations. At 0656, the ships swung to port and steadied up at 28 knots into the gentle southeasterly wind. On her flight deck, the *Enterprise* arrayed her first deckload, comprising ten F4Fs from Fighting Six (including two spares) for CAP and thirty-three SBDs for the strike. The *Hornet*'s deckload was larger: twenty VF-8 F4Fs (ten including spares for CAP, ten for escort), thirty-four dive bombers, and, crowding the stern, six TBDs. Both flight decks buzzed with purposeful activity, as crews swarmed around the blue aircraft, now much less colorful with their red dots and striped tails painted over. Puffs of smoke and flashing propellor blades signaled starting of engines, and pilots waited anxiously in their cockpits. It was 0700, and the enemy carriers (at least two of them) were thought to bear 239 to 240 degrees, distance 155 miles.

Promptly at 0700, plane handlers guided the *Hornet*'s lead fighter into launch position. Carefully assessing the sound of its Pratt & Whitney run up to full power, the Fly I officer waved his flag and sent the Wildcat "clattering" down the deck and into the air. The *Enterprise* responded with a fighter of her own. Thereafter every twenty to thirty seconds another F4F followed and scurried to join division leaders orbiting the task force. First off were the sixteen F4F-4s making up the combat air patrol. Fighting Eight flew in two divisions led by the XO, Eddie O'Neill,

and Lieut. Warren W. Ford. The *Hornet* CAP was to fly high cover ("hi cap")
over the ships; so her F4Fs formed up quickly for a steady climb toward 18,000
feet. The *Enterprise*'s contribution comprised two four-plane divisions under VF-
6's XO, Roger Mehle, and Lieut. (jg) Frank Quady. Mehle's F4Fs flew "lo cap"
near the task force and carefully avoided the strike planes in the process of taking
off and forming up.

Right on the tail of the *Hornet* CAP came the ten VF-8 escort fighters led by
the skipper, Pat Mitchell. His force consisted of:

	1st Division
F-18	Lt. Cdr. Samuel G. Mitchell, USN
	Ens. Johnny A. Talbot, A-V(N)
	Ens. John Magda, A-V(N)
	Ens. John E. McInerny, Jr., A-V(N)
	2nd Division
F-5	Lieut. (jg) Richard Gray, USN
F-9	Ens. C. Markland Kelly, Jr., A-V(N)
	Lieut. (jg) Minuard F. Jennings, USN
	Ens. Humphrey L. Tallman, A-V(N)
	CHAG Escort Section
F-19	Lieut. Stanley E. Ruehlow, USN
F-13	Ens. George R. Hill, A-V(N)

The ten F4Fs got off without trouble, except for the one flown by John McInerny.
His Grumman failed to start. Only when the flight deck officer was about to strike
it below did the balky engine finally catch, as the plane captain desperately jammed
in a last starter cartridge. McInerny firewalled the throttle without going through
even a normal magneto check and made it aloft. In accordance with departure
orders, Mitchell led the escort into a gentle climb to try to conserve fuel while
circling to await the launch of the dive bombers. Then the F4Fs were to join the
SBDs and both wait for the torpedo planes to get off before departing. Even so,
the long climb toward high altitude used considerable fuel, and while the short-
legged fighters orbited, the *Hornet* steamed southeastward into the wind, adding
up to 15 miles to VF-8's mission.

The *Hornet*'s dive bombing force comprised thirty-four SBD-3 Dauntlesses,
apparently half of them armed with 500-lb. bombs and the rest with thousand-
pounders. First to take off were fifteen SBDs from Scouting Eight led by Lt. Cdr.
Walter F. Rodee. Next came the "Sea Hag," Cdr. Ring, and two wingmen from
Bombing Eight, and finally the sixteen SBDs of Bombing Eight proper under Lt.
Cdr. Robert R. Johnson. At Ring's direction, the SBDs assumed "group parade
formation," with Ring's command section at the apex of a giant Vee of Vees and
the two squadrons deployed abreast of one another, VS-8 on the right and VB-8
on the left. Above and behind them the fighter escort took station with Mitchell's
division on the left, Ruehlow's section in the center to guard Ring, and Dick Gray's
division on the right. The SBDs and escorts continued the long ascent to the assigned
altitudes—19,000 feet for the bombers and 2,000 to 3,000 feet more for the fighters.

After the dive bombers took off, the *Hornet* air department brought up on deck
the remaining nine TBD Devastators of Waldron's Torpedo Eight. The squadron
got off in short order, and by 0742, the carrier's deck was empty. At 300 feet
Torpedo Eight effected its rendezvous without delay. Well above them, Ring at
0746 signaled for the group to depart. The *Hornet* aircraft headed west on the

briefed heading of 265 degrees and continued climbing toward the specified altitudes. Waldron's TBDs were to cruise at 1,500 feet. After departure, SBD crews and fighter pilots saw them far below and following behind, keeping in contact because the rate of advance of the still-climbing SBDs was slow. It was fortunate that the *Hornet*'s flight deck was clear. Steve Groves, flying one of the CAP F4Fs, ran into mechanical difficulties and signaled the ship for permission to make an emergency "deferred forced landing." She recovered him at 0754 and scrambled a spare to restore VF-8's CAP to eight.

The *Enterprise*'s launch did not proceed as smoothly as that of her sister *Hornet*. At 0706, the fifteen SBDs of Earl Gallaher's Scouting Six began taking off. The initial six carried only a single 500-lb. bomb apiece, but the last nine added one 100-lb. bomb under each wing. Then came the group leader, Wade McClusky, and his pair of VS-6 wingmen. Finally Dick Best's fifteen VB-6 SBDs took off, laden by the far more potent thousand-pounders. In accordance with the procedures for deferred departure, the thirty-three SBDs circled the task group and formed up during the long, slow climb to 20,000 feet. McClusky waited for his escort fighters and torpedo planes to appear before he, too, departed for the target.

On board the *Enterprise*, plane handlers respotted the flight deck with ten F4F Wildcats and fourteen TBDs. Inexplicably this became a time-consuming process. To McClusky overhead, "action seemed to come to a standstill."[9] In flag plot, Spruance grew increasingly impatient at the slow progress of the launch. It should not have taken so long. The *Hornet* had almost all of her planes aloft, while the *Enterprise*'s second deckload sat on board. The admiral felt the strike had to proceed now even if it meant separating the group. At 0745, the *Enterprise* began signaling McClusky by blinker: "Proceed on mission assigned."[10] The group commander had carefully plotted on his board his estimate of the enemy's course and position, computing the likely point of interception by his planes as bearing 231 degrees, distance 142 miles. He rounded up his SBDs and at 0752 departed on 231 degrees.

Even as Spruance ordered McClusky to depart, the *Enterprise* began launching VF-6's escort force, organized as follows:

1st Division
F-1 Lieut. James S. Gray, Jr., USN
F-2 Ens. Joseph R. Daly, A-V(N)
F-3 Ens. Walter J. Hiebert, A-V(N)
F-4 Mach. Julius A. Achten, USN
F-5 Ens. Ralph M. Rich, A-V(N)
F-6 Ens. Wayne C. Presley, A-V(N)

2nd Division
F-7 Lieut. (jg) John C. Kelley, USN
F-8 Ens. Norman D. Hodson, A-V(N)
F-9 Lieut. (jg) Harold N. Heisel, USN
F-10 Mach. Clayton Allard, USN

Gray's fighters were aloft by 0749, but no one had time to tell him of the change in plans. By the time he formed up the ten F4Fs and headed out in the direction of the enemy, the SBDs (his primary responsibility for escort) had flown out of sight to the southwest. Gray spotted below a torpedo squadron starting out in purposeful fashion without fighter escort in sight, and moved overhead to cover them while still climbing toward his assigned altitude. As Gray later related in

"Decision at Midway," his F4Fs even outpaced the TBDs while in a climb and had to make S-turns to cut down their rate of advance. He apparently hoped to rejoin the SBDs in the target area. Gray's new charges were the TBDs from Torpedo Eight, making up the tail end of the *Hornet* Air Group heading out on 265 degrees.

The last element of the *Enterprise*'s strike group to leave her deck was Torpedo Six. The battered Gene Lindsey refused to be left behind and had to be helped into his cockpit. Along with him, the other thirteen VT-6 TBDs took to the air around 0800 and made a running rendezvous while departing. "The Big E's" launch had taken nearly an hour to complete! Evidence indicates that Lindsey took a heading of 240 degrees for his flight to the target area. Like Waldron, he would stay relatively low and cruise at 2,000 feet.

Circumstances seemed to preclude that Spruance's two strike groups would be able to attack in any coordinated fashion. Indeed, the aircraft had separated into three different groupings during departure. First to leave (at 0746) was the *Hornet* Air Group, flying westward on 265 degrees. Ring's forty-four dive bombers and fighters, in the process of climbing to high altitude, were in the lead. Following along behind them at low level was Waldron's Torpedo Eight, the fifteen TBDs able to keep up for the time being while Ring's planes completed their climb. Overtaking VT-8, but unseen by them, were Gray's ten VF-6 F4Fs. As will be shown, Waldron had no intention of remaining on Ring's course, but would soon find his own way to the enemy. McClusky's thirty-three *Enterprise* SBDs flew a much more southwesterly course than the others, 231 degrees, and departed at 0752. Last of all came VT-6's fourteen TBDs on course 240 degrees. Gray for a time saw a second torpedo squadron a good distance behind him, but they headed away to his left—Lindsey branching off to the southwest on 240 degrees. Thus by 0800 or so, all planes were on their way, an air armada of 116 aircraft: 20 fighters, 67 dive bombers, and 29 torpedo planes. Upon this strike rested American hopes for victory in the Battle of Midway. Its results would be stranger than anyone could have thought.

The Japanese Find Task Force 16

In the growing daylight with the departure of the Midway strike group, Nagumo's *Kidō Butai* settled down to await the results of the attack and the dawn search. Precautionary plans called for the four carriers to ready a second strike force in the event the search turned up American warships within range. On board the *Akagi* and the *Kaga*, thirty-six carrier attack planes armed with torpedoes made ready for launch, while the *Sōryū* and the *Hiryū* made preparations to send thirty-six carrier bombers if necessary. The Japanese combat air patrol had already absorbed nearly a dozen Zeros, and others waited in reserve to replace them. Apparently the Japanese counted on perhaps a dozen Zeros to escort the second strike should it have to go. Meanwhile, the carriers at 0542 scrambled an additional six Zeros for CAP when lookouts noticed Midway-based PBY Catalina flying boats snooping the carrier force.

Warned by PBYs and radar, Midway had every serviceable aircraft aloft well before the Japanese approach. Sent to attack the Japanese carriers were six Grumman TBF-1 Avenger torpedo planes (Torpedo Eight detachment), four Army Martin B-26 medium bombers armed with torpedoes, fourteen Army B-17 Flying Fortresses (diverted from striking the enemy transports), and from Marine Scouting Squadron 241: sixteen SBD-2 Dauntless dive bombers and eleven Vought SB2U-3 Vindicator dive bombers. Divided into four separate groups, the bombers had to attack alone without fighter escort. Ready to defend Midway were eighteen

F2A-3 Buffaloes and six F4F-3 Wildcats from Marine Fighting Squadron 221 (VMF-221), old friends from the Wake relief attempt.

Thirty miles out from Midway, the lead marine fighters tore into the Japanese around 0620. The F2As and the few F4F-3s started with altitude advantage, but the more numerous Zeros were deadly. In a wild succession of small air battles fought all the way back to Midway, the Zeros slaughtered the leatherneck interceptors. For the loss of one or two fighters and a couple of carrier attack planes, the Japanese shot down thirteen F2As and two F4F-3s. Most surviving marine fighters bore scars from the fight, and immediately after the raid, Midway's effective fighter strength stood at only two aircraft. The Japanese lost three or four more planes to the intense ground fire. Thus seven Japanese carrier aircraft (two fighters, one dive bomber, and four torpedo planes) failed to return from the fight, although others were badly shot up. Lieut. Tomonaga's level and dive bombers methodically pounded Midway's defenses. By 0700, they had done what they could, but Tomonaga felt more had to be done to neutralize the island. At 0700 he radioed the flagship, "There is need for a second attack wave."[11]

Tomonaga's message reached Nagumo just ahead of the first wave of attackers from Midway. Shortly after 0700, the Japanese CAP of around twenty-nine Zeros battled the six VT-8 TBFs and four Army B-26 Marauders trying to hit the *Akagi*. The carrier went unscathed, and for the loss of two Zeros, the Japanese shot down five TBFs and two B-26s. Even so, Midway's prompt air counterstrike came as a distinct surprise to the Japanese. Nagumo decided to hit Midway again with the aircraft waiting in reserve. The morning search had proved negative so far, and it appeared likely no American ships lurked close by. At 0715, Nagumo ordered the *Akagi* and the *Kaga* carrier attack planes reequipped with 800-kilogram land bombs in place of aerial torpedoes, while the carrier bombers on board the *Sōryū* and the *Hiryū* would substitute the high explosive (land) bombs for armor-piercing weapons. *Kidō Butai*'s carriers would have to have cleared flight decks anyway, for in ninety minutes they would have to recover planes returning from the first Midway strike. The air officers of the four carriers had to see that some CAP Zeros were recovered and refueled in time to escort the second Midway strike. The Japanese flattops were having a busy time.

While the Japanese rearmed their planes and Task Force 16 suffered the labor pains of its massive launch, a Japanese floatplane on its return search leg made an interesting discovery. The aircraft was the *Tone* No. 4 plane, an Aichi E13A1 Type O reconnaissance floatplane [JAKE], which had departed at 0500 (thirty minutes late) to search 300 miles along a heading of 100 degrees before turning north 60 miles and returning to base. At 0728, Number Four radioed the *Tone*:

> Sight what appears to be ten enemy surface ships, in position bearing 010 degrees distance 240 miles from Midway. Course 150 degrees, speed over 20 knots.[12]

Significantly, the report failed to mention the presence of American carriers. The crew proceeded deliberately and thoroughly to check out the area. As yet the Americans knew nothing of their presence.

News of American ships in range caught Nagumo with his hands full orchestrating the second Midway strike. Realizing the American task force rated top priority, at 0745 he suspended rearming the strike planes with land bombs. (Those armed with the high explosive weapons would be left that way.) The staff proceeded to organize the strike, but with little sense of urgency because they thought no enemy carriers were near. Meanwhile, Midway's air force offered three more diversions for the Japanese. Shortly before 0800, the first group of marine dive bombers, sixteen SBD-2s from VMSB-241, appeared on the horizon. Fearing the inexperience of his pilots, their leader opted for a glide-bombing attack on the *Hiryū*. Unlike Bill Ault's similar ploy at Coral Sea, this maneuver fooled no one. The thirteen Zeros aloft on CAP and six scrambled soon after, together shot down eight SBDs for the loss of one *Hiryū* Zero. That carrier herself suffered no damage. As the SBD survivors departed, fourteen Army B-17 Fortresses attacked the *Sōryū* and the *Kaga*. Sparring with the giant bombers were nine *Sōryū* Zeros newly returned from the Midway strike and three *Kaga* CAP Zeros. Neither side took any losses, nor were the carriers hit. The Army attack ebbed around 0820, and as the B-17s drew away, the second marine dive bombing force, eleven Vindicators, bombed the battleship *Haruna* in the screen. They scored no hits, but lost three SB2Us to a dozen defending Zeros. Midway's brave counterattacks inflicted no damage to the enemy ships, but they helped keep the Japanese off balance.

Forty-five minutes elapsed before Task Force 16 realized it was being snooped by the wily *Tone* No. 4 crew. At 0806, after departure of his strike groups, Spruance brought his ships around to course 240 degrees, speed 25 knots to charge toward the enemy. Nine minutes later, the *Enterprise*'s radar detected a bogey bearing 170 degrees, distance 30 miles. Almost simultaneously, lookouts on board the heavy cruiser *Northampton*, screening the *Enterprise*, eyeballed the intruder bearing 185 degrees, 30 miles out. Lt. Cdr. Dow, "The Big E's" FDO, broke radio silence on the fighter circuit and instructed VF-6 section "Red 17" (Ens. Thomas Provost) to "arrow" 170 degrees for 30 miles for a low-flying bogey. (In early fighter direction terminology, "arrow" meant for the fighters to proceed along a true as opposed to a magnetic compass bearing. Its use compelled the pilots to convert their bearings from magnetic to true and could cause confusion. The difference between magnetic and true directions in the Midway area could lead to discrepancies of 20 or so degrees. The *Yorktown* FDO policy eschewed the use of "arrow" and based orders instead on magnetic bearings or "vectors.")

As ordered, Provost and his wingman hurried out in hopes of ambushing the snooper, but scattered cloud cover at low altitude made that task difficult. At 0820, ship lookouts again spotted the enemy, most likely from sunlight glinting off the aircraft. The two VF-6 pilots were not so fortunate. Simultaneously, the Japanese crew finally obtained a closer look at the American task force. At 0820, the *Tone* No. 4 radioed to base that the enemy force apparently included a carrier. Fuel beginning to run low, the floatplane warned it would soon start home.

Consternation! Nagumo and his staff on board the *Akagi* hurriedly conferred at the news of the American carrier, while their CAP Zeros beat off the last of the Midway-based dive bombers. The Japanese found themselves in a fix. The *Akagi* and *Kaga* carrier attack planes, only partially rearmed with torpedoes, waited in the hangar decks of the two flattops. On board the *Sōryū* and the *Hiryū*, Rear Admiral Yamaguchi Tamon (commanding the 2nd Carrier Division) had thirty-six carrier bombers ready for action, but only a few of them armed with the ship-killing 250-kilogram semi-armor-piercing bombs. The main problem, however, concerned fighter escorts, for only about a half dozen Zeros were ready to go. Most of the rest were on CAP and would have to land for fuel and ammunition before they could serve as escorts. Overhead, aircraft from the first Midway strike group had returned, and they were low on fuel—having been aloft for about four hours.

Rear Admiral Yamaguchi on board the *Hiryū* urged an immediate attack by all available bombers, even without fighter escort if necessary. Perceptively, he desperately wanted to land the first blow in the impending carrier duel. Nagumo was loath to send his bomb-armed carrier attack planes as level bombers against enemy carriers, as they would be most vulnerable to fighter attack. At the prompting of his staff, Nagumo rejected Yamaguchi's advice and adopted the cautious course of delaying the strike until after the recovery of his Midway strike group. He planned to swing northeast to regroup, then at 1030 launch a massive strike of thirty-six carrier bombers, forty-five torpedo-armed carrier attack planes, and twelve Zeros to deal with the American carrier force. All he needed was two hours. At 0837, the four Japanese carriers turned into the wind and began recovering gasoline-hungry CAP Zeros and the Midway strike planes.

While Nagumo made his fateful decision (the one that ultimately lost the Battle of Midway), "Ham" Dow on board the *Enterprise* spent several minutes trying to coach Provost into an intercept of the *Tone*'s cagey No. 4. At 0836, Dow sent reinforcements in the form of Provost's division leader, Quady, and a four-plane division from Fighting Eight. Already, however, the *Tone* No. 4 was opening the range, and it soon disappeared from the radar screen. At 0844, Dow called his fighters back on station. There was a flurry a little later when Dow discovered a bogey to the north. He turned to the *Yorktown*'s Fighting Three and used Brass-field's "Scarlet 19" section to check out the contact. By 0904, Brassfield had found the contact to be friendly and returned to station. Meanwhile, his carrier had made her contribution to the attack on the Japanese carriers.

The Yorktown's Strike Group Departs

While Task Force 17 steamed southwestward at 25 knots, Fletcher on board the *Yorktown* worried about the two enemy carriers that had apparently eluded the Midway search. He delayed launch of the *Yorktown* strike in hopes that further reports would reveal the location of all the Japanese carriers, and in order to close within effective range of his fighters and torpedo planes. Spotted on the *Yorktown*'s flight deck were VF-3 Wildcats ready to reinforce the CAP, as well as the first deckload of strike planes: Massey's twelve VT-3 TBD Devastators and seventeen SBD-3 Dauntlesses from Leslie's Bombing Three. Still in the hangar was Short's "Scouting Five."[13]

Conferring with air advisers Buckmaster, Arnold, and Pederson, Fletcher around 0820 resolved to send part of his strike force to follow up Task Force 16's attack. He was especially concerned not to be caught with his own strike planes on deck should enemy aircraft appear. From monitoring the fighter director circuit, he knew the Japanese had just spotted Spruance's ships. Thus the *Yorktown* would launch the twelve TBDs, VB-3's seventeen SBDs, and six VF-3 fighters as escort, a total of thirty-five aircraft. They had orders to attack one of the two enemy carriers, which Spruance's planes now sought. Held in reserve for a possible second strike was Short's Scouting Five with seventeen SBDs and the six F4Fs of Crom-melin's 2nd Division to escort them.

Thach learned of the new arrangement about forty minutes before his scheduled takeoff, and he was irate. Instead of the eight F4Fs (his 1st Division and McCuskey's section from the 2nd Division) that he had counted on taking, he would now have only the 1st Division. Racing to the bridge to speak with Murr Arnold, Thach explained that his experimental defensive tactics (later known as the "Thach Weave"—see appendix) required multiples of four planes to function effectively. The air officer was sympathetic, but told him that the orders came from above, meaning the captain, and would not be changed. Unfortunately, Thach had not found the time to huddle with his VF-42 pilots to outline his special tactics. He had originally intended for Don Lovelace to instruct them, but after his tragic death, the subject must have slipped Thach's mind. Now he had only a few minutes to work out a new escort plan. He instructed Tom Cheek and wingman Dan Sheedy to take station near the torpedo planes as "close escort." Originally Cheek would have had McCuskey's section as well, but that could not be helped. With the remaining four F4Fs, Thach would fly a few thousand feet above to run interference as the "high escort."

Meanwhile, Arnold and Pederson poured over their charts and studied the fragmentary contact reports. In an effort to permit the strike group to attack in concert without recourse to "deferred departure," which was wasteful of fuel, the two staggered departure times by the three squadrons according to their normal cruising speeds. The slowest would leave first, then the next, and finally the speediest (the fighters), in order to make a running rendezvous on the way to the target. The two also devised a useful means to search for the enemy carrier force. Realizing the original sighting reports were several hours old, they allowed for the time elapsed since then by plotting a direct line along the reported enemy course, which headed into the wind. They marked the farthest point the enemy was likely to reach, considering his need to conduct flight operations and the fact that he would not approach Midway too closely in their estimation. That point proved to be Lat. 30° 00' North, Long. 179° 00' West, which would bear 240 degrees and 150 miles from Task Force 17's 0900 position. The strike group received orders to fly to that point, and if they did not spot the enemy, then turn to the northwest to head back along the reciprocal bearing of the enemy course before turning for home. That way they had an excellent chance of finding the enemy carriers no matter what they did.

Shortly after 0830, the *Yorktown* came left to a southeasterly course into the wind to launch aircraft. First to take off were the twelve TBDs of Torpedo Three. Without much ado, Massey rounded them up and set out directly for the target. Behind Massey came Leslie's seventeen SBDs of Bombing Three, each armed with one 1,000-lb. bomb. Leslie's instructions were to form up his squadron and orbit the ship for twelve minutes after Massey's departure. Because the SBDs cruised at 130 knots in contrast to the TBDs' 100 knots, they could easily overtake the lumbering Devastators before they reached the target area.

Finally at 0905, the carrier depatched the escort, six F4Fs (see list). Happy finally to get into action after their long wait in the ready room, the fighter pilots set their throttles at the F4F-4's most economical cruise for maximum range, giving an airspeed of 140 knots. The target was thought to be perhaps 150 miles away, but the enemy could be much farther. Thach felt confident he could take his short-legged Wildcats out 175 miles, fight, and return. Even so, Leslie acknowledged gratefully that Thach was "really giving a lot."[14] Yorktowners had no illusions as to the combat radius of the F4F-4.

Thus, following the well-ordered launch of the *Yorktown*'s strike, her fighters chased the dive bombers, which in turn overtook the TBDs. Arnold and Pederson figured that the fighters would catch up to the torpedo planes around 0945, and that the group could complete rendezvous before encountering the Japanese. A calculated risk to be sure, but the main consideration for this type of departure

BuNo.	Side No.	1st Division, Fighting Three	
5093	F-23	Lt. Cdr. John S. Thach, USN CO	
5049	F-20	Ens. Robert A. M. Dibb, A-V(N)	
5165	F-6	Lieut. (jg) Brainard T. Macomber, A-V(N)	(VF-42)
5150	F-9	Ens. Edgar R. Bassett, A-V(N)	(VF-42)
5143	F-16	Mach. Tom F. Cheek, USN	
5239	F-24	Ens. Daniel C. Sheedy, A-V(N)	

VF-3's Bill Leonard in F-13 (BuNo. 5244) departs on CAP from the *Yorktown*, 0920, 4 June. (NA 80-G-312016.)

was the short range of both the F4F-4s and the TBDs. The *Yorktown* had utilized this novel type of en-route rendezvous both on 10 March during the Lae–Salamaua raid and on 7 May at Coral Sea. On those occasions it had gone without a hitch. Thach himself was not pleased with the prospect of perhaps missing the TBDs, but fortunately visibility was improving.

Taking off at 0920 as relief CAP were the six F4Fs of Leonard's 3rd Division. He had scheduled himself in that time slot, fully expecting the enemy counterattack to come then. Five minutes later Brassfield brought on board the six F4Fs of his 4th Division for fuel and a little rest. Fletcher changed course to 225 degrees, speed 25 knots to head for Task Force 16 about 15 miles to the southwest. On the *Yorktown*'s flight deck, plane handlers spotted for launch VS-5's seventeen SBDs armed with 1,000-lb. bombs. Ready to go along with them were Crommelin's six F4Fs. With Task Force 16 not in contact, the deckbound group commander Pederson assumed control of the *Yorktown*'s CAP. He would much rather have led the strike. In flag plot, Fletcher waited tensely for news of the other Japanese carriers.

THE ATTACK ON NAGUMO'S CARRIERS

The Sacrifice of Torpedo Eight and Torpedo Six

Better than anyone else in Spruance's air groups, it seems, John Waldron knew where to track down the Japanese flattops. For a time he flew west on 265 degrees behind the rest of the *Hornet* Air Group, glimpsed from time to time by the other *Hornet* planes forging ahead, but finally Waldron swung in a gradual turn to the left to take up a more southwesterly heading.[1] Visibility was somewhat questionable, and that in Waldron's mind might have prevented any kind of coordination with the group even if he had thought they were headed in the right direction— which he did not believe. Now Torpedo Eight was on its own, fifteen TBDs droning along at 100 knots and 1,500 feet above the waves. There was company on high, however, in the form of Jim Gray's ten VF-6 fighters at 22,000 feet. Cruising at 140 knots, his F4Fs swung in wide S-turns to stay along with the much slower torpedo planes. Conditions were such that Gray did not have much trouble keeping the TBDs in sight. He assumed they knew where they were going and devoted most of his attention to watching for the dive bombers or enemy fighters. Waldron had his fighter support, but—irony of ironies—he never knew it was there.

For about an hour VT-8's flight was uneventful. Then an unwelcome visitor happened along. Waldron's flight path had cut across that of the *Tone* No. 4 floatplane on its way back home after shadowing Task Force 16. At 0855 its crew warned Nagumo by radio: "Sight ten enemy attack planes heading toward you."[2] As if prompted by the enemy floatplane seen snooping near the squadron, Waldron deployed the eight planes of his 1st Division abreast into a scouting line to permit them to scan a larger expanse of ocean. Gray and his people at 22,000 feet never eyeballed the enemy seaplane far below. Soon Gray noticed ahead of the TBDs a low-lying cloud bank and later watched them disappear under the whitish mass. It was the last time he ever saw the TBDs. He held Waldron's course, conscious that the enemy ships must be near and Zeros could be above. Suddenly at 0910 Jack Kelley, leader of Gray's 2nd Division, radioed, "There they are at one o'clock down, skipper." Almost dead ahead across the expanse of the cloud bank, Gray spotted ship wakes far off. He continued to head for them and later related, "Our necks were working overtime as our eyes searched every sector for McClusky and Co. and for the highly respected Zeros."[3]

Waldron's chosen course to the enemy had been uncannily accurate, but he could not yet see the enemy ships. Torpedo Eight's scouting line began to drift apart. Concerned, Waldron ordered his formation to close up. He never heard Jack Kelley's report, as the *Hornet* and *Enterprise* planes guarded different radio frequencies. Shortly after 0915, the VT-8 pilots observed smoke ahead on the horizon, and soon Waldron discerned three Japanese carriers. He sent a contact report that never made it back to the *Hornet*, then took his squadron in. Tragically, he never knew of the presence of the ten Grummans overhead. Likewise, far above, Gray thought the TBDs would be able to use the cloud cover to screen their approach, as in the Coral Sea.

Nagumo's *Kidō Butai* at 0918 completed landing the Midway strike planes and a portion of its CAP, then executed a change of course left to a new heading of 070 degrees, speed 30 knots. The Japanese planned to regroup and prepare for the 1030 launch which would smash the American carrier force. Total plane losses up to this point were fourteen: from the Midway strike two fighters, one dive bomber, and eight carrier attack planes missing or ditched, and three fighters lost on CAP.[4] Evidently while the strike force was making its turn, lookouts on board the heavy cruiser *Chikuma* reported enemy torpedo planes to the northeast, distance 35 kilometers. Spruance's first attack was about to commence.

Torpedo Eight went gallantly to its doom. Waldron took his fifteen TBDs down to the wave tops to make a "low approach" in order to keep some of the fighters off. The Japanese were heading toward him, making the deployment of the torpedo planes necessarily swift. Waldron first thought to execute a split attack and motioned Lieut. James C. Owens's 2nd Division to move out to the right. The Zeros responded so fiercely that Waldron recalled Owens and formed his planes tightly in an echelon of divisions—a spearhead aimed at the nearest enemy flattop, which proved to be the *Sōryū*. The Japanese CAP aloft was eighteen Zeros; the *Akagi* and the *Kaga* scrambled an additional eleven. Soon the Zeros had splashed a TBD from the 1st Division. Over the radio Waldron inquired whether a TBD or a Zero had gone in. He was told it was one of his. Again he tried to contact Ring, but there was no answer.

Lt. Cdr. Itaya Shigeru's fighters (the *Akagi*'s for the most part) methodically tore into Torpedo Eight with a succession of shattering attacks from above and behind—wolves ripping into a herd of deer. The TBDs, "flying freight cars bearing the white star,"[5] could only go low and slow. Two more Devastators smacked the water; then a Zero punctured Waldron's left wing tank, flaming the aircraft. The skipper flew into the waves. Finally fighters and antiaircraft fire whittled the formation down to one, the TBD flown by Ens. George H. ("Tex") Gay. He turned slightly to take the nearest carrier (the *Sōryū*) from her starboard side and pulled the torpedo release at 800 yards. Torpedo Eight scored no hits on enemy ships. Five Zeros just scrambled from the *Akagi* jumped Gay not far from his target and sent him into the water. All fifteen TBDs had splashed, and only one man survived—Tex Gay.

During VT-8's attack but totally unaware of it, Gray led his ten fighters toward the Japanese fleet in order to guard the pushover point for the SBDs when they appeared. Strangely it seemed, no Mitsubishis prowled the skies at high altitude, and this puzzled Gray. The fighters arrived in the air space ahead and just out of antiaircraft range of the ships below. He led the Grummans into a lazy circle to the left. This seemed to provoke a few halfhearted antiaircraft shell bursts from the ships that could see them. Because of cloud cover, Gray never did see the whole enemy task force. He tried contacting McClusky, but heard only static in his earphones. To him it seemed best to take station over the enemy fleet for the time being and keep the skies clear for the SBDs he knew had to be coming.

While Torpedo Eight had gone almost straight to the enemy and attacked, Gene Lindsey's Torpedo Six flew southwest along the heading of 240 degrees. Visibility had improved somewhat since McClusky's *Enterprise* SBDs had passed south of VT-6's flight path. Not long after 0930, Torpedo Six observed smoke about 30 miles to the northwest, and Lindsey turned right to investigate. Soon he came upon *Kidō Butai* and discerned three flattops loosely surrounded by heavy cruisers, all of the enemy ships steaming away at high speed to the northeast. Because of the Japanese course change at 0918, they had nearly slipped past Torpedo Six, which was now south of them. Lindsey aimed for the nearest flattop (the *Kaga*), but the rate of closure was agonizingly slow—TBDs at 100 or so knots chasing ships making 30 knots. He decided on a split attack and sent Art Ely's 2nd Division farther to the north to circle around the target's port side.[6] Aloft the CAP comprised twenty-seven Zeros, some about to land. Lookouts spotted the oncoming TBDs at 0938, and two minutes later the *Tone* opened fire with her main battery to direct the Zeros after them. The *Akagi* and the *Sōryū* at 0945 launched seven fighters to reinforce the CAP. During Lindsey's run in, however, his main tormentors would be Itaya's *Akagi* Zeros.

With his ten Grummans, VF-6's Gray continued circling at 22,000 feet over the eastern portion of the enemy striking force, which was hidden sporadically by cloud cover. Neither he nor his pilots had any indication Torpedo Six was even in the area, let alone in a death struggle. They never heard the distress call "Come on down, Jim." Conditions were such that they did not see any attacks on the scattered enemy carriers, spread across many miles of ocean. By 0950, Gray's troops had orbited the target for about a half hour. Glancing at his fuel gauge, Gray was startled to see he had less gasoline than he thought. The F4F-4s, as he had feared, sucked fuel at a higher rate than the old F4F-3As. Yet there was no sign of the SBDs. At 0956, Gray radioed base:

> This is Gray. We are over six destroyers, two battleships, two carriers.[7]

That was the first semblance of a contact that Task Force 16 was able to copy.

Four minutes later, Gray transmitted again:

> This is Gray. We are returning to the ship due to lack of gas. We have been flying over the enemy fleet. They have no combat patrol. There are six destroyers, two battleships, and two carriers. Course about north.[8]

Gray had carefully pondered heading back without attacking. He considered making a strafing run, but thought his machine guns would not be able to do much serious damage. More important was getting his airplanes home so they could be refueled and fight. At 22,000 feet he had the height to copy the *Enterprise*'s YE homing signal on his Zed Baker, but would lose it by diving in. Like fighter pilots at Coral Sea, he had let the strike planes do the navigating while he and his cohorts watched for Zeros. Now he needed that homing signal to get home and did not have the fuel to spare to search for the task force. Also, he was disturbed by the failure of the SBDs to turn up; the skies over the Japanese ships were clear. Feeling he could do nothing else of value, Gray turned for home. Ironically, as the F4Fs departed, the Japanese finally reacted to their presence far above. At 1000, the *Sōryū* launched three Zeros for the express purpose of intercepting the American "horizontal bombing unit" of ten planes, which for so long had lazily circled overhead. These Japanese ended up tackling Torpedo Three when that squadron made contact about ten minutes later.

While the VF-6 pilots had circled unknowingly not far away, Torpedo Six had braved the fierce enemy fighter defense. Both Lindsey and Ely radioed for fighter support, but Gray and his pilots never heard them. As they had with VT-8's attack, the Japanese fighter pilots demonstrated skill and determination in working over the hapless TBDs. One after another the clumsy Devastators took mortal damage and plunged into the sea. Both Lindsey and Ely went down at the head of their men. After 0958, the surviving TBDs finally got close enough to threaten the *Akagi* and the *Kaga*, having traversed the center of the Japanese formation from west to east. Five or six of VT-6's planes launched their fish, but the attack angles were poor because of adroit enemy shiphandling. That and the unreliable American torpedoes assured no hits. The *Akagi* and *Sōryū* Zeros harried VT-6's withdrawal, so the getaway took almost as long as the approach. Five TBDs cleared the hell of *Kidō Butai*; the other nine had splashed. One of the five survivors later ditched, but its crew was eventually rescued.

Drawing away from the slashing fighter attacks and antiaircraft fire, the remaining aircrews of Torpedo Six felt betrayed. They had lacked fighter support, although they definitely had expected an escort. Gray was already heading home, a victim of inexperience and an overly complex plan rendered ineffective when the *Enterprise* Air Group had split. Later escort doctrine eschewed assigning responsibility for two groups of strike planes to the same batch of escorts. As one analyst later wrote:

> Gray stuck to the faulty plan but had every reason to believe it would work out. With experience, we avoided rigid planning and counted on *close escort* as the only escort.[9]

Where Are the Dive Bombers?

It was painfully obvious to both the torpedo crews and the bemused VF-6 escort pilots that Task Force 16's dive bombers had yet to find the Japanese fleet. Torpedo Eight and later Torpedo Six both had encountered enemy carriers seemingly untouched by other strike planes. Yet the *Hornet* and *Enterprise* SBDs had departed along with or ahead of the TBDs and cruised at a faster speed. What had happened to them?

Ring's powerful *Hornet* strike group with thirty-four SBDs, ten F4Fs, and fifteen TBDs had been the first to leave Task Force 16.[10] They flew west (heading 265 degrees), and the SBDs and F4Fs completed the laborious climb to 19,000 feet. Mitchell took his ten protesting Grummans even higher to take station 3,000 feet above and behind the massive SBD formation. The VF-8 pilots had throttled way back to plod along with the SBDs at about 110 knots. Waldron with Torpedo Eight followed for about a half hour, before he turned off to the southwest to find his destiny. Some in the rear of the dive-bomber and fighter formations saw the fifteen TBDs, behind and far below, swing left and head away. At high altitude the *Hornet* flyers found visibility none too good for a look ahead at the ocean. Under the circumstances, Ring felt it wise to deploy his bombers into a scouting line abreast. By sections the SBDs formed into a long line as they spread out laterally—Scouting Eight on the right (north) and Bombing Eight to the south. All kept pace with Ring in the center serving as the guide, but the maneuver exacted a high fuel cost, as the SBD pilots tried—in accordance with peacetime polish—to hold a straight line abreast. Mitchell's fighters remained above and behind out of the way, keeping one eye on the SBDs and the other open for Zeros lurking above.

For the *Hornet* flyers the miles slipped by as they anxiously scanned the horizon and tried keeping good formation. It is not known precisely where Ring expected to encounter the Japanese fleet, but the navigational leg of the outbound flight was very likely 175 miles. Mitchell's VF-8 troops, alert for possible hostiles, counted on the dive bombers to keep track and handle the navigating chores. Having manned planes so early, the escort pilots (with the possible exception of the CO) lacked full navigational dope anyway, even as to the *Hornet*'s Point Option course. Under normal circumstances they expected to accompany the Dauntlesses all the way to the target and back. In the unlikely event they should have to separate, the fighter pilots would have recourse to their Zed Baker receivers to home in the *Hornet*'s YE signals.

Between glances at the SBDs and the skies ahead, most of the VF-8 pilots kept a worried eye on their fuel gauges (now much more reliable in F4F-4s because of factory-fitted fuel tanks). They had never before experienced such fuel consumption in their fighters. By circling more than a half hour before departure (and being drawn miles to the southeast in the process!), the F4Fs had begun the mission with one strike against them. The gas-guzzling climb to 22,000 feet constituted strike two. Now after nearly two hours aloft, their fuel gauge pointers had gone below the halfway mark and started the slide toward empty. Still no enemy ships were in sight, and the SBDs droned on, seemingly oblivious to the plight confronting the shorter-ranged F4F-4s. Strike three loomed as Fighting Eight neared the point of no return, beyond which there would not be sufficient fuel to return home.

In the CO's division, Ens. McInerny kept a close watch on his fuel gauge. Not long after 0900 (as VF-8's flight neared two hours), he concluded that if nothing happened soon, the fighters would be drawn past hope of ever reaching base. Then he did something highly unprecedented for a junior pilot. Easing past his section leader, John Magda, McInerny flew up alongside Mitchell and definitely got the skipper's immediate attention! Pointing animatedly to his fuel gauge, McInerny tried to get Mitchell to understand there was a big problem there. No doubt shaken by the ensign's nerve, if nothing else, the CO waved him back toward his proper slot in the formation and held course. McInerny dropped back, but only for a few minutes. Soon he was again next to the skipper. Mitchell violently gestured for him to get back, but the headstrong McInerny had had enough. He swung round in a wide turn (most likely to the left) to head away to the east. Magda followed

The *Hornet* Air Group attack, 4 June; map by Bowen P. Weisheit.

close behind. In his turn, McInerny happened to see smoke well off to the south-west. He thought it might be enemy ships, but he lacked the fuel to investigate. The inexorable logic of dwindling fuel dictated curtailment of the escort mission just short of the end of the navigational leg of 175 miles. Mitchell turned right to gather the other eight F4Fs and followed through in a right turn to come around to the east behind McInerny and Magda. When they left the SBDs, the F4Fs had flown between 150 and 160 miles from their point of departure.

Some SBD people evidently saw the fighters leave and noted roughly when and where they broke off. After the dive bombers made it back to the *Hornet* and reported, it was surmised that the missing escorts might have tried for Midway. The *Hornet* action report, compiled before the surviving VF-8 pilots could be questioned, noted that VF-8 likely ditched along a bearing of 320 degrees from Midway. That is almost a direct line from Midway to where the fighters were seen to leave the SBDs. Actually the VF-8 escorts ended up far northeast of Midway rather than northwest of there. As for the validity of VF-8's fuel worries, it is interesting to note that when McInerny turned the formation, the F4Fs had been aloft just about two hours. That was almost exactly the amount of time Gray's VF-6 Grummans would fly before he, too, grew aware of his critical fuel situation and thought of starting back immediately. The VF-8 escorts, however, were in worse shape than Gray would be 45 minutes later. At 160 miles out, they were farther from home than Gray would find himself.

The impetuous McInerny got the escort going in the proper direction—east-ward—but the next step was to refine the heading by use of the Zed Baker homers. Given the fickle nature of that device, doing so was not easy. Mitchell tried, but could not tune in the *Hornet*'s YE transmission. Using hand signals, he polled the seven pilots with him, learned that Stan Ruehlow had his Zed Baker working, and motioned him into the lead of the main body. Ahead in sight and off to the right (south) were McInerny and Magda on a parallel course, as they, too, had the homing signal. The F4Fs lost altitude only very gradually as they went downhill. Free from the need of staying with the slower SBDs, the pilots set the throttle for maximum range. What with their shallow descent, their ground speed increased to perhaps 160 knots. So far so good, but the trick was to find the *Hornet* before their fuel ran out. Although they had her direction, they were uncertain as to distance and time to fly.

After VF-8's strange turn-around, the *Hornet* dive bombers with Stan Ring in the lead held the westerly heading of 265 degrees. They neared the intercept area where they expected to find enemy carriers, but no ships appeared. Ring decided to keep going. Unwittingly his flight path carried the group well north of Nagumo's Striking Force. Apparently Ring never heard Waldron's contact report sent around 0920, although at least one of the VB-8 SBDs listened to snippets of VT-8's radio chatter. The group commander faced his moment of truth two hours after departure and some 225 miles out. Anxious observers in the SBDs saw no evidence of the Japanese fleet, and Ring finally led the thirty-four SBDs into a wide left turn in order to head south. A few minutes later, it appears (nothing is certain, because the whole flight of the *Hornet* SBDs remains mysterious) that the group split up.

Ring evidently ended up alone, as his wingmen somehow became separated and probably rejoined Bombing Eight. There may have been considerable confusion trying to close up formations from the scouting line the SBDs had assumed a long time before. Ring set course east directly for Task Force 16. Never having dived, the SBDs had the height to use their Zed Bakers even at that distance. Walter Rodee's fifteen VS-8 SBDs also turned east after only a few minutes on the southerly heading. "Ruff" Johnson with Bombing Eight continued south far longer than the

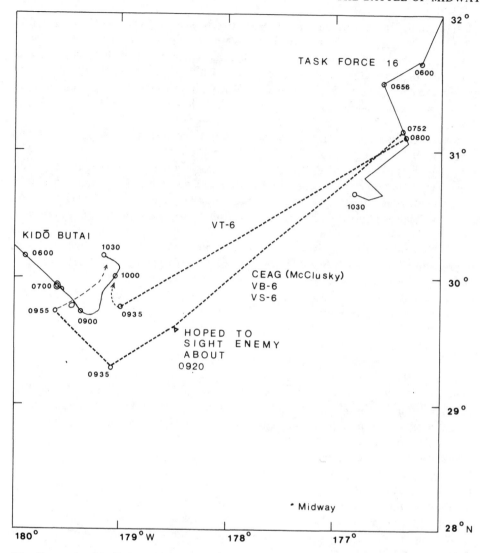

The *Enterprise* Air Group attack, 4 June.

others and searched in the direction of little Kure Island about 60 miles west of Midway. Whatever happened, Spruance's single most powerful strike element—thirty-four SBDs and ten F4Fs—did not attack the enemy! Ring ironically had made the proper decision to turn left at the end of his long westward flight, but he did not fly a long-enough dogleg to the south before turning left again (east) for home. Neither did Rodee. Johnson, however, flew too far south before he thought of swinging east and heading back! The *Hornet* SBDs had the enemy between them but never knew.

For "old" fighter pilot Wade McClusky, the mission so far had not gone smoothly either. First thing that exasperated VF-6's former skipper was the inexplicable delay in completing the *Enterprise*'s launch. Then came Spruance's abrupt orders for the SBDs to depart, leaving them without fighter escort and ruining any chance, it appeared, for a coordinated group attack. Heading southwest on course 231 degrees (and evidently at about 110 knots), his thirty-three SBDs (soon reduced to thirty-two when a VS-6 pilot had to abort) completed the arduous climb to 20,000 feet. McClusky hoped to sight the enemy ships before 0920 (140 or so miles out), but found nothing. He knew he had gone far enough south to account for any Japanese advance; so he altered course slightly to the right (north) to fly west for 15 minutes. At that point if the enemy had still not appeared, he planned to turn northwest until 1000, then fly northeast for a short while before heading straight home. The enemy, he thought, had to be within range of these excursions.

At 0935, McClusky came round to the heading of 315 degrees to fly along the reciprocal bearing of the original Japanese course for 50 miles, before turning northeast at 1000 for the last segment of his search. Fuel was starting to be a problem. Then at 0955, he had the lucky break his careful reasoning deserved. Below, pinpointed by a long white wake, was a Japanese destroyer steaming north–northeast at high speed. McClusky felt certain the tincan was bound for the enemy carrier force. She was the *Arashi*, rushing to rejoin Nagumo after attacking the U.S. submarine *Nautilus* with depth charges. McClusky turned right to parallel the *Arashi*'s track.

The aviators engaged in this deadly drama over the Japanese striking force were not its only uncertain participants. On board Spruance's flagship, the suspense was agonizing, particularly as the hands of the clock swept past 0920 (estimated time of arrival over the target) and neared 1000. Those strike planes were beginning to run out of time! Finally between 0952 and 1000 came Gray's two messages indicating that he, for one, had found the Japanese flattops but was returning home. McClusky himself piped up around 1002 with the most important report of all. With his binoculars he had sighted the Japanese carrier forces about 35 miles to the northeast and radioed the *Enterprise*. Browning, the impulsive chief of staff, grabbed a microphone and at 1008 shouted: "McClusky attack, attack immediately!"[11] But the *Enterprise* dive bombers had to overtake the target, and in the meantime, the *Yorktown* Air Group would fight.

The Yorktown *Strike Group Fights*

Along the flight path to the southwest, visibility had greatly increased in the hour since Task Force 16 airplanes had traversed the area. Bombing Three climbed out of view of Jimmy Thach's VF-3 fighters, which remained closer to the water to be in good position to spot their charges, the TBDs. Leslie's SBDs headed for 15,000 feet and likewise kept a lookout for the TBDs out in front. About a half hour into the flight, Leslie threw the switch electrically arming his 1000-lb. bomb. To his great consternation the bomb dropped free with a lurch of his SBD. Three other VB-3 pilots also unwittingly jettisoned their bombs before the dismayed skipper could tell them to arm bombs manually. Now weaponless, Leslie continued with the mission. Far below, Thach glimpsed a large splash to starboard. Bemused by the strange geyser, Thach thought it might have something to do with submarines.

Almost exactly according to plan, the Grummans overtook Lem Massey's Torpedo Three, and at 0945 Thach had no difficulty making visual contact. Neither did Bombing Three overhead. Thach motioned Cheek to take position close astern and a thousand feet above the torpedo planes.[12] Torpedo Three cruised at 1,500 feet, thereby putting the close escort at around 2,500 feet. Cheek's own cruise of 140 knots was too swift for him to hold station over the 100-knot Devastators. With Sheedy tucked in close formation behind him, Cheek started slow, drifting S-turns back and forth out from the base course in order to cut his actual rate of advance. Himself a former TBD pilot, Cheek noted with professional interest the formation Massey had adopted: a right echelon with Lieut. Patrick J. Hart's 2nd Division of six TBDs stepped down behind the six of Massey's 1st Division to give all twelve rear gunners a free field of fire above and astern. Individual wingmen flew stepped up on their section leaders.

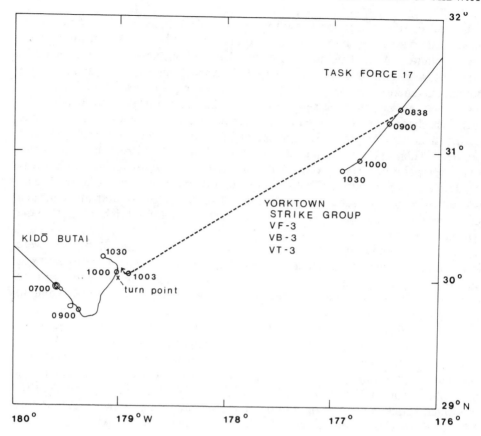

The *Yorktown* Air Group attack, 4 June.

Three thousand feet above Cheek, at around 5,500 feet, Thach took station with his four Grummans, keeping the division deployed in cruise formation to the left, each plane stepped down from the one ahead:

Thach remained in the standard cruise disposition because that was what Macomber and Bassett were used to flying. Neither VF-42 pilot knew about the "beam defense" tactics developed by Thach, which deployed fighter sections split out abreast of each other; but Thach's own wingman, "Ram" Dibb, had some acquaintance with them. Like Cheek, Thach led his division in leisurely S-turns to hold proper position behind the slow TBDs.

As events transpired, the *Yorktown* attackers would not even fly to the end of their navigational leg, where they had been slated to swing northwest had the enemy not turned up. At 1003, Lloyd F. Childers, ARM3c, rearseat man in Mach. Harry Corl's TBD, saw off to his right (the northwest) what he thought was a column of smoke. Corl signaled Massey, on whom he flew wing in the lead section, and VT-3's skipper brought the squadron around to a heading of 345 degrees to approach the enemy. The ships looked as if they were 20 to 25 miles away. Thach noticed the TBDs change course and glanced in the direction they pointed. Sure enough, there were the Japanese. Far above, Leslie with Bombing Three likewise spotted the target.

The enemy ships growing slowly in his windshield, Massey led his twelve TBDs up to 2,600 feet to secure altitude for the so-called high-level torpedo approach. This would permit Torpedo Three to dive in and accumulate more speed than they would have if they stayed "on the deck" the whole way. Cheek also climbed in order to preserve his interval of a thousand feet over the TBDs. At 1010 with the TBDs about 14 miles from the nearest enemy carrier, the heavy cruiser *Chikuma* in the outer screen let loose a salvo from her main battery eight-inchers. The shells bursting near the torpedo planes would help alert the Japanese CAP to their presence and pinpoint their location. Meanwhile, the Japanese carriers began turning northwest away from the new wave of Americans closing from the southeast.

When the Yorktowners first made contact, Nagumo's ships were still maneuvering to avoid the final stage of VT-6's gallant attack. Some Zeros had landed for lack of fuel or ammunition, and others had scrambled; so by 1010, the Japanese CAP comprised thirty-five fighters.[13] Stacked relatively close to the carriers were fourteen Zeros (two from the *Akagi* and twelve, including six just launched, from the *Kaga*), while on board the *Sōryū* and the *Hiryū*, flight deck crews made ready to launch three additional Zeros from each ship. In direct pursuit of Torpedo Six were eight *Akagi* Zeros led by Lieut. Shirane Ayao, *buntaichō*, and three *Sōryū* Zeros under the unit's junior *buntaichō*, Lieut. Fujita Iyōzō. Also ranging out to the southeast, but not engaged with Torpedo Six, were another ten Zeros (four from the *Hiryū* led by the unit commander, Lieut. Mori Shigeru, *buntaichō*; three from the *Kaga*, under PO1c Suzuki Kiyonobu; and the recently launched *shōtai* of three *Sōryū* Zeros that had set out after Gray's fighters). Thus the *Yorktown* Air Group's reception committee numbered no fewer than forty-one Zeros, including six now taking off.

At the sight of the *Chikuma*'s bursting shells, Zeros chasing the remnants of Torpedo Six broke off their pursuit and sought fresh prey. Evidently Lieut. Fujita was the first to eyeball the new wave of intruders. He reported twenty enemy torpedo planes escorted by four Grummans. Zeros converged from several directions to intercept the *Yorktown* group. Most initially took after Thach's four F4Fs at 5,500 feet, while others attacked Torpedo Three and Cheek's close escort near 3,000 feet. None of the Japanese spotted Bombing Three at 15,000 feet, or history might have been different. The survivors of Torpedo Six gratefully withdrew eastward, one of the pilots, Lieut. (jg) Robert Laub, catching sight of two *Yorktown* F4Fs charging in as he headed out. The *Yorktown* torpedo crews and fighter pilots faced the fiercest fight of their lives, one that at great sacrifice would clear the skies for the approach of the dive bombers.

The Ordeal of Thach's Division

The *Chikuma*'s shell bursts seemed almost to materialize Mitsubishis out of thin air. Looking ahead, Thach suddenly discovered he faced desperate odds. By chance he had encountered the majority of the Japanese who had pursued the handful of

VT-6 survivors. So many Zeros charged in his direction that they had to take turns in order to attack. Above and ready to pounce, Thach estimated there were fifteen to twenty enemy fighters, which deployed into a "string formation" in anticipation of making successive individual firing passes.

Unbeknownst to Thach and his troops, danger lurked even closer. A couple of Zeros closed in from below and behind, selecting Edgar Bassett's trailing F4F as their target. The lead Zero took aim and scored swiftly. Bullets ripped into F-9's engine and fuselage. Brainard Macomber, Bassett's section leader, glanced back and was startled to see his wingman had dropped out of formation. As the F4F passed below and to one side of him, Macomber noticed a trail of smoke emanating from its engine. Bassett did not bail out of his aircraft, and Thach saw F-9 erupt in flames just before it struck the water. A veteran of all VF-42's campaigns and with two confirmed kills at Coral Sea, "Red Dog" Bassett had been one of the squadron's most colorful individuals. Joining the Navy in February 1940, he completed flight training and was promoted to ensign in February 1941. His nickname came from his prowess as a "red dog" player. No one ever saw his attacker, who likely was an *Akagi* pilot who had just completed a run on Torpedo Six.

The first Zero to scream in from above singled out Macomber's Wildcat as its target in a high-rear attack. Its gunnery was excellent. From behind his seat, Macomber heard loud noises as 7.7 rounds zipped through his plane's empennage and bounced off the armor plate back of the cockpit. Bullets knocked out his radio and penetrated his aluminum emergency fuel tank, but fortunately F-6's control wires remained intact, and the tank was empty, purged with carbon dioxide.

Confronted with overwhelming fighter opposition, Thach at first thought to nose down, gain speed, and support the torpedo planes. The swifter Zeros never gave him the chance. By the time the F4Fs had descended to 3,000 feet, the Japanese brought them to bay by means of relentless individual high-speed, hit-and-run firing passes. Thach had to break off and maneuver defensively or be shot down. The combat quickly assumed a deadly pattern. Diving in one at a time, each Japanese closed within firing range, opened up with intermittent bursts, then roared past the F4Fs in order to recover below and ahead. A swift zoom climb then put the Zero out of reach and back up above in position to make another run when its turn came. Thach was most impressed with the skill and coordination on the part of his opponents. Essentially, there was a Zero making its run on him at all times. Thach later estimated the interval between successive Zeros to be twenty or thirty seconds. Only very rarely did the Japanese attempt any kind of attack other than above-rear, and this combat refutes criticisms that the Japanese were only tail-chasing dogfighters.

Under pressure, the three VF-3 pilots quickly slid into a near line-astern formation with the trailing planes stepped down behind the leader:

Thach

Dibb

Macomber

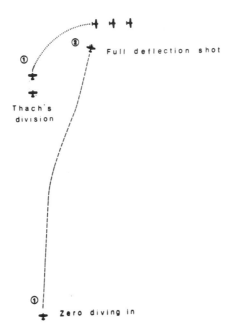

Thach's first countermove.

Thach instinctively knew the best chance for survival lay in maintaining formation and countering each attack. He was too low to dive away and escape, and the pack of Mitsubishis above wanted nothing more than to see the F4Fs split up and run.

Thach's first defensive maneuver was to lead the division into a sharp turn away from the attacker, after he saw the Zero coming in at that moment committed to its run. The turnaway presented the attacker only a full-deflection shot, and for a Zero in a high-speed dive it was difficult to draw sufficient lead. Thach's timing had to be just right to disrupt his opponent's aim. As the trailer, Macomber most often was the target. He watched as each Zero successively slid into its run, moving with deadly grace. Then he called Thach on his dead radio, not realizing it was not functioning. As the Japanese flashed into shooting range, Macomber would jink up and down and from side to side. The line-astern formation permitted some independent maneuvering without risk of collision. Macomber soon discovered that a "short sharp pushover seemed to disconcert [the Japanese] the most since they were all holding positive gee in making their runs and could not easily and smoothly adjust their point of aim downward."[14] Thach timed his turn away about the same time Macomber would begin jinking, all of this depending on where the Zero was in its run. Dibb and Macomber stuck behind Thach in his turns and let him direct all countering moves.

In the beginning Thach hoped to contact Macomber by radio and direct him to split out to the left so the division could deploy abreast and use Thach's "beam defense" tactics. Macomber's radio failure scotched any chance of that. The only formation defensive tactics Macomber knew were what he was taught in VF-42: close line-astern with individual jinking or the Lufbery Circle. Before departure, all Thach had had time to tell Bassett and Macomber was to stay together. ("None of that lone wolf stuff.") Not ever having heard of Thach's tactics, Macomber could not be expected to perceive them intuitively. Under the circumstances, Thach realized that the close formation the F4Fs now flew was a handicap. Being apart so little, the three fighters essentially comprised one target. Thach wanted elbow room to be able to reverse his turn and set up a shot on Macomber's attackers.

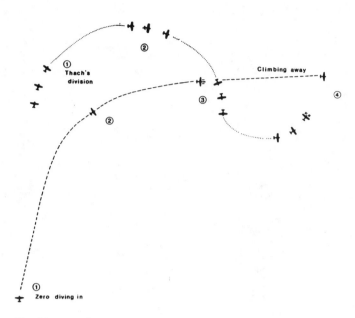

Thach's second countermove.

Each Zero, however, flashed past so rapidly that there was no way he could turn quickly enough to shoot at it. Thach tried loosening the formation, waving Macomber back, but could not establish communication with him. To open the necessary interval between Macomber and himself, Thach even resorted to pulling away while Macomber was preoccupied with a Zero. Just as doggedly, Macomber faithfully obeyed his original instructions and scrambled to regain formation.

After a few excruciating minutes, Thach refined his countermoves to take aim at Zeros when they recovered from their runs. He kept close watch astern and waited until a Mitsubishi had committed itself to the usual rear approach. Just as the enemy was about to loose a burst, Thach led the F4Fs in a sharp turn away from the attacker, ruining the pilot's aim at the last second. Then Thach swiftly reversed his turn, often to find himself with a long-range (400 yards or more) deflection shot on the Zero as it zoomed through the formation with excess speed and climbed straight away. Such shots were snap bursts only, but enough to keep the enemy thinking. One time after Thach had opened the interval between Macomber and himself, a Zero screamed into the inevitable above-rear approach and missed because of the target's quick turn away to the right. Thach then banked left and was surprised to see the Nipponese slow up, evidently as the pilot tried too abrupt a pull out from his dive. This gave Thach a close-range, low-deflection shot from the right rear of the target. He made the most of this rare opportunity and riddled the Zero with a healthy burst as it tried to climb away. Jerking into a stall, the Mitsubishi then fell away toward the water. Thach calmly put a check mark on his knee pad, recording the first of three kills he would score on that mission.

It became obvious rather quickly that Thach could not raise Macomber by radio. Instead, he decided to send Ram Dibb out to the right to take position abreast of him. He radioed Dibb: "Pretend you're a section leader and move out abeam, way out."[15] Dibb dropped out of formation and took station several hundred yards to the right and even with Thach's F4F. Seeing him break away, the Japanese waiting above must have assumed the troublesome Grummans had finally broken under the pressure. The next Zero to dive screamed in after Dibb's lone fighter, seemingly

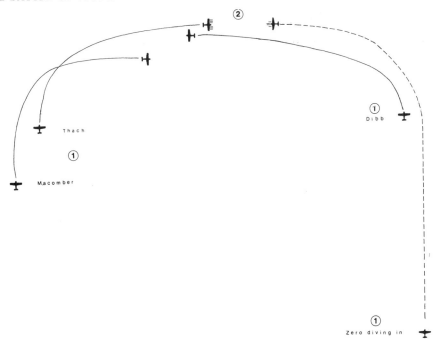

The first test of the weave in combat.

isolated. Dibb saw the Japanese charge in and radioed, "Skipper, there's a Zero on my tail! Get him off!"[16] This was the watchword agreed upon during VF-3's brief introduction to the weave at Kaneohe. Thach told him to swing sharply left, while he turned right to scissor Dibb and his attacker.

Unlike the previous assailants, this Japanese was intent on riding the tail of his quarry. When Dibb turned, the Zero maneuvered to stay behind him, following the F4F in its turn. Thach was ready for this. He came at Dibb head-on in a harrowing approach, dipped underneath his teammate, who just missed him, and lined up for a swift underneath-opposite attack on the Zero. Lines of angry red tracers streaked between the F4F and the Zero. Thach later remarked with a laugh, "I was so mad that I was determined that I was going to run into this bastard because he jumped on my poor, little inexperienced wingman."[17]

Thach had secured the favored position underneath the flight path of his opponent, which let him keep firing longer as the two fighters roared directly at each other. After a certain point the Japanese could not shoot unless he dipped his nose and risked collision. Thach held his run as long as he dared. He walked his .50-caliber bullets up into the Mitsubishi's belly and engine, knocking pieces out of its cowling. The Japanese pulled up his nose as soon as Thach's shells started hitting. Suddenly the engine ignited, then bright flames and thick smoke streamed along the smooth underside of the aircraft. The Zero passed over the F4F, giving Thach a false sensation of great heat as the enemy barely cleared his cockpit. Wrapped in flames, the Zero dived away, and a second check mark appeared on the victor's knee pad.

Dibb was not certain whether Thach wanted him to remain out to the side, so he slipped into line-astern a few times. Thach later explained that his rookie wingman evidently felt "a little lonesome out there."[18] After a couple of swings in and out of line, it dawned upon Dibb that he was supposed to stay split out and that the skipper would support him. Macomber had no idea what Dibb was trying to do, never having learned of Thach's tactics. Primarily the VF-42 veteran had to concentrate on evading each Zero as it came in, and secondarily on remaining in formation. He never was able to see Thach make any of his shots. When Dibb pulled out of line-astern, a bemused Macomber tried at first to split the difference, holding below and between the other two F4Fs. He was highly irritated at Dibb for breaking formation and not following the leader.

The head-on episode with Dibb's attacker assured Thach of the validity of his own tactics. He kept Dibb abreast of him and gradually allowed Macomber to close up behind as his wingman. Thus the roles of Macomber and Dibb were reversed, with Dibb acting the part of the second section leader only because of his earlier knowledge of the weave and his ability to communicate with Thach. The young ensign learned very quickly in his first combat. Thach was not certain whether Dibb knew the proper lookout doctrine for the beam defense formation, that is, to have one section watch the tail of the other. Therefore he kept a gook look on his own tail as well as Dibb's. When he noticed a Zero start a run on Dibb, he waited until the Japanese had committed himself. Then he executed a sharp turn toward his teammate to alert him that an enemy was attacking. In response, Dibb turned toward Thach, and the two scissored. Often the F4F pilots did not have a shot, as the Zero usually did not follow the turn. However, Thach and Dibb brushed Zeros off each other's tail. Sometimes they kept weaving continuously; in other instances they remained split out abreast until a Japanese came in. Dibb absorbed the lookout doctrine very quickly and scissored whenever he saw a Zero nosing up behind Thach and Macomber. When Thach discovered him turning, he would glance back, and, without fail, a Mitsubishi would be charging in from above and behind.

With the weave, both Thach and Dibb had opportunities for good shots at their opponents. On one occasion a Zero executed the usual attack on Dibb, who responded correctly by turning toward Thach as Thach swung toward him. The Japanese held a straight course and did not follow Dibb around. Apparently this Zero pilot also tried too radical a recovery and slowed dramatically. Thach zipped past Dibb, then discovered himself in excellent position to pop the Zero with a good side shot before it could regain momentum and climb out of range. He poured bullets into its fuselage, but this time no flame erupted. Instead the Zero rolled uncertainly over onto its back and spun away crazily for the water, likely with a dead man at the controls. It was Thach's third victory over the Zeros. Dibb hit a Mitsubishi swooping in on Thach and Macomber, firing into the Japanese while it was still astern of the two F4Fs. Thach saw the enemy fighter head for the water. As the trailing plane, Macomber had only one opportunity to shoot. Once after a Zero peppered his tail, Macomber became so furious that he pulled out of formation to fire on his assailant as he climbed away. It was a long shot, but the results were such that Macomber could claim a probable at least.

The Zeros kept Thach and company fully occupied during the approach and attack of Torpedo Three. Thach tried to stay over the TBDs, but the clouds effectively hid them from view, and his opponents had a stranglehold on him. Thach's fight was one of the classic encounters of the Pacific air war. Flown by pilots who kept their cool, Thach's tactics passed the hardest possible test in battle against skilled and determined opponents. Never before had fighters cooperated better in a sustained defensive struggle.

The Fight of the Close Escort

Tom Cheek and Dan Sheedy, the two fighters making up VF-3's close escort, continued making S-turns in a weaving fashion above and behind Torpedo Three

Tom Cheek, 19 Dec. 1941, with VF-2 F2A-3 Buffalo. (Cdr. T. F. Cheek, USN.)

as it approached the enemy fleet. Suddenly a number of large, black shell bursts below and to the left dramatically raised the curtain on another fierce struggle with the CAP Zeros. Quickly looking up, Cheek was startled to see a Japanese fighter emerge from a cloud bank not far ahead of the torpedo planes. Lloyd Childers heard his pilot Harry Corl shout excitedly, "Up ahead! Up ahead!"[19] With a flat-opposite attack, the sleek Zero roared in and fired a snap burst at the lead Devastators. Then the Japanese had to pull up slightly to pass between Massey and Corl on the skipper's right. Evidently planning to make his second run against the right trailing section, the Japanese pulled into a steep, climbing turn to his left.

The impetuous Zero pilot, PO3c Kawamata Teruo, Fujita's No. 3 wingman, did not spot the fighter escort and paid the full price for his negligence. Cheek hauled his F4F into a quick climb and caught the Zero from below and ahead. He walked his tracer's into the Mitsubishi's engine and tender belly, causing it to slow abruptly and stream heavy smoke. Nosing down, the Japanese fell on past Cheek and headed for the water. Two Zeros then appeared poised over the left of VT-3's formation and jumped the lead section. Cheek could not maneuver into a favorable countering position, so he cut loose with a burst ahead of them. Seeing a band of red tracers arc unexpectedly in front of them, the two aborted their attack by a steep climb in order to dive in from another direction.

After the first two encounters, more Zeros happened onto the scene, drawn away from their carriers by the action just as blood attracts bands of marauding sharks. Still ten miles from the release point, Massey responded with what little speed increase he could manage, and by jinking the formation up and down to evade bullets. Cheek swung back over to the right of the TBDs, where he came upon a Zero making a beam attack on the right trailing section (2nd Section, 2nd Division) and brushed the Japanese away. Once again weaving to the left side of the formation, Cheek had occasion to glance back in the direction whence the TBDs had come. He saw a flaming Zero strike the water some distance back, the victim of his first attack. Fujita, his hands full attacking Thach, also observed his No. 3 wingman splash, but he did not know why. Cheek then saw an F4F plunge into the water and sink immediately. He had not seen his wingman since the shooting began and worried that it might have been Sheedy's plane. Sheedy was still flying, however, summoning all his efforts to stay with his wildly twisting section leader. Sheedy hoped he would start the beam defense maneuver taught by Thach at Kaneohe, but Cheek was busy working out shots against the interceptors.

When Cheek turned to look at the torpedo planes, he was surprised to see that his charges had pulled away from him. Massey had nosed down for speed and dipped under the low cloud bank in order to initiate his approach on the nearest flattop. Two Zeros recovering from a firing pass on the right of Torpedo Three next attracted Cheek's interest, and he turned to go after them. Suddenly another Japanese, intent on making a high-astern approach on the trailing TBD section, cut directly in front of his Grumman. Rolling out onto the Zero's tail, Cheek lined up his sights for a low-deflection shot from astern. Just as he was about to press the trigger, the TBD rear gunners converged their fire on the intruder and shot it down. The stepped-down formation permitted all of the rearseat men to take aim on an attacker diving in from straight astern.

His erstwhile victim falling in flames, Cheek tucked into a chandelle to the right. Tracers zipped past his right wing. Cheek turned rapidly left, but the red bands beat him to it, forcing him to reverse course sharply. As he contemplated his course, his opponent charged up close on his tail and peppered the Wildcat's empennage with 7.7-mm bullets. A few seconds later the Zero pilot cut in with his 20-mm cannons. Cheek later recounted:

> I violently kicked the F4F into a vertical left turn and found a Zero tucked in under my tail. My turn had caught him off balance and he was drifting rapidly to the right as I again snapped the Grumman, this time to the right hoping to catch the Zero in a position where I could bring my guns to bear on him.[20]

Cheek definitely was in a jam.

Now Sheedy, scrambling wildly to keep Cheek in sight and start some sort of weave, was surprised to see a Zero pop in between himself and his leader. It was Cheek's tormentor moving in for the kill. Maneuvering to fire, Sheedy found Cheek's F4F also dancing through his sights. He radioed Cheek that there was one on his tail, hoping in this way to get him to turn quickly as Thach had instructed back at Kaneohe. Cheek did roll out of the way, then saw heavy, broad streaks of tracer pass overhead. Looking around, he spotted neither the Zero nor another F4F. But, no matter—for Sheedy had driven the Zero away.

By this time the TBDs had descended almost completely out of view beneath the cloud bank. Cheek noticed that the formation, or at least the 2nd Division, appeared intact except for the No. 12 aircraft—the right wingman in the last section. That TBD spiraled in, while the parachute of one crewman blossomed out in its wake. As a Zero followed the stricken Devastator down, other Japanese fighters were visible above and to Cheek's right. He entered the cloud, hoping to regain visual contact with Torpedo Three when he emerged on the other side. He never saw the TBDs again, and he also wondered how Sheedy was doing.

Cheek's young wingman was behind him, but after driving away the Zero shooting up his leader's tail, Sheedy found himself in deep trouble. One of the seemingly ubiquitous Mitsubishis proceeded to riddle F-24. Bullets punctured the cockpit, wounding Sheedy in his right ankle and shoulder. One 7.7-mm round even cut between him and his seat back, tearing his flight jacket all the way across his back! Most of his instrument panel was shot out as well. Suddenly big holes appeared in the Grumman's wings, as tracers the size of "oranges" whipped past the cockpit. Enemy fire also broke a chain attached to the right front landing gear, causing the wheel to dangle a short way out of the fuselage wheel well. Sheedy's one thought was to follow Cheek into the cloud, there to shake his pursuer and hopefully rejoin his section leader.

Exiting the clouds, Cheek flew into a swarm of Zeros. There was one ahead and to the left on a parallel course; others were off to the right and above him. Of immediate concern, however, was a Zero already well into an opposite attack from ahead of the Grumman. Cheek directed his bullets into his opponent's engine with satisfyingly quick results, as the heavy slugs tore chunks of cowling and penetrated the powerplant. Seeing his fire score so effectively, Cheek broke off the run, rolled out to the left to avoid the smoking Zero as it flashed by, then charged after the second Zero with a side attack. Carefully allowing for proper deflection, Cheek aimed his burst so that the Japanese flying through it was raked from stem to stern. Cutting astern of the target, Cheek sought concealment in a cloud just ahead of him. Then as a precaution to evade pursuit, he changed course and slowly descended through the whiteness, hoping to break into the clear within sight of Torpedo Three. Instead, he discovered himself close to the enemy carrier force. The *Kaga* and the *Akagi* were ahead and to his left, while a third flattop, the *Sōryū*, lay to the north off to his right. Potshots from a screening vessel forced Cheek low over the water while he searched the skies for other aircraft.

Some distance behind Cheek, Sheedy had also entered the first cloud bank, but when he emerged, his leader was nowhere in sight. Looking around, Sheedy saw two Japanese hot on his tail and two others farther back but with the same intentions. He nosed down for speed, aiming to retreat into the clouds. A lone Zero cut around in front of him as if to block his escape. Descending to low altitude, Sheedy turned into a near head-on run with his opponent and at around 400 yards opened fire at the Zero, now barely skimming the waves. After shooting at each other, both fighter pilots turned to avoid a collision—the Zero digging a wingtip into the water and cartwheeling with a violent splash that Sheedy very nearly flew through. Sheedy pulled out very low and moved off as fast as he could. When he had a chance to climb and look around, he found no aircraft in sight. The Japanese ships were a few miles off to his right.

The escort fighters did an excellent job trying to fend off the unexpectedly numerous Zeros until the violence of combat maneuvers separated them from their charges. The closer the aircraft came to the enemy ships, the more intense the action, as more Zeros were drawn into the fight. Soon virtually all the Mitsubishis became embroiled in combat, some pinning down Thach's escorts, but most screaming after Torpedo Three. The F4Fs did as well as they could under the circumstances, and their efforts were appreciated by the hard-pressed VT-3 crews. Childers, one of the three survivors, later wrote:

> I observed the F4F's above us mixing it up with the Zeroes. At one point, when I was not shooting at a Zero, I saw a Zero coming almost straight down, not smoking, smacking the water within a hundred yards of us. So, I knew the F4F's were not losing every encounter, even tho' badly outnumbered.[21]

It appears that the Japanese accounted for one TBD before Torpedo Three broke into the clear under the cloud base and leveled off at 150 feet. Enemy pressure had compelled Massey to dive before he wanted; he had to go lower to protect his squadron from steep high-side attacks. The Devastators soon dissipated the speed accumulated by diving and crawled along at about 110 knots. Zeros quickly found them again. Within a short time, six to eight Mitsubishis at once were slashing in from abeam and ahead, not merely with high-sides and above-rear runs as at Coral Sea. Massey tried to coordinate his approach with Leslie far above, but Leslie could not see him through the cloud cover. At 1020, Massey radioed frantically for additional fighter support, but neither Thach nor Cheek could respond.

Ahead of Torpedo Three, the Japanese carrier captains maneuvered to avoid attack, turning away to the northwest to present their sterns to the oncoming TBDs. This would have given Torpedo Three an extremely poor angle of approach, had Massey pressed his attack. Therefore, he felt compelled to continue northward to take on the fourth carrier (the *Hiryū*), operating several miles north of the main body. This long run to the north roughly paralleled *Kidō Butai*'s base course and gave the Zeros full opportunity to concentrate on the slow, hapless TBDs. Torpedo Three's death ride and Thach's battling F4Fs drew the enemy combat air patrol away from the main force and set the stage for a most dramatic reversal of fortune!

Midway—The Decisive Moment

From the southwest flew the *Enterprise* dive bombers, giving truth to the old saying, "Better late than never." McClusky had thirty-two SBDs, although two from Bombing Six would drop out of formation before the actual dives. Drawing closer to the target, McClusky discerned four carriers and radioed base. He hoped the *Hornet* strike group was nearby to help feast on such a rich crop of targets. His SBDs could handle only two flattops effectively, so he decided to lead Scouting Six against the nearest one and send Dick Best's Bombing Six against another farther east. Still miles to the east, another dive bomber leader took the measure of *Kidō Butai*. Leslie with Bombing Three worked to coordinate his attack with Massey's TBDs, but he could not see what they were doing. Instead, Leslie went after the carrier closest to him, which happened to be the *Sōryū*, and lined up his seventeen SBDs (four minus bombs) for the dives.[22]

On board the Japanese carriers, preparations for the great launch had proceeded apace. The captains only awaited repulse of the latest torpedo attack before commencing the takeoffs of their strike groups. When Massey swung north to chase the *Hiryū*, the flagship *Akagi* at 1020 gave the signal to launch planes. Ten minutes or so later the four flight decks would be cleared of strike planes. Almost simultaneously with her message, her lookouts spotted American dive bombers poised over the *Kaga*! The CAP was totally unprepared for a dive bombing attack. In contrast to the two previous torpedo attacks (VT-8 and VT-6), there were now no fighters held in reserve. All had swarmed eagerly after Torpedo Three or Thach's Wildcats.

McClusky at 1022 pushed over on the *Kaga*, the westernmost of the four carriers. The flattop heeled into a sharp evasive turn, but she could not evade the onslaught of twenty-five SBDs. Gallaher's Scouting Six followed McClusky down, and, by mistake, most of Bombing Six piled on as well. The *Akagi* commenced launching Zeros, holding course into the wind to launch aircraft. Best went after her with five SBDs from Bombing Six. Meanwhile, the first of four bombs slammed into the *Kaga,* preventing the launch of her strike group of three Zeros and twenty-seven carrier attack planes. Flaming aircraft and explosions soon turned the *Kaga*'s

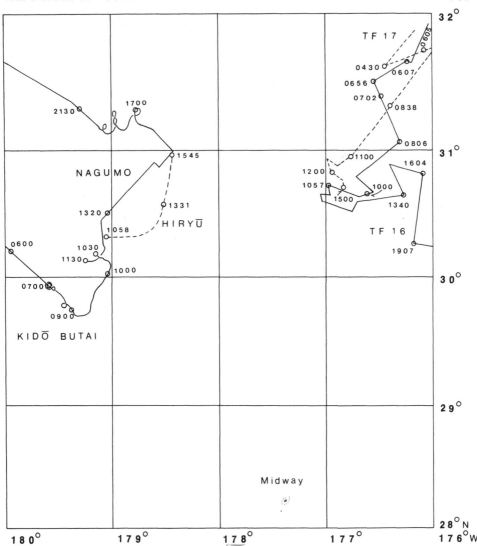

Carrier operations, Midway, 4 June.

flight deck into an inferno and doomed the vessel. The *Akagi*'s time had also come. At 1025, the first Zero started down her flight deck, but Best's five SBDs already hurtled toward her. His pilots secured two 1,000-lb. bomb hits, one detonating in the midst of the eighteen carrier attack planes spotted aft on deck for launch. Like the *Kaga*, the fleet flagship had taken mortal damage.

Leslie with the seventeen SBDs of Bombing Three (only thirteen with bombs) started his dive shortly after McClusky pushed over. The *Sōryū* tried to evade by turning north, but Leslie's pilots smothered her with three 1,000-lb. bomb hits. Four SBDs broke off to attack screening vessels, but without success. The *Sōryū*'s flight deck was destroyed as the gasoline and bombs from her eighteen carrier bombers exploded in the flames. In the hangar, nine armed carrier attack planes helped to torch her vitals. In five minutes the Japanese lost the Battle of Midway.

The SBDs found no interceptors at high altitude, but many Zeros closer to sea level contested their withdrawal. McClusky, after his dive on the *Kaga*, dodged screening vessels as he flew north, then swung east. Outside the screen he picked up an unwanted pair of Zeros that had first tackled Torpedo Three. They chased him for five minutes, enthusiastically shooting up his aircraft and wounding him. His gunner claimed one Zero shot down. Two other VS-6 crews also reported downing one Zero apiece. Lieut. Joe Penland of Bombing Six had helped destroy the *Kaga*, then encountered two Zeros during his retirement. After holing his SBD, the Japanese broke off to go after Torpedo Three, still in the process of attacking the *Hiryū*. Four other VB-6 pilots who had plastered the *Kaga* likewise received attention from Zeros. After flaming the *Akagi*, VB-6's skipper Best spotted four enemy fighters at low level streaking after torpedo planes, but he and his pilots were not molested. It appears that the Japanese CAP intercepted only about one third of the *Enterprise* dive bombers, with the loss of perhaps two SBDs to Zeros or antiaircraft fire in the target area. The *Yorktown*'s Bombing Three was not even bothered by fighters, either during or after its attack.

Nearing the *Hiryū* at about the same time the SBDs rained destruction on the other three enemy flattops, Torpedo Three followed through in its brave, slow attack. Fighters slashed at the little formation, and antiaircraft burst around it, but the squadron was still in relatively good shape. Massey's 1st Division was intact, but Pat Hart's 2nd Division had lost a few aircraft. Massey moved to catch his target in a split attack, sending Hart's division around to hit the carrier from the opposite flank, while he took his division straight in. Fighters swarmed around both groups of TBDs, and one of Hart's planes spun in. Perhaps a mile short of the release point, Massey's aircraft flared up, fell out of formation, and struck the sea in flames. Rad. Elec. Wilhelm G. Esders, Massey's wingman, moved into the vacant lead slot and guided the division toward the target. The five TBDs aimed for the *Hiryū*'s starboard side and launched their torpedoes between 600 and 800 yards out, the actual releases taking place not long after 1030. Esders swung quickly to the right to head away to the east, but most of the other TBD pilots passed ahead of the carrier. The Zeros were relentless, and Esders saw a second TBD from the 1st Division fly into the water. Another 1st Division pilot, Harry Corl, also turned right and sought escape to the east. The others were last seen heading north with a pack of Zeros at their heels. Of Hart's 2nd Division, little is known. The enemy fighters probably annihilated it either before or shortly after the Devastators released torpedoes. Because of the poorly designed aerial torpedoes, Torpedo Three scored no hits on the *Hiryū*.

Throughout the air action, Thach kept glancing toward the Japanese carriers. As the fight progressed, his division worked its way fairly close to one of the flattops. Then shortly after 1022, the first SBDs pushed over, and Thach had a ringside seat at the destruction of three proud enemy carriers, as flames from repeated bomb hits engulfed their flight decks. Only after the Japanese fighter pilots noticed the damage wreaked on their carriers did the attacks on Thach's troops slacken. Nevertheless some Zeros always lurked overhead, even though they did not attack as close together as before. Around 1030, the enemy pulled off entirely, ending the twenty-minute fighter engagement. Searching the sky, the three F4F pilots spotted a lone Zero milling around below them, seemingly an easy mark. Wary of Japanese tricks, Thach carefully looked about. Sure enough, two Zeros waited above screened by the sun, ready to jump the Americans if they took the bait. There were no takers.

Congratulating themselves on still being alive, Thach and his two companions set course for home. Macomber's F-6 had taken heavy damage, but was still flyable. Dibb's aircraft was in good shape, but Thach discovered oil leaking into his cockpit from the engine compartment. F-23's Pratt & Whitney droned smoothly, however. On the way out of the target area, Thach happened upon one of the VT-3 TBDs withdrawing and took station overhead to protect it. A few minutes later he over-took another TBD. The aircraft were those of Esders and Corl. Both TBDs were in pretty bad shape, with numerous bullet holes, oil stains, and tattered fabric. Enemy fighters had wounded both rearseat men. Zeros trailed each more than 20 miles from the drop point, and the TBD pilots had used low altitude and evasive maneuvers to spoil their aim. Childers, Corl's rear gunner, had several times been hit by Japanese bullets. After his .30-caliber machine gun failed to function, he pulled out his .45 Colt pistol and twice blazed away at Zeros as they flashed past. The Zeros had withdrawn before Thach's arrival. Thach stayed with the TBDs until he felt they were safe from wide-ranging enemy fighters. Esders and Corl had throttled back to 85 knots to conserve fuel, and that was just too slow for the Grummans. During the flight back, Corl leaned out his mixture even more to preserve his engine, but Esders forged ahead hoping to reach a friendly flight deck to obtain medical help for his badly wounded rear gunner, Robert B. Brazier, ARM2c. No other VT-3 aircraft survived.

Cheek and Sheedy both were still flying, but alone. Each had to find his own way back home. For Sheedy this was disquieting, as he was on his first flight away from land or out of sight of a carrier. He had only a rudimentary idea where he was. With his instruments shot up and his compass gone, he used the sun to determine approximate direction. It shone over his shoulder on the way out, so he headed toward it on the flight back. His F-24 limped along at 125 knots or so, one wheel dangling and causing considerable drag, but the powerplant soothed his spirit with a reassuring purr.

Japanese records are tantalizingly fragmentary concerning the great CAP action lasting from 1010 to 1045.[23] It was a fast and furious struggle of lone individuals or small groups trying to head off the hard-driving Yorktowners. The defenders had little time to concentrate greater numbers and coordinate interceptions. Yet it is possible in a general way to sketch the strength and losses of the defending fighters. To recapitulate: at 1010, thirty-five Zeros were aloft—fourteen deployed close to the four carriers and twenty-one either directly pursuing Torpedo Six in its withdrawal to the southeast or prowling out in that direction. From 1013 to 1015, the *Sōryū* and the *Hiryū* each launched three fighters, bringing the total engaged to forty-one. Like a magnet attracting iron filings, Torpedo Three and Fighting Three drew the Zeros onto themselves.

The Japanese combat air patrol paid a stiff price for its efforts (not to mention mortal damage to three carriers!). Of the forty-one Zeros, eleven were shot down and three ditched. Of those shot down, two pilots parachuted to safety, but nine others died in battle:

Akagi Fighter Unit	Sea1c Sano Shinpei
Kaga Fighter Unit	Ens.* Yamaguchi Hiroyuki
	PO1c Hirayama Iwao
	PO2c Sawano Shigeto
	Sea1c Takahashi Eiichi
Sōryū Fighter Unit	PO3c Kawamata Teruo
	Sea1c Nagasawa Genzō
Hiryū Fighter Unit	PO1c Hino Masato
	PO1c Tokuda Michisuke

*Special service (promoted enlisted man).

Of the three Zeros that ditched (two *Akagi*, one *Hiryū*) it appears that one ran out of fuel, and the other two splashed because of battle damage. By all odds it had been a terrific fight, with more Zeros lost at one time than in any other action in the war so far.

It is impossible now to assess with any degree of certainty how the losses were inflicted on the Japanese combat air patrol. In at least one case, that of Lieut. Fujita of the *Sōryū* Fighter Unit, Japanese ship antiaircraft fire laced into the low-flying Zero. After a few quick passes against Thach's F4Fs, Fujita had taken after Torpedo Three and ultimately claimed the destruction of three Devastators (including one probable). While returning to his carrier, he encountered SBDs at low level and chased them. At 1025, "friendly" fire ignited the Zero's fuel tanks, and from 200 meters he had to bail out. He survived his fall and was later rescued by the destroyer *Nowaki*. American SBDs and TBDs were definitely another hazard, but it seems unreasonable to assume that they accounted for most of the Zeros. At Coral Sea, the strike planes almost certainly destroyed no intercepting fighters, and it is difficult to see how their record could have changed radically at Midway. Earlier attacks on 4 June by all the Midway land-based bombers and the two carrier-based torpedo squadrons (VT-8 and VT-6) had accounted for the loss of three Zeros to all causes. Regarding the SBDs from 1020 to 1045, fewer than a third of the *Enterprise*'s dive bombers were intercepted, while Bombing Three was left alone. Torpedo Three rear gunners fought hard all the way and shot down at least one Zero. Thus the TBDs and SBDs might have downed a couple of Zeros.

Thach and his pilots were credited with six Zeros shot down and two damaged: Lt. Cdr. Thach, three; Lieut. (jg) Macomber, one damaged; Ens. Dibb, one; Ens. Sheedy, one; and Mach. Cheek, one shot down and one damaged. The magnitude of Japanese losses suggests that VF-3's claims were pretty close to the mark. The *Hiryū* Fighter Unit reported engaging and shooting down nine Grumman fighters as well as torpedo planes and bombers. Lieut. Mori's rump *chūtai* of four Zeros lost one highly experienced *shōtai* leader (PO1c Hino) shot down, while the leader of the *Hiryū shōtai* launched at 1013 (PO1c Tokuda) was also killed. From the number (nine) attributed to the Grummans, it seems likely that the *Hiryū* pilots alternately engaged the F4Fs and the strike planes, assuming that when they repeatedly stumbled on Thach's three F4Fs, they were attacking new opponents. The only other fighter unit claiming Grummans was that of the *Akagi*: two Grummans confirmed destroyed and another probable. The most numerous contingent aloft— and the most dispersed—was that of the *Kaga*. None of the surviving *Kaga* pilots reported fighting Grummans, but four others failed to return. It seems likely that some of these lone Zeros joined battle with either Thach or Cheek and suffered for it. As for the *Sōryū*, Lieut. Fujita's No. 3 (PO3c Kawamata) almost certainly fell to Cheek's guns, and another pilot was killed who might have run afoul of the escorts. Whatever the VF-3 pilots scored, they certainly held their own among far more numerous enemy fighters. Tragically, there were too few F4Fs to protect the torpedo planes.

The Strike Groups Come Back

As the later morning dragged on, those waiting on board the ships of Task Forces 16 and 17 grew increasingly apprehensive. Obviously the Japanese had spotted them, yet no counterattack had come. The American strike planes had departed long before, but vouchsafed so far no definite results. For the CAP it was business as usual, as the F4Fs repeatedly checked out bogeys that proved to be, in most instances, friendly cruiser floatplanes flying inner air patrol. The *Tone*'s No. 4 plane sneaked in and out of the area until finally heading for home around 1000, but the fighters never caught sight of it.

Between 0932 and 0950, Spruance's two flattops rotated their CAP fighters. The *Enterprise* sent aloft four-plane VF-6 divisions led by Hoyle and Rawie, then recovered Mehle's and Quady's eight F4Fs. The *Hornet* contributed four-plane divisions under Bruce Harwood and Lieut. (jg) John Sutherland, but for some reason only landed one of the two original CAP divisions. Thus for the time being, Task Force 16's CAP amounted to twenty F4Fs. To conduct flight operations, the carriers had to break away from the base course (240 degrees) and steam southeast at 27 knots into the slight wind. These high-speed excursions greatly slowed the overall rate of advance to the southwest. Simply put, the carriers would not be where their strike planes expected to find them after returning from the morning's mission. This would prove disastrous for the *Enterprise* SBDs.

There had already been disasters that morning for the ten VF-8 escort pilots flying the balance of their ill-starred strike mission.[24] The first to take off, they were also the first to start back, victims of a critical fuel shortage. In two separate formations the VF-8 pilots headed southeast. McInerny and Magda were out ahead. Trailing a short distance off their port quarter was the main body of eight with Ruehlow in front. The F4Fs no longer bothered to maintain any order or proper distances, and their intervals loosened. Each pilot tried to set his fuel mixture for maximum range and still stay along with the rest. Losing altitude only very slowly, the escorts nevertheless made a fast, downhill return, swifter than they realized. Their Zed Bakers provided only an approximate direction to fly, and in reading the homing beacon, they made a series of gentle turns to the right that curved their flight path more southeast than east the longer they flew. Trouble was, they were not very familiar with the Zed Bakers and had no idea how far they had to fly.

A few minutes past 1000, or about an hour after they left the *Hornet* SBDs, the eight pilots in the main body chanced to sight some ship wakes far off to their left (north). They identified the ships as the Japanese carrier force, their original objective! Not eager to risk capture even though nearly out of fuel, they held their east–southeasterly heading. Tragically, they did not realize they had actually come home or close to it. The ships they glimpsed were not the enemy, but rather Task Force 16. McInerny could have told them differently, but since his track was a little farther to the south than the others, he never saw the ships off to the north. He had thought he spotted the enemy striking force's smoke a whole hour earlier, while he made his turn away from the *Hornet* SBDs. Fighting Eight missed its last chance to reach home plate. Now ahead of the F4Fs lay only desolate ocean and certain ditching. It was another cruel trick of fate on that unhappy mission, and more evil awaited the VF-8 escort.

Not long after leaving the strange ships astern, the escort suffered its first casualty when an F4F finally exhausted its fuel. The pilots all had tried to stretch their gasoline supply, but not all of them had the experience to do that effectively. Neither did all of the airplanes perform identically—some were more economical than others. Flying tail-end Charlie in the ragged line of F4Fs, Ens. Humphrey L. Tallman watched one Grumman ahead of him slow, then nose down in a stall after its engine stopped. He believed its pilot to be his close friend Mark Kelly, and watched with sorrow the F4F's inexorable descent toward the water. Tallman was still too high to see what happened when the aircraft splashed. Instead of Kelly, evidence points to Ruehlow's wingman, Ens. George R. Hill, as the first to go. He was never found. Appointed an aviation cadet in March 1941, Hill received his golden wings and promotion to ensign the following September. Fighting Eight was his only squadron. Leading the pack of eight F4Fs, Ruehlow had seen Hill straggle a few times, only to catch up again. Glancing back a little later, Ruehlow noticed he was gone for good.

Ahead and just off to the south of the main body, McInerny and Magda were next to face their fate, when fuel gauges made it evident both pilots had only a few minutes of flight time left. Conferring by hand signals, the two determined they would ditch,together while they still enjoyed engine power. Circling in, they carefully judged wind and wave conditions (light southeasterly breeze and a mild sea), then set down not far apart. Springing from their cockpits, both secured their liferafts from the little compartments on the dorsal fairings. McInerny inflated his raft without difficulty and stepped in, only to find he had forgotten to cut the lanyard which secured it to the sinking F4F. Both the raft and he were underwater before he managed to break it free. Popping back to the surface, McInerny paddled over to join Magda's raft. What a mission it had been for the exuberant Irishman!

Of the rest of the hapless VF-8 pilots, the next to go as they headed away from the ship contact was Tallman's own section leader, Frank Jennings. His F4F commenced to pop ominously; then the engine quit altogether. Jennings stalled and started down, but Tallman was determined to stay with him in accordance with flight doctrine drilled into him since flight school. A former old line aviation cadet and floatplane driver with VCS-7 on board the cruiser *Tuscaloosa*, Jennings neatly deadsticked into the sea. Tallman made a powered ditching right alongside him. Again, both had time to pop their rubber boats and bring them together—two more dots on a vast and lonely sea. Furious at the whole situation, Tallman spent the next two hours scribbling his report on the rough fabric of his raft.

Fighting Eight's shrinking escort force flew on: the three senior pilots Mitchell, Ruehlow, and fellow "trade school" alumnus Dick Gray, and the two reservist wingmen Kelly and Talbot. Kelly was the first of this group to run out of fuel. He dropped out of formation and was seen to reverse course, as if to get as close to the previously sighted ships as he could. His own F4F down to gasoline vapor too, Talbot followed. Gliding northwest back along the former flight path, Kelly descended close to the water. Talbot tried to radio his friend that he was ditching down wind, but it was too late. Kelly's F-9 plowed into the waves and sank immediately. One of the most promising young pilots in the squadron, Mark Kelly had proudly pinned on his wings in June 1941. Along with Steve Groves (himself fated to die that day), he had spent ten days in May on board the *Monssen* after ditching on takeoff. His was the second life lost on the escort mission. Likewise setting down without power, Talbot splashed about 1030 not far away, but he escaped the cockpit and launched his raft. He was fortunate—he would survive his ordeal.

After their wingmen had fallen away, Mitchell, Ruehlow, and Gray held their southeasterly course for perhaps another quarter hour. Finally one of them ran out of fuel and started down. The other two decided enough was enough and circled to ditch nearby. Stalling his Grumman into the water, Mitchell discovered F-18 sinking out from under him so quickly that he was lucky to escape. Raftless, he bobbed on the sea, supported by his yellow Mae West. When he went in, Ruehlow was jarred by the impact and gashed his head painfully on the gunsight mount. Despite his injury, he scrambled free in time to secure his liferaft before F-19 disappeared into the depths. Dick Gray tried a new tack. Still having engine power, he cranked down F-5's landing gear and eased the Grumman neatly into the sea. He not only grabbed his liferaft, but had the foresight to save his emergency rations as well. Ruehlow and Gray brought their rafts together, picked up the skipper, and worked out a rotation scheme that put a single man in one of the rafts, who then alternated its occupation with one of the two in the second rubber boat.

Thus before 1100, VF-8's ill-fated escort mission had ended with all ten pilots in the water. The mission was doomed by inexperience and errors at many levels of command. First came the horrendous decision to launch the fighters in advance of the other *Hornet* strike planes, compelling the F4Fs to circle and waste fuel. Then the escorts flew close to the extreme limit of their radius of action before turning back. George Hill ran out of fuel only a few minutes after the VF-8 pilots sighted off to the north what they thought was the Japanese carrier force, but which was later determined to be Task Force 16. He might not have made it back to the *Hornet* even if the pilots had turned in that direction. Naval flight doctrine called for the leader to ditch all his aircraft together unless he was certain he could reach base, notify his superiors of the position where the others ditched, and send help. Searchers faced a much easier task locating a group of downed aviators rather than hunting for scattered individuals strewn over a wide area. In this case, patrol planes at Midway had no reason to assume VF-8 was anywhere but northwest of Midway. Once down together, the castaways themselves could team up and help each other, as did happen with the three groups of pilots who managed to ditch simultaneously. The best that can be said about the *Hornet* strike mission in general is that decisive leadership was lacking.

Excitement in Task Force 16 mounted after 1020, when snatches of radio transmission from the strike planes gave hints of the disaster overtaking the Japanese. For the CAP, work beckoned closer to home. The *Enterprise* radar detected another bogey, so Ham Dow alerted his fighters. At 1034, he told Hoyle's VF-6 division to "arrow" 295 degrees, distance 20 miles. Evidently someone eyeballed the contact, for seven minutes later Dow sang out, "Bogey a bandit in cloud, step on it!"[25] Hoyle and his second section under Rad. Elec. Bayers hunted through the overcast, while Dow mustered reinforcements in the form of Rawie's section. The chase was fruitless. The Japanese indeed had found Task Force 16 again. At 1045, the radioman of the *Chikuma*'s No. 5 plane (an Aichi E13A1 Type 0 reconnaissance floatplane [JAKE]) tapped out a sighting report. This aircraft had departed Striking Force at 0855 to amplify the contact originally made by the *Tone* No. 4 plane. Flown by PO3c Hara Hisashi, the *Chikuma* No. 5 would skillfully shadow Spruance for three hours until "Buster" Hoyle took his revenge.

While the VF-6 fighters hunted for the snooper, Task Force 16 swung into the wind to conduct flight operations. The *Hornet* finally landed the four F4Fs from her first CAP launched nearly four hours before. They were almost out of fuel. No *Hornet* strike planes had yet appeared, so Mitscher spotted his reserve CAP of eight VF-8 Grummans for launch to clear the flight deck when Ring's troops returned. The *Enterprise* at 1045 freed up her deck by despatching her relief CAP of eight fighters led by Mehle and Quady. Descending into the landing circle five minutes later were Jim Gray's ten VF-6 escorts—the first planes to return safely from the great mission. Descending gradually from 22,000 feet, Gray zeroed in on the *Enterprise*'s homing signal for a swift and uneventful hop back to the ship. Debriefed by an eager air staff, Gray could offer little information other than the enemy position an hour before. He had not fought, but had to depart before the dive bombers found the target. Spruance had to await the return of his SBDs to learn further of what had happened, but their flight back would be perilous because Task Force 16 would not be where they expected to find it. The ships' rate of advance on the Point Option course (240 degrees) was greatly retarded by the need to head southeast into the wind to conduct flight operations and countermarch back again to the base course. On 4 June the wind gods did not cooperate with the Americans.

Like VF-6s Gray, the *Hornet* SBDs that had elected to try for the ships had the height, never having dived, to use their Zed Bakers to provide a course in the proper direction toward the task force.[26] Rodee and evidently Ring had no trouble coming back. As they passed north of the Japanese carrier force, they spotted towering columns of smoke off to their right (south). The source of the smoke was the three flattops burning, but the SBDs never got close enough to see what caused it. Others later interpreted their sightings as smoke rising from the oil tank fires on Midway, but these airplanes were much too far from the island to see anything happening there. Ring himself flew pretty much a straight course back to the *Hornet*. Not far behind, but not in contact with CHAG, were Rodee's fifteen VS-8 SBDs. The *Hornet*'s radar at 1100 detected these aircraft bearing 260 degrees, distance 59 miles, the range at which they were picked up indicating they still flew relatively high. The *Hornet* cleared her flight deck by launching the relief CAP of eight VF-8 F4Fs under O'Neill and Ford, then made ready to land SBDs. The first to touch down was Ring at around 1118, and within a few minutes Rodee and his troops likewise were on board. Ring and the VS-8 pilots could offer little information, as they had not even seen the enemy. About 1145, four SBDs from Bombing Eight turned up and landed on board the *Hornet*. During the flight back they had somehow separated from the rest of their squadron. For a short while, it appeared that most of Bombing Eight was missing along with all of Torpedo Eight and ten F4Fs from Fighting Eight. This was a staggering loss of thirty-nine planes!

Around 1200 good news reached the *Hornet* from Midway: the naval air station reported that eleven VB-8 dive bombers had made it there safely. As related earlier, Johnson's squadron had searched far to the south after the *Hornet* strike group had split. Finally, when it came time to turn for home, most of the SBDs had trouble tuning in to the *Hornet*'s YE signal. Four of them flew on through to the task force and landed at 1145. Johnson with the other fourteen VB-8 SBDs had to head south for Midway. Fuel was a major problem. Well north of the island, one SBD ran its tanks dry and ditched. Another splashed ten miles northwest of Midway. Johnson's unexpected appearance put the island on alert at 1121, and though he tried to demonstrate his friendly status by jettisoning bombs on the reef, Midway interpreted the gesture as an attack. One SBD ditched in the lagoon, and three were damaged by antiaircraft fire, but Johnson's eleven landed around 1135. Bombing Eight would have to wait there until the hard-pressed Midway ground crews could refuel and rearm the planes for the flight back to the *Hornet*.

The *Hornet*'s entire morning strike mission had been a disaster, distinguished only by the great valor shown by Torpedo Eight. It had cost thirty-one lives, ten F4Fs, three SBDs, and all fifteen torpedo planes, with no measurable loss inflicted upon the enemy.

After smashing two Japanese carriers, the *Enterprise* SBDs individually or in small groups flew eastward toward the briefed Point Option course. They cruised at low altitude, well under the carrier's line-of-sight (VHF) YE homing signal. Perhaps only two or three SBDs had splashed in the actual attack, although at least one or two more ditched shortly afterward. That left perhaps twenty-five SBDs heading for home. low on fuel, some battered. Well behind them, returning at a slower speed, were the five surviving TBDs from Torpedo Six, but one soon went down. As previously related, the *Enterprise* was not at the expected location on her Point Option course. At 1100 she was 44 miles northeast of where her aviators thought she would be. With her flight deck open for business, she awaited her strike planes, but all they saw was vacant ocean.

The *Yorktown* had conducted no flight operations after recovering Brassfield's

VF-3 fighters at 0925. Consequently she was right where her planes hoped to find her when the first of them sighted her around 1100. For two hours Fletcher had held his second SBD squadron in reserve awaiting new reports on the enemy flattops. He knew the *Enterprise* and *Yorktown* groups, at least, had attacked a Japanese force of two or more carriers, but he was far from certain whether all of the enemy carriers operated together. As he saw it, he had two options. One was to send Scouting Five and escort to the target previously attacked in order to mop up. The second was to use the SBDs to search the crucial northwest quadrant to locate without question all of the enemy carriers and ensure sinking them all. At 1106, he advised Spruance of these two options and requested the latest information on the enemy.

The first Yorktowners to make it back from the strike were the seventeen SBDs of Bombing Three. Leslie and his warriors were none the worse for their plastering of the *Sōryū*. At 1115, he received instructions to orbit Task Force 17. The "cool heads" on board the *Yorktown* did not want to break the deck spot of F4Fs and SBDs until absolutely necessary. The air advisors knew VB-3 retained plenty of fuel. One of the SBDs signaled by Aldis light that the squadron had sunk one Japanese carrier—splendid news! Fletcher still lacked the definitive report he so badly wanted. Spruance at 1115 forwarded a position report on the enemy flattops, but that came from old information provided by Gray. Prodded by fresh news of enemy snoopers, Fletcher concluded that it was wisest to launch ten VS-5 SBDs to search the northwest quadrant out to 200 miles. The other seven Dauntlesses, fueled and armed, would be held in ready reserve in the hangar. They could reinforce Bombing Three or the Task Force 16 strike planes for a second attack. On board the *Yorktown*, Murr Arnold's air department rapidly effected the change in plan.

THE JAPANESE RETALIATE

The Hiryū *Alone*

Before the horrified eyes of the mighty *Kidō Butai*, American dive bombers had transformed three of four magnificent aircraft carriers into flaming hulks. Gone was Japanese carrier air supremacy in the Battle of Midway. Only the carrier *Hiryū*, flagship of Rear Admiral Yamaguchi's 2nd Carrier Division, remained unscathed. Assuming temporary command of the striking force was Rear Admiral Abe Hiroaki, commanding 8th Cruiser division (flag on the *Tone*). He detached the light cruiser *Nagara* and six destroyers to tend the stricken flattops, while the rest of *Kidō Butai* (two battleships, two heavy cruisers, and five destroyers) hastened to take station round the precious *Hiryū*.

Both Yamaguchi and his superior Abe determined to carry on with the planned air strike against the American carrier force, located fully three hours before by the morning search. All four carriers had readied strike planes; now only the *Hiryū* could continue the fight. As Yamaguchi and the *Hiryū*'s Captain Kaku Tomeo surveyed their resources, plane strengths appeared meager indeed. On board the *Hiryū* were only thirty-seven operational aircraft: ten Zero fighters (including three of the 6th Air Group), eighteen carrier bombers, and nine carrier attack planes. Scattered aloft were another twenty-seven Zeros from all four carrier air groups, but they could not land for fuel and ammunition until the *Hiryū*'s deck was clear. When the SBD thunderbolt descended on the other flattops, the *Hiryū* had prepared the eighteen carrier bombers and three Zeros for launch. In the hangar, mechanics readied the nine torpedo planes for a possible 1100 launch.

Lieut. Kobayashi Michio, *Hiryū* strike leader
on the first *Yorktown* attack. (NH 81560.)

Yamaguchi resolved to commit his dive bombers immediately as originally scheduled, then follow in an hour or so with a second wave of nine torpedo planes. With
more Zeros available overhead, Kaku beefed up the fighter escort for the first
strike from three to six. For this initial attack, the burden of command fell upon
Lieut. Kobayashi Michio, *buntaichō*, the leader of the *Hiryū* Carrier Bomber Unit.
His eighteen Aichi D3A1 Type 99 carrier bombers carried the usual payloads of
one 250-kilogram bomb apiece. Kobayashi's flyers enjoyed the reputation of being
among the best dive bombers in the Imperial Navy. He personally led the nine
kanbaku making up his unit's 1st *Chūtai*, while the 2nd *Chūtai*'s nine came under
the second *buntaichō*, Lieut. Yamashita Michiji (see unit roster).[1]

Like the *Yorktown*'s Fighting Three, the *Hiryū* Fighter Unit seemed fated by
circumstances to bear the brunt of fighter combat in the carrier exchanges in the
Battle of Midway. Nine Zeros of the 2nd *Chūtai* had flown as escort on the dawn
Midway strike, where their pilots claimed no fewer than eighteen Grumman Wildcats shot down (including four probables) in return for two Mitsubishis damaged.
In the various CAP actions up to 1045, the unit submitted claims for forty-three
American planes destroyed (!), for the loss of four Zeros shot down (including two
veteran *shōtai* leaders) and one plane ditched. The CO, Lieut. Mori, had made
close acquaintance with Jimmy Thach's VF-3 division over the Japanese carriers.
Now from those pilots on deck, the *Hiryū*'s air officer culled out the following six
to comprise the escort or "fighter striking unit" for the first wave:

	1st *Shōtai*
No. 1	Lieut. Shigematsu Yasuhiro (B)
No. 2	PO2c Todaka Noboru
No. 3	Sea1c Yoshimoto Suekichi
	2nd *Shōtai*
No. 1	W.O. Minegishi Yoshijirō
No. 2	PO1c Sasaki Hitoshi
No. 3	PO3c Chiyoshima Yutaka

Roster for First Attack on American Carriers, *Hiryū* Carrier Bomber Unit

Plane	Pilot	Observer or Radioman
	1st *Chūtai*	
	1st *Shōtai*	
*No. 1	Lieut. Kobayashi Michio (B)	W.O. Ono Yoshinori (RM)
*No. 2	PO1c Yamada Kihichirō	PO1c Fukunaga Yoshiteru (RM)
*No. 3	PO3c Sakai Hideo	PO3c Yamaguchi Buichi (RM)
	2nd *Shōtai*	
*No. 1	Lieut. Kondō Takenori (B)	W.O. Maeda Takashi (RM)
*No. 2	PO2c Nakao Nobumichi	PO1c Okamura Hidemitsu (RM)
*No. 3	Sea1c Seki Masao	PO1c Tanaka Kunio (RM)
	3rd *Shōtai*	
*No. 1	PO1c Imaizumi Tamotsu	PO1c Kazuma Rihei (RM)
No. 2	PO2c Tsuchiya Takayoshi	PO2c Egami Hayata (RM)
*No. 3	PO3c Koizumi Naoshi	PO2c Hagiwara Yoshiaki (RM)
	2nd *Chūtai*	
	1st *Shōtai*	
*No. 1	W.O. Nishihara Toshikatsu	Lieut. Yamashita Michiji (B)(O)
No. 2	PO1c Matsumoto Sadao	PO1c Yasuda Nobuhiko (RM)
*No. 3	PO3c Kuroki Junichi	Sea1c Mizuno Yasuhiko (RM)
	2nd *Shōtai*	
No. 1	W.O. Nakazawa Iwao	Ens. Nakayama Shimematsu† (O)
No. 2	PO1c Seo Tetsuo	PO3c Murakami Chikayoshi (RM)
*No. 3	PO2c Kondō Sumio	PO3c Iwabuchi Yoshiaki (RM)
	3rd *Shōtai*	
No. 1	W.O. Nakagawa Shizuo	PO1c Ōtomo Ryūji (RM)
*No. 2	PO2c Ikeda Takazō	PO3c Shimizu Takumi (RM)
*No. 3	Sea1c Fuchigami Issei	Sea1c Nakaoka Yoshinaru (RM)

(B)   *buntaichō*
(O)   observer
(RM) radioman
*Failed to return from mission.
†Special Service (promoted from the ranks).

Leading the escort was the unit's junior *buntaichō*, Lieut. Shigematsu, another representative of that small batch of Naval Academy men upon whom so much depended. A 1938 Eta Jima graduate, Shigematsu had completed flight training (34th Officer Class) in April 1941 and that September had reported to the *Hiryū*. In January 1942 he qualified as a *buntaichō*. His 2nd *Chūtai* had made the Midway strike, and now he was ready to attack the American carrier force with a mixed bag of 1st and 2nd *Chūtai* pilots.[2]

Tight-lipped and grim, arrayed in their bulky kapok life vests, the carrier bomber and fighter aircrews assembled near the *Hiryū*'s island to hear their captain speak before they manned planes. Kaku needed no impassioned rhetoric to stress how vital this mission would be. These men and the torpedo crews who would follow were all that Combined Fleet could now employ against the American carrier force. He cautioned them not to act rashly. The American position was not known precisely, as the last reports were several hours old. Search planes, however, were now combing the critical area, and he expected new information before long. The first aircraft rolled down the flight deck around 1050, and by 1058 the small strike force of twenty-four planes formed up for the flight eastward. Although they did not know it, the Japanese at 1100 were only 91 miles west of Task Force 16 and 95 miles west of Task Force 17.

Kobayashi proceeded out at low level and only gradually gained height. Visibility seemed better close to the water. About a half hour after departure, the Japanese stumbled upon a formation of six American planes which they thought were torpedo planes involved in the strike on the *Kidō Butai*. Shigematsu's six Zeros peeled off to ambush the enemy cruising low over the water. The Americans proved tougher than they looked. In an extended fight, the Japanese shot down no bombers outright, but the American gunners pared the little escort to four Zeros. Both W.O. Minegishi Yoshijirō (2nd *Shōtai* leader) and wingman PO1c Sasaki Hitoshi had their fighters badly shot up, so badly that they had to abort the mission and head back. When they made it home around 1230, Minegishi landed safely on board the *Hiryū*, but Sasaki had to ditch. No doubt highly irritated, the tough Shigematsu gathered his three Zeros and set off after the *kanbaku*, hopefully to catch up before Kobayashi spotted the enemy.

Shigematsu's fight is unsung from the American point of view, although his opponents had to be *Enterprise* dive bombers looking for their carrier. No surviving SBD crews reported fighting Zeros under these circumstances, and it appears none of Shigematsu's tormentors were rescued. Lieut. Charles R. Ware, VS-6 flight officer, had led most of his 3rd Division back to Point Option where the SBDs were seen by other pilots. Thereafter Ware's little group disappeared. It seems likely that Ware's division, perhaps reinforced by a few other SBDs gathered on the way, encountered the Japanese strike group and put up a stout defense against the six Zeros. Then from battle damage or fuel starvation, the SBDs ditched, and their crews were not recovered.

By the time Kobayashi departed on the mission, two Japanese search planes had latched onto the American carrier force. The *Chikuma* No. 5 floatplane continued to transmit accurate reports. At 1100, Abe told its crew to guide the attack unit to the target. Ten minutes later, the *Chikuma* flyers responded that the American force bore 070 degrees and 90 miles from the *Kidō Butai*. Putting in an appearance shortly after 1100 was the *Sōryū* No. 201 aircraft, an experimental Yokosuka D4Y1 Type 2 carrier bomber utilized as a high-speed reconnaissance plane. The *Sōryū* bomber had first checked out an erroneous position report, then was vectored into the proper area. Carefully scouting the vicinity, the speedy recon plane determined that three American carriers lurked in the area. At 1130, the crew attempted to radio their findings, but only garbled messages filtered back to Yamaguchi. At 1132, the *Chikuma* No. 5 aircraft radioed the strike leader: "I will lead you to the target by radio."[3] Nine minutes later, the *Hiryū* rebroadcast for Kobayashi's benefit the report that the American carrier force lay 070 degrees and 90 miles from the *Kidō Butai*. After some anxious searching, Kobayashi had little difficulty in taking up a direct course to the target, which in that case happened to be Task Force 17. The Japanese search planes had done their job well.

By 1130, the *Yorktown* had completed preparations for despatching ten VS-5 SBDs to search in pairs 200 miles to the north and northwest. Fletcher was anxious to locate the remaining enemy flattops or at least clarify the situation. Deck crews struck below the other seven SBDs. Fueled and armed, they constituted a ready reserve. Spotted on the flight deck along with the ten search SBDs were the twelve F4F Wildcats of Crommelin's and Brassfield's divisions. Now that the strike mission had been canceled, all of them could be used as relief CAP for Leonard's six F4Fs presently aloft. Circling overhead were the seventeen SBDs of Bombing Three, recently returned from attacking the Japanese carriers. Still retaining adequate fuel, they orbited patiently, awaiting a clear deck upon which to land. The Yorktowners watched anxiously for the rest of the strike group to appear—the Wildcat fighters and Devastator torpedo planes that would be low on fuel and require swif' .

recovery. At 1133, Task Force 17 turned eastward into the wind, and the *Yorktown* began launching the ten SBDs.

About the time the carrier initiated flight operations, Thach and his two companions Macomber and Dibb made eyeball contact with Task Force 17. Seeing the rest of the strike group begin straggling back, Captain Buckmaster thought it wise to launch all twelve Wildcats on deck to take over the CAP. The *Yorktown* signaled Leonard to bring his F4Fs in for immediate recovery, so they could be refueled and held on standby. The VF-3 pilots waiting on deck and in their ready room received orders to man planes, and the air department had to get them aloft in a hurry. For the fighter pilots, it became a rapid, rather confused launch. Several thought it was a scramble, and they had trouble sorting themselves into proper organization. By 1150, the deck was clear as the last of the twelve F4Fs had taken to the air.

With the *Yorktown* open for business, a number of aircraft queued up taking turns to land. First to come in were two *Enterprise* SBDs returning from the attack on the Japanese carriers. They had wandered into the area while searching for "The Big E" and found the *Yorktown* instead. Lieut. (jg) Wilbur E. Roberts and Ens. George H. Goldsmith of Bombing Six landed on board with very little fuel remaining, and Goldsmith's B-15 was badly shot up. The *Yorktown* almost had another guest in Wade McClusky, but he recognized the *Enterprise*'s sister and headed off for his own carrier miles to the southeast. Following the SBDs were Leonard's six CAP F4Fs, which the plane handlers parked forward, anticipating more landings.

Meanwhile, Thach's little contingent in the landing circle encountered a friend in Cheek, who had made his way back alone. He joined up as number four on Macomber's wing, as the pilots checked each other over to see that their landing gear and tailhooks functioned. First to touch down was Thach, and as soon as his F4F had been parked up deck, he raced up to flag plot to inform Fletcher of the good progress of the battle. Frank Jack learned with pleasure that Thach had positively seen three enemy flattops put out of commission, flames and all. Of the fourth thought to be present, Thach could offer no word. While the two conferred, Spruance suggested by radio that the *Yorktown* locate the targets already attacked and search to the northwest to seek undamaged carriers. Spruance added that he would strike again. From his own returning aviators, he discovered that "The Big E's" planes on their own had knocked out two carriers. Fletcher, of course, had already launched his own search.

While Thach made his way to the admiral, Dibb and Macomber landed safely. Last of the VT escort to come in was Cheek. Alighting on deck, he immediately sensed something was wrong. His tail hook was bouncing over wires rather than engaging one. He was headed for a "crunching contact" with the crash barrier. Uppermost in his mind was avoiding another bounce over the barrier into planes parked forward such as had happened on 30 May when Don Lovelace was killed. Cheek quickly decided what he must do:

> Just feet away from the barrier cables, I jammed the control stick full forward and followed it trying to tuck myself into a ball, my head as close to the cockpit deck as possible. The propellor grabbed one of the snaring wires and the F4F cartwheeled forward to a crashing stop on its back.
>
> I was unhurt but afraid of fire and yelled at the flight deck crew, who I could hear surrounding the plane, "Get this thing to hell off of me!" I was out in a few seconds.[4]

After his bone-shaking stop, Cheek was hurried to the flight surgeon, and told him

Tom Cheek's battered F-16 (BuNo. 5143) struck below in the *Yorktown*'s hangar, afternoon 4 June. (NA 80-G-23979.)

he was okay. Air department personnel swarmed over the inverted F4F, hoisted it onto dollies, and carted old F-16 off to an elevator to be lowered to the hangar deck. Cheek had ripped into numbers four and five wire barriers, rendering the arresting gear inoperable. This forced a temporary halt to landing operations, while crews rerigged the barriers. The ship signaled Leslie's Bombing Three to orbit, but the SBDs still had plenty of fuel. Meanwhile Cheek repaired to the ready room to make his combat report to Thach.

Within a minute or so of when the last CAP F4F lifted off the flight deck, the *Yorktown*'s radar operator, Rad. Elec. Vane M. Bennett, detected unidentified planes bearing 255 degrees, distance 32 miles and closing. Pederson, the FDO, immediately called an alert. The sudden approach of what might be an enemy strike group caught Fletcher in an awkward position. No defending fighters waited at high altitude, as the newly launched CAP worked to sort itself out close to the ships. Thach and Leonard were in the process of landing their F4Fs. At 1152, Pederson ordered Brassfield's division to investigate the contact bearing 255 degrees (M.), distance 32 miles. Himself circling in the proper rendezvous sector, Brassfield established contact neither with his wingman Harry Gibbs nor his other two section leaders, Duran Mattson and Bill Woollen. Two minutes later his pilots still had not appeared, so an exasperated Brassfield had to inform Pederson that his division had not joined up.

Pederson had no recourse but to vector out the individual sections. At 1156 orders went to Brassfield, Mattson, and Woollen to proceed out along the 255-degree heading (M.) to a distance of 20 to 25 miles to intercept enemy aircraft. One of the best in the business, Bennett had warned that the bogeys were climbing, something no friendlies would ordinarily do within sight of their own task force. As mentioned above, the launch had been a strange one for the twelve VF-3 pilots, more in the nature of a scramble than a normal departure because Buckmaster wanted the *Yorktown*'s deck clear to land the strike planes. Then, just after they had become airborne came the urgent steer from the FDO. The two divisions never had a chance to form up. It soon became every section or every man for himself!

Woollen and his wingman Bill Barnes forged ahead, followed by Scott McCuskey (from Crommelin's division) minus his own wingman, Ens. Mark K. Bright, who had not shown up in the rendezvous area when the vector came in. Behind McCuskey and frantically trying to catch up was Gibbs, while division leader Brassfield trailed

Organization of the Combat Air Patrol Defending Task Force 17, First Attack

(I) Fighting Three
2nd Division
F-11 Lieut. (jg) Richard G. Crommelin, USN
    Ens. John B. Bain, A-V(N)
F-3 Ens. Richard L. Wright, A-V(N)
F-25 *Ens. George F. Markham, Jr., A-V(N)
F-21 Lieut. (jg) E. Scott McCuskey, A-V(N)
    *Ens. Mark K. Bright, A-V(N)
4th Division
F-10 Lieut. (jg) Arthur J. Brassfield, USN
F-8 Ens. Harry B. Gibbs, A-V(N)
F-15 Lieut. (jg) E. Duran Mattson, USN
F-22 Ens. Horace A. Bass, Jr., A-V(N)
F-2 Lieut. (jg) William S. Woollen, A-V(N)
    Lieut. (jg) William W. Barnes, Jr., A-V(N)

(II) Fighting Six
3rd Division
F-13 Lieut. Roger W. Mehle, USN
F-14 Ens. Howard L. Grimmell, Jr., A-V(N)
F-17 Ens. Thomas C. Provost III, A-V(N)
F-18 Ens. James A. Halford, Jr., A-V(N)

(III) Fighting Eight
Ford's Division
Lieut. Warren W. Ford, USN
Ens. Morrill I. Cook, Jr., A-V(N)
Ens. George Formanek, Jr., A-V(N)
F-17 †Ens. Stephen W. Groves, A-V(N)

*Not engaged.
†Missing in action.

the four F4Fs from about a mile behind Woollen. Following beneath all of them were Mattson and his wingman, Ens. Horace Bass. These seven pilots faced a furious effort to gain altitude in their fully loaded Wildcats. They did not have much time.

Pederson called in additional help. At 1158, he instructed Crommelin's division to intercept fifty bogeys at "Angels 10" (10,000 feet), bearing 255 degrees (M.) from the Yorktown. The 2nd Division was in disarray as well. Crommelin himself was well aware of how poorly the CAP had performed the month before at Coral Sea because the F4Fs had lacked initial altitude advantage over the enemy dive bombers. He and wingman John Bain started climbing steeply in order to get that height advantage over the attackers. Consequently, the two remained closer to the task force than Brassfield's pilots. One of Crommelin's section leaders, McCuskey, already was charging hard toward the enemy, while Dick Wright, the other, headed out after unsuccessfully trying to locate his own wingman. The two errant wingmen, Mark Bright and George Markham, were among the last of the twelve to take off. By the time they got their bearings, everyone else had disappeared. In desperation they joined together south of the task force and started climbing. Mainly they watched for enemy torpedo planes; they failed to spot the dive bombers coming in, and did not participate in the fight. Thus did the two VF-3 divisions make their entrances piecemeal, but their performance was spectacular all the same.

Handling Task Force 16's CAP, Ham Dow tracked the Japanese raiders on radar as they neared Task Force 17, situated about 30 miles northwest of Spruance's ships. On CAP he had available nineteen F4Fs from both carriers, but for the time being he could count on no reinforcements. Both the *Enterprise* and the *Hornet* were committed to landing the strike planes, which filtered back one or two at a time. Between them the two flattops had twenty-five Wildcats on deck, but they would not be able to launch for thirty minutes. The *Enterprise* ultimately recovered only fourteen of the thirty-two SBDs that had reached the target area (one other had aborted), and most were missing due to the Point Option fiasco. The *Hornet* at first landed only twenty of thirty-four SBDs despatched, but eleven others had taken refuge on Midway.

Dow mustered what troops he could to assist Task Force 17. He made a practice of deploying his CAP at roughly two levels: eight VF-8 fighters at 20,000 feet and the eight VF-6 fighters patrolling under 10,000 feet. Three other VF-8 Wildcats were also aloft, but they ran low on juice and could not be sent. At first Dow thought it best to send the fresh VF-8 contingent to the *Yorktown*'s assistance and retain the *Enterprise* troops in direct defense of his own ships. At 1158, he instructed the "Blue" patrol to proceed out along a heading of 305 degrees to a distance of 30 miles to intercept enemy planes thought to be at 10,000 feet. This would give the VF-8 pilots at 20,000 feet a healthy altitude superiority. Warren Ford acknowledged the transmission and hustled off to the north. At the time his four F4Fs operated west of Task Force 16, significantly closer to the *Yorktown* than the rest of Dow's CAP. O'Neill, VF-8's XO, never answered the vector, and his second section leader, Lieut. (jg) Lawrence C. French, also had a bum radio receiver. O'Neill's wingman, Ens. Carlton B. Starkes, heard the orders clearly and tried to take the lead according to naval flight doctrine. The pilot with the working radio was to take the lead in response to the FDO's orders if the flight leader's radio was not working. O'Neill, however, refused to relinquish the lead to a junior pilot, possibly because French did not appear to have heard anything either. Starkes knew the division was needed somewhere in a hurry, so he contacted French's wingman, Ens. James C. Smith, and the two raced in the direction of the *Yorktown*. Somewhat bewildered, O'Neill and French remained on station over Task Force 16.

In the event the Japanese should turn southeastward toward Task Force 16, Dow deployed his VF-6 fighters in a blocking position between the enemy planes and his ships. At 1158, he warned Mehle and Quady about the bogeys bearing 305 degrees, distance 20 miles, then told Mehle to take station at a point bearing 315 degrees, 20 miles from the *Enterprise*. At 1205, he amplified his instructions, telling them to go only 15 miles out rather than 20. The *Yorktown*'s ordeal was about to begin.

"Come on you SCARLET boys, get them!"[5]
  Oscar Pederson, Yorktown FDO, 1202, 4 June

Keen eyes among the Japanese strike group discerned at 1155 the wakes of an American task force cutting the seas about 25 miles ahead. To attain proper altitude for his bombing attack, Kobayashi led his eighteen *Hiryū* carrier bombers into a shallow climb as they closed the target. His squadron had deployed as two separate Vee-of-Vees formations, with Kobayashi's 1st *Chūtai* leading and Yamashita's 2nd *Chūtai* in echelon to the right. Shigematsu's four Zeros, still smarting from their chastisement by the *Enterprise* SBDs, trailed a few miles back, evidently still trying to catch up. As the Japanese pilots neared the ships, they picked out one enemy carrier surrounded closely by a ring of cruisers and destroyers. Even then, they saw Grummans climbing out to meet them. The survivors noted in their report, "Did not engage these [fighters], but approached the enemy position."[6] This was not a true statement, as the Type 99 *kanbaku* and the Grumman Wildcats soon tangled in one of the strangest dogfights of the war. Kobayashi at 1200 broke radio silence with his first message, to the *Hiryū*:

We are attacking the enemy carrier. 0900. [0900, 5 June, Tokyo time][7]

Brassfield's contingent of VF-3 pilots soon caught sight of the neat formation of enemy planes approaching from ahead and above the fighters. At 1200, he reported to Pederson that eighteen enemy aircraft were heading his way. He estimated he was about 15 miles out and that the Japanese flew two or three thousand feet above him. Brassfield, remembering his 8 May fight at the Coral Sea, had a sense of *déjà vu*, except that here no Zeros seemed to be around. He thought it best to gain more altitude and let the Japanese come to him. While climbing ahead of the oncoming dive bombers, he moved to take favorable position opposite the enemy's right, presaging an effective high-side run when the Japanese passed underneath.

As Brassfield passed 10,000 feet—nearly level with the approaching bombers— he saw the lead Grummans, flown by Woollen and Barnes, attack them from below. The two discovered themselves on an opposite heading and beneath the enemy planes, and by the time they had closed the gap, they were still below the *kanbaku*. To avoid overrunning the target and possibly missing a shot, Woollen pulled up sharply into a low-opposite run and fired from around 300 yards below the 1st *Chūtai*. His tracers and those of Barnes sprayed through the lead formation, causing Kobayashi's bombers to bob up and down individually to evade the bullets from below. For the two F4F pilots it was an awkward angle of attack, so Woollen led Barnes into a climbing turn to the left to recover over the right rear of the enemy formation.

Following some distance behind Woollen's section, McCuskey had just made it to the enemy's altitude when suddenly the oncoming bombers were there! The lead formation of nine bombers appeared to his left, with the second nine beyond and flying at a slightly higher altitude. McCuskey judged there was barely enough space for him to squeeze between the first and second groups of nine. Swinging sharply to his left, McCuskey eased into position for a flat-side run on the lead nine. As his initial target, he singled out the outside bomber in the left Vee. Coming at the Japanese from slightly abaft the beam, he adjusted for deflection and cut loose with a satisfying burst at short range. Under the impact of multiple hits, the *kanbaku* shuddered and flamed up swiftly. The burning bomber filling his view, McCuskey maneuvered slightly to rake the left and center Vees as his momentum drew the F4F behind them. Because of his flat angle of approach, his broad red lines of tracers zipped through the lead enemy formation, certainly disconcerting the crews.

Committed in his plan to cross behind the 1st *Chūtai*, McCuskey rapidly shifted his point of aim in order to walk his bullets into the inside plane of the right Vee. That aircraft's forward motion brought it directly into his sights. He had to hold his run tightly behind the first nine to avoid flying into the second not far beyond. Closing to pointblank range, McCuskey found he had to drop his left wing radically to keep his firing position. This upset his shooting because he was too close to the target to take advantage of the convergence pattern of his guns. Thus he had little more than a snap burst at the inside bomber in the right Vee. Heading out, McCuskey roared within 50 yards of the rear of the right Vee.

Immediately after he cleared the 3rd *Shōtai*, McCuskey was startled to encounter only a few hundred feet ahead two dive bombers making a tight climbing turn to the right. He undertook to match their turn and brought them under fire as they twisted nearly 180 degrees from their original heading. Exactly who of the first nine they were and what exactly they planned to do remains a mystery, but the evidence is very strong the two Japanese pilots were Kobayashi and a wingman breaking out of the lead Vee. At that moment cohesion in the 1st *Chūtai* disappeared; that much is certain from witnesses. The squadron commander might have essayed a right turn to evade the hot tracers McCuskey had tossed in his midst, or possibly he feared the wild Grumman might try to ram. Perhaps he thought he could set up a shot by the 2nd *Chūtai*. Whatever his reason, Kobayashi must have felt the surprisingly aggressive Grummans would have picked off his men one by one if they held neat formation.

McCuskey cut inside the turn of the two carrier bombers and set up a shot. Suddenly he found himself heading directly into the entire 2nd *Chūtai*. As he later put it, "All hell broke loose!"[8] Yamashita's pilots had to break formation or risk collision with the Grumman charging straight at them. Like pins hit by a bowling ball, *kanbaku* peeled off in every direction trying to miss each other and the F4F in their midst. For McCuskey it was a case of "shooting from the hip," as he traded intense, short-range, head-on shots with as many as four bombers before his machine guns quit functioning. After a few seconds of furious flying and shooting, McCuskey fought clear. Still continuing his right turn, he broke into level flight and contemplated the prospect that he had run out of ammunition. It was the vexing problem of reduced ammunition supply in the F4F-4.

Pondering his situation, McCuskey was startled to hear a "ping" as something struck his left wing. Glancing back, he spotted two dive bombers in echelon formation behind him, and they were maneuvering onto his tail! The leader's guns winked tracers at him. His own guns not functioning, McCuskey was in no position to argue. He extended his right turn into a steep spiral, using his superior diving speed to pull away from the two aggressive *kanbaku* shooting up his tail. McCuskey thought his opponents to be the two birds he had followed around into the second group of nine. Perhaps Kobayashi was trying to take revenge on the Grumman that had reduced his formation to a shambles. Recovering near the water, McCuskey looked back to find his tail clear. Also evident was what he called "debris" littering the water beneath the melee. Geysers of water indicated to him that some bomber pilots had dumped their bomb loads. Anxious to rearm, McCuskey tore over to the *Yorktown* well ahead of the actual attack and tried to come on board. The LSO waved him off just as he had done with Bombing Three. Leslie's SBDs retired at low altitude to a point about halfway between the two American task forces. Forced to become an unwilling spectator, McCuskey sheered off out of antiaircraft range to await the results of the strike.

Following not far beind McCuskey was Gibbs. Beginning at 1202, he saw McCuskey "plow right through the middle"[9] of the enemy formation, scattering the dive bombers like tenpins. Gibbs swiftly singled out a target of his own, eased onto its tail, and ripped off a long burst. His .50-caliber slugs soon ignited the Type 99's fuel tanks, and the Japanese spun away in flames. In his first victory, Gibbs could not resist the temptation to follow his victim toward the water. He waited until the bomber splashed before turning back into the fight. Woollen and Barnes also took advantage of the confusion below them and dived after individual Japanese. Each later submitted a claim for one bomber, and Barnes reported damaging two others. Apparently they separated and fought until their ammunition ran low—which did not take long in an F4F-4.

At 1202 as the Japanese formation astonishingly shredded right before his eyes, Brassfield—flying a thousand yards to the right of the Japanese—saw a dive bomber turn toward him. Amazingly the *kanbaku*, still lugging its bomb, initiated a run on the F4F. Shaking off his surprise, Brassfield pitted his six heavy .50-caliber Brownings against the bomber's pair of 7.7-mm guns. The *Hiryū* pilot lost. Reaching out at long range, Brassfield's slugs tore into the bomber. His ardor dampened, the Japanese jettisoned his bomb and dived away to escape almost certain destruction. Brassfield decided not to pursue. He knew the dive bomber was now harmless to the carrier, and he sought Japanese who retained their power to cripple the *Yorktown*. Pulling out, he took station above and between the melee and the task force.

Very soon after, fate gave Brassfield the opportunity to deal a terrible blow to the *Hiryū* Carrier Bomber Unit. At 1203, he saw three dive bombers wring themselves out of the confusion, form up in loose line-astern, and head in purposeful fashion toward the carrier. Apparently one of the Japanese *shōtai* leaders (whose aircraft were distinctively marked with at least one blue stripe on the vertical tail surfaces) had found a couple of wingmen and set off in the direction of the target. Reporting this to the FDO, Brassfield tried to coordinate his attack with another F4F he saw not far away. That pilot concentrated on targets of his own and flew off in another direction. Unperturbed, Brassfield rolled into a high-side run on the lead bomber, coming at the *kanbaku* from the left. The Japanese saw him close in and snapped into a tight climbing left turn to scissor his attacker. This maneuver startled Brassfield for two reasons: first, that he saw an armed dive bomber deflected from its run to counter a fighter, and second, that both wingmen turned to follow the leader in his countermove.

At 300 yards, Brassfield cut loose against his climbing opponent. His long, well-aimed burst tore into the *kanbaku*'s engine and flamed it. Trailing oily black smoke and fire, the Type 99 stalled, then nosed down toward the water. Avoiding his first victim, Brassfield executed a violent wing-over to the left and with a beam attack confronted the second dive bomber in the string. Within 150 yards of the target, he touched his trigger and concentrated his bullets in the fuselage and wingroot—with immediate results, as the *kanbaku* disintegrated in midair. The blast concussion rocked the Grumman with great force. By this time the third Japanese pilot thought it best to find another route to the carrier. He dived at high speed toward

Art Brassfield about 8 June on board the *Hornet*. (From Cdr. John Ford's *The Battle of Midway*.)

the safety of a cloud bank 3,000 feet below. Using his swifter diving speed, Brassfield slipped easily onto the tail of the hapless Type 99 for a good shooting position. A short burst set the bomber ablaze and kept it diving until it splashed. In less than a minute, Brassfield had downed three aircraft by means of his excellent gunnery! Putting his F4F into a zoom climb, he reached 7,000 feet only to find another bomber stalking him from above. As before, Brassfield turned into his assailant's approach for a head-on duel. Opening at 400 yards, the F4F's firepower again proved too much for the Japanese, who broke off the fight by rolling out to one side. Brassfield noticed this opponent no longer carried a bomb.

Obviously something very strange was going on, with dive bombers counterattacking the fighters in a dogfight reminiscent of something out of filmdom's *Wings* or *Hell's Angels*. McCuskey's slashing attack against the 1st *Chūtai* and his near ramming of the 2nd *Chūtai* caused the enemy to break formation and scatter. Their Zero escorts still lagged too far behind to intervene. Despite the melee, the carrier bomber pilots were intent on fighting their way through to the target. None seemed to have jettisoned bombs unless the aircraft sustained damage. Thus the initial phase of the fight saw Woollen, Barnes, McCuskey, Gibbs, and Brassfield intercept the eighteen *kanbaku* and most likely shoot down seven of them. At 1202, lookouts on board the heavy cruiser *Astoria,* nearest to the melee, first noticed eighteen bombers perhaps 17 miles to the west. Intervening clouds then blocked the view, but six aircraft were seen to hit the water before the scattered bombers and F4Fs emerged into sight a few minutes later. Likely the lookouts failed to sight the *kanbaku* that blew up.

After watching his first kill splash, Gibbs regained altitude and headed toward the task force. En route he encountered a lone bomber and charged in from below. Dismayingly, only one of his six Brownings would fire, but he succeeded anyway in winging the Japanese. The *kanbaku* eluded Gibbs by disappearing into a cloud. In the fight Gibbs expended all of the ammunition for his one functioning weapon; so he was out of action. Woollen and Barnes evidently had to withdraw from the action in a less fortunate manner, as they ran into Shigematsu's Zeros. That skirmish was of short duration. Barnes reported damaging one Zero, but both F4Fs had to dive away. They were not pursued.

The 4th Division's trailing section, Mattson and Bass, had raced out along the 250-degree heading in a shallow climb trying to reach the bombers as far out as possible. Apparently the two overran them. One of the *Hiryū* Zeros welcomed Mattson to the battle by diving in from astern and taking him unaware. The first Mattson knew of the attacker's presence was the sight of pieces being shot out of his Grumman's right wing. Loosely trailing his section leader, Bass (one of the VF-3 rookies) surprised the Zero from behind and likely killed the pilot with his first few rounds. The Mitsubishi pitched into a spin and dived into the water. Evidently Shigematsu's escort had passed overhead, and one pilot could not resist jumping a supposedly lone Grumman. It turned out to be a fatal error, leaving only three Zeros in the air.

Mattson continued climbing toward the melee. Suddenly he confronted a lone dive bomber diving in to set up a head-on run on his fighter. Mattson lined up a proper opposite approach and shot back. As his bullets struck the bomber's cowling and engine, the enemy pilot dipped his nose into a steeper dive to flee the stream of tracers. To prevent jamming his guns through a quick pushover into negative G, Mattson rolled over on his back and came at the bomber from abeam. Looking the target over, he was startled to see the Japanese rearseat man facing forward, his cockpit canopy closed and the flexible 7.7-mm Lewis gun tucked away into its housing. Mattson walked his shells from cowling through cockpit, shattering the canopy and instantly killing both crewmen. Following through with his run, Mattson secured position on the bomber's tail until he realized the Type 99 was finished. Almost certainly the *kanbaku* was that of Lieut. Yamashita, *buntaichō* and leader of the 2nd *Chūtai*. He occupied the rear seat as observer/navigator, facing forward rather than to the rear as a gunner normally sat. His pilot was W.O. Nishihara Toshikatsu. Bass got a few licks against this aircraft as well, and afterward joined on Mattson to climb for altitude advantage, but the two located no further targets in the area.

It appears that eight *kanbaku* still toting bombs and perhaps two others without had survived the devastating interception of Brassfield's 4th Division plus Mc-Cuskey. Probably three of the armed dive bombers separately headed eastward toward the *Yorktown*, while five also with bombs (at least four from the 2nd *Chūtai*) regained some sort of formation. The five circled around to the southwest to approach the target from out of the sun. Shigematsu's Zeros after the brief fight with Woollen's and Mattson's sections, also headed toward the ships, probably seeking someone to escort. As for the seven VF-3 pilots, Woollen and Barnes flew at low level after escaping the Zeros and like McCuskey and Gibbs were out of ammunition, while Brassfield, Mattson, and Bass searched for more victims. Certainly they all had done their job!

Crommelin, 2nd Division leader, and Bain his wingman had remained somewhat closer to the task force, using the time to assure altitude advantage. Reaching about 18,000 feet, Bain spied a dogfight below and some distance further out. Crommelin, however, had flushed much closer game. He peeled off to attack. Startled by the disappearance of his leader, Bain turned to follow. Looking down, he saw six or seven thousand feet below a small formation of enemy dive bombers aimed directly at the ships. With Bain tucked in close behind, Crommelin pulled into a long high-side run on the bombers. In the process, the two Grummans picked up plenty of speed before they rolled out to fire. Before takeoff, Crommelin had told Bain to stay with him—a lesson learned after the frequent, unhealthy separations at Coral Sea. Thus on this pass, Bain mainly concentrated on Crommelin's movements instead of shooting. As the tracers zipped past, the *kanbaku* bobbed up and down but did not break formation. Well below their targets, the two VF-3 pilots recovered from the run and zoomed back up for a second try. In the next attack, Bain paid more attention to his marksmanship, but lost contact with Crommelin in the process. Neither pilot saw any bombers fall, so they submitted no claims. They stumbled on the formation of about five Type 99s that still retained their bombs and were intent on doing the *Yorktown* harm.

Bain zoomed up for altitude from which to make a third pass, but Crommelin ran into trouble in the form of Shigematsu and friends. All three Japanese of the Zero persuasion were more than eager to fight. Crommelin's dogfight was very much like the tussle he had experienced on 8 May, except this time he did not get shot down. He charged after one *Hiryū* Zero, poured lead into it, then scored a healthy burst into another Mitsubishi and claimed it. A third Japanese then jumped him and forced him to dive away. By this time Crommelin had run dry of ammunition. Dick Wright, another 2nd Division pilot, also became involved in this scrap. He tangled with a number of Zeros in a wild scramble and reported the destruction of one.

Roaring up from the south were the four Grummans of "Hank" Ford's VF-8 division, which at 20,000 feet enjoyed altitude supremacy over everyone else. Unfortunately it was more difficult to locate targets at that height. Magically, enemy planes appeared below, and Ford took his division into a long dive. He and his wingman, Ens. Morrill I. Cook, Jr., spotted a couple of Zeros disporting around 12,000 feet. At first, things went well for the two VF-8 pilots tasting their first combat experience. Ford put a strong burst into a Zero and claimed it when it spun away out of sight. Separating from his leader, Cook fired successively into two Zeros (or the same one) and thought he had finished both.

Neither VF-8 pilot was reluctant to dogfight with Zeros, and this led to trouble. Ford charged at one Mitsubishi head-on. The two antagonists traded shots, roared past each other, and began scissoring. To his dismay Ford quickly learned firsthand that all he had heard about the Zero's maneuverability was true. The Japanese easily beat him to the turns and worked his way onto the Grumman's tail. Fortunately help was close at hand. Fighting Three's Bain was in position just overhead and had witnessed the whole encounter. The Coral Sea combat veteran dropped swiftly onto the Zero's tail and closed in without being seen. One long burst from Bain's .50-calibers ripped into the target's vulnerable fuel tanks, and the resultant explosion tore the Mitsubishi apart. Bain saw no more Japanese in the area and joined up on a grateful Ford's wing. The air around them was distinctly unhealthy as five-inch shell bursts from the screening cruisers took after the two Grummans.

Ford's second section comprised Ens. George Formanek, Jr. and Ens. Stephen Groves. Instead of Zeros, the two ensigns went after dive bombers—the same little formation that had stood up to Crommelin and Bain. Formanek later reported tangling with nine dive bombers, but likely there were only five. By the time the two VF-8 pilots went in, the battle area had shifted much nearer to Task Force 17, generally within five miles of the *Yorktown*. Shipboard observers saw a dive bomber take damage and fall out of control, ultimately splashing inside the screen and ahead of the *Yorktown*. This phase of the air action remains obscure, but it appears Formanek and Groves shot down one dive bomber on their initial pass. "Cookie" Cook just after his initial tussle with Zeros happened to see a flaming F4F start down toward the water. Formanek later said that antiaircraft bursts did in his wingman.[10] Steve Groves, at any rate, failed to return from this fight. Appointed an aviation cadet in February 1941, Groves had his wings and ensign's stripe that September. He and Formanek later received credit for destroying two dive bombers.

One more aerial obstacle confronted the four survivors in the brave little formation of *Hiryū kanbaku*. Mehle, leading his four-plane division from Fighting Six, had orbited 15 miles northwest of the *Enterprise*. Repeatedly he asked for a vector, and finally Dow released him to aid Task Force 17. Racing northward, Mehle climbed to 12,000 feet en route. Almost over the *Yorktown* he spied the small formation of *kanbaku* deployed in a loose column perhaps 2,000 feet below him. They looked about ready to push over against the carrier. Mehle found himself with a beautiful setup for a high-opposite attack on the enemy leader, and from there he could rake the whole string from fore to aft. Quickly he motioned his four Grummans into line-astern and dived in. Reaching effective range, Mehle lined up his shot and pressed the trigger. Maddeningly, nothing happened desite the fact that he had properly charged his guns. The gunnery system had suffered an electrical failure. He could do nothing but sheer off to give the other three pilots a clear way to attack. Radioing orders for the division to close in, he rolled out to one side to try to fix his guns. Unfortunately the other three did not copy the transmission, and to add to their troubles, antiaircraft fire from the ships threatened to burn up their tails. Mehle's wingman, Howard Grimmell, followed him in his turn as did the second section, "Pappy" Provost and the rookie Jim Halford. Evidently they thought the XO had pulled off to avoid the intense antiaircraft bursts, as the VF-6 pilots had done in earlier battles. In any case, the *Hiryū* carrier bombers escaped unscathed from what might have been a devastating interception.[11]

With the departure of Mehle's Grummans the conflict resolved itself into fourteen men in seven carrier bombers facing the fire power of the *Yorktown*, two heavy cruisers, and five destroyers. The carrier's screening vessels deployed in an irregular circle (radius 1,500 to 2,000 yards) around her. Task Force 17 had observed the approach of the strike group initially on radar and after 1202 by eyesight. Previously the ships had steered 110 degrees while conducting flight operations, but at 1205 they came right to 145 degrees to head away from the oncoming aircraft. Screening ships attained 26 knots, while the *Yorktown* herself worked up to 30.5 knots—"Pretty good for a battered old lady!" At 1206, the *Astoria* astern of the carrier opened fire with her five-inchers on scattered targets some 9,000 yards off. These were F4Fs dogfighting Zeros. The *Astoria* counted three aircraft falling in flames (most likely Groves and two Zeros).

Beginning around 1209, the *Yorktown* lookouts sighted enemy dive bombers closing from astern and off her starboard quarter. High clouds and the sun behind them made the Japanese difficult to discern. Three widely separated dive bombers infiltrated from westward, while farther away, others approached from the southwest. The Japanese dispersed to attack from different bearings, making it extremely difficult for the ship gunnery directors to track targets for the five-inchers. Consequently, mainstays of the defense were the multitudes (for mid-1942) of light antiaircraft guns: 1.1-inch, 20-mm, and .50-caliber. They emitted torrents of ribbonlike tracers with shells deadly within only a few thousand yards.

The initial attack originated from astern of the *Yorktown* and comprised the three lone carrier bombers from the west. At 1210, an anonymous Japanese crew sent the following to the *Hiryū*:

> [Message] Number One. Am bombing enemy carrier. 0910.[12]

This apparently originated from the first *Hiryū* pilot to go in. The *Yorktown* lookouts at 1211 discerned a *kanbaku* diving in steeply from astern. Witnesses later remarked it looked as if this pilot had no intention of pulling out, that he was making every effort to place his bomb on target no matter how much antiaircraft fire he faced. He held his dive to the limit.

As the Type 99 plunged well below a thousand feet and neared the point of bomb release, concentrated fire from the 1.1-inchers clustered round the *Yorktown*'s island chopped the bomber into three large pieces, but the pilot had aimed his projectile true to the mark. His 242-kilogram bomb fell free of the wreckage, and despite tumbling end over end, it struck the *Yorktown* abaft the No. 2 elevator, not far from the No. 4 1.1-inch gun mount aft of the island. A high-explosive bomb (in Japanese terminology, "land bomb"), it detonated on contact and with great force emitted a large, bright reddish sheet of flame that shot more than 60 feet skyward. The blast swept across the aft 1.1-inch mounts and killed or incapacitated most of the crews. Through a jagged 11-foot hole blown in the flight deck, fragments penetrated to the hangar deck below, igniting a dangerous fire. The shattered *kanbaku* splashed in the wake close aboard the starboard quarter, the identities of its brave aviators to remain forever unknown.

Perhaps a minute afterward, the second Type 99 made its run from astern, diving in almost as steeply as the lead plane. This Japanese suffered the same fate—blown to pieces by gunfire at pointblank range. The bomb separated while the aircraft disintegrated, exploding on contact with the wake. Splinters peppered the *York-*

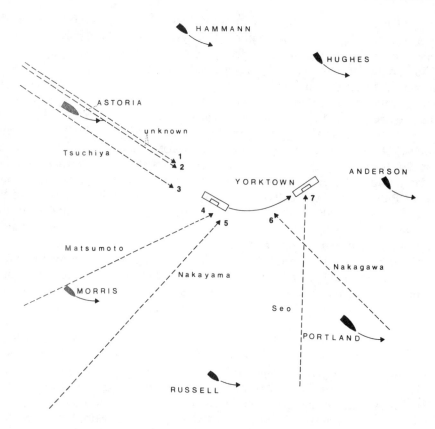

Dive bombing attack on the *Yorktown*, 1211–1214.

town's fantail and started some small fires aft. The bomber also plunged into the wake, its crew also to remain anonymous. Both airplanes had carried "land bombs" which were tactically intended as flak suppression by the first planes to attack, so it is probable they were 1st *Chūtai* aircraft. The identity of a third attacker is known: he was PO2c Tsuchiya Takayoshi, a wingman in the 3rd *Shōtai*, 1st *Chūtai*. Tsuchiya approached the carrier from off her port quarter and pushed over from around 10,000 feet. Holding his descent at a sharp 75-degree angle, he thought he secured a hit amidships with his 250-kilogram "ordinary" (semi-armor-piercing) bomb, but it struck just astern of the *Yorktown*. Tsuchiya escaped at low level, dodging shell bursts and tracers.

Penetrating the screen from the south was the second group of *Hiryū* carrier bombers, four 2nd *Chūtai* aircraft. They fanned out from the loose line-astern in which Mehle had seen them into a ragged line-abreast poised off the *Yorktown*'s starboard side. The *Yorktown* commenced a sharp turn away to port in addition to the radical twisting and turning Captain Buckmaster initiated as each dive bomber attacked. She glided through the water at just better than 30 knots, her screening cruisers and destroyers scrambling to keep station and pour fire onto the diving planes. Some of the *kanbaku* that approached from her starboard quarter or beam finally had to cross round her stern to dive in from her port side. The sketchy reports of the surviving Japanese pilots and American ship narratives give a tentative indication of the order in which the remnants of the 2nd *Chūtai* delivered their attacks on the *Yorktown*.

PO1c Matsumoto Sadao of the 1st *Shōtai* was apparently the first of the 2nd

A *Hiryū* carrier bomber (*circled*) diving toward the *Yorktown*. (NA 80-G-32310.)

Chūtai pilots to go in. Rolling in from 10,000 feet not long after Tsuchiya of the 1st *Chūtai*, Matsumoto started after the *Yorktown*'s starboard quarter, only to round her stern to come against her port quarter instead. Matsumoto prosecuted his dive at 60 degrees or more, trying to hold his aim as the carrier sped away at more than 30 knots. He thought his 242-kilogram bomb hit the target's stern, but it missed astern in her wake. Some American observers reported that the third and fourth dive bombers (Tsuchiya and Matsumoto) did not release bombs, but other saw the near-miss geysers in the wake. Both large splashes were interpreted as the airplanes hitting the water; on the contrary, Matsumoto (as did Tsuchiya) made good his withdrawal.

Following Matsumoto down and similarly crossing from starboard to port was the Type 99 flown by W.O. Nakazawa Iwao with Ens. (Special Service) Nakayama Shimematsu, the 2nd *Shōtai* leader, riding the rear seat as observer. Pilot Nakazawa pushed over from about 8,000 feet, endeavoring to keep his descent steeper than 60 degrees. At 1214, his 250-kilogram "ordinary" bomb penetrated the *Yorktown*'s flight deck amidships only ten feet out from the island. Angling down, it detonated with great force inside the stack uptakes deep in the hull. The blast severely damaged the fireroom uptakes for three boilers (crippling two of them), extinguished fires in the other three boilers, and filled all of the firerooms with thick, black smoke. Only one boiler could be kept in operation, and that temporarily. The *Yorktown*'s speed rapidly dwindled to six knots. She billowed intense black smoke from amidships, quickly losing headway and looking as if she had sustained critical, if not mortal, damage. The hit was a bomber pilot's dream. Nakayama and Nakazawa thought they hit the carrier abaft the island. Given the distractions of the moment, it was a pardonable error!

W.O. Nakagawa Shizuo, 3rd *Shōtai* leader, tried a new tack. He circled well forward of the target and dived in from about 7,500 feet, aiming for the *Yorktown*'s starboard bow. It was a wise move because the *kanbaku* came under considerably reduced antiaircraft fire. Nakagawa executed a high-speed, shallow glide-bombing run. At about 1215, his 250-kilogram semi-armor-piercing bomb hit squarely on

No. 1 elevator forward of the island. It exploded deep inside the ship and set a number of fires that forced, among other things, the flooding of a magazine. The forward aviation gasoline stowage was fortunately protected by CO_2 in the lines and in the dead spaces around the tanks. The *Lexington*'s sacrifice at Coral Sea had pointed to the vulnerability of the fuel systems. Not long after Nakagawa's attack, the seventh and final dive bomber pushed over from off the *Yorktown*'s starboard beam, coming in from 8,000 feet at about a 50-degree angle. The pilot was PO1c Seo Tetsuo of the 2nd *Shōtai*, and his bomb was a near miss close aboard the *Yorktown*'s starboard beam.

Of the seven *Hiryū* carrier bombers to attack the *Yorktown*, three secured direct hits, and two made damaging near misses. Especially impressive to the U.S. Navy were the courage and accuracy of the Japanese pilots. No doubt executed by elite pilots ("the varsity"), the dives were calm, unhurried, and deliberate, with total contempt for antiaircraft fire. American observers swore that they saw most of the Type 99s splash, but Tsuchiya, Matsumoto, Nakazawa, Nakagawa, and Seo individually pressed successful withdrawals at low level unmolested by fighters.

Some Yorktowners who would have liked to see the Japanese really close up (namely through gunsights) were the VF-3 pilots stranded on board by the enemy attack. They took refuge in their battle station, the fighter ready room in the island, but not all of them stayed there. The flight deck officer caught Leonard outside blasting away with his .45-caliber automatic pistol at the dive bombers and chased him in under cover. Particularly disconcerting was the way the *Yorktown* shook and shimmied when the bombs hit. It was not an experience any of the pilots wanted to repeat.

During the actual dive bombings, another *Hiryū kanbaku* maneuvered at low level just outside antiaircraft range of the screen. McCuskey, marking time while awaiting the go-ahead to land, spotted the lone Japanese circling at 500 feet. He carefully charged his guns with the hope they might still have some ammunition and drew up behind the bomber. To his amazement the enemy crew appeared oblivious to his presence. They tried no evasive maneuvers but remained riveted to the spectacle of the *Yorktown* under attack. To McCuskey's disgust, his guns would not fire. Twice he pulled back to work on them, but in vain. Noting some SBDs to the south, he flew over to them to entice one to return and shoot down the "preoccupied" bomber. None of the VB-3 pilots seemed interested, so Mc-Cuskey had to break off. He even contemplated the ramming tactics sketched out on 30 May by Thach, but he realized that if he tried chopping off the bomber's tail at this low altitude, he would never have time to bail out if he crippled his own plane. Besides, the *kanbaku* no longer lugged a bomb and could not harm the carrier. McCuskey thought the crew either photographed the attack or were directing it, so completely did they ignore his presence. Regretfully he had to abandon what he later realized could have been the easiest kill of his career.

Evidence exists to substantiate McCuskey's opinion that the strike commander was in that lone bomber. The *Hiryū* during the attack received a second message using Kobayashi's own call sign:

> Number Two: Fires break out on carrier. 0901 [sic].[13]

Kobayashi's first message (the contact report) and this communication did not get logged in the *Kidō Butai* message file until 1251 and 1252 respectively (local time; Tokyo time was 0951 and 0952 5 June). Kobayashi could not have seen the *Yorktown* damaged until at least 1211 with the first bomb hit. It appears the time given in his second message was garbled in reception—it could have been 0911. His possible presence fits neatly with McCuskey's antics vis-à-vis the oblivious dive bomber. Kobayashi could have lost his bomb because of damage in the melee, as happened to the aircraft that attacked Art Brassfield.

As to the fate of the lone bomber (flown by Kobayashi or not), it fell victim to a pair of VF-6 pilots, Provost and Halford. Splitting off from division leader Mehle in the confusion following the abortive interception, the two spotted a dive bomber flying at 1,000 feet not far from Task Force 17. In succession, the F4Fs executed one high-side pass, and their bullets dropped the Type 99 into the sea. At first they thought their kill was a bomber recovering from its dive on the *Yorktown*, but upon reflection, they later described it as a reconnaissance plane. Apparently Provost and Halford likewise noticed their target had behaved strangely.

In the wake of the attack, the two FDOs had great difficulty reorganizing the CAP. Fighters from all three carriers plus VB-3 dive bombers had scattered round Task Force 17. Some of the fighter pilots mistook Leslie's SBDs for Japanese, as the enemy torpedo planes had yet to put in their appearance. Not long after the last bomb fell on the *Yorktown*, Pederson warned of torpedo planes bearing 060 degrees. Some F4Fs went to investigate what turned out to be SBDs orbiting at 1,500 feet about eight miles south of Task Force 17. Bombing Three experienced tense moments when some VF-6 fighters, probably from Quady's division, dived in with guns blazing. The SBDs quickly took evasive maneuvers, and fortunately the CAP soon realized the error. About the same time, a VF-6 Wildcat jumped one of VT-6's TBDs limping back from the strike on the Japanese carriers. Mach. Stephen B. Smith was most relieved to see the Grumman sheer off before inflicting hits on his battered TBD. Smith had happened upon the *Yorktown* during her trouble and skirted Task Force 17 to the south when he encountered the unexpected opposition.

At 1218, Pederson called for aid from "Red Base." The *Yorktown*'s own fighters were low on ammunition. He had not established contact with Dow's earlier reinforcements, but those Grummans were low on bullets and juice as well. Starkes and Smith, the two strong-willed wingmen from O'Neill's VF-8 division, arrived overhead just as the Japanese withdrew. They decided to circle Task Force 17 and await further orders. The *Hornet* completed landing her SBDs at 1209 and respotted the flight deck for launch. Around 1225, Harwood led five F4Fs aloft on CAP, and Dow sent them to support the *Yorktown*. The *Hornet* then began landing three fighters from her CAP. Meanwhile, the *Enterprise* kept her flight deck open for recovery operations. Not only Smith's TBD, but three other survivors from Torpedo Six anxiously waited to land. "The Big E" brought them on board around 1230, then readied eight Grummans under Hoyle and Rawie as relief CAP. They took off at 1235, leaving the deck free for Bombing Three's SBDs. Ultimately fifteen came on board. Max Leslie and a wingman ended up ditching near Task Force 17.

The last aircraft to return from the strike that doomed three Japanese carriers was the lonesome Grumman flown by Dan Sheedy of Fighting Three. Wounded painfully in ankle and shoulder, Sheedy had reached the area where he had hoped to find the friendly *Yorktown*, but he saw nothing but empty ocean. Following doctrine, he started a square search. On the second leg, two F4Fs from the CAP buzzed him to look him over. He knew now he was close to home. Soon ships appeared on the horizon, including a big carrier with a reassuringly large island structure. She was the *Hornet* and open for business, in the process of taking on board three VF-8 fighters. It was none too soon, as Sheedy's Wildcat was nearly out of fuel.

The *Hornet*'s flight deck aft was clear, as she had just landed three CAP fighters.

At 1229, the wounded Sheedy made his approach, but as he was about to touch down, F-24 skidded to the right. The impact of landing collapsed the damaged right gear, and when the wingtip slapped the deck, all six of the F4F's Brownings cut loose in automatic fire. It was a tragic, devastating two-second burst. The Grumman's tail hook snagged the wire and slewed the aircraft to a stop. Bullets from the wing guns had ripped through the rear of the island structure into spectators watching the landing, then penetrated a one-inch, specially hardened armor plate to wreak havoc in Battle II. The toll was five killed (including Lieut. Royal R. Ingersoll, son of Admiral Royal E. Ingersoll commanding the Atlantic Fleet) and twenty wounded. One VF-8 pilot who had landed just ahead of Sheedy narrowly missed the full effect of the burst. Ens. Henry A. Carey's F4F had cleared the barriers and taxied forward, an ordnanceman up on the wing inquiring of Carey whether he needed ammunition. Suddenly tracers zipped past. Carey heard the firing and ducked beneath the doubtful protection of his armored seatback. He and the ordnanceman were unharmed, but had Sheedy's right gear not failed, Carey's F4F would have taken most of the bullets.[14]

The flight deck crew swarmed rapidly over F-24, helping the wounded pilot out of the cockpit, and assessing the battered Grumman as unserviceable. At the direction of the air officer, they pushed it over the side. Sheedy went to sickbay to have his wounds treated, profoundly remorseful over the incident. There was some concern over whether in his excitement he might have left his gun switches on, but no one was certain what caused the mishap. Japanese bullets had riddled the Grumman, possibly damaging the main switch terminal which armed the machine guns. It is a truism of war that men will die from operational accidents as surely as they will be killed in battle.

Brassfield of Fighting Three happened to join up with some VB-3 dive bombers south of Task Force 17, then swung back toward the *Yorktown*. At 1232, he radioed in, a familiar call, and a minute later Pederson put him to work. The FDO told him to check out a bogey bearing 235 degrees (M.) about 10 to 15 miles out. Brassfield headed to the southwest at 2,000 feet. Eight miles out, he discerned the bogey and recognized it as an enemy dive bomber. Even more interesting, the Japanese circled as if he were going to strafe something on the water. That something proved to be a ditched TBD. This in no little measure spurred Brassfield to the attack. His opponent saw him coming and hightailed it west. Accelerating to 240 knots, the F4F swiftly overtook its quarry. Pederson cautioned him not to pursue too far, but Brassfield really wanted this kill. Its rear gunner anxiously opened fire while the fighter was still over a thousand yards away. At 800 yards, Brassfield squeezed off a ranging burst, closed to 600, then poured a stream of bullets into the *kanbaku* as he roared in. The Aichi started smoking, fell away into a slow turn to the left, and at 1239 smacked the water. It was Brassfield's fourth victory of that flight and the thirteenth dive bomber to go down.

The TBD pilot saved by Brassfield was Bill Esders of Torpedo Three. Using his Zed Baker, Esders had found his way back toward Task Force 17. His fuel gauge read empty, but the battered TBD droned on. He was anxious to secure medical treatment for his badly wounded rear gunner, Robert Brazier. Drawing close to his goal, Esders watched the eighteen enemy dive bombers pass overhead. At 1203, the Devastator's engine finally gave in to fuel starvation, and Esders skillfully ditched about ten miles west of the *Yorktown*. Surprisingly the TBD remained afloat. Inflating the liferaft, Esders gently eased his gunner into it. Not long afterward, Brazier died. Leslie cruising overhead spotted the drifting TBD and dropped float lights to attract attention to the area. Later a Japanese dive bomber made an appearance. Esders watched the enemy plane pass behind the drifting TBD, then turn in his direction as if to make a strafing run. He took no chances and dived under the TBD's wing. Greeting him when he came up for air was the pleasant sight of an F4F emerging from the clouds to chase the Japanese away. Less than an hour later, the destroyer *Hammann* from Task Force 17 rescued Esders unharmed. No one actually saw the Japanese strafe. More likely, the dive bomber crew was curious about the floating aircraft and investigated to see whether it might have been one of theirs. They paid the full price for their curiosity. The only other TBD from Torpedo Three to survive the strike was that flown by Harry Corl and the wounded Lloyd Childers. They came upon the *Yorktown* after she had taken the bomb hits, then swung south to try to reach Task Force 16. What fuel he had gave out; so Corl put the riddled bird into the water. The destroyer *Monaghan* from Spruance's screen soon recovered both men.

Pederson had great difficulty sorting out whose fighters operated over Task Force 17. At 1252 he requested information on the Blue patrol. A minute later Carl Starkes announced he was at 18,000 feet, and Bruce Harwood acknowledged he flew at 12,000. Pederson evidently never copied any of Harwood's messages or knew who he was, but thought Starkes led a full division. Consequently for the next hour he repeatedly vectored Starkes in search of bogeys, and the two VF-8 wingmen Starkes and Smith dutifully carried out orders despite dwindling fuel. At 1253 after her flight deck had been cleared, the *Hornet* launched three additional F4Fs under Jock Sutherland to reinforce Task Force 16's CAP.

Having taken care of the CAP, or so they thought, the two FDOs arranged for the Grummans low on fuel or ammunition to set down on flight decks able to receive them. At 1258, all VF-3 pilots received orders to "pancake" on Blue base (the *Hornet*), but half of them had independently decided that the *Enterprise* was more hospitable. From 1251 to 1304, Brassfield, Gibbs, Mattson, Woollen, McCuskey, and Wright came on board "The Big E," while Crommelin, Bain, Bass, Markham, Bright, and Bill Barnes selected the *Hornet*. Warren Ford and the two surviving pilots of his VF-8 division also took the opportunity presented by the *Hornet*'s open flight deck to descend for fuel and bullets. The *Hornet* accommodated the nine F4Fs between 1316 and 1329. The last to land was VF-3's Barnes, and his guns also discharged automatically, but the bullets zipped over the *Hornet*'s port side without harming anyone.

Ens. Frederick Mears, a back-up pilot in the *Hornet*'s ill-fated Torpedo Eight had remained behind in reserve during the big strike because of lack of aircraft. He narrowly missed getting hit when Sheedy crashed on board. In his book *Carrier Combat*, Mears left a vivid description of the fighter pilots after they landed back on board the *Hornet*. Cdr. Soucek, the air officer, had gone all out to provide the returning pilots with good food and drink, even opening the "admiral's pantry" one deck below the ready rooms:

> The returning pilots crowded into their ready rooms or the pantry gulping lemonade out of paper cups, mechanically stuffing sandwiches into their mouths, and at the same time yammering and gesticulating to each other about their individual adventures. Their hair, when they took off their helmets, was matted with perspiration. Their faces were often dirty, and their cotton flying suits were streaked with sweat. But they were having a good time. They had fought and won and were still alive, and they felt wonderful. All they wanted to do was go right out and fight again.
>
> Many times that day I saw a pilot, with a cup of lemonade in one hand, two sandwiches in the other, and one side of his mouth packed with bread, trying to describe some aerial maneuver, using his hands as opposing planes. It was ridiculous

Claims, 1st Attack on the *Yorktown*

	Dive Bombers		Fighters	
	Conf.	Probable or damaged	Conf.	Probable or damaged
(a) Fighting Three				
4th Division				
Lieut. (jg) A. J. Brassfield	4	2	—	—
Lieut. (jg) E. D. Mattson	1	—	—	—
Lieut. (jg) W. S. Woollen	1	1	—	—
Lieut. (jg) W. W. Barnes	1	2	—	1
Ens. H. B. Gibbs	2	—	—	—
Ens. H. A. Bass	1*	—	—	1**
2nd Division				
Lieut. (jg) R. G. Crommelin	—	—	1	1
Lieut. (jg) E. S. McCuskey	3	3	—	—
Ens. R. L. Wright	—	—	1	—
Ens. J. B. Bain	—	—	1	—
	13*	8	3	3
(b) Fighting Six				
Ens. T. C. Provost	½	—	—	—
Ens. J. A. Halford	½	—	—	—
	1	—	—	—
(c) Fighting Eight				
Lieut. W. W. Ford	—	—	1	—
Ens. G. Formanek	1	—	—	—
Ens. S. W. Groves (MIA)	1	—	—	—
Ens. M. I. Cook	—	—	2	—
	2	—	3	—

*Logged incorrectly as a dive bomber, but said to be a fighter.
**Said to be a VB.

but for [Ens. Robert] Divine and me it was fun to watch because we couldn't help but catch some of their enthusiasm.[15]

Total American fighter claims for the defense of the *Yorktown* amounted to sixteen dive bombers and six Zeros shot down, for the loss of one F4F from Fighting Eight (Ens. Groves, missing in action) (see table). It appears the fighters did shoot down eleven dive bombers and three Zero fighters, while antiaircraft guns accounted for two more dive bombers.

By 1330 that eventful day, the American striking force was trying to recover from the Japanese counterblow that had damaged the *Yorktown*. Total plane losses to that point (not counting aircraft that returned too damaged to fly again) amounted to a staggering sixty-eight planes: twelve fighters, nineteen dive bombers, and thirty-seven torpedo planes. The *Yorktown* drifted broadside to the wind, while repair crews worked frantically to restore power. Fletcher had at 1323 shifted his flag to the heavy cruiser *Astoria*. Spruance sent the heavy cruisers *Pensacola* and *Vincennes* and two destroyers (the *Balch* and the *Benham*). The *Yorktown* could not as yet conduct flight operations. Task Force 17's CAP comprised seven borrowed VF-8 fighters. On board the *Enterprise*, Spruance awaited definite word on the location of additional enemy carriers before he would consent to commit his shattered air groups to a second strike. The Japanese, however, already knew where their adversaries could be found.

The *Yorktown* smoking and stopped because of bomb damage; note the VF-3 F4F-4s spotted forward on her flight deck. (NA 80-G-32300.)

The Hiryū *Tries Again*

With the departure of the first wave, Rear Admiral Yamaguchi and Captain Kaku had labored on board the *Hiryū* to analyze the situation. At 1110, Yamaguchi signaled by blinker to Rear Admiral Abe on board the *Tone* the request that he maintain contact with the enemy carrier force by means of his cruiser and battleship floatplanes. The *Chikuma* No. 5 plane had done sterling service guiding the first strike to the target. However, it could not stay there indefinitely. Yamaguchi had to have up-to-the-minute reports on what the Americans were doing. Below deck, *Hiryū* mechanics swarmed over the nine carrier attack planes capable of making the second strike, while aloft CAP Zeros low on fuel entered the recovery pattern in hopes of landing. Joining them at 1130 was a stray *Akagi* carrier attack plane originally launched at 1015 on search. The *Hiryū* particularly welcomed the newcomer as a bird that could lug a torpedo to the target.

Miles south of the *Hiryū*, the three shattered hulks *Akagi*, *Kaga*, and *Sōryū* drifted while in a losing battle, their crews struggled to stem the flames. Nagumo transferred his flag to the light cruiser *Nagara*. Studying search reports, he learned the enemy striking force lay only 90 miles east. Roused by his staff, Nagumo determined to bring the enemy to surface battle with his warships. At 1156, he ordered his battleships, cruisers, and most of the destroyers to assemble and go after the Americans. The *Nagara* headed northeast to join forces with the ships escorting the *Hiryū*. Excitement ran high at the contemplation of wreaking revenge on the Americans with "Long Lance" torpedoes and big guns.

On board the *Hiryū*, the second wave was ready to go at 1245, but Yamaguchi delayed the launch until he could learn more about the enemy's situation. Reports from Kobayashi's crews had just begun to filter in. The *Hiryū*'s second strike comprised sixteen aircraft: ten torpedo-armed carrier attack planes and six escorting fighters. Personally leading the carrier attack planes was the *Hiryū* Air Group commander, *hikōtaichō* Tomonaga. In the dawn Midway attack, the *Hiryū* Carrier Attack Unit had taken grievous losses, three shot down and one ditched, four others unserviceable from battle damage. Both unit *buntaichō* were casualties, Lieut. Kikuchi Rokurō killed and Lieut. Kadano Hiroharu badly wounded. Thus for this decisive action, the unit had only eight *kankō* operational. Joining them

Lieut. Tomonaga Jōichi, *Hiryū* Air Group
commander. (NH 81559.)

and the group commander's plane was the *Akagi* orphan under W.O. Nishimori
Susumu. Because only two command officers were available to lead the *kankō*,
Tomonaga divided the ten into two *chūtai*, each of five planes (see roster). To-
monaga led the 1st *Chūtai* himself and gave the 2nd *Chūtai* to Lieut. Hashimoto
Toshio, an assistant air officer on board the *Hiryū* who normally flew as Tomonaga's
navigator/observer in the middle seat of his big Nakajima carrier attack plane.

During the Midway raid, a marine fighter had shot up Tomonaga's aircraft,

Organization of the *Hiryū* Carrier Attack Unit, 4 June 1942 Attack on the *Yorktown*

Plane	Pilot	Observer/Navigator	Radioman/Gunner
1st *Chūtai*			
1st *Shōtai*			
#No. 1	Lieut. Tomonaga Jōichi (H)	Ens.* Akamatsu Saku	PO1c Murai Sadamu
#No. 2	PO1c Ishii Zenkichi	PO1c Kobayashi Masamatsu	PO3c Shimada Naoshi
#No. 3	PO1c Sugimoto Hachirō	PO1c Hijikuro Sadami	PO3c Taniguchi Kazuya
2nd *Shōtai*			
#No. 1	W.O. Ōbayashi Yukio	PO1c Kudō Hiromi	PO1c Tamura Mitsuru
#No. 2	Sea1c Suzuki Takeshi	PO1c Saitō Kiyotori	PO2c Suzuki Mutsuo
2nd *Chūtai*			
1st *Shōtai*			
No. 1	PO1c Takahashi Toshio	Lieut. Hashimoto Toshio	PO3c Koyama Tomio
No. 2	PO2c Yanagimoto Takurō	PO1c Ēto Chikashi	PO2c Kasai Kiyoshi
No. 3	PO3c Nagayama Yoshimitsu	PO1c Nakamura Toyohirō	Sea1c Ōbama Haruo
2nd *Shōtai*			
†No. 1	W.O. Suzuki Shigeo	W.O. Nishimori Susumu	PO1c Horii Takayuki
No. 2	Sea1c Nakao Harumi	PO1c Maruyama Taisuke	Sea1c Hamada Giichi

(H) *hikōtaichō*.
#Failed to return.
*Special Service [promoted from enlisted rating].
†*Akagi* aircraft.

puncturing the left wing tank which caught fire. Fortunately for the crew, the slipstream had swiftly extinguished the blaze. After its return, mechanics checked the plane and patched the holes. Just prior to launch, however, when they fueled BI-310, they discovered the metal tank still leaked. There was no time to effect repairs. The quiet Tomonaga cheerfully declined the earnest pleas of his pilots to exchange aircraft with one of them. He joked that the Yankees were only 90 miles away. He could fight and return with the fuel he had. He fully intended to ride BI-310 all the way.[16]

The *Hiryū*'s fighter leader, Lieut. Mori, took charge of the escort. A 1936 Eta Jima graduate, Mori had qualified in March 1939 as a naval aviator and saw combat in China with the 12th Combined Air Group. He was posted in April 1942 to the *Hiryū* after serving as unit commander on board the light carrier *Zuihō*. The morning of 4 June he had survived a series of wild air battles on combat air patrol, including the epic fight with Jimmy Thach. He would soon renew his acquaintance with Fighting Three. His unit took over three Zeros from the 6th Air Group, carried as cargo until they could transfer to the air base to be established on Midway after its capture by the Japanese. That event now would never come to pass. The three fighters replaced *Hiryū* Zeros crippled by battle damage.

Mori's fighter striking force comprised four Zeros flown by *Hiryū* pilots and two from the *Kaga* Fighter Unit, organized as:

	1st *Shōtai*
No. 1	Lieut. Mori Shigeru (B)
No. 2	PO2c Yamamoto Tōru
	2nd *Shōtai*
No. 1	W.O. Minegishi Yoshijirō
No. 2	PO2c Kotani Kenji
	3rd *Shōtai* (*Kaga* Fighter Unit)
No. 1	PO1c Yamamoto Akira
No. 2	PO3c Bandō Makoto

Minegishi had landed on board at 1230 after a shootout with the *Enterprise* SBDs on the *Hiryū*'s first strike. The tough China veteran (who had enlisted in his mid teens in 1931 and earned his wings in 1935) commandeered another Zero and joined the strike. To lead the 3rd *Shōtai*, Mori could not have found a better pilot than the *Kaga*'s Yamamoto Akira. Originally a rating who had qualified for the brutally demanding enlisted flight program, Yamamoto became a flyer in July 1934 and served on board the carrier *Hōshō* the next year. He flew two tours in China, the first (in 1937–38) from the flattop *Ryūjō* and the second (1939–40) along with Mori in the 12th Combined Air Group. He was superbly representative of the high caliber of Japanese carrier pilots early in the war. That morning he and wingman Bandō Makoto had scrambled from the *Kaga* at 1000 during VT-6's attack. The two tangled with a pair of torpedo planes and nine dive bombers, claiming one TBD and four SBDs. Their own flight deck engulfed in flames, they flew over to the *Hiryū*. Now they were going on a mission of the highest importance.

Yamaguchi eagerly awaited news of the first attack. At 1245, one of the *kanbaku* crews transmitted to the *Hiryū*:

> Number One. Enemy carrier is burning. I see no friendly planes in range of visibility. I am homing. 0945 [5 June, Tokyo time].[17]

Five minutes later the experimental Type 2 carrier bomber (the *Sōryū*'s plane No.

PO1c Yamamoto Akira. (Via Dr. Izawa
Yasuho.)

201) returned from its search and dropped a message onto the *Hiryū*'s flight deck.
Yamaguchi thereby learned that its crew had spotted no fewer than three enemy
carriers, identified as the *Yorktown, Enterprise*, and *Hornet*! As confirmation, at
1300 a report from Destroyer Division Four detailed the interrogation of a bailed-
out VT-3 pilot. The prisoner revealed that the American carrier force indeed
comprised the three above-mentioned warships, with the *Yorktown* operating separately. Yamaguchi gathered the flight leaders and told them of the situation. He
instructed Tomonaga to hunt one of the two undamaged American carriers. As he
did with the first strike, the charismatic admiral descended to the flight deck to
shake hands with the aircrews and wish them good fortune.

Around 1315 as the *Hiryū* completed preparations for launch, remnants of the
first strike appeared in the skies overhead. One of the carrier bombers buzzed the
flight deck and dropped a message, informing Yamaguchi that the attack group at
1240 had left an enemy force of five heavy cruisers and one carrier (burning fiercely)
bearing 080 degrees, distance 90 miles from the *Kidō Butai*. Inadvertently Hashimoto rather than Tomonaga got this information, but the *hikōtaichō* would have
little trouble locating the Americans. Led by the Zeros, Tomonaga's small strike
force took off, formed up, and at 1331 departed, taking with them the fervent good
wishes of everyone on board the *Hiryū*. When they left, the actual distance between
the *Hiryū* and Task Force 16 was 112 miles, and that to Task Force 17 only 83
miles.

With the *Hiryū*'s flight deck free, the battered survivors of the first raid came
on board. Only five carrier bombers and one fighter returned; thirteen dive bombers
and three fighters were missing, and another Zero had ditched earlier. Debriefing
the crews revealed only "fragmentary accounts which did not present a very coherent picture,"[18] understandable given what they had endured. The air staff decided perhaps six *kanbaku* had dropped bombs, probably with several hits on an

Enterprise-type carrier that they left burning out of control. The bomber crews claimed the destruction of two enemy Grummans and damage to a third. Shigematsu was the only fighter pilot to survive combat over the enemy carrier.[19] He thought his four Zeros downed five Grummans with two more as probables. The Americans later offered unwitting tribute to the four *Hiryū* fighter pilots by estimating the first strike comprised *eighteen* Zeros escorting the dive bombers.

The CAP Regroups

On board the *Enterprise*, the *Yorktown* fighter pilots wolfed down a hasty lunch, eager to be off again. Quick-talking Scott McCuskey wangled a division of VF-6 pilots and received orders to take over CAP duties over Task Force 17. Flying on his wing was Ens. Melvin C. Roach, while the second section comprised an NAP veteran of Fighting Two, Howard Packard, with Ens. Mortimer V. Kleinmann, Jr. on his wing. McCuskey's ad hoc division took off around 1340. Departing a few minutes later with the same orders were Bill Woollen and Harry Gibbs. Art Brassfield had wanted desperately to go along, but he discovered to his chagrin that the *Enterprise's* plane handlers had struck his Grumman below deck. Meanwhile, "The Big E's" air department respotted the flight deck in order to recover fighters getting low on fuel. At 1350, the carrier landed the eight F4Fs of Mehle and Quady.

McCuskey's troops, followed by Woollen's section, proceeded toward the *Yorktown* and at 1356 assumed the CAP under Pete Pederson's direction. He told them to orbit at 10,000 feet, then released his borrowed *Hornet* fighters. For Carl Starkes, it was none too soon. He and wingman Jim Smith flew on little more than fumes. Bruce Harwood, also from Fighting Eight, had taken five F4Fs over to Task Force 17, arriving before 1300, but Pederson had never made contact and did not know he was there. Once Harwood knew other fighters were on station, he returned to Task Force 16. Beginning at 1409, the *Hornet* recovered Lieut. O'Neill and Lieut. (jg) French. About ten minutes later, their erstwhile wingmen Starkes and Smith moved into the landing circle, eager to come on board. Starkes landed with a bare three gallons of gasoline wetting his tanks, but Smith did not have that much. On his first try, Smith took a waveoff from the *Hornet's* LSO. He paralleled her course before turning for the downwind leg of another approach; but his hungry engine sputtered and died, so at 1422 Smith made an unexpected water landing about 400 yards ahead of the *Hornet*. Scrambling out of his sinking airplane, Smith swam to safety. Four minutes later, the destroyer *Conyngham* brought him on board. About the same time, an *Enterprise* fighter pilot avoided a similar drenching. Bill Holt of Rawie's division had to return to "The Big E" because of engine trouble.

While most of the CAP regrouped, one VF-6 section executed a spectacular interception. Around 1340, Ham Dow detected on radar a bogey bearing 180 degrees, distance 45 miles from the *Enterprise*. That range indicated the contact had to be at a relatively high altitude. Dow alerted section "Red 26" (Buster Hoyle and Mach. William H. Warden). Hoyle's radio was out, but Warden copied the orders and took the lead according to doctrine. He led Hoyle south at 1344, climbing from 11,000 to 14,500 feet on the way. About twenty minutes later, they eyeballed their quarry—a twin-float seaplane cruising perhaps a mile to the west and 200 feet below the two Grummans. It was the *Chikuma* No. 5 plane flown by Petty Officer Hara. The aircraft had cunningly scouted the American carriers for three and one-half hours, a great service to the Japanese, but its luck had finally run out.

Hara swung round to confront the two Grummans and tried to scissor. In the lead, Warden made the first run head-on and directed his bullets into the target's engine. He saw no return fire. Hoyle roared into a near-opposite attack from about 20 degrees off the floatplane's nose. Loosing a ranging burst at 300 yards, he bored in to 100 yards for serious shooting. As Hoyle flashed past, the target had spouted flames and started for the water, the rear gunner managing to bail out. Attached to his parachute harness was a small uninflated liferaft, which a fascinated Hoyle thought was a good idea. The ambush took place at 1409 about 50 miles south of Task Force 16—another remarkable example of the pinpoint interception of solitary targets that the fleet's radar and CAP could execute.[20]

Between 1300 and 1350, chatter on the fighter radio net hinted that the Blue patrol (of the *Hornet*) was low on fuel. At 1350, an eavesdropping Japanese tried to cash in on his knowledge of English and fighter direction vocabulary. With good English pronunciation, he announced, "All Blue patrols return for juice."[21] Essentially this ordered all VF-8 fighters to land back on board for fuel. The idea of an interloper transmitting on Dow's fighter circuit made his hair stand on end! Incensed that the enemy would try such an artful bit of chicanery, Dow quickly piped up, cautioning his CAP: "The bastards are using deception. Beware!"[22] Apparently the enemy made no further attempts to subvert radio traffic on the fighter net. The F4F pilots aloft knew the voices of their two FDOs, and if that failed, there was always recourse to profanity, something no ordinary Japanese linguist could imitate successfully! Still, the incident underscored the need for VHF radios so that the FDOs and pilots could communicate confident of their privacy.

Effectively trapped on board the *Yorktown* while she drifted without propulsion were Jimmy Thach and several of his pilots. Within the ship's vitals, repair crews labored prodigiously to restore the firerooms to operation, while up on the flight deck, carpenter's mates patched the large hole blown in the deck timbers and cleared away debris. Hoping to get some fighters aloft where they could do some good in the event of another Japanese attack, Thach arranged with the captain and air officer for the launch of his F4Fs as soon as the flattop could put sufficient wind over the flight deck. Thach told Arnold he would take aloft any Grumman retaining at least 30 gallons of gas—enough to do a little flying and fighting if need be. Plane handlers had struck Tom Cheek's smashed-up F-16 into the hangar and replaced it with the squadron's spare, F-1. Leonard scheduled Thach for F-1, because the skipper's own Grumman (F-23) had been shot up on that morning's escort of Torpedo Three. Likewise Leonard checked the other eight F4Fs on deck and found all but Brainard Macomber's F-6 ready to go. Macomber was anxious to fly, but Leonard judged F-6 too riddled to take the risk. The air department degassed the two damaged Grummans and secured them aft of the island. This gave Thach eight operational F4Fs which Arnold ordered to be spotted in the center of the flight deck well aft of the island. The VF-3 pilots walked forward along the deck to note the hasty repairs they would have to skirt during a takeoff run.

By 1400 things began looking much encouraging to the men on board the *Yorktown*. Firerooms previously choked by smoke were cleared and readied for operation. As the boilers came back on the main propulsion steam lines, the carrier started maneuvering under her own power. Up the signal halyards were hoisted flags proclaiming "My speed five." The sight of the gallant *Yorktown* steaming under her own power brought cheers from the rest of Task Force 17. In honor of the event, Captain Buckmaster broke a fresh huge American battle ensign. In the next thirty minutes, the *Yorktown*'s speed built up to 19 knots. It looked as if the old lady would again be able to get on with the battle.

On the flight deck, the VF-3 pilots were "downright elated"[23] to sense the ship's movement through the water and feel the freshening breeze pouring down the deck. They manned their aircraft spotted in the following order:

BuNo.	Side No.	Pilot
5174	F-1	Lt. Cdr. John S. Thach, USN
5049	F-20	Ens. Robert A. M. Dibb, A-V(N)
5244	F-13	Lieut. (jg) William N. Leonard, USN
5147	F-12	Ens. John P. Adams, A-V(N)
5142	F-17	Mach. Doyle C. Barnes, USN
5152	F-18	Ens. Milton Tootle, Jr., A-V(N)
5245	F-14	Lieut. (jg) Walter A. Haas, A-V(N)
5080	F-7	Ens. George A. Hopper, Jr., A-V(N)

The spare F4F, Thach's F-1, had already been fueled in the hangar. Arnold directed the remaining Grummans to be fueled now that the risk of fire had abated. The fueling detail began pumping gasoline into Ram Dibb's Grumman in the second spot. The fighters only awaited their drink of fuel and a little more wind, and they would be airborne.

While the *Yorktown* returned to life, the Japanese diligently searched for an undamaged American carrier—and she began to look the part. At 1427 the cruiser *Pensacola*, one of the reinforcements sent to Task Force 17 by Spruance, detected on radar unidentified aircraft bearing 340 degrees, distance 45 miles. She relayed continuous reports to Pederson on board the *Yorktown*. When first alerted, Pederson had six Grummans on CAP overhead, organized as follows:

BuNo.		McCuskey's division	
5153	(3-)F-21	Lieut. (jg) E. Scott McCuskey, A-V(N)	(VF-3)
5222	(6-)F-27	Ens. Melvin C. Roach, A-V(N)	(VF-6)
5075	(6-)F-20	Howard S. Packard, AP1c (NAP), USN	(VF-6)
5236	(6-)F-25	Ens. Mortimer V. Kleinmann, Jr., A-V(N)	(VF-6)
		Woollen's section	
5170	(3-)F-2	Lieut. (jg) William S. Woollen, A-V(N)	(VF-3)
5151	(3-)F-8	Ens. Harry B. Gibbs, A-V(N)	(VF-3)

On the basis of the *Pensacola*'s warning, Pederson at 1429 ordered McCuskey's division to "arrow" because he thought he was dealing with *Enterprise* pilots. McCuskey headed out swiftly at 10,000 feet. He expected to encounter dive bombers, as did the analysts on board ship because the contact was made so far out. Shortly after 1430, the carrier's own radar picked up the bogeys at 33 miles. At 1431, Pederson told Woollen's section to "vector" 340 degrees (M.), distance 20 miles, and seek a large group of bogeys. Woollen and Gibbs charged out at 7,000 feet.

Pederson despatched all the Grummans he had aloft, then flashed a request to Red Base for reinforcements. The two task forces had drawn nearly 40 miles apart, with Task Force 17 west of Spruance's vessels. Any assistance from Task Force 16 fighters would have to get cracking in order to make it on time. In the preceding hour, the *Enterprise* and the *Hornet* had recovered fighters and were in the process of respotting flight decks for the launch of dive bombers. At 1430, the CAP over Task Force 16 comprised the following:

(a) Fighting Six

          Hoyle's division
F-26   Lieut. (jg) Rhonald J. Hoyle, USN
F-12   Mach. William H. Warden, USN
F-23   Rad. Elec. Edward H. Bayers, USN
F-24   Mach. Beverly W. Reid, USN

          Rawie's division
F-21   Lieut. (jg) W. E. Rawie, USN
F-5   Ens. Ralph M. Rich, A-V(N)
F-6   Ens. Wayne C. Presley, A-V(N)

(b) Fighting Eight
Five F4Fs under Lieut. Bruce L. Harwood, USN
Three F4Fs under Lieut. (jg) John F. Sutherland, A-V(N)

On board the two carriers rested an additional thirty F4Fs, but neither vessel would have her deck ready to launch fighters for another twenty minutes. That would be a fatal delay for the *Yorktown*.

Dow alerted Rawie and Bayers leading five F4Fs from Fighting Six and ordered them to arrow 280 degrees, distance 30 miles. Hoyle's section had to remain behind because the two F4Fs had just returned from the long and energetic intercept to the south and needed to conserve fuel. Bayers went over at 10,000 feet, but Rawie's truncated division began climbing during the flight west. He thought he heard orders to climb to 24,000 feet, but it must have been a garbled transmission. At 1437, Dow told Jock Sutherland of Fighting Eight to take his three fighters along a 300-degree arrow out 30 miles. Sutherland held his altitude above 18,000 feet. Dow at 1439 amplified his orders, telling all of the fighters previously arrowed to press on another 10 to 15 miles from their present positions. Having sent eight Grummans, he retained a reserve of seven over Task Force 16.

Approach to the Target

After departing at 1331 from the *Hiryū*, Tomonaga took his small strike force up to 4,000 meters (13,500 feet) for the flight to the American carriers. About 1430, Hashimoto's sharp eyes spotted an enemy task force to the left, distant about 35 miles. He told his pilot, PO1c Takahashi Toshio, to fly up alongside Tomonaga's aircraft so he could point out the Americans to the strike leader. Using hand signals, the two conferred swiftly, Tomonaga breaking radio silence at 1432 with the command, "Take positions in preparation for attack."[24] Swinging left, the *Hiryū* flyers soon discerned what looked like one carrier screened by five heavy cruisers and twelve destroyers. The Americans held course 090 degrees, speed 24 knots according to Hashimoto's estimate. He could see no indication that this carrier was hurt. He assumed, as Tomonaga must, that they had located a fresh target. So far so good.

From 4,000 meters, Tomonaga led his strike planes into a gentle glide to gain speed. They approached the task force from off its port quarter. Tomonaga decided to execute a standard split attack. His 1st *Chūtai* with five torpedo planes would attack the carrier's port side, while Hashimoto's five branched off to the left to sweep around ahead of the target and make their runs from off the target's starboard bow. Accompanied by Lieut. Mori's pair of *Hiryū* Zeros (1st *Shōtai*), Hashimoto took his 2nd *Chūtai* off to the left. Evidently W.O. Minegishi's 2nd *Shōtai* fighters remained with the 1st *Chūtai*, while the *Kaga shōtai* (Yamamoto Akira and Bandō) ranged in between.

McCuskey and the three VF-6 pilots with him flew out as ordered on a heading of 340 degrees. Intermittent cloud cover obscuring the skies below and above them, they kept an especially good lookout for dive bombers and Zero escorts above them. At about 1436, McCuskey copied the startling imperative from Pederson:

> Return buster, you have passed them![25]

"Buster" was fighter direction lingo for flying at maximum sustainable power. Dumbfounded, McCuskey and his pilots swung back around, certain that they had seen nothing above or below them. Actually the Japanese torpedo planes had started to let down just in time, and with their increasing speed they slipped into clouds below the four F4Fs. The enemy was now between McCuskey and the task force. Pederson told him to return, adding that the bogeys were on his left. McCuskey still had no idea what type of planes he was supposed to intercept and could not understand how any dive bombers could have gotten past him. Thus part of the CAP missed jumping the enemy some 20 to 25 miles out. Possibly the error stemmed from confusion over the terms "vector" (proceed on a magnetic heading) and "arrow" (where the pilot himself had to convert the magnetic heading to a true heading). Variation in the Midway region at that time was 10 degrees, allowing for a possible error of 20 degrees if converted wrongly. After this battle the use of "arrow" was abolished.

The Japanese could not evade the next pair of F4Fs to appear on the scene. Woollen's section had departed a few minutes later than McCuskey and took a slightly different heading a few thousand feet lower than he did. Ahead and below, Woollen at 1438 found the enemy torpedo planes already descending past 4,000 feet. Snapping a quick "Scarlet 23 Tally ho!"[26] over the radio, he led wingman Gibbs into a diving attack from 7,000 feet. A long, fast approach by the two Grummans caught the Japanese by surprise. Their quarry turned out to be the five *kankō* of Tomonaga's own 1st *Chūtai*. Singling out a trailing aircraft in the little formation, Woollen swung into a high-side run and soon set the torpedo plane spinning in flames toward the water. Leveling out from his run, Woollen found someone shooting at him. Gunfire ripped his left wing and among other things shot out the port oil cooler. Streaming dense smoke, his Pratt & Whitney engine overheated and began to seize. Woollen, now definitely hors de combat, swung back in the direction of Task Force 17, hoping to stretch his air time in order to ditch ahead of the ships. He never saw the Zero that overtook him in his dive and pumped F-2 full of holes. Not far from the task force, Woollen ditched successfully just after the torpedo attack and broke out his liferaft.

In the first fast dive on the torpedo planes, the speed he attained exhilarated Gibbs following his section leader. Likewise, he rolled out to shoot at one of the Nakajimas below and gave it a good burst. Suddenly a Zero jumped his tail, pouring bullets into the Wildcat's empennage and wings. Gibbs shook off the Mitsubishi before the Japanese could cripple F-8, then climbed back for a second run. Regaining altitude, he could not find the torpedo planes—they were already beyond him—but trouble located him. Again bullets tore into his airplane, this time riddling his engine. Oily black smoke billowed back from the cowling, and there was a sickening loss of power. Gibbs tried gliding back toward the task force about 10 miles off, but F-8 dropped like a brick. Pulling back his canopy, he fired a flare from his Very pistol to attract someone's attention, but while adjusting his controls he inadvertently dropped the signal pistol over the side. Gibbs ditched the Grumman, and before his battered mount sank, he pulled out his small liferaft from behind the cockpit. Enemy bullets had several times holed the rubber boat, and he had to squeeze it tightly to prevent the carbon dioxide from leaking.

So rapid was the fight and the destruction of the three aircraft that Woollen never replied to Pederson's earnest inquiries as to the enemy's altitude. Woollen had shot down one carrier attack plane from the 1st *Chūtai*, but adroit work by Zero escorts Minegishi and Kotani had removed the two Grummans before they could cause any more trouble. The scrap was of such short duration that the two Zeros involved were able to break off and nearly overtake the torpedo planes as they attacked the *Yorktown*. The air action was visible from Task Force 17 about 12 miles away. Observers on board the *Pensacola* and other ships reported three planes falling in flames. Shortly afterward, clouds obscured the enemy flight from view.

On board the *Yorktown*, Thach and his pilots waited restlessly in their cockpits for the signal to launch. News of approaching enemy planes compelled the air department to suspend fueling and shut down the system. Only Dibb's Grumman received additional gasoline before the carrier's fuel lines were drained and purged with carbon dioxide to prevent fires. Leonard's 3rd Division pilots would have to make do with the fuel they had saved from the morning patrol—an average of 30 gallons apiece. Captain Buckmaster held course 090 degrees with the wind blowing from slightly off the carrier's starboard bow—just the way VF-42 used to like it. Spotted well abaft the island, the fighters with their long takeoff run and generally lightened condition would have little difficulty getting aloft despite the *Yorktown*'s reduced speed.

Flight deck personnel surrounding the eight Grummans enthusiastically signaled their support with "Go gettems!" At 1440, the Fly I officer flagged Thach off, and F-1 roared down the flight deck. Waiting behind were Dibb, Leonard, Adams, Tom Barnes, Tootle, Haas, and Hopper.[27] The fighter pilots faced a difficult launch with little time to prepare for combat, what with Japanese planes boring in on the *Yorktown*. There would be no chance to rendezvous, gain much speed, or climb. First it was necessary to crank up the landing gear by hand (twenty-eight turns of the handle), charge and test the guns, accelerate to some semblance of combat speed, and pick out a target—all at an altitude of 200 feet or less in the midst of screening cruisers and destroyers. With a less than fifteen-second interval between each fighter's takeoff, the whole launch lasted a little under two minutes. During the last several takeoffs, Buckmaster commenced turning to starboard to evade torpedo planes charging up his port side. This brought the *Yorktown* fully into the wind.

Tomonaga's 1st Chūtai Goes In

At 1440, the same time Thach sped down the *Yorktown*'s flight deck, Tomonaga radioed his attack planes: "All go in!" Hashimoto's 2nd *Chūtai* already worked its way left to sweep around ahead of the task force. Meanwhile, Tomonaga led his four surviving carrier attack planes directly toward the *Pensacola*. That ship had regained visual contact with the 1st *Chūtai* about nine miles out and at 12,000 yards cut loose with her eight-inch main battery and five-inch antiaircraft guns. The other ships on the *Yorktown*'s port side likewise opened fire. Tomonaga's *kankō* held their swift descent toward the water until they drew within 4,000 yards of the screen. Then he and his pilots leveled out at 200 feet—fleeting targets making

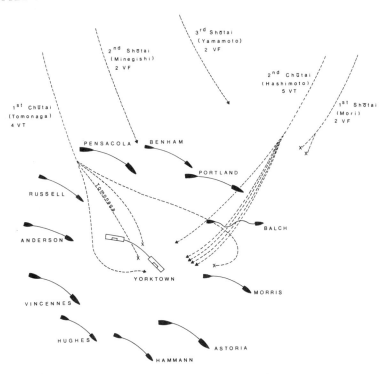

Torpedo plane attack on the *Yorktown*, 1441–1443.

between 180 and 200 knots, extremely swift for torpedo planes. They posed a fire director's nightmare for the American antiaircraft gunners.

Tomonaga's four *kankō* deployed into a very loose Vee, the pilots individually jinking and bobbing to evade the torrents of 1.1-inch and 20-mm tracers streaming past them. The *Hiryū hikōtaichō* aimed for the gap between the *Pensacola* and the destroyer *Russell* astern of her and penetrated the screen about 500 yards astern of the cruiser. The 1st *Chūtai* was perhaps a minute or two ahead of Hashimoto's planes still maneuvering to come around ahead of the ships. As the *Yorktown* turned hard starboard away from him, Tomonaga found himself opposite the carrier's port quarter. This offered a poor angle from which to initiate a torpedo attack. Two 1st *Chūtai* pilots swung to their left to head around toward the *Yorktown*'s port bow, while Tomonaga and a wingman tried the same type of maneuver, but to the right. Thus the 1st *Chūtai* essayed a miniature split attack of its own in hopes of getting in shots at both of the target's bows.

After clearing the *Yorktown*'s flight deck and executing an orthodox turn to the right (as opposed to VF-42's own practice of turning left upon launch), Thach continued in a wide circle to the right, heading back in the direction of the carrier's stern. Startling him was the vision of enemy torpedo planes, lugging menacing 18-foot torpedoes, flying in among the screening cruisers and destroyers. The Japanese he could see had set their sights on the *Yorktown*'s tender starboard quarter as she began turning away from them. Thach headed after one Nakajima moving swiftly low over the water. Enjoying a little altitude advantage, Thach rolled into a flat-side run from right of the target. Coming in very low and close to ensure hits, he poured a long burst into the Japanese as it flashed across his gunsight. Pulling out above and to the left of the *kankō*, he glanced back to see the target's left wing blaze up, burning the metal skin away to such a degree that the wing ribs were exposed. Most surprisingly, the Japanese pilot fought to keep his wings level and made an excellent torpedo drop from off the *Yorktown*'s starboard quarter. Thach was very much dismayed to see the aircraft he had just set aflame press on to drop its torpedo and likely hit the *Yorktown*! Seconds after the pilot had fired his fish, the left wing buckled, and the carrier attack plane spun into the water very close to the carrier's starboard quarter. Shaking off his amazement, Thach himself had to sheer off in the teeth of heavy antiaircraft fire.

The torpedo plane destroyed by VF-3's skipper was none other than that flown by Tomonaga. Thach later noted that his victim sported very colorful tail markings.[28] As the personal aircraft of the *Hiryū hikōtaichō*, Tomonaga's BI-310 bore on its vertical tail surfaces the three broad, yellow stripes denoting his command rank. Thach's account of the brave strike leader's death is corroborated by a Japanese radioman, Sea1c Hamada Giichi in PO1c Maruyama Taisuke's 2nd *Chūtai kankō*. Approaching from the opposite side, Hamada saw the *hikōtaichō*'s aircraft, its command stripes plainly visible, make its torpedo drop. From his angle, Hamada thought he saw Tomonaga crash in the carrier's superstructure, but that is incorrect. Contrary to what Thach thought at the time and to his later relief, Tomonaga's torpedo did not hit the *Yorktown*.

It appears that Tomonaga's wingman who chose to attack the carrier's starboard side dropped his torpedo close aboard her starboard beam, then flew roughly parallel to the *Yorktown*'s course in order to exit the screen close to the heavy cruiser *Astoria*. At that time no other fighters were in position to block its retreat, with the possible exception of Dibb. He had followed Thach's right turn after takeoff, but evidently did not pick out any oncoming torpedo planes. As for this *kankō*, it escaped the screen, but not VF-6 fighters heading up from the south.

The pair of 1st *Chūtai* torpedo planes that swung around toward the *Yorktown*'s port side fell prey to the next two VF-3 pilots to get off. Coming up to the line, Leonard heard the bullhorn announce a torpedo raid coming in, and by the time the flagman sent him off, the *Yorktown*'s port-side five-inchers had begun slamming away at the oncoming torpedo planes. Unperturbed by the concussion, Leonard banked left to clear his slipstream away from the flight deck, then headed for the destroyer *Balch* cruising on station off the carrier's port bow. Behind him, Tomonaga's 1st *Chūtai* had entered the screen and separated into two groups. The *kankō* on the extreme left of the port-side group had come sharply left to parallel the flattop's course in hopes of overtaking the ship and taking a shot off her port bow. The *Balch*'s crewmen were startled to see the Japanese charging directly up her stern. Glancing back in the direction of the *Yorktown*, Leonard spotted the Nakajima heading toward him. As the torpedo plane rapidly neared the destroyer's starboard side, Leonard set up what was essentially a flat-side approach on the target. He fired a long burst as he closed the range and flashed low over the tincan, crossing from port to starboard as he fired. His .50-caliber brass shell cases clattered like hail on the *Balch*'s forecastle. Perhaps wounded by his fire, the Japanese pilot immediately jettisoned his fish close aboard the *Balch*'s starboard side and swung in the direction of the carrier.

The difference in speed between the swift carrier attack plane and the still accelerating Grumman was such that Leonard could not follow through for another gunnery pass. Instead he settled for a stern chase, holding on grimly while he shot from nearly a no-deflection angle from slightly below the target. Soon after leaving the *Balch* behind, the torpedo plane's underside streamed flames and black smoke. About 1,500 yards from the destroyer, the *kankō* splashed in flames well short of the *Yorktown*'s port bow. Leonard was confident his shooting had brought down the Japanese because most of the antiaircraft fire directed at the speedy torpedo plane fell around him instead!

By the time Adams lifted off the flight deck, the *Yorktown*'s antiaircraft guns were all firing in earnest. He turned left slightly, then had to dodge broad, red bands of tracer from her 1.1-inch mounts. Besides the hassle of cranking up his gear, Adams had to contend with a faulty electrical pitch control for his prop. He had to run it up full low pitch manually. Nevertheless, he found a target very quickly after launch, the second of the pair of 1st *Chūtai kankō* that had opted to turn left and aim for the *Yorktown*'s port side.

Unlike Leonard, Adams had neither the speed nor the time to execute a firing pass. For his shot he tailed in directly behind the Japanese, flying into the teeth of intense antiaircraft fire. The Nakajima led him on a merry chase close to the *Yorktown*'s port beam, then released its torpedo. After the drop, the *kankō* continued toward the target, drawing within 50 yards of her port side. The rearseat man stood up and "shook his fist in defiance"[29] at the Yankees. It was the last thing he did. The carrier attack plane suddenly disintegrated in a bright flash and violent explosion. Perhaps Adams's bullets ripped into its fuel tanks or an antiaircraft burst from the ship landed dead on. Whatever the cause, the aircraft was gone, but Adams had no choice but to fly into the blast. He later found debris embedded in the windshield of his F-12. Considering the air space he traversed, Adams was extremely fortunate not to have met a similar fate. Thus of the ill-fated attack of the 1st *Chūtai*, it appears that three aircraft actually launched torpedoes, none of which hit, but only one survived to exit the scene.

The 2nd Chūtai *Strikes Home*

From the northeast, Hashimoto's five torpedo planes bore down on Task Force 17, the *Portland*'s five-inchers taking them under fire around 8,000 yards out. Hashimoto's *chūtai* deployed into a loose Vee and flattened out at 150 feet, moving fast. The fifth VF-3 pilot to scramble, Tom Barnes, was the first to encounter the 2nd *Chūtai*. An experienced pilot, he required little time to orient himself and head in the direction of the bursting AA shells. However, two Japanese fighter pilots had been waiting for just such an action. Lieut. Mori and his wingman, PO2c Yamamoto Tōru, jumped Barnes's F-17 just outside the screen. One after another, the two *Hiryū* Zeros slashed at the slower Grumman beneath them and maneuvering violently to counter each pass. With his quick counterstabs, Barnes thought he damaged the two Zeros.

Frustrated at not finding the enemy, McCuskey's division raced back toward the ships in hopes of overtaking the enemy before they attacked. McCuskey led his four F4Fs into a fast shallow dive toward the *Yorktown* because from the radio chatter he learned the attackers approached at low level. Below him at perhaps 2,500 feet he noticed a couple of Zeros working over what appeared to be one or two F4Fs beneath them. It was just moments after Barnes had first met the challenge of the two *Hiryū* Zeros. Steepening his dive, McCuskey singled out one of the two Mitsubishis. The enemy glimpsed the Grumman screaming in and swiftly hauled into a tight climb to escape in a high loop. At first McCuskey had an excellent setup, as his fast dive drew him close to the Zero before it could climb out of the way. However, he could not shoot that instant because he had not switched on the light for the delicate illuminated N2AN gunsight.[30] Frustrated, he flipped the toggle, but the few seconds of delay compelled him to pull back sharply on the control stick to wrench the F4F into a zoom climb in hopes of staying on the Zero's tail.

His speed kept him with the Japanese long enough to score, and McCuskey continued his accurate shooting even while on his back at the top of the loop. The Zero shredded into flames and spun away toward the water. By this time, F-21 had lost so much speed that McCuskey himself stalled and dropped out of the loop. Recovering from the spin, he got his bearings and climbed to regain altitude advantage.

McCuskey's wingman, Mel Roach of Fighting Six, had followed his leader closely in the dive, but then McCuskey suddenly disappeared into his loop. This was, as McCuskey wryly noted, "the quickest way to get rid of your wingman."[31] Free of the need to guard his leader's tail. Roach charged at the second Zero below and torched it with his first bursts. Both McCuskey and Roach scored on the first pass, killing both Mori, the *Hiryū* Fighter Unit leader, and his wingman, Yamamoto Tōru. Glancing back from the middle seat of his big Nakajima, Hashimoto had watched in horror as two Grummans swooped from a cloud and almost simultaneously flamed both *Hiryū* escorts. Fearful they would next take out his torpedo planes, Hashimoto led his *kankō* into a scrambling left turn to take advantage of some nearby cloud cover. Also witnessing the fatal ambush were the two *Kaga* pilots Yamamoto Akira and Bandō. Unlike Hashimoto, who had a torpedo to deliver, they could retaliate. Eager for a fight, Yamamoto roared in, while his inexperienced wingman Bandō found it was all he could do to keep his leader in sight. Evidently Yamamoto almost immediately latched onto a lone Grumman, Tom Barnes again!

Trailing McCuskey back toward the task force, his second section, VF-6 pilots Packard and Kleinmann, likewise had lost track of him when he suddenly disappeared. Looking around, Packard spied below a Grumman being chased by a Zero; diving in, he traded altitude for speed in order to close the gap. While still well out of range of the target, Packard was startled by heavy bands of tracers passing just over his canopy; Kleinmann had opened up from behind, prematurely forcing Packard to steepen his descent and get out of the way. Somewhat nonplussed, Packard lined up his own shot on the Zero and pressed the trigger when the Japanese drew into effective range. With deadly grace, the Zero rolled left into a tight, climbing turn. Packard pulled into a zoom climb to stay with it, but the twisting Mitsubishi never offered him a good shot. Finally losing speed drastically in the climb, Packard had to level out, and the Japanese responded with a firing pass of his own. Countering with a head-on shot, Packard fired furiously as the Zero roared into range. Flashing past, the enemy climbed back up to regain altitude for another attack. Packard later recounted:

> . . . I was completely out of speed by then, slopping around with about $\frac{1}{4}$ flap, to keep myself positioned so I could meet him gun to gun again. This kept up for 3–4 times. I of course was constantly losing a little altitude all the time. He finally broke off and went away in a long shallow fast dive, to my great relief.[32]

Packard thought his Zero opponent was heading back to his carrier, but Yamamoto Akira had other game in mind.

Meanwhile, after climbing and regaining his bearings, McCuskey spotted some F4Fs in trouble below. He dived on one Mitsubishi and put a good burst into it, certain he had bagged the target as it spun out of sight. His victim was Bandō, and the .50-caliber slugs shattered part of the Zero's windscreen and canopy. Momentarily stunned, Bandō lost control of his fighter and fell perilously close to the sea before he recovered. So far he had not fired a shot on this mission, and with his Zero crippled, he set his own course back to the *Hiryū*.

Yamamoto evidently saw part of the combat between McCuskey and Bandō. Charging in, he tried to come up behind McCuskey's Grumman for an easy shot, but Roach, who had regained contact with his leader, was able to intervene. With a firing pass, he diverted the Zero and brushed it off McCuskey's tail. Caught by overwhelming odds, Yamamoto pulled away and headed off for what would be other adventures with F4Fs.

In the short, sharp scrap, the Japanese had lost two Zeros destroyed and one damaged for the loss of no Grummans. In the wild, low-level dogfight, Yamamoto thought he polished off two or three Americans, but his principal opponent was Packard. As for the Japanese pilot, Packard wrote, "That cookie was good!"[33] He was also highly impressed with the Zero's performance, since the sleek Mitsubishi had dominated the fight. Packard never had the chance to break off and get an altitude advantage of his own. He felt his opponent "in complete charge during the entire dance."[34] Yet Packard got in his own licks and later received credit for damaging the Zero. Upon hearing reports of what befell Packard and Kleinmann on the mission, VF-6's skipper Jim Gray felt it confirmed his fears of the disadvantages confronting F4F-4 pilots when facing Zeros.

Hashimoto's sudden swing leftward into a cloud bank successfully screened his little formation from McCuskey's four F4Fs, but the maneuver jumbled up the chūtai's order. Emerging into the clear, Hashimoto became number three on the extreme left instead of leading the formation. Heavy antiaircraft fire resumed. "Poco" Smith's flagship Astoria, on the opposite side of the screen, tried with her main battery of eight-inch guns to upset the low-flying torpedo planes by shooting in front of them shells set for instantaneous contact. Smith hoped the huge splashes would flip the enemy planes into the sea, but Hashimoto's planes were unaffected by the shell spouts. The massive water columns evidently deceived Barnes, however. Unlike McCuskey, he knew how close the torpedo planes were, and after being freed by Packard's unexpected rescue, he raced after them. He still had time for a few firing passes while and after the Japanese released torpedoes, and he thought he downed two of them. Actually the most he did was damage several, and he probably mistook eight-inch shell splashes as enemy planes smacking the water.

Next to take off from the Yorktown was Milton Tootle. By the time Tootle oriented himself, Hashimoto had entered the screen through the gap between the Portland and the Balch and was curving toward the carrier's port bow. Buckmaster tried to present her stern toward the new group of torpedo planes, but the warship could not turn quickly enough. Tootle headed left in the direction of the AA bursts. Because of the great difference in speed, he also had to settle for a tail position on one of the kankō. Firing furiously with his six Brownings, he followed the Japanese close to the Yorktown. Of all the pilots in the launch, he had the least experience, being fresh out of advanced training. Like Dibb that morning, he was faced with a situation in which he had to learn with lightning-like rapidity.

Getting off ten or fifteen seconds after Tootle was Walt Haas. While he cleared the immediate area of the carrier, the 2nd Chūtai penetrated well within the screen. He turned left after launch and almost immediately picked out the oncoming kankō. Thach, Leonard, and Adams saw the torpedo planes as well, but the Japanese flashed past them before they could do much about it. Still in front of the enemy, Haas was able to set up some sort of shot. By that time the five carrier attack planes had loosened formation as the pilots concentrated on making their individual torpedo runs. Haas made a flat-side run on a group of three or four torpedo planes nearing their drop points off the Yorktown's port side. Singling out the Japanese farthest on the right, he closed in with his trigger down and passed from right to left behind the much faster target. Haas thought he winged his enemy, but did not see it splash. Continuing southeastward in the direction of the destroyer *Morris*, he discovered a lone torpedo plane ahead of him and executed a similar beam attack from right to left past the target. Told later that this *kankō* hit the water on the other side of the carrier, Haas claimed this Japanese. Actually, the aircraft was Hashimoto's own, and he remembered Haas's run, which occurred just before he released his torpedo.

Leaving Haas behind, Hashimoto carefully watched his target, as Takahashi, his pilot, eased down to within 100 feet of the waves. At 600 meters distance from the *Yorktown*'s port bow, Hashimoto launched his torpedo. Three other 2nd *Chūtai* aircraft also dropped their fish, but the release gear in W.O. Nishimori's *Akagi kankō* failed to operate. Hashimoto led four aircraft southwestward ahead of the *Yorktown*'s bow and toward the destroyer *Hughes*. Takahashi asked about the torpedoes, and as Hashimoto turned to look back, he glimpsed the vastly encouraging sight of two heavy geysers, one after the other, towering over the opposite side of the carrier. This meant multiple torpedo hits! PO1c Ēto Chikashi in another *kankō* reported a third geyser as well. Between 1443 and 1444, two torpedoes slammed into the *Yorktown*'s port side, inflicting tremendous damage. The blasts opened rents that flooded three firerooms and also the forward generator room. All electrical power was lost, and all boiler fires were extinguished by the concussion. The ship rapidly reduced speed until she drifted dead in the water. Flooded compartments swiftly inflicted a list to port of 17 degrees, which soon increased to 23, as the *Yorktown*'s flight deck canted at a sickening angle. With her rudder jammed, the carrier would be difficult to tow, and she lacked power to run repairs.

While Hashimoto's four carrier attack planes cut ahead of the *Yorktown*'s bow, Milt Tootle stayed close on the tail of one of them. Hashimoto led his troops toward a gap in the screen between the destroyers *Hughes* and *Hammann*. Suddenly gunfire struck Tootle's F-18 in the engine and set it ablaze in spectacular fashion. His cockpit full of smoke, Tootle had the presence of mind to haul F-18 into a climb so that he could bail out. Reaching 1,500 feet, he leveled off and clambered out on the wing. His F4F was still the target of machine-gun fire from nearby destroyers. Tootle made a successful parachute descent into the sea just south of the task force. The destroyer *Anderson* witnessed his plight and cut out of formation to rescue him. By 1455, he was on the tincan's deck after one of the more remarkable

Hiryū carrier attack planes roar past the *Yorktown* after releasing torpedoes. (NA 80-G-32241.)

Lieut. Hashimoto's 2nd *Chūtai* withdraws after hitting the *Yorktown* twice with torpedoes. (NA 80-G-11639.)

flights of the battle. He thought he destroyed one torpedo plane and also believed that 20-mm cannon fire from one of the screening vessels caused his dunking. Pardonably, the Japanese felt they shot down the Grumman. Hashimoto's radioman/gunner, PO3c Koyama Tomio, submitted a claim for one American fighter, and more than likely that was for Tootle.

The fifth and remaining *kankō* of the 2nd *Chūtai*, the one on the extreme right of the formation, sought escape in a different direction. That Japanese cut instead around the *Yorktown*'s stern and made for the space between the heavy cruiser *Vincennes* and the destroyer *Hughes*. Evidently Adams went after this torpedo plane, but discovered the target too close to the carrier's blazing antiaircraft guns. Instead Adams turned back in the original direction of the attack and looked for a second wave, should it appear.

The eighth and last pilot to take off from the *Yorktown* was George Hopper. Most likely he lifted off the flight deck about the same time Hashimoto neared his drop point. After becoming airborne, Hopper swung left, but the torpedo planes roared past him before he had the knots to do anything about them. Clawing for speed above the wave tops, Hopper flew very close to the *Balch*'s starboard side before he had to sheer up steeply to gain the height to clear her from starboard to port. Just as his F4F pulled up, a Zero streaked in from off the *Balch*'s port quarter. In a near-opposite attack, the Japanese ambushed Hopper with a well-aimed burst. Grumman F-7 nosed down and plowed into the water about 1,000 yards off the *Balch*'s bow. Hopper had little chance to bail out, and from the way his aircraft behaved, gunfire might have got to him. Appointed an aviation cadet in May 1941, Hopper had earned his wings that October before reporting to ACTG Pacific at San Diego. In April, he and his close friend John Bain had gone out to Pearl Harbor to join Fighting Two and ended up in the Coral Sea when the *Lexington* sank. The identity of his attacker is not known for certain, but by process of elimination, he must have been Minegishi or his wingman Kotani. From the evidence, these two *Hiryū* warriors raced to overtake the 1st *Chūtai* after dealing so effectively with Woollen and Gibbs. They entered the screen ahead of the *Pensacola*, and their projected line of flight would have taken them near the *Balch*. At any rate, the two Zeros traversed the task force quickly and exited to the south.

Ens. George A. Hopper, Jr., killed in action 4 June while helping to defend the
Yorktown. (Mrs. G. A. Hopper, Sr.)

Tootle was not the only VF-3 pilot to have trouble with "friendly" antiaircraft
fire. Thoroughly aroused, the ship gunners fired at anything that ventured into
range. Haas found himself the object of the destroyer *Morris*'s earnest attentions,
and 20-mm shells holed F-14's fuselage and wings. Among other things, gunfire
put his flaps out of commission. Adams saw part of the dogfight taking place
northeast of the ships. He tried to join in, but ran afoul of a tincan shooting her
five-inchers directly in his path. The bursts compelled him to pull off. It took some
time before the gunfire cooled among the screening vessels of Task Force 17.

Not long after the actual attack, Thach was flying not far from the stricken
Yorktown and spotted a lone Zero nearby. He tried to surprise it from below and
behind, but his opponent observed his approach. One of the Mitsubishi's patented
loops put the Zero with guns blazing directly onto Thach's tail. His experiences
that harrowing morning uppermost in his mind, Thach was in no mood to challenge
a Zero alone. He found a convenient cloud and disappeared into it. Under the
circumstances, the Zero pilot must have been the pugnacious Yamamoto Akira,
hanging around the target area after disengaging from McCuskey's division.

After shooting down the torpedo plane and trying in vain to catch the others,
Leonard climbed above the cloud base to guard against a possible dive-bombing
attack. Breaking through the scud around 2,000 feet, he saw a Zero almost directly
over the carrier. The Japanese circled in steeply banked turns, no doubt observing
with great interest the damage wrought on the *Yorktown*. Leonard charged in, but
this time Yamamoto (for it could only have been he) acted not at all aggressive.
He headed away at high speed. The information he possessed regarding the crippled
flattop was far too valuable to risk in another tussle with the Grummans. Leonard
could not pursue because of his dwindling fuel supply; he had to conserve it to try
to get to another friendly flight deck. The way the *Yorktown* listed to port, it

seemed certain that she would not be open for business soon, or ever. Shortly after his encounter, Leonard gained a wingman in the person of Barnes. The two circled protectively over the damaged flattop.

South of Task Force 17 some of the reinforcements rushed by Dow encountered retreating torpedo planes and a couple of Zeros, but only the VF-6 pilots saw targets to attack. Sutherland with three F4Fs from Fighting Eight came over at 18,000 feet—too high to discern the enemy flying close to the waves. Rawie's three-plane VF-6 division nearly had the same problem as their *Hornet* counterparts—too much altitude. Rawie had climbed to 17,000 feet by mistake before he learned from radio chatter that the Japanese were making a torpedo attack. Diving in, he had passed 6,000 feet when he spotted a lone enemy torpedo plane hugging the water at 300 feet. The aircraft was two or three miles south of the *Yorktown* and well outside the screen.

The three Grummans screamed in with a high-speed dive, Rawie and Ralph Rich moving to box in the target from both sides. Against the hapless Japanese they made simultaneous high-side runs—Rawie from the left and Rich on the right. Wayne Presley went in flatter to execute a shallow run from abeam. Their first run swiftly got the *kankō* smoking. Rawie and Presley swung around to attain position for a second pass, but Rich beat them to it by boring in from astern. His accurate bursts quickly silenced the rear gunner and "chewed into the left wing at the fuselage like a buzz saw."[35] The carrier attack plane splashed in flames. Watching Rich make his charge, Rawie concluded it was possible to "plow right in and shoot it out"[36] with the rearseat man of a lone torpedo plane. One 7.7-mm Lewis machine gun (such as the enemy had) had very little chance of defeating a fighter's six .50-calibers, provided the Grumman pilot's initial bursts were on target. It appears virtually certain that Rawie's trio accounted for the remaining carrier attack plane of Tomonaga's star-crossed 1st *Chūtai*.

About the same time Rawie's division dealt with the lone *kankō*, Bayers and his wingman Reid, also from Fighting Six, appeared on the scene at 10,000 feet and just southwest of Task Force 17. Seven thousand feet below, Bayers discerned two Zeros, the Japanese section leader circling and his wingman weaving. Rolling into an overhead run, Bayers gained plenty of speed in the long dive. The trailing Mitsubishi caught sight of the Grumman hurtling toward it, and immediately hauled into a steep climb to escape. The enemy section leader failed to react that quickly and presented Bayers with a good shot. He was certain he flamed the Japanese with his bursts, but had no time to linger. Aware that the other Zero lurked above him, Bayers continued on down toward the water and recovered at high speed for a dash over the waves. Ahead of him and drawing away from the task force was an enemy torpedo plane, and Bayers moved in. He put one short burst into it, saw it fall away, and thought he finished it off. At the same time his leader ambushed the two Zeros, Reid spotted two torpedo planes scuttling across the water at 300 feet. Diving in, Reid shot into both of the retreating torpedo planes and was certain he got them.

During their attacks, the two former VF-2 veterans thought they witnessed splashes from a horizontal bombing raid. Actually they saw water spouts churned up by cruiser eight-inch guns firing on the torpedo planes as they withdrew. Like Barnes, Bayers and Reid were deceived in this manner. The two Zeros jumped by Bayers were those of the *Hiryū*'s Minegishi and Kotani. Neither Mitsubishi took more than light damage. Likewise the torpedo planes the two VF-6 pilots roughed up were from Hashimoto's 2nd *Chūtai*. The Nakajimas took hits, but lucky to the end, they kept flying. Hashimoto at 1445 had instructed his radioman, the sharp-shooting Koyama, to send the following message:

I carried out a torpedo attack against an enemy carrier and saw two certain hits.[37]

Five carrier attack planes and four Zero fighters withdrew from the inferno of the American task force; five *kankō* and two Zeros splashed. Hashimoto felt his men had accomplished their mission—seemingly they had crippled the second of three American carriers!

When Hashimoto's torpedoes struck the *Yorktown*, she lost all power and blanked out Pederson on the fighter net. At 1444, Dow on board the *Enterprise* assumed all fighter direction, but he had little notion how the CAP had deployed around Task Force 17. In the *Yorktown*'s vicinity were some eighteen F4Fs from the three fighting squadrons, but they were well scattered. Of immediate concern were the four VF-3 Wildcats (Leonard, Adams, Tom Barnes, and Haas) desperately low on fuel. Over the radio came the order: "When it gets bad, go down and land beside the destroyer."[38] Leonard was not yet ready for that extreme. With three other F4Fs he gathered, he circled the *Yorktown*. It was obvious that "Scarlet base" was in a bad way; the flattop had stopped and now listed radically.

Leonard tried to establish radio contact with Thach, but no go. At 1500, he piped up for the correct vector to base, and Dow replied with the course to Task Force 16. The FDO told all planes low on juice to pancake on Red or Blue base. Evidently all of the fighters over Task Force 17 then headed southeast toward Spruance's carriers. They had an uneventful flight back except for one. Flying low over the water, Haas discovered himself the object of special attention by another Grumman. That F4F roared in with guns blazing and followed through with one pass before the pilot realized that Haas was friendly. He was Dibb, and Haas allowed him to join up for the flight south.

The balance sheet on the attack of the *Hiryū*'s second wave showed ultimately that the Americans lost four VF-3 fighters shot down (Woollen, Gibbs, Tootle, and Hopper, and only Hopper not surviving) in return for claims of twelve enemy torpedo planes and four fighters shot down (see tabulation).

	VT	VT prob. or damaged	VF	VF damaged
(a) Fighting Three				
Lt. Cdr. Thach	1	1	—	—
Lieut. (jg) Leonard	1	1	—	—
Lieut. (jg) McCuskey	—	—	2	—
Lieut. (jg) Woollen	1	—	—	—
Lieut. (jg) Haas	1	—	—	—
Ens. Adams	1	1	—	—
Ens. Tootle	1	—	—	—
Mach. Barnes	2	—	—	2
	8	3	2	2
(b) Fighting Six				
Lieut. (jg) Rawie	1/3			
Ens. Rich	1/3	—	—	—
Ens. Presley	1/3			
Ens. Roach	—	—	1	—
Rad. Elec. Bayers	1	—	1	—
Mach. Reid	2	—	—	—
Packard, AP1c	—	—	—	1
	4	0	2	1

Just after the attack on the *Yorktown*, Spruance's two carriers finally launched relief CAP fighters. The *Enterprise* at 1450 sent aloft four-plane divisions led by skipper Gray and Mehle. The *Hornet* at the same time launched a mixed patrol of eight F4Fs (four from VF-8, four from VF-3) in divisions led by Ford and Crommelin. While they took off, Spruance received the word he eagerly awaited. Someone had located the fourth Japanese carrier!

RETRIBUTION

The Attack on the Hiryū

The search mission despatched by Fletcher hours before finally yielded results. At 1445, almost to the minute when the *Yorktown* was torpedoed, Lieut. Sam Adams from the *Yorktown*'s Scouting Five helped to seal the fate of his ship's tormentor. Along with another VS-5 SBD, he spotted one carrier, two battleships, three heavy cruisers, and four destroyers, and reported them as bearing 279 degrees, 110 miles from his point of origin (the *Yorktown*'s 1150 position). Actually Adams erred 38 miles to the northwest in his estimate, pardonable considering the importance of his achievement. He and his wingman had found the *Hiryū* and her consorts. His sighting report coincided precisely with the arrival of the hapless Nagumo, who at 1445 joined the *Hiryū* formation on board his ersatz flagship *Nagara*.

Adams's sighting report galvanized the air staff on board "The Big E" into action, and they made haste to launch a second strike. Against the advice of Browning, Spruance had awaited definite word as to the target's location before unleashing his carefully husbanded striking force of SBDs. The *Enterprise* had available only twenty-five dive bombers from three squadrons (seven from Scouting Six, four from Bombing Six, and fourteen from the *Yorktown*'s Bombing Three) led by VS-6's skipper, Earl Gallaher. Half of the SBDs were armed with 500-pound bombs; the rest managed the far more potent thousand-pounders. Browning and the staff turned to the vital question of fighter escorts. At 1500, the *Enterprise* had on deck nine VF-6 and three VF-3 F4Fs: aloft were eighteen F4Fs from Fighting Six. The lone Japanese carrier could be expected to wield a strong fighter defense with Zeros left over from her three crippled sisters. Range was not a problem, as the reported distance to the target was only 130 miles. Eight Grummans were fueled and ready to go. Yet the staff, backed by Spruance and Captain Murray, felt the fighters could not be spared. Air defense of the task force had to come first. Spruance planned to launch the dive bombers at 1530.

Unfortunately Browning's staff forgot to forward orders to the *Hornet*, who had monitored the sighting report and waited patiently. Mitscher had prepared a strike of dive bombers, but by 1500 he had received no further instructions. Waiting overhead for a clear flight deck were Lt. Cdr. Johnson's eleven SBDs from Bombing Eight, which had flown up from Midway. Mitscher decided to break the spot of dive bombers on the flight deck and began recovering the VB-8 SBDs at 1510. Also coming on board were Haas and Dibb from Fighting Three and Harwood's five VF-8 fighters.

Leonard arrived over "The Big E" only to find her closed for business, as the air department respotted the deck for launch of the SBDs. The VF-3 pilots would just have to wait, but they were not the only pilots low on gasoline. Warden of Fighting Six anxiously watched his fuel gauge, by no means certain he had enough fuel to make it. At 1525, the *Enterprise* launched eight F4Fs for CAP (divisions led by VF-6's Quady and Brassfield of VF-3) and followed with Gallaher's twenty-five SBDs. During the launch, the *Enterprise* belatedly signaled the *Hornet* to despatch her strike group, less escort fighters. The delay in informing Mitscher squandered any chance of coordinating the two strike groups. About a half hour later, the *Hornet* sent off her strike of sixteen SBDs from both VB-8 and VS-8, led by VS-8's Lieut. Edgar E. Stebbins. On their own, they headed off for the target, said to bear 278 degrees, distance 162 miles.

Finally at 1542, the *Enterprise*'s flight deck beckoned the circling aircraft, and she began landing fighters. Among the first to touch down was Leonard, and as the senior VF-3 pilot yet on board "The Big E," Spruance wanted to see him. The admiral wanted a firsthand report of what had happened to the *Yorktown* and asked Leonard's estimate of the situation. Leonard thought the carrier could be saved and so informed Spruance. Meanwhile, the *Enterprise* landed four other VF-3 pilots (Adams, D. C. Barnes, McCuskey, and last of all Thach) and nine VF-6 aircraft (Hoyle's division, Rawie's division, and the three of McCuskey's division). The only one not to make it was Warden. At 1538, his engine had died before he could land, and Warden ditched F-12 not far from his carrier. The *Monaghan*'s whaleboat soon scooped him up. His would be VF-6's only plane loss during the Battle of Midway.

For the Japanese, the long, exhausting day was far from over. When he learned after 1300 that the Americans had three carriers, Nagumo lost his stomach for a daylight surface engagement. Given American air superiority, they could easily pick off his unsupported ships one by one. The main upshot of Nagumo's abortive sally toward the Americans was to delay the launch of the floatplane search requested at 1130 by Yamaguchi. Between 1300 and 1315, just as Yamaguchi readied his second strike, Abe's staff finally assigned five search planes to cover an arc from 000 to 090 degrees, distance 150 miles. Meanwhile the battleship *Haruna* had launched her own search of three widely scattered floatplanes covering sectors from 040 to 340 degrees, distance 100 miles. Under present circumstances, this search was useless. The *Chikuma* got her first plane (her No. 4 aircraft) off at 1335, but not until 1400 did the *Tone* catapult her No. 3 and No. 4 planes to search along headings of 090 and 070 degrees from the *Kidō Butai*. Two more hours would elapse before the remaining search planes departed. Spruance's staff was not the only one malfunctioning, but the shell-shocked Japanese had a better excuse.

While he awaited word from Tomonaga's strike, Yamaguchi planned the third round. Around 1450 came welcome news that the *Hiryū* crews had found and torpedoed an American carrier, making two down and one to go according to Yamaguchi's scorecard. At 1515, Hashimoto on his way back amplified his report and gave the American position, useful since the Japanese had lost contact at 1400 when Hoyle and Warden had destroyed the *Chikuma* No. 5 aircraft. Yamaguchi hoped to launch his third strike around 1800 so that they could attack at dusk and hopefully neutralize enemy superiority in fighters and antiaircraft defense. Not trusting the tardy searches sent off by the screening ships, Yamaguchi planned to launch the *Sōryū* Type 2 dive bomber an hour before the other planes in order to pinpoint the target and guide the strike group to it. Counting the *Sōryū* No. 201 plane, the *Hiryū* was readying six dive bombers and nine fighters for the third strike. More aircraft might be available, salvaged from whatever Hashimoto brought back.

Hashimoto's return flight was uneventful, his five *kankō* reaching the skies over the *Hiryū* around 1530. The flattop had just landed four CAP Zeros and made ready to launch four as relief CAP. At 1540, the deck was free, and the *Hiryū* carrier attackers came on board. Debriefing the crews, the *Hiryū*'s air staff estimated that they had secured three torpedo hits on a *Yorktown*-type carrier and possibly a fourth hit on a *San Francisco*-type heavy cruiser. The gunners claimed one Grumman definitely destroyed and another as a probable. Five carrier attack planes failed to return, and even those that survived were largely wrecked. Mechanics deemed only one of Hashimoto's planes as to be serviceable. Landing at the same time as the *kankō* were two *Hiryū* Zeros flown by Minegishi and Kotani.[1] Bandō returned with his maimed Zero about an hour later, but Yamamoto Akira was still inbound. Minegishi's cohorts described their air battles as a "fight to the death"[2] with thirty Grummans, but added it was a most confusing struggle. The pilots reported the destruction of seven Grummans and four others as probables. Ultimately Yamamoto received credit for four kills, and three were shared by Minegishi and Kotani. The *Hiryū* Fighter Unit mourned the loss of its skipper, Lieut. Mori, and his wingman Yamamoto Tōru shot down. Of the six Zeros on the mission, three returned to the *Hiryū*, two were lost, and the sixth (Yamamoto Akira) later ditched. The *Hiryū* air officer directed the strike pilots to get some rest before the dusk launch.

Heading eastward after their 1400 departure were the *Tone*'s two floatplanes. Their first sighting report came at 1515 from the No. 4 aircraft, an old friend from the morning. Her crew observed a large American force bearing 102 degrees, distance 120 miles from the point of origin. Cautious as ever, they added five minutes later that there "appears"[3] to be a carrier around 20 miles ahead of the first group. At 1545, the *Tone* No. 3 aircraft chimed in with a report of six heavy cruisers bearing 094 degrees, distance 117 miles from its takeoff point. The two floatplanes continued to snoop the area. Number Four at 1550 made a significant discovery—the Americans still had at least two carriers afloat.

Although contacts, both friendly and suspicious, cluttered his radar plot, Dow kept his CAP busy checking out what they could. At 1600, Task Force 16 had aloft a total of twenty-seven F4Fs from the three fighting squadrons. The Red patrol comprised four-plane divisions under Jim Gray, Mehle, Quady, and VF-3's Brassfield, while the *Hornet*'s Blue fighters consisted of four-plane divisions under Ford and Crommelin of VF-3, and one three-plane VF-8 division under Sutherland. Usually Dow kept the Red patrol looking for bogeys and held the rest in reserve. Fighters investigating one of Dow's bogeys nearly stumbled upon the *Tone* No. 4 aircraft in the process of snooping Task Force 16. The Japanese took refuge in the clouds before the F4Fs could sight them.

The *Tone* No. 3 was not as fortunate. That aircraft was a Nakajima E8N2 Type 95 reconnaissance floatplane [DAVE] of the kind encountered at Wake in February and at Lae–Salamaua on 10 March. An antiquated, open-cockpit biplane sporting one large main float, it nevertheless was highly maneuverable, especially when flown by a good man. The *Tone* No. 3's pilot was one Lieut. (jg) Hasegawa, and he was plenty good. Hasegawa evidently searched the seas around the *Yorktown*. Dow pinpointed him on the screen around 1615 and alerted VF-6 sections led by Mehle and Quady. He told them to arrow 290 degrees out to 20 miles. Ten minutes later he added "Red 1" (Gray) to the chase. At 1626, Gray happened to sight two aircraft ahead and queried Dow as to whether they might be bandits. The FDO responded by rounding up more fighters, including the entire Blue patrol (now down to eight F4Fs). Evidently he thought a Japanese strike group might be lurking out there.

Mehle alleviated Dow's fears at 1629, when he sang out:

> This is Red 13. Bogey is Jap single seat floatplane. We will get him. He is about 5000 feet over me. I will get him this run.[4]

Perhaps a half dozen Grummans had tackled the lone Nakajima, but Hasegawa was no easy target. Utilizing his aircraft's short turning radius and other tricks, he evaded VF-6's lunges no matter what attack they made. Early in the action, Gray's guns jammed on his first pass, and he pulled off to clear them. Relentlessly chasing the Japanese were Quady and two NAPs, Mach. Sumrall and Mach. Achten— both veterans of Fighting Two. Together they made four firing passes on the nimble floatplane before Quady worked his way underneath and shot up into the float. Owing to negative G, Quady's guns malfunctioned, and Hasegawa dived onto his tail. That was the opening Sumrall and Achten needed. They finally got a good shot, and at 1633 they flamed the floatplane. Hasegawa and his gunner were killed.

After pulling clear of the fight to work on his guns, Gray happened upon another floatplane in the clouds nearby. Under the circumstances, this could only have been the *Tone* No. 4, an Aichi E13A1 Type O twin-float monoplane [JAKE]. Gray charged after this quarry, which proved equally elusive. He spent several long minutes chasing the Japanese through the clouds and expended most of his fuel and ammunition. In the end he thought he got it. The *Tone* No. 4 crew, lucky to the end, managed to shake their pursuer and made it back to base. In this fight Gray lacked wingmen, so vital to box in the wily Japanese. Without their help, it was almost impossible to get in a good burst. The *Chikuma* No. 5 plane, shot down by VF-6 at 1410, and the *Tone* No. 3, destroyed by Sumrall and Achten, were the only Japanese cruiser floatplanes lost at Midway.

The *Hiryū*'s time was nearly up. The *Enterprise* strike group took its departure at 1530 and roared off to the northwest. One VS-6 dive bomber had to abort, leaving twenty-four SBDs in the pack. En route, the pilots observed with satisfaction the smoke from the three flattops they had left burning in the morning attack. These derelicts no longer concerned them; they sought the one that had escaped. Fifty minutes after takeoff, the attackers were rewarded by the sight of a Japanese task force steaming on a westerly heading, distant about 30 miles. Gallaher led his dive bombers around to the southwest to stalk the target through the rays of the afternoon sun. Surprise was complete. By 1658, the SBDs had reached the attack point at 19,000 feet and just south of the lone flattop. Gallaher signaled the *Enterprise* pilots to hit the carrier, while VB-3's Lieut. Dewitt W. Shumway was to lead his fourteen *Yorktown* planes against the nearer of the two battleships, which happened to be the *Haruna*.

On board the *Hiryū*, flight deck crews completed preparations to launch the experimental *Sōryū* Type 2 dive bomber to seek the one undamaged American carrier and guide the third strike to it. The attack planes themselves were to depart in an hour. Meanwhile the aircrews enjoyed a brief moment of rest; at Captain Kaku's orders, the *Hiryū*'s crew was served a special supper of sweet rice balls. The *Chikuma*'s lookouts at 1701 glimpsed the terrifying apparition of enemy dive bombers about to pounce on the *Hiryū*. She cut loose with antiaircraft guns to distract the bombers and alert the CAP. Aloft was a mixed CAP of fourteen Zeros (six *Sōryū*, four *Kaga*, one *Akagi*, and three *Hiryū*). Waiting clearance to land was the redoubtable Yamamoto Akira, finally back from the second attack on the *Yorktown*.[5]

Gallaher's Scouting Six pushed over at 1705. From the beginning of the dive and all the way down, Zeros swarmed over them to try to ruin their aim or blast them out of the sky. Kaku brought the *Hiryū* into a radical turn to port. The first two bombs dropped by Scouting Six missed because of the flattop's adroit maneuvering. Back at 19,000 feet, Shumway watched the proceedings with concern. To hell with the battleship! He led Bombing Three against the still unhurt carrier. Three Zeros jumped him in his dive and dogged him most of the way down; likewise other Japanese bedeviled Bombing Three, using all sorts of fancy maneuvers to stay with the SBDs and shoot. Among the many bombs aimed at the *Hiryū*, four in close succession slammed into her forward of the island. The blast blew the forward elevator up against the superstructure and ignited intense fires. The *Hiryū* was doomed. Zeros bagged two VB-3 dive bombers after release. Two Yorktowners went after the original target, the *Haruna*, but missed her. Last to dive in was Bombing Six with only three aircraft. Led by Dick Best, they piled on the now flaming *Hiryū*. Zeros shot down one of the SBDs still in its dive. For the loss of three dive bombers, the Americans had turned the *Kidō Butai*'s last carrier into a sinking inferno.

The *Hiryū* and her consorts were targets of still more attacks before the sun set that fateful 4 June. The *Hornet* strike group, less two SBDs that had to return early, reached the target area about fifteen minutes after the first attack. Already the carrier burned so furiously that Stebbins led his fourteen SBDs against the screening vessels, but secured no hits. The *Hornet* flyers seemingly faced no significant fighter opposition although the Zeros were still there. Happening on the scene about an hour later were three separate formations of Army B-17 heavy bombers totaling twelve aircraft. They bombed the Japanese without scoring any hits, and only one element suffered interception by fighters. By sunset, the last of the fifteen Zeros had either ditched near the burning *Hiryū* or had drifted south to see if any of the other stricken flattops could take them on board. All four Japanese carriers were in extremis, and the Zero pilots made water landings.

The Yorktown's *Travail*

The *Yorktown*'s Captain Buckmaster discovered himself literally powerless to save his ship. The two enemy fish had flooded three firerooms, the forward generator room, and numerous compartments on the port side. Very quickly the flattop took on a list that increased to 23 degrees. No power could be had to counterflood or free her rudder, which had jammed at 15 degrees left. Below deck there were no lights at all, and her crew moved in total darkness. Buckmaster had every reason to believe that the *Yorktown* would inexorably continue to heel over until she capsized and took her 2,000-odd crew with her into the depths. Equally important, he lacked control over what the enemy might do. One more hit and she would surely go down. At 1455, the *Yorktown* raised on the signal hoist the regretful message "Abandon Ship."

Swiftly the *Yorktown*'s crew went over the side in relatively good order. Fletcher instructed his destroyers to approach the battered carrier one at a time and pick up survivors. Five VF-3 pilots—Macomber, Eppler, Evans, Morris, and Cheek—along with the whole enlisted echelon were involved in abandoning ship. The destroyers themselves and their whaleboats carefully combed the waters and recovered rafts full of survivors and individual swimmers. Fortunately the sea was fairly calm and the winds light. The main obstacle facing the swimmers was fuel oil that had streamed out of the *Yorktown*'s torn fuel bunkers. During the operation, a number of alerts sounded for air attack, and the screening vessels churned furiously around the stricken carrier, circling to keep speed up. On one of these curving excursions, lookouts on the destroyer *Benham* spotted Bill Woollen in his raft. She cut out of formation and made the rescue. According to her skipper, Lt. Cdr. Joseph M. Worthington, Woollen shouted as the tincan came close:

> Take your time Captain, I'm in no hurry. This raft won't run out of gas.[6]

Unfortunately Harry Gibbs's partially deflated rubber raft was too far west to be seen by the screening vessels. With mounting concern he watched as the rescue operation proceeded without him. By 1639, the cruisers and destroyers had picked up all of the *Yorktown* survivors they could find, but checked the area once again to make certain. The next move was up to Fletcher, functioning with his staff in the *Astoria*.

On board the *Enterprise*, the flight deck crew made ready to launch a relief CAP of twelve F4Fs—eight from Fighting Six and four VF-3 fighters. Leonard led the VF-3 division with welcome orders to take over the CAP above the *Yorktown*. Once the deck was free, "The Big E" arranged to bring on board F4Fs drawing low on fuel. At 1650, Mehle brought his troops on board, joined by a bemused McCuskey, who had just taken off with the relief CAP ten minutes before. Someone had neglected to replace the gas cap on his fighter, so streaming a trail of raw gasoline, McCuskey had to land immediately. At 1705, the *Enterprise* recovered eight F4Fs led by Quady and Brassfield, and twenty minutes later landed another four-plane division from VF-6. This left nineteen F4Fs from all three squadrons on CAP over the two task forces. Captain Murray wanted to refuel the majority of his fighters and send them aloft before dark to guard against a twilight attack.

For Leonard the flight back to the *Yorktown* was a "sad experience."[7] Arriving shortly after 1700 when the screening vessels secured the last of her survivors, he saw her drifting forlorn and abandoned, the steeply canted flight deck empty of aircraft except for the two VF-3 Wildcats lashed down aft of her island. It was an all too familiar sight:

> I had watched the same scene less than a month before as we CAPPED *Lexington* for the last time in the Coral Sea.[8]

Meanwhile, Fletcher decided to close on Task Force 16 to the southeast and leave the *Yorktown* to her expected fate. He thought that his force, nearest of all to the Japanese, suffered "reduced fighting efficiency" because of "overcrowed conditions and a lack of air coverage."[9] He hoped to be able to transfer all of the survivors to the heavy cruiser *Portland* and return the next morning to see to the carrier. At 1712, the cruisers and destroyers of Task Force 17 steamed away, Fletcher later detaching the destroyer *Hughes* to stand guard over the derelict flattop. Leonard remained over his ship and "ground around and around the old warrior waiting for the worst."[10] Off to the west and from his fish-eye angle, Gibbs could only watch in dismay as the warships left the sea to him and the *Yorktown*.

Leonard and Gibbs were not the only outside observers of the tragic scene. The last pair of Abe's search planes finally scouted the area, although by this time their efforts were largely academic. Not long after 1700, the *Chikuma* No. 2 aircraft spotted an American "*Enterprise*-type" carrier hove to and drifting. The Japanese crew searched the vicinity and noted Fletcher's ships steaming away. This aircraft then headed south after them. About thirty minutes later, the *Chikuma* No. 4 plane likewise stumbled onto the listing *Yorktown* and remained in that location until dark before returning to base.

The *Enterprise* at 1758 cleared her flight deck of twenty F4Fs to serve as twilight CAP, freeing the deck to recover the strike planes expected shortly. Divided into two large gaggles, the fighters deployed with Gray's group to port and Mehle's starboard of Task Force 16. Even as the CAP assembled, the inquisitive *Chikuma* No. 2 aircraft was near. Its crew at 1810 radioed back a sighting report of one carrier, two heavy cruisers, and four destroyers bearing 095 degrees, distance 105 miles from the point of origin. Nine minutes later, they piped up with reports of another American carrier lurking out there. So far so good, but when the crew later returned to the *Chikuma*, they excitedly recounted they had seen no fewer than *five* American flattops, a badly damaged one off to the north and a pack of four operating relatively close together! These tidings thoroughly confused the already hassled Nagumo.

Before the *Chikuma* No. 2 broke contact, the *Enterprise* tagged it on radar as a snooper. At 1819, Dow sent Quady's VF-6 section out 10 miles on a bearing of 355 degrees to bag the bandit seaplane hiding in the clouds. A few minutes later, the FDO provided reinforcements in the form of Achten's section and ultimately added two more sections for the hunt, but the *Chikuma* No. 2 (a Nakajima Type 95 biplane) made itself scarce. Finally at 1840, Dow relented and reined in all Red fighters back on station. The Japanese had already hightailed it back to the *Chikuma*, and—given the deleterious effect their erroneous sighting reports would have on the *Kidō Butai*'s already devastated morale—it was better that they went.

During the chase for the snooper, the *Enterprise* at 1820 started recovering seven F4Fs and also twenty-one SBDs from the strike group. Flying a borrowed VF-3 Wildcat (Tom Barnes's F-17), Rad. Elec. Thomas W. Rhodes of VF-6 had to land because of engine trouble. Distracted, he neglected to lock his landing gear in the "down" position. F-17 had almost come to a stop in the arresting gear, when it crumped on deck. It would require a complete overhaul. With sunset approaching, "The Big E" at 1855 began landing the remaining fighters. Leonard's VF-3 faithful guarded the solitary *Yorktown* until sundown, then ruefully "zoomed her deck one last time"[11] and headed southward toward the *Enterprise*. They landed safely, as did the rest of VF-6. The *Hornet* beginning at 1857 took on board her mixed CAP of four VF-8 and four VF-3 fighters and also landed the fourteen SBDs from her strike. Thus ended flight operations on a most eventful day.

After dark on 4 June, the carrier pilots sought food and relaxation while they exchanged recollections of what had transpired that day. Totally exhausted, some were just happy to find a bunk and sleep. On board the *Enterprise*, Jim Gray and the rest of the VF-6 escort pilots finally learned what had happened to Torpedo Six:

> When news reached us that the torpedo boys had been nearly wiped out the shock was as total as that which one could expect from a death in his immediate family. These were shipmates and dear friends of many years.[12]

The VF-3 pilots who landed on board the *Hornet* bunked in the rooms of Torpedo Eight pilots who had not returned. With success came bitter realization of the cost of victory.

There was no rest yet for the two task force commanders. Spruance with two undamaged carriers gratefully assumed tactical command, when Fletcher, his senior, radioed that he would conform to Spruance's movements. Task Force 17 (minus the *Yorktown*) moved to within visual sighting distance of Spruance's ships. No telling what the Japanese surface ships would do that night. Himself worried about engaging enemy battleships at night, Spruance decided to head eastward for a time, then take position next morning where he could launch air strikes and finish off any crippled Japanese carriers. Should the enemy still try to storm Midway, he would be in position to counter. At 1915, the American warships changed course to 090 degrees. At midnight, Spruance swung north, but a few minutes later a surface radar contact bearing 322 degrees, distance 14 miles, made him suspect the Japanese were hunting him. He detached a destroyer to investigate, then withdrew east. It was a false contact, but Spruance was not taking any chances. Untrained and ill-equipped for night combat, his aircraft superiority would avail him nothing in a night surface engagement with enemy battleships. Fletcher's Task Force 17 also headed eastward. His first order of business was to transfer the *Yorktown*'s crew, make his ships battleworthy, fuel, and then attend to the salvage of the *Yorktown* if indeed she still floated.

SUMMARY FOR 4 JUNE

At the cost of the *Yorktown* crippled and ostensibly sinking, as well as eighty aircraft lost (nineteen fighters, twenty-four dive bombers, and thirty-seven torpedo planes), Nimitz's carrier striking force had destroyed the heart of the Imperial Navy's carrier fleet. Four Japanese flattops with all of their aircraft were either sinking or about to sink because of irreparable damage. The three carrier fighting squadrons, VF-3, VF-6, and VF-8, paid a heavy price in aircraft (six F4Fs shot down, twelve ditched, and one jettisoned over the side), although only five pilots had been killed—fewer than the losses Fighting Two had taken on 8 May at Coral Sea. In contrast to Coral Sea, where the Wildcats had suffered the worst, at Midway the dive bombers and especially the torpedo planes took it on the chin. Many of these losses were due to inadequate fighter protection, for one reason or another.

In a squadron-by-squadron examination, the *Hornet*'s Fighting Eight, curiously, sustained the heaviest losses, in both pilots and aircraft. The main cause was the ill-fated escort mission, accounting for ten F4Fs. As darkness fell on 4 June, all ten escort pilots were missing, including VF-8's skipper and flight officer. The *Hornet* had no inkling of what had happened to them; they were simply listed missing in action. Ultimately Midway-based flying boats would recover eight of the ten. One VF-8 fighter had been shot down defending the *Yorktown* (pilot killed), and another ditched after running out of fuel on CAP duty—pilot recovered. Subtracting the twelve missing planes, Fighting Eight on board the *Hornet* had available fifteen F4F-4s. Claims by VF-8 pilots amounted to three enemy fighters and two dive bombers destroyed.

The *Enterprise*'s Fighting Six suffered the lightest losses of the three: one F4F ditched on CAP, with the pilot promptly recovered. The evening of 4 June, the squadron had twenty-six F4F-4s on hand, apparently all operational. Squadron combat claims totaled nine Japanese planes destroyed (one fighter, one dive bomber, four torpedo planes, and three floatplanes). Although Fighting Six had come through unscathed, there was a lingering feeling of opportunities missed on the crucial day of the Battle of Midway.

Seeing by far the heaviest combat was the *Yorktown*'s Fighting Three. Thach lost five F4Fs shot down (two pilots killed) and another jettisoned. One of the pilots was still in the water and unaccounted for. Squadron claims came to eleven fighters, twelve dive bombers, and eight torpedo planes shot down, for a total of thirty-one Japanese planes. In the course of the day, VF-3's operational F4Fs had split between the two available flight decks. Eight pilots (including the CO and XO) found sanctuary on board the *Enterprise* with seven of the F4Fs operational and one nonfunctioning, and a like number of pilots with eight F4Fs had landed on board the *Hornet*. Six pilots had taken refuge on screening ships after the *Yorktown* had been hit, stranding five F4Fs on the carrier, and the seventh pilot floated in his rubber raft not far from the stricken flattop.

Total fighter claims were:

15 VF   15 VB   12 VT   3 VOS = 45 Japanese planes

Evidence indicates they got:

11 VF   11 VB   5 VT   2 VOS = 29 enemy planes

CHAPTER 16

Midway—The Pursuit

5–6 JUNE OFF MIDWAY

While the exhausted pilots slept, or tried to, an equally tired Spruance thought hard in the early hours of 5 June about how to avoid a possible night counterattack by the enemy and yet position his battered and bruised carrier air groups where they could do some good after daybreak. He withdrew Task Force 16 eastward until 0200, then reversed course westward to approach the Japanese once again. From submarine alerts, he learned of an enemy force bearing down on Midway, and at 0420 came around to the southwest to move into direct support range of the island. The ships glided into a band of bad weather; fog and rain greatly reduced visibility and threatened air operations if those conditions persisted after sunrise. As on the previous day, Spruance relied on Midway-based planes to conduct searches and pinpoint enemy ships. Too few SBDs remained to conduct both searches and follow-up air strikes. Carefully he husbanded what dive bombers he had (his torpedo squadrons had virtually been destroyed), to unleash them should Japanese carriers turn up. The American carrier planes had sunk or maimed four enemy flattops, Spruance knew, but it was within the realm of possibility the Japanese might have a tough old bird like the *Yorktown* out there and back in action. Perhaps a fifth enemy carrier also lurked nearby, something that earlier CinCPac intelligence estimates had warned about.

Dawn found Task Force 16 socked in, so Spruance depended more than ever on Midway's faithful patrol squadrons. At 0630, a PBY radioed a position report for two Japanese "battleships" bearing 264 degrees, distance 125 miles from Midway. They lay within range of his SBDs, but Spruance had to know where enemy flattops were before he committed his strike planes. Ninety minutes later, another flying boat located one burning carrier, two battleships, three cruisers, and several destroyers, bearing 324 degrees, distance 240 miles from Midway. Twenty minutes later, another report reached the *Enterprise*—this one placing an enemy carrier bearing 335 degrees, distance 250 miles from Midway, out in the same area as the burning flattop. Conditions still did not permit immediate flight operations by the American flattops, and Spruance decided to wait a bit longer to see what the far-reaching search planes might turn up.

First scheduled flight operations on board the *Enterprise* that morning involved fighters for the combat air patrol, and "The Big E" readied a dozen F4Fs to go. Among them were six from Fighting Three:

F-1 Lt. Cdr. Thach	F-13 Lieut. (jg) Leonard
F-15 Mach. Barnes	F-12 Ens. Adams
F-10 Lieut. (jg) Brassfield	
F-21 Lieut. (jg) Mattson	

Thach's contingent was warned by the air department to "pack their toothbrushes" and be prepared to land on board the *Hornet*. The evening before, Spruance's staff had assessed the situation and found an excess of F4Fs on board the *Enterprise* and a lack of them on board the *Hornet*. Consequently they decided to shift Thach and most of his *Yorktown* refugees over to the *Hornet*, where he would take command of the composite fighting squadron. Left on board the *Enterprise* were Scott McCuskey and Dick Wright with two VF-3 F4Fs (F-3 and the wrecked F-17).

The twelve CAP fighters started taking off at 0825 from the *Enterprise*, while the *Hornet* remained quiet. For a change, 5 June proved a very quiet day for the fighters. They encountered no enemy aircraft (there were not many left to encounter!), and what snoopers were out (cruiser floatplanes) did not locate Task Force 16. About the most exciting contact came early, at 0900, when the CAP spotted an object floating on the sea. That turned out to be a disabled PBY flying boat from Midway. The fighters alerted Spruance, who sent the destroyer *Monaghan* to the Catalina's assistance.

Later that morning, when Thach's patrol was over, he took the six VF-3 Wildcats over to the *Hornet* and landed on board, where they increased the *Hornet*'s complement of fighters to twenty-nine (fifteen from Fighting Eight and fourteen from Fighting Three). The Yorktowners were made to feel most welcome. Thach assumed command of something designated "VF-3/42/8." Since December he had personally operated from all five of the Pacific Fleet's big carriers: the *Saratoga*, *Lexington*, *Yorktown*, and *Enterprise*, and now the *Hornet*. Quite likely he was the only pilot to do so. Eddie O'Neill, VF-8's own executive officer, went on the sick list. Replacing him as temporary XO was Bruce Harwood, while Warren Ford

VF-3/42/8 on board the *Hornet* about 10 June 1942; *standing l to r*: Bright, D. C. Barnes, Smith, Freeman, Fairbanks, Dibb, Ford, Harwood, Thach, Carey, Sutherland, W. W. Barnes, Brassfield, Markham, Bain, Crommelin, Leonard, Haas; *kneeling*: Dietrich, Mattson, Adams, Cook, Merritt, French, Formanek, Starkes, Sheedy, Stover, Hughes, Bass. (RADM W. W. FORD, USN.)

Task Organization, VF-3,42,8, on board the USS *Hornet*, 10 June 1942

F-1	Thach	F-5	Leonard
F-2	Dibb	F-6	Adams
F-3	D. C. Barnes	F-7	W. W. Barnes
F-4	Bright	F-8	Bass
F-9	Crommelin	F-13	Brassfield
F-10	Bain	F-14	Mattson
F-11	Freeman	F-15	Stover
F-12	Dietrich	F-16	Merritt
F-17	Haas	F-21	Harwood
F-18	Markham	F-22	Fairbanks
F-19	Starkes	F-23	Sutherland
F-20	Smith	F-24	Carey
F-25	Ford	Spare:	
F-26	Cook		O'Neill
F-27	Formanek		French
F-28	Hughes		Sheedy

Source: RADM W. N. Leonard papers.

became flight officer. In the ready room, Thach conferred with his pilots to get acquainted and work out a squadron flight organization. He took the opportunity finally to abolish even an administrative organization in six-plane divisions, as that had ruined his escort plans on the fourth. The composite squadron would have four-plane divisions, composed of pairs whose pilots had flown with each other. Thach did not try to integrate the sections, but kept the different squadron pilots and F4Fs with one another.

By 1100, Spruance had determined to his own satisfaction that the Japanese no longer posed a direct threat to Midway. He changed course to the northwest and bent on 25 knots to pursue the carrier or carriers located that morning by the PBYs. Task Force 16 would not be within range to launch SBDs until well into the afternoon. Meanwhile, Browning, the chief of staff, worked up plans that were to see the SBDs, armed with 1,000-lb. bombs, launched at a range of 275 miles. The orders shocked Wade McClusky and his squadron commanders out of their socks. In the presence of the admiral, they protested most vocally to Browning. Spruance overruled the chief of staff, delayed the launch for an hour, and told the air officers to arm the Dauntlesses with 500-lb. bombs. There was no thought of sending the fighters, given the long flight to the target. For the F4F-4 Wildcats, it was simply out of reach.

The *Hornet* was the first to launch, once Spruance gave the go-ahead. At 1512 she sent aloft a deckload of twelve SBDs from Bombing Eight led personally by Ring, the group commander. Ring set off immediately for the target, said to bear 324 degrees, distance 240 miles. The *Hornet*'s second deckload, fourteen SBDs under VS-8's skipper, Walter Rodee, left at 1543. En route, Ring spotted what he believed was a light cruiser, but pressed on to the target, thought to contain one carrier, two battleships, two cruisers, and five destroyers—the remnants of *Kidō Butai*. Ring took his aircraft out 315 miles, but saw no other enemy vessels. On the flight back he again encountered the "light cruiser," and this time he attacked. His quarry was actually the destroyer *Tanikaze*, detached by Nagumo to ensure that the carrier *Hiryū* had really sunk. The *Tanikaze* skillfully evaded all the bombs. Rodee had worse luck. He flew out to the end of the navigational leg without sighting any Japanese at all. His SBDs, some burdened by 1,000-lb. bombs (despite Spruance's orders), had nagging fuel worries as they droned eastward into the gathering darkness.

Meanwhile the *Enterprise* strike force departed at 1530 after the carrier rotated her CAP. Led by Shumway of Bombing Three, the attack group comprised thirty SBDs from the four squadrons (VB-6, VS-6, VB-3, and VS-5) then operating from the *Enterprise*. On the flight out, Shumway deployed planes from VS-6 and VS-5 into a scouting line abreast to widen the area of search. By 1727, the group had flown 265 miles without turning up any enemy. Recalling the scouting line, Shumway headed for the contact reported by Ring. There she was, the tough little *Tanikaze*, but her wily skipper again avoided any hits and extracted a heavy price from the Americans. Antiaircraft fire shot down the VS-5 SBD flown by Sam Adams, the man responsible for pinpointing the *Hiryū* the previous day.

By the time the first SBDs made it back to Task Force 16, darkness had fallen. The carriers had recovered their CAP fighters and anxiously awaited the return of the dive bombers. Spruance unhesitatingly ordered the carrier landing lights turned on, despite the real danger from Japanese submarines. The SBDs aloft comprised almost the whole of his remaining strike force, none of which he could afford to lose. Some of the pilots faced their first landing at night, but they performed admirably. There were no deck crashes, but VS-8's Lieut. Ray Davis had to ditch for lack of fuel. The *Enterprise* brought on board more aircraft than she had sent off: twenty-eight of her own SBDs and five from the *Hornet*. On her part, the *Hornet* landed twenty of her brood and one from Bombing Six. Altogether it was a magnificent feat for the pilots, the LSOs, and Spruance himself. When the flattops shut down for the night, more than one pilot gratefully quaffed "medicinal" brandy, duly prescribed to help them relax.

The morning of 6 June, Task Force 16 held a westward course for what would be the final act of the Battle of Midway. By 0500, Spruance was more than 350 miles northwest of Midway, too distant to rely solely on searches sent from there. The *Enterprise* at 0500 launched a search mission of eighteen SBDs to cover the 180- to 360-degree semicircle to a distance of 200 miles. Also roused early for CAP were six F4Fs from each carrier. The first important contact flashed in at 0645, when a VB-8 SBD (which had taken off from the *Enterprise*) relayed the position of one battleship, one cruiser, and three destroyers, course 270 degrees, speed 10 knots. Garbled in transmission, the message was received by Spruance as "one carrier and five destroyers."[1] When plotted on the charts, their position was 128 miles southwest of Task Force 16. At 0730, another VB-8 aircraft appeared overhead and dropped a message on the *Enterprise*'s flight deck. This informed Spruance that the pilot had spotted two cruisers and two destroyers. When added to his chart, they were situated 52 miles southeast of the "carrier" contact or even closer to Task Force 16 than the first group reported.

Two separate groups of Japanese ships, including one carrier, appeared to confront Spruance and his staff. Actually, the only Japanese ships in the area sailed together; they were the heavy cruisers *Mikuma* and *Mogami*, badly damaged in a collision with one another early on 5 June, and the destroyers *Arashio* and *Asashio*. They had been part of an abortive attempt to bombard Midway; now they limped westward. Midway-based aircraft had harried them the previous day. Now Task Force 16 swooped down upon them.

Not involved in the search, the *Hornet* was cocked and ready to go. At 0757, she began launching a strike of thirty-four planes:

CHAG	Cdr. Ring	1 SBD-3
Bombing Eight	Lt. Cdr. Johnson	11 SBD-3s
Scouting Eight	Lt. Cdr. Rodee	14 SBD-3s
Fighting Eight	Lieut. Ford	8 F4F-4s

Mitscher specifically provided the fighter escort in the event "previously undetected air opposition was encountered."[2] Thach and the VF-3 refugees remained behind to fly CAP and give their VF-8 compadres their chance at the enemy. Ford's escort force comprised the following:

1st Division
Lieut. Warren W. Ford, USN
Ens. M. I. Cook, A-V(N)
Ens. George Formanek, A-V(N)
Ens. Richard Z. Hughes, A-V(N)

2nd Division
Lieut. (jg) J. F. Sutherland, A-V(N)
Ens. Henry A. Carey, A-V(N)
Ens. David B. Freeman, A-V(N)
Ens. A. E. Dietrich, A-V(N)

With Ring in the lead, the *Hornet* attackers started a slow climb toward 15,000 feet. Meanwhile, at 0815 the *Enterprise* and the *Hornet* began recovering SBDs from the search. The pilot who had made the first contact landed on board the *Hornet* and corrected the erroneous message. Spruance learned no carrier was out there, and at 0850 he advised Ring to that effect.

Ring located the little Japanese task force at 0930 and maneuvered his dive bombers into a good attack position. The *Mikuma* steamed in the lead, and the Americans thought her a battleship. Compared with her maimed sister the *Mogami*, missing most of her bow, the *Mikuma* looked appreciably longer. The *Hornet* SBDs mostly concentrated on the two capital ships, although a few did take after the destroyers. Ring's pilots did well. They claimed three hits on the "battleship," and the *Mikuma* actually did take two or three bombs in her vitals. The crippled *Mogami* sustained two hits, and the destroyer *Asashio* took a 500-pounder on her stern.

Spiraling in with the SBDs, Ford led his eight F4Fs in a strafing run to support the dive bombers. In line abreast, his division of four ganged up on one destroyer, while Jock Sutherland's four machine-gunned the cruiser (presumably the *Mogami*). Sutherland retained a vivid recollection of angry Japanese sailors crowded on her stern shaking their fists in hatred as the Grummans roared past at low altitude. Antiaircraft fire was active, accounting for 2 SBDs (1 VB-8, 1 VS-6). The *Hornet* strike began landing on board their carrier at 1035 after the short hop back from the target. The *Hornet* air department rearmed the dive bombers for a second attack.

The *Enterprise* launched her strike planes at 1045. Taking off first was a relief CAP of eight VF-6 fighters, followed by thirty-one SBDs (from all four VSB squadrons) and twelve escort fighters from Fighting Six. Leading the strike was VS-5's skipper, Wally Short. Short's orders before departure were to attack the same group of ships plastered by the *Hornet*, but once aloft, the *Enterprise* radioed new instructions to seek out and destroy the battleship reported 40 miles ahead of the other target. Almost as an afterthought, "The Big E" despatched the three operational TBDs from Torpedo Six under Lieut. (jg) Laub. He departed with strict orders not to engage if any opposition appeared at all. Spruance would not lose any more torpedo planes if he could help it. On the slow climb to 22,500 feet, Short led the group into gentle S-turns to cut down the rate of advance and allow VT-6's TBDs to catch up. Unfortunately Laub never did establish contact with the dive bombers. Jim Gray, leading the escort fighters, briefly spotted the TBDs at 1211. He tried radioing the strike leader, but failed to raise him.

Twelve minutes after Gray saw the TBDs, he observed the small Japanese task force. The SBDs pressed ahead to search another 30 miles for the mythical battleship, but Gray led his fighters away to take a closer look at the enemy ships below and offer support in case Torpedo Six attacked. Looking over the *Mikuma* and the *Mogami*, Gray likewise thought one of them was a battlewagon. At 1225, he radioed, "There is BB over there!" Three minutes later he added impatiently,"Lets go! The BB is in the rear of the formation."[3] On board the flagship, Spruance was anxious to get on with the attack. At 1235, the *Enterprise* radioed Short: "Expedite attack and return."[4] He could find no ships ahead of the force already sighted, so he came back over the *Mikuma* and the *Mogami*. At 1245, he made ready to attack.

As briefed, Gray waited until the SBDs began to dive, then charged in with his F4Fs to strafe the destroyers. From 10,000 feet, Gray led his division of six F4Fs into a rapid 45-degree dive and barreled in from out of the sun. Responding to the threat, the Japanese tincan heeled over into a tight turn. In close succession, Gray and his pilots opened up with their .50-calibers as they descended below 2,000 feet and held their runs down to masthead level before pulling out. Chunks of metal flew off the destroyer as machine-gun tracers straddled the target and bullets struck home. They ignited a fire and set off a small explosion, visible as the last of the F4Fs rocketed by.

Tackling the other destroyer were six F4Fs led by Buster Hoyle. They approached from off her bow, as the destroyer tried desperately to maneuver out of the way. These VF-6 pilots likewise pressed their runs to within 100 feet of the waves, shot the destroyer full of holes, then in column swung sharply left to avoid the battered *Mogami*. Hoyle climbed to 5,000 feet, then brought his division around for a second try. Their heavy slugs punched more holes into the thin-skinned destroyer, igniting three fires and a satisfying explosion aft. None of the F4Fs sustained any significant damage, but the destroyers *Arashio* and *Asashio* bore souvenirs of the visit. Meanwhile, the SBDs left the *Mogami* and especially the *Mikuma* in a bad way, burning and shattered from more 1,000-lb. bomb hits.

While the *Enterprise* strike planes headed back to their carrier, Ring led a second *Hornet* wave with twenty-four Dauntlesses. Fighters were unnecessary for this attack; so they remained behind on combat air patrol. The task force had closed within 90 miles of the burning enemy vessels, and with the good visibility, Ring's crews at altitude simultaneously beheld the target smoking up ahead and their own ships well astern. At 1415, the *Enterprise* recovered her strike group (except for three SBDs which ended up on board the *Hornet*) and eight CAP fighters. Meanwhile the *Hornet* VSB pilots again gave a good account of themselves. They slammed as many as six 1,000-lb. bombs into the doomed *Mikuma*, besides securing another hit on the *Mogami* and a damaging near miss off the *Asashio*'s stern. In return the *Hornet* flyers took no losses. Spruance still did not know how many enemy ships were out there and what they were. At 1553, the *Enterprise* launched two SBDs for photo-reconnaissance, and they secured superb shots of the bruised and burning *Mikuma* settling into the water. Spruance's analysts saw her for what she was, a *Mogami*-class heavy cruiser. So much for the battleship. They expected her to sink shortly, and she did. The battered *Mogami* and the two destroyers limped off to the west.

The *Enterprise* handled the dusk CAP; at 1629 she launched twelve F4Fs from Fighting Six, two of which had to abort because of mechanical difficulties. The wear and tear of three long days of battle began to tell on airplanes and aviators alike. After sundown, "The Big E" landed her ten fighters and the two recon

SBDs. Now the Battle of Midway was over, as Spruance canceled any further pursuit. The task force had approached within 700 miles of Wake Island, making a Japanese air strike by land-based bombers highly likely the next day if Spruance continued to close on Wake. His destroyers were extremely low on fuel, and the aviators were exhausted. It was time to call it quits. Spruance at 1907 changed course northeast to head for a rendezvous with the fleet oilers *Cimarron* and *Guadalupe*. On board the carriers, the pilots finally realized the desperate battle had climaxed in a fantastic victory for the Allies. The night of 6 June was a time for relaxation and celebration. Liquor appeared from hidden recesses in surprising quantity, and on board the *Enterprise*, at least, the parties were quite lively.

THE LOSS OF THE *YORKTOWN*

During the night of 4–5 June, the *Yorktown*'s survival remained in jeopardy. His Task Force 17 jammed with *Yorktown* survivors, Fletcher had made contact with Task Force 16 and withdrew eastward. Listing steeply as she drifted across the dark seas, the *Yorktown* had only one companion, the *Hughes*, whose skipper had orders to sink the stricken flattop should the enemy appear. Still bouncing in the waves not far away was the partially flooded liferaft of VF-3 pilot Harry Gibbs, shot down by a Zero fighter the previous afternoon.[1] That terrible night Gibbs tried desperately to stay afloat. At dawn he perceived the flattop, also still afloat, and her faithful escort, and it gave him new hope.

To the east, Task Force 17 that morning was busy transferring *Yorktown* survivors, including seven VF-3 pilots (Brainard Macomber, Bill Woollen, Tom Cheek, Harold Eppler, Van Morris, Milt Tootle, and Robert Evans), from the destroyers that had plucked them from the sea to the heavy cruiser *Portland*. On board Fletcher's temporary flagship *Astoria*, Buckmaster collected specialists to make up a salvage team to reclaim the *Yorktown*. When he got them together—a lengthy process—he took the 170 men over to the destroyer *Hammann*. With the survivors crowded on board the *Portland*, Fletcher took the opportunity to fuel his thirsty destroyers from that vessel. Fueling took most of the day; at 1800, Fletcher sent the *Hammann*, *Balch*, and *Benham* to rejoin the *Yorktown*. The rest of Task Force 17 headed south to rendezvous with the oiler *Platte* and also with the big submarine tender *Fulton* coming up from Pearl Harbor to take on the *Yorktown*'s crew.

After dawn that morning, Gibbs had paddled furiously in the direction of the drifting carrier. He tried to raise some response from the tincan's lookouts, but without success. Floating close by was an empty raft that, although oil-soaked, was larger and more seaworthy than his own; so Gibbs switched over. Exhausted, he fell asleep. Later that morning, someone on board the *Hughes* noticed the raft, and she came over to investigate. Her crew recognized Gibbs and at 0938 brought him on deck. In all, he had rowed about six miles. Crewmen asked him how he was. He replied that he was all right—then promptly fainted! Gentle hands took him below deck for food, something to drink, a shower to wash off the salt water, and a comfortable bunk. Gibbs slept until midafternoon, then strolled up on deck for a look around.

Around the drifting carrier there was renewed activity. The fleet tug *Vireo* had joined the little group, and at 1308, she began towing the carrier toward Pearl Harbor. The small tug and her tow could only make three knots or so, but it was a beginning. Gibbs remained on board the *Hughes* and thus became the only *Yorktown* fighter pilot to witness the carrier's curtain scene from start to finish. At 1606 the destroyers *Gwin* and *Monaghan* (with Bill Warden on board) moved round the tug and her charge. Unfortunately the Japanese knew that the *Yorktown* still survived and roughly where she was. A *Chikuma* floatplane happened upon the carrier during the morning and disclosed her position. The Japanese high command gave the submarine *I-168* the mission of finishing her off.

Fletcher on 6 June arranged to divest his warships of the burden of the 2,000-odd *Yorktown* survivors and also to complete fueling of all of the ships. At 0440, the overcrowded *Portland* and two destroyers peeled off to the southeast to meet the *Fulton*. The actual transfer of survivors took almost all day, delayed by a sub scare. Along with the other 2,000 or so Yorktowners, six pilots and 106 enlisted men from Fighting Three went over in coal bags to the friendly sub tender. At the end of the day, the *Fulton* turned south for Pearl at 17 knots with her fill of *Yorktown* people. Meanwhile, Fletcher with the *Astoria* and two tincans met the oiler *Platte* and fueled. That evening he moved to reassemble his scattered task force, but by that time it was too late for the *Yorktown*.

Buckmaster in the predawn hours of 6 June arrived on the scene and started salvage work on board the *Yorktown*. His ad hoc crew initiated counterflooding to reduce the sharp list, attempted measures to restore power, pushed over the side anything reasonably portable (including the two faithful F4F-4s F-6 and F-23 lashed on the flight deck), and even cut away and jettisoned the port-side five-inch guns to decrease topside weight. By early afternoon, things looked much better for the brave flattop. The *Hammann* lay alongside her starboard side, while the *Vireo* chugged away, moving her huge tow slowly but steadily.

Still a guest on board the *Hughes* in the screen, Gibbs around 1330 walked around the destroyer's bridge. Suddenly an alert sounded, and tremendous explosions erupted next to the carrier. With skill and daring, *I-168* had infiltrated the antisubmarine screen and fired a spread of torpedoes. One fish slammed into the gallant *Hammann* and sank her almost instantly. Two others ripped into the *Yorktown*'s starboard side, wreaking fatal damage. The destroyers tried fruitlessly to hunt down the I-boat, while the salvage crew fought to overcome their shock and tried to stem the flooding. It was no use. The men abandoned ship for good at 1550. The *Yorktown* stayed afloat until shortly after dawn on 7 June, when she finally capsized to port. At 0501 with battle flag flying, the magnificent warship slipped beneath the waves. There was nary a dry eye among those who could bear to watch her go, including Ens. Harry B. Gibbs of Fighting Forty-two (temporary duty, Fighting Three).

THE *SARA* BACK TO THE FRONT

The crucial spring of 1942 while the Pacific Fleet fought in the Coral Sea and braced for an onslaught directed against Midway, the *Saratoga* underwent repairs for torpedo damage and also general modernization at Puget Sound Navy Yard. Her air group split between Oahu and San Diego. Knowing he would soon have need of her, Nimitz on 12 May requested that the *Saratoga*'s repairs be expedited so she could sail around 25 May from Bremerton. Her new commanding officer, Captain Dewitt C. ("Duke") Ramsey, was to take her on a trial run to San Diego, there to pick up a cargo of airplanes. By 5 June he was to clear San Diego bound for Pearl Harbor. CinCPac the next day directed that Rear Admiral Fitch upon his return to the West Coast from the South Pacific shift his flag to the *Saratoga* as commander of Task Force 11.

If the *Saratoga* was the forgotten flattop that spring of 1942, the Fighting Two Detachment became the forgotten fighters, detailed as they were to act as her fighter force when she did leave the yards. In mid-February the VF-2 pilots had settled in at NAS San Diego, standing dawn alerts and trying to keep out of the way of the fledgling carrier pilots of the advanced carrier training group operating out of North Island as well. In March, they received orders to ferry aircraft from the East to the West Coast, traveling by commercial airliners from San Diego to New York and there picking up naval planes for the flights back to San Diego. Each VF-2 pilot made a couple of trips. In late March during the midst of the ferrying, Jimmy Flatley left for parts west to take command of Fighting Forty-two on board the *Yorktown*. Taking his place in command of the VF-2 Detachment was Lieut. Louis H. Bauer, formerly Paul Ramsey's flight officer. A 1935 Naval Academy graduate, Lou Bauer had earned his wings in early 1939, reported to Fighting Two, and sharpened his skills as a fighter pilot under such greats as Truman J. Hedding, H. S. Duckworth, Paul Ramsey, and Jimmy Flatley. Likewise in March, the veteran VF-2 NAPs had received welcome promotions. Originally scheduled for warrant rank, Gordon Firebaugh, Theodore S. Gay, and Hal Rutherford obtained commissions as lieutenants (junior grade), while George Brooks became an ensign. Charles Brewer, Patrick Nagle, and Don Runyon fleeted up to warrant rank.

Bauer gradually exchanged his F4F-3As for new F4F-4s and also took over one Wildcat, which seemed a strange bird indeed. On 24 April, the detachment received the first F4F-7 assigned to a West Coast fighting squadron. The F4F-7 was designed as an unarmed, long-range, photo-reconnaissance version of the Wildcat. Fixed-winged, the F4F-7 featured a total of 685 gallons of fuel stored in unprotected tanks, giving it a potential range of 3,700 miles! The prototype had flown nonstop from New York to California, unprecedented for a carrier aircraft. Bauer's new acquisition (BuNo. 5264) was the second of twenty-one to be produced for the Navy. It certainly was not a fighter—gross weight was 10,328 lbs.(!)—and Bauer likely did not know what to do with it.

The *Sara*'s repairs and facelift proceeded more smoothly than expected. Bauer received orders to fly north to be ready to rejoin the ship, and on 12 May the VF-2 Detachment headed for Seattle via NAS Alameda. Meanwhile, Don Lovelace had secured orders to reunite the squadron at Pearl Harbor and took ship for Oahu, unaware that the VF-2 Detachment was at NAS Seattle. On 22 May, the *Saratoga* departed Puget Sound for warmer waters to the south, and Bauer's troops landed on board to serve as air defense if needed. Duke Ramsey made a swift run along the West Coast and reached San Diego early on the 25th. Bauer's pilots flew to NAS San Diego, while the *Saratoga* entered port. She was scheduled for several short cruises off San Diego, both for her trials and to permit carrier qualification landings for the ACTG pilots.

The afternoon the *Saratoga* arrived in port, several VF-2 pilots flew a glide-bomb practice mission to the exercise area about 15 miles south of San Diego. Fred Simpson rolled into his bomb run from about 10,000 feet and dived in at 70 degrees. He released his practice bombs and started to pull out, but his dive had been too fast. Observers estimated his Grumman straining at 350 knots as Simpson tried to recover at 1,000 feet. Pulling 8 to 10 G's, the F4F-4 broke up. First the left wing tore off, then the right. Simpson died on impact.[1] One of the old-guard aviation cadets, Simpson had earned his wings in November 1937 and flew over three years with Bombing Two. In March 1941 he had received a regular commission and his posting to Fighting Two. Fighting Two Detachment went to sea on board the *Saratoga* from 29 to 31 May, then returned to NAS San Diego.

Worried by the impending Japanese offensive against Midway, CinCPac on 30 May told Ramsey to sail as soon as possible for Pearl, even though Fitch, the task force commander, had not yet reached San Diego. Nimitz expected the *Saratoga* to clear Pearl on 6 June and get out to Midway about two days later, there to join Frank Jack Fletcher's Task Force 17 with the *Yorktown*. Ramsey got under way

Often attributed to the *Enterprise*, these Wildcats appear to be former VF-2 Detachment F4F-3As used by ACTG Pacific during carrier qualifications on board the *Saratoga* cruising off San Diego, late May 1942. (NA 80-G-14784.)

early the morning of 1 June and nosed his newly designated Task Group 11.1 past Point Loma and into the Pacific. Already hoisted on board the *Saratoga* was a cargo of four F4F-4s, forty-three SBD-3s, and fourteen Grumman TBF-1 Avengers. At 1310, the *Sara* began landing her air group:

Commander, *Saratoga* Air Group,		
	Cdr. Harry D. Felt	1 SBD-3
Fighting Two Detachment	Lieut. Louis H. Bauer	14 F4F-4, -7
Scouting Three	Lt. Cdr. Louis J. Kirn	22 SBD-3

Bauer's outfit had swelled in May to fourteen with the inclusion of six NAPs who had recently graduated from ACTG, Pacific. The VF-2 Detachment on 1 June comprised:

Old VF-2 hands:
Lieut. Louis H. Bauer, USN
Lieut. (jg) Gordon E. Firebaugh, NAP, USN
Lieut. (jg) Theodore S. Gay, NAP, USN
Lieut. (jg) Harold E. Rutherford, NAP, USN
Ens. George W. Brooks, NAP, USN
Gunner Charles E. Brewer, NAP, USN
Mach. Patrick L. Nagle, NAP, USN
Mach. Donald E. Runyon, NAP, USN

Newly assigned:
Lee P. Mankin, AP1c, NAP, USN
Robert H. Nesbitt, AP1c, NAP, USN
Harold M. O'Leary, AP1c, NAP, USN
William J. Stephenson, AP1c, NAP, USN
Clark A. Wallace, AP1c, NAP, USN
Stanley W. Tumosa, AP2c, NAP, USN

Other pilots, mostly fresh from advanced training, rode the *Saratoga* out to Pearl to join other squadrons. Ramsey set a westerly course at a steady 20 knots.

Missing his new command by a day and a half, Aubrey Fitch on board the *Chester* arrived at San Diego the afternoon of 2 June. The transports *Barnett* and *George F. Elliott* docked at the destroyer base inside San Diego harbor and disgorged the multitude of *Lexington* survivors. The fighter pilots split according to their orders. Paul Ramsey and the original VF-2 hands waited for new assignments, while Scoop Vorse took charge of the VF-3 refugees, trying to get them back out to Pearl to rejoin the squadron. Noel Gayler headed east to become a test pilot. Jimmy Flatley happily reported to NAS San Diego and his nascent Fighting Ten, ready to implement the ideas he had so carefully thought out on the voyage back. Fitch waited until the *Chester* could be refueled and reprovisioned, so he could ride her out to Pearl.

The *Saratoga*'s return to the war zone was uneventful except for some activity on 3 June. At 1026, a radar contact bearing 007 degrees, distance 26 miles afforded an opportunity to practice a CAP scramble. Six VF-2 F4F-4s roared off the flight deck and checked out the bogey, which proved to be an Army B-17 Flying Fortress on a ferry flight to Oahu. At 1215, another contact activated the radar scope, and five fighters took off. A few minutes later, one of the five, NAP Tumosa, lost power at 5,000 feet and tried to get back to home plate for a deferred forced landing. The *Saratoga* was not prepared to recover him, and after circling three times, Tumosa had to put his Grumman into the water. The destroyer *Smith* quickly rescued him unharmed, offering practice of another sort, but at the price of F4F-4 BuNo. 5182.[2]

While the *Saratoga* ate up the miles toward Pearl Harbor, the Pacific Fleet slugged it out with the Japanese at Midway and triumphed in decisive victory. At 0545 on 6 June, the *Saratoga* despatched her air group for fields on Oahu and headed in. She anchored at berth F-2 off Ford Island after an absence of nearly four months. The situation was not nearly as grave as it appeared two days before! With the victory, details of which were very sketchy, the CinCPac staff first thought to send the *Saratoga* out to join Task Force 16 for raids on the newly acquired enemy holdings in the Aleutians. With the second and fatal torpedoing of the *Yorktown* that afternoon, Nimitz decided not to risk an inexperienced carrier and ad hoc air group in combat. He assigned Duke Ramsey a new mission: ferry replacement aircraft to Spruance's carriers, then return to Pearl.

The *Saratoga*'s cruise would provide carrier squadrons long based ashore the chance to stretch their sea legs. Alerted for duty on board the carrier were the outfits that had arrived at Pearl on 29 May: Roy Simpler's Fighting Five, Fighting Seventy-two under Mike Sanchez, and the Torpedo Eight Detachment with Grumman TBF-1 torpedo planes led by "Swede" Larsen. Given the news blackout on Oahu, Simpler's troops, who considered themselves the legitimate *Yorktown* fighting squadron, wondered what was happening to the old lady and were surprised at orders to embark on board the *Saratoga*. Also eager to go were those elements of the *Yorktown* Air Group left on the beach, the "real" Scouting Five and Torpedo Five. With all of the fighters now available, VF-42's Chas Fenton and Vince McCormack, unhappily waiting at Ewa, had to bide their time. They took custody of the sixteen rookie VF pilots who had come out on board the *Saratoga* and maintained a collection of battleworn F4F-3s, survivors of Coral Sea, while they awaited delivery of some F4F-4s. Lou Bauer discovered on reporting in that his own superior, Don Lovelace, had gone out on board the *Yorktown*. Owing to radio silence, he did not know that Lovelace had died on 30 May. Bauer exchanged several of his F4F-4s and gratefully turned over to NAS Pearl Harbor the hybrid

The USS *Saratoga* (CV-3) in Pearl Harbor, 6 June 1942, after her voyage from San Diego. (NA 80-G-10121.)

F4F-7 for the time being. He and eight pilots were to reembark on board the *Saratoga*, relegating most of his rookies to Fenton at Ewa.

On 7 June, Ramsey's redesignated Task Group 11.2 set sail from Pearl with the *Saratoga*, five destroyers, and the oiler *Kaskaskia*. Jake Fitch missed the boat again. His temporary flagship *Chester* had departed San Diego on 4 June and was still en route to Pearl. Around 1100, the *Saratoga* began landing part of her improvised air group. All of those aircraft plus those previously hoisted on board the *Saratoga* totaled 107 (47 fighters, 45 dive bombers, and 15 torpedo planes) organized as shown in the table. His aircraft safely tucked on board, Ramsey set course to the northwest.

Commander, *Saratoga* Air Group,		
	Cdr. Harry D. Felt	1 SBD-3
Fighting Five	Lt. Cdr. Leroy C. Simpler	18 F4F-4s
Fighting Seventy-two	Lt. Cdr. Henry G. Sanchez	20 F4F-4s
Fighting Two Detachment	Lieut. Louis H. Bauer	9 F4F-4s
Scouting Three	Lt. Cdr. Louis J. Kirn	25 SBD-3s
Scouting Five	Lt. Cdr. William O. Burch, Jr.	10 SBD-3s
Ferry Detachment	Lieut. Keith E. Taylor	9 SBD-3s
Torpedo Five	Lieut. Edwin B. Parker	5 TBD-1s
Torpedo Eight Detachment	Lieut. Harold H. Larsen	10 TBF-1s

"HOW GOOD LAND WILL LOOK THIS TIME"

The seventh of June, the day the valiant *Yorktown* gave up the ghost, Task Force 16 with the *Enterprise* and the *Hornet* retired eastward for a vital fueling rendezvous. Other than for normal flight operations (search and inner air patrol), the aviators spent a quiet day trying to pick up the pieces. Spruance's two carriers had on hand a total of 131 aircraft (just over one hundred short of the 4 June figure, including the *Yorktown*) of which 118 (54 fighters, 61 dive bombers, and 3 torpedo planes) apparently were operational. To the southeast, Fletcher spent the day completing his fueling, then headed out to meet Task Group 11.2 coming up from Pearl. That evening, CinCPac issued specific orders for the second phase of the Midway operation. He set a 10 June rendezvous between Fletcher's Task Force 17 (which by that time would include the *Saratoga*) and Spruance's Task Force 16 in order to transfer aircraft from the *Saratoga* to the other flattops. This completed, Fletcher was to turn south for Pearl Harbor.

For Ray Spruance's Task Force 16, Nimitz had other ideas. Concurrent with their assault on Midway, the Japanese had rampaged in the Aleutians and evidently intended to occupy a number of positions in the island chain. The enemy had used strong forces, including carriers, and Nimitz thought the enemy might be up to further mischief in northern waters. Thus Spruance with his two carriers, five cruisers, one light cruiser, eight destroyers, and a fleet oiler was to proceed north to "Point Blow" (Lat. 48° North, Long. 172° West), there on 12 June to rendezvous with elements of Rear Admiral Robert A. Theobald's Task Force 8. Spruance was to come under Theobald's overall command in order to "seek out and destroy enemy forces in the Aleutians."[1] For the aviators, there boded uncomfortable, even perilous flying conditions over cold Alaskan waters renowned for fog, icing, and other noxious forms of bad weather.

The weather on 8 June round Task Force 16 seemed a foretaste of what the pilots could expect in the Aleutians. The *Hornet* lost two SBDs in the poor visibility, one of which found sanctuary on Midway. Good thing the weather was not that way on 4 June when the Japanese first attacked! At 0430, Spruance's ships had begun fueling, destroyers first, from the oiler *Cimarron*. It was their first drink from an oiler in nine days. Later the oiler *Guadalupe* and four destroyers joined up to hasten the fueling. The tincans took the opportunity to transfer aviators they had fished out of the water the past several days. Bill Warden returned to Fighting Six on board the *Enterprise*, while VF-8's Jim Smith made it to the *Cimarron*. That day came definite word of the *Yorktown*'s demise, which saddened everyone and robbed the victory of some of its sweetness.

Fletcher's truncated Task Force 17 (the *Astoria*, the *Portland*, and three destroyers) at 1112 made contact with Ramsey's Task Group 11.2, and early that afternoon, he transferred his flag to the flattop. That accomplished, the reconstituted Task Force 17 steamed northwestward to contact Task Force 16. The *Saratoga* conducted the usual search and inner air patrols, but Ramsey kept his fighters under wraps.

The eighth of June also proved a red letter day for the VF-8 pilots lost on the ill-fated 4 June escort mission.[2] That day PBYs operating north–northeast of Midway finally happened upon some of the rafts and rescued their occupants. One Catalina bellied into the sea to recover the irrepressible John McInerny and section leader John Magda. The two had hoped for an early rescue on 5 June when they happened to see Task Force 16 pass by in the distance (as Spruance headed toward Midway that morning), but no one spotted them. Now flown to Midway, Magda and McInerny looked in good shape and high spirits as they clowned with John Ford's motion picture photographer at the seaplane base. McInerny, however, was deeply worried about the consequences of his turning the fighters back on 4 June, but nothing was ever said to him about it.

A second PBY that day found Frank Jennings and Hump Tallman not too far

(*Left photo*) Ens. John McInerny (*right*) and Ens. John Magda of VF-8 at Midway after their rescue on 8 June by a PBY. (*Right photo*) Ens. Johnny Talbot of VF-8 arriving 8 June at Midway after being picked up by Lieut. (jg) Frank Fisler's PBY. (These photos are stills from Cdr. John Ford's *The Battle of Midway*.)

from where the other picked up Magda and McInerny. As Tallman stepped out of his orange raft, a PBY crewman noticed its interior scribbled with a lengthy message. After ditching, Tallman had set down in detail his recollections of the mission, anxious that it be preserved. Both he and the crewman tried in vain to retrieve the raft, but it floated away and had to be left behind. Also rescued that afternoon was Johnny Talbot, weak from his lonely ordeal. Lieut. (jg) Francis M. Fisler's PBY from VP-51 spotted his raft and whisked him back to Midway for treatment. Still missing were five VF-8 pilots, but Talbot helped point out where they might be.

The morning of 9 June, one of Fisler's sharp-eyed crew spotted the two rafts containing Pat Mitchell, Stan Ruehlow, and Dick Gray. The three were emaciated, tired, sore, sunburned, hungry—and gloriously glad to be alive. The PBY picked them up at a point bearing 047 degrees, distance 131 miles from Midway, and one of the grateful castaways (evidently Ruehlow) presented the crew with a "short snorter," a ten-dollar bill upon which the details of the rescue were written.[3]

For six days the three VF-8 pilots had drifted slowly to the northwest, carried by the current. On 5 June they had several times sighted search planes and tried signaling them with a hand mirror. After dark that day came a really big scare. In the blackness a shark repeatedly nudged both rafts. Finally the bump was violent enough to spill both Ruehlow and Mitchell into the water. Ruehlow actually brushed the shark and gashed his right hand on its rasping skin. He lost no time in making it to Gray's raft, while Mitchell clambered into the now vacant but damaged second raft. The skipper had to lie in the nearly swamped boat with his legs dangling in the water, but very fortunately the shark did not persist in its attacks. On 6 June the three dipped into the survival rations so fortuitously saved by Gray. Even though severely rationed, the food and water did not go far. After another blistering day and cold night in the water-soaked rafts, they secured their first replenishment of fresh water from a rain squall, allowing them to refill their canteen. Rescue came none too soon, as far as they were concerned. The VF-8 pilots spent a few days at Midway, then they were flown back to the naval hospital at Pearl Harbor.

While the VF-8 pilots were recovered, other survivors of the Midway battle made it back to Pearl. At 1530 on 8 June, the submarine tender *Fulton* docked at the submarine base inside Pearl Harbor. There to greet the Yorktowners were Nimitz and the rest of the fleet brass, shaking hands and showing much good cheer. Headed ashore were Macomber and Woollen from VF-42, and from VF-3 came

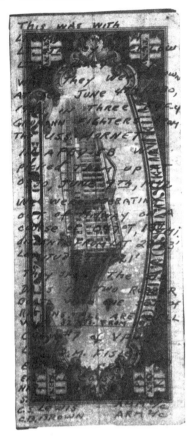 

The VF-8 "short snorter" $10 bill. Obverse legend:

This was with Lt. Comdr. Mitchell, Lt. Stanley Ruehlow, Lt. j.g. Richard Grey (*sic*) when they went down at sea June 4th, 1030, 1942, in three F4F-4 Grumann (*sic*) fighters from the U.S.S. Hornet. In a PBY-5B we picked them up at 0930, June 9th, 1942. We were operating out of Midway on a course of 047° T. 134 mi. distant from Lat. 28° 23' Longitude 177° 21'

They spent the six days in two rubber boats with one set of rations. All are well Wind 32 kts. from 190° T.

Crew #7 of VP-51
Lt. j.g. F.M. Fisler
Ens. Jerry Crawford
Ens. R.L. Cousinslak
NAP Ward AP2c
S.R. Topolski Amm2/c
C.S. Lewis Amm2/c
C.B. Brown Arm2/c

"Short snorter" reverse:

On June 8th, 1942 at 1536 we had picked up Ensign Talbot near the spot we found the other three the next day.

It has been our deep regret that we couldn't find Ens. Kelly and Hill who have been lost near these three other men

R.I.P.

(Source of VF-8 short snorter: Bowen P. Weisheit, Ens. C. Markland Kelly, Jr. Memorial Foundation.)

Cheek, Tootle, Eppler, Morris, and Evans. The seven traveled out to Ewa to join Fenton's contingent. Harry Gibbs came in the next day with the salvage survivors on board the *Gwin* and the *Benham*.

For the carriers, 9 June was a quiet day. The *Enterprise* had the duty, but the fighters did not fly. Jim Smith got back to the *Hornet* while she refueled from the oiler *Cimarron*. Task Forces 16 and 17 made contact the morning of 10 June, for all the good it did them. It was "foggy, foul weather—a day in bed for all hands,"[4] recorded the VF-6 diary. Fletcher and Spruance marked time on a southerly course, waiting for the skies to clear. The *Enterprise* did not get a glimmer of the "floating drydock" (as her pilots unkindly dubbed the *Saratoga*) until late afternoon. The aircraft transfer finally took place the morning of 11 June. To the *Enterprise*, the *Saratoga* flew ten SBDs from Scouting Five (the "real" Scouting Five) and five TBDs from Torpedo Five. The *Hornet* received the nine replacement SBDs of the ferry detachment and the ten Grumman TBF-1s of Larsen's Torpedo Eight Detachment. The TBFs excited special interest, as this was the first time Task Force 16 had seen the big Grumman torpedo planes operate on a carrier. The reinforcements gave Spruance's two carriers a total of 163 aircraft on board (57 fighters, 87 dive bombers, and 19 torpedo planes, not all flyable).

Its mission completed, Task Force 17 by 1100 had turned south for Pearl, while Spruance shaped course north for the next day's rendezvous with Task Force 8 and further combat in Aleutian waters. A few hours later came a welcome reprieve. Nimitz relented and ordered Task Force 16 home. With the Japanese on the run in the Central Pacific, he had no need to risk the carriers in raids on the enemy toehold in the Aleutians. Also on 11 June, the carrier *Wasp* traversed the Panama Canal and reported for duty with the Pacific Fleet. With the loss of the *Lexington* and the *Yorktown*, however, that still left CinCPac with only four fleet carriers—but the Japanese did not have even that many big carriers after Midway!

Steaming southeastward into warmer waters, the two task forces gratefully enjoyed better weather on 12 June. The *Saratoga* that afternoon launched all of her operational fighters. Simpler's Fighting Five and Bauer's VF-2 Detachment (twenty-six F4F-4s all told) flew a welcome gunnery training flight, while Sanchez led nineteen VF-72 fighters in squadron tactical drills. One pilot did not find the exercise much to his liking. At 1447, Lieut. (jg) Robert W. Rynd of VF-72 had engine trouble and ditched. The destroyer *Russell* recovered him unharmed. On board the *Enterprise*, VF-6 pilots handled the last two inner air patrols, but no one minded. They were on their way home!

The morning of 13 June saw a massive fly-in of carrier planes to fields on Oahu. Somewhat ahead of the rest, the squadrons of the *Saratoga* Air Group took off beginning at 0650 and made for NAS Pearl Harbor. Later that morning Task Force 17 entered port. Task Force 16's turn came a little later. The *Enterprise* Air Group flew to NAS Kaneohe Bay, pleased to find there, "a band to meet us and free beer right on the field."[5] The *Hornet* launched her squadrons for MCAS Ewa. Thach's VF-3/42/8 pilots all took care to get into their own squadron's airplanes for the scheduled flight in. When they touched down, Thach and the VF-3 pilots taxied to one part of the field, Harwood's VF-8 troops to another, while Leonard led the VF-42 personnel to a homecoming at the hangar where Fenton, McCormack, and company had set up shop. There was no formal goodby between Thach and the VF-42 pilots who had served him well. There just was not time for that. He flew over to Kaneohe to reunite Fighting Three. Leonard personally did not see him again for two years. That was the way it went. The first phase of the Pacific War was over, but most of the work remained to be done.

CHAPTER 17

The "First Team" Graduates

In the euphoria following victory at Midway, Admirals King and Nimitz took the opportunity to evaluate the state of the carrier air groups upon which so much had depended. With regard to experienced carrier pilots, qualified replacements, and aircraft, CinCPac had operated on a shoestring during the first seven months of the war. Had all of his flattops actually been available, Nimitz would have been hard-pressed to fill out their squadrons, given the small numbers of pilots and planes that trickled westward from the mainland. The fighting squadrons, whose operating strength increased haltingly as the need for their services became more urgent, suffered great turbulence, with planes, pilots, and people shifted here and there as requirements dictated. Manning the three fighting squadrons heading out in late May to Midway took virtually every available fighter pilot in the islands. After Midway, CinCPac had a particularly tired bunch of pilots on his hands, many of whom had persevered with very little rest since the outbreak of the war.

CominCh took the first move to correct the situation. On 11 June, King informed Nimitz that he would assign "service-type aircraft"[1] to the two carrier replacement air groups (Nine and Ten) then in existence and also allot aircraft to others to be created in the near future. Because of production difficulties, modern aircraft were slow in getting to the fleet, and newly formed squadrons often languished with only a few planes. King hoped to ready them for combat as soon as possible. The main obstacle, he noted, was "to provide trained pilot replacements for the carriers now in service and for new carriers." He intended to create a new post: Commander, Carrier Replacement Squadrons, Pacific Fleet, under a rear admiral.

Four days later, King elaborated his thoughts by recommending what should be done with the *Lexington* and *Yorktown* Air Groups, now without flight decks.[2] CominCh wanted to retain the *Lexington* squadrons in commission with the same designations (that is, Fighting Two, Bombing Two, Scouting Two, and Torpedo Two), but transfer up to half the original personnel to other units. Beefed up with new pilots, the old *Lex* squadrons would comprise Carrier Replacement Air Group Eleven, to be organized on the West Coast. Regarding the *Yorktown* squadrons, King proposed essentially the same fate. He thought it best to use former *Yorktown* people to fill out the *Enterprise* and *Hornet* groups as needed, then rebuild the squadrons themselves as components of Carrier Replacement Air Group Twelve, to be formed in the Hawaiian Islands.

Meanwhile, on 13 June, the carriers had returned to port. Nimitz gave his aviators four days off on forty-eight-hour notice. They had a chance to unwind and dispute with the Army Air Force as to who won the Battle of Midway. Nimitz turned to the vital question of carrier pilot replacements. The evening of 15 June he responded with a major policy statement. First, he heartily concurred with the idea of creating a special command to control carrier replacement squadrons in his area and suggested it be organized at NAS San Diego. The replacement situation, CinCPac stressed, grew critical because:

> New aircraft deliveries and new flight school graduates have done little more than balance operational and battle losses of active carrier planes and pilots.[3]

To remain combat ready, the Pacific Fleet's carriers had to be able to draw upon "a reasonable pool of planes and pilots" in the Hawaiian Islands. Nimitz desired expansion of this pool into a functioning carrier replacement air group "as soon as practicable."[4]

Assessing the condition of his own air groups, Nimitz characterized it as "not good" because of "operational fatigue due to long continued intensive operations at sea and heavy battle attrition without reliefs." The only solution was a massive reorganization of the carrier squadrons. Nimitz indicated he would:

> . . . return to mainland for assignment to new squadrons to extent they can now be spared pilots who are the most exhausted, particularly those of *Yorktown* and *Enterprise* groups.[5]

He would have need of his carriers shortly. Plans were brewing in Washington for renewed operations in the New Britain–Solomons area, and CinCPac wanted to remedy the pilot situation swiftly.

Thus in mid-June, Nimitz took steps to rotate home the pilots who had seen the most flying and fighting the past seven months. Such duty took its toll. Physicals taken by VF-42 pilots resting at Ewa showed that nearly all were ten to fifteen pounds underweight and demonstrated other deleterious effects of the strain they endured. Newly formed fighting squadrons as well as the training command vitally required their combat experience for indoctrinating rookie pilots. Nimitz was especially concerned that if he kept the same pilots in battle continuously, they would just be killed off one by one. He wanted to give them the chance to survive a long war. The agency of this reorganization was the administrative office of Commander, Carriers, Pacific Fleet. Rear Admiral Noyes left for the West Coast to assume command of Task Force 18 built around the *Wasp*, which arrived on 19 June at San Diego. Temporarily taking Noyes's place was the head of NAS Pearl Harbor, Captain Shoemaker, a former skipper of Fighting Two.

The powers-that-be moved to reshape the carrier squadrons, disbanding some and beefing up others. The first consideration involved transferring stateside those aviators who had earned a rest. With regard to the fighters, they primarily came from Fighting Forty-two and Fighting Six. Second was to increase operating strength within the fighting squadrons. On board two flattops, fresh fighting squadrons took up residence: Simpler's Fighting Five on board the *Saratoga* and Sanchez's Fighting Seventy-two on board the *Hornet*. The third carrier at Pearl, the *Enterprise*, would keep Fighting Six, but with a different skipper and many new faces. At San Diego, the *Wasp*'s Fighting Seventy-one (VF-71) under Lt. Cdr. Courtney Shands did not figure in the reorganization, as the ship never did come out to Pearl, but sailed on 1 July directly to the South Pacific.

On 16 June, some familiar faces reappeared at Pearl. Arriving on a transport from San Diego were members of VF-3's old team: Scoop Vorse, Bob Morgan,

Marion Dufilho, Bill Eder, John Lackey, Lee Haynes, and Doc Sellstrom. They learned that their old skipper and what was left of the outfit resided at Kaneohe. Thach had released Tom Barnes and Tom Cheek to rejoin their NAP buddies in Lou Bauer's VF-2 Detachment and held the fort with his batch of rookies, some recently arrived and others who had met the test at Midway. Anxious to report, Vorse and Sellstrom went to Ford Island to hitch a ride up to Kaneohe. Two VB-3 SBD pilots gladly obliged. Sellstrom rode in the rear seat of Ens. Bunyan R. Cooner's Dauntless. During the takeoff run from Luke Field, Cooner failed to gain flying speed and clipped a crane parked at the end of the field. The SBD, its tail torn off, bounded into the air, hurtled over a bus on a nearby road, and crashed in flames about a hundred yards beyond. By coincidence, Jim Gray rode on the bus. He ran along with the passengers and other onlookers hastening to rescue the crew. Suddenly he realized that according to standing orders the SBD toted a 500-lb. bomb. Yelling a warning, he dived to the ground just in time to escape the blast of the bomb, which killed Cooner and three would-be rescuers. A dozen others were injured. Sellstrom sustained severe burns and internal injuries. He lingered for five days, but finally died on 21 June.[6] Appointed an aviation cadet on 15 March 1941, Doc first wore his golden wings that September. Posted on 8 December to Fighting Three, he came to be regarded as a fearless and resourceful fighter pilot, both in the 20 February fight and at Coral Sea. Well-liked by his squadron mates, he would be missed.

On 17 June, Fighting Six reopened for business at Kaneohe after the welcome rest. That morning the squadron turned out on "The Big E" for an awards ceremony. Nimitz presented Distinguished Flying Crosses for the 1 February raids to Gray and Rawie of Fighting Six and VF-42's McCuskey and Adams. The next day Gray's pilots resumed gunnery training missions, operating about 15 miles off Oahu's north coast. The pilots took turns making gunnery passes against a towed sleeve at 5,000 feet. Diving in with an overhead run, Ralph Rich's F4F-4 shed its right wing and spun uncontrollably. Rich could not escape and rode his mutilated bird into the water. He was another combat veteran lost in an operational accident. Newly promoted to lieutenant (j.g.), Rich had served with Fighting Six for two years. "He's been in it all," the VF-6 war diary observed.[7]

Early on 19 June, Gray received orders to return the squadron to the *Enterprise* at anchor in Pearl Harbor. Rumor had it that the squadron would be reorganized. Sure enough, Lou Bauer and his nine NAPs reported on board "The Big E." The previous day he had turned over his nine F4F-4s to Fighting Five, and now he had orders assigning him command of Fighting Six in place of Gray, who would be going home. The old Fighting Six ceased to exist. Staying with the squadron were ten pilots who had joined after the war began: Grimmell, Wileman, Halford, Achten, Allard, Reid, Rhodes, Sumrall, Warden, and Packard. For the last seven, it was old home week being reunited with their old mates from Fighting Two. Indeed, Bauer's new Fighting Six was almost a reincarnation of the old Chiefs of Fighting Two, as most of the pilots were NAPs. Bauer rounded up his veterans and some newly arrived pilots to return to Kaneohe and prepare for operations off the *Enterprise*. Leaving the squadron for duty with Fighting Five were six pilots: Daly, Gunsolus, Presley, Holt, Kleinmann, and Roach. Eleven old hands remained on board the *Enterprise* packing and awaiting orders for a thirty-day home leave and new assignments. They were: Gray, Mehle, Hoyle, Quady, Rawie, Kelley, Heisel, Hiebert, Bayers, Provost, and Hodson. The eagerly awaited orders came through on 21 June.

Fighting Forty-two at Ewa was the next to fall under CinCPac's edict. The decision was to disband VF-42 and return all pilots to the States for a rest and new duties. For most it would be the first extended shore duty in nearly a year. The last few days at Ewa had been interesting, particularly for the *Yorktown* survivors whose personal effects went down with the ship. They had few clothes and very little money! The sixteen pilots heading home were: Fenton, McCormack, Leonard, Crommelin, Brassfield, Mattson, Macomber, McCuskey, Woollen, W. W. Barnes, Haas, Wright, Adams, Gibbs, Markham, and Bain. What an enviable record they had made for themselves—victories at Coral Sea and Midway! Final orders decommissioning the unit arrived on 22 June. Fenton the next day turned over six F4F-4s to Fighting Three and the last of his faithful F4F-3s to Marine Air Group 23. Unencumbered, the VF-42 pilots on 24 June boarded the transport *Mount Vernon*, where they met the United States–bound VF-6 contingent and other carrier pilots departing for new assignments. The *Mount Vernon* sailed to San Francisco, arriving in early July, and the aviators split up for a thirty-day home leave.

Fighting Three at Kaneohe also had a change in command. Jimmy Thach's own stateside orders came through on 19 June. He awaited the arrival on Oahu of Butch O'Hare, who formally assumed command of Fighting Three on 24 June, as Thach headed home for a rest and a new mission—spreading the word on how to fight and win in the Pacific air war. Meanwhile, the squadron that had taken VF-3's place set sail on board the *Saratoga*. On 22 June, Roy Simpler's Fighting Five with twenty-seven F4F-4s went out on board the *Sara* as part of Rear Admiral Fitch's Task Force 11 for a week's voyage to Midway, there to deliver army fighters and marine dive bombers to bolster the garrison. Lt. Cdr. O'Hare readied the twenty-seven VF-3 Wildcats to operate out of NAS Maui.

Joining VF-3 late that June on Maui was Fighting Eight. The *Hornet*'s former fighting squadron was in disarray. After the Midway fiasco, it never completely reassembled as a unit. Lieut. O'Neill left for the mainland as soon as the ship docked on 13 June. His orders had come through even before the Battle of Midway. Bruce Harwood retained command at Ewa pending the return of Pat Mitchell from the naval hospital at Pearl. Mitchell, Ruehlow, and Dick Gray had been flown to Oahu to recover from their ordeal in the rafts. On 14 June, the squadron drew fourteen new F4F-4s to replace losses at Midway and restore operating strength to twenty-seven airplanes. Five days later, the powers-that-be changed their collective mind and transferred ten VF-8 aircraft to Mike Sanchez's Fighting Seventy-two, heir apparent to the VF spot in the *Hornet* Air Group. Toward the end of June, Mitchell rejoined the squadron, but only for a day or two. New orders relieved him as squadron commander and assigned him as the *Hornet*'s assistant air officer. He served on board the *Hornet* until she was lost in October, then headed stateside to the training command. Stan Ruehlow took his place as acting CO and flew VF-8's seventeen F4F-4s to Maui. Harwood landed a berth as executive officer of the reconstituted Torpedo Eight on board the *Saratoga*. Fighting Eight's status, on the other hand, was in doubt.

Late in June strange events were taking place in San Diego. Sentiment for the old *Lex* still ran high. In line with ComInCh's stated intention of retaining the *Lexington* Air Group, around 26 June all four squadrons (fighting, bombing, scouting, and torpedo) of Carrier Replacement Air Group Ten were redesignated "Two" in place of "Ten."[8] Thus Jimmy Flatley's Fighting Ten became known as "Fighting Two," ironic because virtually all of the NAP fighter pilots were with Lou Bauer in Fighting Six. On 27 June, VF-2's former skipper, Paul Ramsey, took a temporary job with Advanced Carrier Training Group, Pacific,[9] but two other VF-2 veterans, Fred Borries and Bob Kanze, were posted to Flatley's "Fighting Two." However, the resurrected *Lexington* Air Group was not to be. On 10 July, the authorities restored the numerical designation "Ten" to those squadrons. As of that date Fighting Two ceased to exist, the end of a glorious tradition. Fighting Ten under Flatley's inspired leadership went on to establish its own renown as the "Grim Reapers."

Early in July, Captain Shoemaker implemented the decision to increase fighting squadron operating strength from twenty-seven to thirty-six F4F-4 Wildcats. A few months before, thirty-six fighters on board a single flattop would have been unheard of. The move meant carrier air groups with thirty-six fighters, thirty-six dive bombers, and twelve torpedo planes each. This final reorganization had to take place before impending operations in the South Pacific, and saw a scramble for pilots and aircraft before the *Saratoga* and the *Enterprise* sailed in July for the South Pacific. The burden fell upon the two carrierless fighting squadrons, VF-3 and VF-8.

To O'Hare's dismay, his Fighting Three had in essence become a reserve pool for other units. On 2 July, Dufilho, Haynes, Bass, and Bright said goodby and departed for Fighting Five on board the *Saratoga*. The biggest loss came on 5 July, when XO Scoop Vorse, Ram Dibb, and six newcomers headed off to Fighting Six, taking with them nine F4F-4s to round up Bauer's squadron to thirty-six fighters. That left O'Hare at quiet NAS Maui with eighteen F4F-4s. Reporting for a short time as exec was the *Yorktown*'s former hangar deck officer, the able Lieut. Alberto C. ("Ace") Emerson. However, Emerson and John Lackey left on 11 July for Fighting Seventy-two on board the *Hornet*. So it went. By late July, O'Hare had given up his experienced pilots either to other squadrons (mainly the nascent Carrier Replacement Air Group Twelve) or to the training command. His role in tranquil Hawaii, nevertheless, was extremely valuable. When Flatley's Fighting Ten came out to the islands that September, O'Hare worked closely with him, imparting Jimmy Thach's wisdom on the four-plane division and the "beam defense position" (see appendix on "Thach Weave"). For this reason, Flatley changed from six-plane to four-plane "flights" and used Thach's defensive tactics in combat. O'Hare's next opportunity for combat finally came in the summer of 1943.

If the reorganization altered VF-3's role for the time being, it proved fatal to the unfortunate Fighting Eight also languishing at Maui. Ruehlow on 3 July did his part in supplying pilots to Fighting Five. He sent Dick Gray, Starkes, Stover, and Smith along with nine F4F-4s to bring Simpler's outfit up to thirty-six planes. He also was to go along, but another bout in the hospital due to back injuries spoiled that. Fighting Five had to sail without him. On Independence Day the ax

Unit	CO	Station	Allowance of F4F-4s	On Hand (F4F-4s)
VF-3	Lt. Cdr. O'Hare	NAS Maui	27	18
VF-5	Lt. Cdr. Simpler	*Saratoga*	27	36
VF-6	Lieut. Bauer	*Enterprise*	27	36
VF-71	Lt. Cdr. Shands	*Wasp*	27	30
VF-72	Lt. Cdr. Sanchez	*Hornet*	27	36
VF-8	—	NAS Maui	27	0
VF-10*	Lt. Cdr. Flatley	NAS San Diego	27	16
			189	172

*Designated VF-2 until 10 July.

fell on VF-8. Reassigned to Sanchez's Fighting Seventy-two on board the *Hornet* were ten pilots (Ford, Sutherland, Formanek, Cook, Freeman, Dietrich, Hughes, Merritt, Fairbanks, and Carey) and the last of VF-8's planes, nine F4F-4s. That gave VF-72 its quota of thirty-six fighters. The remaining five VF-8 pilots (Jennings, Magda, Talbot, Tallman, and McInerny) went to other squadrons, notably Torpedo Six. Without pilots or aircraft, VF-8 lingered on the books till 25 August before it was stricken. Ruehlow in late July served with Fighting Three for a short time as exec, then went out to the South Pacific with a welcome berth in Flatley's Fighting Ten.

The fighter situation in ComCarPac on 7 July (see table) reflected the vast changes that had taken place in the previous three weeks.[10] A new "first team" had come into being, leavened for the most part (except for Fighting Seventy-one) with combat veterans, and ready to meet the enemy in battle.

CHAPTER 18

Midway Lessons — The F4F-4 Controversy

The evening of 4 June in VF-6's ready room on board the *Enterprise*, an angry Jimmy Thach compiled a preliminary report for VF-3's morning escort mission over the Japanese carriers. His first, bitter reaction is well worth quoting at length:

> It is indeed surprising that any of our pilots returned alive. Any success our fighter pilots may have against the Japanese Zero fighter is *not* due to the performance of the airplane we fly but is the result of the comparatively poor marksmanship of the Japanese, stupid mistakes made by a few of their pilots and superior marksmanship and team work of some of our pilots. The only way we can ever bring our guns to bear on the Zero fighter is to trick them into recovering in front of an F4F or shoot them when they are preoccupied in firing at one of our own planes.

He squarely stated his exasperation: versus the Zero fighter, the Grumman F4F-4 Wildcat was "pitifully inferior in *climb*, *maneuverability*, and *speed*." Even deleting the armor and self-sealing tanks to save weight would not, in his opinion, "increase the performance of the F4F sufficiently to come anywhere near the performance of the Zero fighter." He concluded his report with a warning:

> This serious deficiency not only prevents our fighters from properly carrying out an assigned mission but it has a definite and alarming effect on the morale of most of our carrier based VF pilots. If we expect to keep our carriers afloat we must provide a VF airplane superior to the Japanese Zero in at least climb and speed, if not maneuverability.[1]

The evident disparity between the F4F-4 and the Zero certainly affected the morale of VF-6's Jim Gray, even though his squadron had not lost a fighter pilot at Midway. Following up his 6 April complaint to Halsey, Gray on 9 June directed a letter to the chief of the Bureau of Aeronautics, routing it through channels (McClusky, Murray, and Halsey). In it he reiterated the basic criticisms of the F4F-4 (climb rate, speed, and maneuverability) and added that it was "urgent a better performing model of this series be produced at once if U.S. Navy pilots are to be given anything approaching an even chance in combat with the enemy."[2] What was needed was not a fighter that surpassed the Zero in all aspects; Gray would be satisfied with a better climb rate than the F4F-4 currently showed to enable the Americans to dictate terms of combat. He noted that those of his pilots who tackled Zeros "were helpless unless the Japanese plane was shot down from above without warning."[3]

Gray concluded his BuAer communication with a statement to the effect that all of the carrier fighting squadron leaders at Midway agreed with him. Certainly most of his superiors did. McClusky endorsed the letter by stating the need for better fighters was "conclusively proven"[4] at Midway. Almost all of the Midway action reports by flag officers and carrier captains contained criticisms of the F4F-4. The *Enterprise*'s George Murray felt the Zeros had "completely out-classed" the F4F-4s,[5] while the *Yorktown*'s postmortem noted: "The fighter pilots are very disappointed with the performance and length of sustained firepower of the F4F-4 airplanes."[6] In their reports, Spruance and Mitscher likewise called for greater range on the part of the fighters.

In his comprehensive report to King, Nimitz reviewed the comments, but tempered the criticisms by noting results:

> 74. *Our F4F-4 is markedly inferior to the Japanese Zero* fighter in speed, maneuverability, and climb. These characteristics must be improved, but not at the cost of reducing the *present overall superiority* that in the Battle of Midway enabled our carrier fighter squadrons to shoot down about 3 Zero fighters for each of our own lost. However much this superiority may exist in our splendid pilots, part at least rests in the armor, armament and leak proof tanks of our planes.[7]

Nimitz seemed to hint that although the F4F-4 appeared outclassed by the Zero, things were not as bad as they looked. He felt one problem was that: "In most engagements our fighters were outnumbered."[8] That could be remedied. On the basis of Midway experience, even twenty-seven fighters per squadron were too few, and the decision to raise operating establishment to thirty-six fighters a carrier precipitated the massive reorganization of the fighting squadrons described in Chapter 17. If the F4F-4s were not equal to Zeros on a one-to-one basis, Nimitz at least would see to it there were more F4F-4s available to fight.

Combat lessons from the Midway fighting seemed to reflect a more pragmatic and flexible approach than for Coral Sea. Regarding the escort missions, those on 4 June were dismal failures due to the inability of the fighters to protect their charges. Strike losses, particularly among the torpedo planes, were catastrophic. At least there now was no doubt that the strike planes had to be escorted:

> The need for adequate fighter escort on every attack mission cannot be over emphasized. Without this support our attack groups are completely at the mercy of Japanese "0" fighters. . . . Adequate fighter support implies not only fighters in sufficient numbers but fighters at least equal to enemy.[9]

Also there would be no question of using indirect escorts or complicated plans such as bedeviled the *Enterprise* Air Group on 4 June. From now on, fighters would closely accompany the planes they would escort. The presence of the new Grumman TBF-1 Avenger torpedo planes somewhat simplified the problem of torpedo escort. No longer would the torpedo boys have to lumber along at low altitude. The TBF was relatively fast, well armored, long-legged, and capable of defending itself in a pinch. Of course, the torpedoes were still inferior, hampering the aircraft's ultimate effectiveness as an antishipping weapon.

Another fundamental problem with the F4F-4 in addition to its performance was providing the Wildcat with enough fuel for the fighters to cruise at a decent speed and take the strike planes all the way to the target and back. As previously described, NAS Pearl Harbor developed a forty-two-gallon drop tank attached underneath the fuselage of the F4F-4. Thach's Fighting Three tested the gimmick in early May and found it adequate, although the pilots worried about the location of the tank. In a takeoff or landing mishap, it would be most vulnerable. By the summer of 1942, the Bureau of Aeronautics opted instead for two fifty-eight-gallon auxiliary tanks, one slung under each wing of an F4F-4. That was the system eventually adopted in place of the forty-two-gallon tanks used in the first stages of the Guadalcanal fighting. The new drop tanks and plumbing added about 750 lbs. to an already overloaded F4F-4. Bill Leonard wryly commented that with its two wing tanks, "the F4F-4 was a *DOG!*"[10]

Fighter direction and combat air patrol were more effective at Midway than they were the previous month in the Coral Sea. Task Force 16 escaped attack altogether, leading the admirals to think that separate carrier task forces operating over the horizon from one another provided the key to combat effectiveness. Henceforth, each carrier would have its own flag officer and screening vessels. Actually, the procedure just fragmented the CAP, as the Guadalcanal carrier actions would demonstrate. The ultimate solution saw multi-carrier task forces allowing for a high integration of the CAP.

The leadership also realized the CAP had to be deployed in layers ("stacked" according to later fighter direction parlance). There would have to be at least two levels of fighters, one on high to guard against dive bombers and the lower to attack torpedo planes and hunt snoopers. At Midway, the high CAP, except for Warren Ford's VF-8 division, was largely ineffective because too much was expected of it. In Mitscher's report, he complained: "Vectoring a fighter from 20,000 feet to 1000 feet and back to 20,000 feet consumes an inordinate amount of fuel."[11] Fighting Eight's CAP had fuel worries all day. Fighting Six analysts thought that a third to half the CAP fighters should be kept at 1,000 feet over the ship and not vectored more than 10 to 15 miles in order to guarantee close defense of the task force. Giving the FDOs much more leeway would be the vastly increased number of fighters embarked on board the carriers. Additional fighters would make the idea of "stacking" feasible. At Pearl Harbor the fleet created a school for FDOs under Lt. Cdr. John H. Griffin, a highly experienced naval aviator (USNA 1925). The school would help to evaluate and disseminate the latest FD doctrine in a profession on which so much depended. Thach summed it up well: "Our aircraft carriers can be kept afloat only by fighters."[12]

The uproar over the F4F-4's performance when compared to the Zero fell heavily upon the shoulders of the Washington bureaucrats, especially the Bureau of Aeronautics. After all, BuAer had approved that variant in the first place and placed contracts with Grumman for the production of hundreds of F4F-4s. On 18 April, the Navy had finalized the deal with General Motors for its newly created Eastern Aircraft Division to produce the FM-1, an exact copy of the F4F-4. Deliveries were expected in late summer 1942. Meanwhile, the Bureau seemed to hedge its bets by contracting with Grumman for an additional 100 fixed-wing F4F-3s with four wing guns. These were supposed to be on hand to meet "intermediate needs,"[13] that is, while awaiting delivery of the new Vought F4U-1 Corsairs and the still-to-be-flown Grumman XF6F-1. Grumman could not get around to making the F4F-3s until early 1943, by which time the whole issue was academic. Safe and serene in its cocoon of production schedules, the Bureau was shocked by the tone of the "severe indictments" and irritated by the "continued implications from the Fleet that the Bureau is not even trying to get better airplanes for them."[14]

The Bureau did recognize some shortcomings in the F4F-4, but felt they were inevitable given the circumstances. Cdr. John B. Pearson of BuAer's Engineering Section stressed in a letter to Jimmy Flatley that the Bureau never claimed the F4F-4 was the perfect fighting machine. Personally he thought the Grumman product "a hastily converted peacetime design,"[15] but because of the crying need for fighters, it was the best that could be provided in the rush for production. The

444

THE BATTLE OF MIDWAY

Bureau seemed to feel guilty about the six-gun battery—its reduced ammunition capacity and additional weight. According to Pearson, the decision for six guns with fewer rounds per gun was "very close" inside the Bureau, the deciding point being the need for standardization in production in view of the British insistence on six guns. However, Pearson maintained:

> After seeing the installation which Grumman cooked up for 6 guns, this Section as well as Armament has realized we made a mistake, but there again it was too late to tamper with production at that time.[16]

Actually, Pearson thought the F4F-4's *volume* of fire was excellent and the whole installation much more reliable now that the jamming problems had been handled. Captain Shoemaker of the Carriers, Pacific administrative office agreed. In a 24 June endorsement to Jimmy Thach's 28 May complaint, Shoemaker suggested that the fighter pilots hold two guns in reserve to prolong their time of firing.[17]

The gun controversy became so heated that the Bureau did decide to "tamper with production." Armament labored to redesign the F4F-4's folding wings to accommodate four guns instead of six and with 430 rounds per gun rather than 240. The resulting aircraft, which included a few other minor changes, tipped the scales about 500 lbs. lighter than a standard F4F-4. The Bureau could not interfere with Grumman's production line, now operating in high gear, but they shocked Eastern Aircraft Division on 14 June by issuing a "Navy change" directing that the eleventh production FM-1 and those following had to feature a redesigned four-gun battery. Eastern, already staggered by a massive conversion from making automobiles to producing aircraft, managed to switch over and hold to its production schedule. The first FM-1 made its maiden flight on 1 September.

The Bureau placed most reliance on the new carrier fighters under development or just entering production. In his letter to Flatley, Pearson prophesied that the Vought F4U-1 and the Grumman F6F:

> . . . are going to be a tremendous advance in performance over the F4F-4. It must be paid for in size, but I believe you will find them outstanding in comparison with the Japanese opposition.[18]

Pearson was right; both F4U and F6F were Zero-smashers. Trouble was they would not be ready to fight until 1943. The F4U-1 Corsair had had a long gestation, the first production aircraft finally flying on 25 June 1942. The Grumman XF6F-1 made its initial test flight on 26 June. Meanwhile the Grumman F4F-4 would be *the* naval carrier fighter until mid-1943, and the pilots would have to make the best of it. The two "Jimmies," Thach and Flatley, would show them the best way to do so.

Setting up shop early that June with his nascent Fighting Ten at North Island, Jimmy Flatley observed with interest the brouhaha between the fleet and BuAer. His first inclination after flying the F4F-4 in March was to side with the others and downcheck the portly -4 as an unworthy replacement of the F4F-3. Then came his first combat at Coral Sea, and he realized that when battling Zeros, the difference in performance between the F4F-3 and the F4F-4 really meant nothing. Individually neither was a match for the nimble Mitsubishi in dogfighting. Because the folding wing feature permitted more -4s to be embarked, that was the way to go. For the past several weeks on his voyage back from the South Pacific, Flatley had reviewed the whole question of fighter tactics and philosophy while drafting a squadron doctrine for Fighting Ten. The post-Midway condemnations of the F4F-4 impelled him to share his thoughts with the rest of the Navy. From the squadron doctrine, he distilled the key points and drafted them into a lengthy letter he entitled "The Navy Fighter."[19] On 25 June, he submitted his treatise to ComCarPac with copies to BuAer, CominCh, and CinCPac. According to the author, it was "the first known attempt to diagnose fighter tactics for our carrier squadrons since the outbreak of the war." In Flatley, the Grumman F4F-4 Wildcat found a champion. He felt strongly that, "Our planes and our pilots, if properly handled, are more than a match for the enemy."

First of all, Flatley emphasized that the basic concepts of aerial combat had changed. The idea of individual fighter-versus-fighter duels—classic dogfighting—was obsolete. Instead, he sought to "eliminate the necessity for individual combat." Formation tactics, teamwork, and mutual support were the keys in overcoming the inferiority of a lone F4F-4 pitted against a Zero. Yet the airplane itself had a number of strong points:

> What the F4F-4 lacks in climb and maneuverability is more than compensated for by its excellent armament, protective armor, protected fuel system, and greater strength. Add to this the inherent superior ability of the [U.S.] navy pilot, particularly as regards using his armament, and the outlook is very favorable.

More succinctly, Flatley noted:

> Let us not condemn our equipment. It shoots the enemy down in flames and gets most of us back to our base.

According to Flatley, it was important to accentuate the positive characteristics of the pilots and aircraft and use them to best advantage:

> Remember the mission of the fighter plane, the enemy's VF mission is the same as our own. Work out tactics on that basis. We should be able to out smart him.

He had great confidence in the Navy's basic philosophy of aviation training and gunnery practices, provided they were properly taught to the rookie fighter pilots. By using proper tactics and teamwork, the fighting squadrons could overcome individual enemy superiority in aircraft performance:

> The answer is to get your planes in the air, find out how best to protect another squadron, how best to maneuver when you are attacked from above. Learn how to attack at high speed, shoot, and keep going in formation. Make your sections stay together under any and all circumstances.

For tactical organization, Flatley recommended retention of six-plane divisions ("flights," as he called them) composed of three two-plane sections, in preference to the four-plane divisions being adopted by the other fighting squadrons. His organization for a twenty-seven-plane squadron would see four six-plane "flights" divided into two twelve-plane "divisions" under the CO and XO respectively, with the remaining three pilots as spares. In opting for his concept of "flights," Flatley stipulated that whenever possible, all six pilots were to train and fight together. He further assigned his pilots so that the third section leader in each flight was an experienced man on whom the flight leader could rely for special tasks.

According to Flatley, the six-plane flight contained the optimum number, offering maximum flexibility for most carrier fighter operations. For attacks against Japanese fighters, he thought two sections (four planes) sufficient for the flight's initial bounce of the enemy fighters from above. The third section could remain overhead as top cover to help any of the F4Fs should they need it. Undoubtedly the 8 May Coral Sea CAP action made a deep impression on him because his four VF-42 F4Fs lacked top cover. On the other hand when facing unescorted bombers, the flight leader could make coordinated runs using all three sections. The first and second sections were to attack from the flanks, the first always from the right and the second from the left of the target. Meanwhile, the third section could attack from astern underneath the enemy formation. He devised drills so that practiced fighter pilots could corner enemy bombers no matter what they did.

Defensively, Flatley instructed his flights to split three ways if bounced from above by Zeros. The wingmen were to stick with the section leaders in all cases. The idea was to disperse the attackers in anticipation of gaining altitude superiority and counterattacking. In this respect, he adopted the basic defensive tactics used by the Royal Air Force and the *Luftwaffe* in Europe. For combat air patrol, Flatley preferred the six-plane flight because he could detach one section to look for snoopers and still have strength on hand for emergencies: In the event the whole flight had to break up to hunt snoopers, each section could take a 120-degree sector. For escort duty, Flatley thought the flight ideal because he could deploy two sections in the sun lane above the bombers—the likeliest avenue of approach by enemy interceptors. The third section would take station above the bombers but down sun, where the section leader could watch the sun lane and warn the others of impending attack. Well advised by his friend Bob Dixon, Flatley made provisions for the fighters to dive in and protect the SBDs during their vulnerable pullouts and recoveries.

As always, pilot morale was vital to Flatley. He noticed the deleterious effect of the F4F-4 debate:

> Let's build the confidence of our fighter pilots by teaching them some tactics rather than breaking down their confidence in themselves and their planes by telling them they can't lick the enemy in those planes. They not only can, but they have, and they will continue to do so . . . .

A realist, Flatley had a big stake in making the F4F-4 work. He knew he would soon take his squadron into combat with that airplane because the vaunted F4Us and F6Fs were months away from being combat ready. Yet his enthusiasm for his tactics and the F4F-4 was not simply to stir up the troops and make them feel better. He sincerely felt his methods would work. He concluded his 25 June letter resolutely:

> Let's take stock of ourselves and get down to work and quit griping about our planes.[20]

Flatley's discussion was masterful and timely. Its effect was immediate and helped clear the air. His primary audience, the fighter pilots, knew Flatley was right, even though some might differ here and there with specific tactical recommendations. By virtue of their training in deflection shooting, emphasis on formation tactics, and use of hit-and-run attacks rather than dogfighting, they continued to face the Zero with confidence. In many instances it was the morale of admirals and Washington functionaries that needed bolstering. Within BuAer, Flatley's letter served to "restore our faith in the good sense of at least a part of our operating personnel,"[21] which was a bit uncharitable to those pilots who were chagrined that the Navy had not provided them with a fighter that could outperform the opposition. Secretary of the Navy Frank Knox was extremely pleased with "The Navy Fighter," and he thought it demonstrated "the kind of spirit that wins wars."[22]

Back in the States on thirty-day leave, Jimmy Thach staying at his home in Coronado had plenty of time to consult with Flatley based at nearby North Island (NAS San Diego). The two, good friends, freely exchanged experiences and ideas and found they differed only on a few tactical matters. Thach much preferred the four-plane division as the primary tactical unit. He thought his 4 June escort mission amply demonstrated the impossibility of keeping three sections together—one was bound to be left out in the cold by enemy pressure. Besides, six planes did not fit with his beam defense tactics (later known as the "Thach Weave"), which had been proved at Midway. Flatley evidently was not ready to accept the weave as more efficacious than his idea of splitting in different directions when the flight was attacked by enemy fighters.

Thach's main brief against the F4F-4 airplane was that he considered it primarily a defensive weapon:

> Our tactics were always purely defensive. They were successful in keeping ourselves from being shot down, but we had little opportunity to use offensive action, which we should be able to use in a fighter.[23]

All of the pilots desired an aircraft capable of seeking out and destroying the enemy under all circumstances, one able to dictate and dominate air combat. That happy event lay in the future with the F4U Corsair and the F6F Hellcat. Meanwhile Thach, like Flatley, felt they could do the job with what they had.

While on leave, Thach worked on a revision of the chapter on fighter tactics and doctrine in the March 1941 edition of *Current Tactical Orders and Doctrine, U.S. Fleet Aircraft, Volume One, Carrier Aircraft USF-74 (Revised)*. This was an official publication issued by Vice Admiral Halsey's headquarters and now much out of date. In his preliminary rewrite, Thach had to expunge each reference to the three-plane section and substitute reference to the two-plane section, four-plane division. He recommended for the present that U.S. naval fighters not enjoying altitude advantage over enemy fighters not attack them except to go to the aid of a friendly plane. Most important, he provided sketches of his beam defense formation and the countermoves he had used so effectively at Midway. He emphasized lookout doctrine and the ways in which enemy attacks could be repulsed.[24] Like Flatley's "The Navy Fighter," Thach's efforts offered the first steps in providing the Navy's fighter pilots concrete tactics to counter fighters with superior speed and maneuverability. No longer was the warning "Don't ever dogfight with a Zero!" the only advice one could offer to embattled F4F pilots. Unusual for an officer so junior in rank, Thach received the Distinguished Service Medal for his leadership of Fighting Three and "his unique system of fighting plane combat teams."[25]

PART IV

Conclusion

The decisive test of tactics and materiel in warfare (as well as of the individuals who use them) can only be actual combat. Often the first enemy bullets have destroyed carefully conceived peacetime doctrine and forced the hardest transition of all to make—from theory to methods that will work. In the seven months following the surprise attack on Pearl Harbor, the U.S. Navy's carrier fighting squadrons took that exacting exam (administered by experts of the Imperial Japanese Navy!) and at great sacrifice earned passing marks, unlike some of the other air forces' fighters. Relying on Jimmy Thach's criterion that only fighters can keep carriers afloat, the Japanese in May–June 1942 lost out, sustaining five carriers sunk in return for two American flattops. Another simple generalization, to be sure, is comparative fighter losses, but there again the U.S. Navy's Grumman Wildcats came out ahead. From February through June 1942, the Navy's fighting squadrons shot down seventeen Japanese carrier fighters (three Mitsubishi A5M4 Type 96 carrier fighters and fourteen Zero fighters, with sixteen pilots killed), while losing to them in aerial combat only ten Wildcats (seven pilots killed).

The foundation of U.S. naval fighter doctrine was deflection shooting, an art that in its complexity only the U.S. Navy possessed; and it was sound. The ability to make deflection shots permitted the Navy's fighter pilots to get the most out of their aircraft. Granted the Grumman F4F Wildcat in all of its various versions was inferior in performance and range to the Mitsubishi Zero, but the Wildcat was stronger, far better protected, and enjoyed superior firepower. Perceptive fighter leaders such as Lt. Cdrs. Thach and Flatley conceived of ways in which the F4F's strong points could be used to defeat the Zero. They took the measure of the enemy even before the first captured Zero was tested in the fall of 1942. The lessons of these first carrier air battles were to go a long way in providing the basis for U.S. naval air superiority in the skies over the Pacific.

APPENDIX 1

The Making of
Carrier Fighter Pilots

U.S. NAVAL FLIGHT TRAINING

In the years preceding the Pacific War, the U.S. Navy drew its pilots from three sources: Naval Academy graduates, selected enlisted men, and specially appointed aviation cadets of the Naval Reserve. The pioneer naval aviators were academy men—regular officers who had volunteered for flight training. In 1925 the Naval Academy added courses in naval aviation and offered the midshipmen some flying experience in dual-control trainers. After graduation from four years at Annapolis, the new ensigns served at sea for one tour, after which they could apply for flight training. A sizable portion of each class did eventually earn the coveted "wings of gold" of a naval aviator. By law, only naval aviators could command carriers, seaplane tenders, and naval air stations, and that induced a number of senior officers to qualify as naval aviators (or observers). Thus the Navy looked to its "trade school" to provide its aviation leaders, from squadron commanders to carrier admirals.

In 1917 the Navy began training petty officers and seamen to qualify as Naval Aviation Pilots (NAP). Congress in 1926 set by law the number of enlisted aviators as 30 percent of the Navy's officer pilots. Early the next year, Fighting Two came into existence as an experiment with mostly NAPs and only a few officers. NAPs performed outstandingly in Fighting Two and other fleet squadrons, but the Bureau of Aeronautics opposed the idea of large numbers of enlisted pilots. Because of low appropriations, the Bureau felt it had enough trouble training sufficient officer pilots, and in 1931 stopped accepting enlisted trainees. However, the growing need for pilots compelled the Navy in 1935 to resume qualifying enlisted men as NAPs. Thereafter they remained a small, but useful part of naval aviation, in December 1941 amounting to about 13 percent of the total pilot strength in the Navy, Marine Corps, and Coast Guard.

Recovering from the doldrums of the Depression, the Navy in 1934 obtained authorization from Congress to increase air strength in the next five years by 2,000 aircraft. Regulars could not supply all the necessary pilots; so under the provisions of the Aviation Cadet Act, the Navy in early 1935 began recruiting qualified men (preferably college graduates) between the ages of twenty and twenty-eight for flight training. First they faced thirty days at a naval reserve air base to test basic flying aptitude; then those who passed trained at NAS Pensacola for one year. Upon graduation they retained the rank of "aviation cadet" for three years' active duty with the fleet. Thereafter they were to be commissioned as ensigns in the Naval Reserve and put on inactive status. The Navy trained many excellent pilots in the program, but troubles soon became apparent. Ranked as they were between warrant officers and ensigns, the aviation cadets were in an anomalous position. Like the NAPs they were restricted in flight operations in that only commissioned officers could lead flights. Pay was also low, considering their qualifications and responsibilities. Many discontented cadets resigned from the Navy to become Army Air Corps officer pilots or to take lucrative jobs in the booming aircraft industry.

By 1939 observers in the Bureau of Aeronautics had become quite worried over the numbers of aviation cadets leaving the service and about the morale of those who remained. New plans loomed for a massive expansion of naval aviation. Consequently the Navy secured the passage in Congress of the Naval Aviation Reserve Act of 1939, calling for 6,000 reservist pilots. It stipulated that all aviation cadets who had completed flight training before 1 June 1939 were to receive immediate commissions as ensigns in the Naval Reserve to rank from their dates of graduation. Their specialty designation would be A-V(N), indicating their status as naval reserve aviators. All aviation cadets then in training and those to follow would likewise become ensigns A-V(N) upon graduation. The term of active duty rose from three to seven years, with opportunity for promotion to lieutenant (junior grade) after three. In early 1941 the Navy offered regular commissions to those old-guard aviation cadets (training completed by 1 June 1939) who had persevered. The act served as the chief vehicle for providing new pilots for the fleet. In June and July 1940, Congress authorized expansion of the Navy's air arm first to 4,500, then to 10,000, and finally to an air armada of 15,000 aircraft. This made it imperative to train huge numbers of pilots to fly them. In December 1941, there were about 6,500 naval pilots (in the Navy, Marine Corps, and Coast Guard), and already close to half were reservists.

Almost all of the pilots in the fighting squadrons as of December 1941 had taken flight training after 1935. The main naval aviation training base was NAS Pensacola, offering both primary and advanced instruction. In late 1938 the Hepburn Board recommended training facilities be greatly enlarged to handle the many trainees expected in the near future. The Navy opened new centers at NAS Jacksonville (December 1940) and NAS Corpus Christi (March 1941).

From the beginning, naval flight training emphasized preparation for all aspects of naval aviation, as pilots transferred from biplane scouts to large patrol planes and back again according to the needs of the fleet. In terms of actual flying hours, the Navy's aviation program in the mid-1930s probably offered the most comprehensive training schedule of all the world's air forces. The 1935 syllabus, for example, outlined a one-year course involving 465 hours of ground school and 300 flight hours. All categories of pilot trainees took the same course. However, students checked out in many different types of aircraft, reducing the time available for concentration for one specific category.

Because of the enormous expansion in the works, Rear Admiral John H. Towers, chief of the Bureau of Aeronautics, recommended in September 1939 that the training syllabus be reduced to seven months, including one month of basic indoctrination. Studies had shown this could be accomplished without significantly reducing the quality of instruction. The new syllabus, which went into effect that October, specified the following:

Primary land planes	14 weeks	74 hours
Basic training (intermediate land planes)	5½ weeks	45 hours
Specialized training	6½ weeks	88 hours
	26 weeks	207 flight hours

The course dictated that during basic training, the instructors would evaluate each student and assign him a specialty: patrol and utility, battleship–cruiser observation, or carrier planes. Those selected for carrier duty went to NAS Miami to check out in fighters, dive bombers, and torpedo planes—the three types of carrier aircraft.

It would be useful to follow an aviation cadet through the flight syllabus in effect in January 1941. Candidates initially spent a month at a naval reserve air base for ten hours of elimination flying, after which they first soloed. At the training base (NAS Pensacola or Jacksonville) came two weeks of indoctrination and then the course itself: thirteen weeks of ground school and a like amount of flight training offering 200 flying hours before graduation. Ground school (full time for the first six weeks and half days thereafter) covered such subjects as navigation, power-plants, structures, and radio code. In Squadron 1 (primary land planes) the students spent sixty-nine hours learning basic flying in sturdy biplanes such as the N3N "Yellow Peril" and Stearman N2S. Next came twenty-eight hours in Squadron 2 (basic training) flying obsolete service types such as 03U and SBU biplanes in formation training. At this point the student learned what specialty he would be given. Squadron 3 involved instrument and blind flying training in NJ and SNJ monoplanes, a total of eighteen hours.

Carrier-bound cadets left their training bases for advanced training of eighty-five hours at NAS Miami. Starting in two-seaters for instruction, the students practiced formation flying, aerobatics, fixed and free gunnery, simulated carrier landings, and night flying in various obsolescent carrier types: Grumman F2F and F3F fighter biplanes, Curtiss SBC and Northrop BT dive bombers, and Douglas TBD torpedo planes. At this time the prospective carrier pilot was a jack-of-all-trades, checking out in VF, VSB, and VT. Graduation came in about seven months, bringing the coveted "wings of gold" and commission as an ensign in the reserve. The only major change in the syllabus before the war occurred in September 1941, when BuAer directed that carrier specialists no longer had to qualify in all three types of carrier aircraft. Henceforth they spent their advanced training in the type of airplane they would fly in squadron service, giving them more of a chance to familiarize themselves with their future duty. The previous practice had facilitated wide flexibility in pilot postings, but the number of naval aviation cadets now permitted specialization early in the training period.

The gold on their chests and the single stripes on their sleeves did not make the newly graduated pilots combat ready. They had first to complete operational training, which involved carrier landing qualification and advanced gunnery and tactics for the fighter pilots. Originally the new carrier pilots trained with fleet squadrons temporarily based ashore at North Island (NAS San Diego) or Norfolk. Each combat squadron periodically went ashore to conduct its own special training and instruct new pilots. By spring 1941, this had become impractical because the demands for the squadrons became too great. On 1 May 1941, the principal carrier command, Aircraft, Battle Force, recommended that special advance carrier training groups be established ashore to qualify pilots for day and night carrier landings and conduct individual training in fixed gunnery and unit tactics. Approval was granted by the Chief of Naval Operations on 28 July, creating two such units: "Advanced Carrier Training Group, AIRBATFOR, U.S. Pacific Fleet" at San Diego and on the East Coast, "Advanced Carrier Training Group, Fleet Air Detachment, NAS Norfolk." Instructors and planes had to come from fleet reserve pools, postponing the creation of six new carrier air groups and the increase of several fighting squadrons from eighteen to twenty-seven airplanes each.

The original ACTG syllabus called for seventy-five flying hours in such areas as tactics, navigation, gunnery and bombing, field carrier land practice, the actual carrier qualification, night flying, and instruments. Organization of the groups proceeded very slowly, as qualified instructors and modern aircraft were in short supply. For example, the fighter pilots did not see any Brewster F2A Buffaloes until late 1941. By that time they had racked up from 70 to 150 flight hours in ACTGs, the long wait before war broke out due to few vacancies in the combat squadrons. Because of a lack of suitable aircraft, instructors, and flight decks, time spent in ACTG was not necessarily very useful. Pacific-based combat squadrons still often had to qualify their new pilots in carrier landings because the San Diego ACTG had few opportunities at carrier flight decks.

Because of these deficiencies, the squadrons still bore most of the burden of operational training. Once in his duty squadron, the rookie had to measure up swiftly to the standards set by his commanding officer. This meant hard work refining gunnery skills and learning practical (as opposed to textbook) tactics. Their greatest failing, according to Lt. Cdr. John S. Thach of Fighting Three, was that the ACTG graduates usually had very little fixed gunnery training. He thought new pilots required fifty hours of gunnery training (camera runs and shooting at towed targets) and thirty to fifty hours of team tactics with their own division and section leaders before becoming combat ready.

Proceeding from the origins and training of individual pilots, it is useful to take a short look at how the fighting squadrons were composed according to experience (see the table). The figures indicate the increasing trend toward aviators trained in 1941 or later. As for experience, the four categories listed above could be characterized as follows:

(a) Wings before 1940: 3,500 to 1,000 flight hours
(b) Wings 1940: 1,000 to 600 flight hours
(c) Wings 1941: 600 to 300 flight hours
(d) Wings 1942: about 300 flight hours

	Wings pre-1940	Wings 1940	Wings 1941	Wings 1942	Total
(1) AirBatFor fighting squadrons, 7 December 1941					
VF-2	16	4	2	—	22
VF-3	5	6	6	—	17
VF-6	7	6	6	—	19
	28	16	14	—	58
	(48%)	(28%)	(24%)		
(2) 1 May 1942 at Coral Sea					
VF-2	5	5	12	—	22
VF-42	6	4	8	—	18
	11	9	20	—	40
	(27%)	(23%)	(50%)		
(3) 4 June 1942 at Midway					
VF-3	7	2	16	2	27
VF-6	4	7	17	—	28
VF-8	7	2	18	—	27
	18	11	51	2	82
	(22%)	(13%)	(62%)	(3%)	

JAPANESE NAVAL FLIGHT TRAINING

The Imperial Japanese Navy pursued a policy for pilot procurement and training radically different from that of the U.S. Navy. The Japanese relied upon enlisted men as the backbone of their aviation program. By January 1940, perhaps 10 percent of the Imperial Navy's roughly 3,500 active pilots were officers: regulars from the Naval Academy, a few reserve officers (college graduates) and some "special service" officers (promoted enlisted men). Unlike the U.S. Navy, the Imperial Navy did not require its carrier captains or air flotilla commanders to be qualified naval aviators; so little incentive existed for those above the rank of lieutenant (junior grade) to take flight training. After graduating from the 3½-year course at Eta Jima (Japan's Annapolis), naval cadets served a year afloat as midshipmen, then were commissioned as ensigns. Then they could volunteer for flight training. Unlike the Americans, the Japanese segregated the different categories of pilot trainees (officer and enlisted) into separate classes for different courses. The regular officers became *kōkūjutsu gakusei* (aviation technical students), and their training programs generally lasted seven to eight months until 1940, when the classes were increased to one year.

Enlisted pilots came from two sources: selected ratings drawn from the fleet and pilot candidates directly enrolled from qualified young men and boys. The first category was originally the more numerous. They were simply "pilot trainees" (*sōjū renshūsei*). Petty officers and seaman under the age of twenty-four could apply for transfers to the aviation branch to become pilots. Competition for these highly prestigious posts was incredibly stiff, with standards extremely high. In early 1937, for example, about 1,500 sailors applied for admittance to the thirty-eighth class of pilot trainees, but only seventy were accepted. Of these seventy, a mere twenty-five graduated. Regular enlisted training classes had commenced in 1920, and for the next dozen years there were only one or two classes a year, graduating twenty to forty pilots each. Beginning in 1933, the number of classes per year rose so that by the mid-1930s, there were as many as six a year until the program was reorganized in 1940.

By 1930, however, the high command had recognized the basic redundancy of preparing a man for a specialty in the surface navy, then transferring him to aviation. The Navy decided to enlist youths between the ages of fifteen and seventeen, give them a basic naval education, then teach them how to fly. The boys had to be primary school graduates and in top physical condition. Because of their tender age and lack of higher education, the program had to take several years. The youths were known as "flight reserve enlisted trainees" (*hikōyoka renshūsei*, abbreviated *yokaren*). The first *yokaren* class convened in June 1930 and completed flight school in May 1933. In 1937 with the creation of a second category of *yokaren*, this program was dubbed *Otsu* or "B." That year, the Navy began accepting boys between 15 and 17 who had completed middle school, classifying them as *Kō* or "A." These increased educational standards meant less time spent in preflight studies. The first *Kō* class was enrolled in September 1937 and graduated from flight training in June 1939.

In the spring of 1940, the Imperial Navy overhauled the entire enlisted program into one system. The two *yokaren* categories "A" and "B" remained the same, but the old enlisted pilot trainee classes were redesignated "C" (*Hei*). In August 1941, belated plans were made to train 15,000 naval pilots. The "A," "B," and "C" classes received numbers in the same serial, and by this time there was little to differentiate in the actual flight training of the three groups. In general, "A" graduates were favored with promotions. By the time pilots from both of the *yokaren* programs received their postings to combat units, they had risen to the rank of aviation petty officer, 3rd class. The earliest *Otsu* graduates had reached the rank of ensign (special service), while veteran enlisted pilots could rise to warrant officer.

Until 1940, naval flight training itself was kept short and brutal, usually seven to nine months, in order to weed out the unfit (particularly among the enlisted pilot trainees). The Japanese favored a policy of quality over quantity and often washed out enlisted men for the slightest infractions. By 1940 with the need for expansion apparent, more time was allowed (without relaxing standards) for the men to learn what they had to know. It was no longer a case of "sink or swim," in a program that still tested the student pilots to the limit. In contrast, the U.S. Navy reduced flight training at the same time from a year to about seven months.

It is most convenient here to describe the Imperial Navy's flight training programs as they were in 1940–41, stressing that the general idea after 1940 was to increase the length of training in order to graduate as many qualified pilots as possible. For primary and intermediate training, the various pilot classes reported after preflight to air groups (kōkūtai) of the 11th Combined Air Flotilla scattered among bases in Japan. By December 1941, seven such air groups were in existence. Primary training lasted six months. The officers accumulated about sixty hours of flight time and the enlisted trainees about forty-four. The principal training plane was an antiquated biplane, the Yokosuka K2Y2 Type 87, a modified version of the British 1914 Avro 504K. After soloing and completion of primary training, the fledgling pilots took intermediate instruction in the Yokosuka K5Y1 Type 93 biplane. Intermediate training lasted four to six months. With their preferential treatment, the officers logged an additional one hundred hours, while enlisted men flew about sixty hours aloft. At this time the instructors determined which specialty the individual students would take up: fighter planes, carrier bombers, carrier attack planes, land-based medium bombers, or seaplanes. This selection process had begun in 1928, much earlier than in the U.S. Navy. Candidates for fighter training had to be particularly skilled, aggressive flyers.

Upon graduating from the 11th Combined Air Flotilla, future fighter pilots reported to either the Omura or Oita air groups on Kyushu for specialized training. They flew obsolete fighters such as the Nakajima A4N1 Type 95 carrier fighter or early versions of the Mitsubishi A5M Type 96 carrier fighter. Their training syllabus included field carrier landing practice and carrier qualification, instrument flying, aerobatics, formation flying, and air combat maneuvers. This last comprised the following subjects: gunnery theory, general principles of air combat, basic attack (single plane combats), formation combat, and attacks against multi-place aircraft. As usual, officers received much more detailed training in tactics than enlisted men because the officers would lead formations after their final qualification in combat units. Operational training for all categories lasted at least three months and encompassed a minimum of 150 flight hours (apparently some 250 for officers). With the end of the operational part, the pilots had completed "Basic Aviation Training," with the officers logging about 400 hours and the enlisted men at least 254.

The second stage, "Joint Aviation Training," began with the posting to the first combat unit, either on board a carrier or in a land-based fighter group. There the new pilots underwent extensive training in gunnery, combat tactics, formations, and carrier operations. As before, officers received much additional attention. By the time they had reached their first squadron, they were lieutenants (junior grade) and close to promotion to lieutenant. Generally the unit held out rookie pilots from combat until the commander deemed them ready. The Japanese themselves estimated it took a year of joint training to qualify new aviators as fully capable fighter pilots. Even during the China Incident (1937–41), the Japanese were able to do this, creating in the end a superbly trained cadre of pilots.

Trouble began when the combat units themselves were committed in heavy battles with much attrition. No other units were in existence to impart at least a part of the skills necessary in joint aviation training. After the outbreak of the Pacific War, the carrier fighter squadrons could not absorb high numbers of green pilots and still remain combat ready. They needed time and tranquil conditions to qualify the rookies, but the strategic situation, such as that with the 5th Carrier Division after the Coral Sea Battle (May 1942), did not permit it. The *Zuikaku* could not participate in the Midway Campaign solely because her air group could not quickly prepare the green replacement pilots assigned to it. No supernumerary squadrons existed to board the carriers once the units already on board had taken heavy losses. At the beginning of the war, Japanese naval air units were extremely good because of a blend of intensive training and prior combat experience. Once the air groups began sustaining losses, they proved extraordinarily brittle. Lacking advance carrier training groups and reserve carrier air groups (such as the U.S. Navy was forming), they could not make their rookies combat ready. Greater American flexibility in training pilots and shifting squadrons and groups from carrier to carrier paid its way in the Pacific War.

APPENDIX 2

Fundamentals of Aerial Fixed Gunnery

"Air battles are won by hitting enemy planes with bullets." So goes an aphorism that underscores the basic mission of fighter planes: to shoot down enemy aircraft as expeditiously and safely as possible. Aerial gunnery was the essential aspect of that function. Indeed, in the words of World War I French ace Georges Guynemer, the fighter was but a "flying gun." In philosophy of gunnery training and marksmanship, the pilots of the U.S. Navy exercised a system superior to those of all of the world's air forces. Here we will discuss the principles of aerial fixed gunnery and demonstrate that superiority on the part of the Navy's flyers.

Central to aerial gunnery was the need to attain the desired firing position vis-à-vis the target within effective range of the shooter's weapons. The maneuvers necessary to set up and make a particular shot became known variously as the gunnery approach, firing pass, or firing run. To complicate matters, aerial targets, other than tethered balloons, possessed forward velocity, often quite swift speeds. If an attacker placed himself directly ahead of or behind the target on the same line of flight, he had but to close within effective range of his guns, aim directly at the target, and his bullets would strike home. This was zero or no deflection, a desirable but very rarely encountered situation.

When a fighter pilot shot from an angle relative to the target's flight path, rather than from directly ahead or astern (zero deflection), he had to aim far enough ahead of his target to compensate for the distance it would travel before his bullets reached it. That was *deflection shooting*. If the pilot in shooting at his target from the side simply aimed his bullets at the enemy airplane, they would miss astern of it. According to Lt. Cdr. James H. Flatley, to make a deflection shot:

> You must shoot at a spot out in space which will be full of airplane when your bullets get there.[1]

This is the same principle employed by a duck hunter when he "leads" his birds, that is, aims in front in order to hit them.

For deflection shooting, the fighter pilot had to determine the correct *lead* or "forward allowance" (to use RAF terminology) to select the proper aiming point ahead of his target in order to hit it. This depended on the target's speed and the angle of deflection, that is, the angle relative to the target's flight path from which the fighter was shooting. The U.S. Navy noted deflection in five basic categories (see diagram). Zero or no-deflection occurred when, as stated previously, the attacker lay dead ahead or astern of the target and required no lead to hit. In a combat situation this was rare, and what appeared at first glance to be no-deflection

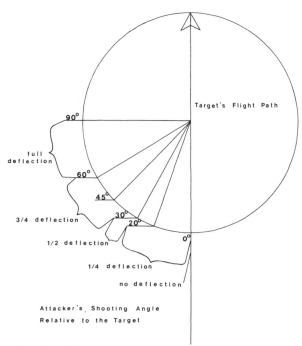

Deflection table.

usually, upon reexamination, turned into a quarter-deflection shot. One-quarter deflection saw the attacker nearing from 0 degree to 20 degrees relative to the target's line of flight; one-half deflection from 20 to 30 degrees; three-quarter deflection from 30 to 60 degrees; and full deflection from 60 to 90 degrees. Naturally the full-deflection shots required the largest lead (forward allowance) to hit the target.

From the early 1920s on, the U.S. Navy taught its pilots the art of deflection shooting. It was a long and arduous process requiring many hours of practice to develop skills for estimating target speed and the proper lead, but the program paid enormous dividends. A pilot trained in deflection shooting was extremely versatile, as he could attack from virtually any angle up to full deflection with a reasonable chance of hitting his target. He would not be restricted to making low-deflection runs from ahead or astern. In the period between 1921 and 1941, aircraft speeds increased nearly four-fold, making it more difficult than ever to set up a proper low-deflection approach. Defending bombers also increased firepower to deal with astern attacks, especially. If a fighter pilot used a low-deflection stern run, then the target's gunners had a low-deflection shot back at him! It proved much safer for fighters to execute deflection shots. The best gunnery runs on bombers saw fighters shoot from sectors poorly covered by enemy defensive fire, such as from the side or above, then break away safely and smoothly in order to end up in position to make another run. Full-deflection approaches gave the fighter pilots tremendous advantage over defending gunners, presenting them with such return fire angles that the gunners faced "one hell of a time finding the lead."[2]

As their basic gunnery guide, the Navy's fighter pilots used the annually revised *Orders for Gunnery Exercises*, which outlined how the pilots would shoot for the record. In preparation for the tests, they trained with camera guns to see if they were reaching the proper aiming points and practiced their runs with live rounds fired at towed sleeves. They put in long hours in gunnery training to sharpen their

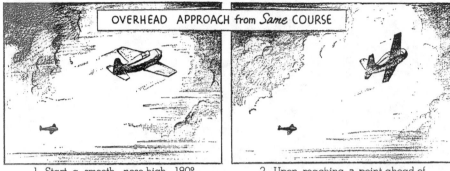

OVERHEAD APPROACH from *Same* COURSE

1. Start a smooth, nose-high, 180°
   turn toward the target . . .

2. Upon reaching a point ahead of
   and in the same vertical plane as
   the target's flight path.

3. . . . . Roll over to inverted flight.

4. Drop the nose on down, then sweep
   it up slightly ahead of the target.

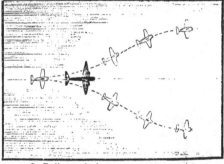

5. You should reach effective range while
   still in a dive of not less than 60°, which
   should flatten out so that you pass the
   target at about a 45° angle.

6. Pull out below, recovering right
   or left of the target's flight path,
   and climb to a second attack
   position.

Overhead approach from the same course.

skills. Man for man, the Navy's prewar pilots had far more practical shooting practice than the pilots of other air forces. The purpose of the *Orders for Gunnery Exercises* was to cover "all of the possible types of approach that a fighter may possibly make in actual combat."[3] The orders specified four basic textbook approaches: overhead, side, opposite, and stern attacks, with variation for the last three depending on whether the fighter approached from above, level with, or below the target's line of flight. Maximum effective range with the Browning .50-caliber machine guns was thought to be in the realm of 400 yards, with the figure of 1,000 feet adopted for training purposes to be used with the concept of mils to help determine angles and ranges. Optimum range was between 200 and 100 yards,

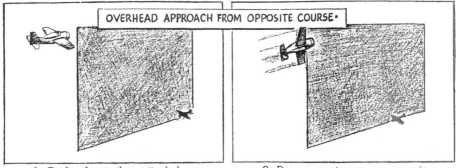

1. Get lined up in the vertical plane containing the target's flight path.

2. Drop your wing as necessary in order to keep the target in view.

3. Upon reaching the desired point execute a half-roll . .

4. Letting the nose drop and the sight sweep ahead of the target.

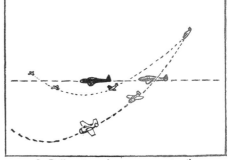

5. Continue in the dive to arrive at the correct firing angle and range, as in the overhead from the same course.

6. Pull out and recover as in the overhead approach from the same course.

Overhead approach from opposite course.

seldom closer than 50 yards because of the difficulty in effecting a smooth break-away from the firing pass. In training, the pilots loaded six rounds per burst for scoring in exercises, but under combat conditions, about fifty rounds per gun were thought sufficient on one firing pass.

The *overhead* approach (see illustrations) was the most complex of all, requiring considerable training to fly smoothly, for it could be deadly. It required an initial altitude advantage for the fighter of at least 2,000 feet and also position well ahead of the target. To start the run, the pilot had to keep close to the vertical plane of the target's flight path, but to one side so he could keep the target in view. The run had two variations, depending on whether the fighter was on the same or the opposite heading in relation to the target. It was easier to begin the run from the same heading as the target. The fighter pilot opened with a nose-high, 180-degree turn toward the target. When he attained position ahead of and in the same vertical plane of the target, he rolled over on his back into inverted flight. It was easy to keep the target in view, and when he reached the proper position directly over the target, he dropped the nose of his aircraft into a near-vertical dive. The fighter dived toward the target at about a 60-degree angle, careful to take the proper lead ahead of the target. The manuals recommended opening fire at 250 yards. The pilot could shoot as long as he could hold the lead; then he would cut just behind the target at about a 45-degree angle, in order to pull out below and astern of the target. With the speed accumulated in his dive, it was easy to break off to one side and zoom back up over the target. Made from an opposite heading, the overhead was a little more difficult because the closing speed with the oncoming target was swift. In this case, the fighter first lined itself up with the target's vertical plane, then dropped one wing to keep the enemy in sight. At the proper time, the pilot then half-rolled to bring himself into inverted flight and proceeded with the attack as previously described.

The fighters liked to use the overhead run, as it offered "the best opportunity to hit a moving plane and at the same time presents opposing gunners with a very difficult shot."[4] By the time an F4F had swung onto its back and was about to start down, there was little the quarry could do to escape. Diving in, the F4F pilot by rolling his ailerons or "corkscrewing" could match any maneuvers taken by the target and shoot without interruption by holding the lead. Usually it took more time for the target to lower a wing and turn, pull up, or dive away than for the fighter to corkscrew and keep the proper lead. Unfortunately, the F4Fs found few opportunities to try overheads on the nimble Zero fighters, but against bombers, the overheads could be devastating. The angle of approach largely evaded return fire and allowed the fighter pilot to shoot into engines and fuel tanks.

The overheads required position well ahead and considerable altitude advantage, and also air space below, at least 2,000 feet, for the fighter to recover. Thus it could not be used against low-flying aircraft. The runs were tricky and took time to learn. Common mistakes saw pilots swinging too wide on their turns and not coming straight down on the target or not having enough altitude advantage to begin with. In both cases, pilots could not pull enough lead without encountering too many G's. Best advice was to roll out and get clear. If a pilot lost sight of his target as he dived in, he was to pull out, regain altitude, and try again.

The *side* approaches (see illustrations) came in three variations, high, flat, and low, depending on whether the fighter shot from above, level with, or below the target's flight path. In principle they were all the same, beginning from position above the enemy, ahead, and to one side. The maneuver basically involved an S-turn toward the target, the pilot swinging in until he was heading in the opposite direction. Then when he reached a point abeam of the enemy, he reversed his turn, following through until he headed roughly in the same direction in which the target was flying. His initial shot was 90 degrees, full deflection, but as he held his run, deflection quickly lessened to three-quarters and finally half-deflection as the fighter was drawn behind and closer to the target's flight path. Naval pilots usually broke away beneath the target before being drawn to one-quarter deflection. Side attacks required careful marksmanship because hits depended on firing within range and holding the correct lead for the deflection as it changed during the firing run.

Most popular were the high-side attacks, best begun from a position 1,200 to 1,500 feet above the target and 3,000 feet ahead, putting the fighter on about a 45-degree angle in front of the target. Starting from a parallel heading, the pilot

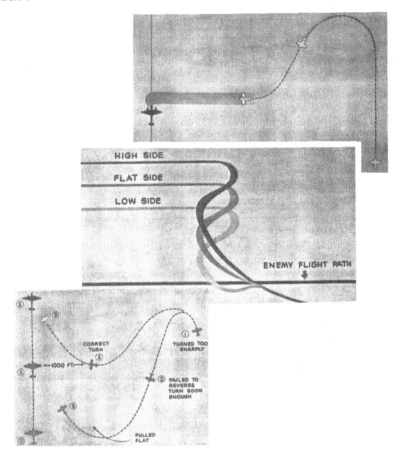

The side approach.

made a nose-high turn toward the enemy on the first hook of the S. Reaching a point even with the target, he started to bank in the opposite direction to reverse his turn. He then found himself about 1,000 feet from the target and 30 degrees above the level of its flight path. While turning, he had to increase speed, take the proper lead, and shoot, the run starting as a 90-degree full-deflection shot with the fighter charging downhill toward the target. Holding the lead dragged the fighter closer to the target's flight path, decreasing the deflection angle from 90 to about 30 degrees as the fighter rapidly closed the range toward the target's quarter. The pilot could either recover on the same side he first attacked or cross over to the opposite side. The high-side provided plenty of speed for a zoom climb to reposition for another attack. Like the overhead, it could not be used against low-flying aircraft because of the need to recover well below the target.

The other two side variants, flat and low, used the same maneuvers as the high-side, but fired from different heights. Flat-side runs began from an altitude advantage 600 to 900 feet, with the eventual firing point within 10 degrees of the target's flight path, a much shallower dive than with the high-side. Low-sides required less altitude advantage, only 400 to 600 feet. The eventual firing point was 20 degrees beneath the target's height, the attacker losing considerable speed because he climbed to make the actual attack. The use of this run was discouraged except in emergencies because the loss of speed made it most difficult to regain position from which to attack again.

Side attacks did not require the altitude advantage necessary for an overhead

1. To start your side approach make a smooth, nose-high turn toward the target.

2. Drop the nose as necessary to keep the enemy's plane constantly in sight.

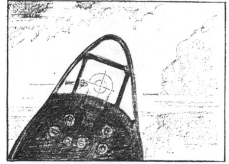

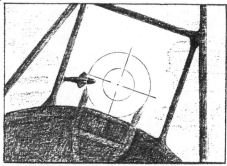

3. As you get to a point almost at the beam of the target, start to bank in the opposite direction to reverse your turn.

4. Increase the throttle, bring up the line of sight and keep it ahead of the target.

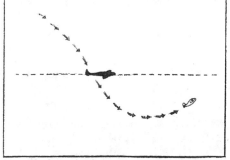

5. When the effective range is reached, let the pipper drift carefully to the point of proper lead.

6. Squeeze the trigger and fire as long as you can hold the lead. Then cease firing.

The high-side approach.

run yet still gave defending gunners great problems because of the rapidly changing deflection, so long as the fighter broke off before encountering one-quarter deflection. Coordinated attacks were easy to orchestrate with side attacks. Naval pilots liked to "bracket the target," with fighters making side attacks from left and right or utilizing opposite or stern attacks. Problems cropped up when pilots did not time their turns properly, ending up too far astern of the target. Pressing an attack under those circumstances endangered the fighter from return fire by rear gunners. Also, if the pilot failed to allot enough lead at the beginning, he would never be able to make up for it. Correctly made, the side approaches permitted accurate shots against bomber engines and other vulnerable spots not normally protected by armor. Like the overheads, they required full knowledge of deflection shooting to be effective.

In contrast, *opposite* (head-on) and *stern* attacks (see illustrations) did not entail much deflection shooting, occurring as they did with the fighter nearly matching the flight path of his opponent. With the opposite or head-on attack, the fighter approached from dead ahead. There were high, level, and low opposite approaches, and of the three, the level was to be avoided because the opponent could likewise blast away with his forward firing guns. No need to be fair in these matters! Naval pilots preferred to come up from below if the target flew above 500 feet in level flight, shooting from 10 to 15 degrees below the target's flight path. They could open up at long range (600 yards) and keep shooting as the range closed quickly. To return fire, the target would have to dip its nose and risk collision. The fighter held its run below the target, passed underneath, and recovered by making a hard, flat turn back in the direction the enemy was heading.

The main problem with head-on attacks was the high closing speed between the attacker and target. Once they had passed, it was difficult to set up another run unless both opponents turned toward each other. Between opposing fighters, head-on attacks were very common, a major defensive maneuver in countering runs. They often avoided long opposite approaches on each other because of the real possibility of being hit by the other's bullets. The more usual short opposites between fighters, as in scissoring, offered little time to shoot because of the high rate of closure.

Classic ever since the earliest days of aerial combat was the stern approach. It gave the fighter pilot who did not know deflection shooting his best shot. Against nonmaneuvering (i.e., surprised) fighters it was deadly, but it could be tricky against more maneuverable planes such as Zero fighters. Against aircraft equipped

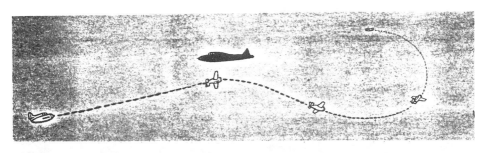

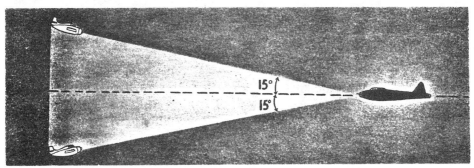

Head-on approach.

with tail gunners, stern attacks were positively dangerous because the gunner had an equally fine shot at the fighter boring in from the rear. As with the side and opposite attacks, there were high, level, and low approaches. Such stern runs could begin from anywhere from behind abeam of the target and lent themselves well to coordination with side attacks.

In coming in from astern, the pilot could make a firing pass and break away, or he could camp on his opponent's tail, matching maneuvers (if he could) until the target was destroyed. Both U.S. and Japanese naval pilots preferred to make their stern attacks in the form of firing passes: first diving in, rapidly closing the range, firing a quick shot, and then breaking away for altitude in order to make another run. For a number of reasons it was dangerous to remain fixed to the tail of a target. If it was a target sporting a rear gunner, the enemy might get lucky. Trying to stay on the tail of a more maneuverable fighter in a classic dogfight situation often meant being outflown by the enemy. Also a fighter twisting and turning on the tail of an opponent made it very vulnerable to attacks by the enemy's teammates. Firing passes, precisely because they utilized only swift shots (albeit from good firing angles), were much safer.

Many things determined which attack a fighter pilot would use in a given situation, including the tactical circumstances, position relative to the enemy, target type, and speed. Best results required good knowledge of enemy pilot and aircraft strengths and weaknesses, but in early 1942, little was known about the Japanese. Fighter leaders had to engage them in battle before they could tailor specific tactics to deal with them. Even so, they trusted the soundness of their training and knew it could be adapted to almost any situation.

The approach from astern is the simplest of all fixed gunnery maneuvers. It gives you a no-deflection shot, and it generally allows for an almost unlimited amount of firing time. This approach is so varied that it cannot be limited to any particular pattern. It may be begun from above, below, or on the same level as the target—in fact, from an infinite number of starting positions. Normally, this approach should be used only against enemy fighters, but under certain circumstances it may be employed against any type of aircraft.

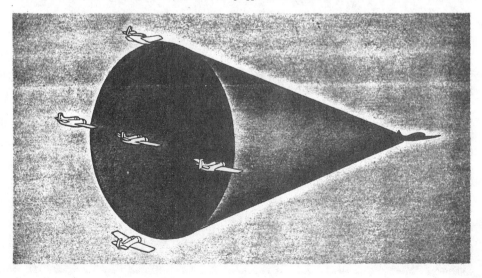

The stern approach.

Given the fast-paced, unpredictable nature of aerial combat, it often was impossible for the pilot to choose the type of attack or counterattack he would make. Perhaps he lacked the initial altitude advantage or speed that would have vouchsafed him such latitude. The Navy's gunnery training with its emphasis on deflection shooting equipped its pilots to make successful attacks from almost any position relative to the target. Once the pilot began his run, he could base his estimate of target speed and deflection on his previous experience in making the four standard approaches. Because of this training, the target presented to him a recognizable aspect in his sights, and he could adjust his lead accordingly. Given Zeros and other nimble enemy aircraft, the naval pilot most often had only a snap burst, full-deflection shot. He had to score with his first bullets or he might not have a second chance to shoot. Thus it was matter of "shooting from the hip," where skill in deflection shooting made most of the difference.

The pilots of the U.S. Navy and Marine Corps were virtually the only fighter pilots trained from the beginning to utilize and regularly succeed in deflection shooting. With the partial exception of the Imperial Japanese Navy, no other air forces during World War II taught their pilots how to make full deflection shots. For the U.S. Army Air Forces, the Royal Air Force, the *Luftwaffe*, the Red Air Force, and all the rest, stern and head-on approaches with their minimal deflection angles comprised the primary attacks. Only a tiny minority of their pilots realized the potential of deflection shooting and taught themselves the techniques, usually after extensive combat experience.

Aside from lack of knowledge of the proper ways to make deflection shots, tangible reasons existed why other air forces had trouble emulating the U.S. Navy. The most important was visibility over the nose of the attacking fighter. When executing overhead and side runs from a full deflection angle (60 to 90 degrees), the attacker had to place his point of aim well ahead of the target, the distance depending on the target's speed. To shoot accurately and obviate risk of collision, ideally the fighter pilot had to see both the target and where his tracers were going; thus both the target and the aiming point should appear in his gunsight. This required excellent visibility over the nose of the attacker's aircraft. Otherwise when allotting sufficient lead for full deflection, the pilot would lose sight of his target when it disappeared under the nose of his own plane.

Among its other qualities, the Grumman F4F Wildcat with its radial engine under a sloping cowling and cockpit installed high over a mid-wing fuselage had the necessary visibility over the nose, a down angle of 6½ degrees required for full deflection shooting. This quality of good vision forward and below evolved also in connection with carrier landings. Thus naval fighter pilots came to expect that attribute as necessary for good shooting and good carrier landings. Land-based fighters often sacrificed visibility for streamlining. Their pilots sat so low and so far back in the aircraft that visibility over the nose was very poor, making deflection shooting extremely difficult even if the pilots knew how to do it.

It is ironic that given its highly advanced gunnery theory and techniques, the U.S. Navy sent its fighter pilots to war with an unsuitable gunsight, a converted Army Air Force design highly inadequate for deflection shooting. Prewar naval pilots depended on the simple ring and pointer or a telescopic sight in the form of a sighting tube stuck through the windscreen. Using the telescopic sight, the pilot had to lean forward, put his head close to the eyepiece, and sight with one eye only. Results were excellent in the simple biplane fighters, but for aerial warfare, the tube sight's field of vision was too low. The original Brewster F2A and Grumman F4F-3 designs called for telescopic sights, but in late 1941 the advent of bulletproof glass windshields forced a change. The new windscreens were not pierced for a tube sight, nor could the squadrons modify them. The Navy had to find another sight quickly.

The 1941 state of the art called for an illuminated, reflector gunsight. With one, a pilot observed the target through a transparent plate of glass situated above his instrument panel. Upon this glass was reflected by electrical illumination the image of a reticle with sighting lines and circles. Ideally such a sight would provide the correct points of aim for deflection shooting and incorporate a mil feature as a range finder to determine effective shooting range. The Navy at the start of the war did not have such a sight of its own. Plans called for the production of the Mark VIII illuminated sight, patterned after one used by the Royal Air Force, but it would not be available until the summer of 1942.

In the interim, the Navy adapted an Army Air Force illuminated reflector sight, the N2A. The original Army version was not designed for deflection shooting, as its "Christmas tree" reticle with horizontal and vertical lines was used for strafing and zero deflection shots from astern or ahead of the target.[5] The Navy's N2AN incorporated a new reticle that reflected onto the glass aiming plate a 35-mil circle, cross-hairs, and an aiming point or "pipper" in the center. The 35-mil circle was good only for about a 50-knot lead, useless in itself for high-deflection shots that could require leads of 250 knots or more. In making such full-deflection shots, it was necessary for the pilots to sight in on a corner of the reflector plate well ahead of the actual 35-mil circle to allow enough lead. In essence they used the circle and pipper more as a reference point, trusting to their training and experience, rather than the gunsight, to determine the proper aiming point. The wonder is that they were able to do it and shoot well despite the gunsight. Shoot well they certainly did! Under the circumstances the range-finding feature was largely useless except for low-deflection shots because with full deflection, the pilot had to shoot before the target could be calibrated within the 35-mil circle.

Other than its reticle, the sight had other definite drawbacks. For illumination it relied on a small high-intensity electric bulb that was prone to burn out or fail at the slightest provocation. Without the bulb, the sight was useless. Bulbs had to be replaced after every flight, and pilots were enjoined to wait till the last minute to switch on the sight. Some even recommended that the sight be switched off between firing runs! Another major problem was the installation of the sight mount itself. Designed as it was for a telescopic sight, the F4F-3's instrument panel had no space for a reflector gunsight. Squadron crews had to move some instruments and jury-rig a mount in the center of the panel. As mentioned repeatedly in the text, the gunsight mount proved hazardous to pilots during ditchings. Fortunately the F4F-4 design made provisions for reflector sights installed at the factory, a much safer arrangement.

After the early battles in the Pacific, the Navy's fighter pilots stressed the need for a sight capable of calculating leads for speeds up to 300 knots, with additional radial lines and circles. After Midway, the fighters were reequipped with the Mark VIII gunsights whose reticle provided two concentric rings at 50 and 100 mils diameters with cross-hairs and a pipper. That was much better than the N2AN sight, but still not precisely what the pilots wanted. It would do until better sights became available.

APPENDIX 3

Fighting Colors, Insignia, and Markings

In aviation studies, it seems that almost more effort and ink are expended in reconstructing how particular aircraft must have looked than in describing what they did in battle. Such research can be elusive and frustrating. Aircraft paint jobs were often temporary and quite arbitrary. Even locating the original directives and technical orders cannot be decisive, for units varied in their rendition of orders regarding markings. For the U.S. Navy in the period Pearl Harbor through Midway, the problem is compounded by a paucity of documents and photographs due to the loss of several carriers. The following is offered only as an outline and general discussion, but even that can be useful. The aircraft were painted the way they were for specific reasons, and it is hoped this aspect will be brought out here.

The color schemes, insignia, and markings of U.S. naval aircraft were in general controlled by the Bureau of Aeronautics (BuAer) and the relevant type commands—for the carrier squadrons, by Commander, Aircraft, Battle Force (ComAirBatFor). The directives in effect in early December 1941 generally followed two BuAer letters: 26 February 1941 and 13 October 1941. The first signaled the end of the Navy's highly colorful squadron markings: tail, fuselage bands, wing chevrons, and cowl colors. It decreed placement of the national insignia on both sides of the fuselage, but removed them from the upper right and lower left wing panels. The second letter (13 October 1941) directed that all fleet aircraft be painted nonspecularly, with all upper surfaces a blue-gray and lower surfaces a light gray, the line of demarcation to be "feathered" or blended indistinctly, so as not to have a clear line of demarcation. This pattern of colors remained in effect after the outbreak of the war and characterized naval aircraft throughout the period under discussion here.[1]

The national insignia was by definition a solid red circle inside a white, five-pointed star, which in turn was inside a blue, circumscribed circle. Prewar painting regulations prescribed the locations of the national insignia as shown in the table.

Aircraft markings involved a number of different sets of letters and numerals to indicate model numbers, service, and aircraft identification. On the tail of each aircraft were letters and digits (by regulation one inch high and one inch wide, with ¼-inch stroke). They revealed the model designation (F4F-3, F4F-3A, or F2A-3), which was placed on the rudder; the bureau number (or individual aircraft acceptance serial number), which was painted on the vertical fin even with the model designation; and finally the service identification. This last one for the carrier fighters consisted of the word NAVY placed just above the bureau number

(1) National insignia on the fuselages of fighters:

Type	Insignia Diameter	Location
F4F-3,-3A	20″	72″ from rudder hinge pin, and placed centrally on fuselage
F2A-3	20″	57″ from rudder hinge pin, and 29″ from lower edge of vertical fin

(2) National insignia on wings (left upper and right lower wing panels only):

Type	Insignia Diameter	Distance, wingtip to star center	Distance, aileron well to star center
F4F-3,-3A			
upper wing	50″	88″	22″
lower wing	44″	77″	23″
F2A-3			
upper wing	40″	73″	21″
lower wing	40″	74″	21″

on the vertical fin. By regulation, the color of these tail markings was to be black, but often they were white.

Included in the category of aircraft markings were the individual squadron designations and plane markings. They consisted of block letters, twelve inches high, located on the fuselage forward of the fuselage stars. First came the squadron number, then the class of squadron (on carriers: F for fighting, B for bombing, S for scouting, and T for torpedo), and finally the individual plane number within the squadron. Thus 6-F-4 would mean the number four aircraft in Fighting Squadron Six.

Variation existed in the fighting squadrons as to the color of the squadron designations and the placement of additional plane numbers on their aircraft. Fighting Squadrons Two and Three used white letters and numerals for their fuselage designations. They also painted small white numerals giving the plane number on both sides of the engine cowling and on each upper wing panel as well. Both squadrons also used white bureau numbers, model designations, and service identifications on the tails of their aircraft. The *Enterprise*'s VF-6 before the start of the war likewise utilized white letters and numerals for all markings, but the trend in that carrier air group was shifting toward black, and at least two of the four squadrons had changed to black, for fuselage markings at least. The color of aircraft markings may have had some relation to which division the carrier was in. Carrier Division One comprised the *Lexington* and the *Saratoga*, while Carrier Division Two consisted only of the *Enterprise* in the absence of the *Yorktown* in the Atlantic.

The outbreak of war on 7 December 1941 saw a number of unfortunate incidents involving misidentification and shooting at friendly aircraft. The worst involved VF-6 the evening of the Pearl Harbor attack, when four of six F4Fs were shot down by American antiaircraft gunners. Consequently, on 21 December on Oahu, representatives of the Army's Hawaiian Department and the Navy's Patrol Wing Two conferred on how to improve and standardize aircraft insignia and markings. They decided first of all to restore the national insignia to both the left and right upper and lower wing panels, and to increase the diameters of the circles to equal the full chord of the wings. They recommended the national insignia be restored to the fuselage wherever it was not so located (for most aircraft, the national insignia would be placed on the rear fuselage), and that the circles be increased to the maximum practical diameter. In accordance with Army Air Corps practice, the conference recommended that the Navy adopt the painting of rudders with seven red and six white horizontal stripes alternately spaced and of equal size.[2]

A day or two after the meeting, the aviation officer on the Pacific Fleet staff wrote up a despatch, sent out by CinCPac, that reported the findings of the conference but added a few changes. The CinCPac message agreed with the use of national insignia on all four wing panels, but specified they should *not* overflow onto the ailerons; that is, they were not as big as the conference recommended. The fuselage circles, according to CinCPac, should be twenty-four inches in diameter, which for most aircraft certainly was not the largest practical diameter. As for the rudder stripes, CinCPac decreed they should be painted with alternate red and white stripes about six inches wide, with red stripes on top and bottom. This meant an odd number of stripes, but not necessarily thirteen!

Without reference to the CinCPac despatch, Cdr. John B. Lyon (AirBatFor structures officer at Pearl) issued on 23 December a comprehensive directive for the carrier squadrons to change insignia and markings.[3] It followed closely the findings of the 21 December conference. Maximum-sized national insignia circles were to be placed on upper and lower wing panels, with the center of the star approximately one-third of the distance from the wingtip to the fuselage. As translated into measurements (by NAS Pearl Harbor) for the fighters, it meant for the F4F-3s and -3As wing circles seventy-three inches in diameter and centered sixty-six inches from the wingtip. For the F2A-3s, the wing circles became sixty-eight inches in diameter and sixty-one inches from the wingtip. In both instances the wing stars overflowed onto the ailerons.

With regard to fuselage stars, Lyon's orders called for them to be increased to the maximum diameter as well. For the fighters this became:

(a) F4F-3,-3As: circles fifty-eight inches in diameter centered thirty inches aft of the trailing edge of the wing
(b) F2A-3s: circles forty-three inches in diameter centered nineteen inches aft of a line with rear hatch cover

This entailed moving squadron designations behind the fuselage circles. As for striped tails, the AirBatFor directive specified seven red and six white stripes evenly spaced between the top and bottom of the rudder. Width of stripes depended on the size of the rudder. For the fighters, this translated to:

(a) F4F-3,-3A: rudder height 67½ inches = 5.2-inch stripes
(b) F2A-3: rudder height 54½ inches = 4.2-inch stripes

The painting orders kept the squadrons busy, and implementation of the scheme took mainly until mid- and late January to complete for those who were doing it. The *Lexington*'s VF-2 and the *Enterprise*'s VF-6 seem to have been the only fighting squadrons to comply with the AirBatFor letter. Paul Ramsey reported on 30 January that his squadron had been repainted, but that was just before he turned over the F2As to the marines. Fighting Six appears to have been the only squadron to take the scheme into combat. Its F4Fs sported the huge wing and fuselage circles. They retained white cowl numerals, but the fuselage code was changed to black, F-(plane number) without the squadron number before it. Jimmy Thach's Fighting Three seems not to have repainted its aircraft at all, except to add thirteen tail stripes. There was much swapping of aircraft between squadrons; so one unit very rarely presented a unified appearance.

In Washington, the authorities at BuAer took steps to comply with the CinCPac

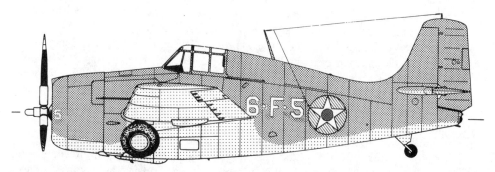

Grumman F4F-3A Wildcat, Bureau Number 3916, 6-F-5 (Fighting Six) as flown on 7 December 1941 by Ens. James G. Daniels III, USN. This aircraft displays the Navy's carrier plane markings and insignia in force at the outbreak of the Pacific War. The evening of 7 December, Jim Daniels was very nearly shot down by American antiaircraft fire over Pearl Harbor which did claim five other VF-6 F4Fs. BuNo. 3916 flew with VF-6 from 26 May 1941 until 17 March 1942 and saw combat in the *Enterprise*'s early raids. Thereafter it was used by VMF-212. (Drawing by Richard M. Hill.)

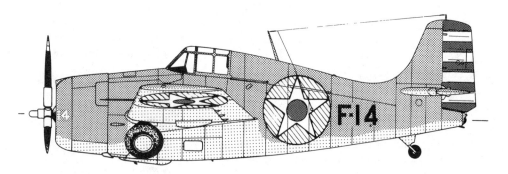

Grumman F4F-3A Wildcat, Bureau Number 3914, F-14 (Fighting Six) as flown on 1 February 1942 by Lieut. (jg) Wilmer E. Rawie, USN. In this aircraft Bill Rawie at 0704 on 1 February 1942 scored the first aerial victory by a U.S. naval or Marine Corps fighter pilot in the Pacific War. Over the island of Taroa in the Marshalls, Rawie shot down the Mitsubishi A5M4 Type 96 fighter flown by Lieut. Kurakane Akira of the Chitose Air Group. This F4F-3A is marked in general accordance with the 23 December 1941 specifications ordered by ComAirBatFor, with large roundels and striped tail. BuNo. 3914 had been flown by VF-6 in the summer of 1941, but was with VF-3 at NAS San Diego on 7 December 1941. It served on board the *Saratoga* during the abortive attempt to relieve Wake Island, but was reassigned to VF-6 on 2 January 1942. Taroa was its first and only combat. On 14 February it was transferred to VF-2 and ended up in VMF-212 on 29 April 1942. (Drawing by Richard M. Hill.)

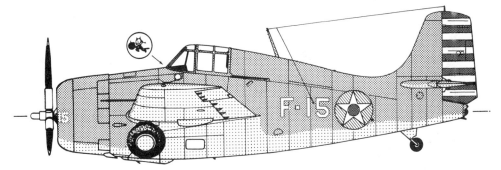

Grumman F4F-3 Wildcat, Bureau Number 4031, F-15 (Fighting Three) as flown on 20 February 1942 by Lieut. Edward H. O'Hare, USN. This is the airplane which "Butch" O'Hare flew on his Medal of Honor flight off Rabaul in which he was credited with five Japanese bombers. Its actual side number has long been in dispute. This side number (F-15) is noted in a contemporary source (Capt. Burt Stanley's diary), and the bureau number comes from O'Hare's own logbook still retained by his daughter, Kathleen O'Hare Nye. Butch also flew 4031 in combat on 10 March 1942 in the Lae–Salamaua raid.

Even aside from its glorious association with Butch O'Hare, 4031 had a most interesting history. Originally assigned to VMF-211, it remained behind at Ewa when the marines left on 28 November 1941 for Wake Island and survived the devastating Japanese attack on Oahu. On 15 December it was transferred to VF-3 and became O'Hare's favorite mount. After VF-3's return to Pearl, 4031 next served with Paul Ramsey's VF-2 at Coral Sea and became one of only six VF-2 F4Fs to survive that battle, taking refuge on board the *Yorktown* on 8 May. Thereafter VF-42 had it until mid-June 1942, when it went to Marine Air Group 23. Used in a training role, it finally became a strike on 29 July 1944. If only this F4F-3 could have been preserved! (Drawing by Richard M. Hill.)

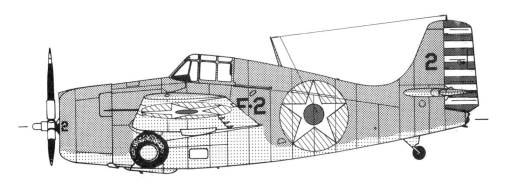

Grumman F4F-3 Wildcat, Bureau Number 2531, F-2 (Fighting Forty-two), as flown on 8 May 1942 by Lieut. (jg) E. Scott McCuskey, A-V(N), USNR. BuNo. 2531 was an early production F4F-3 that operated only with VF-42, being assigned to that squadron even before its formal conversion from VS-41 to VF-42 on 15 March 1941. It served with VF-42 on board the *Yorktown* from June 1941 until the Battle of the Coral Sea in May 1942. Scott McCuskey flew it the morning of 8 May 1942 in the attack on MO Striking Force and shot down a Zero near the carrier *Shōkaku*. Separating from the rest of the VF-42 escort, McCuskey found his way back to Task Force 17 and at 1255, low on fuel, took refuge on board the damaged *Lexington*. There F-2 remained, as the *Lexington* first burned and exploded, then sank. (Drawing by Richard M. Hill.)

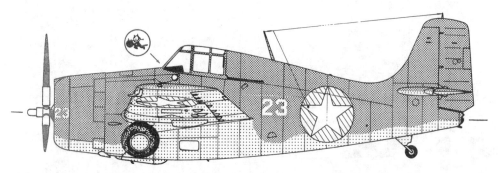

Grumman F4F-4 Wildcat, Bureau Number 5093, F-23 (Fighting Three) as flown the morning of 4 June 1942 by Lt. Cdr. John S. Thach, USN. One of the classic fighter combats of the Pacific War took place the morning of 4 June 1942 at the Battle of Midway, when VF-3's six escorts tangled with the Zeros of the Japanese carrier force. Jimmy Thach flew this aircraft in the action which saw him shoot down three Zeros and first use his "Thach Weave" in combat. His F4F-4 sustained slight damage in its engine during a head-on run with a Zero, but 5093 brought Thach back safely to the *Yorktown*. There it had to be left after the flattop was bombed and later torpedoed by the Japanese. Salvage crews the morning of 6 June pushed 5093 over the side to reduce top weight on board the stricken *Yorktown*, but it was all for naught. The carrier sank on 7 June after being torpedoed by a Japanese submarine. BuNo. 5093 was originally assigned to Fighting Eight on board the *Hornet* and participated in the Tokyo Raid. Upon the task force's arrival at Pearl Harbor, 5093 went to CASU-1 and was allocated on 26 May to VF-3 in the process of fitting out for Midway. (Drawing by Richard M. Hill.)

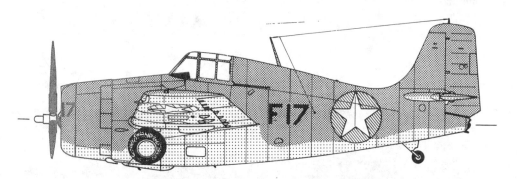

Grumman F4F-4 Wildcat, Bureau Number 5089, F-17 (Fighting Eight) as flown on 4 June 1942 by Ens. Stephen W. Groves, A-V(N) USNR. BuNo. 5089 was part of a batch of eleven F4F-4s allocated on 29 March 1942 to VF-8 at NAS Alameda just before the *Hornet* sailed on the Tokyo Raid. Steve Groves flew this aircraft on combat air patrol the morning of 4 June 1942 at the Battle of Midway and helped defend the *Yorktown* from the attack of the *Hiryū* dive bombers. He was credited with one bomber destroyed, but himself was shot down and killed. Some *Hornet* records and posthumous entries in Groves's own logbook indicate that he was flying BuNo. 5131 at the time of his death, but that is a clerical error. Groves ditched on 1 May in 5131 and was rescued by the destroyer *Monssen*. Strong evidence points to 5089 as the airplane Groves flew on 4 June. (Drawing by Richard M. Hill.)

recommendation and followed it to the letter except for the rudder stripes. On 5 January 1942, the bureau issued a Navy-wide directive. With regard to the wing insignia, it called for circles on all four wing panels to be the maximum diameter *without* overflowing onto the aileron.[4] The fuselage circles were to be twenty-four inches in diameter, and the rudders striped with thirteen alternating stripes (seven red and six white). Squadrons were to effect these changes as soon as possible. This was a big difference from the orders of AirBatFor on 23 December! The 5 January BuAer letter reached Pearl Harbor in mid-February, and Rear Admiral Aubrey W. Fitch forwarded it on 21 February to the fleet. He added: "The retention of the present markings is satisfactory until the next scheduled repainting where there is no fundamental difference between these and those called for above."[5] The days of VF-6's huge wing and fuselage circles were numbered.

From the fall of 1941 into February 1942, the Grumman Corporation at Bethpage, New York continued to paint its production aircraft, particularly F4F-4s, according to scheme 23350-2. This called for finished aircraft to be colored all light gray (necessitating a repaint by receiving units of upper surfaces to blue-gray). Wing circles (on upper left and lower right wing panels only) were fifty inches in diameter, while the fuselage insignia were only twenty inches in diameter and placed low and well aft on the fuselage. The first batches of F4F-4s received at NAS Pearl Harbor in February and March 1942 were marked in this manner. They went first to VF-2 and then in late March to VF-6, which had the distinction of the largest, then the smallest fuselage circles in the fleet.

The Bureau of Aeronautics evidently thought its 5 January letter inadequate for remarking aircraft. On 6 February it issued another that superseded everyone else's orders.[6] The only change involving the national insignia was to increase the fuselage circles to the maximum diameter possible, but not to exceed sixty-five inches. The letter also called for the squadron designations to be painted on the side of the fuselage as before: squadron number, class of squadron (F for fighting), and plane number within squadron. Also the plane number was to be painted "on each half of the wing with the inboard edge of the numeral at a distance from the edge of the fuselage equal to one half over the overall width of the fuselage in plan view."[7] In other words, the numeral was placed on the top and bottom wing panels, where most of the carrier squadrons were already putting it.

The BuAer 6 February directive was interpreted in a number of ways. NAS Alameda on 26 February began providing F4Fs with thirty-six-inch fuselage circles.[8] The Grumman Corporation in late February or early March initiated scheme 23350-4 for the F4F-4s and F4F-7s, which called for blue-gray on upper surfaces, light gray on lower surfaces. Fuselage identifications (bureau number, model number, service identification) were in white. Wing stars (now on all four panels) remained at fifty inches in diameter, and Grumman began putting circles almost that big on the fuselages as well. Striped rudders consisted of six red and five white stripes. It appears that the first F4F-4s received in mid-April at Pearl and delivered to VF-3 were marked in this fashion.

In March and April, the fighting squadrons in the Pacific gradually implemented parts of the 6 February BuAer pronouncement. Fuselage circles especially were affected, their diameters being increased or decreased to a medium size as necessary. The last to do this was VF-6 in mid-May. On 29 April, Rear Admiral Leigh Noyes, shore representative at Pearl for Carriers, Pacific Fleet (the new designation of AirBatFor) directed that squadron numbers and air group commander markings be deleted for security reasons.[9] Except for some of VF-6's F4F-4s, all of the fighting squadrons had long since removed their numbers from their aircraft. Fighting Six complied in its May repaintings.

The reason why the Navy's planes were repainted in the first place involved recognition by friendly forces; but in that regard, the new schemes began to develop problems of their own. On 9 April, Vice Admiral H. F. Leary, commander of the ANZAC Force in Australia and New Zealand, informed CinCPac that in April the Army Air Force units in the Southwest Pacific intended to paint out the red circles in their white stars to prevent confusion. It appears the Aussies were letting go at anything red on an aircraft, thinking it was a Japanese "meatball." Admiral Nimitz agreed, and on 24 April forwarded a recommendation to Admiral King that the red circles and striped tails on naval aircraft be painted out. He requested early action on this from Washington.[10]

Meanwhile, the Army Air Force went ahead with its plans, receiving approval in Washington to standardize insignia of the Army and Navy. On 8 May, the commanding general of the Hawaiian Department passed on to Admiral Nimitz the decision that as of 15 May, all U.S. military and naval aircraft would no longer have the red ball within the stars or striped rudders. The carrier squadrons began repainting their aircraft around 10 May.[11] The rudders were painted blue-gray to match the camouflage scheme. That was the last major repainting of naval combat aircraft for a long time, and the confusion of the first six months regarding aircraft markings was now ended.

APPENDIX 4

Naval Flight Formations and the "Thach Weave"

Inseparably associated with Lt. Cdr. John S. Thach and his Fighting Three is the first use of the famous "Thach Weave" at Midway. Another renowed naval fighter tactician, Lt. Cdr. James H. Flatley, Jr., called it "undoubtedly the greatest contribution to air combat tactics that has been made to date."[1] After 1942, virtually every fighting squadron adopted the weave wholeheartedly, and Army Air Force pilots used it as well. The "Thach Weave" retains its utility today, as American pilots learned in jet duels over North Vietnam, where they had to "rediscover" the tactic. Basically the "Thach Weave" is a means for two or more aircraft to cooperate in mutual lookout and defense against opposing fighters. It is one of the few really important air tactical maneuvers that can be attributed directly to a single innovator who created and first used it in combat. The best way to sketch the origin of the weave is to discuss the development of the fighting squadron combat formations.

Shortly after the outbreak of the European War, the U.S. Navy decided to reevaluate its fighter tactics. In October 1939, Vice Admiral Charles A. Blakely (Commander, Aircraft, Battle Force—ComAirBatFor) directed that two fighting squadrons, Lt. Cdr. Truman J. Hedding's Fighting Two and Lt. Cdr. William L. Rees's Fighting Five, test the concept of using two-plane sections as the basic aviation flight formation. Up to that time the fighting squadrons flew three-plane sections comprising section leader and two wingmen. This formation was cumbersome for single-seat aircraft, as the wingmen had to concentrate mainly on keeping station and preventing collisions with each other in tight turns. This adversely affected their lookout potential, as the fighter pilots were usually busier watching each other than looking for enemy planes.

Test results for the two-plane section were highly favorable, and the pilots were most enthusiastic. The formations turned with ease, and lookout was greatly improved. Once they flew two-plane sections, the pilots could not understand why they had not made the change long before. Going further, Hedding's VF-2 pilots experimented with flying in a stepped-down position behind the leader, the wingman and all successive planes flying below each other. During the tests, the NAPs used their elderly Grumman F2F-1 biplanes, but soon they were to convert to Brewster F2A-2 monoplane fighters. With the single-wing planes, visibility was better looking up than down; hence there was greater efficiency in a stepped-down formation. The use of the two-plane section stepped-down allowed the wingman to cut inside his leader on all turns—easing considerably his staying in formation. This was a very important development.[2]

On 26 March 1940, Blakely authorized Fighting Two and Fighting Five to continue the new formation at least until the completion of the annual cruise that June. That month, Hedding prepared a detailed analysis of his tests, but left for a new assignment before it could be submitted. His successor as VF-2's skipper, Lt. Cdr. Herbert S. Duckworth, was most impressed with Hedding's conclusions and could add a new wrinkle. He thought it was no longer necessary for the division and section leaders to employ the numerous, complicated hand signals to communicate flight orders to their pilots. In most cases, Duckworth found that just rocking his wings was sufficient to signal turns or attacks to his pilots. Inexplicably the new ComAirBatFor, Vice Admiral William F. Halsey, decided that summer to reject immediate adoption of the two-plane section for his fighting squadrons. Despite considerable opposition from above, Duckworth stuck to his guns and retained the formation. He and other enthusiasts kept battling to have the new formation made Navy-wide, but conservatism in the high command prevented that.[3]

From the great air battles fought over Britain and the Continent, some tactical information filtered down to the carrier squadrons in the Pacific. In March 1941, air advisors of the Chief of Naval Operations learned of the Royal Air Force's practice of detaching one or two fighters as "weavers" to cover the rear of the fighter squadron from surprise attack. What OpNav did not know was that the British "weavers" usually did not come back! On 27 March, all carrier squadrons were told to test the weaving method of lookout, nicknamed "Charlie" tactics (or contemptuously, "Ass-end Charlie"). Resulting comments from most of the fighting squadrons were caustic, condemning the practice as a waste of fuel.[4]

In April, Lieut. Thach's Fighting Three came on board the *Enterprise* for sea duty. On the cruise he experimented with the "Charlie" tactics. With his squadron deployed in cruise formation on a steady course (such as escort duty), Thach thought the use of a rear patrol and lookout element had some limited value. He deployed the trailing section slightly above and behind the main formation. Each fighter patrolled independently to watch the blind spot of the divisions. These aircraft executed alternate turns of about 30 degrees to the right and left, steadying down after each turn. There was to be no continuous weaving as practiced by the British. Thach communicated his findings to ComAirBatFor in a letter dated 12 May.[5] In it he also promised further experimentation, indicating his continued interest in lookout doctrine.

Meanwhile, even ComAirBatFor slowly came to the conclusion that the two-plane section was useful. On 7 July 1941, Halsey issued orders that each fighting squadron henceforth would be organized into three six-plane divisions, each composed of three two-plane sections. Rear Admiral A. B. Cook, commanding the Atlantic Fleet air squadrons, likewise on 10 August told the *Yorktown* and *Ranger* fighter pilots to conform to the new organization.[6] It was a year too late, but still most welcome.

Under the new procedure, the six-plane division utilized formations based on the old *USF-74 (Revised)* and other doctrine, but modified to take into account two- rather than three-plane sections. While cruising, the division assumed what was known as the "A-B-C formation" (see sketch), sections deployed stepped up at double the normal open order of 300 feet between sections. When approaching a combat area, the division leader usually formed his planes into echelon with the following planes stepped down behind the leader. This permitted all of the pilots to observe the target and bring their guns to bear. Standard open distance between

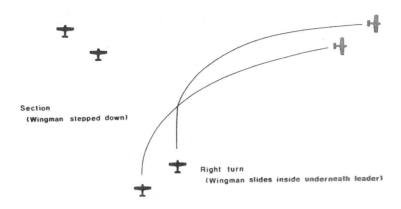

Two-plane section formations and turns.

sections was 300 feet, closed distance 150 feet. The division leader made the tactical decisions, instructing his pilots either to follow for one-division attack in close succession or split to "bracket the target" and hit the enemy from different directions.

The section comprised leader and wingman. In flight, the leader, in concert with

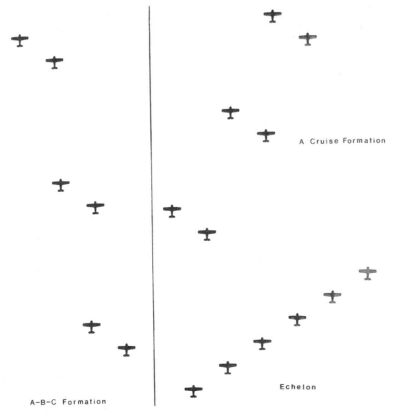

Six-plane division formations.

the division leader's signals, decided what maneuvers the two planes would make, taking care to alert his wingman of what to do and allow for that pilot's need to stay with him. The wingman's main function was to support his leader and protect his tail by unceasing vigilance. It was more important for him to stick with his leader than himself shoot during a firing pass, if shooting would force him to separate. This was a lesson that would have to be learned over and over again by overeager pilots who broke tactical contact in air actions. Generally the section flew in echelon with the wingman stepped down below the leader, but always in a position where his leader could see him. Standard close interval between aircraft was 50 feet, standard open distance 150 feet. Making turns, the wingman was to slide inside and under the leader, greatly minimizing station keeping. In actual attacks, such as a high-side run and subsequent zoom climb, the interval between fighters was to be no more than 250 to 400 yards.

The summer of 1941, Thach's Fighting Three went ashore at NAS San Diego to reequip with Grumman F4F-3 Wildcats. This gave Thach much more opportunity to test new ideas. He liked to simulate various flying formations by laying out matchsticks on the kitchen table of his home in nearby Coronado—often a relaxing diversion before retiring for the night. The next day he would try his ideas in the air. While he was at San Diego, information reached Thach from the Fleet Air Tactical Unit describing the new Japanese Zero carrier fighter. The FATU Intelligence Bulletin of 22 September 1941 gave the Zero a top speed of between 345 and 380 mph (300 to 330 knots), a cruise of between 210 mph and 250 mph (182 to 217 knots), and an armament of two 20-mm cannons and two 7.7-mm machine guns.[7] Thach also may have seen other estimates, emanating from Claire Chennault in China. Chennault possessed firsthand experience in battling the Zero. He rated its top speed at 322 mph (280 knots), but more important, warned of the Mitsubishi's incredible maneuverability and high climb rate (reported variously at 3,500-plus feet per minute, or needing only six minutes to reach 16,000 feet). At any rate, the estimates sketched a formidable opponent, if one gave any credence to them. Thach was inclined to credit the reports he saw, as he felt they appeared to have been written by a fighter pilot. It was not comforting that the potential enemy might already possess a fighter that could outperform the F4F-3s just reaching the squadron.[8]

Faced with the possibility of encountering fighters that were faster, more maneuverable, and swift climbers, Thach began thinking of tactics to overcome these vital advantages. Out came the matchsticks in earnest. He concentrated on developing a cruise formation that would offer protection en route to battle, the time when his fighters would be most vulnerable to surprise attack from above. In dealing with an attacking fighter, the defender has two basic options: turn away and run, or head into his assailant to counterattack or try spoiling his aim. In fighting a Zero such as described, Thach knew it would be suicidal to break away unless the defender had a hell of a long lead. Thus the crux of the problem lay in developing a maneuver in which the defender, in deciding to stay and fight, could line up a shot on the attacker. Because of extensive training in deflection shooting, Thach felt confident his pilots could score hits, even if offered only snap bursts at fleeting targets.

Early on, the matchsticks proved that two sections of four planes, rather than a whole division of six, were best for engaging enemy fighters. Thach's first experiments involved a four-plane division flying close formation. This turned out to be ineffective because the fighters had to maneuver together in almost a tail-chase in order to stay together—little advantage over six planes strung together. Next, Thach decided to split the two sections, placing one farther behind the other. The new formation offered some advantages. In dividing the formation into two distinct elements, Thach compelled the attackers to press the assault against either one or the other section, offering the unattacked section a chance to shoot at the enemy when he recovered from his firing pass. However, the sections still interfered with each other and lacked the freedom to maneuver, still being too close for one section to work out a shot on fighters hitting the other.

Thach made his breakthrough when he decided to deploy the two sections abreast of each other at a distance at least equal to the tactical diameter (turning radius) of the F4F Wildcat. Once he assumed this formation, he saw many opportunities for the defender. Being abreast of one another, the sections had good lookout, particularly over the tail of the opposite pair. Thach evolved a lookout doctrine in which the section on the right watched above and behind the left section, and, similarly, the pair on the left observed the tail of the right section. They could warn each other of imminent attacks by signals, hastened by the fact they were already looking in each other's direction!

In terms of dealing with attacks, all four planes could fire on enemy fighters executing opposite (head-on) attacks. If the enemy charged in from above and behind, one section could turn to shoot at any fighters bouncing the other section. Thach quickly determined that the best procedure was to have the section that spotted an attacker going after the other section, *itself* turn immediately toward the threatened compatriots. This would be the signal to alert the other section and would also get the two counterattacking planes moving in the proper direction for a shot at the enemy. Seeing the other section turn toward them, the section in danger would know they were about to be attacked. Their reaction would be to turn toward the other section and set up a scissors with them. This maneuver would help spoil the aim of the attackers and give the defenders time to work their counter. If the attacker pulled out early, then the unattacked section would get a side shot at him. If the attacker maneuvered to follow his targets around in their turn, then the unattacked section could line up a head-on run. Now this was mutual defense!

Thach was very excited and eager to present his discovery to the squadron. He arranged for a test, taking four planes with him to act as defenders and assigning four other F4Fs under his protege, Lieut. (jg) Edward H. ("Butch") O'Hare, to play the attackers. To simulate the Zero's supposed superior performance, Thach wired the defenders'. throttles so they could not attain full power, giving O'Hare's four a definite advantage. He told O'Hare to try several different types of attacks to see how well his new tactics performed under combat simulation. The results were most encouraging. O'Hare found the maneuvers that Thach's defenders used had both messed up his aim and set up shots by the defenders. He added that it was disconcerting to line up a shot on a target that obviously could not see him screaming in, only to have the quarry swing away at the best moment to avoid his simulated firing! The simplicity of the maneuver lay in the defender's turning to scissor whenever he saw his other section turn toward him. There was no reason to signal or radio each other for warning or instructions. Likewise O'Hare saw the distinct possibilities for return fire by the defenders, no matter how the attackers tackled Thach's new formation. No longer was the "Lufberry [sic] Circle" the "only" defensive formation for fighters. Thach wrote up his findings for Com-AirBatFor, but Halsey's staff declined to recommend the new tactic to other squadrons, probably because they failed to understand its potential. They told Thach he could use it. He spent the remainder of 1941 refining the maneuver with Butch O'Hare when they could find time, but for the time being it remained their personal tactic.

On his first combat tour with Fighting Three, Thach had no opportunity to institute the maneuver because he never encountered enemy fighters. On the escort mission to Lae and Salamaua, 10 March 1942, Thach divided his force into two four-plane divisions, with O'Hare flying the second section in his division all ready for a test; but the Japanese did not oblige. Then in April he lost all of his experienced pilots to other duty and had to rebuild Fighting Three from scratch.

In early May on a gunnery flight from NAS Kaneohe Bay, he introduced the five pilots with him to the rudiments of the maneuver, the "beam defense position," as he called it then. First he strung the division into a tail-chase formation. Making three successive abrupt reversals of course, Thach passed down the line of fighters as if executing a firing pass on the trailing aircraft. After landing, he briefed his pilots, demonstrating how head-on passes could be used by a formation of fighters as a defensive counter. The next few days Thach practiced the weave several times with rookie Ens. Robert A. M. Dibb on his wing and the two NAPs, Mach. Doyle C. Barnes and Mach. Tom F. Cheek, comprising the second section. They worked out the routine. To demonstrate his theory, Thach arranged for two Army Air Force Bell P-39 fighters from the 78th Pursuit Squadron, also at Kaneohe, to make simulated attacks on his four planes. To their chagrin, the Army pilots discovered they could not set up a shot without themselves falling under the guns of Thach's other section.[9] Seven new ensigns joined Fighting Three the third week of May, and Thach had to spend most of his time teaching them the fundamentals of fighter tactics. He had only a few occasions to give them an inkling of how the weave functioned. He was not certain his rookies understood the lookout doctrine; so he told them to radio "There's one on your tail!" to initiate the scissors with the other section.

Given the hectic preparations to flight at Midway, Thach had no opportunity to introduce his borrowed VF-42 pilots to the weave. He had hoped to fly escort with two divisions, both groups of four led by pilots familiar with the weave (himself and Tom Cheek) who could coach the other two pairs by radio. That did not work. The first combat use of the weave is described fully in Chapter 15 of this book. It proved an enormous success under the harshest of conditions. Thach was able to keep his division together with the weave after the loss of one fighter, and the F4Fs destroyed perhaps four Zeros without further loss to themselves. After his experience at Midway, Thach was more than ever a "believer," and sought to spread the word to the other fighting squadrons. That summer while on leave, he labored to set down his maneuver in an easily understood form. He incorporated sketches (reproduced here) of the maneuver in a revision of the fighter chapter in *USF-74*. In an important interview conducted on 26 August at BuAer, Thach stressed that with his maneuver it was possible to keep a four-plane division together and fight as a team:

> The left section can watch the tail of the right section and vice versa, you can protect each other by continual motion toward and away from each other . . . firing opposite approaches, shooting Japs off each other's tails.[10]

That is just what he and his pilots did at Midway.

Two of Thach's disciples were posted in June and July to the reorganized Fighting Six under Lieut. Louis H. Bauer. Serving on board the *Enterprise*, Fighting Six on 7–8 August saw much combat in the skies over Guadacanal, engaging in several

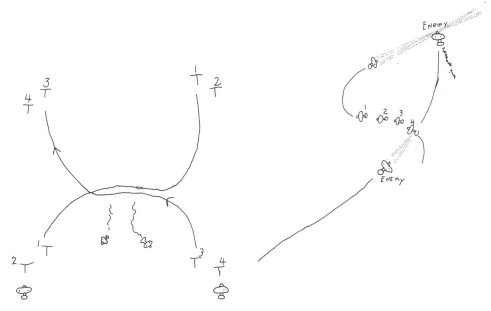

Thach's own diagrams (Aug. 1942) of his second countermove (*right*) and the weave.

sharp fights with Zeros, suffering the loss of four F4F-4s out of ten. In the *Enterprise* action report, it was acknowledged, as on previous occasions, that the F4F-4 was no match for the Zero fighter in a dogfight. The report noted the best countermove for F4Fs was for:

> . . . each plane of the two plane element to turn away then turn immediately toward each other and set up a continuous "scissors." Thus when a Zero bears on one of the F4F's, the other F4F is in position to fire on a Zero.[11]

This appears to have been a sort of "bastard" version of the weave involving only the two aircraft of a section, rather than a whole division. It would be less effective because the F4Fs had not split out to begin with. Starting in close formation, both fighters using the procedure outlined above would have lacked sufficient room to turn again toward each other for a proper scissors. Probably a product of insufficient understanding of Thach's tactic, the "bastard" weave as described lacked any reference to the vital lookout doctrine devised by Thach. There is no record that Fighting Six ever tried either the version listed above or the actual weave in action.

Meanwhile Jimmy Flatley took command of the new Fighting Ten and was eager to apply his own tactical ideas and combat experience from the Battle of the Coral Sea. A thoughtful, outstanding fighter leader, Flatley compiled a detailed squadron doctrine revolving around the use of six-plane "flights." Conferring with Thach in July, Flatley found his ideas fully agreed with his close friend's doctrine except for the use of four-plane divisions and the weave. Flatley thought his own system was superior. In September, Fighting Ten went out to Oahu and trained at Kaneohe, where Lt. Cdr. O'Hare's Fighting Three also operated. Flatley worked closely with O'Hare, who had the chance to demonstrate the weave aloft in the course of many practice missions. Butch ably sold his man, and Flatley became fully convinced of the value of the maneuver. Early in October before embarking on board the *Enterprise*, Flatley made the four-plane flight the basis of his squadron organization and instructed his pilots on the fundamentals of the weave.

On 26 October during the carrier Battle of Santa Cruz, the weave was used for

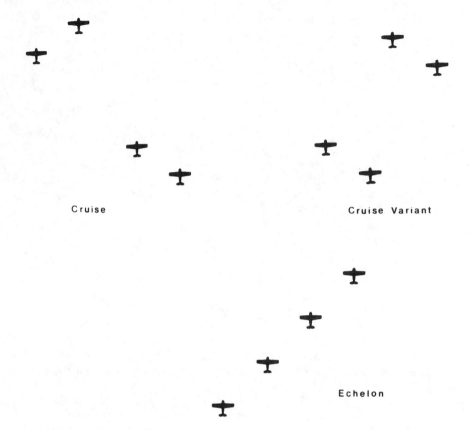

Cruise   Cruise Variant

Echelon

Four-plane division formations.

a second time in combat, this time by Flatley personally. He led eight VF-10 F4F-4s on a long escort mission, but Zeros jumped the strike group not far from the American carriers. One of Flatley's flights, led by Lieut. (jg) John A. Leppla of Scouting Two fame, dived in to engage Zeros, but these planes were themselves ambushed by more Japanese. Two F4Fs, including Leppla's, were shot down, but the two survivors. Ensigns Willis B. Reding and Raleigh E. Rhodes, used the weave to fend off more numerous Zeros until Rhodes's engine failed. He bailed out, and Reding managed to return to base. Meanwhile after destroying one Zero, Flatley's four fighters continued the mission, escorting the strike planes to the target and back. Returning to the *Enterprise* under intense attack, the strike group had to wait until "The Big E" could take them on board. Circling in the area, low on fuel and ammunition, Flatley's flight fell under Zero attack, and VF-10's skipper initiated the weave. The four F4F pilots sustained the weave at only 50 percent power and shook each Zero as it came in. The Japanese were not eager to face the maneuver and pulled off after only a few runs. The four F4Fs landed safely back on board their carrier.

In his action report for Santa Cruz, Flatley devoted a large section to the maneuver, dubbing it for the first time the "Thach Weave." He sent a short message of congratulations to Thach as well. Flatley in his report wrote that the "Thach Weave" was "absolutely infallible when properly executed." He thought the weave was "offensive as well as defensive."[12] Two or four F4Fs working as a team could blunt attacks by more numerous enemy fighters and secure excellent shots. The maneuver could be used by bombers as well as fighters, but would require training and perfect timing to make the weave effective. He enthusiastically recommended that the Navy provide training of the "Thach Weave" for all combat squadrons.

Flatley also provided detailed comments on techniques to be used by F4F-4s in executing the "Thach Weave." The fighter pilots were to deploy abreast whenever they expected to encounter Zeros. One section was to fly slightly higher than the other. Whenever the enemy attacked one section, the two elements were to turn toward each other for a scissors—the high section in a shallow dive and the low section in a gentle climb. As soon as the fighters under attack swung past their other pair, they were to turn immediately in the opposite direction. Flatley felt it was necessary to reverse turns promptly after scissoring and not let the weavers swing too widely out of support range. Meanwhile, the section not under attack could set up a shot on the Zero and head back after firing or after the enemy had drawn away. The two elements were to maintain the weave while they faced direct attack. Flatley warned the pilots not to let the F4F-4's speed drop below 140 knots.

The question of escort tactics came to the fore again, and Flatley felt the weave provided the answer. He recommended the escort fighters take station ahead of and about 1,500 feet above the strike planes. If enough fighters were available, they could fly a similar formation behind the attack planes. If ambushed, both elements were to dive in toward the bombers to cut short any Zeros making runs on them; then the escort was to commence weaving over the bombers. Flatley thought the weave provided the best protection for the strike planes:

> . . . just your presence over the formation with two units (sections or 4-plane flights) weaving so that someone is always heading toward each flank, will detour the enemy and will keep you in a position to take head-on shots.[13]

The whole thing boiled down to mutual support and how best to bring this about.

Flatley's acceptance and enthusiastic endorsement of the "Thach Weave" helped set the stage for its rapid adoption by naval fighting squadrons in subsequent months. Thach himself labored long and hard in late 1942 and early 1943 to produce a series of training films and booklets presenting all of the fundamentals of naval fighter doctrine, including hit-and-run offensive tactics and the "Thach Weave." Together they spread the word.

APPENDIX 5

Japanese Combat Methods

In the Imperial Navy's carrier fighter pilots, the U.S. Navy faced aviators who to a surprising degree reflected much of their own philosophy and tactics of air fighting. Today the common opinion of the Zero pilots wrongly holds them as "individualistic" and "exhibitionistic," with tactics that "never evolved beyond World War I style dogfighting."[1] This is a great disservice to the elite pilots of 1941–42. Like their counterparts in the U.S. Navy, they relied mainly on hit-and-run tactics, predicated around deflection shooting and teamwork, without merely trying to ride their opponents' tails in a dogfight.

During operational training and squadron exercises, the Japanese flew many hours of formation practice and mock combat. Early on, they learned to act as part of a team within the three-plane *shōtai* or section, flying formation, initiating attacks, and defending against them in concert with the rest of the *shōtai*. In contrast, the U.S. Navy put greater emphasis on individual gunnery training built around Individual Battle Practice (IBP), where the pilot flew the four classic gunnery approaches for the record and engaged in single combat with another fighter. In mock combat, the Japanese trained as formations, first matching three planes against three, then three versus six, finally up to a nine-plane *chūtai* (division) battling another nine. In the months prior to Pearl Harbor, the carrier pilots trained intensely:

> Emphasis was placed on keeping formation during aerial combat and training was conducted until the least skillful of the fighter pilots flying three planes to a formation could ably cope with six enemy planes.[2]

The basic tactical unit was the *shōtai* of leader and two wingmen, and the Japanese flew two main types of formations. The first was the "route" or cruise formation, adopted in flight to and from the combat area. It consisted of the standard Vee formation with the two wingmen flying between 30 and 45 degrees off the leader's two quarters:

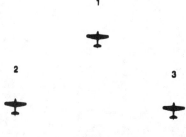

The aircraft flew about at the same level with 50 meters of interval between leader and wingman. This was the same formation as flown by the U.S. Navy before going over to the two-plane section.

When the fighter leaders anticipated action, they deployed their Zeros into much looser combat formations. One variant put the *shōtai* into left or right echelon, increasing the interval between planes to 100 or even 200 meters. Often the two wingmen weaved raggedly in short S-turns to increase lookout behind:

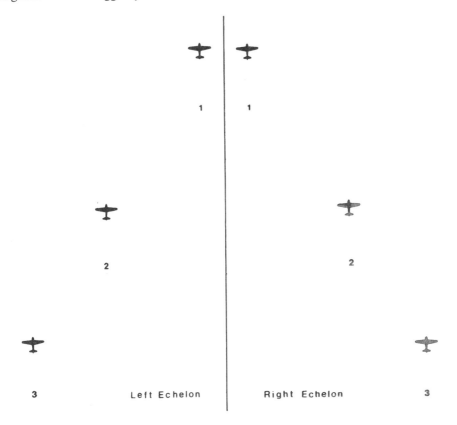

Other times the *shōtai* adopted a formation in principle the same as the U.S. Navy's A-B-C formation, increasing the interval in the Vee for one wingman to 200 meters and the other to 300 meters (as shown on page 488). The key difference between the Japanese *shōtai* and the three-plane Vees (or "Vics" as the RAF called them) was that the Zeros assumed loose formations before entering combat. That gave the Japanese room to react and follow their leader's movements. This was a far cry from the constricted RAF Vics, used until after the Battle of Britain.

Shōtai deployment for attack naturally depended on the tactical circumstances, but the Zeros liked to use firing passes in succession from above-rear or high-side, depending on the opposition. The *shōtai* formed into line-astern, well spaced out with intervals of 500 meters or more. Charging in one at a time, each Zero would roar within range, fire, then pull out underneath and ahead of the target in order to climb away out of reach. As one completed its run, another would be coming in, keeping the target under constant attack. Experienced Japanese pilots seldom sat on the tail of an enemy fighter for an extended shot, unless the attacker was very sure another enemy fighter would not jump him. Sometimes the *shōtai* leader brought his two wingmen up abreast of him and deployed well apart to bracket a

1

2

3

single target and box it in. Zeros then either alternated in making passes from the side, or if the leader did stay on the target's tail, his two wingmen took great pains to watch his tail. At other times, a leader placed one wingman above the fight as top cover, while he and the other wingman dived in.

To function effectively, the *shōtai* required three excellent pilots well trained in its arts. The prewar Japanese carrier pilots had practiced together, and the extreme maneuverability of their Zeros permitted the *shōtai* to remain a coherent entity even through wild combat. They often achieved remarkable coordination with gunnery runs. The key factors were training and experience. In 1941–mid-1942, the pilots enjoyed excellent training and experience. If that was lacking, the *shōtai* broke down in combat much more easily than the U.S. Navy's formations, which required far less effort to fly. In 1943 the lack of experienced pilots compelled the Imperial Navy to adopt the 2–2 formation of two-plane *buntai* comprising a four-plane *shōtai*. The theory was that only the *shōtai* leader, in that case, had to be experienced.

Chūtai or division formations likewise came in two varieties, route and combat. The cruise or route formations usually placed the three *shōtai* Vees in echelon, one behind the other. In combat, a *chūtai* often adopted an A-B-C type deployment, its componental *shōtai* at different heights and intervals to facilitate lookout astern. Japanese training exercises envisioned the *chūtai* leader as manipulating his nine planes in battle, such as sending one *shōtai* on each side of a target in order to bracket or retaining one *shōtai* above as top cover. Many times a *chūtai* formed into one long "string" to execute successive gunnery runs, such as happened on 4 June 1942 at Midway. Usually combat was such that each *shōtai* was on its own after the *chūtai* leader made his initial deployment.

In common with the U.S. Navy, the Imperial Navy taught its pilots deflection shooting, but the Japanese did not utilize the technique to its greatest advantage. They used reflector gunsights, but the Zero fighter itself lacked sufficient visibility over the nose to see the proper lead for full-deflection attacks against speedy targets. Some pilots cranked up their seats, putting their heads just beneath the cockpit canopy in order to sight along the top of the engine cowling, sufficient to make nearly a full-deflection shot in a steep overhead attack, but their shooting was less certain and the pilot certainly less comfortable than in an F4F Wildcat. Japanese high-side attacks generally saw the pilots shooting at half deflection and less, rather than full deflection as with the U.S. Navy. The measure of experienced Japanese was their ability to estimate deflection angles and ranges with or without the sights. The veterans honed their shooting eyes and improved their deflection shooting considerably. Problems included the slow-firing, low-velocity cannons, and the fact that at higher speeds the Mitsubishi A6M2 Zero was not a good gunnery platform. Rapid acceleration in dives caused a deterioration of control due to stiff ailerons. The point of aim tended to wander, and the pilots could not use the ailerons to roll or corkscrew in to match target maneuvers in an overhead run. In addition, too abrupt a recovery, such as pulling into a steep climb close to the target, lost speed quickly and set up the Zero for a counter-shot if the target could bring its guns to bear.

Defensively, the Zero pilots depended on mutual lookout and support between aircraft in a *shōtai* or *chūtai*. The standard defensive maneuver to counter an attack from above and behind was to pull into a tight, climbing turn, usually to the left. This offered an attacker a full-deflection shot and started the Zero climbing away. While the individual under attack made his counter, the other Zeros in his *shōtai* climbed to attack the enemy from other directions. If a Zero pilot found an opponent close on his tail and knew his mount was more maneuverable than the enemy's, he often pulled into a loop and ended up right on the attacker's tail. A variant of this maneuver was to pull up sharply, stall ("almost stopping in mid air"), let the enemy go by, and jump on his tail. At this time the Japanese were not averse to turning into attackers for head-on runs. They were confident in starting a scissors because they knew they could turn inside their opponents and work their way onto the other's tail.

In general, the Imperial Navy's fighter pilots used excellent tactics, based on the advanced concepts of hit-and-run attacks and deflection shooting. Ironically, these commendable tactics sometimes lacked suitability for the aircraft they flew. The Mitsubishi A6M2 Zero was a consummate dogfighting machine, but not so good as a hit-and-run fighter. As hit-and-run tactics depended heavily upon high-speed control, this was a great drawback. The later versions, the A6M3 and A6M5 with their shorter wing spans, were far better in this regard. The second area where the Zero was deficient was as a gunnery airplane. Because of somewhat reduced visibility over the nose (when compared with the Grumman F4F Wildcat), full-deflection shots were difficult to make. The F4F pilots were not the only ones learning the facts of war in the Pacific and making adjustments. The Americans happened to adjust faster.

APPENDIX 6

List of U.S. Navy Fighter Pilots

Pilots in Fighting Squadrons Two, Three, Forty-two, Six, and Eight
7 December 1941–6 June 1942

	Name	Age*	Rank**		Squadrons
1)	Achten, Julius A.	26	Mach.	USN	VF-2,6
2)	Adams, John P.	22	Ens.	USNR	VF-42,3
3)	Allard, Clayton	24	Mach.,	USN	VF-2,6
4)	Allen, Eric, Jr.	25	Lieut. (jg)	USN	VF-6
5)	Bain, John B.	21	Ens.	USNR	VF-2,42,3
6)	Baker, John D.	26	Ens.	USNR	VF-42
7)	Baker, Paul G.	31	Lieut. (jg)	USN	VF-2
8)	Barnes, Doyle C.	29	Mach.	USN	VF-2,6,3
9)	Barnes, William W., Jr.	27	Lieut. (jg)	USNR	VF-42,3
10)	Bass, Horace A., Jr.	26	Ens.	USNR	VF-3
11)	Bassett, Edgar R.	27	Ens.	USNR	VF-42,3
12)	Bauer, Louis H.	30	Lieut.	USN	VF-2,VF-2 Det.
13)	Bayers, Edward H.	32	Lieut. (jg)	USN	VF-6
14)	Borries, Fred, Jr.	29	Lieut.	USN	VF-2
15)	Brassfield, Arthur J.	31	Lieut. (jg)	USN	VF-42,3
16)	Brewer, Charles E.	28	Gunner	USN	VF-2, VF-2 Det.
17)	Bright, Mark K.	22	Ens.	USNR	VF-3
18)	Brooks, George W.	29	Ens.	USN	VF-2,VF-2 Det.
19)	Bull, Richard S., Jr.	28	Lieut.	USN	VF-2
20)	Carey, Henry A., Jr.	21	Ens.	USNR	VF-8
21)	Carmody, Harry T.	28	AMM1c	USN	VF-2
22)	Carter, Homer W.	22	AOM1c	USN	VF-2,6
23)	Cheek, Tom F.	24	Mach.	USN	VF-2,6,3
24)	Clark, Howard F.	27	Lieut. (jg)	USN	VF-3,2
25)	Cook, Morrill I., Jr.	23	Ens.	USNR	VF-8
26)	Corbin, Frank T.	34	Lt. Cdr.	USN	VF-6
27)	Criswell, David W.	24	Ens.	USNR	VF-6
28)	Crommelin, Richard G.	24	Lieut. (jg)	USN	VF-42,3
29)	Daly, Joseph R.	23	Ens.	USNR	VF-6
30)	Daniels, James G., III	26	Lieut. (jg)	USN	VF-6
31)	Davenport, Wayne E.	23	AMM1c	USN	VF-2,3
32)	Dibb, Robert A. M.	20	Ens.	USNR	VF-3
33)	Dietrich, Alfred E.	22	Ens.	USNR	VF-8
34)	Dufilho, Marion W.	25	Lieut. (jg)	USN	VF-3,2
35)	Eder, Willard E.	25	Lieut. (jg)	USNR	VF-3,2
36)	Eppler, Harold J. W.	24	Ens.	USNR	VF-3
37)	Evans, Robert C.	23	Ens.	USNR	VF-3
38)	Fairbanks, Henry A.	21	Ens.	USNR	VF-8
39)	Fenton, Charles R.	34	Lt. Cdr.	USN	VF-42
40)	Firebaugh, Gordon E.	30	Lieut. (jg)	USN	VF-2,VF-2 Det.
41)	Flatley, James H., Jr.	35	Lt. Cdr.	USN	VF-2,VF-2 Det., 42,10
42)	Flynn, David R.	27	Ens.	USNR	VF-6
43)	Ford, Warren W.	26	Lieut.	USN	VF-8

	Enlisted	To 7/42 Awarded Decorations***	To 7/42 Confirmed Victories	Total Confirmed Victories****	Remarks
1)	1935	—	0.5	1.5	NAP; Ret. 3/64 as Lieut.
2)	1941	2 NC, 1 DFC	2.0	2.0	Ret. 7/72 as Capt.
3)	1936	—	0.0	0.0	NAP; K. 3 Aug. 42 in VF-6
4)	1934	—	0.0	0.0	USNA1938; DOW 8 Dec. 41 in VF-6
5)	1941	2 NC	2.0	2.0	Ret. 9/61 as Cdr.
6)	1941	—	0.0	0.0	MIA 7 May 42 in VF-42
7)	1929	NC	3.0	3.0	NAP; MIA 7 May 42 in VF-2
8)	1933	NC	3.0	3.0	NAP; MIA 24 Aug. 42 in VF-6
9)	1940	NC, DFC	1.0	1.0	Ret. 12/72 as Cdr.
10)	1941	NC	1.0	1.0	KIA 24 Aug. 42 in VF-5
11)	1940	NC	2.0	2.0	KIA 4 June 42 in VF-3
12)	1931	—	0.0	1.25	USNA1935; Ret. 7/65 as Capt.
13)	1928	NC	2.333	4.333	NAP; Ret. 8/58 as Capt.
14)	1931	—	0.0	0.0	USNA1935; Ret. 7/61 as Capt.
15)	†1937	2 NC	6.333	6.333	Ret. 7/69 as Capt.
16)	1934	—	0.0	3.0	NAP; Ret. 11/59 as Capt.
17)	1941	—	0.0	9.0	KIA 17 June 1944 in VF-16
18)	1935	—	0.0	2.25	NAP; Ret. 2/56 as Capt.
19)	1932	DFC	0.0	0.0	USNA1936; MIA 8 May 42 in VF-2
20)	1941	DFC	0.0	7.0	Lt. Cdr. USNR 10/45
21)	1931	—	0.0	0.0	NAP; Ret. 7/54 as Lt. Cdr.
22)	1936	—	0.0	1.0	NAP; Ret. 8/60 as Lt. Cdr.
23)	1935	NC	1.0	1.0	NAP; Ret. 7/56 as Cdr.
24)	1934	2 DFC	0.5	0.5	USNA1938; MIA 8 May 42 in VF-2
25)	1941	NC, DFC	2.0	2.0	KIA 26 Oct. 42 in VF-72
26)	1923	—	0.0	0.0	USNA1927; Ret. 7/49 as Capt.
27)	1941	—	0.0	0.0	K. 1 Feb. 42 in VF-6
28)	1934	2 NC	3.5	3.5	USNA1938; K. 14 July 45 in VF-88
29)	1941	—	0.0	2.0	Lt. Cdr. USNR 10/45
30)	†1938	DFC	1.0	1.0	Ret. 7/70 as Capt.
31)	1938	—	0.0	0.0	NAP; Ret. 12/58 as Lt. Cdr.
32)	1941	NC	1.0	7.0	K. 29 Aug. 44
33)	1941	DFC	0.0	1.333	Ret. 4/56 as Lt. Cdr.
34)	1934	—	0.0	2.0	USNA1938; KIA 24 Aug. 42 in VF-5
35)	1939	NC, DFC	1.5	6.5	Ret. 7/65 as Capt.
36)	1941	—	0.0	0.0	Killed in accident
37)	1941	—	0.0	0.0	Ret. 4/62 as Lt. Cdr.
38)	1941	—	0.0	3.0	Lt. Cdr. USNR 10/45
39)	1925	—	0.0	0.0	USNA1929; Ret. 7/59 as RAdm.
40)	1929	—	0.0	0.0	NAP; Ret. 4/57 as Capt.
41)	1925	NC	2.0	4.0	USNA1929; Ret. 5/58 as VAdm.
42)	1939	—	0.0	0.0	Ret. 7/71 as Capt.
43)	1933	DFC	1.0	2.0	USNA1937; Ret. 7/57 as RAdm.

Name	Age*	Rank**		Squadrons
44) Formanek, George, Jr.	22	Ens.	USNR	VF-8
45) Freeman, David B., Jr.	23	Ens.	USNR	VF-8
46) French, Lawrence C.	30	Lieut. (jg)	USN	VF-8
47) Gadrow, Victor M.	28	Lieut. (jg)	USN	VF-3
48) Gay, Theodore S., Jr.	34	Lieut. (jg)	USN	VF-2, VF-2 Det.
49) Gayler, Noel A. M.	26	Lieut.	USN	VF-3,2
50) Gibbs, Harry B.	21	Ens.	USNR	VF-42,3
51) Gray, James S., Jr.	27	Lieut.	USN	VF-6
52) Gray, Richard	29	Lieut. (jg)	USN	VF-8
53) Grimmell, Howard L., Jr.	23	Lieut. (jg)	USNR	VF-6
54) Groves, Stephen W.	24	Ens.	USNR	VF-8
55) Gunsolus, Roy M.	20	Ens.	USNR	VF-6
56) Haas, Walter A.	29	Lieut. (jg)	USNR	VF-42,3
57) Halford, James A., Jr.	22	Ens.	USNR	VF-6
58) Harwood, Bruce L.	31	Lieut.	USN	VF-8
59) Haynes, Leon W.	27	Ens.	USNR	VF-3,2
60) Hebel, Francis F.	29	Lieut. (jg)	USN	VF-6
61) Heisel, Harold N.	28	Lieut. (jg)	USN	VF-6
62) Hermann, Gayle L.	26	Lieut. (jg)	USN	VF-6
63) Hiebert, Walter J.	25	Lieut. (jg)	USNR	VF-6
64) Hill, George R.	23	Ens.	USNR	VF-8
65) Hodson, Norman D.	21	Ens.	USNR	VF-6
66) Holt, William M.	24	Ens.	USNR	VF-6
67) Hopper, George A., Jr.	22	Ens.	USNR	VF-2,42,3
68) Hoyle, Rhonald J.	27	Lieut. (jg)	USN	VF-6
69) Hughes, Richard Z.	23	Ens.	USNR	VF-8
70) Jennings, Minuard F.	26	Lieut. (jg)	USN	VF-8
71) Johnson, Howard L.	27	Lieut. (jg)	USN	VF-3
72) Kanze, Robert F.	26	AP2c	USN	VF-2
73) Kelley, John C.	25	Lieut. (jg)	USN	VF-6
74) Kelly, C. Markland, Jr.	25	Ens.	USNR	VF-8
75) Kleinmann, Mortimer V., Jr.	21	Ens.	USNR	VF-6
76) Knox, Leslie L. B.	25	Lieut. (jg)	USNR	VF-42
77) Lackey, John H.	28	Lieut. (jg)	USNR	VF-3,2
78) Lemmon, Rolla S.	26	Lieut. (jg)	USN	VF-3
79) Leonard, William N.	25	Lieut. (jg)	USN	VF-42,3
80) Lovelace, Donald A.	35	Lt. Cdr.	USN	VF-3, (VF-2 orders)
81) Macomber, Brainard T.	25	Lieut. (jg)	USNR	VF-42,3
82) Magda, John	23	Ens.	USNR	VF-8
83) Markham, George F., Jr.	25	Ens.	USNR	VF-2,42,3
84) Mason, Newton H.	22	Ens.	USNR	VF-3,2
85) Mattson, E. Duran	24	Lieut. (jg)	USN	VF-42,3
86) McClusky, Clarence W., Jr.	39	Lt. Cdr.	USN	VF-6
87) McCormack, Vincent F.	25	Lieut.	USN	VF-42
88) McCuskey, E. Scott	26	Lieut. (jg)	USNR	VF-42,3
89) McInerny, John E., Jr.	26	Ens.	USNR	VF-8
90) Mehle, Roger W.	26	Lieut.	USN	VF-6
91) Menges, Herbert H.	24	Ens.	USNR	VF-6
92) Merritt, Robert S.	21	Ens.	USNR	VF-8
93) Mitchell, Samuel G.	37	Lt. Cdr.	USN	VF-8
94) Morgan, Robert J.	28	Lieut. (jg)	USN	VF-3,2
95) Morris, Van H.	22	Ens.	USNR	VF-3
96) Nagle, Patrick L.	24	Mach.	USN	VF-2, VF-2 Det.
97) O'Hare, Edward H.	27	Lt. Cdr.	USN	VF-3

	Enlisted	To 7/42 Awarded Decorations***	To 7/42 Confirmed Victories	Total Confirmed Victories****	Remarks
44)	1940	DFC	1.0	5.0	KIA 24 Apr. 44 in VF-30
45)	1941	DFC	0.0	1.0	Ret. 7/65 as Capt.
46)	†1936	—	0.0	0.0	Ret. 7/62 as Capt.
47)	1931	—	0.0	0.0	USNA1935; K. 22 Dec. 41 in VF-3
48)	1926	—	0.0	1.25	NAP; Ret. 7/55 as Cdr.
49)	1931	3 NC	5.0	5.0	USNA1935; Ret. 9/76 as Adm.
50)	1941	NC, DFC	2.0	2.0	D. 1970 as Capt.
51)	1932	2 DFC	3.0	6.0	USNA1936; Ret. 1/66 as Capt.
52)	1932	—	0.0	2.0	USNA1936; Ret. 7/60 as Cdr.
53)	1940	—	0.0	4.0	Ret. 7/68 as Cdr.
54)	1941	NC	1.0	1.0	KIA 4 June 42 in VF-8
55)	1941	—	0.0	0.0	Ret. 7/62 as Lt. Cdr.
56)	1940	2 NC	4.833	4.833	Ret. 6/58 as Capt.
57)	1941	DFC	0.5	3.5	Ret. 11/59 as Cdr.
58)	†1935	—	0.0	0.0	KIA 24 Oct. 44 on *Princeton*
59)	1941	NC, DFC	0.5	1.5	Lt. Cdr. USNR 10/45
60)	†1936	—	0.0	0.0	DOW 8 Dec. 41, in VF-6
61)	†1937	—	0.0	0.0	Ret. 10/59 as Capt.
62)	†1937	—	0.0	0.0	K. 25 May 42 in VF-6
63)	1940	—	0.0	1.0	K. 30 Oct. 43
64)	1941	—	0.0	0.0	MIA 4 June 42 in VF-8
65)	1941	—	0.0	0.0	Ret. 7/72 as Capt.
66)	1940	—	0.0	0.0	MIA 9 Aug. 42 in VF-6
67)	1941	—	0.0	0.0	KIA 4 June 42 in VF-3
68)	1934	2 DFC	1.0	1.0	USNA1938; Ret. 5/57 as Capt.
69)	1941	DFC	0.0	4.0	Ret. 7/62 as Cdr.
70)	†1938	—	0.0	0.0	K. 18 Nov. 47 as Cdr.
71)	†1937	—	0.0	0.0	MIA 28 Mar. 43
72)	1936	—	0.0	2.392	NAP; Ret. 7/65 as Cdr.
73)	1934	—	0.0	2.0	USNA1938; KIA 11 Nov. 43 in VF-33
74)	1940	—	0.0	0.0	MIA 4 June 42 in VF-8
75)	1941	—	0.0	2.0	Lt. Cdr. USNR 10/45
76)	1939	NC	1.0	1.0	MIA 7 May 42 in VF-42
77)	1939	DFC	0.5	0.5	K. 6 Oct. 45
78)	†1937	NC	1.5	4.5	MIA 24 June 44 as CAG-50 (*Bataan*)
79)	1934	2 NC	3.0	5.0	USNA1938; Ret. 7/71 as RAdm.
80)	1924	DFC	0.5	0.5	USNA1928; K. 30 May 42 in VF-3
81)	†1938	2 NC	1.0	1.0	Ret. 9/59 as Capt.
82)	1941	—	0.0	4.0	KIA 8 Mar. 51 as CO, VF-191
83)	1941	—	0.0	0.0	Ret. 4/54 as Cdr.
84)	1941	—	0.0	0.0	MIA 8 May 42 in VF-2
85)	1935	NC	1.0	1.0	USNA1939; Ret. 6/44 as Lt. Cdr.
86)	1922	NC, DFC	0.333	0.333	USNA1926; Ret. 7/56 as RAdm.
87)	1933	NC	1.833	1.833	USNA1937; D. 28 Apr. 70 as Capt.
88)	†1938	2 NC, DFC	6.5	13.5	Ret. 7/65 as Capt.
89)	1941	—	0.0	0.0	Lt. Cdr. USNR 10/45
90)	1933	DFC	1.333	5.333	USNA1937; Ret. 7/70 as RAdm.
91)	1939	—	0.0	0.0	KIA 7 Dec. 41 in VF-6
92)	1941	—	0.0	3.0	Ret. 7/62 as Cdr.
93)	1923	—	0.0	0.0	USNA1927; Ret. 7/57 as Capt.
94)	1934	NC, DFC	1.5	1.5	USNA1938; Ret. 7/68 as Capt.
95)	1941	—	0.0	2.0	Lt. Cdr. USNR 10/45
96)	1936	—	0.0	0.0	NAP; MIA 7 Aug. 42 in VF-6
97)	1933	MOH	5.0	7.0	USNA1937; MIA 26 Nov. 43 as CAG-6 (*Enterprise*)

Name	Age*	Rank**		Squadrons
98) O'Neill, Edward J.	33	Lieut.	USN	VF-8
99) Packard, Howard S.	23	AP1c	USN	VF-2,6
100) Palmer, Fitzhugh L., Jr.	28	Lieut.	USN	VF-8,9
101) Pederson, Oscar	37	Lt. Cdr.	USN	VF-42
102) Peterson, Dale W.	21	Ens.	USNR	VF-3,2
103) Plott, Roy M.	26	Lieut. (jg)	USN	VF-42
104) Presley, Wayne C.	25	Ens.	USNR	VF-6
105) Provost, Thomas C., III	29	Lieut. (jg)	USNR	VF-6
106) Quady, Frank B.	26	Lieut. (jg)	USN	VF-6
107) Raby, John	34	Lt. Cdr.	USN	VF-8,9
108) Ramsey, Paul H.	36	Lt. Cdr.	USN	VF-2
109) Rawie, Wilmer E.	26	Lieut. (jg)	USN	VF-6
110) Reid, Beverly W.	24	Mach.	USN	VF-2,6
111) Rhodes, Thomas W.	25	Rad. Elec.	USN	VF-2,6
112) Rich, Ralph M.	24	Lieut. (jg)	USNR	VF-6
113) Rinehart, Clark F.	31	Lieut. (jg)	USN	VF-2
114) Roach, Melvin C.	24	Ens.	USNR	VF-6
115) Rowell, Richard M.	25	Ens.	USNR	VF-3,2
116) Ruehlow, Stanley E.	30	Lieut.	USN	VF-8
117) Runyon, Donald E.	28	Mach.	USN	VF-2,VF-2 Det.
118) Rutherford, Harold E.	37	Lieut. (jg)	USN	VF-2,VF-2 Det.
119) Sellstrom, Edward R., Jr.	25	Ens.	USNR	VF-3,2
120) Sheedy, Daniel C.	25	Ens.	USNR	VF-3
121) Simpson, Fred H.	26	Lieut. (jg)	USN	VF-2,VF-2 Det.
122) Smith, James C.	26	Ens.	USNR	VF-8
123) Stanley, Onia B., Jr.	27	Lieut. (jg)	USNR	VF-3
124) Starkes, Carlton B.	27	Ens.	USNR	VF-8
125) Stover, Elisha T.	21	Ens.	USNR	VF-8
126) Sumrall, Howell M.	29	Mach.	USN	VF-2,6
127) Sutherland, John F.	26	Lieut. (jg)	USNR	VF-8
128) Talbot, Johnny A.	21	Ens.	USNR	VF-8
129) Tallman, Humphrey L.	21	Ens.	USNR	VF-8
130) Thach, John S.	36	Lt. Cdr.	USN	VF-3
131) Tootle, Milton, Jr.	21	Ens.	USNR	VF-3
132) Vorse, Albert O., Jr.	27	Lieut.	USN	VF-3,2
133) Warden, William H.	24	Mach.	USN	VF-2,6
134) White, George A.	25	AMM1c	USN	VF-2
135) Wileman, William W.	24	Ens.	USNR	VF-2,6
136) Wilson, John W.	27	Ens.	USNR	VF-3
137) Woollen, William S.	27	Lieut. (jg)	USNR	VF-42,3
138) Wright, Richard L.	23	Ens.	USNR	VF-42,3

Notes:
   *Age as of 7 December 1941.
  **Highest Rank attained by 6 June 1942.
 ***Decorations: MOH   Medal of Honor
                    NC   Navy Cross
                    DSM   Distinguished Service Medal
                    DFC   Distinguished Flying Cross
****Total Victories: based on research by Frank Olynyk.
   †Original Aviation Cadet program (1935–39).

	Enlisted	To 7/42 Awarded Decorations***	To 7/42 Confirmed Victories	Total Confirmed Victories****	Remarks
98)	1927	—	0.0	0.0	USNA1931; Ret. 2/57 as RAdm.
99)	1937	DFC	0.0	1.0	NAP; Ret. 7/57 as Cdr.
100)	1932	—	0.0	2.0	USNA1936; Ret. 7/61 as Capt.
101)	1922	—	0.0	0.0	USNA1926; Ret. 2/61 as RAdm.
102)	1940	NC, DFC	1.5	1.5	MIA 8 May 42 in VF-2
103)	†1937	—	0.0	0.0	Ret. 8/57 as Cdr.
104)	1941	DFC	0.333	3.333	MIA 16 Sept. 43
105)	1939	DFC	0.5	0.5	Killed in accident
106)	1934	—	0.0	2.0	USNA1938; KIA 11 May 1945
107)	1925	—	0.0	2.0	USNA1929; Ret. 5/49 as RAdm.
108)	1923	NC	3.0	3.0	USNA1927; Ret. 10/66 as VAdm.
109)	1934	2 DFC	1.333	1.333	USNA1938; Ret. 7/62 as Capt.
110)	1935	NC	2.0	2.0	NAP; MIA 24 Aug. 42 in VF-6
111)	1937	—	0.0	3.0	NAP; Ret. 2/65 as Cdr.
112)	1939	NC	0.333	0.333	K. 18 June 42 in VF-6
113)	†1937	DFC	0.0	0.0	MIA 8 May 42 in VF-2
114)	1941	DFC	1.0	3.0	MIA 12 June 44
115)	1939	2 DFC	1.0	1.0	MIA 8 May 42 in VF-2
116)	1931	—	0.0	3.0	USNA1935; Ret. 7/65 as Capt.
117)	1934	—	0.0	11.0	NAP; Ret. 7/63 as Cdr.
118)	1924	—	0.0	0.0	NAP; K. 12 Jan. 43 in VF-6
119)	1941	NC	4.5	4.5	D. 21 June 42 in VF-3
120)	1941	NC	1.0	1.0	Ret. 1/63 as Cdr.
121)	†1936	—	0.0	0.0	K. 26 May 42 in VF-2 Det.
122)	1940	—	0.0	0.0	MIA 24 Aug. 42 in VF-5
123)	†1937	DFC	0.5	0.5	Ret. 7/69 as Capt.
124)	1940	DFC	0.0	6.0	Ret. 7/62 as Cdr.
125)	1940	DFC	0.0	4.5	MIA 17 Feb. 44 in VF-5
126)	1934	DFC	0.5	1.5	NAP; Ret. 12/57 as Cdr.
127)	†1938	DFC	0.0	3.0	Cdr. USNR 10/45
128)	1940	—	0.0	0.0	Ret. 10/65 as Lt. Cdr.
129)	1940	—	0.0	0.0	Ret. 7/65 as Capt.
130)	1923	2 NC, DSM	6.0	6.0	USNA1927; Ret. 5/67 as Adm.
131)	1941	NC	1.0	1.0	Lt. Cdr. USNR 10/45
132)	1933	NC, DFC	2.5	11.5	USNA1937; Ret. 1/59 as RAdm.
133)	1936	—	0.0	0.0	NAP; Ret. 3/66 as Lieut.
134)	1936	—	0.0	0.0	NAP; Ret. 3/58 as Cdr.
135)	1941	NC	1.0	1.0	KIA 13 Sep. 42 in VF-5
136)	1940	—	0.0	0.0	KIA 20 Feb. 42 in VF-3
137)	†1938	2 NC	4.5	4.5	Ret. 7/63 as Capt.
138)	1940	NC, DFC	1.5	2.0	D. 28 Mar. 52 as Cdr.

APPENDIX 7

Bureau Numbers of Fighter Aircraft in Squadrons Embarked November 1941–June 1942

1) Fighting Squadron Two

Cruise 5–13 December 1941 on *Lexington*

18 F2A-3s:	01526, 01529, 01531, 01533, 01535, 01536, 01538, 01540, 01543, 01544, 01547, 01549, 01551, 01554, 01557, 01558, 01560, 01564

Loss at sea: 5 Dec. 01544 (Clayton Allard, AMM1c)

Cruise 14–27 December 1941 on *Lexington*

21 F2A-3s:	01526, 01528, 01529, 01530, 01531, 01533, 01535, 01536, 01538, 01539, 01540, 01543, 01547, 01549, 01551, 01554, 01557, 01558, 01560, 01564, 01565

Loss at sea: 26 Dec. 01529 (H. L Rutherford, ACMM)

Cruise 29 December 1941–3 January 1942 on *Lexington*

17 F2A-3s:	01526, 01528, 01530, 01531, 01533, 01535, 01538, 01539, 01540, 01543, 01547, 01549, 01551, 01554, 01558, 01560, 01564

Loss at sea: 29 Dec. 01540 (Lieut. (jg) F. Borries)

Cruise 7–16 January 1942 on *Lexington*

17 F2A-3s:	01526, 01528, 01530, 01531, 01533, 01535, 01538, 01539, 01543, 01547, 01549, 01551, 01554, 01558, 01560, 01562, 01564

Cruise 15 April–8 May 1942 on *Lexington*

20 F4F-3s:	1865, 3973, 3975, 3976, 3978, 3979, 3981, 3982, 3986, 3987, 3991, 3993, 4003, 4005, 4011, 4014, 4016, 4021, 4031, 4035
1 F4F-3A:	3964

Loss 7–8 May: 3964, 3976, 3978, 3979, 3981, 3982, 3986, 3987, 3993, 4003, 4005, 4011, 4016, 4021, 4035

Landed on *Yorktown*: 1865, 3973, 3975, 3991, 4014, 4031

2) Fighting Two Detachment

Cruise 9–15 February 1942 on *Saratoga*

9 F4F-3As:	3925, 3956, 3957, 3958, 3961, 3962, 3967, 3968, 3969
1 XF4F-4:	1897

Cruise 1–6 June 1942 on *Saratoga*

13 F4F-4s:	5154, 5166, 5177, 5182, 5185, 5226, 5227, 5229, 5230, 5233, 5238, 02064, 02066
1 F4F-7:	5264

Loss at sea: 3 June 5182 (S. Tumosa, AP2c)

Cruise 7–13 June 1942 on *Saratoga*
9 F4F-4s: 5154, 5166, 5185, 5233, 02066, 02072, 02078, 02080, 02081

3) Fighting Squadron Three

Cruise 8–15 December 1941 on *Saratoga*
8 F4F-3s: 3976, 3978, 3979, 3983, 3985, 3986, 3991, 4026
2 F4F-3As: 3914, 3936
1 XF4F-4:   1897

Cruise 16–29 December 1941 on *Saratoga*
10 F4F-3s: 3976, 3978, 3979, 3983, 3985, 3986, 3987, 3991, 4026, 4031
2 F4F-3As: 3914, 3936
1 XF4F-4:   1897
    Loss at sea: 22 Dec. 3985 (Lieut. (jg) V. M. Gadrow)

Cruise 31 December 1941–13 January 1942 on *Saratoga*
11 F4F-3s: 3976, 3978, 3979, 3983, 3986, 3987, 3989, 3991, 4021, 4026, 4031
1 XF4F-4:   1897
2 F2A-3s: 01536, 01557

Cruise 31 January–26 March 1942 on *Lexington*
17 F4F-3s: 3976, 3978, 3979, 3983, 3986, 3987, 3989, 3991, 3995, 3996, 3999,
                 4004, 4009, 4012, 4021, 4026, 4031
1 F4F-3A: 3954
    Losses in combat: 20 Feb. 3995, 4026
    Transfers at sea: 14 Mar to VF-42: 3983, 3996, 3999, 4004, 4009, 4012
    2 F4F-3s from VF-42: 1864, 1865

Cruise 30 May–13 June 1942 on *Yorktown, Hornet*, and *Enterprise*
27 F4F-4s: 5049, 5050, 5066, 5080, 5093, 5142, 5143, 5144, 5145, 5146, 5147,
                 5148, 5149, 5150, 5151, 5152, 5153, 5165, 5167, 5168, 5169, 5170,
                 5171, 5239, 5243, 5244, 5245
    Losses 4–7 June: 5080, 5093, 5143, 5145, 5146, 5150, 5151, 5152, 5165, 5170,
                 5239
    Final disposition on 6 June: on *Enterprise*—5142, 5169; on *Hornet*—5049, 5050,
                 5066, 5144, 5147, 5148, 5149, 5153, 5167, 5168, 5171, 5243, 5244,
                 5245

4) Fighting Squadron Forty-two

Cruise 6 January–6 February 1942 on *Yorktown*
18 F4F-3s: 1860, 1861, 1864, 1865, 1870, 1879, 1883, 1886, 2522, 2526, 2527,
                 2528, 2529, 2530, 2531, 2532, 2537, 3972
    Losses at sea: 8 Jan. 2529 (Ens. W. S. Woollen)
                 12 Jan. 1886 (Ens. W. A. Haas)
                 14 Jan. 1860 (Ens. R. L. Wright)

Cruise 16 February–27 May 1942 on *Yorktown*
17 F4F-3s: 1861, 1864, 1865, 1870, 1879, 1880, 1883, 2522, 2526, 2527, 2528,
                 2530, 2531, 2537, 3972, 4010, 4013
    Transfers at sea: 14 Mar. to VF-3 1864, 1865
    6 F4F-3s from VF-3 3983, 3996, 3999, 4004, 4009, 4012
    Loss at sea: 14 Mar 4009 (Ens. W. A. Haas)
    Loss at sea: 1 Apr. 4012 (Ens. J. P. Adams)
        Status   1 May 1942:

19 F4F-3s: 1861, 1870, 1879, 1880, 1883, 2522, 2526, 2527, 2528, 2530, 2531,
                    2537, 3972, 3983, 3996, 3999, 4004, 4010, 4013
    Losses 4–8 May: 1883, 2527, 2528, 2531, 3972, 3999

5) Fighting Squadron Five

Cruise 7–13 June 1942 on *Saratoga*
18 F4F-4s: 5137, 5141, 5163, 5190, 5191, 5192, 5195, 5196, 5198, 5199, 5200,
                    5201, 5202, 5205, 5207, 02014, 02041, 02044

6) Fighting Squadron Six

      Status 27 November 1941:
17 F4F-3As: 3906, 3907, 3908, 3909, 3910, 3912, 3915, 3916, 3917, 3920, 3922,
                    3923, 3925, 3926, 3935, 3937, 3938
2 F4F-3s: 3982, 3988

Cruise 28 November–8 December 1941 on *Enterprise*
    13 F4F-3As, 2 F4F-3s
    Transfer at sea: 28 Nov. to VMF-211 3988
    Losses over Pearl Harbor, 7 Dec. 3906, 3909, 3935, 3938

Cruise 8–16 December 1941 on *Enterprise*
13 F4F-3As: 3907, 3908, 3910, 3912, 3915, 3916, 3917, 3920, 3922, 3923, 3925,
                    3926, 3937
2 F4F-3s: 3973, 3989

Cruise 19–31 December 1941 on *Enterprise*
11 F4F-3As: 3907, 3908, 3910, 3915, 3916, 3917, 3920, 3922, 3925, 3926, 3937
3 F4F-3s: 3973, 3981, 3982
1 F2A-3:   01562
    Loss at sea: 31 Dec. 3907 (Ens. J. C. Kelley)

Cruise 3–7 January 1942 on *Enterprise*
15 F4F-3As and F4F-3s drawn from:
14 F4F-3As: 3908, 3910, 3912, 3914, 3915, 3916, 3917, 3920, 3922, 3923, 3925,
                    3926, 3936, 3937
3 F4F-3s: 3973, 3981, 3982

Cruise 11 January–5 February 1942 on *Enterprise*
13 F4F-3As: 3908, 3910, 3912, 3914, 3915, 3916, 3917, 3920, 3922, 3923, 3926,
                    3936, 3937
5 F4F-3s: 3973, 3975, 3981, 3982, 4035
    Loss at sea: 1 Feb. 3937 (Ens. D. W. Criswell)

Cruise 14 February–10 March 1942 on *Enterprise*
10 F4F-3As: 3910, 3912, 3915, 3916, 3917, 3922, 3926, 3932, 3936, 3966
7 F4F-3s: 3973, 3975, 3981, 3982, 4000, 4002, 4017
    Losses at sea: 21 Feb. 3932 (Ens. N. D. Hodson)
                 24 Feb. 4017 (Ens. J. R. Daly)

Cruise 8–25 April 1942 on *Enterprise*
22 F4F-4s: 5045, 5048, 5051, 5052, 5054, 5055, 5056, 5059, 5060, 5062, 5063,
                    5067, 5068, 5070, 5071, 5073, 5074, 5075, 5077, 5079, 5082, 5084
5 F4F-3s: 2532, 3994, 3997, 4000, 4002

Cruise 30 April–26 May 1942 on *Enterprise*

27 F4F-4s: 5045, 5048, 5051, 5052, 5054, 5055, 5056, 5059, 5060, 5062, 5063, 5067, 5068, 5070, 5071, 5073, 5074, 5075, 5079, 5082, 5084, 5173, 5174, 5175, 5176, 5178, 5179

    Losses at sea: 15 May 5173 (Ens. W. M. Holt)
                  25 May 5060 (Lieut. (jg) G. L. Hermann)

Cruise 28 May–13 June 1942 on *Enterprise*
27 F4F-4s: 5045, 5051, 5052, 5054, 5055, 5056, 5062, 5063, 5067, 5068, 5070, 5071, 5073, 5075, 5082, 5084, 5174, 5178, 5179, 5180, 5222, 5224, 5228, 5232, 5234, 5235, 5236

    Loss at sea: 4 June 5062 (Mach. W. H. Warden)

7) Fighting Squadron Seventy-two

Cruise 7–13 June 1942 on *Saratoga*
20 F4F-4s: 5197, 5208, 5209, 5210, 5211, 5212, 5213, 5214, 5215, 5216, 5226, 5227, 02000, 02001, 02002, 02003, 02004, 02005, 02006, 02012

    Loss at sea: 12 June 02005 (Lieut. (jg) R. W. Rynd)

8) Fighting Squadron Eight

Cruise 31 March–25 April 1942 on *Hornet*
30 F4F-4s: 5086, 5089, 5090, 5092, 5093, 5095, 5096, 5109, 5110, 5112, 5113, 5114, 5115, 5116, 5117, 5118, 5119, 5121, 5122, 5123, 5124, 5125, 5126, 5127, 5128, 5129, 5130, 5131, 5132, 5133

Cruise 30 April–26 May 1942 on *Hornet*
27 F4F-4s: 5086, 5089, 5090, 5095, 5096, 5109, 5110, 5112, 5113, 5115, 5116, 5117, 5118, 5119, 5121, 5122, 5123, 5124, 5125, 5126, 5127, 5128, 5129, 5130, 5131, 5132, 5133

    Losses at sea: 1 May 5131 (Ens. S. W. Groves)
                2 May 5095 (Ens. C. M. Kelly)

Cruise 28 May–13 June 1942 on *Hornet*
27 F4F-4s: 5086, 5089, 5090, 5096, 5109, 5110, 5112, 5113, 5115, 5116, 5117, 5118, 5119, 5121, 5123, 5124, 5125, 5127, 5128, 5129, 5130, 5132, 5133, 5181, 5237, 5240, 5241

    Losses 4 June: 5086, 5089, 5109, 5113, 5115, 5116, 5117, 5118, 5119, 5123, 5132, 5237

Notes

THE EARLY OPERATIONS

1 INTRODUCTION TO WAR

The Fighting Squadrons: Missions, Men, and Aircraft

General sources on the military/political background include:

Gordon Prange, *At Dawn We Slept*; Husband E. Kimmel, *Admiral Kimmel's Story*; testimony and documents in U.S. Congress, 79th Cong., 1st Sess., *Pearl Harbor Attack*; for Task Force 8's Wake mission, WD ComAirBatFor; William F. Halsey and J. Bryan III, *Admiral Halsey's Story*: Robert D. Heinl, *The Defense of Wake*.

1 VADM Halsey testimony 2 Jan. 1942 in *PH Attack*, Part 23, 608.
2 Text with private diary of Lieut. (jg) Wilmer E. Rawie, USN.
3 Ltr. Putnam to Col. C. A. Larkin 3 Dec. 1941, in Heinl, 9.
4 For background of VF-6, Ltr. CNO to CO VF-31, "Historical data, forwarding of" (25 Sept. 1964), in Capt. O. B. Stanley papers; also U.S. Navy, Bureau of Navigation, *Register of Officers*, 1935–41, and in William T. Larkins, *U.S. Naval Aircraft 1921–1941*.
5 Career information on McClusky and other officers mentioned in this book from U.S. Navy, Bureau of Navigation, *Registers of Officers* and also from *Navy Directories*, dates 1926–1941.
6 In 2-F-15, Bureau Number 01544.
7 History of VF-2: William A. Riley, "The Chiefs of Fighting Two," *Journal of the American Aviation Historical Society* (Fall 1969) 145–52; Earl E. Smith, JOC, USN, "Fightin' Two," *All Hands* (May 1951) 59–63; Larkins; corresp. with VADM H. S. Duckworth, Capt. G. E. Firebaugh, Cdr. T. F. Cheek; muster rolls of VF-2, in National Archives, Record Group 24.
8 Smith, 62.
9 On the F2A see James V. Sanders, "The Brewsters of Fighting Two," in *JAAHS* (Fall 1969) 153–59; Chris Shores, *The Brewster Buffalo*, Profile Publications, No. 217; NA RG-72, Bureau of Aeronautics Correspondence, VF2A-2, VF2A-3. For Grumman F4F Wildcat: Frank Greene, *History of the Grumman F4F "Wildcat"*; Barrett Tillman, *The Wildcat in WWII*; NA RG 72, BuAer Corresp., VF4F-3; for self-sealing fuel tanks, Capt. E. H. Eckelmeyer, Jr., USN "The Story of the Self-Sealing Tank," *U.S. Naval Institute Proceedings* (Feb. 1946) 205–19.
10 Compiled from Aircraft Status Reports in NA RG 313, U.S. Fleet, Aircraft, Battle Force, Corresp., A4-1(1).

Air Raid on Pearl Harbor

Basic sources for Pearl Harbor Attack, Prange, Walter Lord, *Day of Infamy*; for operations of Task Force 8, see WD ComAirBatFor, Action Reports (listed in bibliography), "The War Record of Fighting Six" (Dec. 1941–June 1942, unofficial war diary), Lieut. Clarence Dickinson, *The Flying Guns*; for Task Force 12, WD ComScoFor, WD ComCruScoFor, WD USS *Lexington*.

1 WD ComAirBatfor, 7 Dec. 1941.
2 Ibid.
3 VADM Halsey testimony, 2 Jan. 1942, *PH Attack*, Part 23, 612.
4 Capt. J. M. Shoemaker testimony, 3 Jan. 1942, Ibid., 731.
5 "War Diary" of Lieut. (jg) J. G. Daniels III, 7 Dec. 1941.
6 VF-6 Aircraft Trouble Report (Ens. H. H. Menges), 3 Jan. 1942, in NA RG 72, BuAer Corresp. VF4F-3; Ltr. Officer Commanding Intelligence Field Unit to NAS Pearl Harbor, "Burned American Aircraft" (14 Dec. 1941) in RG 313, ABF, L11-1.
7 VF-6 Aircraft Trouble Report (Lieut. (jg) E. Allen), 3 Jan. 1942, in NA RG 72, BuAer Corresp., VF4F-3; Allen was a strong swimmer on the Naval Academy swim team.
8 VF-6 Aircraft Trouble Report (Lieut. (jg) F. F. Hebel), 3 Jan. 1942, in NA RG 72, BuAer Corresp. VF4F-3.
9 VF-6 Aircraft Trouble Report (Ens. D. R. Flynn), 13 Jan. 1942, in NA, BuAer Corresp., VF4F-3.
10 WD ComCruScoFor 7 Dec. 1941.
11 The *Lexington*'s (and the *Saratoga*'s) turbo-electric drive could be reversed at full power; more conventional steam-driven turbines (as in the other carriers) could only be reversed at one-third power.

Pearl Harbor Aftermath

General sources include war diaries, and the *CINCPAC Greybook*, also known as "Captain Steele's Running Estimate and Summary, 7 December 1941 to 31 August 1942"; it is the war diary of the War Plans section on CinCPac staff and absolutely invaluable for the strategic picture.

1 VF-6 War Record, 8 Dec. 1941.
2 Ltr. Capt. James Seton Gray, USN (Ret.) to *USNI Proceedings* (Dec. 1981) 91.
3 Ibid.
4 For Japanese submarine operations see: Japan. War History Office, *Senshi Sōsho*, Vol. 38, *Chūbu Taiheiyo Hōmen Kaigun Sakusen*, Part 1 (Central Pacific Naval Operations to May 1942), a part of the Japanese Official History, 326–31; also Zenji Orita and J. D. Harrington, *I-boat Captain*, 38–39.
5 WD ComCruScoFor 8 Dec. 1941; *Lexington* WD 8 Dec. 1941.
6 CO *Lexington* to CarDiv 3 112010 of December 1941 (transmitted actually on 13 Dec. 1941), from Franklin Delano Roosevelt Library Map Room Files, copy via Dr. Lloyd Graybar.

The Sara to the Front

General sources are WD ComCarDiv One, *Saratoga* Log

1 Personal diary of Lieut. (jg) O. B. Stanley, Jr.
2 Plane strengths in: Materiel Officer, San Diego to BuAer 11 Dec. 1941, RG 313, ABF, A4–1(1) Aircraft Status Reports.
3 ComAirBatFor to BuAer 22 Oct, 1941, RG 313, ABF, VF4F-3.
4 For VF-3 history, see CNO to CO VF-31 (25 Sept. 1964), in Stanley papers; U.S. Navy *Registers* and *Directories* 1923–41; Larkins.
5 Personal Diary of Lt. Cdr. Donald A. Lovelace, 10 Dec. (11 Dec.) 1941.

2 THE WAKE ISLAND OPERATION

Principal sources: WDs, Action Reports, Operations Orders, *CINCPAC Greybook*; *PH Attack*; Dr. Lloyd J. Graybar, "American Pacific Strategy after Pearl Harbor: The Relief of Wake Island" *Prologue* (Fall 1980) 134–50; S. E. Morison, *The Rising Sun in the Pacific*; Heinl; *Senshi Sōsho*, Vol. 38. Part 1.

Initial Moves

1 Stanley diary.
2 CinCPac Operations Order 39-41 to CTF-14 (15 Dec. 1941).
3 WD ComScoFor 16 Dec. 1941.
4 VF-6 War Record, 16 Dec. 1941.

The Disappointment

1 Later elucidated in USS *Lexington*, Air Defense Doctrine (28 Dec. 1941), in RG 313, ABF, A16-3.
2 Prange, 576, indicating that one of Freuler's kills accounted for the bombardier credited with destroying the *Arizona* on 7 Dec.
3 "Estimate of Capt. McMorris . . . 22 December 1941," in *CINCPAC Greybook*, 81.
4 Message OpNav to CinCPac 221706 of Dec. 1941 in *CINCPAC Greybook*, 72.
5 CinCPac to OpNav 280417 of Dec. 1941, in ibid., 120.
6 Lt. Cdr. John S. Thach, Interview at BuAer, 26 Aug. 1942, 2.
7 Graybar, 146; this is an excellent analysis of the relief attempt.
8 Lovelace diary 22 (23) Dec. 1941.
9 VF-6 War Record, 22 Dec. 1941.
10 Morison, *Rising Sun*, 242–54.
11 CTF-14 to CinCPac, "Report of Operations 16 December–29 December 1941"; Fletcher that morning of 23 Dec. was in fact about where CinCPac expected him to be. Pye assumed Task Force 14 that morning to still be about 500 miles from Wake; actually it was 430 miles out when Wake surrendered—see VADM Pye's very important testimony on 9 January 1942 in *PH Attack*, Part 23, 1063.
12 Morison, *Rising Sun*, 252.

3 INTERREGNUM

The Weeks of Futility

Outline of operations in WDs (now including ComCruBatFor WD), *CINCPAC Greybook*.

1 Text of Memo on 21 Dec. 1941 Conference in *PH Attack*, Part 24, 1487.
2 ComAirBatFor to AirBatFor, "Exterior Painting of Fleet Aircraft for Ready Identification" (23 Dec. 1941), in RG 313, ABF, F39.
3 Card in VF-6 War Record.
4 Ibid., 6 Jan. 1942.
5 *Senshi Sōsho*, Vol. 38, Part 1, 331–34.
6 Action Report, CO USS *Lexington* to CTF-11, "Attack upon enemy submarine by *Lexington* planes January 10, 1942" (15 Jan. 1942) and endorsements by CTF-11 (16 Jan. 1942) and CinCPac (28 Jan. 1942).
7 Foster Hailey, *Pacific Battle Line*, 59.
8 *Lexington* action report (15 Jan. 1942).
9 Hailey, 60.
10 *Senshi Sōsho*, Vol. 38, Part 1, 327.
11 Lovelace diary, 11 Jan. 1942.
12 Ibid.
13 Ibid., 16 Jan. 1942.
14 Based on Aircraft Status Reports in RG 313, ABF, A4-1(1).

The Samoan Operation

General sources include *CINCPAC Greybook,* WD ComCruScoFor (now RADM Frank Jack Fletcher), *Yorktown* Log; Pat Frank and Joseph D. Harrington, *Rendezvous at Midway.*

1 For VF-42 history: U.S. Navy *Registers* and *Directories*, 1928–41, Larkins, Ltr. Lt. Cdr. V. F. McCormack to Lt. Cdr. C. R. Fenton (16 Oct. 1942) in Capt. W. S. Woollen papers; corresp. with RADM O. Pederson and RADM W. N. Leonard.
2 Leonard corresp.
3 Mat. Off. San Diego to BuAer, 6 Jan. 1942, RG 313, ABF, A4-1(1).
4 Leonard corresp.
5 Ltr. CO USS *Yorktown* to CNO 8 Jan. 1942; VF-42 Aircraft Trouble Report (Ens. W. S. Woollen) 9 Jan. 1942; both in RG 72, BuAer Corresp., VF4F-3.
6 VF-42 Aircraft Trouble Report (Ens. W. A. Haas) 14 Jan. 1942, in ibid.
7 VF-42 Aircraft Trouble Report (Ens. R. L. Wright) 15 Jan. 1942, in ibid.
8 ComInCh to CinCPac 021718 of Jan. 1942, in *CINCPAC Greybook,* 122.
9 Rawie diary, 11–17 Jan. 1942 entry.
10 Edward P. Stafford, *The Big E*, 33.
11 VF-6 War Record, 15 Jan, 1942.

4 THE 1 FEBRUARY 1942 RAIDS

General sources include WDs, Action Reports, *CINCPAC Greybook,* U.S. Navy, Office of Naval Intelligence, "Early Raids in the Pacific," *Senshi Sōsho*, Vol. 38, Part 1, 372–403, Halsey and Bryan, Dickinson, Stafford, Frank and Harrington.

Approach to Battle

1 Leonard corresp.
2 CinCPac to CTF-8, 17 280311 of Jan. 1942 in *CINCPAC Greybook,* 193.
3 VF-6 War Record, 27 Jan. 1942.
4 Ibid., 28 Jan. 1942.
5 Rawie diary, 29 Jan. 1942.
6 *Senshi Sōsho*, Vol. 38, Part 1, esp. 384–85; Hata Ikuhiko and Izawa Yasuho, *Nihon Kaigun Sentōkitai*, 83–84.
7 For Japanese aircraft, see Rene Francillon, *Japanese Aircraft of the Pacific War*, Masatake Okumiya and Jiro Horikoshi. *The Zero Fighter*, and Robert C. Mikesh and Rikyu Watanabe, *Zero Fighter*.

Task Force 8 in the Marshalls

1 Rawie diary, 31 Jan. 1942.
2 Copy with Rawie diary.
3 Handout, Intelligence Information, Marshall Is. (Jan. 1942), in ibid.
4 Leonard corresp.
5 VF-6 Aircraft Trouble Report (Ens. D. W. Criswell), 3 Feb. 1942, in RG 313, ABF, VF4F-3.
6 Keith Wheeler, *The Pacific is my Beat*, 47.
7 Ibid.
8 Rawie diary, 1 Feb. 1942; for Atake's account, see his biography in Hata and Izawa, 213.
9 Original in Rawie diary.
10 Cdr. E. B. Mott, "Narrative, U.S.S. Enterprise, Pearl Harbor to Guadalcanal" (22 March 1944).
11 Action report, CO TF-8 to CinCPac, "Action in the Marshall Islands, 1 February 1942" (9 Feb. 1942), 4; Daniels Diary, 1 Feb. 1942.
12 Action report, CEAG to CO USS *Enterprise*, "Attacks made by *Enterprise* Air Group on Northern Marshall Islands, Report on" (4 Feb. 1942), 9.

13 BuAer Ltr. 11 March 1942, in RG 72, BuAer Corresp. VF4F-3/F41.
14 Action report, CTF-8 to CinCPac (9 Feb. 1942), 2.
15 VF-6 War Record, 1 Feb. 1942.
16 Action report, Lt. R. H. Best to CO VB-6 (2 Feb. 1942).

The Yorktown's Strikes

1 ADM J. J. Clark in his *Carrier Admiral,* 85, accuses Fletcher and Buckmaster of abandoning the crew of that ditched airplane. Clark evidently was not aware that Fletcher had despatched the three destroyers to look for the downed aviators. Clark later voiced his displeasure of Fletcher's "inaction" to Admirals King and Towers, another example of Fletcher's reputation being smirched by those who did not know all of the facts.
2 Frank and Harrington, 61.
3 Ibid., also Clark (with Clark G. Reynolds), 85.
4 Lieut. E. S. McCuskey, USN, "Ace High," *Colliers* (Aug. 8, 1942) 41; also Capt. E. S. McCuskey interview, July 1974.

Return to Pearl

1 Rawie diary, 2 Feb. 1942.
2 E. B. Potter, *Nimitz,* 40.

5 THE BATTLE OFF BOUGAINVILLE

Basic sources include WDs, Logs, Action Reports, *CINCPAC Greybook, Senshi Sōsho,* Vol. 49 *Nantōhōmen Kaigun Sakusen,* Part 1 (Southeast Area Naval Operations to the beginning of operations to recapture Guadalcanal), 89–92; *Early Raids in the Pacific;* interview (Oct. 1974) with ADM J. S. Thach, corresp. with VADM H. S. Duckworth, RADM A. O. Vorse, Capt O. B. Stanley, Jr., Capt W. E. Eder; Lovelace and Stanley diaries; J. S. Thach, "The Red Rain of Battle," *Colliers* (5 Dec. 1942).

1 Lovelace diary, 22 Jan. 1942; VF-3 Aircraft Trouble Report (Ens. L. W. Haynes), 23 Jan. 1942, RG 72, BuAer Corresp., VF4F-3.
2 Stanley diary.
3 Lt. Cdr. J. S. Thach, BuAer Interview (26 Aug. 1942), 2.
4 Stanley diary.
5 Ibid.
6 Lovelace diary, 19 Feb. 1942.
7 Lieut. (jg) O. B. Stanley Flight Log, Stanley papers.
8 See especially U.S. Navy, ComAirBatFor, *Current Tactical Orders and Doctrine, U.S. Fleet Aircraft, Volume One, Carrier Aircraft, USF-74 (Revised),* March 1941; U.S. Naval Administration in World War II, DCNO (Air) Essays in the History of Naval Air Operations, Carrier Warfare, Part III "History of Naval Fighter Direction"; corresp. with Duckworth, Thach, and Leonard.
9 Thach, BuAer Interview, 23.
10 Lieut. Noel A. M. Gayler, Interview at BuAer, 17 June 1942, 19. Like Thach's interview, this one of Gayler is extremely useful for the historian of fighter operations.
11 Thach interview, Oct. 1974.
12 Stanley diary.
13 On the Type 1 land attack plane, Francillon, 378–87.
14 Correspondence with Dr. Hata Ikuhiko, who kindly checked for me the records of the 4th Air Group.
15 Stanley diary.
16 Duckworth corresp.
17 Stanley diary.
18 Ibid.
19 Thach interview, Oct. 1974.

20 Thach, BuAer Interview, 3.

21 Action Report, U.S. Aircraft Action with the Enemy, Bombing Two (20 Feb. 1942), Report of Lieut. W. E. Henry.

22 Cited in unpublished thesis by Midshipman John O. Donelon, "Edward Henry O'Hare," copy kindly furnished by Mrs. Kathleen O'Hare Nye. Donelon's account is a good biography of Butch O'Hare based largely on the papers and clippings held by the O'Hare family.

23 Sources on O'Hare's fight include Donelon, John Field, "How O'Hare downed 5 Jap Planes in One Day," *Life* (13 Apr. 1942) 12–18, Stanley Johnston, *Queen of the Flat-tops*, O'Hare family papers, including his flight log; first-person Japanese accounts, which are most valuable if used with caution, are in the newspaper *Japan Times & Advertiser*, 9 and 14 March 1942.

24 *Japan Times & Advertiser*, 14 March 1942.

25 Ibid.

26 Ibid., 9 March 1942; Mori is identified by Dr. Hata as pilot who ditched in Simpson harbor.

27 Ibid., 14 March 1942; for Ono's account, see ibid. 9 March 1942.

28 Morison, *Rising Sun*, 267.

29 Field, 18.

30 Ono's account, *Japan Times & Advertiser*, 9 March 1942; apparently only three of his crew survived to be rescued, as natives on Nuguria later reported a barge took off the three, see Capt. R. J. Bulkley, *At Close Quarters* (Washington, D.C.: Government Printing Office, 1962), 154.

31 Thach, "Red Rain of Battle," 37.

32 CTF-11 to CinCPac, "Report to Action of Task Force Eleven with Japanese Aircraft on Feb. 20, 1942" (24 Feb. 1942), 4.

33 CTF-11 to CominCh, CinCPac 232146 of Feb. 1942, *CINCPAC Greybook*, 253.

34 CTF-11 to CinCPac 232208 of Feb. 1942, in ibid., 234.

35 For VF-2 Detachment, see VF-2 WD, *Saratoga* Log, corresp. with Capt. G. E. Firebaugh and his flight log.

6 THE *ENTERPRISE*'S CENTRAL PACIFIC RAIDS

Return to Wake Island

General sources: WDs, Action Reports, *Early Raids in the Pacific*, Stafford, Dickinson, Wheeler, Halsey and Bryan.

1 VF-6 Aircraft Trouble Report (Ens. N. D. Hodson) 22 Feb. 1942, in RG 313, ABF, VF4F-3.

2 Wheeler, 78.

3 Ibid., 81.

4 Ibid., 83.

5 Ibid., 81.

6 VF-6 War Record, 24 Feb. 1942.

7 VF-6 Aircraft Trouble Report (Ens. J. R. Daly) 25 Feb. 1942, in RG 313, ABF, VF4F-3.

8 CEAG to CO USS *Enterprise*, "Attacks made by *Enterprise* Air Group on Wake Island—Report on" (26 Feb. 1942), 8.

9 CO USS *Enterprise* to CinCPac, "Report of Action on February 24, 1942 (Zone Minus Twelve) against Wake Island" (8 Mar. 1942), 2.

10 CEAG to CO USS *Enterprise* (26 Feb. 1942), 9.

11 CO USS *Enterprise* to CinCPac (8 Mar. 1942), 4.

A Visit to Marcus

1 VF-6 War Record, 3 Mar. 1942.

2 Ibid., 5 Mar. 1942.

3 Ibid.

4 CO USS *Enterprise* to CinCPac, "Report of Action on March 4, 1942 (Zone Minus Eleven) against Marcus Island" (9 Mar. 1942), 4.

5 CEAG to CO USS *Enterprise*, "Attacks made by *Enterprise* Air Group on Marcus Island—Report on" (6 Mar. 1942), 4

6 2nd Endorsement (CinCPac) to CO USS *Enterprise* to CinCPac (9 Mar. 1942).

7 Ibid.

8 Halsey and Bryan, 23.

7 THE LAE–SALAMAUA RAID

General sources: WDs, Action Reports, Logs, *CINCPAC Greybook*, *Senshi Sōsho*, Vol. 49, Part 1, 107–29; John B. Lundstrom, *The First South Pacific Campaign*.

Gathering the Forces

1 ComANZAC to CinCPac 250100 of Feb. 1942, in *CINCPAC Greybook*, 254.

2 CTF-11 to CinCPac 260458 of Feb. 1942, in ibid., 255.

3 Stanley diary.

4 Ibid.

5 Lovelace diary, 4 March 1942.

A Change of Targets

1 Thach, "Red Rain of Battle," 37.

2 Ibid., 38.

3 Thach, BuAer Interview, 4.

4 *Lexington* Summary for 10 March 1942 Attack (Stanley papers).

5 Thach, "Red Rain of Battle," 38.

6 Ibid.

7 Leonard corresp.; Pederson corresp.

8 CTF-11 to CinCPac, "Cruise of Task Force Eleven from Jan. 31 to Mar. 26, 1942" (26 Mar. 1942), 11–12.

9 *CINCPAC Greybook*, 267.

10 Gayler, BuAer Interview, 13.

Withdrawal and the Lexington *Home*

1 Lieut. (jg) A. J. Brassfield to Mat. Off., ABF, 14 Mar. 1942, in RG 313, ABF, VF4F-3.

2 VF-42 Aircraft Trouble Report (Ens. W. A. Haas), 15 Mar. 1942, ibid.

3 Leonard corresp.

4 Stanley diary.

5 The first official change issued by BuAer for lap and shoulder belts was issued on 18 June 1942; see Greene, 42.

6 Cited in Donelon, 10.

8 THE TOKYO RAID

Preliminaries

1 Lieut. George F. Markham, "We Meet the Enemy," *The Scoop* (Nov. 27, 1943) 1, 6; also interview with Cdr. Markham.

2 On F4F-4s and Martlets, see Greene, Tillman, and an interesting analysis by a former Fleet Air Arm pilot: Eric Brown, *Wings of the Navy*, 40–51; also U.S. Navy, BuAer, *Naval Aircraft Record of Acceptances 1935–1946*.

3 Officer-in-charge, Fleet Aircraft Technical Unit to Chief, BuAer (11 Dec. 1941), RG 313, ABF, VF4F-4.

4 CO VF-3 to CO USS *Saratoga*, "XF4F-4 Service Tests" (13 Jan. 1942), in ibid.

5 Chief, BuAer to ComAirBatFor, ComAirLant (4 Feb. 1942), in ibid.

6 ComAirBatFor to VF Squadrons (10 Feb. 1942), in ibid.

7 VF-6 War Record, 28 Mar. 1942.

8 CO VF-6 to ComAirBatFor, "F4F-4 Airplane—Performance of" (6 Apr. 1942), in RG 72, BuAer Corresp., VF4F-4.

9 2nd Endorsement to VF-6 Ltr. of 6 Apr. 1942, CO USS *Enterprise* to ComAirBatFor (7 Apr. 1942), in ibid.

10 Ibid.

11 VF-6 War Record, 7 Apr. 1942.

The Advent of Fighting Eight

1 For the history of VF-8, RG 24, VF-8 Muster Rolls, *Hornet* WD and Log, Clark G. Reynolds and E. T. Stover, *The Saga of Smokey Stover, from his Diary*, George Gay, *Sole Survivor*, Alexander R. Griffin, *A Ship to Remember: The Saga of the Hornet*, Theodore Taylor, *The Magnificent Mitscher*; the research of Bowen P. Weisheit (including flight log of Ens. C. Markland Kelly, Jr.), corresp. with J. F. Sutherland, Henry A. Carey, and Cdr. Carlton B. Starkes.

2 Stover, 14–15.

3 Lieut. Frederick Mears, *Carrier Combat*, 24; this is an excellent contemporary narrative which gives the flavor of carrier service in 1942 and was obviously based on a detailed, accurate diary. The author was killed in action in 1943.

4 Ibid., 25; also ACTG, PAC Aircraft Trouble Report (Ens. R. A. M. Dibb), 25 Mar. 1942, in RG 72, BuAer Corresp., VF4F-3.

Six Hundred Miles from Tokyo

General sources include WDs, Action Reports, Halsey and Bryan, Stafford, Carroll V. Glines, *Doolittle's Tokyo Raiders*, Mitsuo Fuchida and Masatake Okumiya, *Midway: The Battle that Doomed Japan*.

1 VF-6 War Record, 8 Apr. 1942.

2 CinCPac to PacFlt 100505 of Apr. 1942, in *CINCPAC Greybook*, 347; at the same time Fletcher became Commander, Cruisers, Pacific Fleet.

3 VF-6 War Record, 13 Apr. 1942.

4 Narrative, Lieut. Robin M. Lindsey, USN (17 Sept. 1943).

5 Ibid.

6 Rawie diary, also Action Report Lieut. (jg) W. E. Rawie to CEAG (18 Apr. 1942).

7 Ibid.

8 Ibid.

9 Ibid.

10 Ibid.

11 CO USS *Enterprise* to CTF-16,"Report of Action in Connection with the Bombing of Tokyo on April 18, 1942" (23 Apr. 1942).

12 ComCarPac Endorsement of *Enterprise* report.

13 CinCPac Endorsement of *Enterprise* report.

14 ComCarPac to BuAer 260130 of Apr. 1942, in CinCPac Message File.

15 Rawie diary, 25 Apr. 1942

THE BATTLE OF THE CORAL SEA

9 PRELUDE TO BATTLE

The Yorktown in the Coral Sea

General sources: WD ComCruScoFor (later ComCruPac), *Yorktown* Log, *CINCPAC Greybook*, Report ComCruPac to CinCPac, "Operations of Task Force 17 in the Coral Sea Area March 16 to April 20, 1942, Statement to clarify erroneous impressions gained at CINCPAC headquarters" (23 June 1942), WD ComCruTF17, VADM William W. Smith, *Midway: Turning Point of the Pacific*, Lundstrom.

1 CinCPac to ComANZAC, CTF-17 131535 of Mar. 1942, in *CINCPAC Greybook*, 288.
2 Leonard corresp.
3 CominCh to CTF-17 301930 of Mar. 1942, in *CINCPAC Greybook*, 322.
4 Adams in Bureau Number 4012, another of the F4F-3s received from VF-3 on 14 Mar. 1942.
5 CominCh to CTF-17 311455 of Mar. 1942, in *CINCPAC Greybook*, 324.
6 Mears, 22.
7 Ltr. McCormack to Fenton (16 Oct. 1942), Capt. W. S. Woollen papers.
8 McCuskey corresp.
9 ComCruPac to CinCPac (23 June 1942).
10 Leonard corresp.
11 On VF-42's fuel tank woes, following messages all from CinCPac Message File: CTF-17 to CominCh, CinCPac 140147, CTF-17 to CinCPac 160126, CinCPac to CTF-17 162023, Mat. Off. CarPac Pearl to *Yorktown* 162125, Mat. Off. CarPac Pearl to BuAer 170538, all of Apr. 1942; also Ltr. Mat. Off. CarPac Pearl to BuAer 2 May 1942, in RG 72, BuAer Corresp., VF4F-3.
12 Copies of Bureau of Navigation despatches in VADM J. H. Flatley, Jr. papers, kindly furnished by RADM J. H. Flatley III, USN.

> General sources on Fighting Two: *Lexington* WD, Johnston, *Queen*, interview with VADM P. H. Ramsey, Oct. 1974, interview with Cdr. G. F. Markham, corresp. with Cdr. J. B. Bain.

10 OPENING SHOTS

Coral Sea Preliminaries

> General sources on the Battle of the Coral Sea include WDs, Action Reports, *CINCPAC Greybook*, *Senshi Sōsho*, Vol. 49, Part 1, 227–336, U.S. Naval War College, *The Battle of the Coral Sea May 1 to May 11 Inclusive, 1942. Strategical and Tactical Analysis*, Morison, *Coral Sea, Midway and Submarine Actions May 1942–August 1942*, Johnston, *Queen of the Flat-tops*, Lundstrom.

1 Despatches in Flatley papers; Stanley Johnston, *The Grim Reapers*, 21–24; this book is a good source on Jim Flatley at the Coral Sea.

Tulagi Strike

> In addition to general sources cited above, corresp. with RADM Pederson, RADM Leonard, Capt. McCuskey, and Capt. J. P. Adams.

1 WD ComCruTF17, 4 May 1942.
2 Ibid.
3 McCuskey corresp.
4 Ibid.
5 Adams corresp.
6 McCuskey corresp.
7 Along with most of the *Hammann*'s crew, Enright, Kapp, and Jason were killed on 6 June 1942 when the *Hammann* was torpedoed while alongside the *Yorktown* during the Battle of Midway.

Gathering Storm

1 VF-42 U.S. Aircraft Action with the Enemy Report, 5 May 1942.
2 McCuskey corresp.
3 For a detailed discussion of the 6 May 1942 question, see my article "A Failure of Radio Intelligence" in *Cryptologia* (Apr. 1983), 97–118.

The Inscrutable Enemy

> General sources on the Imperial Japanese Naval Air Force include U.S. Strategic

Bombing Survey, Report 63 "Japanese Air Weapons and Tactics," and Report 64 "Japanese Air Power," Masatake Okumiya and Jiro Horikoshi, *Zero!* and their *The Zero Fighter,* Fuchida and Okumiya, *Midway,* Francillon, and detailed discussions in various volumes of *Senshi Sōsho.*

1 On the Type 99 carrier bomber, Francillon, 271–76.
2 On the Type 97 carrier attack plane, Francillon, 411–16.
3 For the Zero fighter, see Okumiya and Horikoshi, *The Zero Fighter,* Robert C. Mikesh and Rikyu Watanabe, *Zero Fighter,* Francillon, 362–77.
4 Okumiya and Horikoshi, *The Zero Fighter,* 62.
5 Ibid.
6 Unit histories and background on pilots in Hata and Izawa—if only there were such a study for U.S. naval fighter pilots! See also *Senshi Sōsho,* Vol. 49, Part 1, 187–92 for details on the Japanese carriers at Coral Sea.

11 7 MAY 1942

The Battle off Misima

In addition to basic sources cited above, corresp. with VADM Duckworth, RADM Pederson, RADM A. O. Vorse, Capt. B. T. Macomber, Capt. W. A. Haas, Cdr. G. F. Markham, Lt. Cdr. E. D. Mattson.

1 *Senshi Sōsho,* Vol. 49, Part 1, 276.
2 Fighter Director, USS *Lexington,* "The Battle of the Coral Sea. Report of Action 7–8 May 1942 by Fighter Director."
3 Ibid.
4 On escort doctrine in early 1942, see *USF-74 (Revised),* comments in various action reports; also Leonard corresp.
5 *USF-74 (Revised),* 120.
6 Ibid.
7 "Memo for all VF-2 Pilots" (n.d., c. Dec. 1941), Flatley papers.
8 *USF-74 (Revised),* 126.
9 VF-42 U.S. Aircraft Action with the Enemy Report, Lieut. (jg) R. G. Crommelin, 7 May 1942.
10 CO VB-2 to CO USS *Lexington,* "The Battle of the Coral Sea" (14 May 1942), 3.
11 VF-2 U.S. Aircraft Action with the Enemy Report, Lt. Cdr. P. H. Ramsey, 7 May 1942.
12 VF-42 U.S. Aircraft Action with the Enemy Report, Lt. Cdr. J. H. Flatley, 7 May 1942.
13 Macomber corresp.
14 Flatley 7 May 1942 action report.
15 VF-42's air battle reconstructed from individual "Pilot Comment" sheets in Flatley papers, Macomber corresp., Johnston, *The Grim Reapers,* 27–28; Hata and Izawa, 52, 271.
16 Ens. W. A. Haas, Pilot Comment sheet, 7 May 1942, Flatley papers.
17 Flatley 7 May 1942 action report.
18 Hata and Izawa, 271.
19 For the correct Dixon quote, see ComDesRon One (CTU 17.2.4) to CominCh, "Engagement with Japanese Forces 7–8 May 1942" (22 May 1942), 2. The oft-quoted "Scratch one flat-top! Dixon to carrier, scratch one flat-top!" publicized in Johnston, *Queen of the Flat-tops,* 181, is in error.

Afternoon Reassessment

1 For Crace's fight, see TF-44 action report and G. Hermon Gill, *Royal Australian Navy 1942–1945,* 49–50.

The Japanese Dusk Attack

Along with basic sources cited above are the VF-42 individual pilot comment sheets and corresp. with RADM Pederson, RADM Leonard, Capt. Macomber, Capt. McCuskey, and Cdr. Markham, also with Mr. Takeshita Takami of the War History Office.

1 Leonard corresp.
2 Johnston, *The Grim Reapers,* 29.
3 Bill Wileman was one of the few individuals (the only U.S. carrier fighter pilot) to fly in the first three carrier battles—with VF-2 at Coral Sea, VF-6 at Midway and Eastern Solomons. He went with VF-5 to Guadalcanal and was killed in action on 13 Sept. 1942. Another iron man among carrier VF pilots was Howard Packard. He served with VF-2 until March 1942, then fought with VF-6 at Midway and Eastern Solomons, and came out with Jimmy Flatley's VF-10 in time for the Battle of Santa Cruz.
4 *Senshi Sōsho,* Vol. 49, Part 1, 292.
5 Ibid.
6 Lieut. (jg) W. S. Woollen, Pilot Comment sheet, 7 May 1942, Flatley papers.
7 *Lexington* Fighter Director Report.
8 Ens. R. L. Wright, Pilot Comment sheet, 7 May 1942, Flatley papers.
9 Leonard corresp.
10 Ibid.
11 The source of the highly exaggerated Japanese losses (eleven ditched, etc.) is an immediate postwar interview of VADM Hara Chūichi done by him without benefit of documents.
12 CTF-17 to CinCPac 071024 of May 1942, CinCPac Message Files.
13 *Senshi Sōsho,* Vol. 49, Part 1, 297.
14 Ibid.

12   THE CARRIER BATTLE OF 8 MAY

The Searches

1 Composite of garbled message in USS *Yorktown,* "List of Dispatches and Signals sent, read, and intercepted on May 8, 1942," an enclosure in CO USS *Yorktown* to CinCPac, "Report of Action of *Yorktown* and *Yorktown* Air Group on May 8, 1942" (25 May 1942); this is an extremely valuable source for reconstructing the air actions.
2 *Senshi Sōsho,* Vol. 49, Part 1, 306.

The Attack on MO Striking Force

General sources in addition to those cited above include Frank and Harrington, corresp. with VADM Duckworth, RADM Vorse, Cdr. J. B. Bain (*Lexington*); RADM Murr Arnold, RADM W. O. Burch, RADM Leonard, Capt. McCuskey, Capt. Woollen, Capt. J. P. Adams, Cdr. J. H. Jorgenson (*Yorktown*); from Japan, corresp. with Okajima Kiyokuma, Dr. Hata Ikuhiko, and Mr. Takeshita Takami; through the courtesy of Col. Raymond Toliver, USAF (Ret.), the 8 May 1942 diary entries of Iwamoto Tetsuzō; also BuAer interviews of Lt. Cdr. W. O. Burch (3 Sept. 1942) and Lieut. N. A. M. Gayler (17 June 1942).

1 *Yorktown,* List of Dispatches, 2.
2 Ibid.
3 Ibid.
4 CO VS-2 to CO USS *Lexington,* "Report of Action, Scouting Squadron Two on May 8, 1942 in Coral Sea."
5 Leonard corresp.
6 Ibid.

7 Important sources on the Japanese CAP include *Senshi Sōsho,* Iwamoto diary, Oka-jima corresp., and information from Dr. Hata.

8 *Yorktown,* List of Dispatches, 8.

9 Lt. Cdr. W. O. Burch, Interview at BuAer, 3 Sept. 1942, 6.

10 CinCPac 1st Endorsement to CO TF-17 to CinCPac, "The Battle of the Coral Sea, May 4–8, 1942" (27 May 1942).

11 To borrow a phrase from another well-acquainted with Zeros, Claire Chennault, *Way of a Fighter* (New York: Putnam, 1949), 58.

12 VT-5 U.S. Aircraft Action with the Enemy, Lt. Cdr. J. Taylor, 8 May 1942.

13 *Yorktown* 8 May action report (26 May 1942).

14 VADM Hara Chūichi interview at Truk, November 1945 ("Truk Report").

15 Minami died 25 Nov. 1944 on a Kamikaze Mission in the Philippines; he was an ensign in the 201st Air Group; Hata and Izawa, 203.

16 Bain corresp.

17 Iwamoto diary, 8 May 1942, furnished by Col. R. T. Toliver.

18 CO USS *Lexington* to CinCPac, "Report of Action—The Battle of the Coral Sea, 7 and 8 May 1942" (15 May 1942).

19 An excellent fighter pilot, Okabe was generally involved in the actions where U.S. aircraft actually were shot down and likely did much of the damage.

"Hey Rube"

In addition to sources mentioned above, corresp. with RADM A. O. Vorse, Capt. W. E. Eder, Cdr. G. F. Markham (*Lexington*); Capt. S. B. Strong, Capt. A. J. Brassfield, Capt. B. T. Macomber, Capt. W. A. Haas, Lt. Cdr. E. D. Mattson (*Yorktown*); also A. A. Hoehling, *The Lexington Goes Down,* and Johnston's two books.

1 *Yorktown,* List of Dispatches, 9; "Hey Rube" was added to the fighter director vocabulary on 26 April 1942 (see OpNav to PacFlt 251500 of April 1942 in CinCPac Message Files) because the British Admiralty originally used 'Shadally," a British slang expression (?), which no one in the U.S. Navy knew.

2 Ibid., 10

3 Ibid.; another source, the radio log in CTG 17.2 (ComCruDiv 6) to ComCruPac, "Engagement with Japanese Force 7–8 May, 1942, in Coral Sea" (28 May 1942), 7, recorded Sellstrom's shout as "There's a whole God damned bunch of them behind you, skipper."

4 Ibid., 11.

5 Ibid.; according to CTG 17.2 radio log, Ramsey said, "There are heavy bombers protected by fighters. We are going to engage the bombers right now."

6 Eder corresp.

7 Okumiya and Horikoshi, *Zero!,* 147.

8 Ibid.

9 CTG 17.2 action report (28 May 1942), 3–4.

10 *Yorktown,* List of Dispatches, 12.

11 Brassfield corresp.

12 The Gunnery Officer, USS *Lexington* to CO USS *Lexington,* "Action fought in the Coral Sea with the Japanese Navy 7–8 May 1942" (30 May 1942), 3.

13 Air Officer to CO USS *Lexington,* "Report of Air Engagement and Subsequent Sinking of the *Lexington,* 8 May 1942" (20 May 1942), 3.

14 Brassfield corresp.

15 Mattson corresp.

16 Leonard corresp.

17 *Yorktown,* List of Dispatches, 12.

18 Ibid., 13.

19 Flatley 7 May action report.

20 VF-42 U.S. Aircraft Action with the Enemy Report, Lieut. (jg) R. G. Crommelin, 8 May 1942.
21 Johnston, *Queen of the Flat-tops,* 228.
22 Macomber corresp.
23 *Senshi Sōsho,* Vol. 49, Part 1, 315.
24 *Yorktown,* List of Dispatches, 13.
25 Brassfield corresp.

Return of the Strike Groups

1 CTF-17 to CinCPac 080204 of May 1942, CinCPac Message File.
2 *Yorktown,* List of Dispatches, 24.
3 Ibid., 25
4 Ibid.
5 Ibid., 29
6 CTF-17 to CinCPac 080346 of May 1942, CinCPac Message File.
7 *Yorktown,* List of Dispatches, 32.

The Loss of the Lex

1 *Yorktown,* List of Dispatches, 31, 32.
2 Ibid., 35.
3 Johnston, *Queen of the Flat-tops*, 259–60.
4 VF-2 Muster Rolls, RG 24; VF-42 lost in the attack on the *Yorktown* Paul C. Meyers, AOM3c, USN.
5 Leonard corresp.
6 CinCPac to CTF-17 080703 of May 1942, CinCPac Message File.

13 CORAL SEA AFTERMATH

"We are all short of oil, running like hell."

Sources include WD ComCruTF-17, W. W. Smith, and VADM W. G. Schindler, "The Finale of the Battle of the Coral Sea," furnished by VADM Schindler.

1 Diary of Lt. Cdr. Phillip H. Fitzgerald, 9 May 1942; RADM Fitzgerald papers; he was gunnery officer on board the *New Orleans.*
2 Leonard corresp.
3 CinCPac to CTF-17 090117 of May 1942, in *CINCPAC Greybook*, 452.
4 *Senshi Sōsho,* Vol. 49, Part 1, 327.

Task Force 16's Anabasis to the South Pacific

Sources: WDs ComCarPac, *Enterprise, Hornet*; *CINCPAC Greybook*, Lundstrom.

1 CinCPac Operations Plan 23-42 to CTF-16, 29 Apr. 1942.
2 Stover, 26; Cdr. Harwood as air officer on board the light carrier *Princeton* was killed on 24 Oct. 1944 while bravely leading a damage control party before the *Princeton* had to be abandoned.
3 Rawie diary, 1 May 1942.
4 VF-8 Aircraft Trouble Report (Ens. S. W. Groves) 12 May 1942, in RG 313, ABF, VF4F-4.
5 Stover, 27.
6 VF-8 Aircraft Trouble Report (Ens. C. M. Kelly) 12 May 1942, in RG 313, ABF, VF4F-4; Kelly was an All-American lacrosse player at the University of Maryland.
7 Stover, 27.
8 VF-6 War Record, 3 May 1942.
9 Rawie diary, 4 May 1942.
10 Ibid., 5 May 1942.
11 CTF-16 to CinCPac 120137 of May 1942, in CinCPac Message File.

12 VF-6 War Record, 13 May 1942.
13 CinCPac to CTF-16 140319 of May 1942, in CinCPac Message File.
14 For the background of the "secret despatch," see Lundstrom, 154–58.
15 VF-6 Aircraft Trouble Report (Mach. J. A. Achten) 15 May 1942, in RG 313, ABF, VF4F-4.
16 *Senshi Sōsho*, Vol. 49, Part 1, 255–56.
17 VF-6 Aircraft Trouble Report (Ens. W. M. Holt) 15 May 1942, in RG 313, ABF, VF4F-4.
18 VF-6 War Record, 15 May 1942.

"Desire you proceed to the Hawaiian area"

General sources: WDs (now including ComCarDiv One), W. W. Smith, Lundstrom.
1 Message CinCPac to CTF-16 160307 of May 1942, CinCPac Message File.
2 CinCPac to CominCh 140741 of May 1942, *CINCPAC Greybook*, 466.
3 Leonard corresp.
4 WD ComCruTF-17, 26 May 1942.
5 *Senshi Sōsho*, Vol. 43, *Middowe Kaisen* (Midway Sea Battle), 114–15.
6 Halsey and Bryan, 106.
7 VF-6 War Record, 18 May 1942.
8 Ibid., 20 May 1942.
9 VF-6 Aircraft Trouble Report (Lieut. (jg) G. L. Hermann) 26 May 1942, in RG 313, ABF, VF4F-4; also WD *Ellet*.

Coral Sea Combat Lessons

1 Flatley 7 May action report.
2 Ibid.
3 Ibid.
4 Ibid.
5 CO *Yorktown* action report (25 May 1942), 22.
6 Ibid., 23.
7 Ibid., 26.
8 CO VT-2 to CO USS *Lexington*, "The Battle of the Coral Sea, Report of" (10 May 1942).
9 CO VS-2, "Report of Action, Scouting Squadron Two on May 7, 1942 in Coral Sea."
10 Gayler BuAer Interview, 11.

THE BATTLE OF MIDWAY

General sources on the Midway campaign include WDs, Action Reports (listed in bibliography), U.S. Naval War College, *Battle of Midway, including the Aleutian Phase June 3 to June 14, 1942. Strategical and Tactical Analysis*; U.S. Navy, O.N.I., *The Japanese Story of the Battle of Midway*; *Senshi Sōsho*, Vol. 43, *Middowē Kaisen*. Important studies of the battle are: Fuchida and Okumiya; Morison, *Coral Sea, Midway and Submarine Actions*; Walter Lord, *Incredible Victory*; Gordon Prange, *Miracle at Midway* (which is based heavily on the excellent Ph.D. dissertation by Robert E. Barde, *The Battle of Midway: A Study in Command*); Thaddeus Tuleja, *Climax at Midway*. For the individual U.S. carriers, see Frank and Harrington, Stafford, and Griffin. Personal accounts include W. W. Smith; RADM C. W. McClusky, "Historical Commentary," Thach, "The Red Rain of Battle," *Colliers* (12 Dec. 1942) 16–17, 44–46; Dickinson; Capt. James S. Gray, "Decision at Midway"; Rawie diary; Gay; Mears; and Stover. On commanders at the battle, see Potter; Hiroyuki Agawa, *The Reluctant Admiral: Yamamoto and the Imperial Navy*; Thomas B. Buell, *The Quiet Warrior: A Biography of Admiral Raymond A. Spruance*; and Taylor.

14   GETTING READY FOR MIDWAY

The Reorganization of Fighting Three

> Main sources: Thach, BuAer interview, VF-3 documents in Leonard papers, corresp. and interviews of ADM Thach, RADM Pederson, RADM Leonard, Cdr. T. F. Cheek, Cdr. D. C. Sheedy.

1   Leonard corresp.
2   Ltr. ComCarPac (Admin.) to CO VF -3 (9 May 1942); Report CO VF-3 to ComCarPac (20 May 1942), in RG 313, ABF, VF4F-4.
3   Memo Capt A. C. Davis to CinCPac 21 May 1942, in *CINCPAC Greybook.*

The Carriers in Port

1   Stover, 28.
2   Ibid., 29.
3   Lord, *Incredible Victory*, 33.
4   ComCarPac to CO VF-6, VF-8 (27 May 1942) in RG 313, ABF, VF4F-4.
5   Leonard corresp.
6   Ibid.; on Don Lovelace, corresp. with his wife, now Mrs. Helen Skaer; Thach interview; corresp., with E. D. Mattson.
7   Ltr. CO VF-3 to Chief, BuAer, "Armament of Carrier Based Fighter Aircraft" (28 May 1942), RG 313, ABF, VF4F-4.
8   Leonard corresp.

Midway—The Waiting

1   Text with Rawie diary.
2   Task Force 16 Plan of the Day, 2 June 1942, in ibid.
3   Ibid., 2 June 1942.
4   Lt. Cdr. Clarence C. Ray, Interview at BuAer, 15 July 1942.
5   Text in Gay, *Sole Survivor*, 319.
6   Ibid.
7   Capt. James S. Gray, "Decision at Midway," 7.
8   Ibid.

15   THE BATTLE OF 4 JUNE

The Opening Moves

1   U.S. carrier aircraft strengths from action reports and Memo to RADM Noyes, 3 June 1942, RG 313, ABF, A4-1(1), Aircraft Status Reports.
2   Japanese carrier aircraft strengths from *Senshi Sōsho*, Vol. 43, 140; their carrier action reports, and for 6th Air Group, Hata and Izawa, 113–14.
3   ComCarPac (TF-16) WD.
4   Ibid.
5   Ibid.
6   Ibid.
7   Mears, 52.
8   Students of Midway are greatly indebted to Bowen P. Weisheit of the Ens. C. Markland Kelly, Jr. Foundation. A marine aviator in World War II, Weisheit set out a few years ago to learn as much as he could about the *Hornet* Air Group in the Battle of Midway. His conclusions, based on all available documents and lengthy personal interviews with key participants, present a totally new picture of the *Hornet's* participation at Midway. Mr. Weisheit has most generously shared his research with the author. His complete findings will be the subject of a forthcoming study in collaboration with this author.
9   RADM C. W. McClusky, "Historical Commentary," 18.

10 Ibid.
11 Message File in *The Japanese Story of the Battle of Midway*, 14.
12 Ibid., 15.
13 For the *Yorktown*'s launch, corresp. with RADM Arnold, RADM Pederson, RADM Leonard, Capt. Macomber, Capt. McCuskey, Cdr. Cheek; Thach interview, Oct. 1974.
14 Lord, *Incredible Victory*, 154.

The Attack on Nagumo's Carriers

1 Weisheit research—his interviews with Capt. Troy Guillory (VB-8) and Capt. Humphrey L. Tallman (VF-8), both of whom watched VT-8 follow the air group out on 265 degrees, then turn left to the southwest.
2 Message File, *Japanese Story*, 16.
3 Gray, "Decision at Midway," 9.
4 For Japanese plane losses to this point, see action reports and *Senshi Sōsho*, Vol. 43, 302, 317–18.
5 Mears, 68.
6 For VT-6 in addition to the above cited sources (especially Barde), see personal account contained in B. R. Jackson and T. E. Doll, *Douglas TBD-1 "Devastator,"* 40–41.
7 "Fighter Director," June 4, 1942, enclosure with ComCruTF-17 to CinCPac, "Report of Action 4 June 1942" (12 June 1942); this source along with Fighter Director School, Navy Yard, Pearl Harbor, "Battle of Midway Island" (3 Apr. 1943), gives the basic CAP dialogue vital for the reconstruction of air actions at Midway.
8 "Fighter Director."
9 Leonard corresp.
10 For the *Hornet* SBDs and F4Fs, see Weisheit research; also interviews with Capt. Tallman and John E. McInerny, Jr., corresp. with Henry Carey. Barde also contains useful information on the *Hornet* SBDs.
11 Fighter Director School, 8.
12 In addition to already cited sources, the *Yorktown* Air Group fight is based on Thach BuAer interview, Thach interview, Oct. 1974, corresp. with Macomber, Cheek, Sheedy, Childers, and Esders, and Esders's 6 June 1942 action report.
13 For Japanese CAP, see their carrier action reports, *Senshi Sōsho*, 327–33; *Japanese Story*, and Hata and Izawa for unit histories, list of losses, and biographical accounts.
14 Macomber corresp.
15 Thach interview, Oct. 1974.
16 Ibid.
17 Ibid.
18 Ibid.; R. A. M. Dibb was killed in a flying accident on 29 Aug. 1944, see Frank Olynyk, *USN Credits for the Destruction of Enemy Aircraft in Air-to-Air Combat World War 2*, xvi.
19 Childers corresp.
20 Cheek corresp.; also interview with Sheedy.
21 Childers corresp.
22 For the controversy of SBDs and targets, see above all Lord, *Incredible Victory*, 289–95, and also Tillman, *The Dauntless Dive Bomber of World War Two*, 73–78.
23 See note 13.
24 Weisheit research; also corresp. with Capt. S. E. Ruehlow.
25 Fighter Director School, 9.
26 Weisheit research; Barde, also corresp. with Henry Carey.

The Japanese Retaliate

1 On the *Hiryū* carrier bombers, see *Senshi Sōsho*, Vol. 43, 347–54 including roster, *Japanese Story*, *Hiryū* action report, Fuchida and Okumiya, Prange, *Miracle*.

2 For the *Hiryū* fighters, sources in note 1, also Hata and Izawa.

3 Message File, *Japanese Story*, 22.

4 Cheek corresp.

5 Fighter Director; for VF-3's part in intercepting the VBs: corresp. and/or interviews with RADM Pederson, Capt. A. J. Brassfield (and his June 4, 1942 action report), Capt. McCuskey, Capt. Woollen, Cdr. Bain, Cdr. Markham, Cdr. Esders (and his action report of 6 June 1942). Dr. Barde kindly furnished a copy of his interview in March 1967 with Capt. H. B. Gibbs.

6 *Hiryū* action report, in "Battle Report of Battle of Midway" (WDC 160985B), 30.

7 Message File, *Japanese Story*, 22.

8 McCuskey interview, July 1974.

9 Gibbs interview by Barde, March 1967.

10 Information on VF-8's obscure role in the CAP over the *Yorktown*: corresp. with RADM Ford, Cdr. C. B. Starkes, H. A. Carey; also Stover, 31. Morrill Cook was killed on 26 October 1942 at Santa Cruz, and George Formanek on 23 Apr. 1944 over Hollandia, New Guinea.

11 RADM R. W. Mehle interview, Feb. 1975.

12 Message File, *Japanese Story*, 23.

13 Ibid.

14 Mears, 56–57, Sheedy interview, Carey corresp., also Ltr. CO USS *Hornet* to Bureau of Ships (12 June 1942), in RG 313, ABF, L11-1(1). The other four men killed in the unfortunate accident were: Plat. Sgt. William B. Ignatius, USMC, Pfc Fred W. Cummings, Jr., USMC, Pvt. Lowell E. Humfleet, USMC; and Elmer A. Meyer, Sea2c USN.

15 Mears, 58–59.

16 For *Hiryū* torpedo attack, see *Senshi Sōsho*, Vol. 43, 355–62; *Hiryū* action report; *Japanese Story*; and especially Dr. Hata Ikuhiko, "Kaeri zaru Tomonaga Raigekitai (1942 6.5)" (The Tomonaga Torpedo Attack Unit Departs), *Kōkūfan* (Jan. 1976) 118–23; Dr. Hata also provided additional information based on interviews with Hashimoto Toshio and Bandō Makoto.

17 Message File, *Japanese Story*, 24.

18 Fuchida and Okumiya, 192.

19 Shigematsu Yasuhiro flew two sorties from the *Junyō* at the Battle of Santa Cruz, 26 Oct. 1942, and died in action on 8 July 1944 as *hikōtaichō* of the 263rd Air Group in a combat mission southwest of Guam, Hata and Izawa, 242.

20 In addition to the VF-6 reports, corresp. with Lieut. William H. Warden and Dr. Hata.

21 Fighter Director School, 19.

22 Ibid.

23 Leonard corresp.

24 Message File, *Japanese Story*, 26.

25 Fighter Director School, 19; also McCuskey interview, July 1974.

26 Fighter Director School, 23; for this fight, Woollen interview, July 1973; Gibbs interview by Barde.

27 Also on VF-3's launch, corresp. or interviews with Thach, Leonard, Haas, and Adams, and Mrs. George A. Hopper, Sr.

28 Thach interview, Oct. 1974.

29 Lord, *Incredible Victory*, 219; also interview with Edward R. Mendoza, formerly a Sea1c with VF-42, who witnessed the incident.

30 For the problems of the N2AN sight, see appendix.

31 McCuskey interview July 1974; corresp. with Cdr. H. S. Packard and information from Dr. Hata, who interviewed Bandō.

32 Packard corresp.; Tom Barnes was very grateful for his rescue!

33 Ibid.

34 Ibid.

35 Rawie diary, also corresp.
36 Ibid.
37 Message File, *Japanese Story*, 26.
38 Fighter Director.

Retribution

1 Minegishi Yoshijirō as an ensign died in ground combat on Roi, Feb. 1944, and Kotani Kenji was lost in a flying accident in 1945, Hata and Izawa, 278, 293.
2 *Japanese Story*, 46.
3 Message File in ibid., 27.
4 Fighter Director.
5 Promoted to ensign, Yamamoto Akira was killed on 24 Nov. 1944 over Yachimata, Japan, while intercepting the first B-29 strike from the Marianas against the homeland, Hata and Izawa, 212.
6 RADM J. M. Worthington, "A Destroyer at Midway," *Shipmate* (Jan. 1965) 6.
7 Leonard corresp.
8 Ibid.
9 ComCruPac to CinCPac, "Action Report, Battle of Midway" (14 June 1942).
10 Leonard corresp.
11 Ibid.
12 Gray, "Decision at Midway," 10.

16 MIDWAY—THE PURSUIT

5–6 June off Midway

1 CTF-16 to CinCPac, "Battle of Midway" (16 June 1942).
2 CO USS *Hornet* to CinCPac, "Report of Action" (13 June 1942).
3 Dialogue on 6 June is included in Ltr. RADM Raymond A. Spruance to ADM Chester W. Nimitz (8 June 1942).
4 Ibid.

The Loss of the Yorktown

1 See especially Gibbs interview by R. E. Barde; Lord, *Incredible Victory*; and Frank and Harrington.

The Sara *Back to the Front*

Sources include: *Saratoga* WD, Log; *CINCPAC Greybook*; WD ComCarDiv One; WD NAS Pearl Harbor; corresp. with Capt. G. E. Firebaugh and Capt. H. S. Brown.
1 VF-2 Det. Aircraft Trouble Report (Lieut. (jg) F. Simpson) 26 May 1942, in RG 313, ABF, VF4F-4.
2 VF-2 Det. Aircraft Trouble Report (S. W. Tumosa, AP2c) 3 June 1942, in ibid.

"How good land will look this time"

1 CinCPac to CTF 8, 16, 17, 080429 of June 1942, in *CINCPAC Greybook*, 556–57.
2 Weisheit research; also conversations with Capt. Tallman and J. E. McInerny; corresp. with Capt. Ruehlow; Barde.
3 Original in archives of Ens. C. Markland Kelly, Jr. Foundation.
4 VF-6 War Record, 10 June 1942.
5 Ibid., 13 June 1942.

17 THE "FIRST TEAM" GRADUATES

1 CominCh to CinCPac 111922 of June 1942, *CINCPAC Greybook*, 580.
2 CominCh to CinCPac 151300 of June 1942, ibid., 582.
3 CinCPac to CominCh 152201 of June 1942, ibid., 582–83.

4 Ibid.

5 Ibid.

6 WD, NAS Pearl Harbor 16 June 1942; VF-6 War Record, 16 June 1942.

7 VF-6 Aircraft Trouble Report (Lieut. (jg) R. M. Rich), RG 313, ABF, VF4F-4.

8 See RG 313, ABF, A4-1(1) Aircraft Status Reports, June–July 1942.

9 In July, Ramsey became CO of Carrier Replacement Air Group Eleven.

10 RG 313, ABF, A4-1(1), Aircraft Status Report, 7 July 1942.

18 MIDWAY LESSONS—THE F4F-4 CONTROVERSY

1 VF-3 U.S. Aircraft Action with the Enemy Report, Lt. Cdr. J. S. Thach, 4 June 1942.

2 CO VF-6 to Chief, BuAer, "F4F-4 Airplane, Undesirable Characteristics of" (9 June 1942), in RG 72, BuAer Corresp., VF4F-4.

3 Ibid.

4 Endorsement to CO VF-6 Ltr. (9 June 1942).

5 Ibid.

6 CO USS *Yorktown* to CinCPac, "Report of Action for June 4, 1942 and June 6, 1942" (18 June 1942), 15.

7 CinCPac to CominCh, "Battle of Midway" (28 June 1942).

8 Ibid.

9 CO USS *Enterprise* to CinCPac, "Battle of Midway Island, June 4–6, 1942, Report of" (8 June 1942).

10 Leonard corresp.

11 CO USS *Hornet* to CinCPac, action report (13 June 1942).

12 Thach, interview at BuAer, 26 Aug. 1942.

13 Ltr. Cdr. J. B. Pearson to Lt. Cdr. J. H. Flatley (15 July 1942), in Flatley papers.

14 Ibid.

15 Ibid.

16 Ibid.

17 First endorsement to VF-3 Ltr. 28 May 1942, ComCarPac (Admin.) to Chief, BuAer, 24 June 1942, in RG 72, BuAer Corresp., VF4F-4.

18 Pearson to Flatley, 15 July 1942; Flatley papers.

19 CO VF-10 to ComCarPac, "The Navy Fighter" (25 June 1942); copy from Cdr. J. H. Jorgenson papers.

20 Ibid.

21 Pearson to Flatley, 15 July 1942; Flatley papers.

22 SecNav to CO VF-10, 29 July 1942; in Flatley papers.

23 Thach, interview at BuAer, 26 Aug. 1942.

24 Thach's rewrite of *USF-74 (Revised)* fighter chapter in Lieut. James S. Gray, Jr., "A to N for the Fighter Pilot," NAS Pensacola, Jan. 1943; in Cdr. G. F. Markham papers.

25 Citation for DSM in Howard Mingos, *American Heroes of the War in the Air*, 69; this is a useful source for award citations for about 90 percent of the U.S. naval pilots who earned decorations in 1941–42.

APPENDIXES

1 THE MAKING OF CARRIER FIGHTER PILOTS

Sources include U.S. Naval Administration in World War II, DCNO (Air) Essays in the History of Naval Air Operations: "Aviation Personnel, 1911–1939," "Aviation Training, 1911–1939," and "Aspects of Aviation Training, 1939–1945"; Turnbull and Lord, *History of United States Naval Aviation*; documents in BuAer Corresp. (RG 72), P11-1; also for a good summary of 1941 syllabus, see NAS Pensacola and Jacksonville, *Flight Jacket*, 1941 (yearbook of reservist pilots); for interesting accounts of prewar aviation training, Guyton, *Air Base* and Winston, *Dive Bomber*.

For Japanese naval aviation training, see Hata and Izawa; Okumiya and Horikoshi, *Zero!*; Saburo Sakai, *Samurai*; U.S. Strategic Bombing Survey, Report 64, "Japanese Air Power."

2   FUNDAMENTALS OF AERIAL FIXED GUNNERY

Document sources include: Lieut. (jg) J. S. Gray, Jr. "VF Gunnery School Pamphlet, 1941," in RG 313, ABF, A5-1; Combat Doctrine, Fighting Squadron Ten (Lt. Cdr. J. H. Flatley, Jr.) (July 1942), in Cdr. J. H. Jorgenson papers; Lieut. J. S. Gray, Jr., "A to N for the Fighter Pilot," NAS Pensacola, Jan. 1943, in Cdr. G. F. Markham papers; BuAer, "Gunnery Approaches," Fixed Gunnery and Combat Tactics Series No. 2 (Sept. 1943), issued under aegis of Cdr. J. S. Thach.

1 Lt. Cdr. Flatley, Combat Doctrine, Fighting Squadron Ten, July 1942.
2 Thach interview, Oct. 1974.
3 Cited in Gray, "VF Gunnery School Pamphlet, 1941."
4 Flatley, Combat Doc., VF-10.
5 For N2A and N2AN sights, see War Dept., Technical Manual TM 1-495, "Aircraft Machine-Gun Sights" (26 Mar. 1941); Gray, "VF Gunnery School Pamphlet, 1941."

3   FIGHTING COLORS, INSIGNIA, AND MARKINGS

Based primarily on documents in RG 313, ABF, F-39 files; photographs of the period.

1 For details on insignia and markings at start of war, U.S. NAS Alameda, "Local Process Specification No. 15a" (15 Dec. 1941), in RG 313.
2 Text in *PH Attack*, Part 24, 1487.
3 ComAirBatFor to AirBatFor, "Exterior Painting of Fleet Aircraft for Ready Identification" (23 Dec. 1941), in RG 313; for implementation, U.S. NAS Pearl Harbor, "U.S. Navy Aircraft Identification Marks" (26 Dec. 1941), in RG 313.
4 Chief, BuAer to all Stations, Ships, Units concerned with Naval Aircraft, "Exterior Painting, Insignia, and Markings of Fleet Aircraft" (5 Jan. 1942), RG 313.
5 ComAirBatFor to AirBatFor, "Exterior Painting, Insignia, and Markings of Fleet Aircraft—Modification of Instructions Concerning" (21 Feb. 1942).
6 Chief, BuAer to all Stations (etc.), "Exterior Painting, Insignia, and Markings of Fleet Aircraft" (6 Feb. 1942), in RG 313.
7 Ibid.
8 NAS Alameda, "Local Process Specification No. 15a—addendum No. 1d and 2" (23 Feb. and 26 Feb. 1942), in RG 313.
9 ComCarPacFlt to CarPacFlt, "Exterior Painting, Insignia, and Markings of Carrier Aircraft" (29 Apr. 1942), in RG 313.
10 CinCPac to CominCh 250135 of April 1942, in CinCPac Message Files.
11 ComGenHawDept to CinCPac, 082050 of May 1942, in CinCPac Message File.

4   NAVAL FLIGHT FORMATIONS AND THE "THACH WEAVE"

Main sources include ADM J. S. Thach, Oral History (copy of preliminary draft supplied by ADM Thach); *USF-74 Revised* (March 1941); Lt. Cdr. Flatley, Combat Doctrine, Fighting Squadron Ten (July 1942).

1 CO VF-10 to CO USS *Enterprise*, "VF Squadron Ten Action Reports for October 25 and 26, 1942" (31 Oct. 1942), Encl. B.
2 CO VF-5 to ComAirBatFor (19 Feb. 1940); CO VF-2 to ComAirBatFor (29 Feb. 1940), RG 313, ABF, A16-3.
3 Strong recommendations for adoption of two-plane sections in CO VF-5 to ComAirBatFor (28 May 1940) and CO VF-2 to ComAirBatFor (31 May 1940), in ibid.
4 "Charlie" principle in OpNav Confidential Ltr. A16-3(5) of 5 Mar. 1941 and ComAirBatFor Endorsement of 27 Mar. 1941, in ibid.
5 CO VF-3 to ComAirBatFor, "Fighting Plane Tactics" (12 May 1941), in ibid.

6 ComAirBatFor to CO VF-6, 2, 3 (7 July 1941); ComAirAtlFlt to CarDiv 3 (10 Aug. 1941), in ibid.

7 Fleet Air Tactical Unit, San Diego, Report of Air Operations, Summary 25-41, "New Type O Fighter" (22 Sept. 1941) in ibid., which seems to refute notion that the U.S. Navy did not know anything about the Zero before Pearl Harbor; perhaps few heeded the warnings.

8 Development of "Thach Weave," Thach Oral History and interviews/corresp. with author.

9 Cheek corresp.

10 Thach, BuAer interview (26 Aug. 1942).

11 *Enterprise* Action Report for Battle of Eastern Solomons, 24 Aug. 1942.

12 Flatley VF-10 report for 25–26 October 1942, Encl. B.

13 Ibid.

5 JAPANESE COMBAT METHODS

Main sources: contemporary U.S. action reports; Pacific Fleet Intell. Bull. 8-42 (12 June 1942); 10-42 (16 Oct. 1942); Hq, AAF, Intelligence Report, January 1945– No. 45-101, "Japanese Fighter Tactics"; CNO, Div. of Naval Intell., Air Intell. Group, OPNAV-16-V #E538, "Japanese Fighter Doctrine" (20 Feb. 1945).

1 Thomas G. Miller, Jr. *The Cactus Air Force*, 208.

2 *Japanese Monograph*, No. 113, "Task Force Operations," 10.

Sources

I) LIST OF PARTICIPANTS CONSULTED (ALL NOW RETIRED FROM THE SERVICE):

Captain John P. Adams, VF-42, -3
Rear Admiral Murr Arnold (*Yorktown*)
Commander John B. Bain, VF-2, -42, -3
Captain Arthur J. Brassfield, VF-42, -3
Captain H. S. Brown, VF-5
Rear Admiral William O. Burch, VS-5
Henry A. Carey, Jr., VF-8
Commander Tom F. Cheek, Jr., VF-2, -6, -3
Lieutenant Colonel Lloyd F. Childers, USMC, VT-3
Kenneth Crawford (*New Orleans*)
Captain James G. Daniels III, VF-6
L. A. DeSalvo, VB-2
Rear Admiral Robert E. Dixon, VS-2
Vice Admiral H. S. Duckworth (*Lexington*)
Captain Willard E. Eder, VF-3, -2
Commander Wilhelm G. Esders, VT-3
Captain Gordon E. Firebaugh, VF-2
Rear Admiral Phillip H. Fitzgerald (*New Orleans*)
Rear Admiral Warren W. Ford, VF-8
Captain David B. Freeman, Jr., VF-8
Captain Lawrence C. French, VF-8
Admiral Noel A. M. Gayler, VF-3, -2
Captain James S. Gray, Jr., VF-6
Captain Walter A. Haas, VF-42, -3
Commander Richard Z. Hughes, VF-8
Vice Admiral Andrew McB. Jackson (Bureau of Aeronautics)
Commander John H. Jorgenson, VS-5
Rear Admiral Edwin T. Layton (CinCPac Staff)
Rear Admiral William N. Leonard, VF-42, -3
Captain Brainard T. Macomber, VF-42, -3
Commander George F. Markham, Jr., VF-2, -42, -3
Lieutenant Commander E. Duran Mattson, VF-42, -3
Captain E. Scott McCuskey, VF-42, -3
John E. McInerny, Jr., VF-8
Rear Admiral Roger W. Mehle,. VF-6
Edward R. Mendoza, VF-42

Captain Robert J. Morgan, VF-3, -2
Okajima Kiyokuma, *Zuikaku* Fighter Unit
Commander Howard S. Packard, VF-2, -6
Rear Admiral Oscar Pederson, VF-42
Vice Admiral Paul H. Ramsey, VF-2
Captain Wilmer E. Rawie, VF-6
Captain Stanley E. Ruehlow, VF-8
Vice Admiral Walter G. Schindler (Task Force 17 Staff)
Commander Daniel C. Sheedy, VF-3
Captain Burt Stanley, VF-3
Commander Carlton B. Starkes, VF-8
Captain Stockton Birney Strong, VS-5
William F. Surgi, Jr., VF-42
John F. Sutherland, VF-8
Captain Humphrey L. Tallman, VF-8
Admiral John S. Thach,. VF-3
Rear Admiral Albert O. Vorse, Jr., VF-3, -2
Lieutenant William H. Warden, VF-2, -6
Captain William S. Woollen, VF-42, -3
Allen R. Wright, Royal Air Force

II) DOCUMENTS

The two principal repositories of documents utilized in this work are the Operational Archives Branch, Naval Historical Center and the National Archives and Records Service.

The Operational Archives Branch contains the action reports, war diaries, message files, interviews, operations orders, tactical publications, and biographical files. They are superbly organized and readily accessible. Below is given a list of the major action reports and other documents consulted.

a) Action Reports

CTF-8 (VADM William F. Halsey) to CinCPac, "Operations of Task Force Eight on 7 December 1941" (18 Dec. 1941) (encl., reports of *Enterprise*, CEAG, VB-6, VF-6, VS-6).

CTF-11 (VADM Wilson Brown) to CinCPac, "Operations of Task Force Eleven , Dec. 14–27, 1941" (26 Dec. 1941).

CTF-14 (RADM Frank Jack Fletcher) to CinCPac, "Report of Operations 16 Dec.–29 Dec. 1941" (28 Dec. 1941).

CO USS *Lexington* to CTF-11, "Attack upon enemy submarine by *Lexington* planes January 10, 1942" (15 Jan. 1942).

CTF-8 (VADM Halsey) to CinCPac, "Action in the Marshall Islands, 1 February 1942" (9 Feb. 1942) (encl. reports of *Enterprise*, CEAG, VB-6, VF-6, VS-6, VT-6).

CTF-17 (RADM Fletcher) to CinCPac, "Report of Engagement January 31, 1942" (9 Feb. 1942) (encl. report of *Yorktown*)

CTF-11 (VADM Brown) to CinCPac, "Cruise of Task Force Eleven from Jan. 31 to Mar. 26, 1942" (26 Mar. 1942).

CTF-11 (VADM Brown) to CinCPac, "Report of Action of Task Force Eleven with Japanese Aircraft on Feb. 20, 1942" (24 Feb. 1942) (encl., reports of *Lexington*, VB-2, TG 11.4, *Patterson*).

CO USS *Enterprise* to CinCPac, "Report of Action on February 24, 1942 (Zone Minus Twelve) against Wake Island" (8 Mar. 1942) (encl., reports of CEAG, VB-6, VF-6, VS-6, VT-6).

CO USS *Enterprise* to CinCPac, "Report of Action on March 4, 1942 (Zone Minus Twelve) against Marcus Island" (9 Mar. 1942) (encl., reports of CEAG, VB-6, VF-6, VS-6).

CTF-11 (VADM Brown) to CominCh, "Report of Attack on Enemy Forces in Salamaua–

Lae area, Mar. 10,1942" (25 Mar. 1942) (encl., reports of CTG 11.5 (*Lexington*) and *Yorktown*).

CO USS *Enterprise* to CTF-16 (VADM Halsey), "Report of Action in Connection with the Bombing of Tokyo on April 18, 1942" (23 Apr. 1942).

ComCruPac (RADM Fletcher) to CinCPac, "Operations of Task Force 17 in the Coral Sea Area, March 16 to April 20, 1942. Statement to Clarify Erroneous Impressions Gained at CINCPAC Headquarters" (23 June 1942).

CTF-17 (RADM Fletcher) to CinCPac, "The Battle of the Coral Sea May 4–8, 1942" (27 May 1942).

CTG 17.5 (RADM Aubrey W. Fitch) to CTF-17, "Action Report—Coral Sea—May 7–8, 1942)."

CO USS *Lexington* to CinCPac, "Report of Action—The Battle of the Coral Sea, 7 and 8 May 1942" (15 May 1942).

Also for the *Lexington*: reports of Executive Officer, Air Officer–Air Operations Officer, Fighter Director, Navigator, Engineering Officer, Gunnery Officer, VB-2, VF-2, VS-2, VT-2; and Preliminary Loss Report (15 June 1942).

CO USS *Yorktown* to CinCPac, "Attack made by *Yorktown* Air Group on Enemy Forces in the Tulagi and Gavutu Harbors" (11 May 1942).

CO USS *Yorktown* to CinCPac,"Air Operations of *Yorktown* Air Group against Japanese Forces in the vicinity of the Louisiade Archipelago on May 7, 1942" (16 May 1942).

CO USS *Yorktown* to CinCPac, "Report of Action of *Yorktown* and *Yorktown* Air Group on May 8, 1942" (25 May 1942).

CYAG to CO USS *Yorktown*, "Air Operations of *Yorktown* Air Group against Japanese Forces in the vicinity of the Louisiade Archipelago on May 8, 1942."

CO USS *Yorktown* to CominCh, "U.S. Aircraft, Action with the Enemy, Report of, 2–8 May 1942" (26 May 1942).

Bureau of Ships, Navy Dept., "U.S.S. *Yorktown* (CV-5) Bomb Damage Coral Sea 8 May 1942, War Damage Report No. 23" (28 Nov. 1942).

Cdr. W. G. Schindler, Memorandum to CinCPac, "Notes on the Coral Sea Action May 4–8, 1942" (22 May 1942).

CTG 17.2 (RADM Thomas C. Kinkaid) to ComCruPac, "Engagement with Japanese Force 7–8 May, 1942, in Coral Sea" (28 May 1942) (encl., reports of the *Minneapolis* and *New Orleans*).

CTU 17.2.2 (RADM W. W. Smith) to CinCPac, "Action Report" (17 May 1942) (encl., reports of the *Astoria*, *Portland,* and *Chester*).

CTU 17.2.4 (Capt. A. R. Early) to CominCh, "Engagement with Japanese Forces 7–8 May 1942" (22 May 1942) (encl., reports of the *Phelps, Dewey,* and *Aylwin*). (ComDesRon One report).

CO USS *Hammann* to CinCPac, "Report of Action May 4, 1942 near Tulagi, Solomon, Island," with "Enclosure A: Report of Rescue of *Yorktown* Aviators from Guadalcanal Island" (11 May 1942).

CTU 17.5.4 (Capt. G. C. Hoover) to CominCh, "Action Report of May 7, 1942," "Action Report in the Coral Sea, 8 May 1942" (18 May 1942) (encl., reports of the *Morris, Hammann, Anderson*, and *Russell*).

CO Allied Naval Forces, Southwest Pacific Area to CominCh, "Task Force Forty-four Attack by Torpedo Bombers and High Level Bomber Aircraft 7 May 1942" (26 May 1942) (Report of TG 17.3, RADM J. G. Crace, RN).

CO USS *Neosho* to CinCPac, "Engagement of U.S.S. *Neosho* with Japanese Aircraft on May 7, 1942, Subsequent Loss of U.S.S. *Neosho*, Search for Survivors" (25 May 1942).

ComDesPac to SecNav, "Sinking of the U.S.S. *Sims* (DD-409) by Japanese Bombers in the Coral Sea on May 7, 1942" (8 July 1942).

CinCPac to CominCh, "Battle of Midway" (28 June 1942).

ComCruPac to CinCPac, "Action Report, Battle of Midway" (14 June 1942).

CO USS *Yorktown* to CinCPac, "Report of Action for June 4, 1942 and June 6, 1942" (18 June 1942) (encl., Executive Officer's Report, War Damage Report).

ComCruTF-17 (RADM W. W. Smith), "Report of Action 4 June 1942" (12 June 1942) (encl., reports of the *Astoria* and the *Portland*).

CTG 17.4 to CominCh (Capt. A. R. Early) to CominCh, "Report of Action June 4, 1942) (4 June 1942) (encl., reports of DesDiv Four, the *Morris, Russell, Anderson*, and *Hughes*)

CO USS *Hughes* to CinCPac, "Operations in connection with the U.S.S. *Yorktown* from time of abandonment until sinking" (11 June 1942).

CO USS *Hammann* to CinCPac, "Action Report 4–6 June 1942" (16 June 1942).

CTF-16 (RADM R. A. Spruance) to CinCPac, "Battle of Midway" (16 June 1942).

Personal Ltr. RADM Raymond A. Spruance to ADM Chester W. Nimitz (8 June 1942).

CO USS *Hornet* to CinCPac, "Report of Action" (13 June 1942) (encl. include "VF-3 Partial Bag").

CO USS *Enterprise* to CinCPac, "Battle of Midway Island, June 4–6,1942, Report of" (8 June 1942); "Air Battle of the Pacific, June 4–6, 1942, Report of" (13 June 1942) (plus reports for VB-6, VF-6, VS-6, VT-6 (Lieut. (jg) R. E. Laub); VF-3, VB-3, VS-5).

ComCruTF-16 (RADM Thomas C. Kinkaid) to CTF-16, "Report of Action June 4, 1942" (11 June 1942) (encl., reports of the *Pensacola* and the *Vincennes*).

CTG 17.4 (Capt. A. R. Early) to CTF-17, "Japanese Torpedo Plane Attack on U.S.S. *Yorktown* during Battle of Midway, June 4, 1942, Report of" (12 June 1942) (encl., reports of the *Balch* and the *Benham*).

CO NAS Midway to CinCPac, "Battle of Midway, 30 May–7 June 1942" (18 June 1942).

CinCPac to CominCh, "Personal Account of Attacks on Japanese Carriers June 4, 1942" (11 June 1942) (forwards Cdr. R. A. Ofstie Memorandum on interview with Ens. George H. Gay, USNR, VT-8, 7 June 1942).

WDC 160985 "Battle Report of Battle of Midway" (includes Battle Reports of the *Akagi, Kaga, Sōryū,* and *Hiryū*).

b) War Diaries

War Plans Division, CinCPac Fleet Staff, *"CINCPAC Greybook,"* Volume I (7 Dec. 1941–31 Aug. 1942).

Commander, Aircraft, Battle Force (later Commander, Carriers, Pacific Fleet) (VADM W. F. Halsey) (Task Forces 8 and 16) (Nov. 1941–June 1942).

Commander, Scouting Force (VADM Wilson Brown) (Task Force 11) (Dec. 1941–Mar. 1942).

Commander, Cruisers, Battle Force (RADM H. F. Leary) (Task Force 14) (Dec. 1941–Jan. 1942).

Commander, Cruisers, Scouting Force (RADM J. H. Newton to 31 Dec. 1941; RADM Frank Jack Fletcher) (Task Force 12; Task Force 17).

Commander, Cruisers, Pacific Fleet (RADM Fletcher) (Task Force 17) (April 1942).

Commander, Carrier Division One (Rear Admiral Aubrey W. Fitch) (Task Group 14.1; Task Force 11) (Dec. 1941; Apr.–June 1942).

Commander, Cruisers, Task Force 17 (RADM W. W. Smith) (Mar.–June, 1942).

Ships: *Lexington, Saratoga, Enterprise, Hornet, Chester, Aylwin, Ellet, Conyngham, Maury, Monaghan, Patterson, Barnett,* and *Fulton*.

Naval Air Station Pearl Harbor

Squadrons: VB-8 (May–June 1942); VF-2 (Dec. 1941–Mar. 1942); and VF-8 (Mar.–May 1942).

c) Interviews and Narratives

Bureau of Aeronautics Interviews: Lt. Cdr. Clarence C. Ray (15 July 1942), Lt. Cdr. William O. Burch (3 Sept. 1942), Lt. Cdr. John S. Thach (26 Aug. 1942), and Lieut. Noel A. M. Gayler (17 June 1942).

U.S. Army Air Forces Interview: Lt. Cdr. Edward J. O'Neill (29 June 1942).

Narratives: Cdr. E. B. Mott (22 Mar. 1944), Lieut. Robin M. Lindsey (17 Sept. 1943), and Lieut. George H. Gay (12 Oct. 1943).

At the National Archives are the administrative files of the U.S. Navy's Bureau of Aeronautics (Record Group 72) and U.S. Fleet, Records of Naval Operating Forces (Record Group 313). In the second record group are the files of the Commander, Aircraft, Battle Force (later Commander, Carriers, Pacific Fleet) for the period 1941–42. Filed by year, they are organized according to the Navy Filing Manual. They are cumbersome to examine, but contain very useful documents. Record Group 24 (Bureau of Naval Personnel) contains ship logs and muster rolls.

d) Deck Logs (RG 24)

Lexington, Saratoga, Yorktown, Enterprise, and *Hornet.*

III) UNPUBLISHED STUDIES AND PERSONAL DIARIES

Barde, Robert E., *The Battle of Midway: A Study in Command.* Ph.D. dissertation, University of Maryland, 1971.

Donelon, Midshipman John O., "Edward Henry O'Hare." Research Paper, U.S. Naval Academy, 1963.

Gray, Capt. James S., Jr., "Decision at Midway" (1963).

U.S. Army, Headquarters Far East Command, Military History Section, Japanese Research Division. *Japanese Monographs*, particularly:

No. 113. "Task Force Operations (November 1941–April 1942)."

No. 118. "Operational History of Naval Communications (December 1941–August 1945)."

No. 120. "Outline of Southeast Area Naval Air Operations, Part I (December 1941–August 1942)."

U.S. Army Air Forces, Historical Division. *The AAF in Australia to the Summer of 1942.* Historical Study No. 9.

U.S. Naval Administration in World War II:

DCNO (Air) Essays in the History of Naval Air Operations, Carrier Warfare, Part III, "History of Naval Fighter Direction" (1946).

"Aviation Training, 1911–1939."

"Aviation Personnel, 1911–1939."

"Aspects of Aviation Training, 1939–1945."

U.S. Naval War College. *The Battle of the Coral Sea May 1 to May 11 Inclusive, 1942. Strategical and Tactical Analysis* (NavPers 91050), Newport, 1947.

———. *Battle of Midway, including the Aleutian Phase June 3 to June 14, 1942. Strategical and Tactical Analysis*, Newport, 1948.

U.S. Navy, Bureau of Aeronautics. *Naval Aircraft Record of Acceptances 1935–1946.* (NavAer 15838).

U.S. Navy, Chief of Naval Operations, Aerology Section. "The Battle of the Coral Sea" (Apr. 1944).

———, Fighter Director School, Navy Yard, Pearl Harbor. "Battle of Midway Island" (3 Apr. 1943).

———, Office of Naval Intelligence. *Combat Narratives.*

"Early Raids in the Pacific, February 1 to March 10, 1942" (1943).

"The Battle of the Coral Sea" (1943).

"Battle of Midway June 3–6, 1942" (1943).

"The War Record of Fighting Six, December 7, 1941 to June 21, 1942," presented by Cdr. James S. Gray, Jr. to United States Naval Academy.

Personal diaries

Lieut. (jg) James G. Daniels III, Nov. 1941–Feb. 1942, furnished by Capt. J. G. Daniels, USN (Ret.).

Iwamoto Tetsuzō, Lieut. (jg), IJN, Entries for 7–8 May 1942 (translated), kindly furnished by Col. Raymond T. Toliver, USAF (Ret.).

Lt. Cdr. Donald A. Lovelace, 7 Dec. 1941–2 Apr. 1942, furnished by Cdr. Donald A. Lovelace II.

Lieut. (jg) Wilmer E. Rawie, 28 Nov. 1941–6 June 1942, furnished by Capt. W. E. Rawie, Ret.

Lieut. (jg) O. B. Stanley, Dec. 1941–Mar. 1942, furnished by Capt. O. B. Stanley, Ret.

IV) BOOKS AND ARTICLES

Abbazia, Patrick. *Mr. Roosevelt's Navy: The Private War of the U.S. Atlantic Fleet.* Annapolis: Naval Institute Press, 1975.

Agawa, Hiroyuki. *The Reluctant Admiral: Yamamoto and the Imperial Navy.* Tokyo: Kodansha, 1979.

Brown, Captain Eric, RN. *Wings of the Navy.* London: Jane's, 1980.

Belote, James H. and William M. Belote. *Titans of the Seas.* New York: Harper & Row, 1975.

Buell, Thomas B. *The Quiet Warrior: A Biography of Admiral Raymond A. Spruance.* Boston: Little, Brown, 1974.

Burns, Eugene. *Then There Was One.* New York: Harcourt, Brace and Co., 1944.

Clark, Admiral J. J., with Clark G. Reynolds. *Carrier Admiral.* New York: John Day, 1967.

Coale, Lt. Cdr. Griffin B. *Victory at Midway.* New York: Farrar and Rinehart, 1944.

Dickinson, Lt. Clarence E. *The Flying Guns.* New York: Scribner's, 1942.

Dull, Paul S. *A Battle History of the Imperial Japanese Navy (1941–1945).* Annapolis: Naval Institute Press, 1978.

Eastern Aircraft Division. *A History of Eastern Aircraft Division, General Motors.* Linden: William E. Rudge's Sons, 1944.

Eckelmeyer, Capt. Edward H., Jr. "The Story of the Self-Sealing Tank," *U.S. Naval Institute Proceedings* (Feb. 1946), 205–19.

Field, John. "How O'Hare downed 5 Jap Planes in One Day," *Life* (13 Apr. 1942), 12–18.

Forrestel, VADM E. P. *Admiral Raymond A. Spruance, USN: A Study in Command.* Washington, D.C.: GPO, 1966.

Francillon, R. J. *Japanese Aircraft of the Pacific War.* London: Putnam, 1970.

Frank, Pat and Joseph D. Harrington. *Rendezvous at Midway: USS Yorktown and the Japanese Carrier Fleet.* New York: John Day, 1967.

Fuchida, Mitsuo and Masatake Okumiya. *Midway: The Battle That Doomed Japan.* Annapolis: Naval Institute Press, 1955.

Gay, George. *Sole Survivor.* Naples, Florida: privately printed, 1979.

Gill, C. Herman. *Royal Australian Navy 1939–1942.* Canberra: Australian War Memorial, 1957.

——. *Royal Australian Navy 1942–1945.* Canberra: Australian War Memorial, 1968.

Glines, Carroll V. *Doolittle's Tokyo Raiders.* Princeton: Van Nostrand, 1964.

Gray, Capt. James Seton, USN. "Comment." *U.S. Naval Institute Proceedings* (Dec. 1981), 90–91.

Graybar, Lloyd J. "American Pacific Strategy after Pearl Harbor: The Relief of Wake Island," *Prologue* (Fall 1980), 134–50.

Greene, Frank L. *History of the Grumman F4F "Wildcat."* Bethpage, New York: Grumman Aircraft Engineering Corp., 1962.

Griffin, Alexander R. *A Ship to Remember: The Saga of the Hornet.* New York: Howell Soskin, 1943.

Guyton, Boone T. *Air Base.* New York: Whittlesley House, 1941.

Hailey, Foster, *Pacific Battle Line.* New York: Macmillan, 1944.

Halsey, FADM William F. and J. Bryan III. *Admiral Halsey's Story.* New York: McGraw Hill, 1947.

Hata, Ikuhiko. "Kaeri zaru Tomonaga Raigekitai" (The Tomonaga Torpedo Attack Unit departs), *Kōkūfan* (Jan. 1976), 118–23.

Hata, Ikuhiko and Izawa Yasuho. *Nihon Kaigun Sentōkitai* (Japanese Naval Fighter Units). Tokyo: Kantosha, 1975.

Heinl, Col. Robert D. *The Defense of Wake*. Washington, D.C.: GPO, 1947.

_____. *Marines at Midway*. Washington, D.C.: GPO, 1948.

Hoehling, A. A. *The Lexington Goes Down*. Englewood Cliffs: Prentice Hall, 1971.

Holmes, W. J. *Double-Edged Secrets*. Annapolis: Naval Institute Press, 1979.

Hoyt, Edwin P. *How They Won the War in the Pacific*. New York: Weybright and Talley, 1970.

_____. *Blue Skies and Blood*. New York: Eriksson, 1975.

Jackson, B. R. and T. E. Doll. *Douglas TBD-1 "Devastator."* Fallbrook: Aero, 1973.

Japan: War History Office. *Senshi Sōsho* (War History Series).

Volume 38. *Chūbu Taiheiyo Hōmen Kaigun Sakusen*, Part One (Central Pacific Naval Operations to May 1942). Tokyo: Asagumo Shimbunsha, 1970.

Volume 43. *Middowē Kaisen* (Midway Sea Battle). Tokyo: Asagumo Shimbunsha, 1971.

Volume 49. *Nantōhōmen Kaigun Sakusen*, Part One (Southeast Area Naval Operations to the beginning of operations to recapture Guadalcanal). Tokyo: Asagumo Shimbunsha, 1971.

Jentschura, Hansgeorg et al. *Warships of the Imperial Japanese Navy 1869–1945*. London: Arms & Armour Press, 1977.

Johnston, Stanley. *Queen of the Flat-tops*. New York: Dutton, 1942.

_____. *The Grim Reapers*. New York: Dutton, 1943.

Kimmel, Husband E. *Admiral Kimmel's Story*. Chicago: Regnery, 1955.

Larkins, William T. *U.S. Naval Aircraft 1921–1941*. Concord: Aviation History Publications, 1961.

Lord, Walter. *Day of Infamy*. New York: Holt, Rinehart, 1957.

_____. *Incredible Victory*. New York: Harper & Row, 1967.

Lundstrom, John B. *The First South Pacific Campaign: Pacific Fleet Strategy December 1941–June 1942*. Annapolis: Naval Institute Press, 1976.

_____. "A Failure of Radio Intelligence: An Episode in the Battle of the Coral Sea," *Cryptologia* (Apr. 1983), 97–118.

Mayborn, Mirch. *Grumman Guide Book*. Dallas: Flying Enterprises Pub., 1976.

McClusky, RADM C. Wade, "Historical Commentary," in *Midway Battle Manual*. Baltimore: Avalon Hill, 1964.

McCuskey, E. Scott. "Ace High," *Colliers* (Aug. 8, 1942), 18–19, 41.

_____. "How We Beat the Zero," *Flying* (Sept. 1944), 29, 94–100.

Mears, Lieut. Frederick. *Carrier Combat*. New York: Doubleday, Doran, 1944.

Mikesh, Robert C. and Rikyu Watanabe. *Zero Fighter*. New York: Crown, 1981.

Miller, Thomas G., Jr. *The Cactus Air Force*. New York: Harper & Row, 1969.

Mingos, Howard. *American Heroes of the War in the Air*. New York: Lanciar, 1943.

Mizrahi, J. V. *Carrier Fighters*, Volumes I and II. Northridge: Sentry Books, 1969.

Morison, Samuel E. *History of United States Naval Operations in World War II*.

Volume III. *The Rising Sun in the Pacific, 1931–April 1942*. Boston: Little, Brown, 1948.

Volume IV. *Coral Sea, Midway and Submarine Actions May 1942–August 1942*. Boston: Little, Brown, 1950.

Naval Air Stations Pensacola and Jacksonville. *Flight Jacket*. 1941.

Okumiya, Masatake and Jiro Horikoshi. *Zero!* New York: Dutton, 1956.

_____. *The Zero Fighter*. London: Cassell, 1958.

Olynyk, Frank J. *USN Credits for the Destruction of Enemy Aircraft in Air-to-Air Combat World War 2*. Aurora: privately printed, 1982.

Orita, Zenji, with Joseph D. Harrington. *I-Boat Captain*. Canoga Park: Major Books, 1976.

Pawlowski, Gareth L. *Flat-tops and Fledglings*. New York: Castle, 1971.

Polmar, Norman. *Aircraft Carriers*. New York: Doubleday, 1969.

Potter, E. B. *Nimitz*. Annapolis: Naval Institute Press, 1976.

Prange, Gordon W. *At Dawn We Slept*. New York: McGraw-Hill, 1981.

_____. *Miracle at Midway*. New York: McGraw-Hill, 1982.

Reynolds, Clark G. *The Fast Carriers: The Forging of an Air Navy*. New York: McGraw-Hill, 1968.

_____. *Famous American Admirals*. New York: Van Nostrand Reinhold, 1978.

Reynolds, Clark G. and E. T. Stover. *The Saga of Smokey Stover, from his Diary*. Charleston: Trad Press, 1978.

Riley, William A. "The Chiefs of Fighting Two," *Journal of the American Aviation Historical Society* (Fall 1969), 145–52.

Sakai, Saburo. *Samurai*. New York: Dutton, 1957.

Sanders, James V. "The Brewsters of Fighting Two," *Journal of the American Aviation Historical Society* (Fall 1969), 153–59.

Sherman, Frederick C. *Combat Command*. New York: Dutton, 1950.

Shores, Chris. *The Brewster Buffalo*. No. 217. London: Profile Publications.

Smith, Earl E., JOC, USN. "Fightin' Two," *All Hands* (May 1951), 59–63.

Smith, VADM William W. *Midway: Turning Point of the Pacific*. New York: Crowell, 1966.

Stafford, Edward P. *The Big E*. New York: Random House, 1962.

Stillwell, Paul (ed.). *Air Raid: Pearl Harbor!* Annapolis: Naval Institute Press, 1981.

Taylor, Theodore. *The Magnificent Mitscher*. New York: Norton, 1954.

Thach, Lt. Cdr. John S. "The Red Rain of Battle: The Story of Fighter Squadron Three," *Colliers*, (Dec. 5, 1942) 14–15, 36–38, (Dec. 12, 1942) 16–17, 44–46.

Thorpe, Donald W. *Japanese Naval Air Force Camouflage and Markings*. Fallbrook: Aero, 1977.

Thruelsen, Richard. *The Grumman Story*. New York: Praeger, 1976.

Tillman, Barrett. *The Dauntless Dive Bomber of World War Two*. Annapolis: Naval Institute Press, 1976.

_____. *The Wildcat in WWII*. Annapolis: Nautical & Aviation, 1983.

Tuleja, Thaddeus V. *Climax at Midway*. New York: Norton, 1960.

Turnbull, Capt. Archibald D. and Clifford L. Lord. *History of United States Naval Aviation*. New Haven: Yale University Press, 1949.

U.S. Congress, 79th Congress, 1st Session. *Pearl Harbor Attack: Hearings before the Joint Committee on the Investigation of the Pearl Harbor Attack*. 38 Parts. Washington, D.C.: GPO, 1946.

U.S. Navy, Bureau of Navigation: *Navy Directory of the U.S. Navy and U.S. Marine Corps Officers*. Washington, D.C.: GPO, 1926–1942.

_____. *Register of Commissioned and Warrant Officers of the U.S. Navy and Marine Corps*. Washington, D.C.: GPO, 1926–1942.

U.S. Navy, DCNO (Air). *United States Naval Aviation, 1910–1970*. Washington, D.C.: GPO, 1970.

_____, Office of Naval Intelligence. *The Japanese Story of the Battle of Midway*. Washington, D.C.: GPO, 1947. (Translation of parts of First Air Fleet, Detailed Battle Report No. 6, Midway Operations, 27 May–9 June 1942.)

U.S. Strategic Bombing Survey. Report 63, "Japanese Air Weapons and Tactics," Washington, D.C.: Military Analysis Division, 1947.

_____. Report 64, "Japanese Air Power," Washington, D.C.: Military Analysis Division, 1946.

Wheeler, Keith. *The Pacific is my Beat*. New York: Dutton, 1943.

Winston, Robert A. *Dive Bomber*. New York: Holiday House, 1939.

Worthington, RADM J. M. "A Destroyer at Midway," *Shipmate* (Jan. 1965), 4–8.

Index

534